BY THE PEOPLE?

For Eileen &
Ralph.

10/20/22

For Eileen &
Khalah,

10/50/55

BY THE PEOPLE?

THE 2020 U.S. PRESIDENTIAL ELECTION AND
THEFT OF AMERICANS' RIGHT TO SELF-RULE

DANIEL ALAN BRUBAKER

Dedicated to the memory of
Mark Fransdal,
Wendell Fransdal,
Chris Gibson,
and Hugh Gibson

[T]ruth will ultimately prevail where pains is taken to bring it to light.

— GEORGE WASHINGTON

Lawful elections are the heart of our freedoms. "No right is more precious in a free country than that of having a voice in the election of those who make the laws under which, as good citizens, we must live. Other rights, even the most basic, are illusory if the right to vote is undermined." Wesberry v. Sanders, *376 U.S. 1, 10 (1964). Trust in the integrity of that process is the glue that binds our citizenry and the States in this Union.*

— STATE OF TEXAS ET AL. V. COMMONWEALTH OF
PENNSYLVANIA, STATE OF GEORGIA, STATE OF
MICHIGAN, AND STATE OF WISCONSIN (2020)

We have put together, I think, the most extensive and inclusive voter fraud organization in the history of American politics.

— JOE BIDEN, OCTOBER 4, 2020

Here is what we know. Using the COVID-19 pandemic as justification, government officials in the defendant states of Georgia, Michigan, and Wisconsin, and the Commonwealth of Pennsylvania ... usurped their legislatures' authority and unconstitutionally revised their state's election statutes. They accomplished these statutory revisions through executive fiat or friendly lawsuits, thereby weakening ballot integrity. Finally, these same government officials flooded the Defendant States with millions of ballots to be sent through the mails, or placed in drop boxes, with little or no chain of custody and, at the same time, weakened the strongest security measures protecting the integrity of the vote—signature verification and witness requirements.

— STATE OF TEXAS ET AL. V. COMMONWEALTH OF PENNSYLVANIA, STATE OF GEORGIA, STATE OF MICHIGAN, AND STATE OF WISCONSIN (2020)

If elections are conducted outside of the law, the people have not conferred their consent on the government. Such elections are unlawful, and their results are illegitimate.

— JUSTICE REBECCA GRASSL BRADLEY, WRITING FOR THE WISCONSIN SUPREME COURT MAJORITY IN TIEGEN V. WISCONSIN ELECTIONS COMMISSION, JULY 8, 2022

CONTENTS

ATTENTION

The clock is ticking. **On September 3, 2022, most evidence of wrongdoing in the 2020 election can—and failing legislative intervention, surely will —be legally** *destroyed.* 52 U.S. Code 20701 says:

> Every officer of election shall retain and preserve, for a period of twenty-two months from the date of any general, special, or primary election of which candidates for the office of President, Vice President, presidential elector, Member of the Senate, Member of the House of Representatives, or Resident Commissioner from the Commonwealth of Puerto Rico are voted for, all records and papers which come into his possession relating to any application, registration, payment of poll tax, or other act requisite to voting in such election, except that, when required by law, such records and papers may be delivered to another officer of election and except that, if a State or the Commonwealth of Puerto Rico designates a custodian to retain and preserve these records and papers at a specified place, then such records and papers may be deposited with such custodian, and the duty to retain and preserve any record or paper so deposited shall devolve upon such custodian. Any officer of election or custodian who willfully fails to comply with this section shall be fined not more than $1,000 or imprisoned not more than one year, or both.

Truth is the foundation of justice. If those who have been working overtime to prevent real scrutiny of the 2020 presidential election are successful in blocking full forensic audits until September 2, 2022, then Americans will forever lose crucial information, and those asserting that the 2020 election was "safe and secure" will achieve a desperately-awaited milestone in evading exposure and possible prosecution. We all can make a difference, but we have a short window.

This book is published about three weeks before the September deadline. There is therefore no time to waste in demanding that legislative action be taken to—under these extraordinary circumstances—preserve all records pertaining to the 2020 election longer so that they may be properly audited.

U.S. Capitol switchboard:
(202) 224-3121
Operators will connect you to the office of your representative or senator.
Don't be scared; you will likely only speak to a staffer.
I suggest saying something like the following:

"I do not wish to live in a country where I cannot trust the elections to be honest.
The 2020 election has not been audited. It must be.
Please support legislation to immediately order the extended preservation of all
2020 election materials and equipment for another two years, and to require full
forensic audits in every state, so that we can be assured
that we still live in a self-governing country.
Thank you."

SOME IMPORTANT TERMS

I've tried to write clearly in these pages, so that all kinds of people can read this book. Maybe you are young; maybe the U.S.A. is not the culture of your birth; or maybe English isn't your first language (even though you may be highly educated). Maybe you just have limited time. I wrote this book for you, too. Since I want to communicate with everyone, here is a short list defining some especially important terms as they are used in this book.

autocracy (*n.*): Rule by those who have seized power for themselves by force or other means. A person who rules in such a way is called an *autocrat*.

checks and balances (*n.*): A design for government that creates accountability and naturally reduces corruption by separating powers, creating competing interests that keep each other under control. In the United States, for example, the power to make laws is given to Congress (the Legislative Branch), but the President (the Executive Branch) can veto a proposed law. Also, the people can replace any elected representative if they do not like what is being done. So, Congress and the President exercise checks and balances on each other, and the people by way of their voting and lobbying power exercise another important check and balance. The fear of getting voted out also should give politicians incentive to behave. Furthermore, state and local governments exercise checks and balances on the power and actions of the federal government. In fact, there are many checks and balances that exist in the American system of government, and preserving or restoring these is important to protect self-government.

democracy (*n*.): Rule by the people. The United States' government is based upon a democratic model, but with the important difference that we affirm some rights as God-given (or "inalienable") and therefore not revocable by even a very large majority vote. For this reason, it is more accurate to describe the United States as a *constitutional republic*.

justice (*n*.): The equal application of just laws to all people. Neither rich nor poor are favored, nor does any other consideration interfere with the application of an even standard. Justice requires the righting of wrongs, with the one who did the wrong being punished and/or making restitution. Justice is rarely perfect in this world, but it can be found and ought to be pursued. Justice is always preceded by truth. Where truth has not prevailed, or where truth has been suppressed, there is no justice.

plenary (adj.): Total, absolute. (See Chapter 3)

progressivism (*n*.): The belief that people are basically good (i.e., not universally sinful), and that government is capable of solving most or all social problems. Progressivism tends toward growth of government and the centralization of power, with checks and balances removed or subverted and lawmaking powers often invested in unelected bureaucrats or committees. Those who recommend or favor the heavy hand of progressivism often do so with an implicit assertion that those in government are somehow more informed, enlightened, or moral than the rest of society. Progressives often excuse arbitrary suppression of individual rights by suggesting that doing so serves the "greater good." Early progressive presidents included Woodrow Wilson and Franklin D. Roosevelt. Roosevelt's forcible internment of American citizens of Japanese descent during World War II is an example of the progressive "greater good" belief system in action.

self governance (*n*.): A situation in which people rule themselves. In self-governing societies, the people's will is typically carried out by representatives who make and administer laws by temporarily exercising limited powers that have been delegated to them by the people. Checks and balances serve as a safeguard against abuse of power by elected representatives. Self governance is the opposite of autocracy, progressivism, or other authoritarian tyrannies. It does not exist without honest and transparent elections, or where laws are made by unelected bureaucrats.

truth (*n.*): What is.

PREFACE

We each have a limited time here and must choose how to make use of that time. In early 2021, I felt burdened to write a serious summary of the events that had recently occurred surrounding the U.S. presidential election. Competent in research but lacking advanced formal training in statistical analysis, constitutional law, or political science, I decided to write as a citizen investigator.

The world is at a crossroads, with the United States at the center.

I understood from the start that this book will face two possible outcomes. Either it will be ignored, or it will see severe scrutiny and withering criticism, both from those who read it but dislike its conclusions and from those who don't read it and do not care to be bothered by the material it presents. While I prefer not to be ignored, I also intend my work to stand up under scrutiny and be free from careless error. Aware of the need for checking by someone without strong American political preferences, I reached out to an overseas colleague who agreed to help me by reviewing my data and reasoning. I have also run this material by a number of others. That is to say, I've taken care to solicit both friendly and critical review.

I've included a lot of information in this book, intending it to be useful for both reading and reference. However, Chapter 3 is the fulcrum in its presentation of three essential facts. First, certain nonlegislative and therefore illegal purported changes to election rules selectively favoring Joe Biden occurred in the states of Georgia, Michigan, Wisconsin, and the

Commonwealth of Pennsylvania—among others. Second, we know the relative makeup of presidential votes among those ballots received outside the legal parameters.[1] Third, if we were to back out the relative numbers of votes for both candidates received outside the parameters designated by standing law from the tallies, the outcome goes to Donald Trump in all four instances. These facts give us everything needed to conclude beyond reasonable doubt, and even before a glance at other factors (such as fraud), that the 2020 election was in fact won by Donald Trump.[2]

The integrity of the 2020 election result therefore fails on account of purported nonlegislative changes to election rules that led to illegal votes being counted far in excess of the margin of alleged victory in each battle-ground state. This argument has nothing to do with fraud. So, please read and enjoy the content to follow, but do not let discussions about how much voter fraud took place, how much of it is provable beyond doubt, and so forth, cloud the picture. Election fraud and voter fraud are contemptible crimes that—given the huge opportunities afforded by drop boxes, mail-in voting, and the relaxation of signature verification—only a naïve individual could assume were not massive in 2020. Fraud compounds the conclusion and is incredibly important, but is secondary to my argument.

Accepting Elections: 2000, 2008, and 2016

Until recently, the American people maintained a tradition—after exhausting the orderly processes for recounts, runoffs, audits, and so forth —of accepting and honoring the results of even the most bitterly fought election. As the saying goes, we "live to fight another day," knowing that self governance requires the common consent of those governed to the rules of fair play. We choose order and fairness over the need to win every contest, calculating that the benefits of self governance outweigh the discomfort of occasional rule by those with whom we disagree.

Cracks began to form in this tradition following the contentious 2000 contest in which George W. Bush ultimately prevailed over Al Gore. That election came down to Florida, which Bush won by a margin of fewer than 600 votes. The mandatory statewide machine recount, required by Florida law, confirmed Bush's victory. The Florida Supreme Court ordered another recount, which was begun before being struck down by the U.S. Supreme Court in a 7-2 ruling.[3] The second majority found that the recount would have applied different standards to different election precincts, and thus would have violated the Constitution's requirement that laws must be applied evenly.

Jeb Bush, George W. Bush's brother, was Florida's governor. In fact, once the election was certified in Florida by Jeb's Secretary of State, Katherine Harris, there was no constitutional scenario under which Al Gore was going to be declared the winner. Even so, claims that the election was stolen were advanced and maintained.[4] Doubt had been sown, and a portion of Americans lost trust in the American election franchise.

The 2008 election of Barack Obama was decisive, but not pristine.[5] Except for voting by mail and drop boxes, many of the factors we will discuss concerning 2020 were present in various degrees in 2008, including control of news and information by gatekeepers, dishonesty in media, and such. Fraud, driven largely by the now-defunct "community organizing" group ACORN—an organization to which the Obama campaign had given $800,000[6]—was one of the major scandals that resulted in a number of people going to prison or admitting guilt.[7]

Illegal activities notwithstanding, it is not likely that the fraud accounted for the margin of Obama's significant 2008 victory. The biggest issue for Obama's ability to be president was whether he was a "natural born citizen" of the United States as the Constitution requires.[8] While any U.S. citizen may be elected to Congress or hold other high office, such is not the case for the U.S. presidency. Given reports by his family members —and by Obama himself—that he was born in Kenya, that his father was not a U.S. citizen at the time, and other factors, the concern was not contrived. Obama's own literary bio, used from 1991 to 2007, read, "Barack Obama, the first African-American president of the Harvard Law Review, was born in Kenya and raised in Indonesia and Hawaii. The son of an American anthropologist and a Kenyan finance minister..."[9] Although Panama-born John McCain was required in 2008 to submit his birth certificate and have his eligibility question adjudicated by the U.S. Senate, similar concerns about Obama were met with ridicule, stonewalling, and accusations of racism.[10] The Supreme Court declined to rule.[11]

Controversies about the 2000 and 2008 elections notwithstanding, the American tradition of accepting election results was completely cast aside by many on the American left after Donald Trump's 2016 victory over Hillary Clinton. Refusal to acknowledge Trump's legitimacy emerged immediately and with great fanfare amid multiple rallies in Washington, D.C., across the United States, and even around the world. These included the Women's March (January 21, 2017) and "Not My President's Day" (February 20, 2017).[12]

Popular support for rejecting Trump was garnered *via* allegations of "Russian collusion" and interference in the election on behalf of Trump by foreign powers. Such allegations were uncritically validated by most major pro-Clinton media outlets. During 2016, the Clinton campaign presented paid opposition research, (the "Steele dossier") to the U.S. Justice Department as though it were intelligence from a foreign source. The Obama Justice Department apparently never asked where the information had been obtained. This material of tainted provenance became the sole basis for a FISA[13] warrant of permission to spy on the Trump campaign. The fact that it was being taken seriously by the FBI was then "leaked" to media who reported these facts during the 2016 election in order to damage Trump politically.

The Russians'—and others'—likely possession of the contents of Hillary Clinton's illegal and unsecured private email server (the use of which certainly constituted a violation of the Espionage Act,[14] for which others would have been prosecuted[15]) was leveraged by Trump during a presidential debate with the former Secretary of State. At that time, in order to emphasize the point that Clinton had recklessly and illegally endangered U.S. national security during her tenure as Secretary of State, with rhetorical flair he invited Russia to share with the U.S. what Hillary Clinton and her lawyers had illegally hidden. Clinton's emails as Secretary of State were property of the United States, but she and her lawyers had destroyed them in 2014 and 2015.

The Clinton campaign, aided by major partisan news outlets, deflected the blow by accusing Trump of having publicly asked the Russians to hack Clinton's email server.[16] But they purposely missed Trump's point, since, by the time of the debate, Clinton's email server had already been wiped clean with BleachBit, destroyed by Clinton herself and at her own admission.[17] It was therefore no longer open to hacking. Trump had merely been calling America's attention to the fact that the Russians and every other foreign power engaged in intelligence gathering against the United States *already had* this information, and that such was only the case because Clinton in her recklessness had essentially delivered it to them on a silver platter.

Did Vladimir Putin prefer Trump over Clinton? As it happens, I was traveling in St. Petersburg, Russia, in 2016 and found that some shop-keepers and others on the street were quite enthusiastic about the prospect of a Trump victory. I did not initiate the conversations—they did so, naturally, after learning that I was an American. I recall one young man's eyes lighting up when asking me if I liked Trump. At the time, Trump was even featured on coffee mugs, sometimes with his face next to Putin's, at sidewalk kiosks. I bought one such mug as a souvenir before leaving St. Petersburg.

Such experiences are obviously anecdotal and cannot be taken as evidence that the Kremlin wished for Trump to prevail over Clinton. Yes, there is a cultural preference in Russia for the "strong man," but from a geopolitical and strategic standpoint, it seems at least plausible that a Clinton administration might have more solidly bolstered Russian interests and aspirations on the global stage. Some, of course, have asserted that others were more interested in sowing a general doubt among Americans, eroding the process and trustworthiness of U.S. presidential elections, resulting in chaos and infighting, rather than any particular electoral outcome in 2016. In my opinion, such a scenario might be closer to the truth. This point would be relevant once we fast-forward from 2016 to consider the 2020 election.

The 2016 election took many off guard. Trump's signature campaign promise had been to build a wall the length of the porous U.S. southern border as a means of ensuring prospective immigrants entered in an orderly and lawful fashion. In an electoral victory that shocked those in positions of bureaucratic security, many of whom seemed unaware how deeply Americans felt about the need for equality and fairness in immigration, Trump carried the 2016 election. Fury from the American and global left was immediate and did not abate during Trump's term as president. Formal campaigns to impeach President Trump (based initially upon the fraudulent and now infamous Steele dossier[18]) were launched January 20, 2017, the very day of Trump's inauguration.

"The Most Secure Election in American History"

The 2020 situation was different from all prior elections in some important respects. First, all kinds of people had been changing the election rules who had no business doing so. Second and largely as a result of the aforementioned rule changes, opportunity for manipulation and fraud was pushed to an unprecedented level in terms of coordination, scale, and deflection of scrutiny. Nearly 2/3 (64.1%) of all votes were cast early, and more than 2/5 (41.1%) of all votes were cast by mail[19]—both levels the highest in American history, and the latter dramatically so. Voting by mail is illegal in many countries and severely limited in many others because such a system is known to be one of the most vulnerable to fraud, as will be discussed in detail later in this book. Furthermore, and perhaps accordingly, voter turnout in 2020 was allegedly "the highest in 120 years when measured as a percentage of the voting-eligible population" (66.7%), some twenty million more votes were recorded (for a total of 159,633,396) than any prior election in American history, and the lackluster Joe Biden was the first presidential candidate ever to have more than 80 million votes counted to his credit.[20]

Following the 2020 presidential election, Democrat partisans seemed to find themselves at a loss to refute claims that Trump had won.[21] Rather, they resorted to ridicule, labeling this assertion the "Big Lie," and attacking the character or intelligence of anyone who dared question the official result. Their predicament seemed an outworking of poetic justice, in that it was truly a conundrum of Democrats' own making, for they had been the ones hiding or destroying paper trails and other evidence. It was Democrats, not their opponents, who went back on their promise to comply with the Supreme Court's order to segregate absentee ballots received past the legal deadline of 8:00 p.m. on Election Day in Pennsylvania.[22] It was Democrats, not their opponents, who refused to allow poll watchers to observe the counting before later claiming such blocking was an "honest mistake."[23] It was Democrats, not their opponents, who insisted upon pushing through administrative changes to election rules in swing states (the subject of Chapter 3), removing so many important safeguards against fraud during the months leading up to the election.

Indeed, at every turn, it was Democrats who removed clarity, security, and certainty from the 2020 election process. Those who claim victory in such a fashion may express anger or frustration at subsequent doubts about the election, but they ought not complain. If they had wished for the public to accept the results, they might have allowed the public to see that the process was not corrupted, and they might have made an effort to avoid acting guilty.

During the 2020 general election, the rule of law was set aside as millions of Americans in swing states cast votes at times and in manners not authorized by law. Many did so following the misleading directions of their state authorities, but the point remains that no one has a right to cast a vote outside the legal parameters. If an election is held on Tuesday, with the law stating that ballots must be received by close of polls, and a registered voter shows up to vote on Wednesday, she should find the polls closed. Despite being a legal voter, she has no right to make her vote count outside the times set by her state legislature.

Yet in 2020, election laws were bent and revised with neither the consent nor the involvement of the governed *via* their state legislatures, despite the fact that the United States Constitution places the sole power for determining the time and manner of elections in the hands of those governing bodies. Ballots received after legal deadlines were counted. Mail-in ballots from people not legally eligible to vote by mail were counted. Ballots delivered in envelopes whose signatures did not match that of the registered voter were counted. And so forth. These matters will all be discussed in the coming pages.

When any person—whether citizen or noncitizen, registered or unregistered, resident or nonresident—casts a vote in an illegal manner, that vote is *illegal* and must not be counted. The conduct of the 2020 election was therefore a usurpation of the people's sovereignty and the outcome of that election was the installation of a usurper[24]—Joe Biden—in the White House.

Concerning Ad Hominem Attacks

Mocking and ridicule are not an answer to serious questions, particularly those of such weight to our system of self governance as the honesty and integrity of our elections. However, in the months following November 2020, Americans watched intelligent and accomplished individuals, some of them recognized experts in their fields, being "canceled" by a mob for suggesting unapproved views or lines of inquiry. Such has happened even to some raising the most basic and reasonable of questions about the election's conduct and outcome. Today, "troublesome" people are too often dismissed out of hand or attacked personally. What's worse, they frequently face professional consequences and, adding insult to injury, even their integrity and intelligence are assaulted. Character assassination awaits the enemies of The Narrative.

It is true that some people are careless with data. But, this phenomenon is not tied to a particular political ideology. The major difference today is the growth in the number of people no longer interested in seeing any evidence at all. What matters to such people is only whether you agree with their preference, and, if not, then you are (in their view) wrong or even dangerous. The humble and open mind—that is to say, the scientific mind —is no longer welcomed or valued.

Laughing hyenas are everywhere. It has been my experience in other spheres of life that *ad hominem* attacks (an attack upon a person's character) is often a sign that the attacker is in a weak position. Generally speaking, the more vicious and visceral the ad hominem attack, the more vulnerable the attacker.

Means, Motive, and Opportunity

American government rests upon a demand that the American people must "trust the system." However, the system is not *owed* trust, and so many people have been told that it is. It only should be trusted if it actually is trustworthy. Everyone wants an honest election, citizens are told. Voter fraud is a myth, citizens are told. Voting machines are secure, citizens are told. There is a chain of custody from the casting of ballots to the certification of the election results, citizens are told.

And yet, noncitizens who live in the United States by the tens of millions are regularly—and in some parts of the country, systematically— registered to vote.[25] Many noncitizens and other ineligible individuals *do* vote, despite it being a felony to do so,[26] even if the precise number is disputed.[27] Furthermore, voter fraud and election fraud exist beyond noncitizen voting. Because of the enormous amount of money and power at stake in connection with political office and political influence, there are many entities, often well-funded and well-positioned, who also have ample motive to commit voter fraud or election fraud. Those with motive to commit fraud include political parties, candidates, corrupt businesses, political organizations, unions, and even some individual voters.

Furthermore, new technologies have brought with them new opportunities for exploitation by people with bad intentions. Data breaches and computer hacks are so common that there are entire multi-billion dollar industries dedicated to combatting such actions. And, because the efforts to stop these activities before they occur are not ironclad, there are other industries dedicated to addressing the aftermath of hacks and compromised data. Companies devote enormous sums to information technology staff to maintain data security in a constantly changing and hostile environment. Given such realities, it stands to reason that national elections in the leading nation of the free world—with all the power and money at stake, and with so many who dream of subduing or subverting her—would similarly be serious targets for attack and manipulation by nefarious actors from within and from without. When the opportunity exists, and especially when potential benefits outweigh the risk or cost of being caught, some portion of those who believe the end justifies the means will commit fraud.

Serious questions have been raised regarding the conduct and outcome of the 2020 election that now demand truthful and complete answers, particularly in light of the perfect storm of means/motive/opportunity that was created and fed in 2020:

Likely more than 35 million noncitizens lived in the United States, making up fully 10% of the population at the time of the 2020 election. Not a single one of those individuals is eligible to vote in a U.S. national election. Were ineligible people permitted to vote in 2020? Did they do so? If so, how many?

Did electronic voting machines report all votes as they were actually cast? Are reports and alleged statistical evidence of formulaic skewing of the data baseless, and if so, what is the evidence supporting that conclusion?

Electronic chain-of-custody: Was vote data transmitted over the internet on election night at some point prior to election certification? If so, why? How may the American people be assured that this data was not manipulated?

Physical chain-of-custody: How many opportunities existed in key states to exploit vulnerabilities in the chain-of-custody of physical ballots, thumb drives, or voting equipment? How many of these opportunities resulted from illegal changes to election laws made by entities other than the state legislatures?

Interference in the vote count: How many ballots were scanned multiple times in key states? How many fake ballots—such as mail-in ballots lacking the creases that would exist on any ballot mailed in the required ballot envelope—were counted?

Why This Discussion Really Matters

Using Nazi Germany and Stalinist Russia as her primary subjects, in her book *The Origins of Totalitarianism,* Hannah Arendt lays out in concrete and practical terms how totalitarian movements take hold over societies.[28] Her analysis is from a secular perspective, lacking recognition of that essential cornerstone of American liberty and justice for all—the assertion that some rights are inherent and inalienable because they come from God, rather than from human government. Nevertheless, her observations about the way totalitarianism advances are rooted in personal experience.

Although the names have changed when we turn our attention to the recent developments in the United States, particularly surrounding the 2020 election, many of the parallels between our current state and the conditions that immediately preceded both of the above totalitarian takeovers cited by Arendt should set off alarms:

> The elevation (or perhaps, re-elevation) of race as a sorting and dividing principle[29]

> Open disregard for law and legal institutions and the ideological justification of lawlessness[30]

> A "vague, pervasive hatred of everybody and everything"[31]

> The decline of the nation-state and the end of the Rights of Man,[32] which are replaced with the will of the mob, and affirmation of individual rights supplanted by vague assertions of the "collective" good[33]

> No real way to hold government accountable or undo unlawful acts: "Nothing which was being done, no matter how stupid, no matter how many people knew and foretold the consequences, could be undone or prevented."[34]

> A loss of rights and government protection for certain categories of people[35]

The points listed above are not an exhaustive summary of Arendt's analysis. But, at a time when the American left and the institutions under their influence are successfully "canceling" dissenters on a large scale, dividing people by race and other traits rather than uniting them as Americans, flouting laws with no one—not even the highest Court of the land—to stop them, removing rights even to bodily autonomy, and claiming that even the most obvious physical or scientific realities do not reflect anything objectively true, they ought to be enough. With every limiting principle having been suspended or removed, we now teeter on a dangerous precipice. And, if the United States—whose Constitution[36] was the first, and remains the clearest, political affirmation of self governance stemming from certain God-given individual rights—falters, we will pull much or all of the rest of the world with us.

What Can Be Done?

This book is longer than I originally intended, and even now there is a great deal of information that has not been included. The first step toward addressing a problem is to understand it. But, I felt it necessary and helpful to write at least what you find in the following pages as a presentation of the situation and problems resulting therefrom. Only after doing that do I offer a multi-point list of suggestions (Chapter 14, "What Now?").

With a likely pretender having been inaugurated and installed in the White House, we are now in uncharted waters with (I am told) no remaining non-extreme[37] constitutional remedy aside from the political process of impeachment or waiting until the next election. One thing that can and must be done, and which bears mention up front, is the appointment of a special counsel to investigate the Biden family dealings, for which Mark Levin issued a call on Sunday, April 3, 2022.[38]

Ultimately, the problem is far more grave than the matter of a single election. What can be done when there is no longer any check on lawlessness, when there is no longer a mechanism for correcting the usurpation of the people's power to protect their elections from fraud and manipulation?

As we seek to remedy existential threats to liberty, we should consider unintended consequences. We *must* set ourselves to restoring checks and balances, limiting the powers of our representatives and other government institutions to their constitutional confines. How such a task can be accomplished given the present situation should be a topic of intense national soul-seeking and action. I have openly supported a constitutional solution in the form of an Article V convention of states,[39] and I do believe that it is one of the few orderly avenues left open to us. Given recent events, however, I do now wonder if we even have time to go down that road.

Let us not forget, these are moral questions. The law of the jungle— that is, "might makes right"—will ultimately prevail when any people reject God. There is no doubt in my mind that (despite our many flaws) it was willingness to acknowledge God, to seek to humble ourselves, and to conform this nation to His laws and justice as understood from the Bible, that led to the many blessings of this place that even Americans who do not acknowledge Him enjoy today.

The story is told by Aesop of a countryman who owned a goose that laid a golden egg once every day. This countryman began to grow rich off these eggs but, becoming greedy and impatient, killed the goose in order to get all the eggs at once. Of course, he found that not only were there no remaining eggs to be had once he cut the goose open, but the goose was dead. Applying the analogy, I believe it appropriate to consider the United States as the goose, and all her people, including those who in future hope to benefit from her blessings—our children and grandchildren and future immigrants—as the countryman. The caretakers ought to reflect before killing the goose.

Courage, Not Surrender

Open-minded readers who value honest elections will find many details in the coming pages disturbing and disheartening. But the spirit of the American people is strong, and I yet believe we have a sense of justice and a zeal for the restoration of self governance. We can repair what is broken, but it will not be easy. If we do nothing, then this nation may be lost—overtaken by a mob led by the same petty tyrants who today rule us as busybodies, transforming the nation, its institutions, and our children before our eyes.

I've not written much original in the following pages. The main argument and focal point of the book was clearly stated in the Texas lawsuit of December, 2020 discussed in detail in Chapter 3, and it has been developed and restated by others since. My task here, therefore, is not to claim credit for original thought but to give a clear and careful summary to a world in which many people remain confused about the facts, battered by misinformation and even by stonewalling from the guilty parties and their allies.

This book is personal to me. I love America. I love the promise that her liberty was intended to hold for everyone—a great promise only attainable so long as government is limited and the people rule rather than being ruled. I was indignant to see that promise slipping away from *all* Americans throughout 2020. Our system of checks and balances was designed to thwart the schemes of abusers and cheaters. Yet at the end of 2020, door after door for rectification or redress slammed shut. Since most Americans have a strong sense of justice, I know I'm far from alone in this sentiment.

For more than a year and a half after that tumultuous time, I refrained from publicly making anything close to the claim that "Trump won," even though I sensed that it was true. Rather, I put my nose into books and data, and started writing. I hope that readers will recognize the care I took, and similarly give its measured conclusions the attention I believe they deserve.

Although readers will discern my views of people and events, this book is not about whether Donald Trump is a good person or a bad person, nor is it about whether Joe Biden is a good person or a bad person. This book is about whether the sovereignty of the American people was infringed in the 2020 election. I believe that it was.

Although I have a PhD in another specialized but mostly unrelated subject, as mentioned already I write here as a citizen investigator. The principles of research, sound reasoning and the scientific method are universal and apply across subjects. My conclusions come from research, from experience as an engaged American (including as an election worker), from contacts and discussions with people from a range of backgrounds and beliefs (some of them with a great deal of expertise in the matters being discussed and some of them actually quite close to the events being described), and from my own critical thinking and analysis of the data.

Some might certainly dismiss this book simply because they do not like its insinuations or its conclusions. Nothing will change the situation for such individuals, and frankly, I have not written for unthoughtful people hardened in their prejudices. This is not to say that anyone who challenges the facts or conclusions in these pages is necessarily unthoughtful, but there is a large difference between those who read and consider with humility and those who simply have no interest in even hearing a viewpoint that may challenge their beliefs or assumptions. As Thomas Paine wrote, "To argue with a man who has renounced the use and authority of reason, and whose philosophy consists in holding humanity in contempt, is like administering medicine to the dead."[40]

I expect the assertion that the 2020 election process was illegally altered to render victory for Joe Biden to be one day generally acknowledged. However, this book was written during a period when expressing doubt about the certainty of his victory was cause for serious reprisal including exclusion from polite society, professional harm, job loss—even violence. While I enjoy being liked, I have always been more interested in truth than the approval of polite society. As to the other factors, I'd rather stand for what's right than let injustice reign under threats from bullies.

Fixing what is broken first requires calling things by their names. I've been direct in the following pages because I believe we don't have time for playing around the edges. However, this book is not meant to be a compilation of so-called "red meat" for conservatives. Readers desiring uncritical validation of every claim supporting one side will not find such in the following pages. Neither is this book—I earnestly hope—a piece of sophistry, forcing the facts toward a desired conclusion. Readers will discover that where there is doubt or uncertainty, I have noted as much.

I present, in other words, a curated assessment. These are not (I believe) sour grapes or the rantings of a sore loser, but an effort to help people understand and set right something that has gone very wrong.

Please note that, despite much care and concentrated effort in its preparation, I remain painfully aware that this book is not complete. In particular, there is some repetition of topics, parts needing further refinement, topics needing more development and people and topics unmentioned despite deserving to be included. But for the urgency of the topic, I would have addressed these all, and I ask your patience with these shortcomings. I sincerely hope this work will yet be of some benefit to you and others, that time will show its merits to outweigh its flaws, and that all doubtful claims were appropriately tempered and qualified.

There are pivot-points in history at which ordinary men and women must rise to meet challenges they did not choose and remedy wrongs they did not invite. Today, people of goodwill must stand up in love of neighbor. It is in such a spirit that I offer this book, intended as a meaningful service.

DB, Lovettsville, April 2022

N.B. — The single most common complaint from my advance readers was the fact that I have employed endnotes instead of footnotes. Like myself, they wanted to see comments and references without having to constantly flip pages. Unfortunately, this book is typeset using a software called Vellum which, despite my many pleas, still has no capability for footnotes. So, I apologize for the trouble and do hope that you will still check the endnotes, as there is substantive material contained within them. Should Vellum make this vital improvement in the future, I expect to quickly reformat this book and issue a second edition.

---

1. Many states altered their election laws prior to November 3, 2020. Alterations made by the state legislative process are legitimate. The focus upon extra-legislative changes in the four states mentioned here follows the argument of the Texas lawsuit discussed in Chapter 3, but is not meant to suggest that these four states were the only ones where the plenary power of the legislatures was usurped.
2. By "won," I here mean the candidate chosen by the voters who cast ballots within legal parameters. Biden, it is true, "won" by clearing the necessary procedural hurdles to be inaugurated. If that is all that matters, Americans should brace for a repeat in every future election.
3. Michael Levy, "United States presidential election of 2000." *Britannica*.
4. Aaron Bandler, "5 Things You Should Know About How Al Gore Lost The 2000 Election," *Daily Wire*, October 21, 2016; Mark R. Levin, "The Rule of Law," *National Review*, November 13, 2000. Levin has explained on his national radio show that there is no scenario under which Gore was going to be declared the winner of the 2000 election. When doing so, he emphasizes that the U.S. Supreme Court did not need to get involved; Congress could have resolved the matter. In that case, George W. Bush would unquestionably have still emerged as the legitimate winner because the majority of the state delegations were Republican. The only twist from how events in fact played out would have been the probability that Joe Lieberman (Gore's running mate) would have become vice president to Bush, because the vice president's office would have been adjudicated in the Senate, where there was a 50/50 split and Al Gore—the sitting Vice President—would have cast the tie-breaking vote in favor of Lieberman as vice-president.
5. Andrew Gelman, "Election 2008: what really happened," *Statistical Modeling, Causal Interference, and Social Science* (Columbia University), November 5, 2008.
6. "Obama's ACORN Connection To Voter Fraud," *CBS News*, October 14, 2008.
7. "18 Former ACORN Workers Have Been Convicted or Admitted Guilt in Election Fraud," *Fox News*, December 23, 2015; John Fund, "More Acorn Voter Fraud Comes to Light," *Wall Street Journal*, May 9, 2009.

8. The question of Barack Obama's birthplace was raised by some who—probably wrongly—interpreted the term "natural born citizen" to mean simply "one born on U.S. soil." In 2016, similar questions were raised about Senator Ted Cruz during his presidential campaign. Although much has been made of Obama's actual birthplace, the true constitutional eligibility issue related to the office of president is probably whether his parents were U.S. citizens when he was born. Even a person born *on* U.S. soil to one or more noncitizen parents may not be a "natural born" citizen, despite being an actual citizen under current laws. In May of 2013, I raised the matter to David Sawyer, Southeast Texas Regional Director of the Cruz campaign, when I met with him for lunch in Houston. He answered that the campaign believed Sen. Cruz would be eligible to the office of president if he ever chose to pursue it. Allegations that Barack Obama was born outside the United States were first advanced against him by Hillary Clinton in the 2008 Democratic primaries, a fact of which Donald Trump reminded audiences when campaigning against Clinton.

The precise meaning of term "natural born citizen" in the Constitution is best discerned from discussion at and following the time of its writing, but it has never been tested by the Supreme Court. The question probably does not turn upon place of birth, but rather citizenship of the parents at the time of birth. As an historical and political precedent, the First Congress passed a measure in 1790 that defined children of U.S. citizens 'born beyond the sea, or out of the limits of the United States' to be natural born.

9. Joseph Farah, "Who was the first 'birther,'" *WND*, August 3, 2022,

10. Long after assuming the presidency, Barack Obama did produce a digital image of a Hawaiian long form birth certificate. Forensics experts alleged that the image presented was a digital forgery, a composite. By that time, however, it did not not much matter: the waters had been so muddied by rhetoric and doubt that it was hard for most Americans to know whom to believe. People took sides largely based upon political preference. Jerome Corsi, PhD, wrote the main books discussing the evidence. During his 2012 run for president, Donald Trump himself was famously skeptical and a vocal supporter of what was labeled by its critics as the "birther" movement. Jerome R. Corsi, *Where's the Birth Certificate? The Case That Barack Obama Is Not Eligible To Be President* (New York: WND Books, 2011); Jerome R. Corsi, *The Obama Nation* (New York: Threshold Editions, 2008), xxiv.

11. Tim Jones, "Court won't review Obama's eligibility to serve," *Chicago Tribune*, December 8, 2008.

12. "The Women's March, 2017," *Smithsonian National Museum of American History*; Trymaine Lee, Andrew Rafferty, and Corky Siemaszko, "America Gives Trump an Earful at 'Not My President's Day' Rallies," *NBC News*, February 20, 2017.

13. FISA = Foreign Intelligence Surveillance Act. Generally speaking, this law allows surveillance under some circumstances (e.g. when espionage or terrorism is suspected) between foreign actors or where a foreign actor is one of the parties. The Fourth Amendment to the U.S. Constitution generally protects United States citizens from surveillance unless a court issues a warrant. The secret FISA court exists to allow very sensitive matters to be investigated without tipping off the subjects who may already be monitoring ordinary channels.

14. 18 U.S. Code 37 § 793 (f): "Whoever, being entrusted with or having lawful possession or control of any document, writing, code book, signal book, sketch, photograph, photographic negative, blueprint, plan, map, model, instrument, appliance, note, or information, relating to the national defense, (1) through gross negligence permits the same to be removed from its proper place of custody or delivered to anyone in violation of his trust, or to be lost, stolen, abstracted, or destroyed, or (2) having knowledge that the same has been illegally removed from its proper place of custody or delivered to anyone in violation of its trust, or lost, or stolen, abstracted, or destroyed, and fails to make prompt report of such loss, theft, abstraction, or destruction to his superior officer—shall be fined under this title or imprisoned not more than ten years, or both." I thank Mark Levin for his on-air legal discussion on this section of the U.S. Code while the Clinton email server matter was happening, and also to several friends with security clearances—unnamed here—who assured me that they or anyone else would have gone to jail for committing a fraction of what Clinton did.

15. The decision not to prosecute Hillary Clinton followed a June 27, 2016 meeting on the tarmac of the Sky Harbor International Airport, Phoenix, between then Attorney General Loretta Lynch and Clinton's husband, former President Bill Clinton. Interestingly, at the time of that meeting, my wife and I were steps away visiting a clinic over which she had

some administrative authority just outside the chain link fence at the edge of the tarmac. We were shocked to hear news of the event being reported later that day. *Judicial Watch*, "FBI Finds."

16. Tessa Berenson, "Donald Trump Calls on Russia to Hack Hillary Clinton's Emails," *TIME*, July 27, 2016; Michael Crowley, and Tyler Pager, "Trump Urges Russia to hack Clinton's email," *Politico*, July 27, 2016.

17. "BleachBit 'stifles investigation' of Hillary Clinton," *BleachBit.org*, August 25, 2016.

18. The Steele Dossier is the collection of opposition research commissioned by the Hillary Clinton campaign that was presented to the FBI and to the American people as though it had come from a neutral intelligence source.

19. James M. Lindsay, "The 2020 Election by the Numbers," *Council on Foreign Relations*, December 15, 2020.

20. Ibid.

21. Tovia Smith, "They believe in Trump's 'Big Lie.' Here's why it's been so hard to dispel," *NPR*, January 5, 2022. "Countless recounts, courts, commissions, and private contractors — including Republicans — have all dismissed former President Donald Trump's claims that the election was stolen. But a new NPR/Ipsos poll shows that two-thirds of Republican voters and just over one-third of all voters still believe it."

22. Alex Swoyer, "Supreme Court orders Pennsylvania to segregate late ballots," *Washington Times*, November 6, 2020.

23. Jordan Lancaster, "Philadelphia City Commissioners Say They Are Investigating After Video Allegedly Shows GOP Poll Watcher Getting Kicked Out Of Polling Place," *Daily Caller*, November 3, 2020; "Fact Check: Clarifying video of poll watcher being turned away in Philadelphia," *Reuters*, November 3, 2020.

24. By using this term, I do not mean to suggest that Joe Biden single-handedly seized the presidency nor that he was the one who consciously orchestrated the events which resulted in his accession to the office. In coming pages, it will be understood that the operation was large and involved breakdowns at many levels and the active participation of many individuals.

25. "Noncitizens, Voting Violations and U.S. Elections," *Federation for American Immigration Reform*, July 2020.

26. Ibid.; Jesse T. Richman, Gulshan A. Chattha, and David C. Earnest, "Do non-citizens vote in U.S. elections?," *Electoral Studies* 36 (2014): 149-157.

27. Chelsey Cox, "Fact check: Claim that voting noncitizens affected 2020 election outcome is unverified," *USA Today*, November 19, 2020.

28. Hannah Arendt, *The Origins of Totalitarianism* (New York: Harcourt, Inc., 1976).

29. Ibid, 185-221.

30. Ibid, 243.

31. Ibid, 268.

32. Ibid, 267-302. By "rights of man," Arendt did not mean rights that were God-given—see pages 290-291—but rather that there exist among civilized peoples certain rights that ought to be beyond the reach of popular opinion, including such things as the opportunity to work and the right to hold property (268). The particular problem of stateless persons that existed in post-World War I Europe at this point looms large in Arendt's writing, and ultimately reveals the problem of tying the Rights of Man to the existence of nation-states. Jews, she notes, were *minorité par excellence*. The Nurenberg Laws had created a distinction between full citizens and nationals, paving the way for "all nationals of 'alien blood'" to "lose their nationality by official decree." This distinction set a course that eventually led to the extermination camps. What begins in laws that are not equal for all, says Arendt, ends with the deprivation of legal status for all citizens and rule by an omnipotent police (288-291). I will not here discuss Arendt's philosophy of rights and their origin; the point here is merely to note her list of signs that a society is descending into totalitarianism.

33. Ibid, 299. For example, in the words of Hitler, "right is what is good for the German people." Arendt observes, "this predicament is by no means solved if the unit to which the 'good for' applies is as large as mankind itself. For it is quite possible … that one fine day a highly organized and mechanized humanity will conclude quite democratically—namely by majority decision—that for humanity as a whole it would be better to liquidate certain parts thereof."

34. Ibid, 267. In this case, Arendt cites the instability and suffering caused by massive inflation as creating the pre-conditions for such overreach.

35. Ibid, 294-296. A "condition of complete rightlessness was created" (i.e., by the creation of second-class citizenship) "before the right to live was challenged" (i.e., *via* the deportation and execution in concentration camps).

36. The U.S. Constitution is rooted, to be clear, in the Hebrew Bible's and New Testament's assertions about the nature of God and the nature of man—such as the universality of human sinfulness, and the blessings that follow when a people live according to the moral code delineated by the Ten Commandments (Exodus 20:1-17) and its derivative laws, as well as the particular blessings that come when some or all people aspire to fulfill the first and second greatest commandments (Matthew 22:36-40)—which assertions are not entirely consistent with the lessons of history.

37. At the base of our system of government lies the assertion that a people have the right to dissolve the political bands which have connected them with another. However, it was also understood by the founders that such a course should not be undertaken for light and transitory reasons; evils should rather be borne so long as they are bearable. There may come a day for dissolution of this nation, but I believe that the American people should first show patience and diligence, making every effort to restore and fortify their system of self governance.

38. Randy DeSoto, "Levin Calls for Special Counsel to Investigate 'Corrupt' Biden Family, Says AG Garland Cannot Be Trusted," *Western Journal*, April 6, 2022.

39. There are two constitutional ways to amend the U.S. Constitution. The first is *via* amendments proposed through Congress and ratified by the states, and the second is through a "convention of states" by which the people propose amendments. In both cases, after proposal, three-quarters of the states (that is, 38 states) are required to ratify any given amendment before it will become part of the Constitution. In spite of the fact that the second avenue for amendment has never yet been employed, it must be emphasized that both means for amendment are equally "constitutional" and lawful. The reason for the existence of the latter means of amendment was the recognition by the founders that Congress would not propose amendments limiting its own power, and the people and the states thus needed some way to do so apart from the initiative of Congress.

40. Thomas Paine, *Common Sense, Together with The American Crisis* (Norwalk: Easton Press, 1994), 123.

ACKNOWLEDGMENTS

I owe thanks to a number of people for their assistance.

The following kindly answered my inquiries, corresponded or spoke with me, some at length. Several were good enough to share with me additional sources and information: Daryl Brooks, Gary Clemens, Margot Cleveland, Lt. Col. Jay N. DeLancy, John Droz, Garland Favorito, Sebastian Gorka, Geary Higgins, John Lott, Col. John Mills, Shelley Oberlander, Joshua Pratt, Ivan Raiklin, Lt. Col. Tony Shaffer, and Kelli Ward.

Professional editing was provided by Leah Garber and Emma Armbrust. The index was professionally prepared by Vickie Jacobs. I am also grateful to friends and colleagues who read the book prior to publication and offered helpful corrections and suggestions: Avigail Brubaker, Rivka Brubaker, Will Estrada, Jon Garber, Dave Garver, Steve Heyl, Robert W. Kerr, John Langlois, Stephen McRoberts, Todd Miller, Chris Rogan, Elizabeth Smith, E.W. Jackson, Ivan Raiklin, and Ibn Warraq.

I've found few commentators as clear, informed, and insightful as former Chief of Staff to the U.S. Attorney General and current author and radio host, Mark Levin.[1] My real-time understanding of events was sharpened by attention to his discussions, both in ways that can be—and therefore are—properly referenced, and also in broad themes and emphases; thus my additional general acknowledgment here. I had the unexpected pleasure of speaking briefly with Mark on September 17, 2021, while working on this book at a local McDonald's where I occasionally go to write. I told him of it and showed him a draft of its cover.

Some individuals spoke with me in confidence. They know who they are, and I thank them. Since I feel strongly about giving appropriate credit, if and when the climate around the topic of this book becomes less volatile, and if any of these people so wish at a later date, I shall be happy to acknowledge them by name.

It is a plain fact that I would not have been able to write this book—at which I have now labored for more than a year—but for the support of my family (particularly my wife, Latha) and my subscribers and followers on the Quran manuscript topic and at my YouTube channel *Variant Quran*, who patiently endured a delay in new material as I worked on this book. This project is a departure from my main professional topic, but in life we need to sometimes raise our eyes to the horizon and change course for a season before returning to the "day job." I therefore thank these various partners for their patience and flexibility, their trust, and their words of encouragement along the way.

My gratitude to the foregoing having been duly expressed, any flaws or shortcomings in this book remain my own. And finally, the views and opinions expressed in the following pages are not necessarily those of any of the people who kindly offered me assistance.

---

1. As of the time of this writing, Levin's recently-published book, *American Marxism*, has already been through seventeen printings, selling over a million copies in a short span of time, and has not only made the top of the New York Times bestseller list, but is the top book of 2021 and the #1 book across all platforms. His prior books have been similarly successful and influential. Paul Bedard, "Mark Levin smashes 1M sold for *American Marxism*, top 2021 book," *Washington Examiner*, September 23, 2021.

DISCLOSURE

Having opinions does not mean that one cannot come to sound and well-supported conclusions. It does mean that the author should take extra care to ensure that his judgment has not been clouded.

This book is published in the full light of day. It is not underhanded, but rather my best effort to present facts and my analysis, fully footnoted and sourced, left open for you the reader to consider.

I was never a starry-eyed cheerleader for Donald Trump. By saying this I do not mean to cast aspersions on those who were, because they turned out to be mostly right. But I came with a critical eye and was initially concerned. In fact, I resigned from the board of an organization over its early support of Trump in the 2016 primaries. But—and this distinction is important—I was not a "never Trumper."[1] I am an American who wants what is best for this country, and at the time I felt my legitimate questions and concerns had not yet been answered.

Like many Americans, I became a strong supporter of Donald Trump gradually. Prior to his nomination, I had written articles and social media posts that were thoughtfully critical, including an opinion piece touching upon his profession of Christian faith in light of some of his then-recent actions and words.[2] Also, I had raised a concern that he was (as nearly as I could see) unproven in his support for the good policy principles that he was then publicly embracing. Mr. Trump had to my knowledge given support—over the course of many years as a businessman—to some Democrat candidates and elected politicians, people who openly opposed many of the principles he was espousing. For me such facts were red flags, and the questions, "Donald Trump: Authentic? Trustworthy?" seemed reasonable in 2015.

My earlier doubts, however, were quickly allayed once he took office. Few times in my life was I happier to have been wrong. President Donald J. Trump, for whom I cautiously voted in 2016, proved true to his good campaign promises and thus received my enthusiastic support in 2020.

I have not ever spoken to Donald Trump nor (to my knowledge) any of his family members. I do hope one day to do so.

The above having been stated, please remember that the deepest issues being raised and discussed in this book are not ultimately about Donald Trump or Joe Biden. They are far more important than any single election or any particular candidate. Politicians come and go. But, once a precedent has been set that allows cultural and governmental elites to get away with using emergencies as an excuse to break the law—tipping elections in favor of their preferred outcome—we may as well do away with elections altogether. So, regardless of one's feelings about any of the 2020 candidates, Americans must weigh the future consequences of failing to mend the major breach that was opened and exploited in 2020.

---

1. "Never Trumper" was a label describing a person who was committed to opposing Donald Trump no matter how well he performed as president.
2. Any candidate's real faith is relevant, as it will indicate the ideas and principles that guide him or her. It is wise to seek signs of moral character and integrity—that is, of grounding in good principles beyond self—in candidates. However, the biblical qualifications for pastor or elder of a church are higher and/or different from those for president or other high office. Indeed, many people fully qualified to be a pastor would make terrible presidents, and vice versa.

INTRODUCTION

On May 28, 2021, Republicans in the United States Congress successfully blocked a Congressional inquiry into the January 6 Capitol riot, and were promptly and loudly accused of attempting to hide the truth of what happened.

The irony of the moment was rich: America had just witnessed more than a year of stonewalling by most of the major institutions of American society (see Chapter 2)—including the dominant social media platforms Twitter and Facebook and the world's largest internet search engine, Google—of key reporting and information that was extremely relevant to the national election but harmful to candidates Joe Biden and Kamala Harris. Yet now the *victims* of the stonewalling—Republican members of Congress and their constituents—were being blamed for wanting to hide "the truth."

Prominent among the many well-documented stories that the afore-mentioned alliance of gatekeepers had vigorously suppressed for months was an eminently newsworthy account: Joe Biden's son, Hunter, had allegedly influence peddled to the Ukrainian energy company Burisma Holdings. This news had come to light *via* the contents of a laptop that Hunter had failed to retrieve from a computer repair shop. The story was thoroughly reported in the bombshell October 14, 2020 *New York Post* article detailing how an email stored on this laptop revealed that Hunter had introduced a top adviser at the Ukrainian firm—which by that time had been paying Hunter up to $50,000 a month for about a year to sit on their board, despite the fact that Hunter had no special qualifications for the job apart from being the son of a sitting U.S. Vice President—to his father, then-Vice President Joe Biden.[1]

The meeting between Burisma's Vadym Pozharskyi and Vice President Biden apparently occurred in Washington, DC in April of 2015. Less than one year afterward, Vice President Biden directly threatened government officials in Ukraine that he would withhold U.S. aid funding to their country if they did not fire anti-corruption prosecutor Viktor Shokin, who was at the time investigating Burisma.[2]

Furthermore, as the Post was already reporting in October of 2020, Joe Biden himself was not only apparently in on the deal—Hunter's May 13, 2017 email noted that 10% was reserved for "the big guy." Former partner Tony Bobulinski, one of the email's original recipients, confirmed by late October of 2020 that Joe Biden was indeed "the big guy." Joe Biden himself claimed that he had "never spoken to my son about his overseas business dealings," a statement almost certainly shown false by the laptop emails as well as other details about the elder Biden's travels with Hunter.[3] The White House, still under criticism over it in 2021, continued to assert that Joe Biden had not lied.[4] In February of 2022, Devon Archer—who served with Hunter on the board of Burisma—was sentenced to prison for fraudulent issuance and sale of tribal bonds.[5] Hunter was unconnected to the matter for which Archer was convicted, but the situation reminded the public of the unresolved issues with Burisma.

A surfaced 2018 voicemail from Joe Biden to Hunter, discovered on a cellphone backup preserved on the laptop, was publicized in late June of 2022. In the voicemail, Joe Biden says, "Hey pal, it's Dad. It's 8:15 on Wednesday night. If you get a chance, just give me a call; nothing urgent. I just wanted to talk to you. I thought the article released, it's been online, it's going to be printed tomorrow in the Times, was good. I think you're clear. And, anyway, um, if you get a chance, give me a call."[6] The former vice president was referencing a December 2018 New York Times article on Hunter's May 2017 private meeting at a Miami hotel with an emissary of Chinese energy tycoon Ye Jianming.[7]

News of the voicemail spurred renewed calls for a special counsel into the Biden family dealings.[8] As they had done with the laptop in 2020, pro-Democrat media outlets ABC, NBC, CBS, CNN, MSNBC, the New York Times, and the Washington Post all declined to cover the story.[9]

The Washington Times in September 2020 reported the Ukraine/Biden situation thus:

> In April 2014, President Obama made Mr. Biden the point man in Ukraine, after the Russian invasion, to persuade leaders to rid the country of rampant corruption.
>
> The next month, Hunter Biden showed up on the board of directors of the energy company Burisma Holdings, which the State Department

considers corrupt, as it does its oligarch owner, Mykola Zlochevsky. Hunter Biden's business partner, Devon Archer, already had secured a spot.[10]

In other words, by all appearances, the son of the 2020 Democratic nominee *for president of the United States* had been selling influence in the form of access to his father, at that time the sitting Vice President of the United States. Joe Biden, after receiving 10% of the haul, apparently returned the favor by using his official powers—in this instance, control of the purse strings of U.S. foreign aid—and directly threatened to withhold $1 billion in American aid to Ukraine unless a particular prosecutor was removed from the investigation in which his own son, and possibly the elder Biden as well, could be implicated. And these actions by Vice President Biden occurred after he and his son had accepted large amounts of money from one of the main targets of that very same investigation: the Ukrainian energy company Burisma Holdings.

Yet, in the waning days of the election year, Hunter's emails were either ignored or downplayed as suspect by national news outlets, and stories about them were actively suppressed on social media and by Google.[11] On October 19, 2020, a supposedly nonpartisan letter signed by 51 individuals billed as former intelligence officials cast doubt upon the authenticity of the Hunter Biden laptop and emails, and stated that "our experience makes us deeply suspicious that the Russian Government played a significant role in this case," enabling Politico to run a story under the bold headline, "Hunter Biden story is Russian disinfo, dozens of former intel officials say," and giving social media giants cover to suppress or discredit the New York Post story by posting warning messages whenever it was shared.[12]

Observed the Post two years later:

> Keep in mind [the October 19 letter] was written ... five days after The Post published its first story. Neither Joe Biden nor Hunter Biden had denied the story, they simply deflected questions. Didn't these security experts think that if this was disinformation, the Biden campaign would have yelled to the heavens that the story was false?[13]

Why had the signatories of the October 19 letter been "deeply suspicious" that the emails were genuine? The New York Post offered an answer: "Because they hurt Biden's campaign, that's evidence enough."

The now-disgraced signatories of the October 19 letter—many of them Democrat partisans and/or open critics of Donald Trump—included:

Jim Clapper | Mike Hayden | Leon Panetta | John Brennan | Thomas Finger | Rick Ledgett | John McLaughlin | Michael Morell | Mike Vickers | Doug Wise | Nick Rasmussen | Russ Travers | Andy Liepman | John Moseman |

Larry Pfeiffer | Jeremy Bash | Rodney Snyder | Glenn Gerstel | David B. Buckley | Nada Bakos | Patty Bradmaier | James B. Bruce | David Cariens | Janice Cariens | Paul Kolbe | Peter Corsell | Brett Davis | Roger Zane George | Steven L. Hall | Kent Harrington | Don Hepburn | Timothy D. Kilbourn | Ron Marks | Jonna Heistand Mendez | Emile Nakhleh | Gerald A. O'Shea | David Priess | Pam Purcilly | Marc Polymeropoulos | Chris Savos | Nick Shapiro | John Sipher | Stephen Slick | Cynthia Strand | Greg Tarbell | David Terry | Greg Treverton | John Tullius | David A. Vanell | Winston Wiley | Kristin Wood

Nearly one year after the election, Politico finally admitted that it had confirmed the laptop and the emails were indeed genuine.[14] It was purposely too little and too late; Joe Biden had already taken up residency at the White House. And in any event, Biden was still being shielded from the story by all major U.S. media outlets even if they could no longer sustain the categorical denial.[15] Media malfeasance will be discussed further in Chapter 2.

The long-overdue admission brought renewed discomfort to the Biden administration. In March of 2022, White House Press Secretary Jen Psaki was asked by reporter Philip Wegmann, "The New York Times has authenticated emails that appear to have come from a laptop abandoned by Hunter Biden in Delaware. The President previously said that the New York Post story about this was 'a bunch of garbage' and that it was a 'Russian plant.' Does he stand by that assessment?"[16] Psaki deflected by noting that the younger Biden "doesn't work in the government." Unfortunately, whether her boss, Joe Biden (who is implicated on the laptop), happens to work for government was not asked as a follow-up.

Would the negative information about Hunter really have mattered? A post-election poll of 1,750 Biden voters in seven swing states commissioned by the Media Research Center revealed that 17% would have abandoned Biden had they known the facts about one or more of eight news stories that they had not heard of, one of them having been this one. In fact, more than 45% of those surveyed

> said they were unaware of the financial scandal enveloping Biden and his son, Hunter (a story infamously censored by Twitter and Facebook, as well as ignored by the liberal media). According to our poll, full awareness of the Hunter Biden scandal would have led 9.4% of Biden voters to abandon the Democratic candidate, flipping all six of the swing states he won to Trump, giving the President 311 electoral votes.[17]

Democrat accusations that Republicans were trying to hide the truth— after Republicans and others had been fighting for months against an actual conspiracy by television, print, and social media, and even some federal agencies, to suppress the flow of information to the public about the Hunter Biden scandal and also about the election itself—thus rang hollow. As Matt Vespa put it, "There was an October Surprise in 2020. The media just suffocated it with a pillow."[18] Fox News' Jesse Watters astutely observed:

> "…and that's how you rig a vote: run the October Surprise a year *after* the election."[19]

Meanwhile, in the months following the certification and inauguration of Joe Biden, the narrative of a January 6, 2021 "insurrection" from the right, let alone one incited by President Trump himself, had been falling to pieces before the eyes of the nation. America had observed those strange two hours through the filter of the national media, with up-close and dramatic photographs. But, despite the regimented lockstep of talking points breathlessly repeated for months in major media, by mid-2021 a somewhat milder picture involving little evidence of coordination[20] and a relatively small number of violent instigators—among whom were alleged FBI informants[21]—began to emerge.

Republicans who stymied the proposed Congressional inquiry into January 6 were objecting not to truth, but to Democrats' efforts to use taxpayer dollars to prop up a crumbling political narrative of an "insurrection" not rooted in fact. A central problem was that the investigating institutions and processes had been compromised: during these events and in the years just prior, Americans saw formerly-neutral institutions of their federal government employed multiple times for partisan ends. By 2021, Republicans had good reason to believe that the proposed investigation would amount to little more than setting the fox to guard the henhouse, shielding the guilty and blaming the innocent.

Reports began to emerge late in 2021 that FBI informants had been among those who planned a kidnapping of Michigan Governor Gretchen Whitmer in mid-2020,[22] and subsequently that more than a dozen such informants—some of whom may have previously helped plan the Michigan operation—were also at the center of the small number of people planning and executing violence at the Capitol on January 6.[23] Such revelations seemed to raise legitimate questions about whether either crime would have become reality at all were it not for instigation from within the FBI, and whether the FBI was being used to create incidents that could be publicly blamed on Donald Trump and his supporters as a political stunt. The agency had been alerted to possible January 6 trouble in advance,[24] and Trump himself had asked for more Capitol security.[25] Yet, the FBI did not take appropriate steps to fortify the Capitol area on the 6th.

Given multiple egregious instances of obvious politicization of the FBI in recent memory,[26] Americans could fairly question whether the more sensational aspects of both the Whitmer kidnapping plot and the events at the Capitol on January 6 might represent more what the left imagines or wishes the American right to be than what it actually is.

At a Senate Judiciary Committee hearing on January 12, 2022, the following exchange occurred between Senator Ted Cruz and Jill Sanborn, executive assistant director of the national security branch of the FBI:

Cruz: "How many FBI agents or confidential informants actively participated in the events of January 6?"

Sanborn: "Sir, I'm sure you can appreciate that I can't go into the specifics of sources and methods ..."

Cruz: "Did *any* FBI agents or informants actively participate in the events of January 6, yes or no?"

Sanborn: "Sir I can't answer that."

Cruz: "Did any FBI agents or confidential informants commit crimes of violence on January 6?"

Sanborn: "I can't answer that, sir."

Cruz: "Did any FBI agents or FBI informants actively encourage and incite crimes of violence on January 6?"

Sanborn: "Sir, I can't answer that."

Cruz: "Ms. Sanborn, who is Ray Epps?"

Sanborn: "I'm aware of the individual, sir. I don't have the specific background of him."

Cruz: "Well, there are a lot of people who are understandably concerned about Mr. Epps. On the night of January 5, 2021, Epps wandered around the crowd that had gathered, and there is video out there of him chanting, 'Tomorrow, we need to get into the Capitol ... into the Capitol.' This was strange behavior, so strange that the crowd began chanting, 'Fed! Fed! Fed! Fed! Fed! Fed!' Ms. Sanborn, was Ray Epps a Fed?"

Sanborn: "Sir, I cannot answer that question."

Cruz: "The next day, on January 6, Mr. Epps is seen whispering to a person, and five seconds later, five seconds after he is whispering to a person, that same person begins to forcibly tear down the barricades. Did Mr. Epps urge them to tear down the barricades?"

Sanborn: "Sir, similar to the other answers, I cannot answer that."

Cruz: "Shortly thereafter, the FBI put out a public post, listing—seeking information on individuals connected with violent crimes on January 6." [Cruz displays picture of FBI media post] "Among those individuals, on the bottom there, is Mr. Epps. The FBI publicly asked for information identifying, offering cash rewards for information leading to the arrest. This was posted, and then, some time later," [Cruz displays picture of subsequent FBI media post] "magically, Mr. Epps disappeared from the posting. According to public records, Mr. Epps has not been charged with anything. No one has explained why a person *videoed* urging people to go to the Capitol, a person whose conduct was so suspect the crowd believed he was a Fed, would magically disappear from the list of people the FBI was looking at. Ms. Sanborn, a lot of Americans are concerned that the Federal Government deliberately encouraged illegal and violent conduct on January 6. My question to you, and this is not an ordinary law enforcement question; this is a question of public accountability: Did federal agents or those in service of federal agents actively encourage violent and criminal conduct on January 6?"

Sanborn: "Not to my knowledge, sir."

Only one person[27] is known beyond doubt to have been killed on January 6 in relation to the events at the U.S. Capitol:[28] unarmed 35-year-old U.S. Air Force veteran Ashli Babbitt, who minutes before had been talking, joking, and laughing with several of the MPD officers and who mere moments before her death had desperately tried to stop rioter Zachary Alam from breaking the window, shouting, "Stop! No! Don't! Wait!"[29] All three other individuals who died at the Capitol that day were Trump supporters, and each of their deaths has been reasonably alleged to be the result of misconduct by Capitol Police or other authorities.[30]

Babbitt was shot climbing through the broken window of a door beyond which was the hallway leading to the Speaker's Lobby. After review of the video and interview of other witnesses, some close to Babbitt now believe she did not know where the hallway beyond the door led but had been trying to move away from a situation that she perceived to have suddenly turned sour. Husband Aaron Babbitt states, "After repeatedly forcing myself to watch the murder of my wife, I have come to my own conclusion that Ashli came to a point of realization that she was in a very bad situation and the police weren't acting appropriately to what she was witnessing."[31]

Babbitt was shot to death inside the Capitol building by Capitol Police officer Lt. Michael Byrd as she was climbing through a barricaded interior hallway window, broken moments before by Alam.[32] Lt. Byrd was later cleared in the shooting by the Capitol Police,[33] and the Justice Department announced on April 14, 2021 that no charges would be brought against him, but his identity was officially kept confidential for months following the event.[34]

Beyond the killing of Ashli Babbitt, and the other three deaths mentioned above, 140 Capitol Police officers were injured,[35] and some Capitol grounds and facilities were damaged. Early hyperbolic estimates of $30 million in damage (e.g. CBS News[36] and NPR[37]) were moderated down to $1.5 million by June.[38] Regardless of the amount, the violence and destruction were quickly condemned by all sides, including conservatives.[39] President Trump's was among the voices condemning the violence, something he had neither proposed nor supported.[40] However, the President's critics sought more than a condemnation of the violence. What they really seemed to need was a solution to (or a distraction from) the major problem they had in the form of Trump's complaint, which to many Americans appeared to be righteous and valid. They needed—and demanded—for Trump to back down on his claims of fraud and a stolen election. Trump was unwilling. He had not made up the concerns that he was expressing, and to back away from them would have been dishonest and a betrayal of the American people who are owed transparent and lawful elections.

Accordingly, the following day the President said in a video filmed outside the White House, "I know your pain. I know your hurt. We had an election that was stolen from us." The remarks infuriated those who saw in them a justification for the riotous behavior and the breach of the Capitol.[41] Trump was offering no such justification. He had not called for, suggested, nor condoned such violence. But his critics asserted that Trump's steady refusal to "accept the results of the election" led naturally and necessarily to expressions of violence such as what had appeared at the Capitol.

Why would Democrats believe that violence was a natural and necessary result of Trump's claim that the election was stolen? One answer may be found when considering leftist justifications for all kinds of violence in recent history, including the BLM and Antifa riots across the nation in 2020. Many on the American left—who regularly assert, for example, that poverty leaves people no choice but to cross the border illegally, or to steal, or to engage in terrorism—often seem to not grasp how any person in a difficult life circumstance, or even with a perceived or actual grievance, could be expected to choose not to resolve matters with violence or lawbreaking, particularly when doing so might allow an injustice to stand.[42]

In my observation, Trump bristled at calls to apologize for his words because there was no causal link between those words and the violence that was carried out by a few key instigators on January 6.[43] One does not apologize for something one did not do. While Trump's critics essentially demanded that he agree with their view of events and their causes, he chose a different path.

As the nation contemplated and debated its direct causes, virtually no one at any place on the American political spectrum condoned the violence itself. Over subsequent weeks, several hundred people were arrested in connection with the events, and the U.S. Justice Department initiated and expedited what it called the biggest investigation in its history.[44]

However, some saw raw politics rather than dispassionate pursuit of the facts in these actions.[45] Supporting this view was the fact that left-leaning partisans and bureaucrats simultaneously fought to hide thousands of hours of January 6 surveillance footage at the U.S. Capitol from public visibility,[46] claiming it to be either irrelevant or a compromise of security.[47] Those arguing for transparency and public release argued that the video would undermine the left's dramatic narrative of "insurrection."[48] Meanwhile, the FBI's extensive criminal investigation was now admitting that it found no evidence that Trump was directly involved in organizing Capitol riot violence, and little evidence of an organized plot to overturn the election results.[49] It is important to understand that the FBI's investigation had all the appropriate standards of evidence applied. The January 6 congressional hearings, in contrast, were not a criminal investigation but a show trial. They did not apply legal standards.

The partisan nature of calls for investigation of January 6 was further highlighted by the general lack of concern from the same people for thousands of officers injured and more than $2 billion in damage from the BLM riots over the summer of 2020.[50] Perhaps Democrats had been less worried by those riots since the brunt of that violence, looting, and destruction did not threaten bureaucrats' power but "only" family and minority owned businesses and residents of urban areas, many of whom were driven to desperation, bankruptcy, and even closure.[51]

Indeed, Democrat reactions to the Floyd riots had extended far beyond lack of concern for the violence, and into explicit approval. In an August 2020 interview with Stephen Colbert—months into these riots and still during their height—Kamala Harris herself said of the protests,

[T]hey're not going to stop. They're not gonna stop, and that's ... they're not ... this is a movement, I'm telling you. They're not gonna stop. And, **everyone beware**. Because they're not gonna stop. They're not gonna stop before Election Day in November, and they're not gonna stop after Election Day. And that should be—**everyone should take note of that**, on both levels. That this isn't ... they're not gonna let up, and they should not. And we should not.[52]

News agencies and fact checkers were quick to declare in the final weeks before the election that Harris had been referring to the *protests*, not the riots.[53] If she meant to refer only to the nonviolent protests, one wonders why she would have included the warnings, "everyone beware," and "everyone should take note of that." Why would everyone need to "beware" of nonviolent protests? So, in my observation Snopes, Reuters, and the Associated Press once again exposed their bias in the "fact checking" of this statement.

Of course, Harris' endorsement of the BLM riots were apparently rooted in two assumptions. First, that the rioters' cause was just, and second, that destruction, assault, and/or killing of civilians somehow served a greater good.

And clearly, Harris had a different opinion of the cause or causes that motivated the rally at the Capitol on January 6, 2021, in the context of which a small number of people acted violently and with some people physically harmed (but no one killed by any rioter). However, one need only imagine President Trump stating during or soon after the events of January 6, "They're not gonna stop. And, everyone beware. They're not gonna let up, and they should not," to discern the hypocrisy of the American left, including major media and other institutions that expressed selective outrage.

For the overwhelming majority of attendees of the January 6 rally at the Capitol who were not violent, the emotion manifested seems to have been an expression of a deep sense of concern that the nation had been violated and that the perpetrators were about to get away with it.[54] They were indignant at what smelled to them like grave injustice on a national scale. And, while there were indeed many with reason to believe that voter fraud and election fraud had shifted the result, a great many more understood that Democrat partisans' illegal structural changes to the election process *via* lawfare and bureaucratic maneuvering in the swing states was the core issue, likely to be repeated and perfected if not checked.

Further, with its refusal to even hear the Texas case (see Chapter 3), the Supreme Court had sealed off the penultimate built-in pressure release valve for the peaceful redress of grievance in our nation. If the Court had heard that case and found *against* the Plaintiffs—indeed, even if the Court had declined to hear the case based upon the merits rather than alleged lack of standing—the situation in January could have been different.

But the Court shrunk from its duty, and a huge swath of Americans were rightly left wondering who, then, would ever address such a matter. If no entity has standing to address an unlawfully conducted election *prior* to its occurrence, because no harm has yet been done, and no entity has standing *after* its occurrence, then there is then no reasonable avenue for remedy, the American people (including those who would wish to repeat a strategy of extra-legislative rule changes favoring Democrats in every future American election) can only conclude that there is no legal avenue for righting such wrongs and thus no hope for ever stopping future strong-arming of elections. This frustration is what many of the Capitol rally-goers, even the vast majority who did not participate in the violence, may have been sensing that day.

The diverse crowds gathered at the National Mall on January 6—and probably a significant number of those who walked into the Capitol itself —were generally zealous and enthusiastic. There were admittedly some strange people among them, including the now-famous bare-chested man wearing face paint, a bear skin and buffalo horn hat, Jake Angeli, and a number of people with apparently freshly purchased camo gear who were prominently parading around through the crowd, who all seemed absolutely bizarre to even the most ardent Trump supporters. These were not their own, but rather seemed to reflect a contrived image of what people on the left might fancy a Trump supporter to be: simply crazy.

Another strange presence was that of John Sullivan ("JaydenX"), who had denounced Trump the previous summer and participated openly in multiple Antifa and BLM riots, and whose own video footage from January 6 seems to show him arriving in the National Statuary Hall, "shouting, 'It's our house, motherf__ers!'—near the very front of a group of rioters determined to enter the House chamber."[55] Though Sullivan was at the front when Ashli Babbitt was shot, he was quickly released without bail after initial arrest,[56] even as others with far more minor involvement remained in jail throughout 2021 under abusive and even inhumane conditions,[57] raising further serious questions about something beyond a simple narrative of an "insurrection" by Trump supporters. The truth may be more complicated, and at the moment it seems impossible to rule out the theory expressed by J. Michael Waller:

> Another 14,000 hours of Capitol Police video remain hidden. When released, they will show that the attack on the Capitol was not an insurrection, but a small, high-visibility operation planned and executed to exploit a large and unsuspecting crowd as cover.[58]

On April 6, 2022, a ruling by federal judge Trevor McFadden dealt a major blow to the narrative of a January 6 "insurrection," when he found Matthew Martin—who had entered the Capitol—not guilty on all charges. Martin had argued that a U.S. Capitol Police officer had waved him into the building, and video supported the claim. The ruling was seen as a watershed moment, as hundreds of others, many or most of whom have asserted that they were also allowed in by officers, face similar charges.[59]

Kangaroo Court

Having failed in their bid for a full congressional committee, House Democrats moved to "Plan B," creating a select committee to investigate the events of January 6. The committee was composed of seven Democrats and two Trump-critical Republicans: Liz Cheney and Adam Kinzinger.

It is true that in August of 2016 Cheney said the nation needed to unite behind Donald Trump (as the lesser of two evils, she made sure to emphasize) since, "In Wyoming there's no question for us that Hillary Clinton would be ... far, far worse than Donald Trump."[60] However, after grudgingly admitting that members of her party should vote for her party's nominee in 2016, it was not long before she once again wore the label "Never Trumper,"[61] and at a crucial point in the 2020 election season Cheney uncritically spread false reports concerning alleged Russian bounties on U.S. forces in Afghanistan as an apparent means of harming Trump and justifying an extended military presence in the country.[62] The false story she helped to spread became the basis for Joe Biden's accusation during the September 29 presidential debate that Trump was "Putin's puppy"—a statement that the New York Times "fact check" of the debate then dutifully declared "true." Was it all worth it for Cheney? By mid-2022, she had only twenty-six percent support among Wyoming Republicans, with her Trump-backed primary challenger Harriet Hageman riding thirty points higher at a cool fifty-six percent.[63]

For his part, Kinzinger had been supporting Trump's opposition for years. Mark Levin commented in December of 2020:

> In 2010 he runs as a Tea Party-backed candidate; within 12 months he abandons the Tea Party; in 2016, after Trump is the GOP nominee for president, he announces he's not voting for him, making way for a possible Hillary presidency. For the next four years he hounds the president, and becomes a frequently quoted media darling. That is, he's a full-fledged Never Trumper.[64]

Both Cheney and Kinzinger evidently decided Trump's guilt and complicity by the day after the events of January 6, and quickly announced their intention to vote for Trump's second impeachment. Both joined all Democrats on the losing side of the vote to create the original congressional committee, and both also voted for the January 6 select committee.

The January 6 committee's first public hearing occurred June 9, 2022. The hearings were scheduled for broadcast and timed to conclude weeks before the midterm elections. It opened with a statement from the committee's chairman, Bennie Thompson, who used his time to compare January 6 to the lynching of black people in the south. Thompson, interestingly, voted not to certify electors for George W. Bush on January 6, 2004. Mercedes Schlapp tweeted about this irony on June 7:

> Reminder that the January 6 committee is being led by Rep. Bennie Thompson, who voted to overturn the 2004 election, Rep. Jamie Raskin, who voted to overturn the 2016 election, and Rep. Adam Schiff, who claimed for years that he had proof of Russian collusion.[65]

Some defenders of Thompson stated that it was not the same thing because his vote not to certify wouldn't have affected the outcome of the election. However, were they insinuating that if it *had* the ability to affect the outcome of the 2004 election, he would have refrained because that would have been a bridge too far? We can never know, but I find it unlikely. After Thompson came Liz Cheney, who among other things stated decisively that,

> On the morning of January sixth, President Donald Trump's intention was to remain president of the United States despite the lawful outcome of the 2020 election, and in violation of his constitutional obligation to relinquish power.[66]

Cheney did not state how she learned the contents of Donald Trump's mind that morning, but it is remarkable news. I had guessed that the president woke up hoping to finally have orderly redress of wrongs, and had no knowledge that he actually intended not to relinquish the White House. Unfortunately, Rep. Cheney failed to reveal her source for this bombshell revelation.

Republicans placed no members on the committee. Evidently uncomfortable with the possibility that any member might competently cross examine witnesses, House Leader Nancy Pelosi rejected two of Minority Leader McCarthy's five nominees, Reps. Jim Jordan (OH) and Jim Banks (IN). In response to Pelosi's rejection, Leader McCarthy pulled all Republican nominees, stating, "Unless Speaker Pelosi reverses course and seats all five Republican nominees, Republicans will not be party to their sham process and will instead pursue our own investigation of the facts."[67] The

circumstance arguably caused the committee itself to be improperly constituted, since the enabling language, House Resolution 503, states, "The
Speaker shall appoint 13 Members to the Select Committee, 5 of whom
shall be appointed after consultation with the minority leader."[68] As such,
other powers, such as the ability of the committee to subpoena witnesses,
were suspect. Rep. Mark Meadows filed a lawsuit against the committee on
December 8, 2021, challenging its legitimacy as unconstitutional and in
violation of House Rules.[69] As of this writing, the lawsuit remains ongoing.

Meanwhile, however, the committee acted as though it were properly
constituted and legitimate. It called witnesses, and when some failed to
appear, it issued subpoenas. Among those who chose not to appear was
former Trump White House advisor, Peter Navarro, who among other
things led the effort to pass the U.S.-Mexico-Canada Agreement to replace
NAFTA. Navarro was arrested at Reagan National airport, just as he was
getting ready to board a flight to speak at a conference, and "frogmarched"
to the federal courthouse in handcuffs the day after he promised to
impeach Biden if Republicans retake Congress. The humiliating display
was clearly designed for dramatic political effect. Navarro lives right next to
the FBI and ordinary procedure would have been to first make a phone call
asking him to come in. Said Navarro of the incident, "I was a distinguished
public servant for four years. No one ever treated me in this fashion."[70]

Also choosing not to appear was former White House strategist Steve
Bannon, who asserted, among other things, that a congressional committee
has no oversight of the Executive branch and that he could not be
compelled to testify about conversations covered by it. Bannon's defiance
angered Pelosi and placed her in an awkward position. To great fanfare,
Bannon was convicted of criminal contempt of Congress in mid-2022.
However, the defense had not been permitted to call all nine members of
the January 6 committee for testimony during the trial. The Speech and
Debate Clause ordinarily protects members of Congress from being
compelled to testify in court. However, since these particular members
were the ones who had pursued this prosecution of Bannon, it was argued
that they should not be allowed to hide behind the Clause in this case and
that Bannon had been denied a fair trial. U.S. District Judge Carl Nichols
appeared to agree and opened the door to a revisitation of the matter.[71]

In the wake of his conviction, Bannon called for a new January 6
committee: "We need a commission or committee on January 6. It's got to
be with the new Congress, with Republicans in charge—we got to get to
the bottom of the intelligence failures, FBI involvement, DHS involvement,
the intelligence services—what happened to the Pentagon and the
National Guard." Unlike the current committee which shut out Republicans, Bannon insisted that the new one should grant Democrats adequate
representation.[72]

The committee's evident overreach stretched into other national concerns. As the Supreme Court's decision to overturn Roe v. Wade was immanent, the committee made an obvious effort to embarrass and intimidate the only black member of the Supreme Court, Clarence Thomas, by going after his wife, Ginni, an outspoken conservative who had expressed independent opinion favorable to Trump. Mrs. Thomas, 65, who had been at the January 6 rally at the Capitol, was "invited" by the committee and initially indicated that she would appear.[73]

The process of the January 6 committee was designed not for justice but to selectively call witnesses, doctor evidence, and dramatize the events.[74] It had no representation from the opposition, no opportunity to call other witnesses, and no provision for cross-examination of witnesses.[75] As such, the committee was pure political theater, a sham, and we need discuss it no further here.

Tail Wagging the Dog

The logic of self governance—which is principally realized through free, honest, and lawful elections—rests upon two premises: first, that people have the right to choose their leaders, and second, that the collective wisdom of the citizens tends more often to be correct than would other more authoritarian or autocratic means of selecting leaders. A self-governing nation is one that may be described as a people with a government, rather than a government with a people. The sovereign in the U.S.A. is her people.

On August 26, 2021, Kabul's Hamid Karzai Airport was bombed shortly following Biden's disastrous withdrawal and loss of Afghanistan to the Taliban on the eve of the 20th anniversary of the 9/11 attacks. Thirteen U.S. soldiers and dozens of civilians were killed in the August 26 bombing, the deadliest terrorist attack on Americans in more than a decade.

By the time of the attack, the Biden Justice Department had fast-tracked and was setting the stage for the early 2022 prosecution, just ahead of the all-important midterm Congressional elections, of those who were still being detained in connection to the January 6 events.[76] At the time of the big push for prosecution of the Capitol rioters, Khalid Sheikh Mohammed—one of the alleged masterminds of the 9/11 attacks—still languished in prison, having by then awaited trial from his cell in Guantánamo for more than eighteen years.[77]

Also in mid-2021, John Hinckley, Jr. became the first presidential assassin or attempted presidential assassin in United States history to escape swift execution or life in prison when he was granted unconditional release scheduled for June 2022. In 1981, Hinckley had made a near-successful attempt to eliminate one-third of the United States government when he shot President Ronald Reagan, whom the American people had recently chosen in one of the biggest electoral victories in American history.[78]

Juxtaposing the release of Hinckley, Jr. with the imprisonment of some Trump supporters who had walked into the Capitol on January 6 unaware of the violence of a relative few at the front, the message from the Biden administration seemed clear: future would-be presidential assassins can take heart that as long as they target Republicans, they may get off easy. However, those caught demanding clarity concerning the questionable election of a Democratic administration should expect to experience the full and swift fury of the institutions of the U.S. federal government.

By summer of 2021, Donald Trump had yet to concede the 2020 election to Joe Biden.[79] As such, Trump became the only modern non-inaugurated presidential candidate to not concede the election to the inaugurated candidate.[80] Trump's critics have ridiculed and cajoled him and his supporters for such a lack of "decorum,"[81] saying his failure to concede was "damaging"[82] and doing "harm to America's democracy and Constitution."[83] But such criticism rang hollow in its context. Surely, affirming an illegally-conducted election and ignoring the Constitution is what would harm America's democracy—not the reverse.

In fact, the 2020 U.S. election was not the first in which significant numbers of the American people were deeply concerned about fraud and had a sense that the process had been compromised. Mollie Hemingway has noted the history of Democratic responses to outcomes of presidential elections they lost since the 1990s, culminating in an all-out refusal by many to accept the legitimacy of Donald Trump's election in 2016. Further, Hemingway notes (as have many others) the serious and real documented problems with the integrity of our state, local, and national elections as far back as 1960.[84]

But, as already mentioned, 2020 was different, and time is already revealing and confirming the qualitative and quantitative disparities. Foremost among these was that for the first time in American history, the power to change election rules was successfully seized on a massive scale in multiple swing states by those with no constitutional right to do so. This situation is the main complaint of the Texas lawsuit that will be discussed in Chapter 3.

The second difference of the 2020 election was the degree of coordination among the major gatekeepers of information flow, who placed their thumbs on the scale in favor of Biden—a *de facto* loss of a free press. These shaped public opinion about the candidates, suppressing information damaging to Biden while validating and amplifying spurious or distorted reports damaging to President Trump. During and after the election, the power of social media and big media gatekeepers was steadily leveraged to gaslight[85] the public in ways that rival the operations of George Orwell's fictional Ministry of Truth. Even today, many in social media and on Wikipedia persist in suppressing unapproved voices or facts *via* such mechanisms as "independent fact checkers." Given the legal immunity granted to social media platforms under section 230 of the United States Code, the need to address this matter is both serious and urgent. It forms the subject of Chapter 2.

A third major difference was scale. Time tested methods for perpetrating and hiding fraud make discovery more difficult. But the extent and nature of cheating can be discerned and estimated to a certain degree by applying reason to the available data, remembering that fraud which is captured and prosecuted is typically only the tiny tip of a much larger iceberg. Although not central to my main argument, Chapter 4 maps out and contemplates the lay of the land in the area.

Finally, there was the cover-up. Part of the 2020 cover-up, as already mentioned, was the plausible deniability gained from making a meaningful or conclusive post-mortem very difficult. The other part was the stonewalling of any investigation that might expose those who should go to prison and unseat those wrongfully certified. Despite the fact that Donald Trump and the RNC won a stunning 73.3% of the 2020 election-related lawsuits that were decided on their merits (See Chapter 9), the dismissal of other lawsuits by way of standing or jurisdiction technicalities—which in some of the cases were merely a pretext used by judges to avoid having to rule on the intensely controversial issues—was spun by Biden propagandists to signify that Trump and his supporters had no case. The resulting narrative that "there is nothing to see here; the courts have ruled against Trump" became pivotal to Biden allies' campaign to block substantive investigations. Stonewalling of investigation is the topic of Chapter 9.

Americans' deep suspicion about the election was shown in a late November, 2020 Rasmussen poll, which reported that many believed votes were stolen by the Biden team.[86] Democrats troubled by suspicion of the election's legitimacy may blame themselves, since they and their party's operatives blocked transparency and election integrity measures in 2020. From this fact alone, the optics strongly suggest nefarious activity. The almost comical disharmony between the evasive maneuvers of those claiming victory during and after the election, and their subsequent breathless assurances that it was "the most secure in American history,"[87] will be discussed further in Chapters 1 and 8.

Every four years, the presidential election is said to be "most important of our lifetime." In ways this contention always makes sense, since each election ideally represents a crossroad, a choice between two different futures. However, I am not alone in believing the prospect of a continued Donald Trump presidency was especially threatening to a large coalition of political players, globally and on both sides of the American political aisle. They *had* to get him out, and there was no low to which they would not stoop in order to do so. I discuss this assertion as a framing principle in Chapter 12.

---

1. Emma-Jo Morris, and Gabrielle Fonrouge, "Smoking-gun email reveals how Hunter Biden introduced Ukrainian businessman to VP dad," *New York Post,* October 14, 2020. Ukrainian businesspeople were not the the only ones who apparently managed to compromise the Bidens. In January 2022, Peter Schweizer revealed that his year-long research had found a staggering $31 million was paid to the Biden family while Joe Biden was vice-president, and continuing when he became president, from individuals linked to the highest levels of Chinese intelligence. "Biden's connection to China: Peter Schweizer," *Life, Liberty & Levin (Fox News),* January 24, 2022.

2. "'Smoking gun' emails reveal alleged meeting between Joe Biden and Ukrainian company," *Sky News,* October 15, 2020.

3. Michael Goodwin, "Hunter biz partner confirms email, details Joe Biden's push to make millions from China: Goodwin," *New York Post,* October 22, 2020.

4. Steven Nelson, "Psaki claims Biden didn't discuss business with Hunter — despite docs that suggest otherwise," *New York Post,* July 9, 2021.

5. "Devon Archer Sentenced To A Year And A Day In Prison For The Fraudulent Issuance And Sale Of More Than $60 Million Of Tribal Bonds," United States Attorney's Office, Southern District of New York, February 28, 2022; Ben Feuerherd, "Hunter Biden's pal sentenced to prison for role in fraud scheme," *New York Post,* February 28, 2022.

6. Joshua Rhett Miller, and Miranda Devine, "Voicemail indicates Joe Biden knew of hunter deals with 'spy chief of China,'" *New York Post,* June 27, 2022.

7. Bruce Golding, "'Huge integrity test': Calls for action as Biden voicemail reveals he knew of Hunter China deals," *New York Post,* June 28, 2022; Brooke Singman, and Adam Shaw, "Hunter Biden requested keys for new 'office mates' Joe Biden, Chinese 'emissary' to CEFC chairman, emails show," *Fox News,* December 12, 2020.

8. Margot Cleveland, "Joe Biden's Voicemail To Hunter Means It's Time To Appoint A Special Counsel," *Federalist,* June 29, 2022.

9. Brian Flood, and Nikolas Lanum, "ABC, NBC, CBS, CNN, MSNBC ignore voicemail Joe Biden allegedly left for Hunter Biden on business dealings," *Fox News,* July 8, 2022.

10. Rowan Scarborough, "Hunter Biden Burisma payments detailed in Treasury Department reports," *Washington Times,* September 30, 2020.

11. Allum Bokhari, "'Joe Biden Corruption' trends on Google—but Google whitewashes auto-complete suggestions," *Breitbart,* October 28, 2020.

12. Natasha Bertrand, "Hunter Biden story is Russian disinfo, dozens of former intel officials say," *Politico,* October 19, 2020; Jim Clapper et al., "Public Statement on the Hunter Biden Emails," October 19, 2020.

13. "Spies who lie: 51 'intelligence' experts refuse to apologize for discrediting true Hunter Biden story," *New York Post,* March 18, 2022.

14. Ryan Lizza et al., "Politico Playbook: Double trouble for Biden," *Politico,* September 21, 2021.

15. "One year later, The Post's Hunter Biden reporting is vindicated — but still buried," *New York Post* (Editorial Board), October 12, 2021.

16. Steven Nelson, "Psaki won't defend claim Post's Hunter Biden laptop scoop was 'Russian plant,'" *New York Post,* March 17, 2022.

17. Rich Noyes, "Special Report: The Stealing of the Presidency, 2020," *MRC Newsbusters,* November 24, 2020.

18. Matt Vespa, "Here's How Many Biden Voters Would Have Bolted from Joe If the Media Did Their Job," *Townhall,* November 28, 2020.

19. "'Watters' World' on Democrats' power grab propaganda, border crisis," *Fox News,* October 4, 2021.

20. Mark Hosenball, and Sarah N. Lynch, "Exclusive: FBI finds scant evidence U.S. Capitol attack was coordinated - sources," *Reuters,* August 20, 2021.

21. Bonchie, "The FBI Admits to Having Informants at January 6th Protest," *RedState*, September 25, 2021; Ian Schwartz, "Greenwald: FBI Involvement In Capitol Riot Not A 'Crazy Conspiracy Theory,' This Is What They Do," *Real Clear Politics*, June 18, 2021.

22. Barnini Chakraborty, "FBI informants had bigger role in Whitmer kidnap plot than thought: report," *Washington Examiner*, July 21, 2021.

23. Pat Droney, "New court filings show FBI had at least 12 'informants' in Whitmer 'kidnap-ping' plot," *Law Enforcement Today*, July 22, 2021; Steve McCann, "So Much Evidence that January 6, 2021 was a Calculated Set-Up," *American Thinker*, July 13, 2021; Arthur Bloom, "Of Course The FBI Was Infiltrating January 6 Groups," *American Conservative*, June 22, 2021; Tucker Carlson, "Tucker Carlson: Government agents may have helped organize the Jan. 6 Capitol riot," *Fox News*, June 16, 2021.

24. Chris Mills Rodrigo, "Parler says it alerted FBI to threats before Capitol riot," *Hill*, March 26, 2021.

25. "Trump asked for more security on Jan 6 and was ignored, memo confirms | American Agenda on Newsmax," Newsmax TV, December 6, 2021, YouTube video; Jan Wolfe, "Trump wanted troops to protect his supporters at Jan. 6 rally," *Reuters*, May 12, 2021.

26. Joseph E. diGenova, "The Politicization of the FBI," *Imprimis*, vol. 47, no. 2 (February 2018).

27. I emphasize the word "only" not to diminish the tragedy, but to correct the lie repeated by some media that multiple people were killed that day or as a result of the events at the Capitol. Only one killing is confirmed. The circumstances surrounding the deaths of several others, such as medical events possibly set off by police action, are unconfirmed. Beyond that, a single Capitol Police officer—Brian Sicknick, himself a Trump supporter—died the following day, also from a medical condition apparently unrelated to the events.

28. For months after the details of the day were well known, a number of journalists and news organizations repeated that *six* (or five) people had been killed (or "lost their lives") in the riots, apparently padding a narrative of violent insurrection. Although details were known soon after the events, nearly a year later USA Today's editors allowed their "fact checker" McKenzie Sadeghi to claim that "the Jan. 6 attack on the Capitol ... *resulted in four deaths*." McKenzie Sadeghi, "Fact check: Trump repeats false claim that Pelosi rejected request for National Guard ahead of Jan. 6," *USA Today*, December 16, 2021. (emphasis added).

29. Joseph M. Hanneman, "Babbitt Tried to Stop Attack on Capitol Speaker's Lobby, Video Shows," *Epoch Times*, January 19, 2022.

30. Media reported that 34 year old Rosanne Boyland of Kennesaw, Georgia was trampled to death. Subsequent reports and video showed that she lost consciousness while pinned beneath a pile of other protesters. CPR was attempted by fellow protestors Jake Lang and Ronald McAbee, but DC Metropolitan Officer Lila Morris allegedly struck Boyland repeat-edly on the head with a steel baton while she lay unconscious. Despite the Department's Internal Affairs Bureau ruling that Morris' use of force on the unconscious woman was "objectively reasonable," some alleged the blows caused Boyland's death. The coroner's report, initially withheld from the family, declared her cause of death an overdose of Adder-all, a prescription medication that Boyland had been taking for about 10 years. If so, it would be a remarkable coincidence that such death from overdose happened simultaneous to the victim being crushed unconscious and beaten in the head with a steel baton.

The other two deaths that day were those of Benjamin Phillips of Bloomburg, Pennsyl-vania, 50—who died from a stroke after a stun grenade thrown by Capitol Police into the crowd on the south side lawn area outside the Capitol building reportedly struck him before detonating feet away (bystander Chris Alberts states he was prevented from adminis-tering CPR to Phillips by a Capitol Police officer, who also refused to administer CPR on COVID policy grounds)—and Kevin Greeson of Athens, Alabama, 55—who died of a heart attack after collapsing when a crowd control grenade exploded near him.

Joseph M. Hanneman, "Police Beating of Unconscious Trump Supporter Was 'Objec-tively Reasonable,' Department Rules," *Epoch Times*, February 15, 2022; Tayler Hansen, "Capitol Offense: The Ugly Truth Behind The Five Deaths From January 6th and 7th," Substack. January 27, 2022; Alexandra Hutzler, "2 People Who Died at Capitol Riot Died of Natural Causes, Medical Examiner Rules," *Newsweek*, April 7, 2021; Julia Terruso, "He orga-nized a bus of Trump supporters from Pa. for 'the first day of the rest of our lives.' He died in Washington," *Philadelphia Inquirer*, January 7, 2021; Israel Salas-Rodriguez, "DEADLY SCENE: Who was Kevin Greeson?," *Sun*, January 7, 2021.

31. Hanneman, "Babbitt Tried to Stop."

32. "Report names Capitol Police officer as shooter of Ashli Babbitt," *World Tribune,* July 8, 2021; Paul Sperry, "Naming the Capitol Cop Who Killed Unarmed Jan. 6 Rioter Ashli Babbitt," *Real Clear Investigations,* July 7, 2021; Ibid.

33. Rich Schapiro, Anna Schecter, and Chelsea Damberg, "Officer who shot Ashli Babbitt during Capitol Riot breaks silence: 'I saved countless lives,'" *NBC News,* August 26, 2021.

34. Hanneman, "Babbitt Tried to Stop."

35. "140 Officers were Injured in Capitol Riot," *Police,* January 28, 2021.

36. Rebecca Kaplan, "More than $30 million needed for Capitol repairs and new security after assault, officials say," CBS News, February 24, 2021.

37. "The cost of repairing damages from the attack on the U.S. Capitol and related security expenses have already topped $30 million *and will keep rising.*" (emphasis added). Bill Chappell, "Architect Of The Capitol Outlines $30 Million In Damages From Pro-Trump Riot," *NPR,* February 24, 2021.

38. Spencer S. Hsu, "Jan. 6 riot caused $1.5 million in damage to Capitol — and U.S. prosecutors want defendants to pay," *Washington Post,* June 3, 2021; U.S. Department of Justice, *Re: United States v. Jacob Chansley Criminal Case No. 21-cr-003 (RCL),* Channing D. Phillips, July 15, 2021, 7.

39. Ted Cruz, among the most conservative members of the Senate and a supporter of President Trump, tweeted at 3:07 p.m. on January 6, 2021, "Those storming the Capitol need to stop NOW. The Constitution protects peaceful protest, but violence—from Left or Right—is ALWAYS wrong. And those engaged in violence are hurting the cause they say they support." Donald Trump, Jr. tweeted at 2:17 p.m., "This is wrong and not who we are. Be peaceful and use your 1st Amendment rights, but don't start acting like the other side. We have a country to save and this doesn't help anyone." Mark Levin tweeted at 3:24 p.m., "Anyone breaching the Capitol Building should immediately stand down. We don't know who these people are. That will have to be determined. People came to protest peacefully. And that is their constitutional right. But we condemn and must condemn anyone who acts lawlessly, period." Tom Fitton of Judicial Watch tweeted at 1:51 p.m., "Stop the violence!" Actor Kevin Sorbo tweeted at 3:16 p.m., "To those storming the capitol building: Please be careful, do not act like ANTIFA. Respect the police and know they are mostly on our side, they are simply trying to do their job," and at 4:46 p.m., "They don't look like patriots to me..." Fuzzy Slippers, "Republican and Conservative Leaders Condemn Capitol Hill Violence," *Legal Insurrection,* January 6, 2021.

40. Nicholas Reimann, "Trump's Changing Stance On Jan. 6 Attack—From Condemning Rioters To Backing 'Protest,'" *Forbes,* January 6, 2022.

41. Rob Crilly, "Trump under pressure to condemn violence after his supporters attack Capitol," *Washington Examiner,* January 6, 2021.

42. Jesus' instruction to turn the other cheek when wronged in certain ways (e.g. Matthew 5:38-39) and biblical reminders that vengeance belongs to God (e.g. Deuteronomy 32:35, Romans 12:9) guides and tempers many Christians. It doesn't mean action, even occasionally violent action, in pursuit of justice is never appropriate, but it does recommend restraint—and give hope—to victims. Such logic of forbearance centered in individual agency often confuses those lacking such perspective. The nonviolent resistance movements of Mohandas K. Gandhi and Dr. Martin Luther King, Jr. were influenced by the example of Jesus. Although self-identified Christians exist on both the left and the right of the American political spectrum, I observe that a biblical ethic of human agency is today more common on the right, and alien to many on the left except as a matter of pragmatic strategy.

43. Laws in some countries against "incitement to hatred" (and such) tend to absolve those committing crimes of violence by blaming someone other than the perpetrator. The patronizing and insulting nature of asserting that some people have no control of their own actions if "provoked" is regularly lost on these laws' supporters. Ultimately, blaming "provocative" speech becomes a tool for suppression of speech. Such control is usually the true purpose of such laws.

44. James Bovard, "The Coming 'January 6' Train Wreck," *The American Conservative,* July 22, 2021; "FBI investigation into January 6 becomes largest in FBI history," *Yahoo!news,* May 25, 2021.

45. Julie Kelly, "Capitol Investigation Seeks to Criminalize Political Dissent: The government's response to the January 6 melee isn't about justice. It's about partisan retribution and revenge. And the consequences will be disastrous," *American Greatness,* March 15, 2021.

46. Libby Emmons, "Gaetz, Greene call on FBI to release 14,000 hours of footage from Jan 6," *Post Millennial*, September 27, 2021; Rich Welsh, "Rep. Gosar Holding Press Conference Calling on DOJ to Release 14,000 Hours of Video Footage of January 6 at the Capitol," *RPW Media*, July 27, 2021; Kyle Cheney, "Capitol Police provided more than 14,000 hours of Jan. 6 footage to lawmakers," *Politico*, March 29, 2021.

47. William Moloney, "Has the FBI demolished Democrats' insurrection narrative about Jan. 6?," *Hill*, August 25, 2021.

48. "Judicial Watch: U.S. Capitol Police Tell Federal Court January 6 Disturbance Videos Are Not Public Records," *Judicial Watch* (Press Release), August 20, 2021.

49. Bryan Metzger, "FBI finds no evidence that Trump and his allies were directly involved with organizing the violence of the Capitol riot: report," *Yahoo!News*, August 20, 2021.

50. Pat Droney, "Thousands of cops were injured, over $2 billion in damage during Floyd riots. Where are the 'congressional hearings?,'" *Law Enforcement Today*, July 28, 2021; Brad Polumbo, "George Floyd Riots Caused Record-Setting $2 Billion in Damage, New Report Says. Here's Why the True Cost is Even Higher," *Foundation for Economic Education*, September 16, 2020.

51. Brian Flood, "Minnesota newspaper lists over 360 local businesses destroyed by riots," *Fox News*, June 30, 2020; David Harsanyi, "I know first-hand how looters can crush a family's dreams," *New York Post*, June 5, 2020. (5/25/22); Leticia Miranda, "First came a pandemic. Then, looting. Small businesses pick up the pieces as their debt mounts," *NBC News*, June 4, 2020; Melanie Gray, "Businesses and bystanders feeling pain of George Floyd riots," *New York Post*, May 30, 2020.

52. Lizzy Murica, "VP Candidate Kamala Harris chilling interview about BLM riots: 'They're not gonna stop. And they should not,'" *Law Enforcement Today*, August 30, 2020. (Emphasis added)

53. "Fact check: Kamala Harris said she supports protests, not 'riots', in Late Show clip," *Reuters*, October 29, 2020; Ali Swenson, "Kamala Harris said protests should continue, not riots," *Associated Press*, October 8, 2020; Nur Ibrahim, "Did Kamala Harris Say Protests Are 'Not Gonna Let Up, and They Should Not'?," *Snopes*, October 7, 2020.

54. Daniel Brubaker, "Democrats to America: 'You'd better put some ice on that,'" *danielbrubak er.com*, November 11, 2020 .

55. Robert Mackey, "John Sullivan, Who Filmed Shooting of Ashli Babbitt in Capitol, Detained on Federal Charges," *Intercept*, January 14, 2021.

56. Jordan Boyd, "Federal Judge Releases BLM Capitol Rioter Without Bail," *Federalist*, January 17, 2021.

57. Louie Gohmert et al., "The Tyrannical Treatment of Jan. 6 Prisoners Is a Threat to Our Democracy," *Epoch Times*, November 4, 2021; Julie Kelly, "A January 6 Detainee Speaks Out," *American Greatness*, July 22, 2021.

58. J. Michael Waller, "'A small number of extremists': Capitol Police video will show that January 6 was not an insurrection," *Center for Security Policy*, September 28, 2021.

59. Elizabeth Nolan Brown, "January 6 Defendant Who Says He Thought He Was Allowed in Capitol Beats Charges," *Reason*, April 7, 2022; Andrew Millman, and Casey Gannon, "Man who said January 6 was 'magical' acquitted in US Capitol riot case," *CNN*, April 6, 2022.

60. "Liz Cheney Endorses Trump; Rips 'Felon' Hillary," *Newsmax*, August 12, 2016.

61. Todd Beamon, "Rand Paul Slams Liz Cheney as 'Never Trumper' Amid Twitter Rift," *Newsmax*, September 12, 2019.

62. Tristan Justice, "Liz Cheney Was A Primary Culprit Of Spreading Fake News On Russian Bounties To Undermine Trump," *Federalist*, April 16, 2021.

63. Jason Lemon, "Liz Cheney's Chances of Beating Trump-Backed Harriet Hageman in Wyoming," *Newsweek*, May 28, 2022.

64. Rudy Takala, "Mark Levin Savages 'Pathetic' Rep. Kinzinger: 'Full-Fledged Never Trumper,'" *Mediaite*, January 1, 2021.

65. Mercedes Schlapp, Twitter post, June 7, 2022, 12:29 p.m..

66. Liz Cheney, Twitter post, June 10, 2022, 2:45 p.m..

67. Annie Grayer, and Jeremy Herb, "McCarthy pulls his 5 GOP members from 1/6 committee after Pelosi rejects 2 of his picks," *CNN*, July 21, 2022.

68. "H.Res.503 - Establishing the Select Committee to Investigate the January 6th Attack on the United States Capitol," United States Congress, June 28, 2021.

69. Joel B. Pollak, "Pollak: Mark Meadows' Lawsuit Could End the January 6 Committee," *Breit-bart*, December 9, 2021; Meadows v. Pelosi (1:21-cv-03217).

70. Joel Pollak, "FBI Arrests Peter Navarro One Day After He Vows To Impeach Biden," *Breitbart*, June 3, 2022; Wendell Husebø, "Report: Peter Navarro Handcuffed At Airport And 'Frogmarched' To The Courthouse," *Breitbart*, June 3, 2022.

71. Harper Neidig, "Judge: Bannon can argue to throw out contempt charges after conviction," *Hill*, July 27, 2022.

72. Ryan King, "Bannon calls for new Jan. 6 committee to deliver 'crushing blow' to Democrats," *Washington Examiner*, July 22, 2022.

73. Virginia Chamlee, "Ginni Thomas Might Get a Jan. 6 Subpoena: 'Hope It Doesn't Get to That,'" *People*, July 25, 2022; Penny Starr, "Lawyer: Ginni Thomas Will Not Testify Before January 6 House Committee," *Breitbart*, June 29, 2022; Jon Levine, "Ginni Thomas to 'clear up misconceptions' about role to Jan. 6 committee," *New York Post*, June 18, 2022; Kevin Daley, "Conservative activist talks to the Free Beacon about her work and her husband, Supreme Court justice Clarence Thomas," *Washington Free Beacon*, March 14, 2022.

74. Kristina Wong, "January 6 Show Trial: Liz Cheney Omits Exculpatory Phrase While Quoting Trump—'Go Home With Love And Peace,'" *Breitbart*, June 10, 2022; Sean Davis, "During January 6 Hearing, Schiff Doctored Text Messages Between Mark Meadows And Rep. Jim Jordan," *Federalist*, December 15, 2021.

75. David Bossie, "Jan. 6 committee abusing its power," *Washington Times*, January 31, 2022.

76. Spencer Hsu, "Justice Dept. calls Jan. 6 'Capitol Attack' probe one of largest in U.S. history, expects at least 400 to be charged," *Washington Post*, March 12, 2021.

77. Aleem Maqbool, "Guantanamo Bay: In a courtroom, just feet away from 9/11 suspects," *BBC News*, September 12, 2021.

78. Mark Levin, *Mark Levin Show,* September 28, 2021.

79. Brian Freeman, "Trump: I Have Not Conceded 2020 Election," *Newsmax,* June 22, 2021.

80. Amy McKeever, "No modern presidential candidate has refused to concede. Here's why that matters," *National Geographic,* November 8, 2020.

81. Nellie English, "'Donald wants a participation trophy': Even GOP pundits are mocking Trump for being a sore loser," *Front Page Live,* November 12, 2020.

82. Noah Feldman, "Comment: Trump's refusal to concede is legal; and damaging," *HeraldNet,* November 13, 2020; Uri Friedman, "The Damage Will Last," *Atlantic,* November 27, 2020.

83. Noah Feldman, "By not conceding, Trump is doing extraordinary harm to America's democracy and Constitution," *Print,* November 20, 2020.

84. Mollie Hemingway, *Rigged: How the Media, Big Tech, and the Democrats Seized Our Elections* (Washington, D.C.: Regnery, 2021), vii-ix, x.

85. The term "gaslighting" comes from the 1944 film "Gaslight," and refers to psychological manipulation involving telling a person repeatedly that reality does not match what they've seen and heard, while also denying them external confirmation of their true memories. The intended—and often actual—effect is victims beginning to doubt their own memory, even their own sanity.

86. "Election Integrity: 62% Don't Think Voter ID Laws Discriminate," *Rasmussen Reports,* April 13, 2021; Michael Austin, "Poll: The Majority of Likely Voters Now Believe Cheating Impacted the Results of the 2020 Election," *The Western Journal,* June 11, 2020.

87. Tom Wolf, "U.S. Election was 'most secure in American history' Federal Agency says;" "Joint statement from Elections Infrastructure Government Coordinating Council & the Election Infrastructure Sector Coordinating Executive Committees," Cybersecurity and Infrastructure Security Agency, November 12, 2020.

1

SOMETHING'S NOT RIGHT

They muddy the water, to make it seem deep.

— FRIEDRICH NIETZSCHE

Throughout 2021 and into 2022, some partisans regularly and condescendingly referred to any suggestion that Biden was not the true winner in 2020 as "the Big Lie." The term struck me as rather insecure, and somewhat more so every time I heard it. It almost seemed that those using the label hoped its frequent repetition would mystically cause the facts recommending a different conclusion to disappear.

The "Big Lie," however, did not go away. It lingered as many Americans who knew that a terrible wrong had been done—even if they'd not yet quantified it—continued to ask questions, sift through data, contemplate, and observe with unabated interest the unfolding of various audits and investigations around the country.

On January 6, 2022, one year after the rally and riot at the Capitol, Joe Biden delivered a speech in the Capitol's Statuary Hall, swinging out in evident frustration and visible anger at the stubborn accusations of his illegitimacy expressed by Donald Trump and believed by millions of Americans. Biden's enormous insecurity in his position was rather evident throughout his speech. In one statement that seemed to beg the question, Biden (making obvious reference to Donald Trump) said,

> You can't love your country only when you win. You can't obey the law only when it's convenient. You can't be patriotic when you embrace and enable lies.[1]

In a further comment—the tragic irony of which his own partisans might have missed—Biden said, "I will defend this nation and allow no one to place a dagger at the throat of democracy." He then said of Trump,

> He's not just a former president. He's a defeated former president, defeated by a margin of over 7 million votes.[2]

Was this inaugurated occupant of the Oval Office protesting too much? Were his words of blame justified?

Seeds of Doubt

Late on election night—which will be discussed in more detail in Chapter 7 —millions of Americans went to sleep believing that Donald Trump had won, and were shocked in the morning to learn that results had shifted dramatically in every swing state during the small hours of the morning, to render a completely different result.[3] As early as November 5, 2020, with those bizarre events of election night fresh in the consciousness of the nation, Ken Starr was predicting that 2020 may come to be "viewed as the election where the ultimate results are called into question" because of "the lack of integrity or the appearance of the lack of integrity in the process."[4]

I have already noted the enormous and widespread introduction of *opportunity* for compromise of the election process in 2020, and this theme should be kept in mind throughout. I have also noted that it was Democrat operatives who pushed for the removal of processes which would have assured Americans that the election was honest. As will be seen in greater detail in Chapter 3, every last one of the major increased opportunities for fraud in 2020 shared one thing in common: it was pushed by partisans of the eventual alleged victors, Joe Biden and Kamala Harris.

There are features of the 2020 election that some view as "red flags," or a clear indication of problems. In this chapter, I pause to present a selection of these.

The items discussed over the next several pages could be taken together as "probable cause." Probable cause is a legal standard for measuring whether further inquiry is warranted in a criminal case.

The existence of probable cause is not a determination that a person of interest is guilty. Rather, it is an assessment that there is enough evidence to support an inquiry. Probable cause is more than a mere gut feeling; it is the next step, an indication that there is reason to believe that the gut feeling of something being wrong may be caused by more than mere indigestion.

The Temperature of the Nation

To say that there was a steady media drumbeat—throughout his presidency and growing to a crescendo in 2020—accusing Donald Trump (and by extension his supporters) of being racist,[5] stupid,[6] incompetent,[7] bigoted,[8] out-of-control,[9] brash, mentally unstable,[10] and any number of other negative attributes, would be a gross understatement. Non-stop repetition of such accusations, amplified by all the major leftist media institutions and coupled with suppression of alternate points of view by the gatekeepers of information (see Chapter 2), surely had an impact upon public opinion.

The phenomenon of apparent triggered rage at every Trump action and tweet—even mere mention of his name—was so dramatic that Trump partisans mockingly assigned it a label: Trump Derangement Syndrome (TDS).[11] In an article two weeks prior to President Trump's inauguration, Bernard Goldberg cited vomiting, a need for cupcakes or therapy dogs or coloring books or designated areas for "breathing space," and other measures, as evidence of TDS.[12] The possibility that TDS (which included symptoms similar to those of "Beatlemania" decades prior, albeit caused in the current instance by fear and loathing rather than adoration) could be an actual clinical syndrome—rather than merely "a malicious slur term used to discredit and delegitimize criticism of President Trump"—was not ruled out by psychology professionals.[13]

Chris Cillizza, noting that a similar epithet had been used during the prior two administrations, suggested the phenomenon was likely "a function of increased polarization—not to mention our national self-sorting—at work in the country today."[14] But was that all? Goldberg noted that manifestations of TDS—which included "anti-Semitism, religious slurs, overt racism and talk of punishing people for who they are and what they believe"—were different from what had been seen in critics of Obama, and bore alarming similarity to warning signs that a 90-year old Holocaust survivor had seen before in Nazi Germany.[15] My reference to Hannah Arendt's work on totalitarianism in the Preface ("Why This Discussion Really Matters," page *xxxi*) also speaks to this matter.

But despite all of the above hostility, Trump saw remarkable growth in support among some of the very demographics to which he had been supposedly (if one believed the breathless pronouncements repeated on seemingly endless loop in major media) most hostile. In the 2020 election, Donald Trump increased his performance by six percentage points among black men, and by five percentage points among Hispanic women[16] when compared to his winning performance in the 2016 presidential election. Trump also won all but one of the counties that had until then been bellwethers (I will define this term in a moment).

Facts such as those listed above seemed not to square with the loss by Donald Trump of both the electoral and popular votes by an enormous margin. In this chapter we will make a general survey of features of the reported 2020 outcome that some suggested to be, even if circumstantial, incongruous with a Biden victory.

Things That Make You Go "Hmm"

Most public polls indeed showed Biden with a comfortable lead in the final days before the election of 2020. Why, then, would a Trump loss not have been the more reasonable outcome?

There are several reasons to believe that the polls in 2020 were just wrong. Why? For one thing, "cancel culture," which aggressively and ruthlessly pursued the personal and professional destruction of people holding unapproved opinions, was by then in full flower.[17] This environment led to an enormous partisan disparity in terms of perceived freedom to share one's views. A poll by the CATO Institute during the summer of 2020 revealed that 58% of staunch liberals reported feeling they could say what they believe, and that this was the *only* group of Americans for whom a majority felt such safety. Fully 64% of moderates, 77% of conservatives, and 77% of strong conservatives agreed with the statement "The political climate these days prevents me from saying things I believe because others might find them offensive." Such fear of sharing one's opinions represented a significant increase from 2017, just three years prior.[18]

These concerns were not merely about approval in social settings; they touched upon Americans' basic need to make a living. In 2020, 50% of strong liberals reported supporting the *firing* of Trump donors. 44% of all Americans under 30 years of age supported firing executives if they donated to Trump. Nearly one third (32%) of employed Americans reported being "personally worried about missing out on career opportunities or losing their job if their political opinions became known." The disparity of such worry was most pronounced among the most highly educated: 60% of Republicans with postgraduate education were worried their political views could harm them at work, versus 25% of similarly educated Democrats.[19]

Such an environment is probably more than enough to explain why polls did not match the reality of the election. When I was asked to answer questions about political support in 2019 and 2020 on incoming phone calls, I found myself instantly on guard. I could not be sure who this person was, or whether the information would be used against me. This very concern caused me to decline to participate in at least one such survey. Certainly, this would have been the case for others less bold than I, and more so among those who supported Trump.

There was also growing support for Trump among many Americans between 2016 and 2020. While some may have abandoned him, a significant number of formerly skeptical Americans found themselves pleasantly surprised by his performance in terms of keeping campaign promises that most other politicians were unwilling to tackle despite their own campaign promises, and accomplishing other good policy objectives. Trump had won in 2016 with the half-hearted support of many Republicans who had preferred other candidates and whom Trump had yet to fully convince. Millions of these skeptics turned into serious supporters as they watched now-President Trump—in spite of failing to reduce spending—follow through on one campaign promise after another, and observed the results of his leadership at home and abroad.

To the joy of his supporters and the dismay of his opponents, Trump's first-term accomplishments were extensive. Selections follow:[20]

Moved the U.S. Embassy in Israel from Tel Aviv to Jerusalem (February 2018), as promised, and over loud objections of naysayers;[21] took action to recognize Israel's sovereignty over the Golan Heights;[22] implemented a temporary ban (upheld by the Supreme Court) on travel to the U.S. from countries with high levels of terrorist activity and inadequate means for screening travelers;[23] ISIS driven out of all the territory they formerly held in Iraq and Syria;[24] more than five million Americans were lifted off of food stamps in the first part of Trump's term; presided over a dramatic unemployment reduction: at or below 4% for 26 straight months, reaching the lowest rate in nearly fifty years;[25] the number of blue-collar jobs grew at the fastest rate in over three decades; Hispanic-American unemployment (April 2018-February 2020) fell to its lowest rate in history; African-American (January 2017-March 2020) and Asian-American (May 2018, April and June 2019) unemployment reached all-time record lows; women's unemployment (October 2017-February 2020) reached its lowest rate in 65 years; Veteran unemployment reached a 20-year low (September-October 2017, July, October-November 2018, February-May, September-October, December 2019); youth unemployment (May 2017) reached its lowest point in nearly half a century; unemployment for Americans without a high school diploma hit its lowest point in history; unemployment for disabled Americans reached its lowest point in history; median income for Hispanic-Americans surpassed $50,000 for the first time ever; the official poverty rates for African-Americans and Hispanic-Americans reached the lowest levels ever recorded; manufacturing, consumer, and small business confidence reached record highs; created the Space Force;[26] passed and signed Right to Try legislation to give critically ill patients access to more life-saving cures;[27] responded quickly and decisively to reports of poor service quality at V.A. hospital;[28] made the United States energy independent (exporting more oil than it imported) for the first time in more than 70 years;[29] withdrew the United States from the Paris Climate Accord;[30] canceled the anti-coal (so-called) Clean Power Plan;[31] signed a bipartisan Criminal Justice Reform bill into law;[32] presided over peace and de-escalation with a belligerent North Korea, including a stop to nuclear and ballistic missile testing, a release of American hostages, and the return of remains of fallen soldiers;[33] withdrew the United States from the Iran Deal—which would have guaranteed Iran a path to nuclear weapons—and imposed tough sanctions;[34] made the United States the first country to recognize Juan Guaidó as the interim president of Venezuela;[35] completed construction of 458 miles of the promised Wall along the Southern border[36] and implemented the successful "stay in Mexico" policy for refugees, as a means of preventing mass-release of un-vetted asylum seekers into the American interior;[37] passed significant tax cuts for Americans that increased tax revenues by increasing prosperity.[38]

What Happened With the Bellwether Counties?

The United States has over three thousand counties. A very small handful of these are—or have historically been—very special with respect to elections. Bellwether counties are those rare places that fluctuate reliably between parties and presidential candidates in apparent harmony with the overall mood of the nation. Some bellwethers do so rather dramatically, in contrast to most of the nation which tends to be more habitually partisan. The behavior of bellwethers has fascinated political scientists for years.

There are nineteen bellwether counties in the United States, or at least there were until 2020. In that year, Joe Biden and Kamala Harris allegedly destroyed the records of eighteen of them. If Biden and Harris' win was authentic, then out of over 3000 U.S. counties, there today remains only a single bellwether: Clallam County, Washington.

The remaining eighteen,[39] in each of which the winning presidential candidate had prevailed in every election since the 1970s (seven of them since the 1960s, two the 1950s, and one since 1948) were carried by Donald J. Trump in 2020. In twelve of these counties, Trump's win over Biden exceeded 10%. In five of them, Trump beat Biden by over 20%. In two, Trump's victory margin was greater than 27%. *Every single one of these counties voted for Barack Obama and Joe Biden in both 2008 and 2012.* If Trump was truly the pariah that he was made out to be, and if Biden's candidacy were really such a juggernaut as the American people were led to believe, why then would this shift not have been reflected in at least a few of these eighteen counties in 2020?

With a total turnout of 78%, Donald Trump won Ottawa County by a margin of 61% to 38%, improving his 2016 return by four points. ... [I]n this year's election voters in leading bellwether counties didn't just come out for Donald Trump marginally; they backed him in droves. ... In Westmoreland County, Virginia—a small, rural community south of Washington, DC that's failed to be a bellwether only twice since 1928, and is home to twice the number of African Americans than the national average—[Trump] beat Mr Biden by 16 points.[40]

Such results have many observers scratching their heads. Is it possible that all these counties which had so consistently swayed this way and that—mirroring the nation's pulse—for half a century or longer, would have gone so strongly against the prevailing candidate (Joe Biden, *whom they had supported in 2008 and 2012),* in 2020? Yes, it is possible; almost anything is possible. Indeed, ten of these eighteen counties last deviated from the nation's choice for president, simultaneously, 44 years ago (1976), choosing Gerald Ford in the election he lost to Jimmy Carter.[41]

But ten of nineteen is not the same as eighteen of nineteen, and the more salient question is therefore whether it is likely, or even plausible, that such an overwhelming proportion of these counties bucked the trend in 2020. Could it be just one more indication that these were strange political times? On a case by case basis, analysts have furnished theories to explain the deviation of these bellwethers in 2020. To be fair, 2020 was no ordinary year. Whatever the case, the matters should be considered soberly and in light of all the evidence.

Vigo County

One of the more remarkable examples among the bellwethers was that of Vigo County, Indiana, which prior to 2020 voted with the rest of the nation in every presidential election except for two (1908 and 1952) since 1888.[42] Not long after the 2020 election, the Associated Press published a fascinating analysis by Claire Galofaro of the strange case of 2020 deviance. Vigo County, Galofaro notes, "long had some mysterious mix of quirky politics, demographics, geography, religion, labor and luck so that it had become America's most reliable presidential bellwether."[43] And, to be quite clear, Vigo County is no hard and fast hotbed of conservatism:

> [F]or generations [Vigo County's] conservative tilt on social issues was balanced by left-leaning idiosyncrasies. There are four colleges in Terre Haute, a remarkable number for a city its size. It is the birthplace of Eugene V. Debs, a champion for workers' rights who ran for president as a socialist five times in the early 20th century. The county's blue collar workforce was heavily organized and union halls dotted the city. ...

[In 2020,] Trump won in Terre Haute by 15 percentage points, holding his margin of victory in 2016.[44]

As noted, Vigo County has followed the country in its presidential choices almost perfectly since 1888. It seems the county was almost prescient of the national mood, beginning to swing away from Obama's policies, while still giving him the win, in 2012:

When Obama came to town, people packed a school gymnasium and screamed like he was a rock star. The county had from 1960 to 2004 voted within 3 percentage points of the national vote, but it broke that streak to vote overwhelmingly for Obama, who won this county by 16 percentage points. That margin narrowed considerably in 2012, when Obama won Vigo County by just a few hundred votes.[45]

So, what happened to Vigo County in 2020? Galofaro reports the story of Ken Warner. Undoubtedly anecdotal, Warner's trajectory is yet not unlike that of others about whom we have heard:

Warner, 64, has toggled between Republicans and Democrats, and wasn't terribly excited about Trump in the 2016 primary. Warner remains uneasy about the president's personality. He cringed when Trump antagonized governors during the pandemic and hurled childish insults at people such as the late Sen. John McCain, R-Ariz.

But he grew more enthusiastic about Trump throughout his presidency. He cheered for Trump's economic policies. He supported the tax cuts, the tariffs and his tough stance on China. ...

"I think his tweets were part of his downfall," Warner said. "But the people that voted for Trump didn't vote for him for his personality. They voted for results."[46]

In other words, people like Warner in a county that strongly supported Obama in both his first and second terms actually *grew* in their support for Trump, building to real enthusiasm in 2020. Warner was unfazed by Trump's tweets, but was very impressed with Trump's policies and accomplishments. Is it possible that Warner saw something in Trump that the rest of America just did not see, that the rest of the nation turned away from Trump even as bellwether Vigo County went sharply in the other direction with even stronger support for him?

The case of Vigo County is only one example, and it must be remembered that political science is not a hard science, since it is impossible in an open system to control for all variables. The most important thing to ponder is whether such deviations in 2020 from historical trends is the most reasonable explanation for the outcome. "Most reasonable" of course, is not the same thing as "theoretically possible." In terms of *theoretically possible* explanations, there seem to be only three:

If Joe Biden Actually Won in 2020

Explanation #1: *Those 18 counties have changed.* Counties are comprised of people, people change over time, and in the aggregate, changes in sentiment can affect the overall culture of a county. One of several factors that can hasten such a change is migration: have a great number of people with a different temperament moved into the county, and/or have many people who formerly contributed to the county being a bellwether relocated to another part of the country? Another factor that could have such an effect is generational: Are young people voting for the first time in 2020 more strongly pro-Trump and/or were those who are no longer voting (for example, those who have died) more left-leaning? Confirming the "counties have changed" theory would require case by case study. Among the considerations would be *trajectory*: Have many of these counties been trending conservative in the 8 years since they voted for Obama and Biden in 2012?

Explanation #2: *America has changed.* The United States is not set in stone. For better or for worse, our society is evolving, and the bellwether counties are changing with it. America's partisan divide has been increasing.[47] As this trend continues, it may be increasingly unlikely that *any* counties in any part of this nation will fluctuate back and forth between political parties over the decades the way that some bellwether counties have done during the last century. Is it possible that these eighteen bellwether counties have finally fallen victim to the partisan calcification that has long since hardened much of the rest of the country?

If Donald Trump Actually Won in 2020

Explanation #3: *Those 18 counties retained their long record of siding with the winning presidential candidate for one more election cycle,* and the deviation of the bellwethers from the official outcome should have been a red flag alerting the nation to the fact that something was amiss with the certified results.

An Odd Way For Innocent People to Act

As a general rule, those with nothing to hide tend not to fear the light. In 2016, the Department of Homeland Security (DHS) issued a list of steps that should be taken to help safeguard the right of every American to have their vote counted. Among them:

Have backup paper ballots on hand if voting systems fail to start up, as happened during the South Carolina presidential primaries in January 2008. Paper doesn't fail to boot up. Nor can a paper ballot be hacked from a server abroad once it is marked by the voter.

Have paper copies of poll books, if e-poll books are used.

Have paper copies of voter registration lists.

Ensure that vote counting systems are not connected to the Internet. Some vendors have put wireless capacity in their voting systems to make reporting easier. These need to be turned off.

Curtail all Internet voting. Ballots cast by email or through an Internet portal are vulnerable to hacking.

Run robust post-election audits, cross-checking vote tallies counted by computer with manual counts of paper ballots.

Conduct reconciliation procedures to ensure that the number of voters who cast ballots squares with the number of votes to be tallied.[48]

This list assumes electronic voting systems, and we should question that premise.[49] Divorcing elections from tangible objects is probably not wise. There is a principle here: **If the voting system cannot be understood by the average citizen, then they cannot be expected to trust it.**

Marked paper ballots with security features to show that the number of marked ballots on hand in a precinct after an election match the number of registered legal voters who appeared to cast them, and that have been kept secure through a chain of custody which has, at all times, been safe from tampering by anyone who might wish to influence the election, are easy for any citizen to understand. That is to say, a regular person can conceptualize not only the idea of marking a ballot, but also the process of counting it onsite and recording the result in a record book with witnesses, and then putting it into a secure container which is then locked and kept safe from tampering for future reference or audit. If regular people were to watch such a process of voting and counting happening, they would be able to see if someone was cheating. And, if any regular person was asked, he or she would be able to explain how, at least in concept, to determine that something is wrong: for example, the secure container of ballots was missing from the precinct for one hour on election night, or an unauthorized person was seen on camera entering the room and accessing the box. Safeguards can also be implemented in the virtual space, but the problem is that reliance upon experts is required to even understand that something *has* happened, that some compromise *has* occurred.

To put it simply, there are two circumstances under which it would not be immediately obvious that some breach has taken place in any election:

1. There is a *physical* breach in the chain of custody that is outside the view of the public because the process has either not been well-designed or protocols have not been followed

2. There is a *virtual* breach in the system that is outside the view of the public because the public does not have the technical ability to even understand when a breach has occurred and when it has not

The difference between the two situations is that true transparency can be achieved in the first, while it is much more difficult—if not impossible—to achieve in the second (particularly if there are no paper ballots that have been physically counted and recorded at the precinct and preserved rigorously through chain of custody) because technical experts would be required to even tell the public whether the situation was secure.

A crucial consideration is the time factor. As we saw in 2020, all that is necessary for election manipulators to carry the day is to successfully run down the clock with plausible deniability. When the American people must rely entirely upon the word of technocrats, many of them with financial interest in the "reliability" of voting technology and in the future flow of money to be made by securing victory for those politicians favored by the voting technology companies and/or likely to continue, protect, and expand massively lucrative government contracts to these companies, there is simply too much at stake, too many opportunities for interference, and not enough time to get to the bottom of it before tremendous damage is done by the certification of a false result.

Self governance cannot exist without fraud-resistant elections. The tendency in technology toward ever-increasing ease and convenience stands at cross-purposes with the objective of elections, which must prioritize reliability and a true outcome above all other considerations. When honest elections are the objective, more high-tech bells and whistles are not necessarily better. Multiple systems and processes designed to stop fraud by either making it visible when it occurs or by discouraging it in the first place were set aside as "unnecessary" or even resisted vigorously by Democrat partisans in 2020 and afterward.[50] George Soros-supported ThinkProgress ran a story "New study confirms that voter ID laws are very racist."[51] The study that it cited, however, had a deeply flawed methodology. Among the flaws, it interpreted a reduction in voting turnout among some racial groups when more strict voter ID laws were in place as evidence that the voter ID law itself was racist.

With the advent and growing use of electronic voting systems, and the involvement of the internet in updating voting machine software and potential transmission of voting results, enormous new risks for compromise of the process and its outcomes have arisen. Several years ago, I discovered through casual conversation that the man seated next to me on a flight was in the business of electronic voting machines and technologies. Fascinated, I asked him many questions, and he was an obvious advocate for the technology. We talked about all the steps that are taken to make sure that the tabulations are correct and that the vote is secure. But ultimately, when I probed about the theoretical possibility that someone with the technical ability could influence the counts or the outcome, he admitted with some reluctance that it was true. He added that such a thing did not really happen, and I took note that the basis for his assertion was that the people designing and running these systems "would never do that." In other words, it all came down to a requirement to trust the people running the technology and a fundamental belief that people in the technology sector are somehow above the temptation to cheat or manipulate results.

It became obvious through clues in the conversation that this man was sympathetic to the Democratic Party. I sensed that he revealed this leaning with an assumption that I was as well.

A matter so important as self governance should not rest upon a demand that we simply trust that the people running the technology are not up to something nefarious. There must be a way to see what is going on, and to recognize and correct when something has gone wrong—and the best way remains old-fashioned in-person physical balloting with upgraded security features as needed.

In 2019, the Cyber Policy Center at Stanford University released its report with recommendations for maintaining and enhancing the security of the 2020 U.S. presidential election and future elections in light of the increasing presence of electronic methods and equipment in the voting picture. Among other things, the report recommended requiring that all vote-counting systems provide a voter-verified paper audit trail, and assessing the security of computerized election-related systems in an adversarial manner.

As with the DHS list mentioned above, the assumption of the Stanford University report is that computer election systems will be employed. Again, I recommend against this assumption. Blockchain technology (a shared and public database or ledger keeping records that cannot be altered once they are in place) holds some promise to address these challenges in the future, but there remains a serious question about whether even in such a scenario transparency to ordinary people can be achieved. Using electronic technology for other parts of the process, such as compiling and keeping records of vote tabulations and results that are primarily recorded in a paper record-book with signatures at the precinct level on the day of the election, and backed up by preserved paper ballots, remains (in my opinion) the best system.

However, in 2020, voting machines and voting by mail—both susceptible to compromise—were heavily employed across the nation. Furthermore, when those who raised questions about the election's integrity asked for full forensic audits, they were rebuffed at almost every turn by Democrats, Democrat allies, and even by a few Republicans.

A common objection to full forensic audits is that conducting them "undermines trust in democracy." For example,

> Baseless lies about widespread voter fraud and false allegations of a "stolen" 2020 presidential election have inflamed mistrust in democracy and provided the political fuel for hundreds of proposals across the country to enact new barriers to voting. These efforts to undermine the election have been especially conspicuous in Arizona, where voter fraud conspiracies are behind a state Senate–led push to conduct a partisan "audit" of votes cast in Maricopa County, which was won by President Joe Biden.[52]

Notice that the above excerpt presents five opinions as though they are established facts: 1) "Maricopa County ... was won by President Joe Biden," 2) that those seeking audit were engaged in "efforts to undermine the election," 3) that widespread voter fraud is "baseless" and 4) a "lie," and that 5) allegations of a stolen election are "false." Such insertion of opinion into purported news reporting related to the election, the audits, January 6, and subsequent events is sadly not limited to the obviously partisan papers; in researching this book, I have found it repeatedly from Reuters, the Associated Press, Forbes, and others.

Typically, however, regular and rigorous audits serve to strengthen trust in the entity being audited, at least if it is indeed trustworthy. Those who pursued audits in 2020 were not asserting at the beginning that widespread fraud occurred; they had good reason to suspect that it had and sought to investigate its extent, if any. And the wholesale and immediate rejection of any meaningful consideration by those in charge is what undermines democracy. Those seeking an audit do not distrust democracy, even if they might distrust the people who ran this particular election under conditions more vulnerable to fraud than ever before.

Furthermore, our entire system of government, with its checks and balances at every turn, rests upon the principle of mistrust. If people were not sinful, there would be no need for *any* election security, *any* locks on bank doors, *any* walls or armed guards around homes of celebrities or dignitaries, or *any* restrictions on who should be around children. The idea that we need to just "trust democracy" and not worry about checking up on processes is a nice sentiment, but it is without question a fairy tale.

The above argument is, in fact, an example of a common logical fallacy called the "false choice" or "false dilemma." It wrongly asserts that there are only two options—in this case:

1. accept every democratic election result (no matter how shadily conducted) as true, or else you
2. mistrust the very institution of democracy

But there are other possibilities, like trusting democracy when it is conducted transparently and with integrity, when people are allowed to vote only once, when people ineligible to vote are prevented from doing so, when there has been a secure chain of custody to prevent tampering with the results, and so forth.

The basic argument of such people seems to be: "We should not check for fraud, because fraud did not occur." The website quoted above levels *ad hominem* attacks at concerned citizens, labeling the audit team a "sham" and stating, without evidence, that allegations the election might have been rigged are "lies."[53] Such resistance to post-election forensic audits, however, calls into doubt claims that the 2020 election was the "most secure in U.S. history." It was also interesting that the very same Democrats who had just spent four years of virtually nonstop allegations that the Russians had interfered with the previous presidential election now asserted, without even blushing, that the U.S. election of 2020 was the most secure and trustworthy election in the nation's history.

In fact, it was known that major problems existed in states that decided the election. In a 2019 audit of the Pennsylvania Statewide Uniform Registry of Electors (SURE), Democrat former Auditor General Eugene DePasquale found, among other things, "tens of thousands of potential duplicate and inaccurate voter records," "weaknesses in the ... maintenance of voter records in SURE," and "potential areas of improvement related to computer security." Further, the audit admitted that DePasquale's office "was unable to determine with any degree of reasonable assurance that the SURE system is secure and that Pennsylvania voter registration records are complete, accurate, and in compliance with applicable laws, regulations, and related guidelines."[54]

The Hasty Anointing

There was also something very different about how the election *decision* unfolded in 2020. One red flag can be seen by comparing events following election night in 2020 to those of 2000. Daryl Brooks, who was a poll watcher in Philadelphia on November 3 and was with Rudy Giuliani when the Associated Press called the election for Joe Biden, notes:

> What was ironic was how the media covered those 37 days from November 7th to Gore's concession. They were thorough and in-depth about everything ... I was glued to the TV the whole time. I knew all of Florida's counties, the lawyers' names, the types of lawsuits that were being filed and counter-filed, and the exact vote count, minute by minute. It wasn't until after a fair and thorough coverage of this entire 37-day event that the media officially predicted Bush the winner. ...
>
> [C]ontrast that to today. ... Instead of reporting the different lawsuits that were being filed, evidence of voter fraud, and the problems with the voting machines, they declared that ... Joe Biden was the winner. It took them only 4 days, and the recount had not even begun. And if you questioned their conclusion, they called you a right-wing nut, conspiracy theorist, or a racist. Plus, the mainstream media, along with other social media platforms, censored dissenting opinions. ...
>
> What got me so angry was the media did nothing at all to cover the massive voter fraud that went on in the election. There was no reporting on the investigations, allegations of fraud, proof of election illegitimacy, or even the ongoing lawsuits filed by Trump and his team. Instead, the media was calling Trump an obstructionist for not allowing Biden to make his transition team. ...
>
> Back in 2000, all I heard on the news was how every vote counted and the legitimacy of democracy had to be upheld. It was all about fairness in the votes and how every voice counted. Jump 20 years later to 2020, and none of that mattered any longer. Once the media declared Biden the winner, that was the end of the story. Any suggestion of voter fraud or ballot tampering was considered heresy.[55]

Brooks' choice of the word "heresy" is interesting and matches my own experience and observation of the time period. The assertion that Biden had won quickly became a sort of orthodoxy that could not be questioned without danger of excommunication. People asking even the most obvious questions were not welcome in polite company—they were branded heretics and canceled. Even more telling, the orthodoxy was not being defended with evidence but rather with bandwagon assertions that good people, smart people, non-racist people all agreed that the election was over and that Joe Biden won.

On November 11, 2020, I wrote in an article titled, "Democrats to America: 'You'd better put some ice on that'":

> One week after Election Day, 2020, the United States still have no official declaration of a projected winner of our presidential contest. However, this fact has not prevented the media from crowning a preferred victor: Joe Biden. And, many are insisting with great stridency that the rest of us fall in line.
>
> Beginning early Wednesday, November 4, Biden and/or Harris have stepped up to the mic several times, posturing as though they have won. Most of the institutions and media of American society, including Fox News, are happily playing along, calling Joe Biden the "president elect."
>
> Throughout the latter part of last week, many of us have been admonished fiercely and/or mockingly by liberal friends that "It's over," and that we need to just "accept the result," because "the American people have spoken, and they chose Biden and Harris."
>
> Hold on, there. Have they? In fact, whether what we are hearing is actually what the American people have spoken is *precisely* the question that needs a real answer ... This election has been anything but transparent. We've seen this chaos coming for months, as Democrats have been moving furiously, in the election lead-up, to change rules, removing the very safeguards that were designed to prevent fraud.[56]

Of course, for all anyone knew at the time, it could have been the case that Joe Biden won. However, the lighting-fast and sweeping assertions that there was no doubt about it, accompanied by a stunning lack of curiosity about the oddities and serious allegations of fraud and misbehavior in Philadelphia and other areas around the swing states, accompanied thenceforward by an almost comedically predictable quick characterization of every lawsuit brought by the Trump team as another attempt to "overturn the results of the election," did not seem to match the way one might expect real winners to act.

Like many others, political commentator and former CNN host Lou Dobbs, evidently sensing the magnitude of the problem, was indignant. Interviewed by Devin Nunes on Fox, Dobbs spoke frankly:

> We all lived through this. ... What I'd like to know is, "What in the hell is the Republican Party doing to defend and to ..." I mean, why not just say, "We're not going to accept the results of this election." It's outrageous. Why would we put up with it?

Nunes replied, "In order to win these battles, we have to have a place that we can communicate. And, that's the challenge. And so you ask, 'So what are we doing now?' That's why millions of Americans are flooding over to Parler. They're flooding over to Rumble..."

Dobbs, however, suggested that going to Parler and Rumble is not a solution to the current crisis: "Good Lord. With all due respect, congressman, and I respect the hell out of you. But pushing Parler and Rumble is not an answer to what I'm asking. ... On either one of those, I would hope that there would be more interest in the content than in the messenger."

Nunes agreed, "This election should not be called. But, what's happening out there because of the media putting out this narrative, is..."

Dobbs interjected, "But what are you doing, and what is the party doing, to make sure that it isn't called? I see so little animation in the Republican party on this. It's as if it's just another day at the store, when in fact, I believe, the fate of the Republic hangs in the balance here. Don't you?"

Dobbs' became one of three Fox hosts, along with the network itself, named in a multibillion dollar defamation suit filed by voting technology company Smartmatic. His long-running Fox show, Lou Dobbs Tonight, was canceled by the network three months later.[57]

Other Facts Suggesting Something Wrong

In a July 2021 Op-Ed, Lieutenant General (Ret.) Michael Flynn presented ten facts from the 2020 election that he suggests should give us pause. His summary bears serious discussion and consideration.

The first fact noted by Flynn is the matter of the bellwether counties already discussed, to which he adds that, "since 1936 ... Luzerne County of the Commonwealth of Pennsylvania ... has gone to the winner of Pennsylvania," adding that, "In 2016 and 2020, Trump won that county handily. Any Republican winning Luzerne County in that time frame (since 1936) has also never failed to carry the state of Michigan."[58] Yet, we are told that Joe Biden won both Pennsylvania and Michigan in 2020 despite Trump winning Luzerne. Did Joe Biden thus end the county's 84-year record?

Second, in addition to the bellwether counties, Flynn notes that four bellwether *states*—Ohio, Iowa, North Carolina, and Florida—have been won by the same presidential candidate in thirteen national elections since 1896, and each and every time that all four of these states aligned on a candidate, that same presidential candidate also won the election. Put differently, these states have not historically aligned—they all aligned in only thirteen out of thirty-one elections over 124 years—but in 100% of those years that they *did* align, they aligned in support of the actual winner nationally. *All four of these states were won by Donald Trump in 2020.* Is it possible that Biden ended the century-and-a-quarter record concerning the alignment of these four states?

Third, Flynn notes that incumbents generally win a second term, and when they don't, there are typically early warning signs. Lack of party enthusiasm and unity around an incumbent president—as represented in the presidential primary during a re-election year—has historically served as a *prerequisite* to the loss of re-election. Since the start of presidential primaries in 1912, the only four incumbent presidents who have lost re-election also fared poorly in their primaries.

- Herbert Hoover (1932): 36.0%
- Gerald Ford (1976): 53.3%
- Jimmy Carter (1980): 51.1%
- George H.W. Bush (1992): 72.8%

In contrast, the biggest Republican landslide re-elections during the same time frame showed high approval from the party in the primary:

- Dwight Eisenhower (1956) 85.9%
- Richard Nixon (1972) 86.9%
- Ronald Reagan (1984) 98.8%

So, how did Donald Trump fare in his 2020 primary? The answer is that he had tremendous support from his party, winning the Republican primary with 94.0%, making his incumbent popularity within the party second only to that of Ronald Reagan in 1984. *Never before in U.S. history has an incumbent Republican with such tremendous primary support from his own party lost re-election.*

The picture becomes even more bizarre when contrasted with Joe Biden's performance compared to the other 2020 Democratic primary candidates. Biden was not swept to victory in the Democratic primaries. In fact, he was "trounced ... in Iowa, New Hampshire and Nevada—the traditional indicators of general election viability." Furthermore, he picked as his running mate Kamala Harris, another primary candidate so deeply unpopular that she had been one of the first to drop out.

Fourth, Flynn presents incumbent vote gain as an indicator of outcomes, noting that, "[s]ince 1892 ... only six presidents have lost re-election. All six had fewer total votes in their re-election campaigns than in their initial campaigns." By contrast, "All incumbents who gained votes won re-election. In 2020, Trump gained a record 11 million votes. For perspective, former President Barack Obama *lost* 4 million votes nationally in 2012 and still won re-election." In other words, it has been possible to win re-election with fewer votes than the first round, but losing re-election *while gaining* votes has not happened in 128 years. Is it possible that Biden and Harris were such immensely inspiring candidates that they were able to break a century-and-a-quarter trend that delivered re-election to every single incumbent who gained national votes?

Fifth, Flynn notes that trends in voter registration by party within a state tend to indicate the direction that state is headed with respect to the presidential candidate. "As far back as records are publicly available, three of the key states in the 2020 election—Pennsylvania, Florida and North Carolina—have moved in favor of the same party that made overall registration gains since 2000. In Pennsylvania, from 2012 to 2016, 60 of 67 counties trended more Republican in registration, suggesting a major GOP gain ...—consequently, Pennsylvania flipped for Trump in 2016." Following this pattern, we would expect that if Biden won Pennsylvania, we would also have seen Democrats outpace Republicans in terms of voter registration in Pennsylvania over the intervening years. The opposite was the case—by a very wide margin. Writes Flynn, "from 2016 to 2020, 60 of 67 counties became [even] more Republican in registration ... with the GOP registering roughly 242,000 net new voters, compared to just 12,000 for Democrats." Is it possible that Biden actually won Pennsylvania despite his party not only having lost it in 2016, but having been outpaced by Republicans in voter registration during the intervening four years *by a factor of twenty to one*?

Sixth, Flynn discusses House of Representatives down-ballot voting as a normal indicator of success at the top of the ticket:

> When Obama won a landslide victory in 2008, the Democrats took 14 U.S. House seats away from Republican incumbents, while only losing five seats. When Reagan was elected in 1980, the Republicans gained a net of 34 seats. When Reagan was re-elected, Republicans clawed back a net of 16 House seats from the 26 lost in the 1982 midterms. *In 2020, with Trump at the top of the ticket, Republicans knocked out 13 incumbent Democratic seats, while not losing a single Republican seat.* Common sense suggests a Biden electoral landslide would have taken at least [one] Republican seat with it.

Not only does common sense suggest it, but the pattern of history does as well. Is it possible that Biden actually won an electoral landslide while not gaining a single House seat for his party—and in fact losing more than a dozen?

Seventh, Flynn discusses the odd divergence of Florida in 2020 from Michigan and Pennsylvania. He notes that "[s]ince 1932, Florida's trajectory has correlated perfectly with the trajectory of Michigan and Pennsylvania as a reflection of working-class political sentiment. In every single election since then, if Florida became more Republican from the previous election, Michigan and Pennsylvania did exactly the same." Trump won Florida in

2020 by a significantly larger margin than he did in 2016. Yet, despite Republicans' aforementioned 20:1 registration advantage in Pennsylvania in 2020, "both Pennsylvania and Michigan charted a separate direction from Florida for the first time in nearly a century." Is it possible that Biden was able to inspire working-class voters in Michigan and Pennsylvania so as to overcome significant Republican headway in those states while failing to do the same in Florida?

Eighth, Flynn presents the situation of Trump's massive, and in a number of cases record-breaking, net vote gains over his 2016 performance in key areas while still apparently losing out to Joe Biden in those very areas by an even more massive vote gain by the latter. Maricopa County, Arizona is discussed as an example. Nearly two-thirds of Arizona's votes come from Maricopa County. Maricopa County, notes Flynn, "has not voted for the Democratic nominee since it supported Harry Truman in 1948. In 1996, Bob Dole became the first Republican in nearly 50 years to lose Arizona, but he still won Maricopa County." Trump won Maricopa County in 2016, and added about 248,000 votes in 2020—a Republican record for net additional votes there. Yet, we are told that Joe Biden gained even more, some 338,000 net new votes from the number garnered by Hillary Clinton in 2016. In other words, the lackluster Biden raked in a number of votes *"nearly three times higher than the all-time previous [record] high Democratic vote gain ... by John Kerry in 2004."*[59] Observes Flynn, "Similar record high vote totals and increases for Trump were also eclipsed in 2020 in ... Georgia, Michigan, Pennsylvania, Wisconsin, Nevada and Minnesota." Clearly, Donald Trump was tremendously popular in these states and built upon his net numbers after his 2016 win. Factors such as demographic change, migration in and out of these counties, and people just changing their minds about the candidates are real things that occur all the time and must be weighed into the equation. The question Flynn and others have asked is whether the performance of Joe Biden and Kamala Harris, eclipsing Trump's gains in those places, makes sense. Chapter 4 will more closely examine Maricopa County, in relation to the findings of the Arizona audit that were released on September 24, 2021.

Ninth, Flynn looks at the movement in sentiment among minority voters. In 2020, Trump earned more than 25% of the non-white vote, a level of support among minority voters seen only one other time since Richard Nixon's 1960 campaign. Trump's gains among this group of Americans caused him to win "counties [in 2020] that had been in the Democratic column for decades ..., perhaps most notably, ... Miami-Dade County, Florida." In light of this remarkable movement among minority American voters toward Trump in 2020, Flynn states, "[t]he absence of millions of core Democratic base minority voters raises considerable questions as to how Biden was able to surpass Obama's popular vote record by 12 million [votes]."

Finally, Flynn notes that the post-election behavior of the media, politicians (Democrat in particular), and others does not match their rhetoric about 2020 being "the most secure presidential election in U.S. history." He notes that in 2016, "with narrow margins in Pennsylvania, Michigan and Wisconsin, Trump's camp had no concern over recounts or potential audits in any of those three states that decided the election." Biden's certified margins of victory in both Pennsylvania and Michigan are much larger than Trump's 2016 margins in those states, but the opposition from the left to full forensic audits, whether statewide or in certain counties, does not seem consistent with the steady "most secure election ever" drumbeat.

> If Biden's team was 100 percent confident they won the election fair and square, then they should feel there is nothing to hide. Audits confirming his certified totals would certainly solidify his administration and simultaneously deal an embarrassing defeat to election skeptics.[60]

Rather than invite audits, however, the left has stonewalled them and increased the volume on their "most secure election in U.S. history" claim. Indeed, Democratic secretaries of state have been taking extreme actions to prevent audits, with the Colorado secretary of state, Jena Griswold, going so far as to effectively ban audits in her state.[61]

Although these many features—even when taken together—fall short of conclusively proving a dishonest election, I suggest that only the most uncurious or willfully blind person could fail to find them deeply troublesome.

Trend and Statistical Analysis

Following the election, Seth Keshel aggregated summaries of various statistical trends pointing toward fraud. Keshel's website, electionfraud20.org, comprised a clearinghouse of lightly-curated data and analysis from a variety of sources. Much of its content was the product of volunteer effort, often by experts but usually lacking double-blind peer review.[62] Some is highly technical.

Trend analysis considers election patterns over time, takes note of anomalies or significant deviation from a trend. Deviation alone is not proof of fraud, since there may be a rational explanation. But, deviation from the trend can be a clue.

Some 2020 election trends—such as the case of the bellwether counties —are discussed in detail elsewhere in this chapter. Below are summarized two such trend analyses.

"Battle for the Largest Counties"

Keshel points out that Democrats are over time winning fewer and fewer—but more populous—counties in the United States, while Republicans are winning more and more counties overall. In 2016, Donald Trump won 2,623 counties across the country, up from George W. Bush's 2,438 (2000) and 2527 (2004) and George H.W. Bush's 2,292 (1988). Meanwhile, Joe Biden won only 537 U.S. counties in 2020, down from Obama's 873 (2008) and 694 (2012) and Bill Clinton's 1,514 (1992) and 1,524 (1996). This result probably shows a general trend of increasing political polarization between urban and rural areas in the United States.[63]

Biden's 537 in 2020 represents only 17% of all U.S. counties; all the rest went to Trump. In order to win in this way, Biden needed to not merely win those counties by a little; he had to drive up the tallies in those areas and achieve total domination. And, what Keshel reports is that Biden had an *average* of 109,703 in every single county that he carried in 2020, up from an average of 64,866 for Obama in 2012 and 56,991 for Obama in 2008, and a stunning *five times more* than the per-county average of 20,168 and 21,999 for Clinton in 1992 and 1996 respectively.

So far, there is nothing particularly difficult or nefarious about the numbers cited above apart from questioning the plausibility of the enormously high level of voter turnout that allegedly occurred in those counties that Biden won. However, the analysis continues. There was also a massive increase in the total number of votes cast in the United States in 2020, up from just over 136 million in 2016, to 158.2 million in 2020. But the single most striking aspect to me about the data is that the total increase in Democrat votes in 2020 was 15.5 million, with 9.94 million of these votes coming in from large counties with over 200,000 votes in the election.

The total increase in Democrat votes in Democrat areas in 2020 was nearly 11 million. This number was only slightly over 2 million in 2016. Remember, these are Democrat areas, whose voters were highly motivated to defeat Trump and elect Clinton in 2016. Yet somehow, these areas came up with nearly 11 million *more* Democrat votes in 2020. Is it reasonable?

Another factor to remember is the precincts and counting in heavily Democrat areas is run by Democrats. A Republican working in connection with the elections will not be seen within miles of many of these areas. In other words, the checks and balances are missing. If there was nefarious activity, it is certainly possible or likely that those present would "look the other way."

The main point here is that there was an enormous increase in Democrat votes in 2020, at the same time as the United States saw 64+% mail-in voting nationwide, drop boxes everywhere, early voting at an all time high, reports of ballots carried across state lines, dead of night changes in tallies on Nov 3-4, and so forth.

The 2020 "Voting Rate" Blowouts

Keshel also presents what he calls the "curious case of the 2020 'voting rate' blowouts." The voting rate blowout was an increase in voter turnout that deviates drastically from what is statistically reasonable to expect.

By the end, voter turnout for the 2020 general election was 66.8%, the highest for a presidential election in 28 years—and this alleged turnout happened in the midst of COVID-19.[64] Keshel presents charts that purport to show evidence of fraudulent elevation of the voting numbers not consistent with reason, but I cannot properly discuss those here for two reasons: First, I am not a statistician, and second, the units of measure were not labeled on the charts I was able to reference. For those who are technically inclined, you may find a visit to his data and calculations rewarding.

Dominion

Allegations of changed votes *via* electronic voting machines were prominent in 2020. These allegations were voiced by President Trump[65] and others.[66] Three major voting machine vendors at this time dominate the market: Election Systems and Software, Dominion Voting Systems Corporation, and Hart Intercivic.[67]

In 2020, voting machines manufactured and run by Dominion Voting Systems Corporation, a Toronto company with headquarters in Denver, CO, were used in North Carolina, Nevada, Georgia, Michigan, Arizona, and Pennsylvania, all pivotal states where questions were raised about possible interference with the election.

One reason for concern is the political bias of people driving such endeavors. I have noted that the people I've encountered who are in the electronic voting systems business tend to lean left. My experience in this matter is limited and anecdotal, but any conflict of interest in a person working with the design, function, or deployment of electronic voting technologies should be deemed relevant and important.

The problem makes sense on two fronts. First, someone choosing to start a company typically has a passion for the business that is rooted in some deep personal reasons. There are few more potentially impactful positions, in terms of power and money, than those occupied by the founders and boards of electronic voting systems companies. A founder has a vision. A board has an obligation to the shareholders. Where does the money come from that drives an increase in profits to electronic voting systems companies? It comes almost exclusively from government contracts. If both major political parties are equally supportive of a major move away from paper systems and into electronic voting machines, then —at least on the level of corporate profitability—the voting machine company has no conflict of interest between their purported mission (i.e., efficient and accurate election operations that yield a true result) and their business interests (shareholder value and profitability).

However, if one political party pushes a major move toward electronic tabulation and the use of voting machines instead of paper ballots, a company that designs, manufactures, and sells such machines will naturally favor that party. If the same company has involvement in the elections, there exists a serious conflict of interest. Such incentive to lean toward and accommodate the political party likely to best serve their business interests, combined with the means and opportunity which are both held by voting machine companies—creates a perilous circumstance.

Turning our attention back to Dominion Voting Systems, the company has a number of concerning ties to Washington figures—not all of them Democrat, but none of them (so far as I can find) conservative. Its constituency appears to be Democrat operatives, including those on the very far left, and some influential career Republicans who are often called "establishment" by their conservative critics. Dominion is reported to have links to the Clinton Foundation, Georgia's Governor Brad Raffensperger (who allegedly put up roadblocks to election transparency and audits in his state in 2020 and during the subsequent inquiries),[68] to House Speaker Nancy Pelosi, and to Republican Senate Majority Leader Mitch McConnell. Dominion has also worked with firms tied to George Soros and Robert Mueller. Furthermore, Dominion sources some components of its equipment from China, which raises other concerns.

In fact, a former ambassador appointed by President Obama, William Earl Kennard, sits on the board of the company that acquired Dominion in 2018. After any such acquisition, the acquired company's board is no longer independent but is effectively subject to the oversight and will of the parent company. On November 6, 2020—that is, mere days after the election, and at the very moment that Dominion was coming under serious national scrutiny—Kennard was also named to the board of WarnerMedia parent AT&T, which owns CNN. As such, he has influence in national media that, combined with his fiduciary duty to Dominion, would create an incentive to protect Dominion from scrutiny and anything that would harm Dominion's business success.

Specifically referencing "concerns about whether [Dominion's system]... is safe from fraudulent or unauthorized manipulation," Texas barred the use of Dominion Voting Systems in 2020, as it had already done twice before. Ryan Vassar, general counsel for the Office of the Attorney General, wrote of the Dominion system in November of 2019, "Both during and after the examination, the examiners raised specific concerns about legal compliance, including numerous technical and mechanical issues. Because these concerns at minimum suggest the system is not suitable for its intended purpose ... and does not operate efficiently and accurately, I do not recommend the Dominion Democracy Suite 5.5-A be certified at this time."[69]

Software Updates, Thumb Drives, Online Assistance

The 2020 election included credible reports, some of which will be mentioned in more detail later in the book, of software updates immediately prior to Election Day, the movement of thumb drives (sometimes without chain of custody) and their connection to voting machines, and the provision of online assistance with voting machines by voting machine companies during the election. The first two items could have a reasonable explanation, but the problem is that there is no way to verify that the noncheating explanation is the *true* explanation.

In the last case, that of online assistance with a voting machine, the problem is that these machines are not supposed to have capability for internet connection *at all*.

In fact, an exposé investigation by NBC News aired January 10, 2020, sought to check up on years of assurances from officials that electronic systems were never on the internet. The piece documents the work of Kevin Skoglund, Andrew Appel, and eight other independent security consultants who suspected that the official story was not true. Together, they constructed a tool to scour the internet to "see if the central computers that program voting machines and run the entire election process at the precinct level were online."[70] What they found should concern every American: *over thirty-five voting systems were accessible online*, and the specialists believe that they only found a portion of the total.

According to Appel,

> Once a hacker starts talking to the voting machine through the modem, the hacker cannot just change these unofficial election results, they can hack the software in the voting machine and make it cheat in future elections.[71]

Dominion Voting Systems, Election Systems & Software, and Hart InterCivic, the three biggest U.S. voting machine companies, have admitted that they put modems into some of their tabulators and scanners, ostensibly to relay unofficial results quickly to the public. Why a quicker relay of unofficial results to the public is worth risking the actual integrity of an election to the malicious attacks of hackers outside the system or cheaters inside the government is not entirely clear. Said Appel,

Modems in voting machines are a bad idea. Those modems that ES&S [and other manufacturers] are putting in their voting machines are network connections, and that leaves them vulnerable to hacking by anybody who can connect to that network.[72]

The Navarro Report

In late 2020 and early 2021, Peter Navarro issued a report in three sequential volumes on findings of election irregularities. In it, he discusses six dimensions of election irregularities across the six battleground states. These include outright voter fraud, ballot mishandling, process fouls, Equal Protection Clause violations, voting machine irregularities, and statistical anomalies (1. significant changes in absentee ballot rejection rates compared to previous elections, 2. excessively high voter turnout—at times exceeding 100%, 3. statistically improbable vote totals based upon party registration and historical patterns, and 4. unusual vote surges). He also discussed the two-pronged strategy that Democrats played out in 2020, which he together calls "stuff the ballot box": 1) Dramatically increase absentee and mail-in ballots in battleground states, and 2) Dramatically decrease ballot verification. In the third volume, Navarro brings all the evidence together to settle on some reasonable quantification of what happened. He finds that in all the battleground states, the margin of error due to vote irregularities and illegalities is many multiples of the official margin of victory: Arizona, twenty-four times the margin; Georgia, fifty-one times the margin; Michigan, 2.8 times the margin; Nevada, six times the margin; Pennsylvania, twelve times the margin; and in Wisconsin, twenty-six times the margin of victory. Taken together, Navarro finds that the total margin of popular vote victory is approximately one-tenth of the margin of error in those six states.

I do not elaborate further on Navarro's substantial and freely available report here, but encourage readers to view it directly.[73]

DOJ Classify Canvassing as Voter Intimidation?

One way to discern fraud after the fact is to *canvass*, that is, to go door to door post-election and find out whether people who are reported by the state to have cast a vote actually did so, whether people who did vote are not recorded as having done so, and so forth. Canvassing is particularly important given the increased potential for fraud that accompanies the expansion of mail-in voting. Canvassing is a lot of work, and takes time.

Canvassing related to the 2020 election seems to have turned up disturbing information in several states. Some of the canvassing results and reports have come under criticism for flawed methodology. Methodology is how a study is conducted. A scientific study must be designed in such a way that the results can be trusted. Even professionals are susceptible to drawing unwarranted conclusions, and this is one reason peer-review exists. One of the most difficult parts of writing this book has been sifting through claims, looking for their support (which in some cases is not included with the discussion) and evaluating whether the claims are well founded. The uncritical acceptance of a flawed analysis helps no one.

In Arizona, the Maricopa Forensic Audit originally included voter canvassing to interview voters about whether and how they actually voted to see if this information matches the official records. Biden's United States Department of Justice quickly exerted major pressure against the canvassing portion of the audit, stating that it would amount to "voter intimidation." In Colorado, canvassing has revealed that approximately 5% of ballots in Mesa County may have been cast by faked or "phantom" voters, and Weld and Pueblo Counties may have had even higher rates of the same. Canvassers there have discovered residents who say that they did not vote in the election but for whom official records show that a vote was submitted.

In Georgia, canvassing directed by Matthew Braynard revealed that 18.39% of a sample of the 138,029 voters that the state marks as having requested and been sent absentee ballots, but did not return it, did not actually request a ballot, and 33.29% of the same sample from the 138,029 voters who report having sent in their absentee ballots are recorded in the state's database as having not returned an absentee ballot. 1.53% of a repre- sentative sample of 138,221 registered voters who changed addresses and were recorded as having voted said they did *not*, in fact, vote, and 20,312 absentee or early voters were not residents of Georgia when they voted. Finally, this canvass revealed that 1,043 early or absentee ballots were cast by voters in Georgia who were registered with a postal box disguised as a residential address, and that at least 234 individuals in Georgia voted in the 2020 election in multiple states.[74] Stephen Ansolabehere, in a 49-page response to Braynard's report, alleged that the survey upon which its claims are based "is riddled with errors and biases that render it invalid for purposes of drawing inferences about the quantities at issue here." Ansolabehere, however, does not challenge Braynard's claims that ballots were sent to Georgians who did not request them (this is illegal), or that registered voters who returned absentee ballots may not have had them counted.

Since canvassing would present a wonderful opportunity for those who assert that the 2020 election was honest to discredit the "Big Lie" (in this context, the claim that Trump won the 2020 election), it seems odd that *anyone* would oppose it. The burden to explain why they are opposed should rest upon those who do oppose it. The rest of us do not need to be ashamed for wanting to know that our election system is working properly and fairly—indeed, it is the solemn duty of all Americans to do so. As elsewhere in this chapter, I suggest that we ought to focus a great deal of attention upon those people who consistently throw up obstacles to one process after another designed to prevent election fraud or voter fraud. We need to be asking, relentlessly, *"Why are you opposed to investigation and shining the light into these things?"* and *"Surely, if everything is on the up-and-up, you would not be afraid of an audit, because it would only demonstrate even more conclusively that the elections are every bit as reliable as you claim—right?"*

Smoke and Fire

It is not wrong to want transparency in government, and the familiar saying, "Where there is smoke, there is fire," may apply here. Is it possible that there is a reasonable explanation for all the circumstances above existing alongside a legitimate victory for Joe Biden in 2020? Taken together, these details should give us pause, even before the material contained in the rest of this book enters the picture.

Something was also not right in the narrative and aftermath concerning the events of January 6. American Democrats, joined by some anti-Trump Republicans—who persisted in posturing as though they wanted to get to the bottom of January 6—however, resisted inquiry into some of the very important questions around that day. Julie Kelly has listed a number of questions for Nancy Pelosi that have long been left unanswered—indeed *unasked*—by major media. Among them:

- Why were requests made by USCP [United States Capitol Police], a federal agency under the purview of Congress, for extra security ahead of January 6 denied?
- Why did law enforcement (including USCP and D.C. Metro Police) show up wearing full riot gear including gas masks and batons?
- Who authorized police to attack the peaceful crowd with flashbang grenades, sting balls, and tear gas around 1:00 p.m.?
- Have any police officers been charged with assault?
- Who seeded the lie that Brian Sicknick was killed in the line of duty, and who told the *New York Times* he was murdered by a Trump mob with a fire extinguisher?
- Who were the officers caught on tape allowing protesters into the building?
- Who opened the doors on the upper west terrace at approximately 2:30 p.m. at the direction of an unknown USCP officer?

- How much damage did the building sustain? The architect of the Capitol originally claimed $30 million in damages. But in court filings, the government claims the building only sustained approximately $1.5 million in damages.
- On January 7, Nancy Pelosi called the Capitol riot an "armed insurrection." How many people have been charged with carrying a firearm into the building?
- How many Americans have been charged with sedition?
- Who are the anonymous "proud members of the United States Capitol Police" threatening to withhold security from members of Congress who did not support a commission?
- How many "white supremacists" have been identified by law enforcement?[75]

Many of these questions, and others, were left unasked by the January 6 Committee itself. John Solomon observed,

> House Democrats' marquee summer show of primetime investigative hearings ended Thursday night where it began: unable or unwilling to answer essential questions about the Jan. 6 Capitol breach. Chief among them: If Donald Trump wanted to incite violence that fateful day, as his critics suggest, then why did he order the Pentagon to have a large military force ready to quell a disturbance? And why did a Democrat-led Congress turn down the assistance of pop National Guard troops in the face of intelligence warnings about violence?[76]

Solomon further points out that the partisan committee scrupulously barred any questions about what House Speaker Pelosi knew and when she knew it, and that Secret Service agents who were in the limousine with the President were never called by the committee to testify about whether allegations by White house aide Cassidy Hutchinson that Trump had tried to force the limousine to the Capitol were true. Nor were those who were in charge of Capitol security that day exposed to questioning concerning their response to pre-event warnings from the FBI and Homeland Security about potential violence.

> "It's the first time this has happened in my lifetime since McCarthyism, and it's despicable," said famed Harvard law professor Alan Dershowitz, a lifelong Democrat who voted for Biden in 2020. "The idea that they would interview this witness and allow her to testify to hearsay about the president jumping toward the wheel, without first asking eye- and ear- witnesses. I've never heard of a lawyer doing that in my 16 years of practicing law. ... It's not only unethical, it's not only unfair, it's bad lawyering."[77]

Former federal prosecutor David Sullivan also offered comment on the way the January 6 hearings were conducted, without cross-examination, clearly scripted, and without any opportunity for Republicans to bring other evidence or witnesses: "Legal scholars are very troubled by the way these hearings are being conducted. There is no due process. For people who don't have an agenda to promote, these [hearings] are Stalinist. And I hate using that term."[78]

QUESTIONS

1. List some of the major indications that something was not right about the 2020 election. Can you think of reasonable explanations for them? Which explanations do you find unconvincing, and why?

2. Why do security measures exist in the first place? Can you think of any reason Americans should assume large-scale fraud did *not* occur after the alleged winners managed to relax anti-fraud procedures in 2020, with more than 41% of all ballots in the nation cast by mail? Why do you suppose the national media did not report *details* of the various legal challenges to the 2020 election, as they did in 2000?

3. In what ways are electronic voting systems vulnerable to compromise? In what ways are they lacking in transparency? What conflicts of interest do electronic voting companies have? What conflicts of interest do those who purchase electronic voting technologies have?

---

1. Chelsey Cox et al., "Jan. 6 review: Biden blasts Trump in speech, Dick Cheney hailed in surprise Capitol visit for ceremony," *USA Today*, January 7, 2022; Joey Garrison, "Biden unleashes a year's worth of anger at Trump in Jan. 6 speech, blasting him as an undemocratic liar," *USA Today*, January 6, 2022.

2. Ibid.

3. "Presidential Election Results," *Fox News*, https://www.foxnews.com/elections/2020/general-results.

4. Talia Kaplan, "Ken Starr: 2020 election may be remembered as one 'where the ultimate results are called into question,' *Fox News*, November 5, 2020.

5. Hayes Brown, "Trump crams one more racist policy into his final days as president: Even on his way out, Trump continues to place white people's grievances over national security," *MSNBC*, November 24, 2020; Kevin Liptak, "Trump defends honoring racists in monument debate," *CNN*, July 1, 2020; Meagan Vazquez, "Trump leans into racist rhetoric and downplays violence against Black Americans," *CNN*, July 14, 2020; Joe Concha, "CNN, MSNBC say 'racist' more than 1,100 times regarding Trump 'go back' tweet since Sunday," *Hill*, July 16, 2019; Kevin Liptak, and Kaitlan Collins, "Trump denies racist tweets were racist," *CNN*, July 15, 2019; John Blake, "There's a sobering truth to Trump's racist tweets that we don't like to admit," *CNN*, July 15, 2019; David A. Graham et al., "An Oral History of Trump's Bigotry," *Atlantic*, June 2019; David Rutz, "CNN's Powers: All Trump Supporters Are Racist," *Washington Free Beacon*, November 18, 2018; David Leonhardt, and Ian Prasad Philbrick, "Donald Trump's Racism: The Definitive List, Updated," *The New York Times*, January 15, 2018.

6. Matthew Walther, "How can Trump be so stupid?" *Week*, August 17, 2017.

7. Anthony L. Fisher, "Trump is an incompetent, conspiracy theory-pushing liar who puts

Americans' lives at risk," *Business Insider Nederland*, September 16, 2020; Alexander Nazaryan, "Trump's incompetent presidency is succeeding despite itself," *CNN*, June 18, 2019; Steve Chapman, "Donald Trump is a profoundly incompetent president." *Chicago Tribune*, June 7, 2017; Conor Lynch, "Yes, Donald Trump is an incompetent buffoon — but he's still a major threat to democracy," *Salon*, June 11, 2017.

8. David Freed, "The First U.S. General to Call Trump a Bigot," *Atlantic*, June 22, 2020; John Hendrickson, "Are You Going to Vote for a Bigot?," *Esquire*, August 23, 2016; Colin Campbell, "Barbara Walters to Donald Trump: 'Are you a bigot?'," *Business Insider*, December 8, 2015.

9. Steve Benen, "Why an out-of-control president raged through a cringe-worthy debate," *MSNBC*, September 30, 2020; Eugene Robinson, "Opinion: Trump is spinning out of control. We must stop pretending otherwise," *Washington Post*, October 17, 2019; Michal Kranz, "'This is not going to end well': Trump's friends and allies are worried he's spiraling out of control — and they say this time is different," *Business Insider*, March 4, 2018; Julia Glum, "Trump Is Out of Control and 'Spiraling Down Into Paranoia,' Says His 'Art of the Deal' Ghostwriter," *Newsweek*, October 11, 2017.

10. John Gartner, "Mental Health Professionals Declare Trump is Mentally Ill And Must Be Removed," (Petition). (70,423 signatories on date of reference)

11. Chris Cillizza, "What is 'Trump Derangement Syndrome' - and do you have it?" *CNN*, July 20, 2018. "Trump Derangement Syndrome (TDS) is a mental condition in which a person has been driven effectively insane due to their dislike of Donald Trump, to the point at which they will abandon all logic and reason." (Urban Dictionary, as quoted in the cited article.) "TDS is, in the eyes of its adherents, the knee-jerk opposition from liberals (and Never Trumpers) to anything and everything Trump does. If Trump announced he was donating every dollar he's ever made, TDS sufferers would suggest he was up to something nefarious, according to the logic of TDS. There's nothing—not. one. thing.—that Trump could do or say that would be received positively by TDSers."

12. Bernard Goldberg, "It's Worse Than Bush Derangement Syndrome," *RealClear Politics*, January 3, 2017.

13. Rob Whitley, "Is 'Trump Derangement Syndrome' a Real Mental Condition?," *Psychology Today*, January 4, 2019.

14. Cillizza, "What is."

15. Goldberg, "It's Worse."

16. Ashitha Nagesh, "US election 2020: Why Trump gained support among minorities," *BBC*, November 22, 2020.

17. It is true that the practice of "canceling" was not wholly novel. Indeed, it bore similarity to the ancient practice of ostracization, or the exclusion of a person from society as a means of enforcing conformity, which originated in Athens—the birthplace of democracy. The problem with the modern manifestation of the practice in the form of "cancel culture" was the fact that it became a tool for protecting political doctrine from criticism, and indeed for protecting weak ideas from being exposed as such. For this reason, cancel culture ought not be viewed as a positive development in American society.

18. Trump was so demonized, and the social and even professional consequences of failing to join in this demonization so tangible, that many Americans reported self-censoring and keeping their support of the President to themselves. Critics, meanwhile, had little reason to keep quiet. The phenomenon, multiplied across American society, created an illusion of popular disapproval of Trump that was far greater than actual disapproval, and a similar illusion of popular support for the policies and candidates of the left. Emily Ekins, "Is Cancel Culture Real? New Poll Says Americans Are Self-Censoring: Nearly a third of Americans are afraid for their jobs," *National Interest*, July 26, 2020; Emily Ekins, "Poll: 62% of Americans Say They Have Political Views They're Afraid to Share," *Cato Institute*, July 22, 2020.

19. Ibid.

20. The following list—adapted and updated—is based upon Sebastian Gorka, *The War for America's Soul* (Washington, D.C.:Regnery, 2019). 176-182.

21. The Jerusalem Embassy Act became law in 1995, but opponents continued to insist that moving the U.S. embassy to Israel's capital would start a war. Trump fulfilled the law, and no war broke out.

22. "'Trump Heights': A symbol of US shift on Mideast policy," *Times of Israel*, October 20, 2020.

23. "Executive Order Protecting the Nation from Foreign Terrorist Entry into the United States," White House, January 27, 2017.

24. Courtney Kube, Carol E. Lee, and Josh Lederman, "U.S. troops to leave Syria as President Trump declares victory over ISIS," *NBC News*, December 19, 2018; Robin Simcox, "Did Trump Really Beat ISIS?," *Heritage Foundation*, January 28, 2018.

25. "Civilian unemployment rate," U.S. Bureau of Labor Statistics; "US Unemployment Rate by Month," https://www.multpl.com/unemployment/table/by-month.

26. Jim Garamone, "Trump Signs Law Establishing U.S. Space Force," U.S. Department of Defense, December 20, 2019.

27. Allie Malloy, "Trump signs 'Right to Try Act' aimed at helping terminally ill patients seek drug treatments," *CNN*, May 30, 2018.

28. "Trump signs bill to fund veterans medical care program," *PBS*, August 12, 2017; Tyler O'Neil, "17 VA Scandals Before Trump's Reform Bill," *PJ Media*, June 28, 2017.

29. "Trump Has Just Achieved What Every President Since Nixon Had Promised: Energy Independence," *Investor's Business Daily*, December 7, 2018.

30. Matt McGrath, "Climate change: US formally withdraws from Paris agreement," *BBC*, November 4, 2020; "President Trump Announces U.S. Withdrawal From the Paris Climate Accord," White House, June 1, 2017.

31. "Trump Administration Rolls Back the Clean Power Plan," *Yale Environment 360*, August 21, 2018.

32. Chris Mills Rodrigo, "Trump signs criminal justice overhaul," *Hill*, December 21, 2018.

33. Adam Withnall, "Donald Trump greets American hostages released by North Korea as they touch down on US soil," *Independent*, May 10, 2018; "Trump On North Korea Missile Launch: 'We Will Take Care Of It'," *CBS News*, November 28, 2017.

34. Tessa Berenson, "President Trump Pulls U.S. Out of 'Defective' Iran Nuclear Deal," *Time*, May 8, 2018.

35. Jason Lemon, "Who Is Juan Guaidó? Trump Officially Recognizes Venezuela's National Assembly Leader As 'Interim President,'" *Newsweek*, January 23, 2019.

36. Claire Hansen, "How Much of Trump's Border Wall Was Built?," *U.S. News and World Report*, February 7, 2022.

37. Suzanne Gamboa, and Julia Ainsley, "Trump administration starts 'remain in Mexico' policy in El Paso, Texas," *NBC News*, March 20, 2019.

38. "Go Figure: Federal Revenues Hit All-Time High Under Trump Tax Cuts," *Investor's Business Daily*, October 16, 2018.

39. In order of margin of Trump victory over Biden: Juneau, WI (29.65%); Marquette, WI (27.68%); Ottawa, OH (23.78%); Warren, IL (20.42%); Shiawassee, MI (20.27%); Washington, ME (20.25%); Bremer, IA (16.39%); Hidalgo, NM (15.29%); Sawyer, WI (13.56%); Vigo, IN (12.77%); Van Buren, MI (12.47%); Essex, VT (11.58%); Richland, WI (9.88%); Valencia, NM (8.57%); Westmoreland, VA (8.32%); Wood, OH (7.74%); Otsego, NY (5.14%); and Cortland, NY (1.99%).

40. Stephen Starr, "US election result: Why the most accurate bellwether counties were wrong," *BBC News*, November 27, 2020.

41. There are some interesting parallels between 1976 and 2020, and Joe Biden is in many ways similar to Jimmy Carter in his foreign policy, economic philosophy, and so forth. Could it be that these counties that rejected Carter in 1976 also rejected his successor, Joe Biden, in 2020, and for similar reasons?

42. That is, thirty-one out of thirty-three elections prior to 2020.

43. Claire Galofaro, "America's bellwethers crumbled in aligning with Trump in '20," *ABC News*, November 18, 2020.

44. Ibid.

45. Ibid.

46. Ibid.

47. Carroll Doherty, "Key takeaways on Americans' growing partisan divide over political values," *Pew Research Center*, October 5, 2017; "The Partisan Divide on Political Values Grows Even Wider: Sharp shifts among Democrats on aid to needy, race, immigration," *Pew Research Center*, October 5, 2017.

48. Karen Hobert Flynn, and Pamela Smith, "Commentary: Why voting systems must be as secure as the U.S. power grid," *Reuters*, August 17, 2016.

49. Philip B. Stark, "There is no Reliable Way to Detect Hacked Ballot-Marking Devices," University of California, Berkeley, August 21, 2019; Matthew Bernhard et al., "Can Voters Detect Malicious Manipulation of Ballot Marking Devices?" University of Michigan and The Harker School.

50. Brianna Lyman, "Democrats Are Desperate To Brand Voting Integrity Measures As 'Racist' Suppression," *Daily Caller*, July 8, 2021; Matt Margolis, "Five Things Democrats Could Do To Convince Us They Don't Want Widespread Voter Fraud," *PJ Media*, June 20, 2021.

51. Ian Millhiser, "New study confirms that voter ID laws are very racist," *ThinkProgress*, February 17, 2017.

52. "The Arizona Senate's Partisan Audit of Maricopa County Election Results," *American Oversight*, updated March 2, 2022.

53. "Arizona Sham 'Audit' E-course," *American Oversight*, June 7, 2022,

54. Rob Shearer, "Rob Shearer: What a PA Democrat's election system audit found," *Broad and Liberty*, October 13, 2021.

55. Daryl M. Brooks, and Stephen Martino, *37 Days: The disenfranchisement of a Philadelphia poll worker*, Independently published, 2020.

56. Brubaker, "Democrats to America."

57. AP Archive, "Fox cancels 'Lou Dobbs Tonight' after a decade," February 11, 2021.

58. Michael Flynn, "Gen. Flynn Exclusive: 10 INDISPUTABLE FACTS on the 2020 Election That Argue for Audits," *Western Journal*, July 30, 2021. Unless otherwise noted, all remaining quotations in this section are from this article. Extensive quotation by permission of *The Western Journal.*

59. Ibid. Emphasis added.

60. Ibid.

61. "Colorado Secretary of State's Office Adopts Emergency Rules for Voting Systems," *Office of Colorado Secretary of State Jena Griswold,* June 17, 2021.

62. While peer review is always preferable, and should be pursued on this topic, the short time-frame and highly politicized nature of the subject make it difficult to demand at this early stage.

63. Seth Keshel, "The Battle for the Largest Counties," *Election Fraud At A Glance*, Updated September 9, 2021.

64. William H. Frey, "Turnout in 2020 election spiked among both Democratic and Republican voting groups, new census data shows," *Brookings Institute*, May 5, 2021.

65. President Trump wrote on Twitter: "Report: Dominion deleted 2.7 million Trump votes nationwide. Data analysis finds 221,000 Pennsylvania votes switched from President Trump to Biden. 941,000 Trump votes deleted. States using Dominion Voting Systems switched 435,000 votes from Trump to Biden." Jessica McBride, "Dominion Voting Systems: Glitch, Clinton Tie Cause Scrutiny in 2020 Election," *Heavy*, December 18, 2020.

66. Vivek Saxena, "Witness testimony describes how Dominion took over Georgia voting machines remotely during election," *BPR*, December 9, 2020; Andrew Mark Miller, "Democratic senators warned of potential 'vote switching' by Dominion voting machines prior to 2020 election," *Washington Examiner*, November 13, 2020.

67. McBride, "Dominion."

68. "Georgia Lawmaker Wants Sect. of State Brad Raffensperger Investigated After Ballot Audit Fraud Allegations," *USA Features News*, July 15, 2021; Pamela Geller, "Report: Raffensperger Launches Intimidation Campaign Against Election Whistleblowers in Georgia," *Geller Report*, July 10, 2021.

69. Brad Johnson, "Texas Rejected Use of Dominion Voting System Software Due to Efficiency Issues," *Texan*, November 19, 2020; Ryan Vassar, *Letter from Ryan Vassar to Mr. Keith Ingram, Director of Elections, Texas Secretary of State*, Letter, November 4, 2019.

70. Kevin Monahan, Cynthia McFadden, and Didi Martinez, "Online and vulnerable': Experts find nearly three dozen U.S. voting systems connected to the internet," *NBC News*, January 10, 2020.

71. Ibid.

72. Ibid.

73. Peter Navarro, "The Navarro Report," 2021.

74. Matthew Braynard, "Expert Report of Matthew Braynard," https://cdn.factcheck.org/Upload edFiles/BraynardReport.pdf.

75. Julie Kelly, "20 Questions for Nancy Pelosi About January 6," *American Greatness*, July 5, 2021.

76. John Solomon, "Trump gave order to 'make sure' Jan. 6 rally was 'safe event,' Pentagon memo shows," *Just The News*, July 22, 2022.

77. Ibid.

78. Ibid.

2

SUPPRESSION OF NEWS AND INFORMATION

W hat is the meaning of a "free press" when true but politically damaging information is systematically hidden from the general population by those who would be harmed by it?

We began the last chapter with discussion of what Joe Biden and the Democrats had been calling the "Big Lie." In this chapter, we will consider some of the forces and mechanisms that helped to suppress the flow of information in service of an approved narrative. Many of the entities involved, to be sure, were private companies. However, problems of corruption and potentially illegal activities related to the election remain to be investigated.

One recent trend that Americans ought to note with special alarm is the use of private information gatekeepers by Democrats in government, both elected and unelected, to enforce political narratives favorable to the interests of the Party and its candidates and policy preferences, sometimes with use of taxpayer funds. During a press briefing on July 15, 2021, White House Press Secretary Jen Psaki stated that the Biden Administration was actively involved in limiting content on Facebook:

> We are in regular touch with the social media platforms, and those engagements typically happen through members of our senior staff, but also members of our COVID-19 team. Given as [Surgeon General] Dr. Murthy conveyed, this is a big issue of misinformation, specifically on the pandemic. In terms of actions that we have taken, or that we're working to take, from the Federal Government, we've increased disinformation research and tracking. Within the surgeon general's office, *we're flagging problematic posts for Facebook that spreads this information.*[1]

Psaki's admission came after Biden was in office and in the context of the COVID-19 pandemic. The Biden administration used the pandemic as a pretext for working hand-in-hand with privately-owned Facebook to flag "problematic" social media posts. The administration's argument in defense of such action would have probably cited a compelling need to do so in the interest of public health. However, political involvement of the social media giants—including Facebook and its founder Mark Zuckerberg—and traditional media giants over the preceding year and a half had been anything but nonpartisan.

U.S. law prohibits government employees from using their official position or government resources for their personal benefit or for the benefit of others.[2] The seeming or alleged influence over media and gatekeepers of information by partisans inside government seeking to preserve and expand their own power by limiting and shaping the free availability of information is therefore highly troublesome.

Yet, during the 2020 election social media giants Google, Facebook, Twitter, and others, all now more or less open cheerleaders and activists for Democrats and leftist causes, maintained and increased their advocacy. Using biased search algorithms, left-leaning "fact checks," shadow-banning,[3] and other means, they variously suppressed information and opinions complimentary to Trump or damaging to Biden and Harris, while amplifying even false information critical of Trump or complimentary to Biden and Harris. Although certain cultural and legal obstacles prevented total elimination of conservative speech, these voices were systematically disadvantaged by powerful information gatekeepers. One would not be incorrect to state that social media companies were by now fully engaged as a sort of private-sector Pravda[4] for the American left.

This bias of the major media and social media companies was no secret to the public. A poll of 1000 likely voters between May 21 and May 26, 2020 revealed an enormous majority (60% versus 31%) believed some members of the media wanted a shutdown to drag on as long as possible so that it would hurt Trump's chances in November.[5]

Abuse of an Overly Broad Legal Protection

While publishers such as news media may be sued for harm caused by their editorial decisions, U.S. law, Section 230, exempts internet platforms from these liabilities. Section 230's express purpose for such exemption is to shield these platforms from lawsuits when they block or screen "offensive material," with the law specifically mentioning the protection of children from explicit or lewd content and empowerment of parents to that same end. Section 230 states that "[n]o provider or user of an interactive computer service shall be treated as the publisher or speaker of any information provided by another information content provider," and that no such provider or user "shall be held liable on account of any action voluntarily taken in good faith to restrict access to or availability of material that the provider or user considers to be obscene, lewd, lascivious, filthy, excessively violent, harassing, *or otherwise objectionable*, whether or not such material is constitutionally protected."[6]

With its inclusion of the term "otherwise objectionable," this law effectively clears any internet service provider to escape being sued for any restriction of content. If challenged, all a Twitter or a Facebook would need to do is say they found the content "objectionable," and they will be immune to liability.

Ironically, there remains question whether Section 230 has actually protected children from exposure to lewd or inappropriate content online, but there's little doubt that it has facilitated extensive manipulation and censorship of news and information by private parties acting as publishers but evading the legal accountability that should accompany such a role.

Bias of the "Fact Checkers"

Social media platforms leveraged in-house or third-party "fact-checkers" as a means of lending a veneer of respectability to the insertion of ideological bias. The power of such control to shape public perception in the direction of the fact-checkers' personal preference or template, at what approached a population level, can hardly be overstated. These entities, while sometimes eliminating false, misleading, or unsubstantiated claims, as often or perhaps even more often suppressed, distorted, or discredited mountains of unquestionably true information that either harmed Democrats or supported Republicans. As such, the fact-checkers cumulatively constituted something akin to Orwell's fictional "Ministry of Truth."

Fact checkers today exist in the employ of social media platforms, news organizations, and independently. Most fact checkers wish to be seen as neutral and present themselves as such. A rather humorous example of the bias toward Joe Biden and against Donald Trump can be observed in the (so-called) fact checking conducted by The New York Times in relation to the September 29, 2020 presidential debate:

- Biden: "He's Putin's puppy." (referring to Trump) NYT rating: True
- Trump: "We believe in law and order." NYT rating: False
- Trump: "I'm OK with electric cars." NYT rating: False
- Trump: "I want beautiful clean air." NYT rating: This is misleading
- Trump: "We use airports." NYT rating: False

- Trump: "H1N1. You were a disaster." (referring to Biden's handling of the H1N1 virus as Vice President) NYT rating: False
- Trump: "Every year I get the call. California is burning." NYT rating: False
- Trump: "They said it would take a miracle to bring back manufacturing." NYT rating: This is false
- Trump: "The mayor of Moscow's wife gave your son $3.5 million." NYT rating: This is misleading
- Trump: "They're sending millions of ballots all over the country. There's fraud. They found them in creeks." NYT rating: This is exaggerated.[7]

Fact Checking the Fact Checkers

One problem with many or most of the "fact checkers" in 2020 was that their purpose was enforcement—not elimination—of bias by their declaration of claims as "true," "mostly true," "mixed," "mostly false," "false," or "pants on fire!" One major fact checking operation is PolitiFact, a project of the Poynter Institute. PolitiFact's self-description reads, "PolitiFact is a nonpartisan fact-checking website to sort out the truth in American politics. PolitiFact was created by the *Tampa Bay Times*, a Florida newspaper, in 2007. In 2018, PolitiFact was acquired by the Poynter Institute, a nonprofit school for journalists."[8]

Who funds PolitiFact? Facebook and TikTok are listed as major 2021 donors. After its acquisition and initial grant from Craig Newmark (to be discussed below), PolitiFact received its first major grant of $200,000 from the Knight Foundation in 2010. According to reporting on the PolitiFact website, the Knight Foundation donated a total of $542,500 in the first seven years, but has not donated since 2017. In 2013, the Democracy Fund stepped up with a gift of $162,500, and by 2020 had donated $1.3 million. This makes the Democracy Fund the single largest donor to PolitiFact. On my preliminary review of the Democracy Fund website's statement of mission and values, I judge it to be a solid organization, committed to justice and its necessary components including free inquiry and free speech including a free and independent press, dignity of all people, and constitutional checks and balances.[9] As such, I am disappointed to observe that the activities of PolitiFact do not live up to the stated principles of the Democracy Fund—in fact, I note that they tarnish what might otherwise be a solid reputation.

In 2015 and 2016, the Bill and Melinda Gates Foundation gave just shy of $200,000, but have not given since.

It appears that PolitiFact got its first major push with a 2010 grant from Craigslist. Craig Newmark, the founder of Craigslist, is a philanthropist who seems to support Democrats; he volunteered for Obama in 2008, and supported Joe Biden in 2020.[10] From 2017 through 2021, Craig Newmark Philanthropies gave $279,500 to PolitiFact.

In 2020, Craig Newmark Philanthropies donated $100,000, Democracy Fund donated $75,000, Google donated $50,000.

PolitiFact checks have come up multiple times in my own searches, which tells me that they are either frequently referenced or they are favored by the search engines—perhaps both. It would be unsurprising if Facebook and Google both favored PolitiFact, considering that both of them are major donors.

Is Politifact a fair arbiter of truth? Hardly. It takes very little effort to observe the strong Democrat and/or progressive slant. While it is true that it sometimes finds false statements from people on the left, these tend to be either so obvious as to be undeniable, or else of little real consequence. In contrast, Politifact publishes completely unqualified sweeping statements that are either untrue or are not known to be true. One such statement is on an August 16, 2022 post concerning "decertification of 2020 ballots." In it, Politifact makes the statement, "there wasn't widespread fraud in the election."[11] But, this fact is simply not known, because not a single full forensic audit has been done. Therefore, Politifact has overreached the evidence.

We will discuss fact checkers in the context of several of the major internet platforms in a moment; in this chapter, it is only possible to provide the briefest of introductions for the sake of illustrating why the fact checkers have come to present what truly may be called a threat to self governance or, if you prefer, a threat to democracy.

Democracy, or government by the people, presumes a baseline ability of the people to have access to information and the means to discover—if they so wish—whether a given claim is true or false. This reality is why the First Amendment, which protects speech, the free exercise of religion, and the freedom of the press, is so crucial to the American system of government. All these are necessary for an environment of free inquiry and the flow of information required in order for the people to know what is happening in their locality, in their nation, and with their leaders.

The growth of the internet giants and increasing consolidation of the control of the flow of information into the hands of a relative few gatekeepers has created a problem. Every dictator and totalitarian regime in history has understood that the control of the flow of information is power, and that absolute or critical-mass control of information is more powerful than honesty, integrity, or actual political accountability. Corruption makes no difference if nobody ever hears of it, or if people can be made to believe that a whistleblower is a kook or a liar.

Americans for the most part now understand that the fact checkers are mostly biased, because they've seen suppression of information known for certain to be true, as well as presentation of information known to be false as though it were true. Even by 2016, a full 62% of American voters indicated that they believed the fact checkers to be biased.[12] The problem is that in many ways, it does not matter. Knowing something is not true when half the nation who want it to be true believe it, or when the control of information prevents you from even being able to discover for sure what *is* true on that point, leaves many people in a state of virtual helplessness. So, this problem urgently needs to be addressed.

CNN

As Fox News increasingly secured the middle ground viewership and worked its tagline "fair and balanced," CNN over the decade preceding the 2020 election gradually abandoned the trusted "just the facts" news portion of the market and moved more unapologetically into political advocacy for the left.[13]

During the 2020 election, the wheels of political advocacy were in motion at CNN and other major networks. Charlie Chester, a technical director at the network, was secretly recorded by Project Veritas in early 2021, openly admitting that CNN had used "propaganda" to help get Joe Biden elected president. Chester stated, among other things, that "fear really drives numbers." He said COVID-19 was "Gangbusters with ratings... Which is why we constantly have the death toll on the side...It would make our point better if [the COVID death toll] was higher." Chester also said, "Look what we did, we [CNN] got Trump out. I am 100 percent going to say it, and I 100 percent believe that if it wasn't for CNN, I don't know that Trump would have got voted out." In fact, Chester admitted that he came to CNN because he "wanted to be a part of that." He also said, "Our focus was to get Trump out of office, right? Without saying it, that's what it was."[14]

Under current law, political advocacy in terms of causes and principles is not inappropriate for news. However, there are laws governing campaign contributions when it comes to rendering of goods and services to a candidate or campaign. Resources (such as advertising or air time) expended in advocacy for a particular candidate is considered an in-kind contribution and is subject to laws governing required reporting and contribution limits. According to the Federal Election Commission (FEC):

> An in-kind contribution is a non-monetary contribution. Goods or services offered free or at less than the usual charge result in an in-kind contribution. Similarly, when a person or entity pays for services on the committee's behalf, the payment is an in-kind contribution. An expenditure made by any person or entity in cooperation, consultation or concert with, or at the

request or suggestion of, a candidate's campaign is also considered an in-kind contribution to the candidate.

The value of an in-kind contribution—the usual and normal charge—counts against the contribution limit as a gift of money does. Additionally, like any other contribution, in-kind contributions count against the contributor's limit for the next election, unless they are otherwise designated.[15]

The problem with different standards in prosecuting such matters is that it is not fair to those who play by the rules, and the result can be a dramatic unfair advantage for cheaters. In 2022, the FEC concluded that Hillary Clinton's 2016 presidential campaign and the Democratic National Committee evaded campaign law that would have required the expenditure to be reported by wrongly labeling opposition research against Donald Trump as "legal services." The FEC agreed with the statement, "By intentionally obscuring their payments through Perkins Coie," that is, the law firm hired by the DNC, who contracted Fusion GPS, which paid former British spy Christopher Steele to compile the now-infamous Steele dossier, "and failing to publicly disclose the true purpose of those payments, HFA and the DNC were able to avoid publicly reporting on their statutorily required FEC disclosure forms the fact that they were paying Fusion GPS to perform opposition research on Trump with the intent of influencing the outcome of the 2016 presidential election."[16]

Whether the existing law strikes the right balance or not is a question for another day, but whatever the law is, failing to apply it evenly to all sides is unjust. In the case of CNN and other media outlets that engage in open advocacy for Democrat candidates, it is damaging to democracy to let them evade the campaign donation and activity rules that everyone else has to follow.

Furthermore, self governance as a just system that stops the tyranny of the few can only exist when the people who are self-governing have a reasonable opportunity to learn the facts needed to make informed decisions. For more than two centuries, and until only recently, one of the stark differentiating factors between various totalitarian regimes around the world and the United States has been a commitment, in the latter, to freedom of speech including freedom of the press. This affirmation of a robust marketplace of ideas has been undermined in recent years, and a new paradigm was set in place by a conspiracy of technocrats and politically interested and powerful news industrialists.

News Organizations and Reporters

Partisanship of major media in the United States is nothing new, nor is it disharmonious with the United States' founding principles. The First

Amendment's protection of freedom of the press was originally conceived in an environment of a proliferation of partisanship in various media. The idea was that a vigorous environment of free discourse would allow all ideas and assertions to be cross-examined in full view of the public. If one newspaper asserted something as true that was demonstrably false, that newspaper would gain a reputation for being untrustworthy or dishonest. Like so many other dimensions of our national structure, freedom of the press and a marketplace of ideas set up yet another system of checks and balances that ultimately served to naturally maximize truth and foster the pursuit of knowledge.

The problem over the past century, however, has been the capture of more media, and the channels through which information is found and flows, by the American left. The result has been something that is a de facto anticompetitive business practice—and it harms the American public while also setting the stage for tremendous abuse of political power.

The intimidation or suppression of reporters and news organizations, particularly those that are otherwise competent and trusted, yet who begin asking questions and probing sources that threaten to expose the left, has recently become increasingly common. Furthermore, as already noted, even agencies of the federal government have been implicated in such political activities. The textbook case in recent years was the targeting of Tea Party groups by the Lois Lerner-led IRS under President Obama.[17] One of the most exemplary instances since has been the FBI's clandestine intrusion into the work and personal computers of CBS News investigative journalist Sharyl Attkisson.[18]

News organizations have never been free from bias, but there was a time not so long ago when at least a semblance of adherence to professional standards of reporting was maintained. Today, such standards have been cast to the wind by many formerly trusted major outlets. Examples of utter falsehood brazenly reported as truth by the likes of the New York Times, the Washington Post, CNN, MSNBC, CBS, and others over just the last two years could fill volumes, and it is not the purpose of this book to catalogue them. In his book *Unfreedom of the Press* (Threshold Editions, 2019), Mark Levin chronicles the descent of the press as an institution into "objectivity." The trajectory he describes is a movement from a time which the American press made no pretense of being partial—but as a baseline promoted the good principles of America's founding—to a situation today brought upon us by "progressives" in which a facade of "objectivity" masks a deep and hostile leftist partisanship, in many cases completely unmoored from truth. Today's press no longer affirm the goodness of the nation's 1776 founding principles laid out in the Declaration of Independence, instead dogmatically asserting that diversity and "multiculturalism" are the ideal and truth is relative. If truth is relative, of course, there is no truth. In practice, the press of today has no real interest in diversity, as it presses its boot on the neck of dissent from its program of leftism.

One current example from the disgraced Washington Post demonstrates the complete and carefree abandon of truth and journalistic standards. On March 12, 2022, the Post published an article by Gregory S. Schneider headlined "All 133 Virginia school superintendents urge Youngkin to scrap tip line and content policy." The article begins,

> All 133 Virginia public school division superintendents have urged Gov. Glenn Youngkin (R) to scrap the "tip line" set up to let parents complain about teachers and principals and have asked him to stop his campaign against the teaching of "divisive" content in schools.[19]

The problem? First, Virginia does not have 133 superintendents. Second, the article discusses a letter sent by one person, the executive director of the Virginia Association of School Superintendents, Howard Kiser, opposing newly-elected Governor Youngkin's policy of opposing the recent implementation of racist pedagogy in Virginia schools. The letter, as it turns out, was merely approved by the Association's 12-member board. The headline's clear and bold claim—repeated in the article's opening sentence—that "all 133 Virginia public school division superintendents" urged the governor against his policy is therefore flatly false. This is not only due to the fact that the state does not have 133 superintendents, but also because the superintendents that do exist did not sign Kiser's letter, nor is it evident that they actually support its assertions. What, then, is the basis for the outrageous claim of this screaming Washington Post headline? According to the article, "Kiser...said he was writing *on behalf of* the 133 school officials and later said he *had not heard 'any dissent'* from superintendents.'"[20]

Imagine that you belong to a professional association. The director of that association *personally* decides he wants to support a racist policy, but he wishes to use *your* name to give the appearance of widespread support. He drafts a letter endorsing the racist initiative, and puts your name on it. When asked later by people if you really endorsed such a thing, he responds "Well, I did not hear any dissent from [your name]!" This is exactly what Kiser appears to have done, and the Washington Post joined in the effort, publishing a propaganda piece with an open lie in its headline and opening sentence. In the process, he dragged the name of many Virginia public schools superintendents through the mud.

Four days after the article's publication, and having been called out on the outrageous overreach by Luke Rosiak and others, the Washington Post had not altered its original headline.[21]

Twitter

On October 14, 2020, Twitter locked the account of the United States White House Press Secretary, Kayleigh McEnany. Why? Because she shared the now-famous—and vindicated—New York Post story about Hunter Biden and Ukraine.[22]

News About Trump and Biden

Twitter took sides against Donald Trump, freely allowing verifiably false information about him to be spread widely, while protecting Joe Biden from even scrupulously verified true information that would have been damaging to his campaign. Technically, a platform is not to engage in editorial activity, but is rather to be a public square, a place where speech is free. Thus, the problem was not so much the permitting of false information about Trump as it was the selective censorship of reporting that would have allowed citizens to make their own properly-informed assessment after access to various data sets.

Trump Himself

Donald Trump joined Twitter in 2009 and favored it as a way to communicate directly with the nation, since it allowed him to circumvent the filter of an often hostile media. Trump's extensive use of the platform throughout his presidency frustrated his critics, who regularly accused him of propagating lies and disinformation. Trump tweeted conversationally, casually, and frankly. He was unconcerned about even making mistakes.[23] Furthermore, Trump used Twitter to share news that was being actively suppressed on other social media and search engines such as Facebook and Google. In this way, millions of people saw news and perspectives that they otherwise would not have encountered. They also learned of his schedule and his perspective on events, and they were able to observe his direct interactions with many people. Despite Twitter's pronounced leftist bias,[24] it seems that the President's significant profile—watched by some 88 million followers—made it difficult for the social media giant to take broad restrictive action against him throughout his presidency.

During 2020, and especially after the election itself, Twitter became more bold, blocking—for example—Trump's criticism of election night irregularities such as early morning reduction of his vote counts and elevation of Biden's in swing states.[25] Even prior to the election, the anti-Trump bias of Twitter's censors was being noted by conservatives. For example, when Trump mocked CNN by posting a re-edited version of a well-known viral video in which two toddlers, one black and one white, ran to greet each other and then parted ways after exchanging hugs in New York City, showing the last part of the video—in which the children have parted ways —and suggested in his tweet that CNN might have selectively edited and captioned it "Terrified toddler runs from racist baby," Twitter labeled it "manipulated media."[26]

For the first time in American history, a sitting president was banned from posting on two major social media platforms.[27] On January 8, 2021, Twitter placed Donald Trump's account under a lifetime ban. Instantly, all of the President's thousands of prior tweets disappeared and were no longer accessible.[28] Twitter also blocked the President's attempts to tweet from an alternate account. Over the prior week, Twitter had removed several of the President's tweets. The lifetime suspension was praised by Democrat politicians such as Virginia Senator Mark Warner who called it "overdue."[29] Twitter underscored that its ban was permanent, with its Chief Financial Officer Ned Segal stating one month later, "when you're removed, you're removed...our policies don't allow people to come back." Thus, even if Trump were to run for office again, he would not regain access to communication by Twitter.[30]

Twitter, which is supposedly a platform, played a tremendously influential role by exerting editorial influence over content throughout 2020. Among other things, the social media giant famously blocked the New York Post's October 6, 2020 Hunter Biden story, barring users from sharing it. Using that article as pretext, Twitter also locked the Post out of its own Twitter account for more than two weeks when the paper did not delete the now-vindicated offending tweet.[31]

Rep. Steve Scalise later pressed Twitter CEO Jack Dorsey about the platform's evident political editorial double standard while Dorsey testified before Congress. Scalise pointed out that Twitter not only allowed a January 9, 2021 Washington Post article falsely accusing President Trump of urging Georgia's lead election investigator to "find the fraud" in the state's presidential vote—an error for which the Washington Post was forced to make an extensive correction—but that Twitter months later persisted in actively applying filters favoring Biden and falsely maligning Trump. Said Scalise:

> There are tweets today...that still mischaracterize it even in a way where the Washington Post admitted it's wrong, yet those mischaracterizations can still be retweeted. Will you address that and start taking those down to reflect what even the Washington Post themselves has admitted is false information?[32]

Dorsey declined to give an affirmative answer.

Twitter's evidently partisan editorial practices, which advanced false reporting while suppressing what was true, facilitated the quick second impeachment of Trump, just as it had facilitated the ostensible election of Biden, by inhibiting reporting of information damaging to Joe Biden prior to the election, while allowing spurious negative articles about Trump to be shared and retweeted widely. Such double standards continued long afterward.[33]

On July 7, 2021, Donald Trump, Linda Cuadros, and the American Conservative Union brought a civil rights action against Twitter, Inc., and Jack Dorsey for allegedly violating the Plaintiffs First Amendment rights. The suit was filed on behalf of the class which consisted of "[a]ll Twitter platform Users ... who have resided in the United States between June 1, 2018 and the time of filing who had their Twitter account censored by Twitter or Dorsey, and were damaged by such."[34]

Censoring of Conservatives and Trump Supporters

Immediately after Twitter suspended President Trump's account, a number of conservative and celebrity accounts on Twitter reported that thousands of their followers disappeared. James Woods said, "Twitter, the 'public forum' for free speech, has deleted 15,000 followers from my account in the last few hours." Later, he reported that Twitter had removed a total of 137,000 of his followers over a two-day period. Thousands of indignant Twitter users fled the platform over this news, joining competing platform Parler. The big internet players tried desperately to block the exodus. Google removed the Parler app from its app store, and Apple threatened to do so as well.[35]

Wikipedia

While the crowdsourced online encyclopedia Wikipedia has long been hated by college professors trying to teach good research skills, the platform has become a warehouse of a tremendous quantity of information. As of this writing it claims to receive some 1.7 billion unique device views per month.[36]

Wikipedia's gatekeepers, however, selectively block information while presenting biased articles to unsuspecting users visiting a topic page, under an aura of neutrality. Administrators seem to enforce an ideological slant across the platform, suppressing even obviously true statements of fact if they run afoul of a leftist worldview or agenda. While many—myself included—have long observed this trait of the platform, a recent experiment run by Steven Crowder seems to lay it bare.[37]

When introducing his experiment, Crowder first notes the following about Wikipedia's protocols:

- Some pages have a "semi-protected" status and are not universally open to editing; only those who have ten prior *successful* edits can edit such a page.
- The "Joe Biden" and "COVID-19" pages have "extended protection." The account of anyone editing those pages must be more than 30 days old and already have at least 500 successful edits on Wikipedia.
- The "COVID-19 pandemic in mainland China" page has "full protection" status, meaning that you must be an administrator to edit it. There are only 1,000 administrators in the whole world. Wikipedia describes administrators as censors whose duties include "deletion of articles deemed unsuitable, protecting pages (restricting editing privileges to that page), and blocking the accounts of disruptive users.[38]

To calibrate expectations, Crowder first reviews examples from Wikipedia's own guide for making neutral edits. First is the sentence, "Donald Trump made many false or misleading statements during his campaign and presidency, to a degree unprecedented in American politics." Wikipedia presents this sentence as a good example of a "Neutral" statement because, it states, "Wikipedia's content should reflect that of reliable sources, even when it differs from a view held by a large portion of the general public."

The next example statement Crowder shares from Wikipedia's guide is, "Princess Diana died in a Paris hospital in 1997 after being injured in a tragic car crash." Given the example about Donald Trump, one might expect the Diana sentence to likewise qualify as "neutral." However, Wikipedia classifies it "Not Neutral," reasoning, "Even though her death is almost universally considered tragic, using the word tragic is still an inappropriate instance of editorializing." The logic is a bit hard to reconcile with the prior sentence about Trump, but we move on.

The next statement reviewed by Crowder in Wikipedia's guide is, "The New York Yankees are one of the greatest baseball teams in history." Wikipedia classifies this statement as "Not Neutral," explaining, "Calling something the greatest is an example of peacock language, which it is best to avoid. You should show instead of tell, using verifiable facts; it would be much better to instead write The New York Yankees have won 26 World Series championships—almost three times as many as any other team."

The Wikipedia guide did not state why—when it came to accusing Donald Trump of making "many false or misleading statements ... to a degree unprecedented in American politics"—Wikipedia did *not* consider it necessary to "show instead of tell."

After reading the guide and studying its examples, Crowder decided to test the system by making edits that were objectively sound, factual, and completely free of opinion. On a Wikipedia page about the minimum wage in the United States, he discovered the following statement:

> Economist Paul Krugman advocated raising the minimum wage moderately in 2013, citing several reasons, including:
> · The minimum wage was below its 1960s purchasing power, despite a near doubling of productivity;
> · The great preponderance of the evidence indicates there is no negative impact on employment from moderate increases; and
> · A high level of public support, specifically Democrats and Republican women.

Noting that the article presented only a leftist opinion and lacked balance (for example, from the Chicago school of economics), Crowder's team added the following statement as an edit:

> American economist, novelist, and senior fellow at Stanford University's Hoover Institution Thomas Sowell has often criticized the practices around minimum wage laws. In his book Basic Economics, he states:
> "Unfortunately, the real minimum wage is always zero, regardless of the laws, and that is the wage that many workers receive in the wake of the creation or escalation of a government-mandated minimum wage, because they lose their jobs or fail to find jobs when they enter the labor force. Making it illegal to pay less than a given amount does not make a worker's productivity worth that amount—and, if it is not, that worker is unlikely to be employed."

Now, Thomas Sowell is one of the most qualified and accomplished economists alive, and has written as much or more on the topic of the minimum wage than nearly anyone else. However, Crowder reports that this edit was removed within a day, with the following explanation:

> Hello, I'm TylerBurden. I noticed that you added or changed content in an article, Minimum wage in the United States, but you didn't provide a reliable source. It's been removed and archived in the page history for now ...

It was a remarkable statement. Sowell and his alma mater—the University of Chicago, are formidable. But, Sowell is black, and Krugman is white —could this fact have something to do with why the Wikipedia censor excluded him as not "a reliable source"? I certainly hope not.

Next, Crowder reports making an edit to the Wikipedia page, "Transgender youth." On that page he found this statement under a section titled "Societal and legal attitudes":

> For individuals who are minors, if their parents consent, they are able to begin puberty blockers at a young age and later receive cross-sex hormones and then transitional surgeries upon turning 18 years of age.

To this, Crowder and team made the following addition, referencing a well-known court case related to the topic:

> The topic is far more controversial in cases where parents agree neither on the diagnosis of gender dysphoria, nor upon medical interventions that may include hormone blockers and invasive surgery. The case of one such 7 year-old child made international headlines due to how both parents wholly disagreed on both premises. In this case, which originates in the state of Texas, the child's legal mother (though not the biological mother), Dr. Anne Georgulas maintained that James was a girl, while the father Jeff Younger argued that the child had instead been persuaded of this over time *via* positive reinforcement such as gifts, attention, and toys, and displayed very few of those behaviors in his presence. The legal case was fought between 2016-2021, with the most noteworthy occasions including in 2019 when Judge Kim Cooks decided that the parents would have joint rights on all medical and psychological decisions, and must both agree to medical procedures. The decision was reversed in 2020, when Judge Mary Brown effectively reversed the previous decision. This granted Georgulas full authority to begin transitioning James into a girl, but most importantly, the sole say in the administration of hormone-based interventions and surgical procedures.

Crowder's edit avoided any comment on whether transitioning a child was good or bad. Indeed, it avoided rendering any moral judgment at all. Crowder's edit merely recorded a very public dispute relevant to this topic that had recently played out in the American courts. However, this substantive contribution was taken down by Wikipedia's editors. Crowder was informed that it was a "neutral point of view violation."

Next, Crowder's team turned to an article on George Floyd. There, he found the following statement:

> The medical examiner found that Floyd's heart stopped while he was being restrained and that his death was a homicide, caused by "cardiopulmonary arrest complicating law enforcement subdual, restraint, and neck compression", though fentanyl intoxication and recent methamphetamine use may have increased the likelihood of death. A second autopsy, commissioned by Floyd's family, also found his death to be a homicide, specifically citing

asphyxia due to neck and back compression; it ruled out that any under-lying medical problems had contributed to Floyd's death, and said that Floyd being able to speak while under Chauvin's knee does not mean he could breathe.

Crowder's team, noting that the prosecution in the Chauvin trial had tried to debunk the idea that drugs played a significant role or even a primary role in Floyd's death, made an edit stating that the prosecution's

point fails to consider that a person who dies of overdose may have also consumed the substance on more than one occasion (i.e., prior to the poten-tially fatal dose), and relies on the presupposition that there was only one administration of fentanyl.

The claim is hard to deny. It is first a plain fact that a person who dies of an overdose may have consumed the same substance multiple times prior, and second it is true that the prosecution was relying on a particular presupposition. Both are mere reports of fact that ought to be uncontrover-sial. However, this edit was also taken down, with the explanation, "There is a strong consensus against including this content." A consensus? Where? Perhaps there is a general agreement among the gatekeepers, or perhaps this editor just produced a lazy excuse for transforming the supposedly neutral platform into a vehicle for his own bias.

Either way, it is the problem Crowder set out to expose and it is the problem we are discussing in this chapter. Crowder observes that the phrase "there exists a strong consensus" is quite literally an all-purpose excuse that could be used by anyone to discredit anything they don't like or find uncomfortable.

Next, Crowder turned his attention to the actual election audit that took place in Maricopa County, Arizona. The Wikipedia article refers to the audit as "the result of a conspiracy theory." Apparently, the editors saw no bias in that statement! He noted the following statement on that page:

Attorney General Mark Brnovich stated that the Maricopa County Board of Supervisors violated state law by not complying with election audit subpoena. The Maricopa Board of Supervisors countered by claiming that it was not illegal to ignore a subpoena, because the Senate lacked the power of enforcement when not in legislative session. Senate President Karen Fann, who issued the subpoena, applauded the finding saying "the Senate is pleased to see the attorney general stand strong enforcing the laws of our state, regardless of who is breaking those laws".

Having observed that the article never mentions that it is illegal to refuse a subpoena, Crowder simply added,

> According to the Arizona statute § 41-1153 Disobedience of subpoena as legislative contempt "If a witness neglects or refuses to testify, the senate or the house may, by resolution entered in the journal, commit him for contempt."

In other words, Crowder merely quoted, word for word, the actual law. However, once again the Wikipedia gatekeepers rejected his edit, saying, "maybe true, but we can't use it because it relies on interpretation of a primary source, namely a statute." Where, exactly, was Crowder's interpretation in the above statement?

Next, Crowder turned to an article on "Stop Asian Hate." This article, he says, made reference *only* to white perpetrators of crimes against Asians, and blamed Asian Hate on "Trumpism." To make it less deceptive, Crowder made an edit contributing crime statistics:

> Though it might appear that many of these events are driven by President Trump's messaging about Covid-19 reported origins in China, a 2008 San Francisco Police Department survey found 85% of physical assault crimes consisted of a black attacker and an Asian victim. This suggests that Asian hate is neither a new, nor mostly-white phenomenon. In addition and according to the Bureau of Justice statistics, black or African Americans commit 28% of crimes against Asian victims, which is a higher proportion than any other race.

At a moment when Trump and his supporters stood accused of something awful by his critics, such details would seem important. However, Wikipedia editors canceled the edit, saying that these statements—whose *only* references are a police survey and official U.S. Bureau of Justice statistics—are "based on an opinion piece." What did they mean? Are official government statistics "opinion"?

Next, Crowder's team turned to an article about the 2021 shooting in Boulder, Colorado, in which a Syrian-born gunman shot and killed ten people, including an off-duty police officer. The Wikipedia article failed to list all the celebrities who used the shooting as a pretext for calling for an end to white supremacy before they learned that the shooter was not white. Crowder's edit added,

> On March 22, before the suspect's identity was made public, the Indian American race and inclusion editor of *USA Today*'s Sports Media Group, Hemal Jhaveri, reacted to the shooting on Twitter, inaccurately saying, "It's

always an angry white man. Always." She later expressed "regret" for the "careless error of judgement" in sending the tweet, and deleted it. By March 26, Jhaveri had been fired by *USA Today*, with her attributing this to the tweet and its promotion by alt-right Twitter users "as an example of anti-white bias and racism against whites". *USA Today* did not directly comment on her firing, instead stressing their commitment to "diversity, equity and inclusion". American Congresswoman and member of The Squad (United States Congress) Rashida Tlaib also mischaracterized the shooter's identity, as evidenced by the March 23rd Twitter message that read: "We need courage to take on white supremacy + gun violence"

Within twenty-four hours, Wikipedia gatekeepers had taken it down, stating, "doesn't appear to be notable, and no secondary source anyway."

Next, Crowder turned to the article about public figure Ron DeSantis, the current governor of Florida. Crowder noticed that it heavily emphasized negative assertions about Florida under DeSantis. Regarding COVID-19, it said, "But by August 2021, amid a record in new cases within the state, Florida become (sic) the state with the highest per capita hospitalizations for COVID-19."

Crowder's team added, "As of January 19th, Florida's hospitalization rate was half of that in Washington D.C. and it had fallen to twelfth in the nation behind states such as New York and Maryland which still have mask mandates in-place." This was a perfectly factual statement and easily verified. Wikipedia editors, however, removed it, citing "neutrality."

Next, he turned to the article on the Texas Heartbeat Bill, and found that it merely talked about how bad the bill was. Nowhere in the entire article did it even state the *reason* for the bill. The reason behind any legislative action is, of course, important to understanding its history. As the article stood, it read in part,

> A study produced by researchers at the University of Texas at Austin claims that the bill would prohibit 80% of abortions in Texas and would disproportionately affect black women, lower-income women, and women who live far away from facilities that provide abortion care.

Crowder's team left the above statement in place, modifying only the last few words:

> from facilities...that are more prepared to offer procedures for late-term abortions, such as Dilation and evacuation. This procedure differs from Intact dilation and extraction and is characterized by the cervix being dilated while the fetus and all other products of conception are removed *via*

suction, though sometimes requiring the dismemberment of the fetus prior to extraction.

This edit was taken down by Wikipedia editors with no explanation given whatsoever.

These examples provide some illustration of how Wikipedia's gate-keeping directs the course of what is seen to be true and reliable among its billions of monthly users around the world. Page visitors don't encounter what is deleted, only what is allowed to remain.

At the beginning of this section, it was mentioned that many articles on Wikipedia can only be edited by those who have 10 (or 500) *successful* edits. You can now see how even a very evidence-driven individual who knows how to present factual material can be excluded from making substantive contributions to many of the most important and influential articles on the massive Wikipedia platform. Of the nine very thoughtful and factual edits made above, not a single one was successful; Crowder or someone like him would not be able to edit "semi protected" articles, much less any with "extended protection." Those pages seem to be reserved for individuals who exhibit a leftist slant and therefore are able to rack up the requisite number of "successful" edits.

Wikipedia co-founder Larry Sanger, interestingly, is not unaware of the problems highlighted above. He said,

> When we are getting the news, when we are learning, or when we are just trying to get some basic information, we—being free individuals—want to make up our own minds. And if we don't, then there's something wrong with us, I think. And in situations in which that happens, well, the word for that is propaganda, when it's systematic, and that's really what we're dealing with on Wikipedia. ... If only one version of the facts is allowed, then that gives a huge incentive to wealthy and powerful people to seize control of things like Wikipedia...in order...to shore up...their power."[39]

As Crowder's experiment shows, those who would offer balance on certain topics, even an alternate and eminently factual perspective, seem to be systemically blocked and silenced.

Facebook and Mark Zuckerberg

Suppression of news and information harmful to the further advance of leftist objectives, by the internet and social media giants, was not new in 2020. Facebook had been allegedly engaged in blacklisting and suppressing conservative news and perspectives since at least 2016, actively altering its "trending topics" *via* the human intervention of its own "news curators."

According to online media company Gizmodo, who conducted a study of the matter by talking directly to the people involved with Facebook's news aggregation service (as reported in the Federalist),

> They were ... told to select articles from a list of preferred media outlets that included sites like the New York Times, Time, Variety, and other traditional outlets. They would regularly avoid sites like World Star Hip Hop, The Blaze, and Breitbart, but were never explicitly told to suppress those outlets. They were also discouraged from mentioning Twitter by name in headlines and summaries, and instead asked to refer to social media in a broader context.
>
> News curators also have the power to "deactivate" (or blacklist) a trending topic—a power that those we spoke to exercised on a daily basis. A topic was often blacklisted if it didn't have at least three traditional news sources covering it, but otherwise the protocol was murky—meaning a curator could ostensibly blacklist a topic without a particularly good reason for doing so.[40]

At that time, for example, "Planned Parenthood" was the #1 trending topic on Facebook, following the organ-harvesting coverage resulting from citizen journalist David Daleiden's clandestine filming which exposed the taxpayer-funded operation of organ harvesting and sale by agents of Planned Parenthood.[41] Yet, Facebook labeled the trending topic, "U.S. State inquiries into organization show no criminal evidence, report says."[42] And, at the top of the "trending" topic list were two posts by Planned Parenthood's official Facebook page, the first one with "a puny 2.6 thousand likes" and the next with just over 3,000 likes. Both downplayed or sidelined the big story. These posts were followed by others with a relatively small number of likes and shares, that similarly emphasized that investigations (in states where Planned Parenthood did not have a fetal tissues donation program in the first place) did not turn up any evidence of wrongdoing.

> By contrast, LifeSite's one story about today's eye-opening video has over 50,000 likes and shares on Facebook, and growing by the second. Breitbart's article about the video ... has over 20,000 likes and shares. LiveActionNews's story has 10,000. Young Conservatives has more than 18,000.[43]

By 2020, then, Facebook had long been in the business of influencing the public perception of news and trending topics and had had at least four additional years to refine its methods, presumably with greater precision and in such a way as to be less detectable to a public wanting the straight facts.

Through most of 2020 and the first part of 2021, Facebook engaged in actively shaping public opinion by blocking or flagging stories that supported President Trump's assertions or that reflected favorably upon him. This phenomenon covered a range of topics, from the Hunter Biden laptop story, to the suggestion that COVID-19 had its origins in a lab in Wuhan, China. Although Facebook presented its actions as attempts to protect the public from the proliferation of "false news,"[44] many expressed the opinion that the Facebook censors did not hold truth as an ideal, but were pursuing partisan political objectives.[45] At the end of May, 2021, Facebook ended its ban on posts related to the alleged origin of the COVID-19 virus in the face of mounting evidence supporting both an engineered origin and placing that origin in a particular Wuhan lab. Conservatives, indignant over many months of being banished to the digital wilderness by Facebook censors over even the mere discussion of such matters, were quick to condemn Facebook for this belated admission that they had been wrong.[46]

One of the most egregious examples of Facebook censorship that undoubtedly affected the outcome of the 2020 election was the platform's suppression of the October 2020 New York Post story detailing the contents of Hunter Biden's laptop. As details of that story have already been discussed, there is no need to go over it more here. However, Facebook played a significant role in killing the story, effectively doing the very opposite of "saving democracy."

The election-influencing operations of Mark Zuckerberg in 2020 was not limited to the manipulation of information flow. His multi-million dollar pro-Biden election tampering scheme involving strings-attached support for "safe" election operations involving greatly increased use and selective placement of ballot drop boxes in Democrat-heavy areas, and increases in Democrat-heavy mail-in voting, and other strategic changes to election administration that all favored Biden and Harris, will be mentioned in the following chapter.

Suppression of Dissent in Public Opinion

Coordination among the gatekeepers of information flow in the service of the Biden/Harris ticket was not something entirely new. Fully leveraging the power of social media to go directly to the voters had been pioneered by the Obama presidential campaign during the 2008 election cycle,[47] so President Trump's famous use of the power differed only in degree and style. But in 2020, the outright and apparently coordinated activism, including the extreme degree and near-complete unanimity of the supposedly neutral platforms against one candidate (Trump) and in support of another (Biden) on the part of these gatekeepers themselves, reached dramatic new heights.

The willingness to silence political opponents, embraced in the instance of Trump from April 12 to 18, 2021 by 49% of Americans (81% of Democrats and 11% of Republicans) who supported his lifetime ban from the Twitter platform (50% opposed the ban),[48] is a remarkable and concerning development in the American political landscape. The change in attitude coincides with a recent erosion in American support for the First Amendment protections of free speech[49] that has also found expression in so-called "cancel culture" and "de-platforming" campaigns.

Google

As the world's largest internet search engine, Google wields tremendous power over the flow of information. We cannot survey it completely here but must be content to touch on some highlights.

There is today significant evidence that Google's bias is not coincidental.[50] The institutional culture at Google, as well as its leadership, has become uniformly Democrat/left, and this shift occurred particularly following the 2016 U.S. presidential election. Senior Google engineer Gregory Coppola tells that he has observed this shift. During the 2016 election, "'every tech company, everybody in New York, everybody in the field of computer science basically believed that' anyone who supported Donald Trump was a racist. Inconveniently for himself, Coppola kind of liked Trump."[51]

In July of 2017, Google employee James Damore famously circulated an internal memo titled "Google's Ideological Echo Chamber: How bias clouds our thinking about diversity and inclusion," calling for viewpoint diversity—and was promptly fired.[52]

First Page Results

When someone conducts a search on Google, the algorithm instantly ranks the often millions of results and presents only the tiniest fraction at the top of that list—that is, on the first page seen by the user. The expectation of users is generally that the most relevant results will automatically appear at the top of the list, with relevance calculated by some combination of key words, number of times a source has been referenced online or shared on social media, and so forth. And indeed, this is how searches originally were ranked. But, since at least 2016, Google appears to have been manipulating search results on controversial or political topics.[53]

Indeed, behavioral psychologist Robert Epstein reports, "in 2016, biased search results generated by Google's search algorithm likely impacted undecided voters in a way that gave at least 2.6 million votes to Hillary Clinton (whom I supported). I know this because I preserved more than

13,000 election-related searches conducted by a diverse group of Americans on Google, Bing, and Yahoo in the weeks leading up to the election, and Google search results—which dominate search in the U.S. and worldwide—were significantly biased in favor of Secretary Clinton in all 10 positions on the first page of search results in both blue states and red states."[54]

Search Suggestions and Autocompletion

Autocomplete is a list of suggestions shown in a dropdown menu while typing in a search bar. Having faced criticism for their unsubtle apparent advocacy for Hillary Clinton in 2016, Google announced in 2020 that it would be disabling autocomplete for some political search terms.[55] However, Google's protection of the Democrat candidate seemed as obvious as ever in the critical month before the election, failing to show "Joe Biden corruption," or "Joe Biden Burisma" in its autocomplete options, despite these terms spiking enormously in Google's search trends and showing prominently in autocomplete suggestions of other search engines. A Google search that began "Joe Biden cor" would, rather, display the suggestion "Joe Biden Corvette."[56] This anomaly seemed to replicate a pattern observed in 2016, when Google appeared to be protecting candidate Hillary Clinton.[57]

Google News

As a growing number of people get their news through what are called "aggregators," the role of those who curate news stories, gathering them from various corners of the internet and presenting them in one place, is also powerful. Google News is, of course, one of the major such aggregators, and—as expected, it exhibits a strong bias, measured by one analysis as leaning 70% toward left and left-leaning sources, with only 4% of its sources from right or right-leaning individuals or outlets.[58]

Subverted Government Agencies

Four years earlier, some will remember that rumors of Trump being under investigation related to the fraudulent Steele dossier were abounding as Trump ascended to office, yet FBI Director James Comey allowed the President to endure mockery and political damage by refusing to confirm his report that Comey had told him on three separate occasions that he was not under investigation. The truth of the matter—that Trump was never under investigation, just as Trump claimed, and that Comey had indeed told him on three separate occasions that he was not under investigation (January 6, January 27, and March 30, 2017)—did not come out until that summer.[59] Meanwhile, Trump had endured vicious and steady accusations of being a liar for making the claim. There is no requirement or protocol that would have prevented the FBI director from publicly confirming that any citizen was *not* under investigation, if in fact they are not. Comey obviously knew this and knew that his refusal to confirm would be taken as tacit evidence that the President was being investigated.

Contrast Trump's treatment to the very delicate handling of the *actual* investigation into Hunter Biden, which government offices went to great lengths to literally hide from public view so as to not hurt Joe Biden's prospects in the election. Delaware's U.S. Attorney David Weiss took care to prevent his ongoing investigation into Hunter Biden from being revealed to the public during the 2020 election:

> By last summer, the probe had reached a point at which investigators could have issued grand jury subpoenas and sought search warrants that might have revealed its existence at a time when many of then-President Donald Trump's supporters were seeking to draw attention to Hunter Biden's actions. Weiss, however, decided to delay taking any actions that were likely to make the existence of the Hunter Biden probe public.[60]

Weiss was not alone in his protective maneuvers on Joe Biden's behalf. Attorney General William Barr was also actively engaged in hiding the story.[61]

Called Out

In April of 2022, the University of Chicago's Institute of Politics and the Atlantic magazine hosted a conference titled "Disinformation and the Erosion of Democracy." During a question and answer period, freshman Christopher Phillips asked CNN anchor Brian Stelter,

> You've all spoken extensively about Fox News being a purveyor of 'disinformation,' but CNN is right up there with them. They pushed the 'Russian collusion' hoax; they pushed the Jussie Smollett hoax; they smeared Justice Kavanaugh as a rapist, and they also smeared Nick Sandmann as a white supremacist, and—yes—they dismissed the Hunter Biden laptop affair as 'pure Russian disinformation.' With mainstream corporate journalists becoming little more than apologists and cheerleaders for the regime, is it time to finally declare that the canon of journalistic ethics is dead or no longer operative? All the mistakes of the mainstream media, and CNN in particular, seem to magically all go in one direction. Are we expected to believe that this is all just some sort of random coincidence, or is there something else behind it?[62]

Rather than admit that the young man was correct in noting that CNN had gotten it wrong on every item that Phillips listed, or apologizing and promising to work to do better, Stelter answered,

> I think you are describing a different channel than the one that I watch, but I understand that that is a popular right-wing narrative about CNN.[63]

Satire—The Greatest Threat of All

For millennia humor has been a powerful tool for criticism of political opponents, policies, and positions. The political cartoon, witty song or verse, or clever label expressing irony or reproach have all served to sharpen, refocus, and challenge ideas and people.

As with much else discussed in this chapter, political satire from the right came under attack and suppression by the gatekeepers in relation to the 2020 election and its aftermath. Often, satirical clips which added (for example) sound effects such as the sound of crickets, or the overlay of music, were blocked by social media companies as "fake news." Even actual video of Joe Biden mis-speaking by stating plainly "We can only re-elect Donald Trump," was marked by Twitter as "disinformation," and a "partly false" label, with the suggestion that he didn't really mean to say what he said.

One-sided suppression of such commentary, however, betrays more than a lack of sense of humor on the part of Twitter and other gatekeepers. They fear the power of the meme, the hashtag, the political cartoon and the viral video clip. As one writer notes,

> Today's media and political gatekeepers aren't concerned that people will find these clips misleading; they are rightly concerned that they will be effective. Political satire works because it challenges those in power while using humor to draw people into the discussion.[64]

Elon Musk To The Rescue

In early 2022, billionaire Elon Musk, a supporter of free inquiry and exchange of ideas, surprised the world by making a move to buy Twitter for $41 billion. The reaction from within Twitter and from powerful people around the world was telling, to say the least. Those who disliked free speech and free thought made numerous attempts to derail the deal.[65]

As the scenario played out over the next several months, after Twitter eventually was obligated to accept Musk's offer since it was higher than the current share value and doing so would likely have constituted a breach of fiduciary duty to the shareholders, Musk then asked for evidence supporting key representations by Twitter upon which his offer had been based—namely the percentage of Twitter accounts that were fake, or "bots." The company had claimed that such accounts were fewer than five percent of the total; Musk said that he had reason to suspect that the number was significantly higher. When Twitter balked at Musk's assertion, Musk withdrew his offer—prompting Twitter to threaten to sue him to force completion of the sale.[66]

Experts suggested that Twitter had little likelihood of prevailing for various reasons.[67] Meanwhile, commentators also noted that the very thing Musk sought—verification of the number of real accounts—would be part of any discovery as part of such a lawsuit.[68] It was suggested that the highly intelligent Musk was playing with them every step of the way as a means of publicly exposing the company. Although left-leaning technocrats in Silicon Valley and Washington alike were not amused,[69] others expressed gratitude and admiration to Musk for his initiative.

QUESTIONS

1. List benefits and dangers of free speech and free flow of information. List benefits and dangers of censorship and suppression of unapproved views. Under which system can a true but unpopular view be publicly presented and defended? Under which is a false and harmful view more likely to go unopposed and be widely believed?

2. What is a gatekeeper? In what ways did news agencies and social media gatekeepers suppress information in 2020? How did Facebook, Google, and Twitter affect what was seen to be true, false, or not seen at all by most people in 2020?

3. Describe examples of "fact-checker" bias listed above. Give examples of Wikipedia bias. What about Wikipedia's process made such bias possible and caused it to multiply over time?

---

1. Ian Schwartz, "WH's Psaki: 'We're Flagging Problematic Posts For Facebook That Spread Disinformation," *RealClearPolitics*, July 15, 2021. Emphasis added.

2. "Misuse of position and government resources," United States Department of Justice, https://www.justice.gov/jmd/misuse-position-and-government-resources.

3. "Shadow-banning" is the practice of blocking or limiting content from a user in such a way as to be not noticeable by the user.

4. *Pravda* was the official newspaper of the Communist Party of the former Soviet Union, and today of the Russian Federation. Its name has become popularly synonymous with the concept of an unfree press that disseminates propaganda favoring the party in power, and suppresses information unfavorable to that party.

5. "Breaking MRC Poll: Majority of Voters Believe Media Hope Shutdown Hurts Trump Reelection," *NewsBusters*, June 9, 2020.

6.   "47 U.S. Code § 230 - Protection for private blocking and screening of offensive material," *Legal Information Institute* (Cornell University). Emphasis added.

7.   "Fact-Checking the First 2020 Presidential Debate," *New York Times*, September 29, 2020.

8.   "Who Pays For PolitiFact?" https://www.politifact.com/who-pays-for-politifact/.

9.   "Who We Are," *Democracy Fund*. https://democracyfund.org/who-we-are/.

10. Michela Tindera, "Biden Extends Lead Over Trump In Race For Billionaire Donors," *Forbes*, May 29, 2020; Gillian Reagan, "Craig Newmark, Tech Genius, Is an Obama Man," *Observer*, October 29, 2008.

11. Sherman, Amy, "'Send your postcards to 5 key states to decertify fraud' in the 2020 election," *PolitiFact*, August 16, 2022.

12. "Voters Don't Trust Media Fact-Checking," *Rasmussen Reports*, September 30, 2016.

13. Brent Baker, "Washington Examiner's 'Liberal Media Scream' With the MRC's Assessment," *MRC*, July 18, 2022.

14. Emily Jacobs, "CNN staffer tells Project Veritas network played up COVID-19 death toll for ratings," *The New York Post*, April 14, 2021.

15. "How to report in-kind contributions," Federal Election Commission.

16. Zachary Stieber, "Clinton Campaign, DNC Misreported Opposition Research as Legal Services: FEC," *Epoch Times*, April 28, 2022.

17. Miles Terry, "President Obama's IRS Scandal: Seven Years & Counting," *American Center for Law and Justice*, accessed October 1, 2021; M.D. Kittle, "Conservative Groups Targeted in Lois Lerner's IRS Scandal Receive Settlement Checks," *Daily Signal*, January 11, 2019; Stephen Dinan, "Judge approves $3.5 million settlement from IRS to tea party groups," *Washington Times*, August 9, 2018; Peter Overby, "IRS Apologizes For Aggressive Scrutiny Of Conservative Groups," *National Public Radio*, October 27, 2017; Bernie Becker, "Conservative groups sue Holder over Tea Party targeting," *Hill*, May 29, 2013; Lauren French, "IRS knew of tea party targeting," *Politico*, May 11, 2013.

18. Attkisson, Sharyl, "Justice Dept. still ignoring 7 years of questions re: illegal spying on investigative reporter Sharyl Attkisson—and others," *Sharyl Attkisson*, June 10, 2020. https://sharylattkisson.com/2020/06/justice-dept-still-ignoring-7-years-of-questions-re-illegal-spying-on-investigative-reporter-sharyl-attkisson-and-others/; Haines, Tim, "Sharyl Attkisson: How Government Illegally Spied On Journalists And Doctored Documents," *Real Clear Politics*, January 14, 2020; Ron Johnson, "Letter to Attorney General The Honorable William P. Barr and Federal Bureau of Investigation Director The Honorable Christopher A. Wray," *United States Senate Committee on Homeland Security and Governmental Affairs*, January 8, 2020.

19. Gregory S. Schneider, "All 133 Virginia school superintendents urge Youngkin to scrap tip line and content policy," *Washington Post*, March 12, 2022.

20. Ibid. Emphasis added.

21. Gabe Kaminsky, "Virginia Superintendents Group Did Not Consult Members Before Issuing Letter Slamming Youngkin's Policies On CRT, DEI," *Daily Wire*, March 15, 2022; "Two separate Washington Post reporters, @valeriestrauss & @SchneiderG, gave readers false information & refused to correct it. The idea that 'all 133 superintendents' in VA favor CRT was always absurd. Somehow smaller outlets were able to figure that out." Luke Rosiak, Twitter post, March 15, 2022, 1:48 p.m..

22. Victor Morton, "Kayleigh McEnany Twitter account locked," *Washington Times*, October 14, 2020.

23. "Trump's 'covfefe' tweet sparks confusion on social media," *CBS News*, May 31, 2017.

24. Michael Austin, "Five Left-Wing Lies That Twitter Refuses To Fact-Check," *Western Journal*, August 19, 2020; John Bowden, "Twitter CEO Jack Dorsey: I 'fully admit' our bias is 'more left-leaning.'" *Hill*, August 18, 2018.

25. Queenie Wong, "Trump's tweets blocked for election misinformation still spread to other sites," *CNET*, August 25, 2021.

26. Jack Davis, "Watch the Blatantly Satirical Video Trump Posted That Twitter Has Labeled 'Manipulated Media,'" *Western Journal*, June 19, 2020. CNN, obtusely missing the point of Trump's satirical post—that CNN regularly slanted its reporting in such a way as to disingenuously portray Trump and his supporters as racist—replied to the President that they had in fact reported the baby video as it happened.

27. Admittedly, social media platforms are a relatively recent innovation, but the event remains remarkable. Larry Elder, "Twitter Permanently Bans Trump. Why Do Hillary Clinton, Jimmy Carter, Harry Reid Get a Pass?" *Daily Signal*, January 21, 2021; Fred Lucas, "Facebook Extends Its Ban of Trump to 2 Years or More," *Daily Signal*, June 4, 2021.

28. Thanks to an archive maintained off the Twitter platform, all of Donald Trump's tweets can still be accessed. "Trump Twitter Archive v2," http://www.thetrumparchive.com.

29. Ben Collins, and Brandy Zadrozny, "Twitter permanently suspends President Donald Trump," *NBC News*, January 8, 2021.

30. "Twitter says Trump ban is permanent—even if he runs for office again," *Guardian*, February 10, 2021.

31. Noah Manskar, "Jack Dorsey says blocking Post's Hunter Biden story was 'total mistake'— but won't say who made it," *New York Post*, March 25, 2021.

32. Ibid.

33. Jordan Boyd, "Twitter Allows Actual Hacked Doxxing of Freedom Convoy Donors After Censoring Hunter Biden Reporting," *Federalist*, February 16, 2022.

34. "Trump et al. v. Twitter, Inc. et al.," *Unicourt*.

35. Peter Aitken, "Conservatives, others claim Twitter removed thousands of followers," *Fox News*, January 9, 2021.

36. "Wikipedia:About," Wikipedia, https://en.wikipedia.org/wiki/Wikipedia:About.

37. Steven Crowder, "Exposed: Wikipedia's Bias Tested and Proven! | Louder with Crowder," January 27, 2022, YouTube video, https://www.youtube.com/watch?v=Iv7s_ydrdHE.

38. Ibid.

39. Ibid.

40. Quotation from Gizmodo in "Surprise! Facebook Blacklists Trending Topics And Conservative News Outlets," *Federalist,* May 3, 2016.

41. Camila Domonoske, "2 Activists Who Secretly Recorded Planned Parenthood Face New Felony Charges," *NPR*, March 29, 2017.

42. "Surprise!," *Federalist.*

43. Ibid.

44. "Working to Stop Misinformation and False News," Facebook/Meta, April 7, 2017, https://www.facebook.com/formedia/blog/working-to-stop-misinformation-and-false-news.

45. "Facebook, Censorship and Political Speech: The problem at hand isn't politically incorrect content that might offend American liberals. It entails covert, fraudulent and often illegal campaigns to manipulate public opinion ahead of elections around the world," *Wall Street Journal*, November 18, 2019.

46. Houston Keene, "Conservatives blast Facebook over sudden decision to end ban on COVID origin posts: Rep. Banks quipped, 'The "Ministry of Truth" admits a mistake! Amazing!,'" *Fox Business*, May 27, 2021.

47. Jennifer Aaker, and Victoria Chang, "Obama and the Power of Social Media and Technology," *Stanford Graduate School of Business,* Case M-321, August 27, 2009.

48. Monica Anderson, "Americans divide on whether Trump should be permanently banned from social media," *Pew Research Center,* May 5, 2021.

49. Phillip Bader, "A shocking 61% of Americans want more restrictions on free speech. Here's why they're dead wrong," *Pacific Legal Foundation,* November 25, 2019.

50. C. Douglas Golden, "Insider Documents Show Anti-Trump Google Employees Wanting To Rig Search Results," *Western Journal*, September 21, 2018; Allum Bokhari, "10 Times Google's Far-Left, Anti-Trump Bias Was Exposed," *Breitbart*, August 28, 2018.

51. Denyse O'Leary, "Google Engineer Reveals Search Engine Bias," *Mind Matters News*, July 27, 2019.

52. Sean Davis, "Read The Google Diversity Memo That Everyone Is Freaking Out About," *Federalist*, August 8, 2017; Lucas Nolan, "Social Justice Warriors Furious As Internal Google Manifesto Slams Company For Political Intolerance," *Breitbart*, August 7, 2017; James Damore, "Google's Ideological Echo Chamber," July 2017.

53. Peter Machera, "If You Don't Want To Use Google's Biased Search Engine, Try This," *Federalist*, April 23, 2021.

54. O'Leary, "Google Engineer."

55. Carlie Porterfield, "Google Will Slash Some Autocomplete Suggestions For Political Searches Ahead Of Presidential Election," *Forbes*, September 10, 2020.

56. Bokhari, "'Joe Biden Corruption.'"

57. Lucas Nolan, "Google Hides Popular Hillary Clinton Health Searches," *Breitbart*, August 30, 2016.

58. "2019 Allsides Google 'Top Stories' Bias Audit," *Allsides*, (6/29/22).

59. Mitchell Shaw, "Comey: Trump Was Not Under Investigation," *New American*, June 8, 2017.

60. Ben Schreckinger, "Hunter Biden's prosecutor rejected moves that would have revealed probe earlier," *Politico*, July 16, 2021.

61. Sadie Gurman, and Rebecca Davis O'Brien, "Barr Worked to Keep Hunter Biden Probes From Public View During Election," *Wall Street Journal*, December 10, 2020.

62. Fox News, "College student who questioned Brian Stelter speaks out," April 8, 2022.

63. Ibid.

64. Brendan Carr, "Twitter Suppresses Speech by Calling It 'Manipulated Media': Imagine going after LBJ's 'Daisy Girl' ad lest viewers think the girl actually died in a nuclear strike," *Wall Street Journal*, March 17, 2020.

65. Tom Slater, "Why Elon Musk has rattled them: His attempted takeover of Twitter has revealed just how terrified the liberal elites are of freedom of speech," *Spiked*, April 15, 2022; Jonathan Rose, and Keith Griffith, "'What are the Kingdom's views on journalistic freedom of speech?' Elon Musk socks it to Saudi prince Twitter shareholder for trying to block his hostile takeover bid," *Daily Mail*, April 14, 2022; Hanna Panreck, "Progressive activists, media pundits react to Elon Musk's Twitter takeover: 'No good will come of this,'" *Fox News*, April 5, 2022.

66. Lucas Nolan, "Read Elon Musk's Letter To Twitter Calling Off $44 Million Buyout," *Breitbart*, July 9, 2022.

67. Winston Cho, "Twitter's Case Against Elon Musk Might Be Tougher Than Expected," *Hollywood Reporter*, July 15, 2022.

68. Kelsey Vlamis, "Elon Musk accuses Twitter of rushing its lawsuit along at 'warp speed' after two months of 'foot-dragging' on providing bot data," *Business Insider*, July 15, 2022.

69. Jordan Boyd, "Corporate Media Is Hating On Musk's Twitter Bid Because They Hate Free Thought," *Federalist*, April 19, 2022; David, Ingram, "Elon Musk has a plan for Twitter. It may scare away users and advertisers," *NBC News*, April 15, 2022.

3

THE TEXAS LAWSUIT

Laws made by common consent must not be trampled on by individuals.

— GEORGE WASHINGTON

Voters who cast lawful ballots cannot have their votes diminished by states that administered their 2020 presidential elections in a manner where it is impossible to distinguish a lawful ballot from an unlawful ballot.

— STATE OF TEXAS V. PENNSYLVANIA, ET AL.

Government is not free to disregard the [Constitution] in times of crisis.

— JUSTICE NEAL GORSUCH

On December 8, 2020, Texas Attorney General Ken Paxton filed a lawsuit[1] against four other states: Georgia, Michigan, Wisconsin, and the Commonwealth of Pennsylvania. For ease of reference, these are together called the Defendant States. Attorneys general of seventeen other states[2] filed a joint brief in support of Texas on December 9, and the lawsuit was also supported by 126 members of the U.S. House of Representatives.

The lawsuit contained three major complaints, which I have edited for readability. The complaints are:

1. The Defendant States violated the Constitution's grant to state legislatures of plenary (that is, absolute) power to decide the rules for appointing presidential electors, and they did so in a way that determined the outcome in Joe Biden's favor.

2. The Defendant States violated the Constitution's Equal Protection Clause by applying different standards for treatment and tabulation of ballots within their states.

3. The actions of the Defendant States violated the Constitution's guarantee of due process to all Americans by lowering the election standards—"with express intent to favor their candidate for President and to alter the outcome of the 2020 election"—in a way that allowed invalid ballots to be counted and valid ballots not to be counted, in many cases in areas with a documented history of election fraud.

A summary of the official results in the Defendant States, as certified, follows:

Georgia

Joe Biden: 2,473,633 (Election Day 373,530; Mail 848,726; Early Voting 1,244,988; Provisional 6,389); Donald Trump: 2,461,854 (Election Day 598,458; Mail 450,522; Early Voting 1,409,331)

Margin: 11,779[3]

Wisconsin

Joe Biden: 1,630,866, Donald Trump: 1,610,184

Margin: 20,682[4]

Pennsylvania

Joe Biden: 3,458,229 (Election Day 1,409,341; Mail 1,995,691; Provisional 53,168), Donald Trump: 3,377,674 (Election Day 2,731,230; Mail 595,538; Provisional 50,874)

Margin: 80,555[5]

Michigan

Joe Biden: 2,804,040, Donald Trump: 2,649,852

Margin: 154,188[6]

It's important to make a few points before we discuss the lawsuit. First, the official margins of victory were: Michigan 154,188, Pennsylvania 80,555, Wisconsin 20,682, and Georgia 11,779. Second, Biden's official margin of victory represented as a percentage of the total number of combined votes for the two candidates was, respectively, 0.2%, 0.6%, 1.2%, and 2.8%.

Although—as we shall see—it is true that the lawsuit cites allegations of voter fraud and electoral fraud within the four Defendant States, fraud itself was not the main point of its argument. The fundamental problem was unconstitutional and biased interference by third parties with the Defendant State legislatures' sole power to determine the manner in which electors are chosen—in this instance laws governing the conduct of elections.

Why State Legislatures Have Total Power In Elections

The United States are a group of individual states—today fifty—that voluntarily formed a union, delegating certain limited powers to a federal government. This federal government was created to serve the states, not the reverse. In presidential elections, Congress may determine only the dates, including the certification deadlines. But the Constitution's Electors Clause (discussed in more detail later) clearly says that *how* electors are chosen by states, how statewide elections—if they are held—are to be conducted, and so forth, is to be left entirely to the state legislatures ... so long as the states' choices in all these things do not violate the Constitution's specific guarantees to citizens and others. For example, states are obligated to uphold the Constitution's guarantee of equal protection of the laws and may not unduly deny any citizen the right to vote, so they cannot pick a system for choosing electors that denies everyone equal protection.[7]

The essential point here is that if anyone else—whether a secretary of state, an election official, or a judge—purports to modify the manner of elections for president or vice president in any way, such action violates the absolute power of the state legislature. That is to say, it is illegitimate.

The Argument In Summary

The lawsuit was prepared under great time pressure and had to incorporate and consider a tremendous amount of data with a looming statutory deadline of December 14 for certification by the states. Throughout this chapter, I will extensively quote or paraphrase the lawsuit, including rearranging its parts as appropriate to minimize repetition. Unless otherwise noted, all direct quotations in this chapter are from the lawsuit's Motion for Leave to File a Bill of Complaint, and text not explicitly inside quotations will include many paraphrases and some direct quotations from that document.

Most cases that come before the Supreme Court reach it after being heard in lower courts which have jurisdiction (that is, judicial authority) over the case. However, because this case was one in which states were suing other states, the U.S. Supreme Court had what is called exclusive jurisdiction—meaning only they had authority to resolve the matter. No other court had the power to hear this case.

The Supreme Court is not required to accept most cases.[8] For this reason Texas filed a "motion for leave to file a bill of complaint," a brief statement of why the case was important and a request for the Court's permission to file their complaint.[9] The motion first summarized what it called the significant and unconstitutional irregularities in the Defendant States.

- Non-legislative actors' purported amendments to States' duly enacted election laws, in violation of the Electors Clause's vesting state legislatures with plenary authority regarding the appointment of presidential electors.
- Differences within the states in their treatment of voters, with more favorable treatment—whether lawful or unlawful—in areas administered by local government under Democrat control whose populations had higher ratios of Democrat voters than other areas of Defendant States.
- The appearance of voting irregularities in the Defendant States that would be consistent with the unconstitutional relaxation of ballot integrity protections in those States' election laws.

Put more simply, Texas claimed that Georgia, Michigan, Wisconsin, and Pennsylvania,

1. Disenfranchised their own legislatures by allowing other parties to effectively change the laws;
2. Treated different parts of their states differently, favoring voters in more heavily Democrat areas; and
3. Manifested the sort of voting irregularities that one would expect if the ballot integrity measures of those states' duly enacted election laws had been unconstitutionally relaxed ... as they indeed were.

All these problems, including even the violations of *state* election law, Texas asserted, "violate one or more of the federal requirements for elections (*i.e.*, equal protection, due process, and the Electors Clause) and thus arise under federal law." By "arise under federal law," Texas was claiming that these matters are not merely concerns internal to the respective states

—a detail relevant to whether the Supreme Court should accept the case. These problems, Texas said, not only genuinely concern the whole nation, but are governed by the federal Constitution. Citing the Supreme Court's own *Bush v. Gore* decision in 2000; it says, "significant departure from the legislative scheme for appointing Presidential electors presents a federal constitutional question." Texas emphasized that the electoral irregularities in this case departed even further from both state and federal law than did those of the 2000 election—in which the Supreme court *did* intervene.

And finally, it asserted that these problems together made it impossible to even know "who legitimately won the 2020 election and threaten to cloud all future elections." Texas emphasized a second time that these are violations of *federal* requirements for elections. They don't just affect voters within the defendant states, but present a serious and legitimate national concern.

The motion concluded by asserting that the listed grievances were *large enough to influence the outcome* of the respective states' appointment of presidential electors, which were in turn large enough to influence the national presidential election: "Taken together, these flaws affect an outcome-determinative numbers (sic) of popular votes in a group of States that cast outcome-determinative numbers of electoral votes."

This outcome-determinative nature of the changes will become clear as we move through a discussion of what each Defendant State did and how many votes were tainted by such actions.

The Gravity of the Situation

Having laid the outline, the Bill of Complaint then opened:

> Our Country stands at an important crossroads. Either the Constitution matters and must be followed, even when some officials consider it inconvenient or out of date, or it is simply a piece of parchment on display at the National Archives. We ask the Court to choose the former.

> Lawful elections are at the heart of our constitutional democracy. The public, and indeed the candidates themselves, have a compelling interest in ensuring that the selection of a President—any President—is legitimate. If that trust is lost, the American experiment will founder. A dark cloud hangs over the 2020 Presidential election.

> Here is what we know. Using the COVID-19 pandemic as a justification, government officials in the defendant states of Georgia, Michigan, and Wisconsin, and the Commonwealth of Pennsylvania (collectively, "Defendant States"), usurped their legislatures' authority and unconstitutionally

revised their state's election statutes. They accomplished these statutory revisions through executive fiat or friendly lawsuits, thereby weakening ballot integrity. Finally, these same government officials flooded the Defendant States with millions of ballots to be sent through the mails, or placed in drop boxes, with little or no chain of custody and, at the same time, weakened the strongest security measures protecting the integrity of the vote—signature verification and witness requirements.

Presently, evidence of material illegality in the 2020 general elections held in Defendant States grows daily. And, to be sure, the two presidential candidates who have garnered the most votes have an interest in assuming the duties of the Office of President without a taint of impropriety threatening the perceived legitimacy of their election.

Deadline Should Not Prevent Justice

A statutory (i.e., set by law) deadline, December 14, loomed at the time of this lawsuit's filing. However, Texas and allies asserted that the deadline should not permit lawless actors to finally force their will upon the nation by setting a false result in stone:

3 U.S.C. § 7 requires that presidential electors be appointed on December 14, 2020. That deadline, however, should not cement a potentially illegitimate election result in the middle of this storm—a storm that is of the Defendant States' own making by virtue of their own unconstitutional actions.

Furthermore, as will be seen in Chapter 7, the December 14 deadline has already been declared to be nonbinding by multiple legal precedents including by the U.S. Supreme Court. The actual deadline under most circumstances is January 6. The last point of the above quotation—that the Defendant States' problem is of their own making—is particularly relevant considering the frustration that developed during the lead-up to the January 6 rally at the Capitol: Georgia, Michigan, Wisconsin, and Pennsylvania were the states that broke the law by changing rules, then blocked poll watchers and other attempts to see what was going on. Blaming concerned citizens, watchdog groups, those who brought the lawsuit, or any person apart from those who advocated, made, and protected these changes is like blaming a victim for being assaulted while protecting the attacker and accomplices. Since doubt existed, blame belonged with those whose illegal actions created the doubt, not to those seeking to verify the process and outcome.

Three Constitutional Clauses

The complaint then addressed the various alleged violations. The first was that of the Electors Clause. Texas "challenge[d] Defendant States' administration of the 2020 election under the Electors Clause of Article II, Section I, Clause 2, and the Fourteenth Amendment of the U.S. Constitution."

The Equal Protection Clause is part of the Fourteenth Amendment, which was passed following the abolition of slavery. Its immediate purpose was to ensure that *all* citizens—expressly including but not limited to former slaves—have the full rights of citizenship under the law, and that all persons, whether citizen or not, have equal protection of the laws. In addition to providing that no state shall deprive any person within its jurisdiction equal protection of the laws, the Fourteenth Amendment also speaks of ways to remedy a denial or abridgment of the right to vote at any election for the choice of electors for president and vice president. Any time there is an unequal application of the laws, it is possible to argue a violation of the Equal Protection Clause.

The Electors Clause says: *Each State shall appoint, in such Manner as the Legislature thereof may direct, a Number of Electors... .*[10] According to the Constitution, no party other than the state legislature has authority to determine the manner in which electors are appointed—not the secretary of state, not a judge, not a precinct captain choosing not to check signatures or deciding to count late-postmarked ballots—nobody.

The Elections Clause says: *The Times, Places, and Manner of holding Elections for Senators and Representatives shall be prescribed in each State by the Legislature thereof, but the Congress may at any time by Law make or alter such Regulations, except as to the Places of chusing Senators.*[11] The Electors Clause, by failing to make provision for Congress to make or alter regulations in the case of presidential and vice presidential elections, thus modifies the Elections Clause when it comes to those two offices.

The lawsuit's central claim, therefore, was that by pretending to waive or otherwise modify the existing state law in a manner that was not adopted by each state's legislature, the Defendant States violated the Electors Clause, the Elections Clause, and the Equal Protection Clause of the U.S. Constitution.

Texas once again stated that the unconstitutional changes opened the door to election irregularities in several forms, and claimed that each of the Defendant States' actions "flagrantly violated constitutional rules governing the appointment of presidential electors. In doing so, seeds of deep distrust have been sown across the country." Texas further assert[ed] that the Supreme Court's attention to the matter "is profoundly needed to declare what the law is and to restore public trust in this election."

Crisis Does Not Cancel The Constitution

The lawsuit reminded the Court that Justice Gorsuch wrote in a concurring opinion—mere months prior—that "Government is not free to disregard the [Constitution] in times of crisis. ... Yet recently, during the COVID pandemic, certain States seem to have ignored these long-settled principles." This case, Texas said, was no different.

Concerningly, there was evidence of coordinated action. "Each of Defendant States acted in a common pattern. State officials, sometimes through litigation," including settling "friendly" lawsuits in which both plaintiff and defendant want the same outcome, and perhaps have even discussed it, but they wish to have the outcome established or legitimized through the legal process. In other instances, officials acted by executive fiat, simply announcing "new rules for the conduct of the 2020 election that were inconsistent with existing state statutes defining what constitutes a lawful vote."

What's more, this apparent coordination was accompanied by apparent steps to block later audit or remedy: "Defendant States also failed to segregate ballots in a manner that would permit accurate analysis to determine which ballots were cast in conformity" with existing legislation "and which were not. This is especially true of the mail-in ballots in these States. By waiving, lowering, and otherwise failing to follow the state statutory requirements for signature validation and other processes for ballot security, the entire body of such ballots is now constitutionally suspect and many not be legitimately used to determine allocation of the Defendant States' presidential electors."

Evidence of Significant Corruption

The Texas suit next listed examples of rampant lawlessness that resulted from the Defendant States' unconstitutional actions:

- Dozens of witnesses testified under oath about the physical blocking and removal of Republican poll challengers; thousands of the same ballots run multiple times through tabulators; mysterious late-night dumps of thousands of ballots at tabulation centers; illegally backdating thousands of ballots; signature verification procedures ignored; and more than 173,000 ballots in the Wayne County, MI election center that cannot be tied to a registered voter.
- Videos of poll workers erupting in cheers as poll challengers are removed from vote counting centers; poll watchers being blocked from entering vote counting centers, despite even

having a court order to enter; suitcases full of ballots being pulled out from underneath tables after poll watchers were told to leave.

- Facts for which no independently verified reasonable explanation yet exists. For example, ... a laptop and several USB drives—used to program Pennsylvania's Dominion voting machines—were ... stolen from a warehouse in Philadelphia. [These] were the *only* items taken, and ... could be used to alter vote tallies; In Michigan, which ... employed the same Dominion voting system, election officials ... admitted [on November 4, 2020] that a purported "glitch" caused 6,000 votes for President Trump to be wrongly switched to Democrat Candidate Biden. A flash drive containing tens of thousands of votes was left unattended in the Milwaukee tabulations center in the early morning hours of Nov. 4, 2020 ...

Supreme Court's Own Order Violated

The lawsuit next reminded the justices that their clear and unambiguous orders to Pennsylvania were brazenly ignored by that state. Remember, once a mail-in ballot is separated from its envelope containing the postmark and the voter's information, it looks just like any other ballot. It has no time stamp or other identifying mark. Therefore, whether large batches of potentially illegal ballots would be identifiable later was of utmost relevance to the question of whether the Supreme Court needed to intervene immediately.

What could be done? If Pennsylvania declined to keep suspect ballots separate, the Supreme Court might step in and immediately rule that the law must be followed in Pennsylvania, and following the law would have harmed Joe Biden. So, Democrat partisan officials in Pennsylvania apparently decided to deceive the Court with a promise to keep the suspect ballots separate for later scrutiny. Relying upon this promise, the Supreme Court narrowly agreed—in a 4-4 decision—to allow the process to move forward.

What happened next was nothing short of stunning: "Remarkably, before the ink was dry on the Court's ... decision, Pennsylvania changed that guidance [i.e., to keep the late ballots separated], breaking the State's promise to this Court." Furthermore, Pennsylvania did not even inform the Supreme Court of the immediate reversal of its promise—in the words of the complaint, "a classic bait and switch."

Real Consequences

Disenfranchisement of voters in other states might be a moot point if the purported changes to election laws could not have reasonably affected the outcome of the presidential election in those states. So, Texas emphasized that the number of absentee and mail-in ballots handled unconstitutionally in Defendant States *greatly exceeded* the difference between the vote totals of the two candidates for President of the United States in each Defendant State.

The complaint concluded by stating that these problems were not mere academic questions. Voters across the nation would be harmed by these states' lawless acts, since voters who cast *lawful* ballots in other states would be disenfranchised if results from states that did not conduct their elections in compliance with the Constitution were counted:

> Plaintiff States and their voters are entitled to a presidential election in which the votes from each of the states are counted only if the ballots are cast and counted in a manner that complies with the pre-existing laws of each state. "[T]he President and the Vice President of the United States are the only elected officials who represent all the voters in the Nation." Voters who cast lawful ballots cannot have their votes diminished by states that administered their 2020 presidential elections in a manner where it is impossible to distinguish a lawful ballot from an unlawful ballot.

Requested Resolution

Texas asked for both *injunctive relief* for the 2020 election—that is, for the Court to address the immediate matter of the Defendant States' lawless acts which were in the process of disenfranchising all American voters— and also *declaratory relief* for all presidential elections in the future—that is, a clear pronouncement that such acts were prohibited in future. "This problem," according to the suit, "is clearly capable of repetition," and "[t]he integrity of our constitutional democracy requires that states conduct presidential elections in accordance with the rule of law and federal constitutional guarantees."

Texas was asking the Supreme Court to prohibit "the use of unlawful election results without review and ratification by the Defendant States' legislatures," and return the matter "to the Defendant States' respective legislatures to appoint Presidential Electors in a manner consistent with the Electors Clause and pursuant to 3 U.S.C. § 2."

Specifically, Texas and the other plaintiff states asked the Court to:

- Declare that the Defendant States administered the 2020 presidential election in violation of the Electors Clause and the Fourteenth Amendment
- Declare that any Electoral College votes cast by such presidential electors appointed in Defendant States were in violation of the Electors Clause and the Fourteenth Amendment and could not be counted.
- Prohibit Defendant States' use of the 2020 election results for the president to appoint presidential electors to the Electoral College.
- Prohibit Defendant States' use of the 2020 election results for the Office of President to appoint presidential electors to the Electoral College and authorize, pursuant to the Court's remedial authority, the Defendant States to conduct a special election to appoint presidential electors.
- If any of Defendant States had already appointed presidential electors to the Electoral College using the 2020 election results, direct such States' legislatures ... to appoint a new set of presidential electors in a manner that did not violate the Electors Clause and the Fourteenth Amendment, or to appoint no presidential electors at all.
- Prohibit the Defendant States from certifying presidential electors or otherwise meeting for purposes of the Electoral College ... pending further order of the Court.

Why Their Actions Violated Equal Protection

Citing precedent, Texas wrote that in a presidential election, "the impact of the votes cast in each State is affected by the votes cast for the various candidates in other States." The constitutional failures of Georgia, Michigan, Wisconsin, and Pennsylvania injured Texas and other states because, "'the right of suffrage can be denied by a debasement or dilution of the weight of a citizen's vote just as effectively as by wholly prohibiting the free exercise of the franchise.'" In other words, contaminating the results with fraudulent or otherwise improper ballots in Georgia, Michigan, Wisconsin, or Pennsylvania actually disenfranchised voters in Texas and the other states by diluting the power of their votes just as if they had been denied the opportunity to vote in the first place.

Essentially, therefore, the four states of Georgia, Michigan, Wisconsin and Pennsylvania denied every citizen of the nation their right to vote.

Only States, And Only The Supreme Court

But who could address such a grievance? The case noted that there was *no one but a state* who could bring certain constitutional claims for adjudication—and that was one such instance. Furthermore, under such circumstances, Texas argues that the courts *owed* the states a "special solicitude in standing analysis," meaning that in determining the right to bring a case, the states must get a benefit of the doubt here. Even more, it would likely be impossible to have an appropriate remedy if the states were to pursue their grievance against any individual officer of any Defendant States (for example, Kathy Boockvar, Pennsylvania's Democrat secretary of state) or any one of the Defendant States alone, because redress in any one state would not alone rectify the harm at the national level. No, it asserted, "This action against multiple State defendants is the only adequate remedy for Plaintiff States, and this Court is the only court that can accommodate such a suit."

> No court—other than this Court—can redress constitutional injuries spanning multiple States with the sufficient number of states joined as defendants or respondents to make a difference in the electoral college.

So, this matter was of a nature that could not be brought by anyone *but* a state, and this case could not be heard by anyone *but* the Supreme Court of the United States. There was a very narrow range of opportunity for addressing the grave problems at issue, and the criteria for doing so were met by the current situation.

Legal Background

Next, the lawsuit laid out the legal background, some of which has already been mentioned. First, the primary authority of the Constitution is emphasized:

> [T]he 'Constitution, and the laws of the United States which shall be made in pursuance thereof ... shall be the supreme law of the land.' U.S. CONST. Art. VI, cl. 2.

Second, the Constitution does not guarantee citizens a right to vote for electors for president: "[T]he individual citizen has no federal constitutional right to vote for electors for the President of the United States unless and until the state legislature chooses a statewide election as the means to implement its power to appoint members of the electoral college." State legislatures may choose to have popular elections for president, but they are not required to do so.

Third, remembering that the word "plenary" means *unqualified and absolute*:

> State legislatures have plenary power to set the process for appointing presidential electors: "Each State shall appoint, in such Manner as the Legislature thereof may direct, a Number of Electors." U.S. CONST. art. II, §1, cl. 2

The Court at this point was reminded that, at the time of the nation's founding, most states—in fact—did *not* choose popular vote as the means of appointing electors, but instead chose electors *via* a vote in the state house. Nor was such practice limited to the time of the nation's founding: "In the second presidential election, nine of the fifteen states that appointed electors did so by direct legislative appointment. ... In the third presidential election, nine of sixteen states that appointed electors did so by direct legislative appointment. ... This practice persisted in lesser degrees through the Election of 1860." Furthermore, the choice of electors by another valid means in the event of a failure to lawfully appoint electors by the day prescribed by law is entirely appropriate:

> Though "[h]istory has now favored the voter," *Bush II*, 531 U.S. at 104, "there is no doubt of the right of the legislature to resume the power [of appointing presidential electors] at any time, for *it can neither be taken away nor abdicated.*" *McPherson*, 146 U.S. at 35 (emphasis added). *cf.* 3 U.S.C. § 2 ("Whenever any State has held an election for the purpose of choosing electors, and has failed to make a choice on the day prescribed by law, the electors may be appointed on a subsequent day in such a manner as the legislature of such State may direct.").

Facts

Having stated the legal background, the motion continued by outlining key facts relevant to the case.

First, the "use of absentee and mail-in ballots skyrocketed in 2020, not only as a public health response to the COVID-19 pandemic but also at the urging of mail-in voting's proponents, and most especially executive branch officials in Defendant States." It stated that, according to Pew Research Center, 65 million votes were cast by mail in 2020, compared to 33.5 million in 2016.

Second, the bipartisan Jimmy Carter and James Baker commission (following the 2000 election) noted that absentee ballots are "the largest source of potential voter fraud."

Third, as valid as it remains today, concern over mail-in ballots is not new: a Washington Post article described how mail-in ballots were part of a plot to deny Lincoln reelection.[12] In fact, it said, "Absentee and mail-in voting are the primary opportunities for unlawful ballots to be cast," and

> As a result of expanded absentee and mail-in voting in Defendant States, combined with [these states'] unconstitutional modification of statutory protections designed to ensure ballot integrity, Defendant States created a massive opportunity for fraud. In addition, Defendant States have made it difficult or impossible to separate the constitutionally tainted ballots from all mail-in ballots.

Every state that decided the 2020 election not only created a massive opportunity for fraud, but subsequently took steps to make it difficult or impossible to separate suspect ballots. A situation of heightened opportunity for fraud should have at minimum been accompanied by *more* diligence to existing processes designed to stop fraud, such as signature verification. However, the Defendant States decided to go the exact opposite direction:

> Rather than augment safeguards against illegal voting in anticipation of the millions of additional mail-in ballots flooding their States, Defendant States *all* materially weakened, or did away with, security measures, such as witness or signature verification procedures, required by their respective legislatures. Their legislatures established those commonsense safeguards to prevent—or at least reduce—fraudulent mail-in ballots.

Fourth, Democrat voters in these four states voted by mail at 2-3 times the rate of Republicans; thus, "[f]ormer Vice President Biden ... greatly benefited from this unconstitutional usurpation of legislative authority, and the weakening of legislative mandated ballot security measures."

Fifth, Texas complied with the Constitution, while these four other states "violated the Constitution in the process of appointing presidential electors by unlawfully abrogating state election laws designed to protect the integrity of the ballots and the electoral process." All of the integrity and careful election handling efforts taken in states like Texas and others would be to no avail if politically motivated officials in other states are permitted to validate an unconstitutional brute-force takeover of the election. Texas and other states *may as well not even conduct elections* if the predetermined outcome is to be that the Constitution does not govern.

Next, the Texas lawsuit turned its attention to the situation in each of the four states being sued. A summary follows.

Pennsylvania

Pennsylvania has twenty electoral votes. Biden's official margin of victory was 81,597. The number of votes in Pennsylvania tainted by the constitutional violations exceeds the margin of votes that separated the candidates.

The following purported changes to election law in Pennsylvania materially affected the election outcome:

"Pennsylvania's Secretary of State, Kathy Boockvar, without legislative approval, unilaterally abrogated several Pennsylvania statutes requiring signature verification for absentee or mail-in ballots. Pennsylvania's legislature has not ratified these changes, and the legislation did not include a severability clause."

On Aug 7, 2020, the League of Women Voters of Pennsylvania and others filed a legal complaint against Secretary Boockvar and other local election officials, seeking "a declaratory judgment that Pennsylvania's existing signature verification procedures for mail-in voting" were unlawful for a number of reasons. While this complaint was filed *against* Pennsylvania Secretary of State Kathy Boockvar (D) and other local election officials, it is important to understand that the action was what is called a "friendly" lawsuit, because the outcome it sought was one that benefited Boockvar's own party and was being pursued by Democrats across the battleground states. It did not seek faithfulness to election law, but rather its relaxation.

What the League of Women Voters sought was unlawful for several reasons. Nonetheless, "The Pennsylvania Department of State," under Boockvar's leadership, "settled quickly with the plaintiffs, issuing revised guidance on September 11, 2020," declaring that "Pennsylvania Election Code doesn't authorize the county board of elections to set aside returned absentee or mail-in ballots based solely on signature analysis by the county board of elections." In other words, Boockvar's office unilaterally decided that county boards of elections could *not* throw out absentee or mail-in ballots just because the signatures did not match the voter signature on record, despite the actual law plainly stating the exact opposite:

"Pennsylvania Election Code, *mandates* that, for non-disabled and non-military voters, all applications for an absentee or mail-in ballot 'shall be signed by the applicant,' [... and second,] Pennsylvania's voter signature verification requirements are expressly set forth"[13] in the law. Boockvar therefore had no constitutional authority to alter election law. This friendly lawsuit from the League of Women Voters, thus, was a ruse under which the Secretary of State was able to do something that benefited her party—relax signature requirements—on the pretense of having had her hand forced by those suing her office. What was the effect?

The Pennsylvania Department of State's guidance unconstitutionally did away with Pennsylvania's statutory signature verification requirements. Approximately 70 percent of the requests for absentee ballots were from Democrats and 25 percent from Republicans. Thus, the unconstitutional abrogation of state election law greatly inured to former Vice President Biden's benefit.

In summary, Democrat Kathy Boockvar illegally used a friendly lawsuit as an excuse to discard the law requiring signatures to match for a category of ballots that were seventy percent Democrat and only twenty-five percent Republican—clearly benefiting her own party.

Boockvar was not the only one who had been imposing her preference for the conduct of the election over the will of the state legislature. A narrow (4-3) majority of the Pennsylvania Supreme Court, in a second friendly lawsuit, *Pa. Democratic Party v. Boockvar,* interfered with the statutory deadline of 8:00 p.m. on Election Day for a county board of elections to receive a mail-in ballot, pretending to change the law by moving that deadline to three days after Election Day. It furthermore imposed a requirement that *even ballots without a postmark* had to be presumed received on time. This meant that—contrary to Pennsylvania law—*any* number of ballots mailed on November 4 or 5 would be counted, so long as they were received by November 6 and postal workers had failed to postmark them.

The Pennsylvania Supreme Court, further, purported to change Pennsylvania law by ruling that ballots with mismatched signatures could not be rejected. CBS News was quick to make this critical announcement to the world just over one week before election.[14]

Pennsylvania law "also requires that poll-watchers be granted access to the opening, counting, and recording of absentee ballots: 'Watchers shall be permitted to be present when the envelopes containing official absentee ballots and mail-in ballots are opened and when such ballots are counted and recorded.' Local election officials in Philadelphia and Allegheny Counties, however, decided not to follow the law for the opening, counting, and recording of absentee and mail-in ballots."

Secretary Boockvar was not finished. Prior to the election, she "sent an email to local election officials urging them to provide opportunities for various persons—including political parties—to contact voters to 'cure' defective mail-in ballots." This process violated Pennsylvania law at several points:

- Section 3146.8(a) requires: "The county boards of election, upon receipt of official absentee ballots in sealed official absentee ballot envelopes as provided under this article and mail-in ballots in sealed official mail-in ballot envelopes ... shall safely keep the ballots in sealed or locked containers until they are to be canvassed by the county board of elections."

- Section 3146.8(g)(1)(ii) limits the counting of mail-in ballots to only those received by eight o'clock p.m. on Election Day.
- Section 3146.8(g)(1.1) requires that the first look at the ballots shall be "no earlier than seven o'clock a.m. on Election Day." *And* the hour for this "pre-canvas" must be publicly announced at least 48 hours in advance. Then, the votes are counted on Election Day.

By taking out the ballots and looking at them before seven o'clock a.m. on Election Day, Boockvar "created a system by which local officials could review ballots without the proper announcements, observation, and security. This entire scheme, which was only followed in Democrat majority counties, was blatantly illegal in that it permitted the illegal removal of ballots from their locked containers prematurely."

Election officials, statewide and local, in Philadelphia and Allegheny Counties, "aware of the historical Democrat advantage in those counties, violated Pennsylvania's election code and adopted the differential standards favoring voters in Philadelphia and Allegheny Counties with the intent to favor former Vice President Biden." In this way, "[a]bsentee and mail-in ballots in Pennsylvania were ... evaluated under an illegal standard regarding signature verification." The complaint emphasizes, "It is now impossible to determine which ballots were properly cast and which ballots were not."

"The changed process allowing the curing of absentee and mail-in ballots in Allegheny and Philadelphia counties"—that is, giving these Democrat majority areas special treatment—is another violation of equal protection.

Additionally, "a great number of ballots were received after the statutory deadline and yet were counted by virtue of the fact that Pennsylvania did not segregate all ballots received after 8:00 p.m. on November 3, 2020." Boockvar, the lawsuit points out, has *no way to prove* "her claim that only about 10,000 ballots were received after this deadline since Pennsylvania broke its promise to the Court to segregate ballots and co-mingled perhaps tens, or even hundreds of thousands, of illegal late ballots."

"On Dec 4, 2020, fifteen members of the Pennsylvania House of Reps led by Rep. Francis X. Ryan issued a report to Congressman Scott Perry (the "Ryan Report") stating that '[t]he general election of 2020 in PA was fraught with inconsistencies, documented irregularities and improprieties associated with mail-in balloting, pre-canvassing, and canvassing that the reliability of the mail-in votes in the Commonwealth of Pennsylvania is impossible to rely upon.' The Ryan Report's findings are startling, including:

- 9,005 ballots with NO Mailed Date.
- 58,221 ballots returned on or BEFORE the Mailed Date.
- 51,200 ballots returned one day after Mailed Date.

"These nonsensical numbers alone," the lawsuit states, "total 118,426 ballots and exceed Mr. Biden's margin of 81,660 votes over President Trump. But these discrepancies pale in comparison to the discrepancies in Pennsylvania's reported data concerning the number of mail-in ballots distributed to the populace—now no longer subject to legislated mandated signature verification requirements."

"The Ryan Report also states:

[I]n a data file received on November 4, 2020, the Commonwealth's Pennsylvania Open Data sites reported over 3.1 million mail in ballots sent out. The CSV file from the state on November 4 depicts 3.1 million mail in ballots sent out but on November 2, the information was provided that only 2.7 million ballots had been sent out. *This discrepancy of approximately 400,000 ballots from November 2 to November 4 has not been explained.*

"These stunning figures illustrate the out-of-control nature of Pennsylvania's mail-in balloting scheme. Democrats submitted mail-in ballots at more than two times the rate of Republicans. This number of constitutionally tainted ballots far exceeds the approximately 81,660 votes separating the candidates.

"This blatant disregard of statutory law renders *all* mail-in ballots constitutionally tainted and cannot form the basis for appointing or certifying Pennsylvania's presidential electors to the Electoral College.

"According to the U.S. Election Assistance Commission's report to Congress *Election Administration and Voting Survey: 2016 Comprehensive Report,* in 2016 Pennsylvania received 266,208 mail-in ballots; 2,534 of them were rejected (.95%). However, in 2020, Pennsylvania received more than ten times the number of mail-in ballots compared to 2016. As explained above, this much larger volume of mail-in ballots was treated in an unconstitutionally modified manner that included:

1. doing away with Pennsylvania's signature verification requirements
2. extending that deadline to three days after Election Day and adopting a presumption that even *non-postmarked ballots* were presumptively timely, and

3. blocking poll watchers in Philadelphia and Allegheny Counties in violation of State law

"These non-legislative modifications to Pennsylvania's election rules appear to have generated an outcome-determinative number of unlawful ballots that were cast in Pennsylvania. Regardless of the number of such ballots, the non-legislative changes to the election rules violated the Electors Clause."

Georgia

Georgia has sixteen electoral votes, which Biden claimed with a margin of approximately 12,670. "The number of votes affected by the various constitutional violations," says the complaint, "exceeds the margin of votes dividing the two candidates."

The settling of "friendly lawsuits" was one means by which voting laws were changed by unauthorized individuals. The compromise settlement agreement included in the supporting materials of the Texas lawsuit is one example. Three Democratic entities (the Democratic Party of Georgia, the Democratic Senatorial Campaign Committee (DSCC), and the Democratic Congressional Campaign Committee (DCCC)) had sued the state to secure a relaxation of ballot treatment procedures.[15] The suit was settled with an agreement to add requirements to existing election law concerning signature verification, making it so difficult to disqualify any absentee or mail-in ballot that many or most ballots lacking matching signatures would be counted—despite being actually illegal to count such ballots under Georgia law.[16]

In fact, a number of purported changes to Georgia law came about by way of such "friendly" lawsuits. The motion complained that Georgia's Secretary of State, Brad Raffensperger took it upon himself to abrogate Georgia's law governing the signature verification process for absentee ballots, and that he did so without legislative approval. Georgia law, it said, "prohibits the opening of absentee ballots until after the polls open on Election Day." But contrary to the law, in April 2020 the State Election Board (which is not the legislature) "adopted Secretary of State Rule 183-1-14-0.9-.15, Processing Ballots Prior to Election Day," a rule which pretended to authorize county election officials to begin processing absentee ballots *up to three weeks before* the day of the election.

Georgia law, it continued, "authorizes *and requires* a single registrar or clerk—after reviewing the outer envelope—to *reject* an absentee ballot if the voter failed to sign the required oath or to provide the required information, the signature appears invalid, or the required information does not conform with the information on file, or if the voter is otherwise found ineligible to vote."[17]

Georgia law also gives absentee voters the opportunity "to 'cure a failure to sign the oath, and invalid signature, or missing information' on a ballot's outer envelope by the deadline for verifying provisional ballots (*i.e.*, three days after the election)." In order to help facilitate such cures so that ballots missing required information can be counted, Georgia law mandates that the relevant election official must notify the voter in writing, and to retain a record of such notification: "The board of registrars or absentee ballot clerk shall promptly notify the elector of such rejection, a copy of which notification shall be retained in the files of the board of registrars or absentee ballot clerk for at least two years."

"On Mar 6, 2020," however, in *Democratic Party of GA v. Raffensperger*, Raffensperger "entered a Compromise Settlement Agreement and Release with the Democratic Party of Georgia,"—and the terms of that agreement materially altered the requirements of the law for checking signatures on absentee ballot envelopes to confirm the voter's identity. It did so "by making it far more difficult to challenge defective signatures beyond the express mandatory procedures" of the law. "Among other things, before a ballot could be rejected, the Settlement required a registrar who found a defective signature to now seek a review by two other registrars, and only if a majority of the registrars agreed that the signature was defective could the ballot be rejected but not before all three registrars' names were written on the ballot envelope along with the reason for the rejection. These cumbersome procedures are in direct conflict with Georgia's statutory requirements, as is the Settlement's requirement that notice be provided by telephone (*i.e.*, not in writing) if a telephone number is available." To top everything, the settlement purported to require state election officials "to consider issuing guidance and training materials drafted by an expert retained by **the Democratic Party of Georgia.**

"Georgia's legislature," however, "has not ratified these material changes to statutory law mandated by the Compromise Settlement Agreement and Release, including altered signature verification requirements and early opening of ballots. ...

Did it make a difference? Claimed the motion, "This unconstitutional change in Georgia law materially benefitted former VP Biden. According to the Georgia Sec. of State's office, former VP Biden had almost double the number of absentee votes (65.32%) as President Trump (34.68%)."

"The effect of this unconstitutional change in Georgia election law, which made it more likely that ballots without matching signatures would be counted, had a material impact on the outcome of the election ... Specifically, there were 1,305,659 absentee mail-in ballots submitted in Georgia in 2020. There were 4,786 absentee ballots rejected in 2020. This is a rejection rate of .37%. In contrast, in 2016, the 2016 rejection rate was 6.42% with 13,677 absentee mail-in ballots being rejected out of 213,033 submitted, which is more than *seventeen times greater* than in 2020 ... If the rejection rate ... remained the same in 2020 as it was in 2016, there would be 83,517 fewer tabulated ballots in 2020. The statewide split of absentee ballots was 34.68% for Trump and 65.2% for Biden. Rejecting at the higher 2016 rate with the 2020 split between Trump and Biden would decrease Trump votes by 28,965 and Biden votes by 54,552, which would be a net gain for Trump of 25,587 votes. This would be more than needed to overcome the Biden advantage of 12,670 votes, and Trump would win by 12,917 votes. ... Regardless of the number of ballots affected, however, the non-legislative changes to the election rules violated the Electors Clause."

Michigan

Michigan has sixteen electoral votes, and Biden's official margin of victory is 146,007. In Wayne County, Biden's margin (322,925) significantly exceeds his statewide lead. Notes the complaint, '[t]he number of votes affected by the various constitutional violations exceeds the margin of votes dividing the candidates."

First, Michigan Secretary of State Jocelyn Benson, "without legislative approval, unilaterally abrogated Michigan election statutes related to absentee ballot applications and signature verification. Michigan's legislature has not ratified these changes, and its election laws do not include a severability clause....

The Michigan Constitution was amended in 2018 to give "all registered voters the right to request and vote by an absentee ballot without giving a reason ... On May 19, 2020, however, Secretary Benson announced that her office would send **unsolicited** absentee-voter ballot applications by mail to all 7.7 million registered Michigan voters prior to the primary and general elections. Although her office repeatedly encouraged voters to vote absentee because of the COVID-19 pandemic, it did not ensure that Michigan's election systems and procedures were adequate to ensure the accuracy and legality of the historic flood of mail-in votes. In fact, it did the opposite and did away with protections designed to deter voter fraud ... Secretary Benson's flooding of Michigan with millions of absentee ballot applications prior to the 2020 general election violated [Michigan law, M.C.L. § 168.759(3), which] limits the procedures for requesting an absentee ballot to three specified ways:

An application for an absentee voter ballot under this section may be made in *any of the following ways:*

(a) By a written request signed by the voter
(b) On an absent voter ballot application form provided for that
purpose by the clerk of the city or township
(c) On a federal postcard application

The Michigan Legislature could have included the Secretary of State as a means for distributing ballot applications, but decided *not* to do so. "Under the statute's plain language, the Legislature explicitly gave *only local clerks* the power to distribute absentee voter ballot applications ... Because the Legislature declined to explicitly include the Secretary of State as a vehicle for distributing absentee ballots applications, Secretary Benson lacked authority to distribute even a single absentee voter ballot application—much less the *millions* of absentee ballot applications Secretary Benson chose to flood across Michigan."

But that was not all. The complaint continues to relate that, "Secretary Benson also violated Michigan law when she launched a program in June 2020 allowing absentee ballots to be requested online, *without* signature verification as expressly required under Michigan law. The Michigan Legislature did not approve or authorize Secretary Benson's unilateral actions."

In Michigan it is illegal to process *any* absentee ballot application without signature verification. "[Michigan law] states ... [that]: 'An applicant for an absent voter ballot shall sign the application. Subject to section 761(2), a clerk or assistant clerk shall not deliver an absent voter ballot to an applicant who does not sign the application.' ... Further, [the law] states in relevant part: 'The qualified voter file must be used to determine the genuineness of a signature on an application for an absent voter ballot", and if 'the signatures do not agree sufficiently or [if] the signature is missing' the ballot must be rejected."

The scale of increase in ballots requested and cast following this illegal policy change was enormous. "In 2016 only 587,618 Michigan voters requested absentee ballots. In stark contrast, in 2020, 3.2 million votes were cast by absentee ballot, about 57% of total votes cast—and more than *five times* the number of ballots *even requested* in 2016....

"Secretary Benson's unconstitutional modifications of Michigan's election rules," therefore, "resulted in the distribution of millions of absentee ballot applications without verifying voter signatures as required by [two different provisions in Michigan law]. This means that *millions* of absentee ballots were disseminated in violation of Michigan's statutory signature-verification requirements." And, the benefit that these illegal changes conferred upon the official winner of the presidential race in Michigan was plainly evident: "Democrats in Michigan voted by mail at a ratio of approximately two to one compared to Republican voters. Thus, former Vice President Biden materially benefited from these unconstitutional changes to Michigan's election law."

The complaint further reported, "Michigan also requires that poll watchers and inspectors have access to vote counting and canvassing," but that, "[l]ocal election officials in Wayne County made a conscious and express policy decision not to follow M.C.L. §§ 168.674-.675 for the opening, counting, and recording of absentee ballots."

Furthermore, just as signature verification requirements under Michigan law were ignored for the *requesting* of absentee ballots, so also were they ignored in their *counting*: "Michigan ... has strict signature verification requirements for absentee ballots, including that the Elections Department place a written statement or stamp on each ballot envelope where the voter signature is placed, indicating that the voter signature was in fact checked and verified with the signature on file with the State. *See* MCL § 168.765a(6) ... However, Wayne County made the policy decision to ignore Michigan's statutory signature-verification requirements for absentee ballots."

And, once again, it made a big difference: "Former Vice President Biden received approximately 587,074, or 68%, of the votes cast [in Wayne County] compared to President Trump's receiving approximately 264,149, or 30.59%, of the total vote. Thus, Mr. Biden materially benefited from these unconstitutional changes to Michigan's election law."

After discussing the illegal guidance, the motion reported election worker testimony confirming that they were trained and instructed to disregard Michigan law concerning signature verification processes. "Numerous poll challengers and an Election Department employee whistleblower have testified that the signature verification requirement was ignored in Wayne County in a case currently pending in the Michigan Supreme Court. For example, Jessy Jacob, a decades-long City of Detroit employee assigned to work in the Elections Department for the 2020 election testified that:

> Absentee ballots that were received in the mail would have the voter's signature on the envelope. While I was at the TCF Center, I was instructed not to look at any of the signatures on the absentee ballots, and I was instructed not to compare the signature on the absentee ballot with the signature on file.

The TCF Center "was the only facility within Wayne County authorized to count ballots for the City of Detroit." Taken together, "[t]hese non-legislative modifications to Michigan's election statutes resulted in a number of constitutionally tainted votes that far exceeds the margin of voters separating the candidates in Michigan."

The complaint next mentioned absentee ballots that were counted in Wayne County without being linked to a registered voter, adversely materially impacting the integrity of the vote: "[T]he Wayne County Statement of Votes Report lists 174,384 absentee ballots out of 566,694 absentee ballots tabulated (about 30.8%) as counted without a registration number for precincts in the City of Detroit. ... **The number of votes not tied to a registered voter by itself exceeds Vice President Biden's margin of 146,007 votes by more than 28,377 votes.**"[18]

How could such discrepancy between the number of registered voters and the number of ballots counted have occurred? Testimony of witnesses supported by some video evidence suggested an answer, that the motion reports "The extra ballots cast most likely resulted from the phenomenon of Wayne County election workers running the same ballots through a tabulator multiple times, with Republican poll watchers obstructed or denied access, and election officials ignoring poll watchers' challenges, as documented by numerous declarations."

The phenomenon of number of ballots cast not aligning with the number of voters who checked in was widespread in Wayne County. "[A] member of the Wayne County Board of Canvassers ... , William Hartman, determined that 71% of Detroit's Absent Voter Counting Boards ('AVCBs') were unbalanced—*i.e.*, the number of people who checked in did not match the number of ballots cast—without explanation."

Failure to either reconcile or explain the discrepancies in so many instances led to concern among those members of the Canvassing Board who were not Democrats. However, those expressing concerns were threatened with violence if they would not certify the "results." The complaint reported: "On November 17, 2020, the Canvassers Board deadlocked 2-2 over whether to certify the results of the presidential election based on numerous reports of fraud and unanswered material discrepancies in the county-wide election results. A few hours later, the Republican Board members reversed their decision and voted to certify the results after severe harassment, including threats of violence ....

"The following day, the two Republican members of the Board *rescinded their votes* to certify the vote and signed affidavits alleging they were bullied and misled into approving election results and do not believe the votes should be certified until serious irregularities in Detroit votes are resolved....

"Regardless of the number of votes that were affected by the unconstitutional modification of Michigan's election rules," the motion concludes in its discussion of this state's actions, "the non-legislative changes to the election rules violated the Electors Clause."

Portions of several of the supporting affadivits quoted in the motion are presented below.

Wisconsin

Wisconsin has ten electoral votes, with an official margin of victory of 20,565. In two Wisconsin counties, Milwaukee and Dane, Biden's margin (364,298) significantly exceeds his statewide lead.

"In the 2016 general election," the motion's introduction of the issues in Wisconsin said, "some 146,932 mail-in ballots were returned in Wisconsin out of more than 3 million votes cast. In stark contrast, 1,275,019 mail-in ballots, nearly a 900 percent increase over 2016, were returned in the November 3, 2020 election."

The motion stated, "Wisconsin statutes guard against fraud in absentee ballots: '[V]oting by absentee ballot is a privilege exercised wholly outside the traditional safeguards of the polling place. The legislature finds that the privilege of voting by absentee ballot must be carefully regulated to prevent the potential for fraud or abuse.'" However, it continued: "In direct contravention of Wisconsin law, leading up to the 2020 general election, the Wisconsin Elections Commission ('WEC') and other local officials," none of which were the Wisconsin legislature, "unconstitutionally modified Wisconsin election laws—each time taking steps that weakened, or did away with, established security procedures put in place by the Wisconsin legislature to ensure absentee ballot integrity ... For example, the WEC undertook a campaign to position hundreds of drop boxes ... including the use of unmanned drop boxes ... The mayors of Wisconsin's five largest cities—Green Bay, Kenosha, Madison, Milwaukee, and Racine, which all have Democrat majorities—joined in this effort, and together, developed a plan to use purportedly 'secure drop-boxes to facilitate return of absentee ballots.' Wisconsin Safe Voting Plan 2020 (June 15, 2020)."

This move to place unmanned drop boxes all over heavily Democrat areas of Wisconsin was apparently massive in scale. "It is alleged in an action recently filed in the United States District Court for the Eastern District of Wisconsin that **over five hundred unmanned, illegal, absentee ballot drop boxes were used in the Presidential election in Wisconsin.**"[19]

"However, **the use of *any* drop box, manned or unmanned, is directly prohibited by Wisconsin statute.**"[20] So, every ballot drop box in Wisconsin was illegal. "The Wisconsin legislature specifically described in the Election Code 'Alternate absentee ballot site[s]' and detailed the procedure by which the governing body of a municipality may designate a site or sites for the delivery of absentee ballots 'other than the office of the municipal clerk or board of election commissioners as the location from which electors of the municipality may request and vote absentee ballots and to which voted absentee ballots shall be returned by electors for any election.'...

"Any alternate absentee ballot site," says Wisconsin law, "'shall be staffed by the municipal clerk or the executive director of the board of election commissioners, or employees of the clerk or the board of election commissioners.' ... Likewise, [Wisconsin law] provides, '[i]n a municipality in which the governing body has elected to establish an alternate absentee ballot site under [Wisconsin law], the municipal clerk shall operate such site as though it were his or her office for absentee ballot purposes and shall ensure that such site is adequately staffed.'" So, unmanned absentee ballot drop-boxes "are prohibited by the Wisconsin Legislature as they do not comply with Wisconsin law expressly defining '[a]lternate absentee ballot site[s]'."

It was not only the issues related to election authorities' power and responsibilities concerning alternate absentee ballot sites that caused the drop boxes to be illegal. It was also the fact that placing a ballot into a drop box was not a valid means of delivering a ballot to the municipal clerk: "In addition, the use of drop boxes for the collection of absentee ballots, positioned predominantly in Wisconsin's largest cities, is directly contrary to Wisconsin's law providing that absentee ballots may only be 'mailed by the elector, or delivered *in person* to the municipal clerk issuing the ballot or ballots.'...

"The fact that other methods of delivering absentee ballots, such as through unmanned drop boxes, are *not* permitted is underscored by Wisconsin Statute § 6.87(6) which mandates that, "[a]ny ballot not mailed or delivered as provided in this subsection may not be counted."[21] Likewise, [Wisconsin law] underscores this point, providing that [Wisconsin law] "shall be construed as mandatory." The provision continues—"Ballots cast in contravention of the procedures specified in those provisions may not be counted. *Ballots counted in contravention of the procedures specified in those provisions may not be included in the certified result of any election.*" [Wisconsin law cited][22]...

"These were not the only Wisconsin election laws that the WEC violated in the 2020 ... election. The WEC and local election officials also took it upon themselves to encourage voters to unlawfully declare themselves 'indefinitely confined'—which under Wisconsin law allows the voter to avoid security measures like signature verification and photo ID requirements....

"Specifically, registering to vote by absentee ballot requires photo identification, except for those who register as "indefinitely confined" or "hospitalized." Registering for indefinite confinement requires certifying confinement "because of age, physical illness or infirmity or [because the voter] is disabled for an indefinite period." Should indefinite confinement cease, the voter must notify the county clerk, *id.*, who must remove the voter from indefinite-confinement status." In each of these cases, the motion cites the specific section of Wisconsin law being referenced.

"Wisconsin election procedures for voting absentee based on indefinite confinement enable the voter to avoid the photo ID requirement and signature requirement." This is clearly an exception made for those who are actually indefinitely confined, e.g. due to a serious actual medical condition. However, "[o]n March 25, 2020, in clear violation of Wisconsin law, Dane County Clerk Scott McDonnell and Milwaukee County Clerk George Christensen both issued guidance indicating that all voters should mark themselves as 'indefinitely confined' because of the COVID-19 pandemic."

Believing the guidance to be "an attempt to circumvent Wisconsin's strict voter ID laws, the Republican Party of Wisconsin petitioned the Wisconsin Supreme Court to intervene. On March 31, 2020, the Wisconsin Supreme Court unanimously confirmed that the clerks' "advice was legally incorrect" and potentially dangerous because "voters may be misled to exercise their right to vote in ways that are inconsistent with [Wisconsin law]."

The brazenness of the WEC was most evident in what happened next. "On May 13, 2020, the Administrator of WEC issued a directive to the Wisconsin clerks prohibiting removal of voters from the registry for indefinite-confinement status if the voter is no longer 'indefinitely-confined.'"

But, "[t]he WEC's directive violated Wisconsin law [which] specifically provides that 'any [indefinitely confined] elector ... no longer indefinitely confined ... shall so notify the municipal clerk.' [Wisconsin law] further provides that the municipal clerk 'shall remove the name of any other elector from the list upon request of the elector or upon receipt of reliable information that an elector no longer qualifies for the service.' ...

"According to statistics kept by the WEC, nearly 216,000 voters said they were indefinitely confined in the 2020 election, nearly a fourfold increase from nearly 57,000 voters in 2016. In Dane and Milwaukee counties, more than 68,000 voters said they were indefinitely confined in 2020, a fourfold increase from the roughly 17,000 indefinitely confined voters in those counties in 2016. ...

"Under Wisconsin law, voting by absentee ballot also requires voters to complete a certification, including their address, and have the envelope witnessed by an adult who also must sign and indicate their address on the envelope ... The sole remedy to cure an 'improperly completed certificate or [ballot] with no certificate' is for 'the clerk [to] return the ballot to the elector[.]' ... 'If a certificate is missing the address of a witness, the ballot *may not be counted.*' ... (emphasis added) ... However, in a training video issued April 1, 2020, the Administrator of the City of Milwaukee Elections Commission unilaterally declared that a **witness address may be written in red and that is because we were able to locate the witnesses' address for the voter**" to add an address missing from the certifications on absentee ballots. The Administrator's instruction violated [Wisconsin law].

The WEC issued similar guidance on October 19, 2020, in violation of this statute as well ....

"In the Wisconsin Trump Campaign Complaint, it is alleged, supported by the sworn affidavits of poll watchers, that canvas workers carried out this unlawful policy," and following its directions, "in Milwaukee used red-ink pens to alter the certificates on the absentee envelope and then cast and count the absentee ballot. These acts violated [Wisconsin law, for example]: (**'If a certificate is missing the address of a witness, the ballot may not be counted'**) ... and, ('If a municipal clerk receives an absentee ballot with an improperly completed certificate or with no certificate, the clerk may return the ballot to the elector ... whenever time permits the elector to correct the defect and return the ballot within the period authorized.') ... Wisconsin's legislature has not ratified these changes [that were made apart from the state legislature by the WEC], and its election laws do not include a severability clause."

Wisconsin's issues raised in the motion, however, did not end there. According to sworn testimony, U.S. Postal Service workers had been fraudulently backdating late ballots with the result that they could be counted under Wisconsin rules: "Ethan J. Pease, a box truck delivery driver subcontracted to the U.S. Postal Service ("USPS") to deliver truckloads of mail-in ballots to the sorting center in Madison, WI, testified that **USPS employees were backdating ballots received after November 3, 2020.** ... Further, Pease testified how a senior USPS employee told him on November 4, 2020 that '[a]n order came down from the Wisconsin/Illinois Chapter of the Postal Service that 100,000 ballots were missing' and how the USPS dispatched employees to 'find[] ... the ballots.' (DOC) One hundred thousand ballots supposedly 'found' after Election Day would far exceed formerly Vice President Biden's margin of 20,565 votes over President Trump."

Electors Clause Was Violated

Having presented the material relating to Pennsylvania, Georgia, Michigan and Wisconsin, the motion returned to its main assertions, the first being that actions of these four states violated the Electors Clause of the Constitution. "The Electors Clause of Article II, Section 1, Clause 2, of the Constitution makes clear that only the legislatures of the States are permitted to determine the rules for appointing presidential electors. The pertinent rules here are the state election statutes, specifically those relevant to the presidential election ... Non-legislative actors lack authority to amend or nullify election statutes."

Under legal precedent, "conscious and express executive policies—even if unwritten—to nullify statutes or to abdicate statutory responsibilities are reviewable to the same extent as if the policies had been written or adopted. Thus, conscious and express actions by State or local election officials to nullify or ignore requirements of election statutes violate the Electors Clause to the same extent as formal modifications by judicial officers or State executive officers ... The actions discussed above [therefore] constitute non-legislative changes to State election law by executive-branch State election officials, or by judicial officials, in Defendant States, in violation of the Electors Clause."

Since the Electors Clause was violated in the listed ways, the motion asserted that electors "appointed to the Electoral College in violation of the Electors Clause cannot cast constitutionally valid votes for the office of President."

Equal Protection Clause Was Violated

Remember that the Equal Protection Clause provides that all persons shall be guaranteed equal protection of the laws and "prohibits the use of differential standards in the treatment and tabulation of ballots within a State." Based upon this fact, the motion now concluded that "[t]he one-person, one-vote principle requires counting valid votes and not counting invalid votes ...[and] ("the votes eligible for inclusion in the certification are the votes meeting the properly established legal requirements")."

The actions described above, said the motion—and it here specified the sections—"created differential voting standards in Defendant States in violation of the Equal Protection Clause." And, it stated that the action set out in—and it here specified other sections— "violated the one-person, one-vote principle in Defendant States."

Why did all these things constitute a valid reason for the Court to intervene? It is because these constitutional violations effectively disenfranchised not only the offending states' own voters, but in fact they disenfranchised all Americans: "By the shared enterprise of the entire nation electing the President and Vice President, equal protection violations in one State can and do adversely affect and diminish the weight of votes cast in States that lawfully abide by the election structure set forth in the Constitution. Plaintiff State is therefore harmed by this unconstitutional conduct in violation of the Equal Protection or Due Process Clauses."

Due Process Was Violated

Finally, we come to the Due Process Clause. "When election practices reach "the point of patent and fundamental unfairness," the integrity of the election itself violated substantive due process." Many legal precedents were listed before the motion continued: "Under this Court's precedents on procedural due process, not only intentional failure to follow election law as enacted by a State's legislature but also random and unauthorized acts by state election officials and their designees in local government can violate the Due Process Clause ... Defendant States acted unconstitutionally to lower their election standards—including to allow invalid ballots to be counted and valid ballots to not be counted—with the express intent to favor their candidate for President and to alter the outcome of the 2020 election. In many instances these actions occurred in areas having a history of election fraud. ...

"The actions set out in [specified sections above]," the motion stated, "constitute intentional violations of State election law by State election officials and their designees in Defendant States, in violation of the Due Process Clause."

Supporting Affidavits—A Selected Summary

The Texas lawsuit was accompanied by several sworn affidavits related to the conduct and results of the election in the four states of Georgia, Michigan, Pennsylvania, and Wisconsin. An affidavit is a statement concerning something about which the one testifying claims to have knowledge and is willing to affirm as true under oath. Filing a false affidavit constitutes perjury, a crime in all U.S. states punishable by time in prison—in some jurisdictions up to a decade—and, usually, serious fines. Just because something is sworn in an affidavit does not mean it is true; perhaps those testifying drew an unwarranted conclusion or misinterpreted what they saw. But strong consequences for perjury are reason to take sworn affidavits seriously.

While many of these affidavits include first-hand testimony of alleged fraud, keep this fact in perspective of the main complaint. Also, if we consider the axiom "where there is smoke, there is fire," we should take appearance of fraud contained in these testimonies as the "smoke" part of the equation: evidence of real harm but perhaps the tip of an iceberg whose dimensions were not yet fully measured or documented at the time the affidavits were given. The following are summaries and excerpts.[23]

Charles J. Cicchetti, Ph.D.

One affidavit is from economist Charles Cicchetti. It involves statistical analysis that—at least as summarized in the lawsuit—seems outrageous. Being neither an economist nor a statistician, I have not been able to understand its highly technical analysis. I have seen it criticized with a general claim that it assumes things about the uniformity of voting populations, either from one presidential election to the next, or within the state during the 2020 election, that cannot be assumed.

Having neither been able to speak to Dr. Ciccetti myself, nor to judge his statement myself, and also guessing that it would fly over the head of most readers, I omit presenting it except to mention that his argument seems to have been at least partly misrepresented inside the lawsuit. In fairness, I withhold judgment. In any event, it is—like the others—only supporting evidence and not indispensable to the constitutional argument.

Monica Palmer

In 2020, Ms. Palmer chaired the four-member Wayne County, Michigan Board of Canvassers. In her affidavit she told how, following reports of fewer ballots recorded than the number of voters according to the poll book, missing absentee ballot applications, and 72% of the absentee precincts in the city of Detroit being out of balance in the August 4, 2020 primary, the board unanimously approved a proposed joint resolution requesting an investigation into that election and the appointment of a monitor to supervise the training and administration of the City of Detroit Absentee Voter Counting Boards for the upcoming November general election. Even the two Democrats admitted a need for course correction.

On November 3 and 4, 2020, Ms. Palmer observed the election process at the TCF Center, and from the 5th through the 17th she was at the Wayne County Canvas nearly every day.

On November 17, the Board of Canvassers was to meet starting at 3:00 p.m., to decide whether or not to certify the November election. The meeting, however, did not begin until 4:46 p.m., and only minutes before it began was she even given a report on the final canvas. Moreover, the report she was given lacked even an executive summary.

During the meeting, Ms. Palmer observed that 70% of Detroit's 134 Absentee Voter Counting Boards did not balance and many of them lacked even an explanation as to why they did not balance. The vice-chair made a motion to certify the vote. Ms. Palmer, noting the earlier concerns from August, voted not to certify the Wayne County elections, causing the motion to fail 2-2. At the public comment period that followed, she notes,

> ... dozens of people made personal remarks against me and Mr. Hartmann. The comments made accusations of racism and threatened me and members of my family. ... After several hours of harsh comments, Wayne County Corporate Counsel Janet Anderson-Davis told me that I had to certify the vote that night. She told the members their role was ministerial and they could not use their discretion on matters like the record being incomplete. We were told that discretion was outside the board's authority.

After being told that I could not use my discretion ... I believed I had no choice but to certify the results despite my desire to oppose certification based on the incomplete record. ... [W]e were presented with a resolution that promised a full, independent audit that would present answers to the incomplete record. *I voted to agree to certify based on the promise of a full, independent audit. I would not have agreed to vote to certify but for that promise of a full, independent audit.*

[The vice-chair] gave me assurances that voting for the certification of the November election would result in a full, independent audit of Detroit's unbalanced precincts....

Later that evening, I was sent statements that Secretary Jocelyn Benson made saying that she *did not view our audit resolution to be binding.*

The Wayne County election had serious process flaws which deserve investigation.[24]

Ms. Palmer concluded by stating that she rescinded her prior vote to certify the Wayne County elections.

William C. Hartmann

Mr. Hartmann was the second member of the Wayne County Board of Canvassers who on November 17 voted not to certify the November 3 election results. Like Ms. Palmer, he stated in his affidavit that he observed the Absentee Voter Counting Boards at the TCF Center, and attended the Wayne County Canvass on an almost daily basis between the election and the November 17 vote to certify.

Mr. Hartmann's affidavit agrees with that of Monica Palmer on details of events related to the certification votes, including the derision and berating (from the two Democrat members of the board, and from the public) that both of them received for failing to vote to certify, the affirmation that Ms. Anderson-Davis told Hartmann he lacked the authority to vote against certification but must vote to certify the election that very night, the assurance from Anderson-Davis that if he did vote to certify, then a "full, independent, and complete audit of Detroit's election" would be conducted, and the subsequent news—received after he finally gave in to pressure and voted to certify—that Michigan Secretary of State Jocelyn Benson had now made a public statement that the promise to audit would not be honored.

Like Ms. Palmer, Mr. Hartmann had been deeply concerned at so many of Detroit's Absentee Voter Counting Boards (he calculates 71%) remaining out of balance even at the moment he was being demanded to affirm the election results as true and correct. Remember, this vote to certify came *two full weeks* after the election, yet the great majority of these crucial results had still not been reconciled, and he said that many of them were even left unexplained.

Hartmann's affidavit also lists several of his misgivings and unanswered questions about the election in Detroit:

> I am ... concerned about the use of private monies directing local officials regarding the management of the elections, how those funds were used and whether such funds were used to pay election workers. I have not received answers to these questions....
>
> Why do the pollbooks, Qualified Voter Files, and final tallies not match or balance? ...
>
> Did the chairperson of each of Detroit's 134 AVCB's (sic) keep logs of shift changes?
>
> Why were republicans (sic) *not* used in signing seals certified at the end of the night on Monday, and Wednesday evening before ballot boxes were documented, closed, and locked?
>
> How many challenged ballots were counted?
>
> Was any information placed directly into the Qualified Voter Files in the AVCB's (sic)?
>
> How many voter birthdays were altered in the pollbooks?
>
> Were ballots counted in TCF that were not reflected in the electronic pollbook or paper supplemental list?
>
> Based on information and belief, there were over 18,000 same-day registrations in Detroit on November 3. Were these new applicants verified as proper voters prior to the tabulation of their ballots?[25]

Hartmann's concerns about private money and outside influence in the election were publicly confirmed three weeks later in an NPR article praising Mark Zuckerberg for "saving" the 2020 election by donating $400 million that was distributed to over 2,500 jurisdictions around the United States. These monies, the article admits, were not isolated to Detroit, but spread around the nation, with apparent concentration of funds in swing states. For example, Chester County, Pennsylvania received $2.5 million from Zuckerberg for the election. Biden's official margin of victory over Trump in Chester County alone was 53,807,[26] fully two-thirds of Biden's statewide official margin of 80,555 votes. The NPR article credits Zuckerberg's investment for the victory, crowing, "Pennsylvania was pivotal to Joe Biden's victory over President Trump, and his win in the state was fueled in part by his success in Chester County. He won it by 17 percentage points—*nearly double Hillary Clinton's margin four years earlier.*"[27]

The matter of the 2020 Zuckerberg-Chan multi-million dollar pro-Biden election influence scheme was the focal point of the 2020 investigative documentary *Rigged* (Dave Bossie, Citizens United) as well as being discussed in the documentary *2000 Mules* (Dinesh D'Souza).

Jessy Jacob

Jessy Jacob, a naturalized U.S. citizen and decades-long employee of the City of Detroit, on furlough prior to the election, was assigned to work in the Elections Department for the 2020 election. In her affidavit, she stated that in September of 2020, she was instructed to fraudulently adjust the date on absentee ballots received after the legal deadline to make them appear as though they were received on time. In later oral testimony, she stated that she and others were similarly directed by supervisors to fraudulently pre-date absentee ballot packets before mailing them to voters, as will be discussed below. She said there were 70-80 workers beside herself processing absentee ballot applications throughout September. Mrs. Jacob stated in her affidavit attached to the Texas lawsuit,

> I directly observed, on a daily basis, City of Detroit election workers and employees coaching and trying to coach voters to vote for Joe Biden and the Democrat party. I witnessed these workers and employees encouraging voters to do a straight Democrat ballot. I witnessed these election workers and employees going over to the voting booths with voters in order to watch them vote and coach them for whom to vote.
>
> During the last two weeks while working at this satellite location I was specifically instructed by my supervisor not to ask for a driver's license or any photo I.D. when a person was trying to vote.
>
> I observed a large number of people who came to the satellite location to vote in-person, but they had already applied for an absentee ballot. These people were allowed to vote in-person and were not required to return the mailed absentee ballot or sign an affidavit that the voter lost the mailed absentee ballot.

Mrs. Jacob also described the nature of the Qualified Voter File (QVF) system, in particular stating that she was instructed to input the name, address, and birthdate of any absentee voter application or in-person registration. She further stated that the QVF system can be "accessed and edited by any election processor with proper credentials in the State of Michigan at any time and from any location with internet access."[28] She went on to say that,

> I worked at the satellite location until the polls closed on November 3, 2020 at 8:00 p.m. and properly completed the entry of all absentee ballots into the QVF by 8:30 p.m.

I then reported to work at the TCF Center on November 4, 2020, at 8:30 a.m. to process ballots. *I was instructed not to validate any ballots and not to look for any deficiencies in the ballots.*

Absentee ballots that were received in the mail would have the voter's signature on the envelope. While I was at the TCF Center, *I was instructed not to look at any of the signatures on the absentee ballots*, and *I was instructed not to compare the signature on the absentee ballot with the signature on file.*[29]

Mrs. Jacob noted that all absentee ballots were required to be entered into the QVF system by 9:00 p.m. on Election Day, November 3, and the purpose of that requirement was "to have a final list of absentee voters who returned their ballots prior to 8:00 p.m. on November 3, 2020—the legal cutoff time for such a ballot to be received and counted." However, on November 4, Mrs. Jacob testified,

I was instructed to improperly pre-date the absentee ballots receive (sic) date that were not in the QVF as if they had been received on or before November 3, 2020. I was told to alter the information in the QVF to falsely show that the absentee ballots had been received in time to be valid. I estimate that this was done to thousands of ballots.[30]

In subsequent testimony before the Michigan House, Mrs. Jacob told of 10,000-14,000 absentee ballot packets per day throughout the month of September being fraudulently backdated at the explicit instruction of supervisors. She further affirmed that during her ballot processor training at Wayne County Community College on September 28-29 (which she audio recorded with permission from the instructor), the instructor told the trainees that, "It doesn't matter if the address is wrong, or the birthdate is missing, or there are no names. You must try and find a birthdate. If the signatures look different, find something about them that's the same. No application should be rejected."[31]

Mrs. Jacob's testimony was discounted by a judge in early November as not credible based upon lack of specificity and the claim that she had not tried to stop the alleged fraudulent actions and only came forward after unofficial results of the voting indicated that Biden would be the winner in the state of Michigan.[32] I agree that a witness needs to provide names and to come forward in a timely manner, but I also have some cultural understanding in this situation, and will discuss the matter for a moment here.

To my understanding, Mrs. Jacob is a Catholic woman, born and raised in Kerala, India. For decades, I have been married into a Christian family from Kerala, very embedded in the Kerala Christian community. I understand the culture and have hundreds of Indian "aunties," "uncles," and cousins. My wife watched Mrs. Jacob's testimony before the Michigan

House—as did I, at a separate time—and we both observed a few items. First, Mrs. Jacob would not have come forward merely to seek attention. Culturally, speaking up as she did would have been extremely difficult. Stepping into the limelight on the unpopular side of a matter of great public controversy is not something that an Indian aunty will do for no reason.

Second, she was certainly torn and conflicted—and it took time to process this conflict. Indian Christians have a strong cultural impulse to respect authority and to be careful not to dishonor or hurt others. If someone like Mrs. Jacob is told to do something a particular way while at work, she will respect that authority. Indeed, her conscientiousness was quite evident from her testimony. So, when her supervisor's instructions to disregard signatures and other ballot deficiencies conflicted with what the state guide book said, her first impulse would have been to trust that the person in authority over her has some new guidance and must be obeyed. That it took Mrs. Jacob a number of weeks to bring the pieces together and then get up the courage to make a public complaint will be no surprise to anyone familiar with the culture.

Third, Mrs. Jacob is clearly not a mean or vindictive person. Her reluctance to provide names—even though she did provide them to Giuliani, apparently—reflects her desire not to get people who otherwise had been kind to her into trouble.

Finally, so far as we were able to discern from her testimony, my wife and I believe that Mrs. Jacob leans Democrat—as is the case with many Indian immigrants to the United States. We do not know whom she supported for president, but she does not fit the profile of a default conservative.

Michigan representatives on the panel hearing testimonies were each permitted one question. One representative chose to ask whether Jessy Jacob was Mrs. Jacob's given name. It was an odd thing to ask, and betrayed —in my view—a great deal of cultural insensitivity. First names (or "good names") in the culture are sometimes novel or a variation on an ordinary spelling. The practice in Kerala is also for a wife to take her husband's first name as her own last name, and children take their father's first name as their last name. These conventions often change in the first generation after immigrating to the United States. For the most part, one can know whether an Indian person is culturally Christian, Hindu or Muslim based upon his or her last name. We don't know what the representative—who seemed to be a Democrat—meant by her question about Mrs. Jacob's name. Was it to insult her? Was it intended as a threat or intimidation, to get her on record in a way that would jeopardize her safety or future job prospects with the City of Detroit?

Mellissa A. Carone

Mellissa Carone was contracted by Dominion Voting Services to do IT (information technology) work at the TCF Center in Detroit, Michigan, for the November 3, 2020 election, and stated, "I arrived at the TCF Center at approximately 6:15 AM November 3, 2020 and worked until 4:00 AM November 4, 2020. I went home to get some sleep, then arrived back at the TCF Center at 10:00 AM in which I stayed until 1:45 PM."

Carone's affidavit was not carefully worded at all points. For example, she stated that during the time referenced above, she witnessed "nothing but" fraudulent actions taking place. The problem is clear. Did she see someone open a door? Sit in a chair? Turn on a light? Say hello to a co-worker? Was every such action fraudulent? Obviously not. Even though reasonable people understood what she meant to say, it would have been better to write with precision, stating (for example) that she witnessed a large number of actions she knew to be fraudulent, or had cause to believe were so.

Carone's report should be viewed critically, of course, but it also should be taken seriously.

After her public testimony, Carone was ridiculed with ad hominem attacks, parodied on Saturday Night Live, and became the subject of mocking internet memes. In a recent interview, she reported that she had been harassed with many death threats, was doxxed (that is, the act of malicious publication of someone's personal details such as address, employer, or contact information) twice (including once by Dominion Voting Systems on CNN on Christmas Eve 2021), and has had to move and change schools for her children three times in the course of a year. Although she took the initiative to contact the FBI with her concerns, she never heard back. However, she discerned after two incoming contacts from a government agent that she herself was under investigation.[33]

Having duly noted its minor problems, following is an excerpt of Carone's affidavit that was included with the Texas lawsuit as supporting material:

> The counters ... were handed a "batch" (stack of 50) of mail-in ballots ... which they would run through the tabulator. The tabulators would get jammed 4-5 times an hour, when they jammed the computer would put out an error that tells the worker the ballot number that was jammed and gives an option to either discard the batch or continue scanning at which the counter should discard the batch, put the issue ballot on top of the batch and rescan the entire batch. I witnessed countless workers rescanning the batches without discarding them first which resulted in ballots being counted 4-5 times.

At approximately midnight I was called over to assist one of the counters with a paper jam and noticed his PC had a number of over 400 ballots scanned- which means one batch was counted over 8 times. This happened countless times while I was at the TCF Center. I confronted my manager, Nick Ikonomakis saying how big of a problem it was, Nick told me he didn't want to hear that we have a big problem. He told me we are here to … assist with IT work, not to run their election.

The adjudication process, from my understanding there's supposed to be a republican (sic) and a democrat (sic) judging these ballots. I overheard numerous workers talking during shift change in which over 20 machines had two democrats (sic) judging the ballots. …

The night shift workers were free to come and go as they pleased, they could go out and smoke from the counting room. This is illegal, as there were boxes and stacks of ballots everywhere, anyone could have taken some out or brought some in, and No (sic) one was watching them.

There was (sic) two vans that pulled into the garage of the counting room, one on day shift and one on night shift. These vans were apparently bringing food into the building because they only had enough food for not even 1/3 of the workers. I never saw any food coming out of these vans, coincidentally it was announced on the news that Michigan had discovered over 100,000 more ballots- not even two hours after the last van left.

When a worker had a ballot that they either could not read, or it had something spilled on it, they would go to a table that had blank ballots on it and fill it out. They were supposed to be filling them out exactly like the one they had received but this was not the case at all. The workers would also sign the name of the person that the ballot had belonged to-which is clearly illegal.

Samuel Challandes and one more young man in his mid-20 (sic) were responsible for submitting the numbers into the main computer. …[M]y manager Nick … was on the floor assisting with IT most of the time …

I overheard Samuel talking to Nick about losing tons of data, they all got on their phones and stepped to the side of the stage. I asked Nick what was going one (sic) and he told me that it was all taken care of and not to worry about it. I fully believe that this was something very crucial that they just covered up.

I was the only republican (sic) working for Dominion Voting, and on the stage there was (sic) many terrible comments being made by the city workers and Dominion workers about republicans (sic). I did not give any indication that I was a republican (sic), I have a family at home and knew I was going to have to walk to my car at the end of my shift. If anyone had an American flag on their shirt or mask, they were automatically deemed to be Trump supporters.[34]

Zachary Larsen

Mr. Larsen, an attorney in private practice in the State of Michigan, formerly served as Assistant Attorney General for eight years from January 2012 through January 2020. In his affidavit, Mr. Larsen noted that he volunteered in September of 2020 to serve as a poll challenger for the Michigan Republican Party's Election Day operations "to ensure the integrity of the vote and conformity of the election process to the election laws of Michigan."

On November 3, he served as a roving attorney and credentialed poll challenger, visiting some 20-30 voting precincts in Lansing, East Lansing, and Williamston. During these visits, he was allowed to visually inspect the poll book without touching it at every precinct where he asked to review it, and was allowed to stand at a respectful distance behind the election officials while yet close enough to read the relevant names and numbers.

In contrast, he noted,

> The following day, on Wednesday, November 4, 2020, I arrived at the former Cobo Center, now known as the TCF Center, in Detroit, Michigan to serve as a poll challenger for the absent voter count occurring in Detroit and arrived between 9:30 and 9:45 a.m. [...After various check-in procedures, credential checks, and a temperature scan,] I was admitted at approximately 10:30 a.m.
>
> When I arrived at a counting table and began to observe the process, I noticed immediately that part of the process ... did not conform to what I had been told in my training and the materials that I had received.

What *should* have been happening, according to the training Mr. Larsen had received, was the following:

> A first election official would scan a ballot. If the scan did not confirm a voter in the poll book, that official would then check the voter against a paper copy "supplemental poll book."
>
> The official would then read the ballot number to a second election official and hand the ballot to that official, who would remove the ballot (while still in the secrecy sleeve) and confirm the ballot number. That second official would then hand the ballot (in the secrecy sleeve) to a third official who would tear the stub off of the ballot, and place the stub in a ballot stub envelope, then pass the remaining ballot to a fourth official.
>
> The fourth official would then remove the ballot from the secrecy sleeve, flatten the ballot to ensure it was capable of processing, and visually inspect for rips, tears, or stains before placing the ballot in the "ballots to be tabulated box." However, if that fourth individual identified a concern, she would place the ballot back in its envelope and into a "problem ballots" box that

required additional attention to determine whether they would be processed and counted.

However, Mr. Larsen stated that the above process was not being observed at the TCF Center. Rather,

> What I observed immediately was that the secrecy of the ballot was not being respected.
>
> Instead, the second official at the table where I was observing was repeatedly placing her fingers into the secrecy sleeve to separate the envelope and visually peek into the envelopes in a way that would allow here to visually observe the ballot and identify some of the votes cast by the voter.
>
> Sometimes, the third official whose job was merely to remove the stub from the ballot would likewise remove the ballot from the secrecy sleeve or otherwise peek to observe the ballot. Sometimes a ballot would be removed completely from the secrecy sleeve and then placed back inside and passed along this process.
>
> I conferred regarding this issue with another challenger at a nearby table, and he indicated he had observed similar irregularities regarding the use of the secrecy sleeves.
>
> When that challenger raised the issue with a supervisor, ... he was immediately asked "why does it matter?" and "what difference does it make?"

Why did it matter? Because the law—designed expressly to ensure that election workers would run the election without influencing its outcome—required it. Larsen wrote,

> [B]oth of us were concerned that the violations of the secrecy of the ballot that we witnessed could be or were being used to manipulate which ballots were placed in the "problem ballots" box.

Larsen continued to describe how, later that morning and at a different table, he observed election workers placing ballots lacking a secrecy sleeve into the "problem ballots" box while those with a sleeve were placed into the "ballots to be tabulated" box.

> I personally observed that several ballots were placed into the "problem ballots" boxed (sic) and marked with a sticky note indicating that they were "problem ballots" merely because of the lack of a secrecy sleeve. When I spoke with a supervisor regarding this issue, he explained that [it was being done] for efficiency.

So, not having a secrecy sleeve somehow made a ballot a "problem" at the second table, but Larsen had observed ballots arriving without a secrecy sleeve placed into the "ballots to be tabulated" box at the first table. This discrepancy

> again raised concerns that some ballots were being marked as "problem ballots" based on who the person had voted for rather than on any legitimate concern about the ability to count and process the ballot appropriately.

Larsen next described an encounter at another table where another Republican challenger had been observing the process. When Larsen asked her if she had observed anything of concern,

> [S]he immediately noted that she had seen many ballots scanned that did not register in the poll book but that were nonetheless processed. Because she needed to leave for lunch, I agreed to watch her table.
>
> As I watched the process, I was sensitive to her concern that ballots were being processed without confirmation that the voter was an eligible voter in the poll book, so I stood at the monitor and watched.
>
> The first ballot scanned came in as a match to an eligible voter. But the next several ballots that were scanned did not match any eligible voter in the poll book.
>
> When the scan came up empty, the first official would type in the name "Pope" that brought up a voter by that last name. I reviewed the running list of scanned in ballots in the computer system, and it appeared that the voter had already been counted as having voted. Then the first official appeared to assign a number to a different voter as I observed a completely different name that was added to the list of voters at the bottom of a running tab of processed ballots ...
>
> I was concerned that this practice of assigning names and numbers indicated that a ballot was being counted for a non-eligible voter who was not in either the poll book or the supplemental poll book. From my observation of the computer screen, the voters were certainly not in the official poll book. Moreover, *this appeared to be the case for the majority of the voters whose ballots I had personally observed being scanned.*[35]

Mr. Larsen described how, because of such concerns, he then moved to a position behind where the first official was conducting her work. He tried to maintain distance in sensitivity to COVID while still being able to visually observe the names on the supplemental poll book and on the envelopes—but distance was difficult to maintain because the tables were arranged in such a way that standing behind one official would place one close to another. He wrote,

> As soon as I moved to a location where I could observe the process by which the first official at this table was confirming the eligibility of the voters to vote, the first official immediately stopped working and glared at me. I stood still until she began to loudly and aggressively tell me that I could not stand where I was standing. She indicated that I needed to remain in front of the computer screen.
>
> I responded, "Ma'am, I am allowed by statute to observe the process." As I did, a Democratic challenger ran towards me and approached within two feet of me, saying "You cannot speak to her! You are not allowed to talk to her." I responded, "Sir, she spoke to me. I was just answering her."
>
> The first official again told me that the only place I was allowed to observe from was the computer screen. A second official at the table reiterated this. I said that was not true.
>
> Both officials then began to tell me that because of COVID, I needed to be six feet away from the table. I responded that I could not see and read the supplemental poll book from six feet away, but I was attempting to keep my distance to the extent possible.
>
> Just minutes before at another table, a supervisor had explained that the rules allowed me to visually observe what I needed to see and then step back away. Likewise, on Election Day, I had been allowed to stand at equivalent distance from poll books in Lansing and East Lansing precincts without any problem. With this understanding, I remained in a position where I would be able to observe the supplemental poll book until I could do so for the voter whose ballots had just been scanned and did not register in the poll book.
>
> Both officials indicated that I could not remain in a position that would allow me to observe their activities and they were going to get a supervisor. This seemed particularly concerning because the Democratic challenger who raised concerns over my verbal response to the official had been positioned behind the second official ... no further away than I was from the first official at that time and had not been stationed at the computer screen as the officials repeatedly told me was the only place that I could stay.
>
> When the supervisor arrived, she reiterated that I was not allowed to stand behind the official with the supplemental poll book, and I needed to stand in front of the computer screen. I told her that was not true, and that I was statutorily allowed to observe the process, including the poll book.
>
> The supervisor then pivoted to arguing that I was not six feet away from the first official. I told her I was attempting to remain as far away as I could while still being able to read the names in the poll book. In an attempt to address her concerns, I took a further step away from the table and indi-

cated I would try to keep my distance, and that I thought I was about six feet away from the first official. The supervisor then stood next to the chair immediately to the left of the first official and indicated that I was "not six feet away from" the supervisor and that she intended to sit in the chair next to the official with the poll book, so I would need to leave.

The supervisor had not been at the table at any time during the process ... Further, the supervisor's choice of chairs was approximately three feet to the left of the first official and therefore in violation of the six-foot distance rule.

Accordingly, I understood that this was a ruse to keep me away from a place where I could observe the confirmation of names in the supplemental poll book. The supervisor began to repeatedly tell me that I "needed to leave" ...

Between 1:30 p.m. and 2 p.m., my colleague and I decided to return to the suite that housed the Republican challengers to get lunch. We left the counting floor ...

Larsen concluded by telling how, when he attempted to return to the counting floor after lunch, he and others with him were denied readmittance because they were already counted as being in the room and no more would be allowed in due to capacity limitations. When the challengers raised the issue to the man at the door that they should not be counted as though they were in the room for capacity purposes when they were not actually in the room, "he refused to discuss any solutions such as confirming the identity of challengers who had been previously admitted."[36]

Andrew John Miller

Andrew Miller was a poll watcher on Election Day, November 3, 2020. His affidavit does not state the location where he was serving in such capacity. He stated,

The table I was at was duplicating ballots and had about 25 ballots to duplicate. One poll worker held the original ballot and a second poll worker duplicated the ballot. The poll worker who duplicated the ballot hovered over the ballot and blocked me from being able to see the duplication process. A third worker was blocking anyone from being able to see this duplication process.

I informed a supervisor that I was denied access to see the duplication process and need to review the ballots for accuracy. I was informed that I "couldn't because the duplication process was personal like voting."

I watched them duplicate 3 or 4 ballots and this happened on each ballot

I watched. I challenged these 3 or 4 ballots and the table worker refused to acknowledge my challenge. ... [t]he poll workers refused to enter my challenge into the computer and also refused to enter my challenge into the poll log.

On both November 3, 2020 and November 4, 2020, I was instructed to back up 6 feet from the table and I was unable to see what was happening with the ballots from 6 feet away from the table. At one point on November 4, a democrat (sic) challenger was standing between myself and the table where the poll worker was processing the ballots. I was instructed to back up 6 feet from the table, however, the democrat (sic) challenger, who stood in between where I was standing and the poll worker at the table, was not told they needed to back up.

I saw roughly 24 computers on November 3, 2020 and every computer I saw had a red error message in the lower right-hand corner saying "update overdue." Additionally, not all of the computers indicated the correct time, with some being off by approximately 5 hours. All computers with the incorrect time were synchronized to show the same incorrect time.[37]

Gregory Stenstrom

Gregory Stenstrom was the sole GOP poll watcher, certified by the Delaware County Board of Elections, for thirty-six precincts in Chester City, Pennsylvania. Of these, he stated that he was able to inspect and observe twenty-two. Wrote Stenstrom,

On November 3rd, I observed poll workers in multiple assigned Chester City polling places [...he lists seven], and several others, provide regular ballots, rather than provisional ballots, to voters who were told they had registered to vote by mail, without making them sign the registration book. I challenged the practice in those precincts where I observed it, and while I was present, they then stopped the practice and began providing provisional ballots. I was informed at each polling location by their respective judge of elections that I was the only GOP poll watcher they had seen in this 2020 election, or any other election they could remember.

Mr. Stenstrom told how, after checking in and taking the elevator to the first floor counting room at the Delco Chester City counting center with his certified poll watcher certificate, he was

denied entry, surrounded by first four (4) Park Police, and then an additional five (5) joined them. I presented my poll watcher certificate, and refused to leave, and was threatened with physical removal and arrest, at which point I was informed there was a separate list for "observers," and I had to somehow get on it. I asked if there were any GOP poll watchers in the building and was informed ... that there were two (2) inside. I asked to speak to them, and one man came out. I asked him how he got on the list and he stated he had volunteered *via* email [...] and that he was leaving shortly. I asked him if he knew what he was supposed to be "watching" and if he could see anything at all, and he stated he had "no idea," and "couldn't see anything from behind the barriers." I went back to the ground floor to figure out how to gain access ....

Stenstrom's statement included photographs of the facility and operations as he observed and described them. Among many other things, he noted that mail-in ballots in green trays were passing through the facility "in multiple directions from multiple points of entry up and down elevators that led from the garage loading dock to the top floor of the building."[38]

Five hours after his arrival at the facility, at approximately 11 p.m., Mr. Stenstrom finally gained entry along with a colleague. He stated,

We were the only GOP "observers" in the room, that was otherwise packed with Democrat employees, volunteers, and poll watchers. I observed a counting room for ballots with counting machines. Trays of ballots came in through three doors that appeared to lead from a back office, a second back office supply room, and doors leading from an outside hallway with separate elevator access from the public elevators and the garage loading dock elevators.

I had no meaningful opportunity to observe any part of the count: the sorting appeared to have been done elsewhere, and the machines were too far away from the observation position to see any part of the mail-in envelopes or ballots. I observed opened ballots going out the second back office closest to the windows in red boxes after handling and sorting by volunteers, some being placed in green boxes, and ballots from the green boxes being placed in scanners by workers, similar to the scanner I had used to vote myself, but was too far away (30 feet) to be sure. I asked the sheriff where the ballots came from, and where the ones that were leaving the room went, and he said he did not know.

I asked Ms. Lorraine Hagan, the elections official in charge of the operations, where the ballots were coming from and how they were being processed. She responded that I was only there to observe, and that I had no right to ask any questions. I said that I wanted to observe the activity in the sequestered room, but she denied my request, stating that the law prohibited access to that room by poll observers. I responded that there is no law denying access to observers, and she then said that it was "a COVID thing." I pointed out that I have a mask on, and so did the people visible through the door when it opened. She then informed me that she wanted to prevent us from "interfering." I responded that I was only there to observe and not to interfere, and to make a statement if I observed something wrong. Ms. Hagan said, "I assure you that everything's fine. There's no fraud going on."

Shortly after this exchange with Ms. Hagan, workers—who appeared to be volunteers—started bringing in semi-opaque bins with blue folding tops that contained clear plastic bags, approximately 10" square, with each bag containing a scanner cartridge, a USB drive, and a paper tape, and when they were brought to the computer tables which contained four (4) computer workstation towers on tables connected to four (4) wall mounted monitors, with one workstation tower in the floor under the tables that was not connected to a monitor, for a total of five (5) computers. A flurry of workers started disassembling the bags and separating out the USB sticks, cartridges, and paper tapes from the plastic bags, and dropping them in open cardboard boxes, with two workers sticking the USB drives into the computers to start the Election Day counts. I immediately objected, and demanded that Mr. McBlain [a lawyer who was also along with them at this point] challenge the process, and he again retrieved Ms. Hagan to hear my objections. I asked *why the returned items had not come with the sealed bags from the judges of elections*, and she explained that they had been taken out of the bags at the three (3) county election "processing centers" by the Sheriffs (sic) who were collecting them for ease of transport, and I stated that that was a break in the chain of custody, to which she shrugged her shoulders. I then asked her why they were separating out the USB drives from the cartridges and paper tapes, which was destroying any forensic auditability and further corrupting chain of custody, and she said "that's how we have always done it," and again stated I had no right to object, interfere, and was only permitted to observe, turned on her heels and walked away. I pleaded with Mr. McBlain to intervene and at least demand that the USB drives remain with the cartridges and tapes in the plastic bags so we would not have to reassemble them during tabulation, and he did nothing.

It is noteworthy that dozens of "volunteer" workers constantly streamed through the counting area unaccosted, with no check of either ID's (sic), or names, as the certified poll watchers were, several still wearing "Voter Integrity" lanyards and badges that had been widely distributed by Democrat poll watchers throughout the day, and they walked about unrestricted, and unaccompanied without any scrutiny, many handling ballots.[39]

Mr. Stenstrom next described how despite his many efforts, he and his colleagues remained confined in a small area where they could essentially see nothing. Pressing the lawyer to pursue meaningful access, Stenstrom said the latter left the roped-off area and returned at approximately 2:30

a.m., stating that he had spoken with the president of the board of elections, and they had agreed to

> allow us access to the "back office" and "locked ballot room" at 9:30 ... the following morning. ... I objected, but reluctantly agreed and left. I believe counting continued through the night because the count had increased, when I returned several hours later, the count on the tally screen was approximately 140,000 for Biden, and 85,000 for Trump and with all Republican candidates of all other races leading their opponents.

As agreed several hours before, Stenstrom, his lawyer, and Leah Hoopes (a Trump poll watcher) returned at 9:30 a.m. He continued,

> The elections officials ignored us for two hours, and at 11:30 AM, Ms. Hagan informed us that she would give a tour of the Chester City counting center to our group and a few Democrat poll watchers. I stated that I did not want a tour of the facility, that I only wanted them to honor their agreement to allow direct access to the sequestered counting room, and was ignored. Ms. Hagan, along with Ms. Maryann Jackson, another elections official, did not allow us to enter the sequestered counting room. Instead they walked us in an approximate 20-foot circle directly in front of the roped off area we had been restricted to, discussing the basics of election balloting but provided no insight into the purpose of the sequestered counting room.
>
> One comment made by Ms. Hagan led me to think that "pre"-pre-canvassing happened in the back room. The comment indicated that all ballots had been checked before going downstairs to the ground floor cafeteria for pre-canvassing, before being brought back to the 1st floor counting area, and entering the main counting room, for accuracy/sufficiency of signature, date, and barcode label, and entry in the Commonwealth SURE system. I specifically asked Ms. Hagan whether the names and signatures were matched, and whether the dates and barcode label were accurate. She replied in the affirmative. I then asked whether the names were checked against the voter registration rolls, and she again answered in the affirmative, indicating that people in the back room did the checking.

Stenstrom said that he saw about ten people in the back room through the door when it was opened. Ms. Hagan confirmed to him that no ballots went through the BlueCrest sorter without first being checked for name, date, signature, and barcode. Stenstrom continued,

> I could see 4000-5000 ballots in bins on the racks next to the BlueCrest Sorter, and I asked both Ms. Hagan and Ms. Jackson in front of the group "If all of the mail in ballot envelopes are checked for completion, as you stated,

then why are there multiple large bins of ballots on the racks next us (sic) between the BlueCrest sorter and ballot extractors labeled 'No Name,' 'No date,' and 'No signature,' on the bins?" The election officials, red faced, declined to answer. At this time, several Democrat observers, including Mr. Richard Shiffer, conferred with myself and Ms. Hoopes and stated that they were now not comfortable with the ballot ingestion process, and the back room, being sequestered from all watcher's (sic) sight, and also wanted to see the back room with us. The bins mentioned above were removed shortly after.

At this time, Ms. Hagan and Ms. Maryann Jackson ended the "tour" to "take a phone call" ... and the "tour" was abruptly ended. I asked Solicitor Parks when that phone call would be done so that we could see the back rooms as promised, and he simply turned around, and walked into the back room without further comment. Ms. Hagan, Ms. Jackson, and Solicitor Parks never returned, and we left ... two (2) hours after having been denied access to the back room.[40]

Stenstrom's lawyer sought and at 9:30 p.m. was granted a court order providing access to the back room, allowing the observers a five minute observation period once every two hours. Stenstrom continued,

I returned the following morning at 8:30 ... with Ms. Hoopes and the sheriff again barred entry despite the court order. ... When I returned to the main room, I saw that some areas had been cordoned off, and John McBlain [Stenstrom's lawyer] unexpectedly came out from the back room and stated that he had conferred with Solicitor Manly Parks and they had mutually agreed to bringing ballots in question out from the sequestered room to the main room so that I didn't have to go into the back room. Mr. McBlain told me that the elections officials were going to bring 4500 of the 6000 total ballots in the back room out to the main room, and leave the remaining 1500 spoiled ballots in the "spoilage room." I made Mr. McBlain confirm multiple times that the "universe" of remaining ballots in the back room that remained to be processed was ... in fact 6,000, and further made him affirm multiple times that he had personally sighted those ballots in the back rooms and storage rooms, and he reaffirmed this multiple times to me.

Mr. McBlain stated that their new plan was to re-tabulate the 4500 ballots by re-filling them out with a pen so that they could be read by voting machines, so we could "see everything." I followed him out of the counting room, and continued to ask him if it was, in fact, legal under election law to cure ballots, and was unconvinced that this was the case, and thought we should challenge it, but he assured me it was "normal" procedure and got on the elevator and left. It was during this time that Leah Hoopes, who had remained behind in the counting room ... observed Jim Savage, the

Delaware County voting machine warehouse supervisor, walked in with about a dozen USB drives in a clear unsealed bag, and she showed me two photos she had been able to surreptitiously take (no photos or camera use was permitted anywhere in the counting rooms despite live streaming cameras throughout the room).

I went back outside to see if I could retrieve Mr. McBlain ... and upon my return to the counting room at approximately 11am, I observed Mr. Savage plugging USB drives into the vote tallying computers. The bag containing those drives was not sealed or secured, and the voting machine cartridges were not present with the drives, and he had no ballots at that time.

I immediately objected and challenged the uploading of votes from the unsecured drives, and retrieved Deputy Sheriff Mike Donahue with my objection, and he went to the back room to retrieve Ms. Hagan. Ms. Hagan informed me that I could only observe the process but I could not make any comments or ask any questions while Mr. Savage was directly in front of us loading USB sticks, and the display monitors above the computers reflected that they were being updated. I responded that I was indeed observing a person plug USB sticks into the computer without any apparent chain of custody and without any oversight. No one stopped the upload, and Mr. Savage was permitted to continue this process and he was then allowed to walk out without any interference or examination by anyone. I called and texted Mr. McBlain throughout the day without success to get him back to the counting center to address the USB issue, and what was now being reported to me by other GOP observers that there appeared to be more additional paper ballots in excess of the 6000 "universe" coming into the office administration area that McBlain had assured me of ....

What happened next is emphasized with bold type and underlining in Stenstrom's testimony. I preserve only the former. Remembering that Stenstrom had earlier confirmed that only 6000 total ballots remained for possible tabulation, note that the total number of votes increased by ten times that much after the USB drive activity of voting machine warehouse supervisor, Mr. Savage:

Approximately one hour after Savage had departed, at 1:06pm, the center published an update on the vote. The numbers moved dramatically as follows: from approximately 140,000 Biden and 85,000 Trump in the morning; to now approximately 180,000 Biden and 105,000 Trump after the 1:06 PM update. (At that 1:06 PM update, ALL Republican candidates who had previous leads were reversed and flipped).

Having seen the USB updates, and now seeing paper ballots in the back office, and other observers reporting that they had seen more ballots as well, I went outside and again called Judge Capuzzi's office and again spoke with his secretary and explained the situation, and [that] McBlain had departed and was unresponsive to calls or texts, and she asked me what I wanted the judge to do. I stated that I wanted him to call to demand his order be enforced, and that I would gladly bring my phone back up and hand it to the Sheriff and Solicitor. She stated that she could not provide any legal advice, suggested I seek legal counsel, and hung up.[41]

At 1:30 p.m. on Thursday, November 5, Stenstrom was informed that he would now be allowed access to the locked ballot room for 5 minutes. He and a Democrat observer were shown back.

On my way to the locked storage room, while passing through what was now referred to as the "back office," I counted 21 white USPS open letter boxes on two racks, on my immediate right after entering the room, labeled "500 ballots" per box. In addition, the approximately 16 cubicles for workers in the same room each contained one box also labeled "500 ballots." for a total of 31 boxes of 500 in that sequestered room. This is the same room that McBlain had stated had 4,500 ballots in it earlier, most of which had been presumably moved to the front of the counting room (and later cured and copied to new ballots) and was supposed to be relatively empty with the exception of "several hundred ballots being processed by workers to update the Commonwealth's SURE system," according to McBlain. This was a ... difference ... of approximately 16,500 ballots in just the "back office."

Just after the two racks with the 21 boxes of 500 unopened ballots each, I observed an open door to a 20'x30' storage room with dozens of semi opaque storage bins with blue folding tops that appeared to have envelopes in them. I could see through to another door that led back into the counting room which was the same door I had seen workers bring red bins full of "spoiled" ballots in the previous evening.

I also saw one shelf just to the left of the locked and secured "ballot room" with 4 sealed boxes. I lifted one box before Solicitor Martin objected that I could not touch anything, and it was heavy, and approximately 30-40 pounds. They appeared to match the description of the boxes described to me earlier by poll watcher Jim Driscoll and another observer with a first name of Paul. If those boxes contained ballots, I estimate that they were about two times the size of the 500-ballot containers, and if full, could have contained an additional 2,500 ballots per box for a total of 10,000.

Ms. Hagan unlocked and opened the "ballot room" ... Sheriff Donahue following us and closing the door behind us. There were multiple racks filled with thousands of unopened mail-in ballots. We were not allowed to take any photos, so I immediately started counting. Labels on some boxes were visible, mostly with names of districts known to trend Republican, including Bethel and Brandywine. I took the following notes at the time:

a. 5 boxes of 500 labeled 10-12

b. 5 boxes of 500 labeled 18-20

c. 1 box of 500 each, labeled 26-28, 50-52, and 58-60.

d. The remaining boxes did not have markings visible and we were not allowed to touch them to determine their origin.

e. Democratic poll watcher Dr. Jonathan Briskin also observed these boxes and confirmed the numbers of ballots, and that the number of ballots was vastly greater than we had been led to believe earlier in the day.

f. I later observed Dr. Briskin working with a fellow female poll watcher drawing a diagram and detailing what he had seen after we were returned to the roped off area in the counting room, and noted it was quite detailed and corroborated what I had observed in the ballot room.

In addition to the boxes of unopened mail-in ballots, I observed another shelf that was packed with open and ripped clear plastic bags with cartridges, green security ties, and a 16"x16"x28" cardboard box labeled "CHAIN OF CUSTODY RECEIPTS." In total, I estimated approximately 18,500 unopened mail-in ballots, which Dr. Briskin uncomfortably concurred with.

So, after being told the "universe of total remaining paper ballots to be counted was 6,000" by Mr. McBlain, the 1:30pm tour, on Thursday, two days after election, and 38 hours after being denied access, and having to obtain a court order, I sighted a total of:

a. 16,500 unopened mail-in ballots in the "back office"

b. 18,500 unopened mail-in ballots in the locked "ballot room"

c. Potentially 10,000 ballots in the sealed 30-40-pound boxes outside of the locked ballot room

d. 4,500 ballots being "cured" in the counting room

e. *For a grand total of 49,500 unopened ballots*

To my knowledge, and according to the tally monitor, and as reported on the web, 113,000 mail-in ballots had been requested, and 120,000 mail-in ballots had already been counted, with an approximate outcome of 18,000 for President Trump and 102,000 for Biden already recorded.

So, Gregory Stenstrom, the *only* GOP certified poll watcher over thirty-six precincts in Chester City, Pennsylvania, was stonewalled by election officials and others in authority as he attempted to carry out his duties. He was long denied access to observe the processes for ballot handling at the Delco Chester City counting center in Pennsylvania after his senses alerted him to concerning practices and circumstances there. After persisting many hours, he and a Democrat observer gained access to a locked storage room which he had noticed as a hub of activity that struck him as unusual. In that room, he reported seeing still-unopened ballots that he estimated to number 49,500. Yet, according to public information, by that time seven thousand more mail-in ballots had *already* been counted than had even been requested. If those 49,500 ballots were also subsequently counted, this would mean approximately 56,500 more mail-in ballots would have been tallied than had been requested. Even assuming that a perfect 100% of the ballots requested were returned by voters—which is never the case —this would be an enormous discrepancy. What can account for this difference? Why were authorities so reluctant to allow Stenstrom to observe what was going on?

Catch-22

The Bill of Complaint was filed on Monday, December 7. On December 9, attorneys general for Pennsylvania, Georgia, Michigan and Wisconsin filed their responses, with each one of them asserting that Texas lacked standing to sue because Texas as a state had suffered no injury from the alleged violations. Early Friday, December 11, Texas filed its reply to those responses.[42] The Supreme Court, in an unsigned ruling (meaning that we don't know which justices agreed to it) in the evening of the same day, declined to hear it, citing lack of standing on the part of Texas and the other plaintiff states, and stating curtly, "Texas has not demonstrated a judicially cognizable interest in the manner in which another State conducts its elections."[43] Justices Alito and Thomas refrained from the ruling, issuing a separate statement, "explaining that in their view the Supreme Court lacks the 'discretion to deny the filing of a bill of complaint in a case that falls within our original jurisdiction."[44]

Margot Cleveland explains that the fact that only two justices expressed the view that the Court lacked the discretion to deny the filing does not mean that other justices did not agree. Rather, she suggests that, "given the compressed time frame for resolution, the other justices may have believed prudence dictated the Supreme Court apply its current precedent and leave reconsideration—and comment—on the procedural question [that is, whether the Court has such discretion when states sue each other] to another day."[45]

In its refusal to hear the various complaints prior to the election, the Supreme Court essentially said, "You don't have standing because you have not been harmed." After the election, the same Supreme Court essentially said, "The election is over, so even though there has been harm, it is a moot point. And furthermore, visiting this case will undermine the legitimacy of those elected and confidence in our elections," and so forth. According to the Court, the right time to address a brute force attack on the people's sovereignty seems to be *never*.

Constitution Left Defenseless

The Supreme Court's one-sentence dismissal carefully navigated around Texas' central complaint. At issue was not really whether Texas had a judicially cognizable interest in how another state conducts its election, but rather whether Pennsylvania, Georgia, Michigan and Wisconsin had violated the three clauses of the Constitution (Equal Protection, Due Process, and Elector's) and harmed Texas as a result.

"But by failing to mention Texas's constitutional claims," writes Cleveland, "and by not providing any reasoning for its decision—omissions likely needed for the court to maintain its near-unanimous agreement—the Supreme Court created the appearance that it does not care about constitutional violations. When the question of standing is considered against Texas's allegations of violations of the Elector's Clause, it is hard to believe the court does. Or, rather, given their refusal to address Texas's Elector's Clause claim, it is hard to believe the justices put the constitutional question above their desire to avoid appearing to meddle in the 2020 election."[46]

In 2000, the Supreme Court stepped into the situation in Florida on precisely the grounds that were so carefully presented in the Texas lawsuit: Florida's Supreme Court had effectively stepped in to alter election rules in a way that violated the Equal Protection Clause, and Rehnquist had acknowledged (in a statement, indeed, cited in Texas' Motion to file bill of complaint) that these actions presented a federal constitutional question. So, really, if the Supreme Court intervened in Florida—and they did—for it not to do so in 2020 when far more numerous and grievous infringements were alleged, made little sense whatsoever.

Cleveland notes that a section of an amicus brief submitted by Citizens United gets to the very heart of the matter:

> When one state allows the Manner in which Presidential Electors be chosen to be determined by anyone other than the state legislature, that state acts in breach of the presuppositions on which the Union is based. Each state is not isolated from the rest—rather, all states are interdependent. Our nation's operational principle is E pluribus unum. Each state has a duty to other states to abide by this and other reciprocal obligations built into the Constitution. While defendant states may view this suit as an infringement of its sovereignty, it is not, as the defendant states surrendered their sovereignty when they agreed to abide by Article II, § 1. Each state depends on other states to adhere to minimum constitutional standards in areas where it ceded its sovereignty to the union—and if those standards are not met, then the responsibility to enforce those standards falls to this Court.

In declining to hear the Texas lawsuit on the basis of standing, Cleveland writes, "the Supreme Court voted not to enforce those standards."[47]

Such a situation, however, should be unacceptable to Americans. If the Constitution is not enforced, it no longer governs. The matter of elections is upstream of everything else in our country since it has a cascading effect upon the course of this nation's history. It is more dramatically the case when the election results in one party control of presidency and both houses of Congress. If, as is sometimes the case, it is the people's choice to give a single party such control, then that is proper. However, a false election seized by brute force *via* constitutional violations, permitted by a Supreme Court lacking sufficient courage and sense of duty to rule on the constitutional question, has in this instance given one-party rule when the people in fact chose divided government.

And this one party, the Democrat, compromised and corrupted by commitments to foreign nations and actors hostile to the United States, hostile to the American principles of liberty and justice for all, and hostile to the widespread prosperity of the American people that has resulted from the application of these principles, has made short work of destruction, preying upon the wealth and livelihoods of many millions of Americans, ripping apart the fabric of civil society by opening the borders to tens of millions of people with no right to enter and no respect for the law, and moving toward granting tens of millions of such people the right to vote. Whereas the best immigrants are always those who love the United States and the principles that made her great, Democrats have selected for the opposite sort of immigrant—those who reject laws. Democrats' intended result is evidently that the stolen election in 2020 will lead to incorporation of millions of these bad citizens (i.e., those who have already demonstrated their disdain for equal application of laws and unwillingness to be governed by the same laws that apply to others) into the pool of those who will cast votes in future elections. That is to say, what we are witnessing is society unraveling before our very eyes in a nation that—since the Supreme Court's delinquency—effectively is no longer governed by a constitution at all.

Update

In July of 2022, Wisconsin's Supreme Court ruled that drop boxes are not allowed under state law, and that they never were allowed, because, in the words of Justice Rebecca Bradley, writing for the majority, "Nothing in the statutory language detailing the procedures by which absentee ballots may be cast mentions drop boxes or anything like them." Writing for the dissent, Justice Ann Walsh Bradley wrote that concerns about safety of drop boxes "is downright dangerous to our democracy."[48] However, her remark is beside the point. If the Wisconsin legislature wishes to pass a law that allows drop boxes, they may do so. Failing any parameters in law that permit them, however, Justice Bradley's personal opinions cannot override the plenary authority of the Wisconsin legislature. Most ballot drop boxes in Wisconsin were illegal in the 2020 election, and therefore the ballots received in them—which were counted ahead of Wisconsin's ten Electoral College votes being assigned to Joe Biden—were illegal to count.

QUESTIONS

1. What was the main argument of the Texas lawsuit? What is "original jurisdiction," and why did it apply to this case?

2. Thinking about the Equal Protection Clause, why did Texas assert that another state treating Democrat areas different from Republican ones was any of its business? How would a Texas voter be harmed if Pennsylvania flipped the state to Biden by unfairly favoring Democrat precincts?

3. Thinking about the Electors Clause, why did Texas argue that the elections in the four other states were not legally conducted after people other than the state legislatures changed the rules? List some ways that rule changes might have affected the outcome.

---

1. State of Texas v. Commonwealth of Pennsylvania, State of Georgia, State of Michigan, and State of Wisconsin (Supreme Court of the United States, 2020).
2. Alabama, Arkansas, Florida, Indiana, Kansas, Louisiana, Mississippi, Missouri, Montana, Nebraska, North Dakota, Oklahoma, South Carolina, South Dakota, Tennessee, Utah, and West Virginia.
3. "November 3, 2020 Results." Georgia Secretary of State Brad Raffensperger.
4. "Official 2020 Presidential General Election Results." Federal Election Commission.
5. "2020 Presidential Election, Tuesday, November 3, 2020, Official Returns," Pennsylvania Department of State.
6. "2020 Michigan Election Results (Official)." The Office of Secretary of State Jocelyn Benson.
7. There are some circumstances under which people can lose the right to vote for a period of time, such as convicted felons. There is a process in each state for the restoration of rights, usually after completion of the terms of a sentence and payment of any required restitution, sometimes with a waiting period afterward, or by an act of the governor. The reasoning here is that felons have temporarily relinquished their civil and political rights by breaking the social contract, grievously separating themselves from submission to common governance by the law of the land, which represents the people's sovereignty.
8. In their dissent, Justices Samuel Alito and Clarence Thomas stated that because the Court had exclusive jurisdiction it was required to take this case. It is also suggested that other justices agreed with this view, but for unspecified reasons did not affirm it.
9. Cleveland, Margot, "6 Thing To Know About Texas' Supreme Court Petition Over 2020's Messed-Up Election," *The Federalist*, December 9, 2020.
10. United States Constitution, Article II, Section 1, Clause 2.
11. United States Constitution, Article I, Section 4, Clause 1.
12. Waters, Dustin, "Mail-in ballots were part of a plot to deny Lincoln reelection in 1864," *Washington Post*, August 22, 2020.
13. Emphasis added.

14. "Pennsylvania high court rules ballots with mismatched signatures can't be rejected." CBS News, October 23, 2020. YouTube video, https://www.youtube.com/watch?v=TeinrGywgQ8.

15. *Democratic Party of Georgia, et al. v. Raffensperger, et al.*

16. "Compromise Settlement Agreement And Release," Perkins Coie LLP and Krevolin & Horst, LLC (Counsel for Plaintiffs) and Office of the Georgia Attorney General and Robbins Ross Alloy Belinfante Littlefield LLC (Counsel for State Defendants). March 6, 2020.

17. Emphasis added.

18. Emphasis original.

19. Emphasis original.

20. Emphasis original.

21. Emphasis original.

22. The Motion states that emphasis has been added to the quoted statute.

23. If you wish to read the affidavits directly, you may do so at https://www.supremecourt.gov/DocketPDF/22/22O155/163048/20201208132827887_TX-v-State-ExpedMot%202020-12-07%20FINAL.pdf.

24. Ibid. Emphasis added.

25. Ibid. Emphasis original.

26. "Chester County Pennsylvania Election Results: Official General Election, November 3, 2020." https://pennsylvania.totalvote.com/resultsSW.aspx?eid=35&type=FED&map=CTY&cid=03.

27. Tom Scheck et al, "How Private Money From Facebook's CEO Saved The 2020 Election." NPR, December 8, 2020. Emphasis added.

28. Ibid.

29. Ibid. Emphasis added.

30. Ibid.

31. "RAW: Full Jessy Jacob testimony before Michigan House alleging election irregularities | Diya TV." Diya TV, December 2, 2020, YouTube video, https://www.youtube.com/watch?v=KmsIs5QemG8. (6/23/22).

32. Olesko, Andy. "Michigan Judge Rejects Challenge to Detroit Election Results." *Courthouse News Service*, November 13, 2020.

33. Carone, Mellissa A. "Interview with Dominion Whistleblower Mellissa Carone from Michigan (VIDEO)." Interview by Joe Oltmann. *PAL Bulletin*.

34. Affidavit of Mellissa A. Carone, State of Michigan, In the Circuit Court for the County of Wayne, November 8, 2020.

35. Emphasis added.

36. Ibid.

37. "Affidavit of Andrew John Miller," November 8, 2020.

38. Declaration of Gregory Stenstrom in Support of Plaintiffs' Motion for Temporary Restraining Order and Preliminary Injunction, November 9, 2020.

39. Italics added.

40. Ibid.

41. Emphasis original.

42. Cleveland, Margot, "The Supreme Court's Rejection Of Texas' Election Lawsuit Failed The Constitution," *The Federalist*, December 14, 2020.

43. Platoff, Emma, "U.S. Supreme Court throws out Texas lawsuit contesting 2020 election results in four battleground states," The Texas Tribune. December 11, 2020.

44. Cleveland. "The Supreme Court's Rejection Of Texas' Election Lawsuit Failed The Constitution."

45. Ibid.

46. Ibid.

47. Ibid.

48. Bauer, Scott, "Wisconsin Supreme Court disallows absentee ballot drop boxes," *AP*, July 8, 2022; Fleetwood, Shawn, "Wisconsin Supreme Court Drops Hammer On 2020 Election Shenanigans: 'Ballot Drop Boxes Are Illegal' Under Wisconsin Law," *Federalist*, July 8, 2022.

4

FRAUD

We find that some non-citizens participate in U.S. elections, and that this participation has been large enough to change meaningful election outcomes including Electoral College votes, and Congressional elections. *Non-citizen votes likely gave Senate Democrats the pivotal 60th vote needed to overcome filibusters in order to pass health care reform and other Obama administration priorities in the 111th Congress.*[1]

Voter fraud and election fraud are crimes of opportunity. When opportunity exists alongside motive and means, fraud will occur. In 2020, opportunity for fraud was increased exponentially in the months before the election thanks to Democrat lawfare (i.e., using the law as a weapon to disadvantage or harm opponents) and bureaucratic maneuvering as discussed in Chapters 3 and 8. A flood of election problems ensued, but sifting reports of election irregularities was challenging, with news and analysis often poorly sourced and tainted by ideology. On all sides of the question, key data or details about methodology were often not shown. While not limited to Democrat partisans, I found lack of rigor, transparency and scientific curiosity especially pronounced among those asserting that no significant fraud existed.

Bold and unqualified statements that the 2020 election was clean, safe, and secure, which began mere days after the election itself, were interesting to hear, but they have since been demonstrated not to have been true, even if the degree is not fully known. Those who made such assertions were either uninformed, deluded or intentionally deceptive.

Voter fraud and election fraud can take a very long time to investigate. When they are widespread, many barriers to investigation exist, because many more people have an interest in muddying the waters. The chaos of 2020, combined with the type and magnitude of extralegal relaxation of anti-fraud measures, means that the principle applies in 2020 more than perhaps any time in past history of the United States. Furthermore, real and meaningful investigations were blocked. As of July 2022, not a single full forensic audit of the election has been conducted in any swing state, some evidence has already been illegally destroyed,[2] and the ballots and equipment that remain will soon be legally shredded and destroyed in September of 2022 unless legislative action is taken to preserve them for a true investigation.

Yet on November 12, 2020, a mere *nine days* after the election, the Cyber-security & Infrastructure Security Agency released the following joint statement of the Election Infrastructure Government Coordinating Council (GCC) Executive Committee[3] and the Election Infrastructure Sector Coordinating Council (SCC)[4], (a total of ten individuals including some apparently representing voting systems companies and also Democracy Works, a non-profit organization that advocated increased mail voting, praised by the New York Times and promoted in a video by former President Obama):

> The November 3rd election was the most secure in American history. Right now, across the country, election officials are reviewing and double checking the entire election process prior to finalizing the result.
>
> When states have close elections, many will recount ballots. All of the states with close results in the 2020 presidential race have paper records of each vote, allowing the ability to go back and count each ballot if necessary. This is an added benefit for security and resilience. This process allows for the identification and correction of any mistakes or errors. **There is no evidence that any voting system deleted or lost votes, changed votes, or was in any way compromised.**
>
> Other security measures like pre-election testing, state certification of voting equipment, and the U.S. Election Assistance Commission's (EAC) certification of voting equipment help to build additional confidence in voting systems used in 2020.
>
> While we know there are many unfounded claims and opportunities for misinformation about the process of our elections, we can assure you we have the utmost confidence in the security and integrity of our elections, and you should too. When you have questions, turn to election officials as trusted voices as they administer elections.[5]

Even if we assumed the above statement is true, and it certainly is not, you should notice the many problems discussed in this book that would pass completely unnoticed by people who were merely concerned to make sure that all ballots received were properly counted. Why? Because there are always ballots received that **should not** be counted—like these two, which are examples of *fraud.*

- Ballots cast by noncitizens or other ineligible individuals, even if registered to vote in their states
- Ballots completed and returned by someone other than the eligible voter

And, there are sometimes (hundreds or even millions of times in 2020) ballots—like this one, which is not usually an example of fraud on the part of the voter despite the votes being illegal—that are improperly received and therefore **should not** be counted:

- Ballots cast outside the times and places prescribed by the state legislatures

Would an election in which every ballot was recorded exactly as marked, without a single one missing, altered, or mis-counted, be "secure" even if millions of such ballots were cast by people whose votes were illegal? The council that issued the above joint statement seems either not to have contemplated such a scenario, or not to have been bothered by it.

"Secure" does not equal "correct." And, an election in which illegal ballots were counted in any appreciable number (no matter how accurately) alongside legal ones should not be considered "secure."

Why This Chapter?

Fraud is not the focus of this book, and (as already stated) it is unnecessary to demonstrate any instance of voter fraud or election fraud in order to establish that Donald Trump likely won the 2020 election. However, my decision to exclude fraud from my methodology does not mean that fraud did not occur or that it is not important. Since the specter of fraud hangs over the 2020 election following the obstruction of transparency and audit efforts in addition to irregularities and problems almost too many to number, this book would not be complete without discussing it.

Is fraud a serious factor in U.S. elections? The answer is an unqualified "yes," and it is a matter that should deeply concern people of all parties who value self governance. Entire books have been written that carefully document the enormous and growing problem of voter fraud and election fraud in the United States. Prominent among these are books by John Fund and Hans Von Spakovsky.[6] The existing documentation on vote fraud is so extensive that focus upon it could overshadow the root issues that enabled fraud to proliferate in the first place.

Was fraud a serious factor in the 2020 election? There are many places one could start with this question, and the matter is thorny and contentious. I maintain—and state in the conclusion of this book—that, given the widespread (and illegal) introduction of opportunities for fraud in 2020, the burden is no longer upon those who say there *was* fraud in the 2020 election to prove their position. Rather, the onus is upon those who say that fraud was nonexistent or negligible to prove their position. Given the enormous opportunity, widespread fraud in 2020 should be assumed until it is ruled out by full forensic audits in every state.

One good place to start is Patrick Byrne's book *The Deep Rig*. The book —self-published and (due to the time-sensitivity of the matter, I expect) not well edited or formatted—seems nevertheless a substantive source. Byrne, an anti-corruption activist who did not vote for Trump, came to be quite close to the action dealing with the problem of election fraud before, during, and after the 2020 election.[7] For those wishing to focus on the specific question of 2020 fraud (including that alleged with respect to electronic voting technologies), Byrne's book is important, both for its in-the-room-where-it-happened quality, and for its presentation of the technical issues.

Attorney General Bill Barr famously stated in December 2020 that he had not seen evidence of fraud "on a scale that could have effected a different outcome in the election."[8] It was wise of him to parse his words, because there is no way he could have known that there wasn't fraud sufficient to have affected the outcome. With all the chaos and uncertainty, with all the legitimate unanswered questions and allegations, and most importantly prior to forensic audits, such knowledge would have been impossible.

Furthermore, Lt. Col. Tony Shaffer informed me that Barr *did* see evidence of fraud sufficient to have affected the outcome, because Shaffer himself provided it to him. Shaffer (at the time the U.S. National Security Advisor) reported that Barr called him on the phone, and he further told me that the Attorney General became very angry with him, even swearing at him, stating that it was his investigation and that Shaffer should not be looking into it, or words to that effect.

In public, Barr also expressed indignation at allegations of 2020 voter fraud or election fraud, telling the January 6 committee that he "had three discussions with the president that I can recall ... I made it clear that I did not agree with the idea of saying the election was stolen and putting out this stuff, which I told the president was bulls***."[9]

Barr's assertion that "you can't live in a world where the incumbent administration stays in power based on its view, unsupported by specific evidence, that there was fraud in the election,"[10] is technically true, but also strikes me as at least somewhat disingenuous for its insinuations about what President Trump was actually claiming. Yes, Trump said publicly that there was a lot of fraud in 2020. Frankly, the overall claim was almost certainly right, but that is beside the point, since the complaint in lawsuit after lawsuit filed by Trump and the GOP was that elections across the country were *conducted illegally*, in violation of the Constitution and with changed rules which threw ballots many times the margin of victory into question and made it impossible to know who had won. Barr is an attorney, and I find it hard to believe that he was not familiar with the Texas lawsuit and the many additional lawsuits that will be summarized in Chapter 9. If he was, then he understood full well that fraud was an important but secondary claim of these parties, including Trump.

While we do not know all the details of the evidently deteriorating personal relationship between Barr and the president which culminated in Barr's firing, we do know that he took steps to sabotage Trump and to protect Joe Biden. The most glaring of these was his shielding of DOJ probes into Hunter Biden from public view during the election, as already referenced in Chapter 2.

Slippery Business

Bill Barr's evident frustration over the sometimes uncritical presentation of dubious studies as though they were unassailable is justified. The same problem dogged me as I have sifted through materials to write this book. At the same time, most people knew that it was an error to hastily and categorically dispense with the serious and obvious problem of fraud, especially in 2020. The findings of Englebrecht and Phillips as documented in *2000 Mules* (discussed below) were not documented at the time of Barr's above-mentioned colorful statements, but they are anything but surprising given what the whole world could see was happening with the drop boxes and expansion of mail-in voting in 2020.

As I have stated already, means, motive and opportunity existed in 2020 at levels perhaps never before seen in American history, and only a naïve individual would state with a straight face that significant fraud did not occur. Furthermore, preventing, tracking, and prosecuting voter fraud and electoral fraud should be a perpetual high priority for any self governing people.

One of the most challenging and frustrating realities about voter fraud and election fraud is that they are "slippery" by design. Much or even most such fraud is conducted in a manner that makes its specific instances unprovable after the fact. How voter fraud and election fraud is perpetrated and how it is covered up are all well known. In most cases, unless the culprits are caught in the act, or the counting and ballot processing work is halted before the built-in steps to destroy the proof of fraud have occurred, plausible deniability can be achieved by the cheaters.

Regular perpetrators of election fraud and promoters of voter fraud are aware of everything above—it is their business to be aware of it—and preserving the processes that systematically destroy evidence is a central part of their activity in every election. In 2020, those who orchestrated cheating on behalf of their preferred candidates would have done so in a fraudster's dream environment of immense relaxation of the exact measures designed and legally implemented to keep elections honest. Many who assert that relaxation of safeguards in 2020 wasn't done for the express purpose of allowing election fraudsters and voter fraudsters to increase their illegal activity while evading detection are probably sympathetic to the fraud itself.

A Real Threat Worth Stopping

Self governance is the primary political right of every American person, *the crown jewel of American citizenship*. Every vote from an unqualified voter—such as a noncitizen, a felon, or any person who has already cast a ballot—and every manipulation of vote tallies by corrupt election officials or other parties, is *disenfranchisement* of all the legal voters. Every illegal vote or manipulation of the tallies diminishes or cancels the vote of those who are actually entitled to it. It is therefore ironic that Democrats so often trumpet fears of voter disenfranchisement as an excuse for removing basic protections designed to prevent illegal voting and to ensure the transparency and accuracy of the election. In fact, it is beyond hypocritical. Democrats know that they are stealing votes when they encourage illegal immigrants or other noncitizens to vote in a national election. They are the ones who are engaged in active voter disenfranchisement. And it must be stopped.

First and foremost, voter fraud and election fraud are crimes of opportunity. They occur when the system is not tight, when the door is left open. In 2020, there were open doors everywhere. The 2020 presidential election was far more vulnerable to fraud, probably by an order of magnitude or more, than any other election in the 235-year history of the United States. These vulnerabilities left ample opportunity for the various types of potential fraud to be discussed below.

With mail voting, there were two main dimensions. First, voting by mail was illegal in many specific instances. Unauthorized expansion in 2020 caused many ballots to be counted that the law expressly forbade. Counting such ballots was illegal regardless of who cast them. Such meddling—apparently driven overwhelmingly by Democrats—surely tipped the field of play.

Second, it has been well established—and acknowledged by Democrats and Republicans alike, as well as by nations around the world—that mail-in ballots are the greatest source of potential voter fraud and election fraud in any election. Furthermore, the increase in vulnerability as the number of ballots cast by mail rises is not linear. Limited election resources which may be able to manage a small number of mail-in ballots with integrity will be inadequate to handle a deluge. Particularly if signature verification rules are suspended (as they were in 2020), deadlines for receipt and postmark requirements are fudged (as they were in 2020), and so forth, a recipe for the least secure election in U.S. history has been studiously followed. Whatever else it might have been, the enormous push by Democrats in 2020 to massively and quickly expand vote by mail was an unprecedented (and, I believe, calculated) opening for major fraud.

What are Voter Fraud and Election Fraud?

Criminal meddling with elections falls into two general categories: voter fraud and election fraud.

Voter fraud (or vote fraud) is fraud by individual voters.[11] Any person who engages in vote fraud is committing theft of the sovereignty of all the citizens; thus, vote fraud is a heinous crime. Vote fraud includes:

- Any noncitizen voting in a federal election
- Any person casting a vote as someone else
- Any person voting more than once in an election
- Vote-selling
- Interference with or misuse of absentee ballots
- Any felon voting before restored eligibility
- Ballot petition fraud
- A false statement on a voter registration
- Voting in a district where one does not live

Election fraud (or electoral fraud) is the illegal interference with the election process.[12] Any person who engages in electoral fraud is committing theft of the sovereignty of all the citizens; thus, electoral fraud is also a heinous crime. Electoral fraud includes:

- Altering the vote count
- Illegal "assistance" at the polls, in nursing homes, etc.
- Buying votes (also known as ballot trafficking)

Voter fraud and electoral fraud both exist and are well-documented.[13] Despite an often-cited statement from the Brennan Center for Justice at the New York University School of Law that "fraud is very rare, voter impersonation is nearly non-existent, and much (sic) of the problems associated with alleged fraud relates to unintentional mistakes by voters or election administrators,"[14] Eric Eggers observes that the Brennan Center's conclusion is only drawn from the fact that prosecutions are rare.[15]

But that is flawed logic. No reasonable person would conclude from a lack of citations or prosecutions for jaywalking that jaywalking therefore hardly ever happens. Despite jaywalking being illegal in most cases, there is simply a lack of political will or priority placed upon its enforcement. One cannot draw conclusions about the actual prevalence of a crime— particularly one so difficult to prove after it has been committed as are many forms of voter fraud and election fraud—by the extent of its actual prosecution. Theft of a vote is many orders of magnitude more grievous than jaywalking (and jaywalking is not a felony), but the lack of will to prosecute it is often similar—and furthermore often made more difficult by stonewalling from within the agencies. On top of all this, Eggers notes that the Brennan Center chose to define voter fraud in such a narrow way that many actual instances of voter fraud are not even counted—and the only point that proves is the unseriousness (or bias) of the Brennan Center itself.[16]

Voter fraud and election fraud have historically been perpetrated by unethical individuals within both major American political parties, though not necessarily in equal measure. Local and state elections, and even elections of tremendous national significance—such as the disastrously consequential 2008 election of Al Franken to the U.S. Senate—have at various times resulted in victory being awarded to the likely actual loser. However, the nature and extent of the fraud, and the degree to which it is embraced at the highest levels of national strategy are almost always difficult to establish because there are so many people inside the system who either have a direct interest in protecting it, or who, alternately, remain skeptical about its existence, scope, or gravity.

Because self governance depends upon honest elections, however, it is appropriate for all United States citizens, regardless of party or affiliation, to care about voter fraud and electoral fraud.

Ballot Harvesting vs. Ballot Trafficking

Some states allow the collection of ballots by third parties, an activity that is sometimes called *ballot harvesting*. In almost every case there are tight restrictions on who can carry a ballot for a voter. Some states restrict it to an immediate family member, and others require written designation. A few, like Hawaii, Oregon and California, make no real limitation on who can carry a ballot for another, so long as money does not change hands for it.[17]

In all fifty states, any ballot becomes illegal if money changes hands in association with its delivery. In no state is payment to private individuals for delivery of ballots allowed. The movement of ballots by paid individuals has a technical legal term: *ballot trafficking.*[18]

Democrat Activists Push For Voter Fraud

In 2016, Gina Rodriguez, an activist for amnesty for illegal immigrants,[19] asked President Obama:

> "Many of the millennials, Dreamers, undocumented citizens—and I call them citizens because they contribute to this country—are fearful of voting. So if I vote, will immigration know where I live? Will they come for my family and deport us?"

Rodriguez has subsequently been involved in the production of various television projects generally advocating for those who persist in breaking immigration law, including one for the CW (CBS/Warner Brothers) called "Illegal," and another called "Have Mercy." The project "Illegal" is based upon the story of actor Rafael Agustín, who learned as a high schooler that he was illegally present in the United States. About the project, Agustín tweeted:

> IT'S OFFICIAL: Gina Rodriguez and I sold our first TV show based on my life as a former undocumented student. Get ready for the first undocumented family on TV!!! #DefendDACA #DREAMers[20]

Agustín is also an activist. About the show, he said, "I always wanted to call it *Illegal* because I wanted to make a statement: 'Listen, we're gonna get rid of this word once and for all.'"[21]

Rodriguez' question to Obama as the 2016 election loomed was thus not about people who are citizens. Why would U.S. citizens be afraid of people knowing that they had voted? Rather, it was a crafted question inviting the sitting president of the United States to reassure those *noncitizens* who were contemplating voting that they would not be found out.

Obama did not refute Rodriguez' rather obnoxious declaration that illegal immigrants—among whom are included the so-called "Dreamers" —are actually citizens (i.e., of the United States), even though they are not. Obama's answer (quoted below) not only failed to clarify and correct, but actually seemed to affirm her statement by falsely suggesting that anyone who votes is automatically a citizen. It is unquestionably illegal for any of the three categories of people that Gina Rodriguez mentions to vote in any U.S. national election.

Were Obama and Rodriguez merely talking theoretically about something that wasn't really an issue in the election? Obviously not. If Obama had believed noncitizen voting was not happening in large numbers, that is, that it had no possibility of influencing the outcome of elections in favor of Democrats, he would have answered, "It's against the law for noncitizens to vote in a national election. If you are not a citizen, you should not vote."

President Obama did not say this—or anything remotely close to it. Instead, he answered,

> Obama: Not true. And the reason is—first of all, when you vote, you are a citizen yourself, and there is not a situation where the voting rolls somehow are transferred over and people start investigating, et cetera. The sanctity of the vote is strictly confidential in terms of who you voted for. If you have a family member who maybe is undocumented, then you have an even greater reason to vote.
>
> Rodriguez: This has been a huge fear presented especially during this election.
>
> Obama: And the reason that fear is promoted is because they don't want people voting. People are discouraged from voting and part of what is important for Latino citizens is to make your voice heard, because you're not just speaking for yourself. You're speaking for family members, friends, classmates of yours in school ....
>
> Rodriguez: Your entire community.
>
> Obama: ... who may not have a voice. Who can't legally vote. But they're counting on you to make sure that you have the courage to make your voice heard.

The mention by Obama in these remarks that some members of the community "can't legally vote," was later presented by careless fact-checkers like leftwing Snopes as evidence that accusations of Obama encouraging illegal immigrant voting were categorically false.[22] But look at his words. Nowhere in his statements does Obama say or even suggest that "undocumented" immigrants can't legally vote. Rather, he says two things: 1) If you have a family member who is "undocumented," then you have an even greater reason to vote (i.e., presumably for those who would enact policies favorable to "undocumented" immigrants), and 2) There exist people who may not have a voice because they can't legally vote.

There are many categories of people who can't legally vote, apart from illegal immigrants: children under the age of 18, immigrants with Green Cards, convicted felons, and others. It is nowhere evident that Obama meant illegal immigrants when he references "family members, friends, classmates" who can't legally vote. So, the clear affirmation that Obama gave to Rodriguez at first is not undone by this reference to other people who can't legally vote. Furthermore, the latter portions of President Obama's comments would be easy to exclude from the sound bite version of his remarks that many noncitizens would hear later. The interview thus served an important purpose for those who wanted to get illegal immigrants to vote.

And guess what? A 2014 study by two Old Dominion University professors found that 6.4 percent of all noncitizens voted illegally in the 2008 presidential election, followed by 2.2 percent in the 2010 midterms.[23] This figure would amount to more than one million noncitizens voting in 2008, with estimates of 80 percent of these votes going to Democrats. No wonder President Obama was courting the illegal immigrant vote again in 2016 on behalf of Hillary Clinton. In a year when the signature campaign issue of one of the candidates, Donald Trump, was addressing illegal immigration by enforcement of immigration laws and control of the borders, such numbers of illegal votes could tip the entire election.

There are some in the United States who believe that illegal immigrants and other noncitizens *should* be able to vote even though the law says otherwise. Americans remain overwhelmingly opposed to noncitizen voting. But the boldness of those who ignore the law rather than following the legislative process to change the law is increasing. Gina Rodriguez and Barack Obama are among them. It is no coincidence that the people who pushed to change immigration laws by executive order in 2012 advocated and cheered extra-legislative changes to election laws in 2020, removing or relaxing election integrity safeguards, and expanding manners of voting most vulnerable to fraud in the key states.

The United States, unlike many other countries, are built not upon a particular race or ethnicity, but upon its citizens' common assent to certain principles. Among these principles is the affirmation that everyone should follow the same laws. Creating a special class of people who are not required to follow the same rules as everyone else is damaging to the cultural fabric and leads to a society that does not affirm equality but rather has different rules for different people. The United States are already adopting tiered society thanks in part to Democrats' rejection of equality for millions of illegal immigrants currently living within U.S. borders. It is an insult to the American people and also to millions of immigrants who followed the rules and waited their turn.

If merely wanting to come to the United States, or feeling that one has the chance of a better future or better economic opportunities inside the United States, qualifies any person to enter, then there are a billion or more other people in the world who should be let into the country at this very moment. Obviously, however, these preferences do not form a sufficient basis for entry.

Unless the American left is prepared to openly admit to the American people that they believe every human being on planet earth should be uncritically admitted to the United States if they wish to enter, they should stop pretending to care about equality and join the rest of Americans in actually affirming it through equal application of just laws.

Why Allegations Must Be Examined

One reason that I have chosen to de-center the matter of vote fraud and election fraud in this book is not because it does not occur, but because it is very difficult for a researcher to confirm claims, and there are false or over-inflated claims mixed in with everything else. The constitutional issue that was the focus of the prior chapter is simply too important to be derailed by the inevitable debunking of some ambitious but methodologically flawed claim of election fraud or voter fraud. Following is one example:

A review[24] by the North Carolina Board of Elections allegedly found, based upon a crosscheck with data from twenty-seven other states, that 35,570 North Carolina voters in 2012 shared the same first names, last names, and dates of birth with individuals who voted in other states."[25] An additional "765 North Carolina residents who voted in 2012 had the same names, birthdays, and final four digits of a Social Security Number (SSN) as people who voted elsewhere."[26] The study also found 155,692 voters with an exact match of first and last name, date of birth, and last four digits of SSN who were registered in North Carolina and another state, with the most recent date of registration or activity being in another state.

Were these the same people? One problem that made research on this book so difficult was the proliferation of sensational-sounding but care-lessly-researched reports in 2020 that, upon closer inspection, were simply not sound in their assertions or conclusions. One example is discussed in the article, "US Election 2020: The 'dead voters' in Michigan who are still alive."[27] The article describes an investigation in which 30 names were chosen at random, plus the name of the oldest person on a list of 10,000 dead people who had allegedly voted in Michigan in 2020. Of the 31, it was discovered that 28 had still been alive at the time of the election, and there were reasonable explanations for the remaining three (two were sons who shared the same name and registration address as their deceased fathers).

The art of stealing elections is probably as old as elections themselves. Election theft is usually carried out stealthily. Election fraud is difficult or impossible to prove after certain steps have been taken in the vote tabulation process. Procedures that erase the tracks of fraudsters are a design feature, to make it unprovable unless it is detected immediately—which most often it is not.

The prime example of such evasion in the 2020 election was the intentional comingling of ballots after their removal from the mail-in ballot envelopes. Although the envelopes in which they arrive carry the voters' details, the ballots themselves have no personally identifying information. Accordingly, the main objective of fraudsters is to get fraudulent ballots counted and then separated from their envelopes. Once this has been done, there is simply no way to identify which ballot came from which envelope. Therefore, even if hundreds of thousands of mail-in ballot envelopes were later to be determined fraudulent, there would simply be no way to correct the tabulation. The only remedy in such a situation would be a new election, and most of the time this costly and disruptive course of action is simply not deemed reasonable.

Furthermore, once the culprits in an illegally conducted presidential election in the United States have managed to get their candidate past the Constitutional hurdle of certification on January 6 following the election, there really remains no further peaceful remedy under the Constitution of the United States—not even a new election. For this reason, any party attempting to get a national presidential candidate into office by brute force will focus all its energies upon ensuring that this candidate is made Constitutionally official before the wider public is able to gather enough information to object to the certification.

In particular, those who support fraudulent outcomes generally take great care to make sure that processes such as failure to keep potentially questionable ballots separated from others are in place. If it seems as though election thieves are thumbing their noses at us and saying, "So, maybe I did cheat! What are you going to do about it?" you are absolutely right. And, unless the American people find *and implement* a solution, the tyrants really do have all of us trapped. Such thievery happens in election after election; in some parts of the country, it has become a science. What is worse, the fraudsters accuse those seeking accountability of being crazy, of being conspiracy theorists. Everyone knows, after all, that elections are secure. There is nothing to see here, and the real problem is you—the person asking the questions.

That point having been made, no lie is perfect. There are lots of moving parts in an election. Furthermore, when it comes to really big lies, the truth can be stretched only so far before cracks begin to show.

Some allegations ought to be dismissed (remember, "dismissed" does not mean an allegation is "untrue" but rather just that it may not be fruitful to pursue for a variety of reasons), while other allegations may emerge as very serious and strongly substantiated.

In any election, there is fraud. If there were no vote fraud or election fraud, then there would be no resistance to audits, voter ID requirements, and so forth. The *only* reason for objecting to such measures is that something is being hidden.

Sometimes voter fraud takes an extended time to be proven, as was the case with the likely false victory given to Al Franken over Norm Coleman in Minnesota's 2008 U.S. Senate race, which singularly paved the way for the transformation of the United States by the passage of Obamacare and —to be sure—many others of Obama's most controversial policy priorities needing legislative confirmation.[28] Sometimes allegations turn out to be unfounded, and at other times real fraud exists but is never discovered or documented.

Circumstances in the United States and abroad during the 2020 election season created numerous opportunities for those who wished to "flood the system," creating so much chaos and doubt that it would be very difficult to unravel nefarious manipulation of the election until it was too late. *As we shall see, these opportunities were in fact seized upon and leveraged by Democrat partisans in 2020 as a means of perpetrating election fraud on a large scale. Aided by a complicit media, the effort was successful in the short term. But, it was not invisible to the public.*

The Compounded Effects of False Elections

It is extremely likely that the Democrats' passage of Obamacare in 2009 happened only with the help of voter fraud in the 2008 election:

> The [...] Minnesota 2008 Senate contest [...,] ultimately decided by 312 votes for Democrat Al Franken, was of critical national importance. It gave Democrats the filibuster-proof super-majority needed to pass major legislative initiatives during President Obama's first year in office. The Patient Protection and Affordable Care Act, for instance, would have had a much more difficult path to passage were it not for Franken's pivotal vote. The MN 2008 Senate race is also the race where the smallest portion of non-citizen votes would have tipped the balance — participation by more than 0.65% of non-citizens in MN is sufficient to account for the entirety of Franken's margin. *Our best guess is that nearly ten times as many voted.*[29]

If, as the authors of the above article in *Electoral Studies* seem to have shown, the 2008 election of Franken was indeed decided by the illegal votes of noncitizens (i.e., voter fraud), then all legislation passed *via* the resulting avoidance of the filibuster represents an absolute theft of sovereignty from the American people.

How Are Election and Voter Fraud Perpetrated?

Mail-in Ballots

Absentee ballots remain the largest source of potential voter fraud.[30]

— COMMISSION ON FEDERAL ELECTION REFORM
(JIMMY CARTER, CHAIR)

"[E]ven many scholars who argue that fraud is generally rare agree that fraud with VBM [i.e., vote-by-mail] voting seems to be more frequent than with in-person voting."[31]

The combination of drop boxes with a flood of absentee and mail-in ballot applications as well as actual mail-in ballots, sometimes sent en masse and sometimes unsolicited by the voter, in 2020 created a perfect storm for rampant fraud, rife with all kinds of opportunity with greatly reduced likelihood of getting caught.

> I work in the District of Columbia. They mailed out absentee ballots to all of their registered voters. I can't tell you how many phone calls I got from people that I know saying that, not only had their ballot arrived in the mail, but five, six, seven ballots, all coming into their apartment, for people who used to live there.[32]

An August 2020 article in the New York Post opens, "A top Democratic operative says voter fraud, especially with mail-in ballots, is no myth. And he knows this because he's been doing it, on a grand scale, for decades."[33]

Voter Interference

Voter interference usually takes the form of poll workers or other individuals exerting illegal influence over a person who is casting a vote or getting ready to do so. Voter interference is not limited to threats or intimidation; it more often takes the form of "assisting" voters at the polling place or when they are filling out an absentee ballot, carrying or displaying campaign materials closer to the polling booths than the legal perimeter, or similar activities. Voter interference can at least be observed and addressed at polling places. One of the problems with voting by mail is that it opens the door for all kinds of illegal influence of innocent voters by pushy or dishonest third parties. And the fact that such influence is illegal is little consolation if it happens anyway and winds up changing the outcome of an election.

Breaks In Chain Of Custody

You may have heard it said that a chain is only as strong as its weakest link. In few situations is that saying truer or more consequential than in the operation of an election. Consider this: You could have a perfectly secure registration process, a perfectly executed voter check-in at the polling places, a perfectly operational balloting system, a perfect collection of voted ballots and elimination of ineligible ballots, a perfect closing procedure, a perfect placement of security zip-ties on all the ballot containers, etc. All these components of a successful and secure election take a tremendous amount of time, energy, planning, and care on the part of many people.

Now, consider that for twenty minutes, an unsealed box of ballots is left unattended somewhere along the way to be tabulated. Or imagine that a thumb drive is inserted into a voting machine at some point during the process. Or that a voting machine's internet capabilities are turned on temporarily for some reason during the election, even for a few minutes—perhaps to download a software "update." All these things are breaks in the chain of custody. It is possible that nothing nefarious happens during that break. But when such breaks in the chain are planned into the process, or inserted into the process when no one is looking, you can imagine the tragic outcome. And, what a waste of an election effort, if the whole thing is spoiled by some cheater who rigs the vote when no one is looking.

Ballot Trafficking

One way that the chain of custody is broken is when ballots are not directly delivered by the voter to the authorities as the law in most states requires. In Wisconsin, for example, the law states that an absentee ballot envelope containing a cast absentee ballot must be "mailed by the elector [that is, the voter], or delivered in person, to the municipal clerk issuing the ballot or ballots."[34]

How Are Election and Voter Fraud Hidden?

Voter fraud is only caught if people want to catch it. It is thus very easy to "hide" noncitizen voting, for example, in places like California. Nobody is even looking for it, because even looking for it in that state (even though noncitizen voting in a federal election is a felony) is politically unpopular.

The same can be said for many parts of the country: voter fraud is often hidden in plain sight.

Similar can be said for election fraud. When a precinct has no representation from the other party at the polling place, or along the way in the course of counting and processing election results, or when it is simply assumed that everything is fine election after election, this is the time that mischief can be done.

I have found in other parts of life that when people complain loudly about being checked on, it can be a sign that there is trouble. Cheating people protest loudly against oversight. Often, they use distraction tactics, such as deflection by ridiculing or teasing those who are making the inquiry. They try to paint you as the problem and try to make you out to be the bad person who is picking on them. They will accuse you of having something personal against them, of being biased against them, anything to take the attention off of them. The situation is more pronounced when a stone that has been left unturned for a very long time is suddenly lifted up. Many precincts have never had much scrutiny. Some precincts are very well protected from scrutiny, either because active blocking is going on, but probably more often it is because nobody on the other side ever makes the effort to go there.

Why Not Suspect Fraud On Both Sides?

To make a fair assessment, one is obligated to ask whether the relaxation of safeguards against fraud could have made voter fraud and election fraud easier not just for Democrats but across the board, and subsequently whether such across-the-board increased ease of fraud is likely to have resulted in across-the-board *actual* increase of fraud at relative parity between the parties.

It is right to consider this question, but I believe that large scale voter fraud and election fraud favoring Donald Trump in 2020 was unlikely and does not fit with the evidence for several reasons.

First, the signs do not point toward intent to commit fraud on the Trump side, while many signs point toward such on the Biden side. In 2020, it was uniformly Democrat partisans who over many months prior to and during the election pushed, agitated for, litigated, funded, maneuvered, and executed the relaxation or outright removal of safeguards against fraud, while it was overwhelmingly Republican partisans who fought to keep lawful anti-fraud measures in place. A scenario of Republican fraud on a large scale does not fit with such observed behaviors.

Second, the relaxation of safeguards was localized to states, cities, and precincts under Democrat control.

Third, in terms of absentee and mail-in voting, through which fraud was most likely to occur on a very large scale, the percentage of votes for Biden was far greater than it was in the general vote. If Republicans had been attempting vote fraud by way of absentee ballots, they were doing a very poor job of it.

Fourth, Democrats have long had a much stronger ground game when it comes to ballot harvesting, achieving near-100% "turnout" in nursing homes, and so forth.[35] The strategies long employed in these contexts were made far easier by the relaxation of ballot scrutiny, relaxation or total removal of signature and witness requirements, backdating of postmarks on late mail-in ballots, and other loosening of legal safeguards. With such barriers to fraud torn down, the fine-tuned machine in many Democrat strongholds would have been turning at full speed.

Every national election has some fraud, and we know from the span of American history that fraud has at times been perpetrated by agents of both major political parties, Republican[36] and Democrat.[37] However, it was Democrats and not Republicans who uniformly resisted calls for audits or close scrutiny of the 2020 election after the fact. Had Republicans engaged in large-scale fraud, they would not have been advocating for such audits or transparency. And furthermore, had Democrats been innocent or had reason to suspect that Republicans were just as guilty, they would have had much to gain politically from such audits. The fact that they still resisted them may be taken as evidence against both these scenarios on the part of Democrats.

Ballot Trafficking in the 2020 Election

In late 2021, news began to emerge that the election integrity organization True The Vote had been conducting a major clandestine operation to investigate ballot trafficking. In its operation, True The Vote collected

> "more than 27 terabytes of geospatial and temporal data—a total of 10 trillion cell phone pings—between Oct. 1 and Nov. 6 in targeted areas in Georgia, Arizona, Michigan, Wisconsin, Pennsylvania, and Texas. The data includes geofenced points of interest like ballot dropbox locations, as well as UPS stores and select government, commercial, and non-governmental organization (NGO) facilities. 'From this we have thus far developed precise patterns of life for 242 suspected ballot traffickers in Georgia and 2020 traffickers in Arizona,' True The Vote's document says. 'According to the data, each trafficker went to an average of 23 ballot dropboxes.'"[38]

In May of 2022, Dinesh D'Souza, in cooperation with True The Vote's Katherine Englebrecht and Gregg Phillips, released the film *2000 Mules*, documenting the apparent large-scale and coordinated fraud that occurred in 2020 around the ballot drop boxes.[39] The film documents how Phillips and Englebrecht's team acquired and analyzed more than a petabyte of geo-location data from cellphones, plus over four million minutes of surveillance videos, in order to investigate a theory about abuse of mail-in ballots and ballot dropboxes across the United States during the 2020 election. What they found was stunning but not surprising: thousands of individuals were documented repeatedly making a travel path between dozens of dropboxes in major urban areas throughout the election period, many in the dead of night—2:00 or 3:00 a.m.—and along the way had also stopped at the offices of campaigns or leftist activist organizations. Many were caught on surveillance cameras photographing ballots before dropping them into the box—a common practice among ballot traffickers who are required to show proof in order to get paid.

Articles emerged almost immediately attacking the film. One such article, disappointingly from the Associated Press, claimed that *2000 Mules* engaged in "flawed analysis" and that cellphone location data "is not precise enough to confirm that somebody deposited a ballot into a drop box."[40]

However, such critics seem not to have watched the movie, for nowhere in it was the claim made that any location data demonstrated that a person dropped a ballot into any drop box. What the researchers did, rather, was to find a pattern of certain individuals visiting dozens of dropboxes a day, and along the way making stops at known Democrat activist offices. It correlated these data with a national database of individuals who had been flagged as having been present at other recent violent protests such as the BLM and Antifa riots of 2020 and discovered many of the same individuals that were visiting these dropboxes had also attended one or more of these riots. It found that hundreds—and in the case of Philadelphia, Pennsylvania, 1,100—of such "mules" were active in these patterns during the election. It also linked the data with official surveillance video, which *did* show individuals dropping ballots into the boxes, sometimes doing so while wearing surgical gloves beginning the day after news had broken that fingerprints had been successfully used to prosecute a local individual for ballot trafficking fraud. The proverbial ostrich with its head in the sand is an appropriate image of any individual who could take such a confluence of data and still claim that it does not "prove" anything.

Advance Warning

In August of 2020, the *New York Post* ran an article[41] detailing a Democrat whistleblower's description of the ways in which he conducted fraud for the Party on a grand scale across multiple elections, for decades. From the article:

[T]he political insider, who spoke on condition of anonymity because he fears prosecution, said fraud is more the rule than the exception. His dirty work has taken him through the weeds of municipal and federal elections in Paterson, Atlantic City, Camden, Newark, Hoboken and Hudson County and his fingerprints can be found in local legislative, mayoral and congressional races across the Garden State. Some of the biggest names and high office holders in New Jersey have benefited from his tricks, according to campaign records The Post reviewed ...

The whistleblower — whose identity, rap sheet and long history working as a consultant to various campaigns were confirmed by The Post — says he not only changed ballots himself over the years, but led teams of fraudsters and mentored at least 20 operatives in New Jersey, New York and Pennsylvania — a critical 2020 swing state.

"There is no race in New Jersey — from city council to United States Senate — that we haven't worked on," the tipster said. "I worked on a fire commissioner's race in Burlington County. The smaller the race, the easier it is to do."[42]

How is it done? This whistleblower described one type of election fraud involving mail-in ballots. The process begins with a blank mail-in ballot received by the voter in a large envelope. This blank ballot itself has no specific security features like a stamp, identifying number, or watermark, and can therefore easily be copied. The more difficult part was the return envelope, which cannot be easily duplicated; for this reason, ballot envelopes needed to be collected from actual voters. In order to accomplish the fraud, this individual would have his operatives fan out, going house to house collecting completed ballots from voters with the offer to mail them in on their behalf as a public service. Having collected many such envelopes, the individual and his colleagues would open the envelopes by steaming them to loosen the glue. Real ballots would be replaced by counterfeit ballots inside the ballot envelope signed by the actual voter. The operation took a maximum of five minutes per ballot, the whistleblower said. Finally, the fraudulent ballots would be dropped into multiple mailboxes around town in order to avoid drawing attention.[43]

The tipster further detailed how some postal workers had historically participated in such scams: "You have a postman who is a rabid anti-Trump guy and he's working in Bedminster or some Republican stronghold. ... He can take those [filled-out] ballots, and knowing 95% are going to a Republican, he can just throw those in the garbage." According to the article, the whistleblower claimed that in some cases, mail carriers were even part of his "work crew," and would hand sifted ballots over to him.[44]

Another well-known venue for election fraud is nursing homes. The article reported the whistleblower as revealing that "hitting up assisted-living facilities and 'helping' the elderly fill out their absentee ballots was a gold mine of votes":

> "There are nursing homes where the nurse is actually a paid operative. And they go room by room by room to these old people who still want to feel like they're relevant," said the whistleblower. "[They] literally fill it out for them."[45]

Next, there is voter impersonation. According to the tipster, he would send operatives to vote in-person at polling stations in states like New Jersey, New York, and much of Pennsylvania, that do not require voter ID. It is a matter of public record when registered voters routinely miss elections; these voters—unlikely to turn up anyway—would be the ones the operatives would impersonate. The tipster said that he would fill out index cards with people's names and districts, then distribute these cards around the city to his operatives to go cast the votes in those places. The fraudulent voters would do their best to duplicate the actual voters' signatures (which appeared on the voter roll). In the rare instance that an actual voter had already been in, the fraudster would just say he or she had made a mistake and leave.[46]

Finally, there was vote-buying. For this, the tipster revealed that homeless shelters provided large opportunities. Votes have been bought for as little as $50, as demonstrated in a 2013 prosecution in Hoboken.

What about the candidates? Were they in on the scam? Usually not, at least when it came to the details. The tipster said that his operations in the Garden State and elsewhere typically proceeded like mafia organizations, with a boss (often the campaign manager) leaving day-to-day management of the soldiers to an underboss (the tipster's role). The candidate was almost always left in the dark to maintain "plausible deniability."[47] As an aside, a good fictional representation of how this sort of operation can (and probably does) play out is nicely portrayed in the recent book, *The Election Heist,* by Kenneth R. Timmerman.

When it came time to count the mail-in ballots, partisans from both parties would oversee the counting, in theory challenging ballots that looked inauthentic based upon non-matching signatures or other irregularities. Fraud operatives would often participate in this counting, and the inside clue that a particular ballot had been one they had fraudulently-altered was a bent corner along the voter certificate; when they saw that bent corner, they would know not to object to that particular ballot. This informant boasted that the bent corner trick had been his own invention.[48]

The warnings contained in the *New York Post* article and others like it, alerting the world to potential fraud on a scale never before witnessed in the United States, came amid many months of major pushes on the part of

Democrats to dramatically increase the use of vote-by-mail, place unmanned ballot drop boxes in key states and precincts, and so forth.

And, with the sudden ten-fold increase in the number of mail-in ballots in circulation in 2020, what was already a serious and known problem for election integrity now became an epidemic .... a veritable candy-land on steroids for the perpetrators of fraud. The situation must have exceeded their wildest dreams: more than double the ballot opportunities existed nationwide over 2016 as a percentage of total votes,[49] while at the same time the possibility of getting caught was significantly reduced because there was just too much mail-in voting going on for law enforcement or integrity measures to be able to interfere.

Selected Additional Fraud Allegations: GA and MI

Following, I list some fraud allegations or investigations. This is not a complete list and I've made no attempt to be exhaustive. Also, these matters continue to develop as investigations proceed.

Since I elsewhere discuss problems, initiatives, and investigations that span multiple states—particularly those related to Mark Zuckerberg and Priscilla Chan (the focal point of the 2022 investigative documentary *Rigged*, by Dave Bossie and Citizens United) and the mail ballot fraud documented in the 2022 film *2000 Mules* (Dinesh D'Souza) mentioned above—those are not extensively detailed for each state below.

There are by now many thousands of affidavits alleging fraud or other irregularities in the election,[50] and dozens upon dozens of lawsuits seeking redress in some form or another (see Chapter 9). Meanwhile, there have been monumental efforts by Democrats and some Trump-critical Republicans to stonewall forensic audits until after the deadline for destruction of 2020 election records. If these individuals succeed in blocking investigations until after that event, they will be able to destroy incriminating evidence in the name of routine housekeeping and be one step closer to "home free."

Georgia

In Georgia, 4,935,487 votes for president were counted in 2020. Of these, a mere 11,779 separated Joe Biden from Donald Trump.[51] Based upon these results, all of Georgia's sixteen electoral votes went to Biden.

While even a victory of a single vote is sufficient to decide an election, serious questions about the integrity of the election in Georgia, and sworn testimony indicating significant voter fraud, have been put forward.

The following factual assertions have been advanced by the election integrity group VoterGA, concerning an analysis of Fulton County:

The team's analysis revealed that 923 of 1539 mail-in ballot batch files contained votes incorrectly reported in Fulton's official November 3rd 2020 results. These inaccuracies are due to discrepancies in votes for Donald Trump, Joe Biden and total votes cast compared to their reported audit totals for respective batches. Thus, the error reporting rate in Fulton's hand count audit is [...] 60%.

One type of error discovered involved duplicate results reporting for batches of ballots. The team found at least 36 batches of mail-in ballots with 4,255 total extra votes were redundantly added into Fulton Co. audit results for the November election. These illicit votes include 3,390 extra votes for Joe Biden, 865 extra votes for Donald Trump and 43 extra votes for Jo Jorgenson.

But it is not simply a case of errors. The VoterGA team found 7 falsified audit tally sheets containing fabricated vote totals for their respective batches. For example, a batch containing 59 actual ballot images for Joe Biden, 42 for Donald Trump and 0 for Jo Jorgenson was **reported as 100 for Biden and 0 for Trump.** The seven batches of ballot images with 554 votes for Biden, 140 for Donald Trump and 11 votes for Jo Jorgenson had tally sheets in the audit **falsified to show 850 votes for Biden, 0 votes for Trump and 0 votes for Jorgenson.**[52]

For example:

When Fulton County, Ga., poll manager Suzi Voyles sorted through a large stack of mail-in ballots last November, she noticed an alarmingly odd pattern of uniformity in the markings for Joseph R. Biden. One after another, the absentee ballots contained perfectly filled-in ovals for Biden — except that each of the darkened bubbles featured an identical white void inside them in the shape of a tiny crescent, indicating they'd been marked with toner ink instead of a pen or pencil.

Adding to suspicions, she noticed that all of the ballots were printed on different stock of paper than the others she handled as part of a statewide recount of the razor-thin Nov. 3 presidential election. And none was folded or creased, as she typically observed in mail-in ballots that had been removed from envelopes.

In short, the Biden votes looked like they'd been duplicated by a copy machine.

"All of them were strangely pristine," said Voyles, who said she'd never seen anything like it in her 20 years monitoring elections in Fulton County, which includes much of Atlanta.

She wasn't alone. At least three other poll workers observed the same thing in stacks of absentee ballots for Biden processed by the county, and they have joined Voyles in swearing under penalty of perjury that they looked fake.[53]

Fulton is one of 159 counties in Georgia. Subsequent to the election, a state judge—convinced by the affidavits of Voyles and several others—ordered that all 147,000 mail-in ballots counted in Fulton County be unsealed and inspected for evidence of counterfeiting. However, the ordered inspection was blocked by the county just before it was to occur, and the storage facility was breached in a strange sequence of events the very next day:

"We have what is almost surely major absentee-ballot fraud in Fulton County involving 10,000 to 20,000 probably false ballots," said Garland Favorito, the lead petitioner in the case and a certified poll watcher who runs VoterGa.org, one of the leading advocates for election integrity in the state.

He said the suspect ballots remain in the custody of the election officials and inaccessible from [sic] public view.

"We have confirmed that there are five pallets of shrink-wrapped ballots in a county warehouse," Favorito said [...]

He and other petitioners were ordered to meet at the warehouse May 28 to settle the terms of the inspection of the absentee ballots. But the day before the scheduled meeting, the county filed a flurry of motions to dismiss the case, delaying the inspection indefinitely. [...]

As part of his May 21 order, Superior Court Judge Brian Amero requested officials to guard the warehouse around the clock until an inspection date can be set. But just eight days later, a breach in security was reported after sheriff's deputies left their post for a couple of hours.

"The front door was [found] unlocked and wide open in violation of the court order," Favorito said.

County officials confirmed that a motion-detection alarm was triggered Saturday, May 29, shortly after the deputies drove away from the building in their patrol cars around 4 p.m. But they said a locked room where the ballots are kept "was never breached or compromised."

Favorito is not convinced, and his lawyer is seeking to obtain the video footage from building security cameras. "How do we know for certain there was no tampering with the ballots?" asked Favorito, who said he did not vote for Donald Trump.[54]

In the previous chapter, we spoke about the myriad and serious election integrity problems with ballot drop boxes. Another problem in Georgia during the 2020 election was the placement of drop boxes that were "largely unregulated and unattended — located outdoors, open 24 hours a day and available for drop-offs until the evening of Election Day, prompting complaints of ballot stuffing and double voting."[55] Georgia was not the only state in which unattended drop boxes presented an enormous opportunity for fraud, but given the slim margin and decisive nature of Georgia's electoral votes, the drop box situation there is a major failing.

Michigan

An investigation conducted by the Michigan Senate Oversight Committee, begun on November 7, 2020, culminated in the release of a report[56] on June 23, 2021. In its executive summary, the report stated that the Committee "found no evidence of widespread or systematic fraud in Michigan's prosecution of the 2020 election." However, the summary promptly qualified this statement with the admission that "this investigation should not be considered exhaustive" and that "every possible investigative avenue was **not** undertaken" by the Committee.[57] The report summary specifically delineated four "severe weaknesses" in Michigan's election system:

1. "[L]ack of clarity in the tabulation of ballots"
2. "[U]nnecessary barriers to ensuring that every lawfully cast ballot is counted"
3. "[I]nconsistent poll worker or challenger training"
4. "[A] system not primarily designed to handle ballots cast absentee or otherwise prior to Election Day."[58]

The Report opened with a letter from the chair, Senator Edward McBroom (R). In this statement he wrote that, while the Committee "found … real vulnerabilities … to the systems," yet, "I feel confident to assert the results of the Michigan election are accurately represented by the certified and audited results." McBroom stated his view that in light of the Committee's findings, "another audit, a so-called forensic audit, is not justifiable." He did admit, however, that this recommendation might change "if genuine issues are shown in Arizona's audit or from continued investigation here."[59]

Following is a summary of the issues noted and discussed in the Michigan Senate Oversight Committee Report. I have arranged these in order of what I consider to be most concerning.

Deceased and Non-residents Voting

The Committee investigated the claims that were presented to it and found most of them to be false. As an example, from a list provided to the

Committee of over 200 people in Wayne County believed to be deceased but to have cast a ballot, only two instances turned out to be votes attributed to a deceased voter and neither one was nefarious. In the first, a clerical error had checked in a man who had the same name as his 118-year-old deceased father who had lived at the same residence. In the second, a 92-year-old woman had legally submitted her completed absentee ballot in advance of her death four days before the November 2020 election. This vote ought to have been discounted. The Report continued, however, to state that, "Notably, research showed the secretary of state and clerks were able to discover and remove approximately 3,500 absentee ballots submitted by voters while they were alive but died before Election Day."[60]

Examples are given of other instances, including claims by the widow of a man who had passed away in 2013 that he was recorded as having voted. The Report said that Senate staff "searched the state database with the information provided by the individual and were not able to find her husband in the database," suggesting that he had been removed from the database and therefore his identity could not have been used to vote in 2020. However, the Report, which was concluded in 2021, did not account for the possibility that the man's name might have been removed from the database after the election.

The report also addressed an allegation that a husband and wife who had moved out of state saw documentation online that they had voted in Michigan during the 2020 general election. Upon researching the matter, the Committee found that the couple had indeed been mailed an absentee ballot application and are still registered to vote, but that "the local clerk did not receive returned and completed absentee ballot applications in these voters' names."[61]

Unsolicited Absentee Voter Ballot and Application Mass Mailings

The Report stated that "Citizens across the state were left confused and frustrated by the arrival of applications for long deceased family members, those who have moved to other states, or persons never present at that address."[62] It found that the lists chosen for these mailings by the state's Bureau of Elections were often old and ones that had been previously purged. This fact would raise serious questions as to how and why they were used in 2020 in the first place. The Report also noted that the mailing did not appear to have a mechanism for returning to, or even informing, the secretary of state of undeliverable applications. What, then, would have happened to undeliverable applications?

The Committee observed that, despite a court having ruled that pre-election mass mailings were permitted, "there were significant communications between the department [i.e., the office of the Secretary of State] and Rock the Vote, a group which tends to target young persons and those with more left ofcenter (sic) political leanings."

The Report addressed a claim made by the group Voter Integrity Project[63] that "289,866 illegal votes" had been cast. It explained that the group had arrived at this number by calling 1,500 voters and asking them if they'd received a ballot without asking for it. Sending an unsolicited ballot to any voter would have been illegal in Michigan. Apparently the group received a number of affirmative answers, which were then extrapolated in consideration of the total state population to arrive at the number 289,866, the projected number of Michigan residents who would have received unsolicited ballots. The Report noted that

> Throughout discussions with these individuals, as well as others who claimed they had received an unsolicited ballot, it became clear that many equated receiving an absentee ballot application with receiving an absentee ballot. [...] **There was no evidence presented to the Committee indicating that hundreds of thousands of** <u>absentee voter ballots</u> **were mailed to Michigan voters without previously being requested.**[64]

The Report further noted that "while it may not be lawful to send ballots without first receiving an application, voting this ballot is not an illegal action by a lawful voter and it is not indicative of fraudulent or illicit behavior of the voter nor of an illegitimate vote."[65] However, this statement further reinforces my emphatic statement at the beginning of this chapter: The sending, perhaps selectively (since we have already seen the Report's admission that the Secretary of State had "significant communications" with Rock the Vote), of unsolicited ballots which were then cast by lawful voters when other lawful voters of possible different political leanings did not receive unsolicited ballots, would represent a de-facto change to election law or an illegal activity or even illegal interference in the conduct of the election that could have changed the election's outcome, *while at the same time supporters of the outcome might truthfully claim that it was neither voter fraud nor election fraud.* Such a concern would be grave, and in my view the matter deserves further scrutiny.

Tempering these concerns somewhat was the Report's observation that a large-scale fraudulent utilization of the ballots of others, undetected, would be difficult given the systems in place which would, it said, have caught some or all second attempts at voting.[66] But again, actual voter fraud is only one of the concerns in a scenario of possible mass, and possibly selective, solicitation of voters to request an absentee ballot. The greater concern is the potential influence, on the election outcome, of such a voter turnout campaign itself—with a possible coordination between the office of the Secretary of State and advocacy groups such as Rock the Vote.

The Report furthermore acknowledged that the mailing of unsolicited applications "to the former Michigan addresses of those who moved out of state and applications sent to the new addresses of former Michigan citizens now registered to vote in another state constitute a real and virtually undetectable potential for fraudulent activity."[67] The Report recognized that,

> [T]here is essentially *no mechanism in place to prevent counting votes from those who may be also registered and vote in another state*, whether done by themselves or the recipient of an application at their former Michigan address. As there are *no efficient or established procedures to confirm or detect this*, it is not possible for the Committee to report on any occurrences or to have confidence no such actions occurred. However, with *mass mailings of absentee ballot applications being mailed across state lines to many who no longer reside or vote in Michigan and to thousands of former addresses in Michigan*, the situation must be addressed to ensure that those individuals are voting only once in an election, are doing so only in the state of their residence, and that no one is impersonating them at their old address. *The serious, potential outcomes of these vulnerabilities versus the minor effort to request an application make a strong and compelling necessity to not provide such applications without a request from a voter—as was standard practice until this past year.*[68]

Personal Experience

In 2016, I served as an election worker (not a poll watcher) at the John W. Tolbert Jr. Elementary School in Leesburg, Virginia. Over the course of the day, I came to understand that the precinct chief, and many of my fellow poll workers, were Democrats. In fact, out of nearly a dozen people, I was the only one who apparently did not lean Democrat. As the day went on, people came and voted and we ran the check-in and the machines following our training.

I made several observations about the processes that day. The first was that, after the polls had closed and the closing procedures were in process, myself and most of the others were told by the election judge, "You all must be tired; everyone sign a page of Avery labels, and you can go home." While others did exactly that, I said, "No thanks; I'll stay until the end."

The Avery labels were the ordinary stickers often used to print addresses and attach to mailings. The first thing to observe is that the volunteers were asked to sign a whole sheet of labels, which would then be stuck to the lids of plastic bins to give the impression that their closure had been witnessed by the person who had signed the label.

The second thing I noted was that the Avery labels served virtually no purpose on the plastic bins. They barely stuck on, and could be easily removed and reapplied. In fact, I saw this done in the ordinary process of closing out the precinct. There was nothing nefarious when I witnessed it; someone just needed to re-access a bin. But the incident made clear that someone could easily get into the bins at a later point without any sign. In other words, the Avery labels did not seal the bins and provided only an impression of security.

Zip ties were also used to seal containers. As I recall, these were also of little real help in some cases, because of the nature of the containers. Since I was a newcomer, and did not know how the process was "supposed" to be conducted, I just watched as we wrapped up the day. But in my observation, this process was about as loose and un-secured as any fraudster could possibly wish.

I am not alleging actual interference with the vote at the Tolbert Elementary precinct that night in 2016. What I am presenting to you is an example of the reality of an atrocious and completely un-secure system that could be easily manipulated by those with fraudulent intentions. Was Loudoun County cutting corners on security measures, was it simply a poorly designed process, or were the un-secure systems there on purpose? Whatever the case, "plausible deniability" is a big problem that makes it difficult to document nefarious activity.

In my observation, the American people have been encouraged to place far too much trust in those running the show. But honest elections do not run on trust; they run on transparency, processes designed to anticipate and prevent corruption of the result, and actual oversight.

Following is the national conversation I observed in 2020 and the period following:

The People: We want honest elections.
Elites: Elections are honest.
The People: If elections are honest, then surely you won't mind having processes in place to stop cheating.
Elites: You are racist.
The People: But, you said elections were honest. If they really are already honest, then safeguards won't change the outcomes—but they will assure people that their elections can be trusted. Wouldn't that be good?
Elites: You are crazy. And conspiracy theorists. And stupid. If you knew how our processes worked, you would not have these concerns.
The People: If they are so secure, can we have transparency so that people can watch the entire process?

Elites: No. We are going to keep poll watchers from watching, kick everyone out for key moments, and refuse voter ID.

The Prior Election

When Trump won the election in 2016, the American political establishments on both sides of the aisle expressed shock and dismay.[69] However, Hillary Clinton's supporters took a small degree of solace in the claim that at least their candidate had won the popular vote, which, according to the official counts, she had.[70] Donald Trump, however, boldly asserted that millions of fraudulent votes had been cast for his opponent, and that his true margin of victory (if vote fraud were known and eliminated) not only included the popular vote, but did so by a significant and comfortable margin.[71] For such claims, the President was ridiculed and scoffed by many,[72] including some inside his own party.[73]

Abuse Of The Elderly And Mentally Incapacitated

A perennial problem in elections is fraud perpetrated in nursing homes. In 2010, as reported in Psychology Today and referencing a Fox News report, a voter named Montgomery Jensen "says he and his wife saw a group of mentally incapacitated individuals ushered through the voting process by mental health staff, who told some of the group who they should vote for and, in some cases, filled out ballots on their behalf. ... Jensen suggested that the county officials processing the ballots were aware that some had been cast by mentally incapacitated people who may not be legally eligible to vote."[74]

In Texas, social worker Kelly Reagan Brunner was charged with 134 felony counts involving 2020 election fraud, related to theft of votes of the mentally incapacitated. According to the Attorney General of Texas, "Brunner submitted voter registration applications for 67 residents without their signature or effective consent, while purporting to act as their agent."[75]

These are just a couple examples. I did not go out searching to make an exhaustive or comprehensive list of 2020 election fraud, because this book is not about election fraud. But it will be helpful to remember that observed or prosecuted fraud is always merely the tip of the iceberg. And the more chaos exists, the more confusion around the process, and particularly the more safety precautions designed to prevent or catch fraud in the first place are removed from the *process*, the more of that iceberg remains invisible under the water.

What Is (And What Isn't) A Forensic Audit

When an audit is downstream from the corruption of data, the fraudsters have nothing to fear. Consider the following chart:

$$A \rightarrow B \rightarrow C$$

Let's say that A is all the legitimate *voters* at start of an election, B is the *number of votes* recorded in each precinct by the end of the election counting, and C is the *election outcome* after all the votes are added together, electors are assigned and so forth.

Now, let's imagine that somehow the number of votes, B, is not correct because of an error, or because someone voted twice, or because an ineligible person voted, or because someone surreptitiously added votes for one candidate or subtracted them from another—or both. This happened *before* point B, that is, somewhere between points A and B. We can represent this situation thus, with the vertical line showing that the true expression of the will of the people, A, was blocked from reaching point B:

$$A \rightarrow | B \rightarrow C$$

Now, let's imagine that some people at point C say, "Now, wait just a minute. That can't be right. We need to check that this election was correct." "No problem!" the election officials say, "We'll do an audit!" So, the people wait. But what if the election officials' idea of an "audit" is just to go back, check the record books and tallies from point B, maybe recount the ballots, plug them into a calculator, and make sure that they add up to the same numbers that gave result C the first time?

Can you see the problem? Such an "audit" would be meaningless. Unless someone was really bad at counting or adding the first time, the numbers will come out *exactly the same*, or very nearly so, the second time. Why? Because the "audit" failed to check whether the numbers were correct in the first place.

Yet, for the most part that is exactly what happened with the "audits" of the 2020 election numbers that have occurred so far.

Officials in 2020 did not go back and verify that voters who were recorded as voting actually did so. They did not go through and check to see how many people who are deceased or no longer resident in the state were recorded as having voted. They did not (for the most part) go through to check how many people cast more than one ballot—such as mail-in and in-person, or voting in more than one state, or voting under a married name and a maiden name. They did not check to find out how many noncitizens were recorded as voting. They did not allow non-sympathetic experts to check the electronic voting equipment. They did none of these things. What they did, rather, was to re-add all the numbers, or in some cases recount the ballots. But recounting the ballots will give you the same false result if a portion of those ballots were illegally cast, and re-adding machine totals will not tell you whether the machines correctly recorded the numbers in the first place or if the machines recorded votes that were not legally cast by eligible voters.

There is an old saying: "Garbage in, garbage out." Unless the data is correct, the result of the calculation at the end will be wrong. Adding up the same set of manipulated numbers a second time will yield the same false result.

It is extremely important that Americans take note of how some people are behaving around the requests for *actual* audits of the 2020 election, and shielding the upstream data and equipment from examination. Their touchiness about those things should tell you all you need to know.

There are some things to understand before we continue. First, adding up the same set of numbers a second time does *not* constitute a meaningful election audit. In order to discern fraud, an audit requires making sure that the various sets of numbers being added were correct in the first place. That is, it involves digging deeper. Second, an audit is—by its very definition—skeptical. It does *not* assume from the start that everything was OK. Any investigation that starts out with a premise that the subject did everything right is biased and is not a proper investigation. If everything is found to be solid at the end of the investigation, then that is a very good outcome. However, the time for such a conclusion is after the investigation, not before it. Third, the people doing an audit must be free from bias in favor of those being audited. Someone with a conflict of interest in the form of a personal connection or material interest in the well-being of the party being audited must not lead an audit inquiry.

I will return to the topic of *full forensic audits*, in Chapter 14. A full forensic audit has not, to my knowledge, been done for any state or precinct in the 2020 election, and this fact is an indication of the state of U.S. elections.

A Much Needed Public Information Campaign

Many noncitizens do not know that it is a crime for them to vote in a U.S. national election. Some others know but, disagreeing with the law and/or the principles of self governance upon which the United States rest, vote as an act of subversion and defiance. As already discussed, Democrats cultivate and perpetuate both the ignorance and the defiance among immigrants because noncitizen voting benefits Democrats electorally. The right to vote in a federal election, by law, belongs only to U.S. citizens 18 years of age or older. If one hundred million people vote in an election, a single illegal vote disenfranchises *all* the 999,999,999 legitimate voters. Such unethical and self-serving activity disenfranchises every American.

Most noncitizens entered the United States legally, do not want to break the law, and would refrain from voting if they understood that it is illegal and could carry serious consequences for them including jail time, visa revocation, or deportation. Therefore, one of the simplest ways to address the grave problem of noncitizen voter fraud is to clearly and prominently display a public service message informing everyone that noncitizens may not vote in any federal election.

Given the foundational importance of honest elections, and the evident lack of awareness among a significant portion of noncitizens currently living in the United States that it is a crime for them to vote in any federal election, there is eminent reason for federal law to require that an official statement—in multiple languages—be prominently displayed at every polling place, printed on every absentee or mail-in ballot, printed directly on in-person ballot forms and voter registration forms, and in any place where voter registration occurs (such as a Department of Motor Vehicles).

Following is an excellent and appropriate statement for such use, from the Federation for American Immigration Reform (FAIR)[76]:

- Pursuant to 18 U.S.C. § 611, it is a crime – punishable by a fine and up to one year in prison – for an alien to vote in a federal election.
- Pursuant to 8 U.S.C. § 1227, any alien who has voted in violation of any Federal, State, or local constitutional provision, statute, ordinance, or regulation is deportable.
- Pursuant to 42 U.S.C. § 1973gg-10(2) any false statement concerning an applicant's citizenship status that is made on a registration form submitted to election authorities is a crime.
- Pursuant to 18 U.S.C. § 911 knowing and willful false assertions of United States citizenship in order to vote are punishable by up to three years in prison.
- Pursuant to 18 U.S.C. § 1015(f) it is a criminal offense for an individual to make a false statement or claim that he or she is a citizen of the United States in order to register or to vote.

Can you think of any reason that *at least* the following statement should not be prominently posted in every polling place in America? If officials in your state resist it, then you can be certain that your state probably already has large numbers of noncitizens voting—and the officials resisting know it.[77]

IT IS A FEDERAL CRIME FOR ANY PERSON WHO IS NOT A CITIZEN OF THE UNITED STATES TO VOTE IN ANY U.S. PRESIDENTIAL ELECTION.

Es un delito federal que cualquier persona que no sea cuidadana de los Estados Unidos vote en cualquier elección presidential estadounidense.

任何不是美国公民的人在任何美国总统选举中投票都是联邦犯罪。

Isang kriminal na pederal para sa sinumang tao na hindi isang mamamayan ng Estados Unidos na bumoto sa anumang halalan sa pagkapangulo ng Estados Unidos.

Bất kỳ người nào không phải là công dân Hoa Kỳ bỏ phiếu trong bất kỳ cuộc bầu cử tổng thống nào của Hoa Kỳ đều là tội liên bang.

C'est un crime féderal pour toute personne qui n'est pas citoyenne des États-Unis de voter à une élection présidentielle américaine.

إنها جريمة فيدرالية أن يصوت أي شخص ليس من مواطني الولايات المتحدة في أي انتخابات رئاسية أمريكة

미국 시민이 아닌 사람이 미국 대통령 선거에서 투표하는 것은 연방 범죄입니다.

Голосование на президентских выборах в США является федеральным преступлением для любого лица, не являющегося гражданином Соединенных Штатов.

Es ist ein Bundesverbrechen für jede Person, die kein Staatsbürger der Vereinigten Staaten ist, an einer US-Präsidentschaftswahl teilzunehmen.

किसी भी ऐसे व्यक्ति के लिए जो संयुक्त राज्य का नागरिक नहीं है, किसी भी अमेरिकी राष्ट्रपति चुनाव में मतदान करना एक संघीय अपराध है।

Waa dambi federaali ah qof kasta oo aan u dhalan Maraykanka inuu ka codeeyo doorasho kasta oo madaxtinimo ee Maraykanka.

رای دادن در انتخابات ریاست جمهوری آمریکا برای هو فردی که تابعیت ایالات متحده را ندارد ، جرم فدرال محسوب می شود

Amerika Birleşik Devletleri vatandaşı olmayan herhangi bir kişinin herhangi bir ABD başkanlık seçimlerinde oy kullanması federal bir suçtur.

کسی بھی ایسے شخص کے لیے جو امریکہ کا شہری نہیں ہے کسی بھی امریکی صدارتی
انتخابات میں ووٹ ڈالنا وفاقی جرم ہے ۔

É um crime federal para qualquer pessoa que não seja cidadã dos Estados Unidos votar em qualquer eleição presidencial dos Estados Unidos.

米国市民ではない人が米国大統領選挙に投票することは連邦犯罪です。

È un crimine federale per qualsiasi persona che non è un cittadino degli Stati Uniti votare in qualsiasi elezione presidenziale degli Stati Uniti.

ማንኛውም የዩናይትድ ስቴትስ ዜጋ ያልሆነ ማንኛውም ሰው በማንኛውም የአሜሪካ ፕሬዚዳንታዊ ምርጫ ላይ መምረጥ የፌዴራል ወንጀል ነው።

Głosowanie w jakichkolwiek wyborach prezydenckich w USA przez każdą osobę, która nie jest obywatelem Stanów Zjednoczonych, jest przestępstwem federalnym.

Είναι ομοσπονδιακό έγκλημα για κάθε άτομο που δεν είναι υπήκοος των Ηνωμένων Πολιτειών να ψηφίσει στις προεδρικές εκλογές των ΗΠΑ.

זהו פשע פדרלי עבור כל אדם שאינו אזרח ארצות הברית להצביע בכל בחירות לנשיאות ארה"ב

No Good Reason to Resist

A prominent and visible notice to all people present in the United States of the legal requirement that only U.S. citizens may vote in a federal election is an eminently reasonable policy. If any of your elected authorities resist implementing such notification, it is appropriate to ask "Why?" Whatever excuse they give, I suggest that there are only two viable answers:

1. The one resisting has calculated that noncitizens are indeed voting in significant numbers in U.S. national elections and that such people's votes are benefiting his or her preferred candidates or policies.
2. The one resisting believes that, regardless of the actual laws of the land, noncitizens *should* be able to vote in U.S. national elections.

Note that both of the above reasons are tyrannical: they propose to get around the right of the American people to self governance, and replace it with the personal preference of the person who is resisting, by undermining the laws that the American people have painstakingly enacted *via* their elected representatives in the legislative and executive branches.

Temptation to cheat is wired into us biologically[78] and has been translated to reality in nearly every facet of human relationship for millennia. It is for precisely this reason that systems are set in place to ensure integrity in any situation of great consequence. Nobody wants to entrust their care to physicians who cheated their way through medical school; therefore, strict guidelines and tests are set in place to ensure that learning is real and the system of licensure cannot be gamed. Nobody wants to fly in a plane comprised of critical parts made from inferior materials; therefore, safeguards exist to ensure that aircraft parts critical to the safe function of an aircraft are tested and that quality is controlled.

Similarly, people who wish to be self-governed rather than ruled by despots have set in place certain mechanisms to prevent cheating. Cheaters will always look for ways to game the system, in the same way that bank robbers or identity thieves look for opportunities. Vigilance is needed to protect what is valuable.

Concern about election fraud is as old as the institution of democratic elections. Democratic elections are *meant* to reject raw imposition of power. Without honest elections, tyrants will rule.

Shouldn't We Just Trust People?

Those who oppose voting integrity rules often assert that "people don't really cheat," or that if they do, it is in such small numbers as to rarely, if ever, make a difference in the outcome. While it is true that many people reject cheating as a matter of conscience, there are plenty who believe that dishonest means are excusable in pursuit of a goal that they consider worthy or important. Such reasoning is termed "end justifies the means," and in politics, end justifies the means reasoning is far from uncommon. When politicians or their staff and supporters cheat and get away with it, those who don't cheat are left at an immediate disadvantage—even if they are more worthy, and even if they are the actual choice of the people in an election. It is a truism in politics, often proven in the victory of those willing to play dirty over those with integrity, that being better or more correct is not a guarantee of victory. But if we excuse a system that helps cheaters, we must not be surprised to see ourselves ruled by the worst among us.

In the lead-up to the 2020 election, many recognized signs of increased opportunity to cheat being pushed by those who might benefit from such cheating. In 2018, Eric Eggers published *Fraud: How the Left Plans to Steal the Next Election.*[79] Furthermore, the pitch of vocal hatred of Trump, day by day, and even hour by hour, was almost deafening throughout his term and had reached a crescendo by the end.

In the lead-up to the 2020 election, former Assistant to the U.S. Attorney General Mark R. Levin also extensively discussed the machinations of the American Democratic Party that were geared specifically toward enabling unprecedented levels of voter fraud and election fraud in the 2020 election, using COVID-19 and other circumstances as a pretext for sweeping extra-legislative changes to state election laws.

Was there fraud in the 2020 election? Absolutely and unequivocally, yes. How much? The answer is that we do not know exactly, but evidence and common sense both point toward a large amount. This chapter has been a brief survey, not an exhaustive treatment.

What if I am wrong in my statement, and there was no fraud after all? Remember, it does not alter the conclusion of this book.

Seth Keshel's Ten Recommendations

Although many or all of them are discussed or recommended elsewhere in this book, I conclude this chapter with Seth Keshel's list of real steps that can help ensure clean elections. I have edited them for clarity:

1. Voter rolls should be wiped clean and all resident citizens re-registered with appropriate safeguards to prevent illegal or duplicate registrations.
2. There should be a ban on all electronic elections equipment (poll books, voting machines, tabulators).
3. All balloting should be completed with paper and pen or pencil, and ballots given only upon presentation of a valid ID matching the voter registration.
4. Mail balloting should be illegal, with exceptions only for overseas military or associated personnel, legitimately disabled (with appropriate approval and supervision), or individuals or professionals who are unable to vote on Election Day (e.g. doctors, pilots, etc).
5. There should be no early voting. Rather, Election Day voting should be completed with more and smaller precincts as needed.
6. Precincts should be kept to 1,000 voters or fewer.
7. Ballot harvesting should be illegal and punishable by a decade in prison.
8. Election Day should be a state or national holiday, to reduce opportunities for fraud that arise when elections are stretched over a period of weeks, a month, or more.

9. Winners should be announced by midnight. If Florida and Texas can tally more than 10 million votes 90 minutes after polls close, other states can do the same. There is no good reason that Pennsylvania needs 4 days and California needs 4 weeks.

10. There should be a mandatory minimum ten-year prison term for anyone caught restricting access of members of any party authorized to observe election procedure (such as occurred in 2020 at Atlanta's TCF Center), for ballot harvesting, for repeat scanning ballots, or for any other act that distorts a federal election.[80]

Conclusion

At the time of this writing, evidence of apparent fraud in the 2020 has grown to a mountain. Some of it is now being proven. Given the circumstances of the year, the world should expect this evidence to grow in quantity and certainty. I have attempted above only to give a sense of the range of likely fraudulent activity that tainted the election—again, as an addendum and secondary layer to the constitutional problem of ballots cast in illegal time or manner and then improperly counted.

Did voter fraud and election fraud exist in amounts that exceeded the margin of victory for Joe Biden in 2020? The answer seems to be that *we don't know* with scientific certainty, because some evidence was destroyed, and because investigators have been universally blocked from subjecting the remaining evidence to full forensic audits. Because we do not know, it is not possible at this point to base a claim that Trump won upon the amount of fraud. What we do know is that claims of a Biden victory are rife with indications that fraud was rampant, that this conclusion would be quite consistent with a scenario in which safeguards against fraud were enormously relaxed (as they were), and that the evidence presented in the films *2000 Mules* (D'Souza, 2022) and *Rigged* (Bossie, 2022), and the books *Rigged* (Hemingway, 2021), *Justified* (Ward, 2022), and *Our Broken Elections* (Fund and von Spakovsky, 2021) and other investigations and analyses dating to November and December 2020 suggest an enormous illegal national (or at least multi-state) operation to deliver the election to Joe Biden. Whatever it *was*, one thing that seems quite evident is that the 2020 presidential election *was not* "the most safe and secure" election in American history.

QUESTIONS

1. Describe the difference between voter fraud and election fraud. What are some examples of each?

2. What are some factors that make fraud easy to hide and difficult to investigate after the ballots have been counted? If you wanted to cheat, would you rather do so when no one was watching? If you had cheated, would you be happy to hear of an investigation?

3. The author claims that even one fraudulent vote disenfranchises *all* the lawful voters. Why? Would you rather live in a country that does *not* make every effort to stop voter fraud and election fraud, or one that takes the matter very seriously?

---

1. Richman, "Do non-citizens vote." 149-157. Emphasis added. This study had an enormous sample size (*n* = 32,800 in 2008 and *n* = 55,400 in 2010) and estimated at the low end 620,000 noncitizens registered to vote nationwide; at the upper end approximately 3.72 million. The study estimated that at least 38,000 noncitizens, and up to a maximum of nearly 2.8 million, likely cast votes in 2008—with the most likely number of actual noncitizen votes that year being 1.2 million. That was, of course, during a time period where the total number of adult noncitizens in the United States was roughly 19.4 million (the study's estimate). That figure could certainly be significantly higher by the time of the 2020 election.

2. Margot Cleveland, "Whistleblower Videos Capture Pennsylvania Election Officials Destroying Evidence," *Federalist*, November 19, 2021.

3. Namely: Cybersecurity and Infrastructure Security Agency (CISA) Assistant Director Bob Kolasky, U.S. Election Assistance Commission Chair Benjamin Hovland, National Association of Secretaries of State (NASS) President Maggie Toulouse Oliver, National Association of State Election Directors (NASED) President Lori Augino, and Escambia County (Florida) Supervisor of Elections David Stafford.

4. Namely: Chair Brian Hancock (Unisyn Voting Solutions), Vice Chair Sam Derheimer (Hart InterCivic), Chris Wlaschin (Election Systems & Software), Ericka Haas (Electronic Registration Information Center), and Maria Bianchi (Democracy Works).

5. "Joint statement," Cybersecurity and Infrastructure Security Agency. Emphasis original.

6. John Fund, *Stealing Elections: How Voter Fraud Threatens Our Democracy, (Second edition)* (New York: Encounter Books, 2008); John Fund, and Hans Von Spakovsky, *Who's Counting? How fraudsters and bureaucrats put your vote at risk* (New York: Encounter Books, 2012); John Fund, and Hans von Spakovsky, *Our Broken Elections: How the left changed the way you vote* (New York: Encounter Books, 2021).

7. Patrick Byrne, *The Deep Rig: How Election Fraud Cost Donald J. Trump the White House, By a Man Who did not Vote for Him*, Independently published, 2021.

8. Lauren Egan, "Barr says no evidence of widespread fraud, defying Trump," *NBC News*, December 1, 2020.

9. Jerry Dunleavy, "Jan. 6 committee highlights Barr calling Trump fraud claims 'bulls***,'" *Washington Examiner*, June 13, 2022.

10. Ibid.

11. "What Is Electoral and Voter Fraud?," *FindLaw*, last updated March 18, 2020.

12. Ibid.

13. Richman, Chatta, and Earnest, "Do non-citizens vote;" Fund and von Spakovsky, *Our Broken Elections*.

14. "Debunking the Voter Fraud Myth," *Brennan Center*, January 31, 2017.

15. Eric Eggers, *Fraud: How the Left Plans to Steal the Next Election* (Washington, DC: Regnery, 2018). 7-8.

16. Ibid, 9.

17. "Ballot Collection Laws," National Conference of State Legislatures.

18. Unfortunately, some disingenuous individuals and organizations have recently suggested that the term *ballot trafficking* is just a pejorative term of rhetoric that means the same thing as *ballot harvesting*. Even my alma mater, the University of Washington, which to my knowledge even has a law school, has been recently sowing confusion on this distinction, calling ballot harvesting a "deceptive term." It is no such thing; it is a technical term. Mike Caulfield, Kayla Duskin, Stephen Prochaska, Scott Philips Johnson, Annie

Denton, Zarine Khazarian, and Kate Starbird, "The rise of 'trafficking' language in ballot collection narratives," *Center for an Informed Public*, University of Washington, April 30, 2022.

19. "[Rodriguez] was featured last year in the #ImWithHer video saying she supported former Democratic candidate Hillary Clinton 'because she is fighting for immigration reform and fighting to keep our families together.'" Rodriguez in 2017 also tweeted, "We protect DACA because they are human. Because those recipients are HUMAN beings not toys for you to f[*]ck with Donald! #DefendDaca. ..." and "I am staying hopeful that Congress will act decisively in protecting DACA recipients. PROTECT OUR YOUTH #DefendDaca." Jerome Hudson, "Illegal alien sitcoms from actress Gina Rodriguez headed to CBS and CW," *Breitbart*, September 17, 2017.

20. DACA is the acronym for "Deferred Action for Childhood Arrivals," an executive order by President Obama in 2012 that allowed some illegal immigrants who came to the United States as children, but refused to return to the country of their citizenship on reaching adulthood, the opportunity to escape deportation and even to get work permits. DREAMers is a term derived from the DREAM Act, which has failed every attempt at passage through the U.S. Legislature since its introduction in 2001. The bill's name is an acronym for "Development, Relief, and Education for Alien Minors." DREAMers are those illegal immigrants who would have qualified for temporary conditional residency, including a right to work and a special alternate pathway to citizenship apart from the pathway already open to them, but which many so-called DREAMers found too inconvenient, had the act passed and been signed into law. Frustrated that the law remained tremendously unpopular with the American public—most of whom still believe in equality and that everyone should follow the same laws—President Obama's DACA order was effectively an end-run around the constitutional requirement that only Congress can legislate. Strictly speaking, DACA is itself likely illegal: a president can issue pardons to individuals but cannot exempt entire classes of people from the requirements of the law. Based upon such reasoning, even the U.S. Supreme Court let stand an injunction against DACA expansion and the creation of another similar program Obama took *via* executive action called DAPA ("Deferred Action for Parents of Americans") intended to similarly excuse illegal immigrant parents of people with legal status or with DACA protection.

21. Marvin Miranda, "Rafael Agustin: the uniquely American writer redefining the American story," *LA Weekly*, May 31, 2018.

22. Bethania Palma, "Obama Encouraged 'Illegal Aliens' to Vote," *Snopes*, November 6, 2016.

23. John Fund, "Non-Citizens Are Voting." *National Review*, October 30, 2014.

24. Kim Strach, Marc Burris and Veronica Degraffenreid, "Presentation to Joint Legislative Elections Oversight Committee," *North Carolina State Board of Elections*, April 2, 2014.

25. Andrew Johnson, "N.C. Board Finds More than 35K Incidents of 'Double Voting' in 2012," *National Review Online*, April 2, 2014; Strach, Burris and Degraffenreid, "Presentation to Joint Legislative." 33-35.

26. Ibid.

27. Jack Goodman, Christopher Giles, Olga Robinson, and Jake Horton, "US Election 2020: The 'dead voters' in Michigan who are still alive," *BBC*, November 14, 2020.

28. Byron York, "When 1,099 felons vote in race won by 312 ballots," *Washington Examiner*, August 6, 2012; Peter Roff, "Al Franken May Have Won His Senate Seat Through Voter Fraud," *US News And World Report*, July 20, 2010.

29. Richman, Chatta, and Earnest, "Do non-citizens vote." 154. Emphasis added. The authors' extensive survey of 32,800 people in 2008 yielded a percentage of non-citizens that voted in the election. Respondents were asked their preferences concerning both the presidential and congressional tickets. Non-citizen voters in 2008 went 66.7% for the Democratic House candidate, and 20.8% for the Republican candidate. Because of this, the authors determine that each additional noncitizen vote adds an expected 0.459 votes for the Democratic House candidate. Using Current Population Survey (CPS) data, they were able to know the number of noncitizens living in Minnesota, and from this number to then estimate the percentage of such noncitizens whose votes would have been required to secure a victory for Franken based upon the national voting preferences of noncitizen voters in that year as stated above.

30. John Lott, "Heed Jimmy Carter on the Danger of Mail-In Voting," *Wall Street Journal*, April 10, 2020.

31. "Voting by mail and absentee voting," *MIT Election Data and Science Lab*, March 16, 2021.

32. Hans Von Spakovsky, interview in *2000 Mules*, (2022).

33. Jon Levine, "Confessions of a voter fraud: I was a master at fixing mail-in ballots," *New York Post*, August 29, 2020.

34. Steven Kovac, "Election Watchdog Finds 137,500 Ballots Trafficked in Wisconsin," *Epoch Times*, New York/DC Edition, March 30, 2022.

35. Susan Ferrechio, "Wisconsin probe finds 2020 election riddled with nursing home voting fraud: 100% turnout in some facilities," *Washington Times*, March 2, 2022; "Second Interim Investigative Report On the Apparatus & Procedures of the Wisconsin Elections System," Wisconsin Office of the Special Counsel, March 1, 2022.

36. Richard L. Hasen, *Election Meltdown: Dirty Tricks, Distrust, and the Threat to American Democracy* (New Haven: Yale University Press. 2020). 2-6.

37. Andrew Jose, "Dem Rep Pleads Guilty to Mass Voter Fraud: Thousands of Dollars Paid to Crooked Judges," *Western Journal*, June 8, 2022.

38. Matthew Boyle, "Exclusive — True the Vote conducting massive clandestine voter fraud investigation," *Breitbart,* August 24, 2021.

39. John Haughey, "Researcher Featured in '2000 Mules' Documentary Explains How Local Election Fraud Was Grown to National Scale," *Epoch Times*, May 1, 2022.

40. Ali Swenson, "Fact-checking '2000 Mules,' the movie alleging ballot fraud," *The Denver Post*, May 8, 2022.

41. Levine, "Confessions."

42. Ibid.

43. Ibid.

44. Ibid.

45. Ibid.

46. Ibid.

47. Ibid.

48. Ibid.

49. "Voting by mail," *MIT Election Data and Science Lab.*

50. Scott McClallen, "Over 7,000 affidavits delivered to Michigan lawmakers claim election fraud," *Washington Examiner*, June 18, 2021.

51. State of Georgia, Certificate of Ascertainment (Amendment and Re-Certification), December 7, 2020.

52. Andrea Widburg, "It looks as if there was massive election fraud in Fulton County, Georgia," *American Thinker*, July 15, 2021. Emphasis added.

53. Paul Sperry, "Why a Judge Has Georgia Vote Fraud on His Mind: 'Pristine' Biden Ballots That Looked Xeroxed," *Real Clear Investigations*, June 8, 2021.

54. Ibid.

55. Ibid.

56. "Report on the November 2020 Election in Michigan," Michigan Senate Oversight Committee.

57. Ibid., 3. Emphasis added.

58. Ibid., 3.

59. Ibid., 4-5.

60. Ibid., 9.

61. Ibid.

62. Ibid., 10.

63. I contacted Voter Integrity Project in connection with the Report's presentation of these allegations. The group's founder and director, Jay DeLancy, Lt. Col, USAF (Ret), told me that dubious research quoted in the Michigan Senate Oversight Committee Report did not originate with his group but rather he understood it to be from Matt Braynard, a Washington, D.C. political consultant. He says that Newsmax contacted Voter Integrity Project requesting an interview with Mr. Braynard, and Voter Integrity Project helped to facilitate it. Subsequently, there was confusion about Braynard being connected with the group. Mr. DeLancy expressed disappointment at the impact of this misunderstanding, and thanked me for the opportunity to clarify.

64. Ibid., 10. Emphasis original.

65. Ibid.

66. "The Committee concludes this demonstrates a clear vulnerability for fraud that may be undetected, if the actual voter does not vote at all," i.e., if a fraudulent voter casts a vote but the legitimate voter does not. "If the actual voter does vote, it will create turmoil and draw

attention from state and local officials. However, the lack of any such incidents or turmoil in the November 2020 election creates a clear probability that no such efforts were committed to any significant extent." Ibid., 11.

67. Ibid.

68. Ibid. Emphasis added.

69. Scott Malone, and David Ingram, "Despair and introspection on U.S. coasts after Trump win," *Reuters,* November 9, 2016; "Across the world, Shock and Uncertainty at Trump's Victory," *New York Times,* November 9, 2016.

70. "More Americans voted for Hillary Clinton than any other losing presidential candidate in US history." Gregory Krieg, "It's official: Clinton swamps Trump in popular vote," *CNN,* December 22, 2016.

71. "Trump claims millions voted illegally in presidential poll," *BBC,* November 28, 2016. The President tweeted, "In addition to winning the Electoral College in a landslide, I won the popular vote if you deduct the millions of people who voted illegally."

72. Arnie Seipel, "Trump Makes Unfounded Claim That 'Millions' Voted Illegally For Clinton," *NPR,* November 27, 2016; Dylan Stableford, "Trump issues stunning, baseless claim that 'millions' voted illegally," *yahoo!news,* November 27, 2016; Mallory Shelbourne, "Trump claims voter fraud without evidence, says 'I won the popular vote,'" *Hill,* November 27, 2016; Glenn Kessler, "Donald Trump's bogus claim that millions of people voted illegally for Hillary Clinton," *Washington Post,* November 27, 2016; Tom LoBianco, "Trump falsely claims 'millions of people who voted illegally' cost him popular vote," *CNN,* November 28, 2016; Heather Caygle, Burgess Everett, and Kyle Cheney, "Trump repeats debunked voter fraud claim at meeting with Hill leaders," *Politico,* January 23, 2017; Logan, Bryan, "Trump repeats debunked claim that voter fraud caused him to lose popular vote to Hillary Clinton," *Business Insider,* January 23, 2017; Rob Farley, "Fact check: Trump claims massive voter fraud; here's the truth," *USA Today,* January 26, 2017.

73. Darren Samuelsohn, "Republicans tell Trump to quit claiming rigged election," *Politico,* October 11, 2016; Elana Schor, "Sen. Lankford criticizes Trump's false voter fraud allegations," *Politico,* November 28, 2016.

74. Anneli Rufus, "Voter Fraud and the Mentally Disabled: Were mentally disabled Minnesotans 'coached' to vote for certain candidates?," *Psychology Today,* November 2, 2010.

75. "Texas Social Worker Charged With 134 Counts Involving Election Fraud," *CBS DFW,* November 6, 2020; "Limestone County Social Worker Charged With 134 Felony Counts Involving Election Fraud," *Office of Attorney General of Texas Ken Paxton,* November 6, 2020.

76. "Noncitizens, Voting," *Federation for American Immigration Reform.*

77. Permission is granted to copy, quote, or reproduce the contents of the following notice. No warranty is made by the author concerning it.

78. Cheating is also observed in animals at all levels, and forms a core concern of the field of sociobiology. Cheating is a strategy for achieving dominance and asserting one's own interests (and, ultimately, one's own genetic succession) ahead of those of others. See Trivers, Robert, *Social Evolution* (Menlo Park: Benjamin/Cummings Publication Company, 1985).

79. Eggers, *Fraud.*

80. Keshel, Seth, "The Ten Points To True Election Integrity," *ElectionFraud20,* January 10, 2022.

5

BACKGROUND AND CONSEQUENCES

I n 2020, Democrat operatives carried out what may be the biggest and most coordinated attack on American democracy thus far in the 250-year history of the nation.[1] Their actions led to the inauguration of a man whom the people had not chosen, while narrow Democrat control of both houses of Congress was preserved.

Americans sensed something wrong about the election, and the concern was not limited to Biden's political opponents. The inauguration of Joe Biden and Kamala Harris finalized one of the least-trusted U.S. elections ever.[2] As discussed in Chapter 2, throughout 2020 and well into 2021, the Biden and Harris ticket received strong cover from government, establishment media, major segments of big business and big tech, and academia. But, the cover eventually began to crack under its own weight. Ordinary citizens had been instructed for months not to trust their eyes, and many complied for a while. However, widespread and growing censorship of topics or views bothersome to the left, odd behavior by government agencies related to the COVID-19 pandemic, and other factors fed a mainstream sense that the official story was not true or complete.

In this chapter, I briefly discuss events following the election, showing the effects of installing Joe Biden. Then, I present two issues preceding 2020 that provide important context to events of the election year. These are the first impeachment of Donald Trump and the staged assault of Jussie Smollett, which sought to falsely tar Trump and his supporters with guilt for an attack that turned out to be pure fiction. Both illustrate why many Americans lost trust in their institutions and national media, and why they should not be blamed for questioning the official 2020 election narrative.

Immediate Effects of the Biden Presidency

By July 1, 2021, an unprecedented expansion in forced transfer of wealth from high-earning Americans to the bottom 90%, by way of monthly checks mailed directly to citizens, noncitizens, non-workers, and illegal immigrants alike under the euphemism "child tax credit," began.[3] The expansion in payments included a change that made those who do not pay taxes at all eligible for these "credits," while excluding those Americans who (according to the Tax Foundation[4]) pay 75-90% of the taxes.[5] The checks represented a step closer to Democrats' goal of a "universal basic income." Biden hoped to make the monthly wealth transfers permanent,[6] paying more and more people not to work.

Forced wealth transfer was not the only initiative Democrats pressed through after taking complete control. Joe Biden immediately set about unraveling Trump's economic, equality, regulatory relief, energy independence, and national sovereignty policies. On day one—among other actions—he canceled the permit for the Keystone XL oil pipeline, halted construction of the southern border wall, canceled Trump's rules allowing enforcement of immigration laws inside the United States, paused deportations for 100 days beginning January 22, directed the Department of Homeland Security to renew the categorical non-enforcement of immigration law against "Dreamers" that President Obama had begun with his "Deferred Action for Childhood Arrivals (DACA)" program, undid Trump's changes to the census that would have stopped the counting of illegal immigrants from giving more House seats to Democrats, and rejoined the Paris Climate Accord all by executive order. In his first day Biden signed seventeen executive orders—far outpacing Obama (9), Trump (8), George W. Bush (2), and Bill Clinton (3).[7] By the end of April, 2021, fully half of Biden's executive orders had been revocations of prior orders, most of them Trump's.[8]

There was more. Emboldened Democrats used the ongoing COVID-19 pandemic as a pretext for efforts to coerce businesses and individuals, up to and including compelling employee vaccination,[9] requiring vaccination in order to keep a job in healthcare, travel domestically, or enter places of business such as shops, restaurants, schools, courts, and churches, and threatening private businesses with fines or loss of license unless they fired employees declining vaccination.[10]

Throughout Biden's first months in office, concerned parents across the nation petitioned their school boards. These parents opposed placement of sexually explicit books in classrooms and school libraries. They objected to school boards hiding sexual assaults in schools. They resented the implementation of racist and Marxist policies and rubrics in classrooms. They opposed mandatory masking of students during the COVID-19 pandemic, and so forth.[11] In 2021, the Biden administration coordinated with the National School Boards Assocation (NSBA) to request the Federal Bureau of Investigation to begin treating such parents as potential terrorists.[12]

The damage was not merely domestic. By August, on the very eve of the twentieth anniversary of the 9/11 attacks, the Biden administration handed Afghanistan back to the Taliban, together with tens of billions of dollars in U.S. assets, an outcome that would have been unthinkable mere months before. After his mismanaged withdrawal of U.S. troops, the hapless Biden left a large number of American citizens, many pleading for extraction, stranded in a country now controlled by the U.S.'s enemies in the War on Terror. Biden similarly abandoned many Afghan nationals and their families who had risked their lives to help the United States, effectively consigning them to likely execution at the hands of the Taliban. Retributionary attacks ensued with horrifying rapidity and scope.[13] An "amnesty" extended by the Taliban was largely for show; recipients were allowed to live for a while and then killed weeks or months later after attention moved on.

The Biden Administration turned a deaf ear to pleas of stranded U.S. citizens and allies. U.S. citizens were told, "We can't take you out without a passport." When they replied, "We don't have a passport," they were essentially told "too bad." Antony Blinken and Joe Biden subsequently reported to the American people that all U.S. citizens were given an option of leaving, and that those who stayed had chosen to do so. These actions led to some calling Blinken the "Baghdad Bob" of the Afghanistan withdrawal disaster.[14] (The original "Baghdad Bob" was Iraq's information minister from 2001 to 2003, Mohammed Saeed al-Sahhaf. During the U.S.-led invasion of Iraq, he drew ridicule even from the Arab press for his patently untrue public announcements, like "There is no presence of American infidels in the city of Baghdad," at the very moment black clouds of smoke were rising from the capital.[15]) The Biden administration disavowed and abandoned allies who had faithfully but covertly served the U.S. for many years in key operations to be hunted by the Taliban with technical assistance from China, Pakistan, and Russia.

As if the human cost was not enough, Biden's surrender handed the Taliban enormous quantities of equipment, armored vehicles, airplanes, helicopters, weaponry, and munition.[16] The strategic Bagram Air Base and up to an estimated $83 billion worth of high tech equipment, gear, and infrastructure were lost to enemy hands.[17] In the midst of the U.S. withdrawal, a bomb attack at Hamid Karzai International Airport killed 13 U.S. servicemembers and at least 170 Afghans.[18] It soon became known that the attack was carried out by a man released from prison one week prior as part of Biden's withdrawal plan.[19]

In an apparent panic to overshadow the botched withdrawal with some news of victory, the Biden administration oversaw an airstrike in Afghanistan on August 29—presented at first as a successful retaliation for the Kabul bombing. As the Associated Press reported,

> Acting swiftly on President Joe Biden's promise to retaliate for the deadly suicide bombing at Kabul Airport, the U.S. military said it killed two members of the Islamic State group's Afghanistan affiliate with a drone strike in the group's eastern stronghold ... Biden authorized the drone strike ... .[20]

This strike, in fact, killed ten civilians—seven of them children.[21] Meanwhile, the Taliban appeared committed to returning Afghanistan to its prewar form of rule, including punishments and executions demanded by Islamic law.[22]

While he defended the outcome by stating that "nobody could have known" that the Afghan army would fall to the Taliban, even Democratic senator Tim Kaine went on record to state that such was simply not the case.[23] A leaked July 23, 2021 transcript of Biden's 14-minute phone conversation with Afghan President Ashraf Ghani also told a different story and betrayed his conscious attempt to mislead:

> I need not tell you the perception around the world and in parts of Afghanistan, I believe, is that things are not going well in terms of the fight against the Taliban. And there is a need, whether it is true or not, there is a need to project a different picture.[24]

Chairman of the Joint Chiefs of Staff General Mark Milley was also involved in the deception, informing Ghani that he, too, wanted to turn around international awareness that the Taliban had gained the upper hand:

> [T]he perception in the United States, in Europe, and the media sort of thing is a narrative of Taliban momentum, and a narrative of Taliban victory. And we need to collectively demonstrate and try to turn that perception, that narrative around.[25]

World leaders' actions have a cascading effect, and Afghanistan was no exception. While geopolitics are complex and influenced by multiple factors, power dynamics also follow a certain relatively simple human logic. At the time of the U.S. withdrawal from Afghanistan, Russia had already been testing the waters and contemplating an invasion of Ukraine. As if on cue, after seeing Biden's handling of Afghanistan, Russia moved forward and was quickly ready to invade Ukraine.[26] By the second week of

February 2022, the U.S. announced plans to withdraw all personnel from Ukraine's capital of Kyiv.[27] Australia followed suit,[28] and Russia's invasion seemed imminent. Reports emerged that Gen. Mark Milley had warned a closed-door meeting of the House and Senate the prior week that the city "could fall within 72 hours if a full-scale Russian invasion of Ukraine takes place."[29] In the early morning of February 24, 2021, Russian president Vladimir Putin announced during a session of the UN Security Council that Russia was launching a military operation in Ukraine. Bombings began midmorning.[30]

There is a centuries-long history, but also a present material motive behind Russia's current interest in Ukraine: its agricultural output (i.e., food).[31] The Russian government believes that Ukraine is rightly part of their nation. Ukraine's independence since 1991, however, is established and rooted in the same principles of self-determination that underlie the United States' independence. There are also, I am told, geopolitical concerns related to the globalist aims of Klaus Schwab and the World Economic Forum and their "Great Reset." It is true that Biden had known of Putin's desire and preparations to invade Ukraine since at least December of 2021, and had even warned the Russian president that he would pay a 'terrible price' if he did so.[32] The salient point is that after Afghanistan, Putin correctly calculated that the United States under Biden's leadership would not be an obstacle, and only then did Russia move forward in Ukraine.

Back at home, economic problems grew. Inflation in the United States reached its highest level in four decades by the end of Biden's first year in office, and interest rates were also set to rise dramatically.[33] In January of 2022, the Dollar Tree store near our home raised its prices for the first time in more than three decades, from $1 to $1.25—an overnight price increase of 25%. Our youngest daughter, who loves Dollar Tree, nearly cried. What is more, the *sizes* of some items simultaneously shrank. For instance, a 64-fluid ounce bottle of "LA's Totally Awesome Stain Lifter Laundry Detergent" that had cost $1 in December of 2021 was replaced by a much smaller 42-fluid ounce bottle costing $1.25 in January of 2022—nearly a 100% increase in price per ounce.[34] The cumulative effect of such increases—felt every day by Americans in grocery stores, at the gas pump, in services, supplies, and materials—were not the fault of retailers such as the Dollar Tree. The rise in cost of basic necessities of life followed mismanagement and even sabotage of the economy, much of it by Biden and his allies *via* closures and other often unnecessary burdens put on businesses and supply chains throughout 2020 and 2021.

Then, there is illegal immigration. The situation at the southern U.S. border following Biden's halt of construction on the wall, elimination of the Trump-era Migrant Protection Protocols (MPP)—better known as the "remain in Mexico" policy requiring asylum seekers at the southern border to wait in Mexico until they could be processed in an orderly and lawful fashion—and other reductions in border security deteriorated rapidly.[35] Swarms of illegal immigrants almost immediately began flooding into the United States after much lower numbers just months before. A major caravan of "thousands of illegal immigrants from Honduras, El Salvador, Haiti, and other countries, mostly in Central America," was making its way across Mexico toward the United States after breaking through a barricade of Mexican police near the southern Mexican border.[36] The mass had been enticed by Joe Biden's promises of a more "humane" approach to immigration.[37]

Already in March of 2021, record numbers of unaccompanied illegal immigrant minors were being held in Department of Health and Human Services shelters, and political activism disguised as journalism (as practiced, for example, by the Washington Post) were attempting to force their release into the U.S. by reporting that their detention exceeded the legal time limit.[38] Secret flights and chartered buses quietly moved illegal immigrants all around the United States in the dark of night.[39] By August, images of nearly 1,000 illegal immigrants being held under the Anzalduas Bridge in Mission, Texas began to emerge.[40] A month later, the number under that same bridge had swelled to more than 10,503 as the Biden FAA instituted a two week flight restriction over the city which effectively grounded news drones and prevented the public from seeing further aerial photos of the developing crisis.[41]

This surge of illegal crossings followed confirmation by border officials that DHS had encountered 208,887 migrants at the southwestern frontier in August. This was the second month in which more than 200,000 crossed, and the first time of such consecutive month numbers since February and March of 2000.[42]

The situation at the border was tense. Border patrol personnel were beginning to openly express a deep and growing anger against the Biden Administration policies and rules of engagement.[43] A few days after the one-year anniversary of Biden's inauguration, leaked audio of a meeting between DHS Secretary Alejandro Mayorkas and U.S. Border Patrol agents in the Yuma Sector of Arizona revealed the breadth of the illegal immigration crisis throughout 2021 and the near boiling-point frustration of agents. More than *two million* migrants had been stopped while attempting to enter the United States illegally from Mexico in 2021.[44] Among those attempting to illegally cross into the United States at the southern border were increased numbers from all parts of the world, including South America, Russia, India, Turkey, Ukraine, and China.[45]

Meanwhile, the Biden administration was going to great lengths to prevent news of such circumstances from getting out. One exasperated border patrol agent, referring to his observation that his superiors were regularly taking actions to hide the severity of the border crisis from the American public, challenged Secretary Mayorkas,

> "Every time someone important [e.g., a U.S. congressperson] comes here, we rush out. Fifty more busses come in and they take as many people out of here as they can. You guys be saying 'Let's see how it really is down here.' Why do we keep sending as many people out of here as we can before they get here?"[46]

Near the end of March, 2021, Biden appointed Kamala Harris as his border czar to address the migrant surge. Yet, ten months into her tenure in that role, Harris had yet to visit the Southern border, where the crisis was spinning out of control.[47] Despite Democrats' often repeated claim that illegal immigrants are running away from persecution, the fact that Harris' sole actions related to the crisis involved sending financial aid to the source countries[48] suggested that she and her party understood that most illegal immigrants scoffing at U.S. law and jumping the line do so not from political fear but rather personal convenience and financial benefit.[49]

On April 7, 2022, Ketanji Brown Jackson, who not only stated in her confirmation hearings that she was unable to define what a woman is, but also refused to affirm the core assertion of the Declaration of Independence that led to the abolition of slavery when she said, "I do not hold a position on whether individuals possess natural rights," was added as a member of the United States Supreme Court.[50]

The following month, possibly intending to fall back on the Brown Jackson appointment as a defense from accusations of bigotry in his next action,[51] the Biden administration announced a series of twenty-five action plans to make racial discrimination and other types of discrimination the official policy of his executive branch. The administration euphemistically called these discrimination roadmaps "Equity Action Plans."[52] The plans, it was revealed, had been written in part by the Black Lives Matter organization (see more on the BLM organization in the following chapter).[53]

> As an example of the fundamentally unfair and bizarre effects of these 'equity' policies favoring particular groups, a federal agency would give priority to a wealthy Chilean-born neurologist or to a gay dentist over a poor, Italian American factory worker who has fewer resources ... . Equity plans by the Departments of Agriculture, Defense, Education, Energy, Justice, Transportation, the Treasury, and others call for steering contracts and other kinds of federal procurement toward the Administration's favored identity groups. In the context of hundreds of billions of dollars in annual federal contracting and procurement activity, this contact-steering could

damage or benefit countless businesses based on the immutable characteristics of owners and employees, as well as on personal sexual identifications or orientations. An additional consequence could be that contracts are awarded to companies that are unqualified to perform the necessary work, resulting in substandard service delivery for the government—and taxpayers.[54]

In May of 2022, a pro-abortion rights protest group published a map containing the home addresses of the conservative Supreme Court justices Barrett, Kavanaugh, Thomas, Gorsuch and Alito, as well as that of Chief Justice John Roberts.[55] On Wednesday, June 8, 2022, an armed California man, Nicholas John Roske, was arrested near the home of Supreme Court Justice Brett Kavanaugh, and later charged with attempted murder, after making threats against Kavanaugh.[56] The above incidents came after a draft decision indicating the imminent overturning of Roe v. Wade was leaked—the first time in U.S. history such a leak has occurred.[57] It also followed widely publicized incendiary threats, specifically aimed at Kavanaugh and fellow justice Neil Gorsuch, from Senate majority leader Chuck Schumer at a pro-abortion-rights rally on the Supreme Court steps in March of 2022. The intimidation seemed clearly intended to influence the justices in their ruling on the Dobbs case which was poised to overturn Roe v. Wade. The senator shouted,

> I want to tell you, Gorsuch, I want to tell you, Kavanaugh, you have released the whirlwind and you will pay the price! You won't know what hit you if you go forward with these awful decisions![58]

The attempt on Kavanaugh's life came the day before the January 6 select committee aired the day of the prime-time hearing on all major news networks except Fox. The New York Times buried the story of the assassination attempt on page A20, and was promptly criticized.[59] Most understood that, had it been an attack on a liberal justice by a conservative assassin, the story would have been front page and lasted for weeks, and all conservatives loudly vilified by association. More than two days after the arrest, Joe Biden had yet to speak on the assassination attempt, despite making public remarks on the topic of inflation that Friday.[60] The Supreme Court Policing Parity Act, designed to give the justices and their families under attack their own police security details similar to the president's secret service, and in reaction to the violent attacks and ongoing threats, flew through the Senate on Thursday with no objections.[61] However, Speaker Nancy Pelosi declined to bring it to the floor of the House, shockingly insisting that no Supreme Court justices are "in danger over the weekend."[62] Rep. Alexandria Ocasio Cortez even bragged about her role in stopping the bill.[63]

By February 2022, inflation in the United States was measured at 6.4%, the highest in forty years, meaning that the average American household would be spending $5,200 more merely to maintain the same standard as the year prior. This inflation rate was far higher than that of other countries, nearly *three times* the average of other developed countries with which its inflation rates ordinarily align—a divergence that began in early 2021.[64] By June, the U.S. inflation rate had risen to a heart-stopping 9.1%. Why?

Inflation is a choice, the result of monetary policy decisions. In the United States, four factors—all supported or created by the Biden administration—almost certainly drove the increase. First was the enormous quantity of money printed beginning mid-2020 and steadily continuing throughout 2021 and 2022. In major part as a result of the Biden administration's actions,[65] nearly twice as many dollars existed in April 2022 as a mere twenty-eight months earlier. It is a basic principle of economics that sharp increases in money supply lead to inflation.

Second, decisions to flood the economy with "stimulus" money for Americans and businesses inflated the total number of dollars in actual circulation. Such action also leads to inflation. Third, supplies of consumer goods have been constricted, further amplifying the effect. The intrusive and over-reaching policies of the left throughout 2020, 2021, and into 2022 related to the pandemic destroyed businesses and caused lasting disruption to supply chains. Fewer businesses meeting the same demand translates to less competition and less supply, naturally leading to higher prices for those items that are available.

Finally, the price of everything—from food to clothing, manufacturing, and every other consumer product—is affected by the real cost of bringing those products to the consumer. As was mentioned above, Joe Biden immediately canceled the license for the Keystone XL oil pipeline on his first day in office. He followed through with a steady stream of other actions that served to further constrict oil supply in the United States. Specifically, he

- Ended new oil and gas leases (January 27)
- Re-joined the anti-oil Paris Climate Agreement (February 19)
- Raised the "social cost of carbon" (February 27)[66]
- Prohibited oil and gas operations on 30% of U.S. public land (May 7)[67]
- Suspended oil-drilling leases in ANWR, Alaska (June 1)[68]
- Reversed Trump's cuts to "mountains and mountains of bureaucratic red tape" in the National Environmental Policy Act (NEPA) (October 7)[69]

- Proposed a moratorium on oil and gas drilling in Chaco Canyon, New Mexico (November 15)

Even before the February 24, 2022 Russian invasion of Ukraine, the average cost of gas in the United States had already climbed from $2.38 per gallon on the eve of his inauguration to $3.67 per gallon—a 54% increase.[70] By mid-May, 2022, this surge was reaching record and painfully high levels across the country, with the price of regular unleaded topping $4 in all fifty states for the first time in history.[71]

My sister sent me a photo she took of the Union 76 station in Beverly Hills, on May 13, 2022: the price for self-serve regular unleaded was $6.849 per gallon, with full serve premium at a jaw-dropping $8.199 per gallon. This rising cost of gas was not only felt by Americans filling their vehicles to go to work, to church, to school, or to just drive to the grocery store; it was also seen in increased prices for food and other items as truckers had to fill their tanks, maintain their vehicles (as prices on vehicles and vehicle parts were rising dramatically for the very same reasons), and so forth.

Was it all an accident? Astonishingly, some of my left-leaning friends were cheering the high price of gas, just as many of them had done during the Obama administration.[72] In reply to a photo of the Beverly Hills 76 station mentioned above, one commented, "Gas should be this expensive," and another left-leaning friend "liked" the comment.

What about the inflation overall? Economist John Maynard Keynes, a supporter of forceful wealth redistribution by government and thus loved by the American left, once described inflation thus: "By a continuing process of inflation, government can confiscate, secretly and unobserved, an important part of the wealth of their citizens."[73]

Banana Republic

At 6 a.m. on April 28, 2021, the apartment of former New York mayor Rudy Giuliani, a lead attorney for Donald Trump in the election challenges, was raided by federal agents. They seized his cellphone and other devices.[74] Alan Dershowitz days later likened the raid to actions in totalitarian regimes: "In banana republics, in Castro's Cuba, in many parts of the world when a candidate loses for president, they go after the candidate, they go after his lawyers, they go after his friends. That's happening in America now. They're going after Rudy Giuliani." Dershowitz recognized it as political theater designed to harm associates of Trump:

> "A search warrant on a lawyer or a doctor or a priest? You don't use search warrants. You don't use search warrants when people have privileged information on their cell phones and in their computers. You use a subpoena.

The difference between a subpoena and a search warrant is like night and day .... It's just not constitutional."[75]

But that was not all. On Monday, August 8, 2022, the FBI raided Donald Trump's home in Mar-a-Lago. Merrick Garland—whose nomination to the Supreme Court was stalled by Republicans in the final year of the Obama administration and passed over by Trump before Joe Biden appointed him attorney general in 2021—defended the raid of the former president's house, stating that he "personally approved" it. When the administration was pressed to give a reason,[76] an allegation that classified documents were suspected to have been removed from the White House by Trump was forthcoming. Garland on August 11 stated to the press that the Justice Department "does not take such [a decision for an FBI raid] lightly," but that it always seeks to use a "less intrusive means as an alternative to a search, and to narrowly scope any search that is undertaken."[77] The Washington Post shortly after Garland's press conference reported that confidential sources said the raid had been looking for documents related to nuclear codes.[78] However, neither explanation makes sense. Disagreements with the National Archives and Trump had been happening for months, and Trump had been cooperating with the authorities in the process. Why the sudden need for a high profile raid on the home of a U.S. president, while he was not present? Furthermore, if the nuclear code scenario is entertained, are Americans to believe that authorities waited months while *nuclear codes* were at risk before finally going in to secure them? And, what possible motive would Trump have to take such documents with him, anyway?

On a somewhat more rational note, Margot Cleveland contemplated four more likely possibilities. First, that the authorities who ordered the operation were so thoroughly siloed and shielded from the real world that they were oblivious to how the public would actually react. Cleveland asks, "How could the DOJ and FBI not anticipate the visceral reaction a broad swath of America would have to the Biden administration's DOJ initiating a raid against a former commander-in-chief and the Democrat's main political opponent?" The answer is that the FBI has fallen prey to politically correct groupthink, with dissent unwelcome. Cocooned in such an environment, they simply were out of touch with America. Second, Cleveland suspects that those who ordered the FBI raid hoped it might spur protests that could then be manipulated to make Trump supporters look like violent extremists. Third, the raid could have been an attempt to keep Donald Trump from running for office again. Democrat lawyer Marc Elias (the one who had commissioned the Steele dossier) pushed a theory out soon after the raid that Trump could not run again if he had unlawfully concealed records after leaving office. Finally, and in my opinion extremely likely, she postulates a fishing expedition: the Biden FBI could have used the pretext of the raid to rifle through seized documents in the hopes of finding something—anything—that might be spun to support the January 6 committee's flagging campaign to portray Trump as having incited the riots of January 6. Or, for that matter, anything else that could be used to criminally prosecute Trump for something, in order to avert the looming prospect of his return to the White House.[79]

Dystopian Reality

The upshot of everything detailed above is that after installing Joe Biden and Kamala Harris in office, the United States began to feel somewhat like the alternate world that unfolds in the movie *Back to the Future II*, when an elderly Biff Tannen from 2015 hijacks the time machine and delivers an almanac of sporting results to his younger self in 1955. The windfall empowers the younger Biff to make millions betting on winners and to transform the world into a living nightmare—at least for everyone not a friend of Biff Tannen. One tragedy of the situation in the United States after 2020 is that the Biden presidency never needed to happen in the first place, since it was not what the American people chose (see Chapter 3 and Conclusion).

The 2016 Silent Coup Ends In A Whimper

In November of 2021, following five years of gross malfeasance, the Washington Post finally retracted some of its key assertions about the Steele Dossier, a collection of opposition research paid for by the Hillary Clinton campaign which had become the sole basis for the FISA court's grant of a warrant to the FBI for the 2016 surveillance of the Trump campaign on behalf of the eventual president's political enemies.[80]

Media critic Erik Wemple also sharply rebuked CNN for their stubbornly-maintained claims of having independently verified parts of the dossier. Wemple noted that analyst Igor Danchenko—a key source for the dossier—had fabricated one source and used a Democrat operative as another.[81] So persuaded had they been that Trump and his team were dirty, his opponents manufactured a warrant for a fishing expedition. Aside from the enormous irony of the situation—considering that the operation was conducted on behalf of Hillary Clinton, one of the most corrupt figures in modern American politics[82]—the fact that the FISA court could be co-opted by political operatives constitutes, as Mark Levin observed, a "silent coup d'etat" attempt, and "One of the greatest scandals in American history."[83]

We may be variously astonished, disappointed, and outraged that media businesses like CNN and the Washington Post were so late to the party and even then so anemic with their *mea culpas* concerning incorrect reports that competent journalists had known to be so years earlier, but perhaps we should not waste our breath.

Prior Events: The First Impeachment of Donald Trump

Donald Trump, a billionaire businessman in commercial real estate and more recently the star of a reality TV show, was not part of the political establishment. From the start he was recognized, by insider Democrats and Republicans alike, to pose a unique threat—while at the same time pretending to dismiss him as a joke. Donald Trump was, in fact, "the first person without government or military experience ever to be elected president of the United States."[84]

And in another historic first, a U.S. president's political opponents announced their intention to impeach him when he had yet to take a single official action as president. A *Washington Post* article on January 20, 2017, the very day of his inauguration, proclaimed, "The campaign to impeach President Trump has begun."[85]

At inauguration, the impeachment efforts had every appearance of an outcome in search of a reason. Among the early proposed pretexts for removal was the fact that Trump continued to own his hotel and golf course businesses while in office. Another rested upon the "Russian collusion" theory based entirely on the Steele Dossier just mentioned.

One website, impeachdonaldtrumpnow.org—at the time of this writing an archive of the early campaign to remove Trump—lists various alleged grounds for impeachment.[86]

However, neither the initial pretext ("Russian collusion," presumably referenced in point 3 on the above list) nor most of the other theories—being either disconnected from reality in terms of Trump's actions[87] or misinformed concerning the legitimate powers of the office[88]—bore fruit for the President's critics.

A real action seeking removal of President Trump, however, did not take long to materialize. In July of 2017, Democrat Congressmen Al Green and Brad Sherman introduced an impeachment article for "High Crimes and Misdemeanors." Their allegation was that Trump's firing of his FBI Director James Comey on May 9, 2017 constituted an obstruction of justice. No U.S. president is subject to FBI oversight, and any president may hire and fire his agency heads at any time and for any reason. FBI directors serve at the pleasure of the President. There had been nothing inappropriate about Trump firing Comey. In fact, the President's top advisers had urged him[89] to send Comey home far sooner, since he had clearly been working—in concert with outgoing President Barack Obama and Vice

President Joe Biden[90]—to undermine Trump and his policy priorities.[91] It therefore came as no great surprise when this first impeachment resolution failed 58-364 in the House, a poor showing even with Democrats in the slight minority.

By 2019, the picture was different. Democrats had taken control of the House of Representatives in the 2018 midterm election. Even so, Speaker Nancy Pelosi, apparently sensing political danger and possible unintended consequences, rebuffed calls to move forward on impeachment for several months, fearing it "too divisive."[92] In the end, however, she gave in to pressure from within her party and moved forward with an impeachment inquiry.

The would-be impeachers initially pinned their hopes upon a conspiracy theory rooted in materials (namely, the aforementioned Steele Dossier) known to have been fraudulently presented to the FBI as intelligence by individuals with undisclosed connections to the Democratic National Committee and the Hillary Clinton campaign.[93] These materials alleged various sordid claims about the President which, if true, would have indeed been devastating. However, the Steele Dossier was nothing but opposition research and its most sensational claims political fabrications.[94] By November 2021, even CNN was compelled to admit that

> multiple US government inquiries uncovered dozens of contacts between Trump campaign associates and Russians ... .Still, none of it added up to the collusion suggested in Steele's memos. Legitimate questions are now being raised about the dossier—how it was used by Democrats as a political weapon against Trump, how it was handled by the FBI and US intelligence agencies, and how it was portrayed in the mainstream media.[95]

A full description of the development of Democrats' efforts to impeach Donald Trump is beyond the scope of this book, and I mention the above background merely to place some prior context around what was happening when the 2020 election cycle was in motion.

Democrats, ironically, impeached Trump for alleged abuse of the power of the presidency, a charge that was questionable with respect to Trump, but almost certainly true with respect to Joe Biden and Hillary Clinton. In fact, it was ostensibly an actual pursuit of justice in relation to Biden and his family dealings which gave rise to the impeachment inquiry against Trump. It seemed a new twist on the tactic of loudly accusing your political opponent of what you are doing or intend to do. The strategy also appears to have been used in the election itself, as will be discussed further in Chapters 3 and 8. Mark Levin remarked on national-level Democrats' actions in the days immediately following the election,

They believe in flooding the system, create chaos. They've done this in the number of places. Grab power, and then accuse your opponent of misbehavior.

Where does that come from? Two Marxist professors, Cloward and Piven, that was their ideology. The Democrats have embraced this for years and years.[96]

Cloward and Piven, husband and wife, wrote with great fondness of Karl Marx, taking pains to explain why he was right even though his predictions had failed, and to defend Marx and his theories as originally formulated.[97] They decried efforts to extend welfare to only those who were actually qualified for it, on grounds that "low ineligibility levels can be achieved only at the price of keeping much larger proportions of eligible families off the rolls," and mocked efforts to limit "welfare cheaters," characterizing such efforts as "anti-welfare."[98] Cloward and Piven lamented the fact that under efforts to rein in abuse, "the militancy of the welfare poor all but vanished."[99] Elsewhere, they wrote,

> It is our purpose which affords the basis for a convergence of civil rights organizations, militant anti-poverty groups and the poor. If this strategy were implemented, a political crisis would result that could lead to legislation for a guaranteed annual income ... the strategy we propose, is a massive drive to recruit the poor *onto* the welfare rolls ... . Widespread campaigns to register the eligible poor for welfare aid, and to help existing recipients obtain their full benefits, would produce bureaucratic disruption in welfare agencies and fiscal disruption in local and state governments. These disruptions would generate severe political strains, and deepen existing divisions ... . By the internal disruption of local bureaucratic practices, by the furor over public welfare poverty, and by the collapse of current financing arrangements, powerful forces can be generated for major economic reforms at the national level. The ultimate objective of this strategy—to wipe out poverty by establishing a guaranteed annual income—will be questioned by some ... . The ultimate aim of this strategy is a new program for direct income distribution.[100]

Piven's and Cloward's plan is thus to collapse the system in order to force their socialist vision upon Americans. Later in the article just quoted, they insist that efforts to increase opportunity and economic mobility in order to help people become economically competitive is not desirable; they push, rather, for simple wealth redistribution. They argue strongly against requiring attendance of classes or rehabilitation, or work, as conditions for receiving welfare. In short, Piven and Cloward aim to create a growing class of people without hope of improvement and therefore permanently dependent upon government, loyal to those politicians promising to keep and expand such initiatives:

> [L]egislative measures to provide direct income to the poor would permit national Democratic leaders to cultivate ghetto constituencies .... And those seeking new ways to engage the Negro politically should remember that public resources have always been the fuel for low-income urban political organization. If organizers can deliver millions of dollars in cash benefits to the ghetto masses, it seems reasonable that the masses will deliver their loyalties to their benefactors. At least, they have always done so in the past.[101]

The quotation above is not from a conservative critic of the Democrats, but from two committed Marxists whose words have for decades constituted virtual holy writ, almost a procedure manual, for prominent Democrat politicians.

Democrats' first impeachment article against President Trump for "abuse of power" faulted him for seeking to have Ukrainian allies of the United States look into corruption in which former Vice President Joe Biden appeared to have used the power of his office to avoid exposure of corruption in his own family. As already mentioned, Biden's son Hunter was hired by the Ukrainian energy firm Burisma to sit on their board, and paid an enormous monthly sum, with a portion allegedly earmarked for "the big guy," his father. In 2016, Joe Biden forced the removal of anti-corruption prosecutor Viktor Shokin, by threatening to withhold $1B in U.S. aid to Ukraine. He later bragged publicly about his threat and its success in forcing this outcome.[102] Democrat partisans, however, shielded Biden and blamed President Trump for seeking to harm a political rival by encouraging the Ukrainians to get to the bottom of this matter.

Like Hillary Clinton after violating U.S. Code § 793 (f) when Secretary of State[103] and Lois Lerner after using the IRS to target political opponents of the Obama administration,[104] Joe and Hunter Biden—astonishingly—evaded prosecution for their evident corruption and influence peddling. The matter might have been swept completely under the rug had Hillary won the 2016 election, as the Washington machine apparently anticipated. But when Donald Trump won instead, the Bidens, among many others, quickly took steps to protect themselves. Their standard strategy of diversion by loudly accusing the *other* party of what the accusers were actually doing, planned to do, or—as in this case—had already done, was immediately set into motion.

Presidential impeachments in U.S. history

Impeachment is a political process for the removal of a sitting U.S. president. Three presidents have been impeached thus far: Andrew Johnson (1868), Bill Clinton (1998), and Donald Trump (2019 and 2021).

Bill Clinton faced four articles of impeachment in 1998. Two of them succeeded, but *all four* received votes in support of impeachment from members of Clinton's own party. In fact, on each of three of the articles (perjury before the grand jury, perjury in the Jones case, and obstruction of justice), two of which were successful, *five* congressional Democrats voted in favor of impeachment. In other words, Bill Clinton's impeachment was bipartisan, despite the fact that Republicans would have had enough votes to successfully impeach him (at least on the first article) without a single Democrat crossover.

In contrast to the impeachment of Bill Clinton, not one Republican voted to impeach President Trump in 2019. On December 18, Trump was impeached by Democrats alone on two articles. Indeed, while the vote to impeach Trump was entirely partisan, the vote to *not* impeach him was bipartisan. Two Democrats joined Republicans in voting against impeachment on the first article—abuse of power—and three Democrats joined the Republicans in voting against the second article, obstruction of Congress. As such, the first impeachment of Trump was thoroughly partisan. Donald Trump was also the first non-Democrat president to be impeached.[105]

Both articles of impeachment against Trump somewhat predictably—though one must never take such outcomes for granted—failed in the Senate. Trump was acquitted on February 5, 2020.

Why People Doubted the Narrative

On March 10, 2022, actor and singer Jussie Smollett was convicted on five felony counts and sentenced to five months in prison followed by 25 months' probation. He was also fined $25,000 (the statutory maximum) and ordered to pay $120,000 in restitution to the City of Chicago.[106] His crime? In January of 2019, he staged a fake attack upon himself, and then reported to police that it had been done by guys wearing "MAGA" ("Make America Great Again," Trump's campaign slogan) gear, and saying "MAGA country." Fortunately, Smollett was careless and left a long trail of evidence of his lie. His accomplices, the "attackers," were two Nigerian brothers who had worked with him as extras on the TV show *Empire*. He paid them with a $3,500 check.[107]

At Smollett's sentencing, the judge delivered a "scathing 30-minute monologue" which included the following comments,

You've destroyed your life as you knew it. There is nothing any sentencing judge could do to compare to the damage you've already done. ... Your very name has become an adverb for lying.[108]

The case was emblematic of the experience of Trump and his supporters. Smollett had put up a contrived and false narrative about Trump's supporters matching the cartoonish image preferred by the left, and his story was dutifully reported as fact by a partisan media. The slander would have been successful but for Smollett's own incompetence. In the end, the saga exposed a national media eager to portray Trump in a negative light.

Even with clear evidence of guilt (the later December 2021 jury rendered their sweeping verdict in a single day), the charges against Smollett were dropped in 2019. The charges were restored only after appointment of a special prosecutor tasked with finding out *why* the charges were dropped. This scenario became another example of media and government bias, with Democrats (such as Joe and Hunter Biden, Hillary Clinton, Lois Lerner, and Smollett) regularly presumed innocent or not prosecuted, and Republicans (such as Nick Sandmann of Covington Catholic High School,[109] Trump supporters waved into the Capitol by Capitol Police on January 6, or even Trump himself) routinely facing vicious and immediate campaigns of destruction and presumption of guilt. A long succession of such double standards by media and government grated at Americans' sense of fairness.

QUESTIONS

1. List major changes in the United States (for example, in the economy, national security, freedom and protection of civil liberties, or rule of law) after Joe Biden took office. What actions might have contributed to those changes?

2. What was the "Silent Coup" referenced in this chapter? Who contributed to it? What were its effects on its target(s)? What were its effects on the nation?

3. What was the negative "narrative" about Trump and his supporters leveled by his critics? What were some reasons people doubted it? Can you think of other reasons not mentioned above?

---

1. In 2021 and into 2022, the terms "attack on our democracy" and "insurrection" as descriptors of the January 6, 2021 events at the U.S. Capitol became standard talking points of Democrats in major media such as CNN, ABC, MSNBC, and others. As I have already discussed in the Introduction, use of both terms in relation to January 6 was strained and misapplied.

2. "A new poll from Rasmussen indicates that a majority of U.S. voters believe cheating impacted the 2020 election results." Austin, "Poll."

3. "The Child Tax Credit: Legislative History," *Congressional Research Service*, Updated December 23, 2021; Betsy McCaughey, "Democrats Reject Work Ethic, Embrace Freeloaders," *Epoch Times*, December 29, 2021; Steven A. Camarota, "Illegal Immigrants Get $10.5 Billion from Child Tax Credit in Reconciliation; More than Previously Estimated: Illegals with both U.S.-born & illegal immigrant children will benefit, as will recent bordercrossers," *Center for Immigration Studies*, November 9, 2021; Peter A. Schulkin, "Child Tax Credits for Illegal Immigrants," *Center for Immigration Studies*, November 8, 2021; Emil Akan, "COVID-19 Relief Measures Make US Tax System 'More Progressive': Tax Foundation," *Epoch Times*, August 22, 2021.

4. Erica York, "Summary of the Latest Federal Income Tax Data, 2020 Update," *Tax Foundation*, February 20, 2020.

5. Adam Michel, "In 1 Chart, How Much the Rich Pay in Taxes," *Heritage Foundation*, March 3, 2021. Figures are based upon federal income taxes and adjusted gross income earned in 2018. The bottom 50% of earners pay only 3% of all the nation's income taxes.

6. Tom Ozimek, "Biden Says Next Month's Child Tax Credit Payments 'Just the First Step' as He Seeks to Make Benefit Permanent," *Epoch Times*, June 22, 2021.

7. Alice Ollstein, Arjun Kakkar, and Beatrice Jin, "The 17 things Joe Biden did on Day One: Through executive orders, he overturned Trump's policies—and started making his own," *Politico*, January 21, 2021; "Biden sets to work on reversing Trump policies with executive orders," *BBC News*, January 21, 2021.

8. John T. Woolley, and Gerhard Peters, "Biden in Action: the First 100 Days," *American Presidency Project*, April 30, 2021.

9. David Marcus, "Biden introduces door-to-door vaccination effort," *New York Post*, July 6, 2021; Erin Schumaker, "New 'medical freedom' law outlaws requiring COVID-19 vaccine to access public spaces," *ABC News*, July 26, 2021; Steven Nelson, "Biden orders federal workers to get COVID vaccine or submit to testing," *New York Post*, July 29, 2021; "Inslee issues proclamation requiring vaccination for most state employees, health and long-term care workers," Office of Washington Governor Jay Inslee, August 9, 2021; Maria Caspani, and Julia Harte, "New York City mandates COVID-19 vaccine for teachers in largest U.S. school district," *Reuters*, August 23, 2021; Olivia Cavallaro, "As Expected, Biden Administration Now Pushing Forced Vaccinations Following FDA Approval of Pfizer Jab," *Christianity Daily*, August 24, 2021.

10. "Path out of the Pandemic: President Biden's COVID-19 Action Plan," White House; Brittany Bernstein, "Biden Announces Plan to Require Large Companies to Mandate COVID Vaccines," *National Review*, September 9, 2021; "Biden's Desperate COVID Overreach," *National Review,* September 9, 2021; Remarkably, open discussion of firing employees who refuse COVID-19 vaccination began within weeks of the vaccine first becoming available to the public: MacKenzie Sigalos, "Yes, your boss can fire you if you refuse to get a Covid (sic) vaccine," *CNBC*, December 7, 2020.

11. I was among the parents in Loudoun County, Virginia who were regularly petitioning the school board. Loudoun County Public Schools were the tip of the spear in the national discussion around these matters. An LCPS father, I spoke at the now-famous June 22, 2021 meeting at which two citizens were arrested after public comment was shut down.

12. Burk, Eric, "Virginia School Board Association Withdraws from National Association that Asked Biden to Use Federal Agencies to Respond to Threats," *Virginia Star*, November 23, 2021; Boyd, Jordan, "Ridiculous AP 'Fact Check' Claims School Boards Association Didn't Ask Biden To Label Parents As 'Domestic Terrorists,'" *Federalist*, October 6, 2021; Ali Linan, "Texas sues Biden for education memo labeling parents 'domestic terrorists,'" *Herald Banner*, March 4, 2022; National School Boards Association, Letter to Joseph R. Biden, September 29, 2021. In February of 2022, months after the NSBA scandal, reports emerged about threats of violence against school board members, including photographs of notes received by mail. Of course, no elected public servant should face a credible threat (much less the reality) of violence. Reports I reviewed failed to mention whether notes received by school board members had been subjected to forensic analysis or otherwise judged authentic, although Reuters confirmed that "these threats often come from people out of state with no connection to the districts involved." My strong suspicion is that the worst were sent by leftist groups or individuals (perhaps teacher unions or others) to support a narrative of dangerous parents. Such events happen in Loudoun County periodically

during election season, as flyers purporting to be from the KKK or some white supremacist group appear on doorsteps, leading to local papers reporting a "resurgence of white supremacy in Loudoun County," which is then blamed on conservatives. Gabriella Borter, Joseph Ax, and Joseph Tanfani, "School boards get death threats amid rage over race, gender, mask policies," *Reuters*, February 15, 2022.

13. "'No Forgiveness for People Like You' Executions and Enforced Disappearances in Afghanistan under the Taliban," *Human Rights Watch*, November 30, 2021; Yaron Steinbuch, "US volunteer claims Taliban beheaded boys ages 9 and 10 in Afghanistan," *New York Post*, September 15, 2021; Will Berkovitz, "Afghan allies in hiding, executed in the street — Jewish people know this haunting story," *USA Today*, September 9, 2021; Krayden, David, "Former Navy SEAL Who Killed Bin Laden Claims Taliban Are Torturing Families Of Afghans Allies 'Before They Cut Their Heads Off,'" *Daily Caller*, September 9, 2021; Siddharthya Roy, and Richard Miniter, "Taliban kill squad hunting down Afghans—using US biometric data," *New York Post*, August 27, 2021; Robert Spencer, "13 Americans Killed in Kabul: 'We did it, Joe!,'" *Frontpage Mag*, August 27, 2021; Liz George, "Biden Admin gave Taliban a list of American, Afghan evacuees' names: Politico," *American Military News*, August 26, 2021; Anna Coren, Sandi Sidhu, Abul Basir Bina, and Hilary Whiteman, "The Taliban knocked on her door 3 times. The fourth time, they killed her," *CNN*, August 18, 2021; Toby Luckhurst, "Taliban 'carrying out door-to-door manhunt,'" *BBC News*, August 15, 2021; David Williams, and Mark Nicol, "Military translator, 30, who helped US soldiers in Afghanistan is beheaded by the Taliban sparking new alarm for the interpreters left as the West withdraws," *Daily Mail*, July 25, 2021.

14. "Blinken: 100 U.S. citizens in Afghanistan want to leave," *Yahoo News US*, September 13, 2021; Katelyn Caralle, "Antony Blinken rejects comparison of Afghanistan to Saigon and blames 'inability of Afghan security forces' for Taliban takeover as Republicans say the buck stops with Biden," *Daily Mail*, August 15, 2021.

15. Michael Starr, "Herein 'Lies' the Tale of Baghdad Bob," *New York Post*, April 9, 2003.

16. Emily Crane, "The cost of the Afghanistan war: Lives, money and equipment lost," *New York Post*, August 31, 2021; Rebecca Kheel, "Billions in US weaponry seized by Taliban," *Hill*, August 21, 2021; Adam Andrzejewski, "Staggering Costs—U.S. Military Equipment Left Behind In Afghanistan." *Forbes*, August 23, 2021; Lee Brown, "Taliban has billions in US weapons, including Black Hawks and up to 600K rifles," *New York Post*, August 20, 2021. Some of Biden's supporters argued that his hands had been tied by Trump's negotiated deal with the Taliban to withdraw by April 2021. However, the claim seems to fail on at least two counts: First, Biden did not, in fact, keep Trump's deal, but rather arbitrarily extended the deadline by four months, a decision that angered the Taliban and precipitated a re-escalation of hostilities on the part of the latter after 18 months of relative peace. Second, Biden had clearly not felt constrained to keep other deals cut by Donald Trump (Paris Climate Accord, Iran Deal, etc.), and, therefore, his decision to follow through on the Afghanistan withdrawal must be owned by him. We will now never know how Trump would have handled the matter. However, even critical observers admitted that Trump would have first seen to the safety of Americans and Afghan allies, to the extraction of all equipment and weaponry prior to an ultimate withdrawal, and that the "Art of the Deal" author would have held his negotiating partners to their commitments using a combination of carrot and stick.

17. Struan Stevenson, "Taliban's windfall from U.S. withdrawal: $83B in weapons." *United Press International*, September 20, 2021.

18. John Friberg, "Investigation on Abbey Gate Bombing HKIA August 2021," *Afghan Report*, February 5, 2022.

19. Jon Dougherty, "Bomber who killed 13 U.S. soldiers at Kabul airport released from Bagram prison by Taliban thanks to Biden's plan; report," *BizPacReview*, September 20, 2021.

20. Lolita C. Baldor, and Robert Burns, "US drone strike kills 2 Islamic State members in Afghanistan," *Associated Press*, August 27, 2021.

21. Caitlin Doornbos, "DoD Inspector General Launches Investigation into Kabul Drone Strike that Killed 10 Civilians," *Stars and Stripes*, September 24, 2021; Robert Burns, "Pentagon admits deadly Kabul strike was an error," *Associated Press*, Septermber 17, 2021.

22. Kathy Gannon, "Taliban official: Strict punishment, executions will return," *Associated Press*, September 23, 2021.

23. Houston Keene, "Dem Sen. Tim Kaine rips Biden admin's claim that nobody forecasted rapid Afghanistan fall," *Fox News*, September 14, 2021.

24. "Excerpts of call between Joe Biden and Ashraf Ghani July 23," *Reuters*, August 31, 2021; Rob Crilly, and Ariel Zilber, "As Biden repeats claim that 'nobody could have known' Afghan Army would collapse, bombshell transcript from July reveals he pressured Afghan President Ghani to create 'perception' Taliban wasn't winning 'WHETHER IT'S TRUE OR NOT.'" *Daily Mail*, August 31, 2021.

25. Ibid.

26. Holly Ellyatt, "Russian forces invade Ukraine," *CNBC*, February 24, 2022.

27. Margaret Brennan, and Christina Ruffini, "U.S. preparing to withdraw all personnel from Ukraine capital within 48 hours, sources say," *CBS News*, February 13, 2022.

28. "Australia to withdraw staff from Kiev embassy," *Teletrader News*, February 12, 2022.

29. Vivek Saxena, "Gen. Milley claims Ukraine capital Kyiv would fall within 72 hours of Russian invasion: report," *BizPacReview*, February 6, 2022.

30. "LIVE Russian attack on Ukraine: Number of reported casualties rises, EU prepares massive sanctions," *Norway Today*, February 24, 2022; "Ukraine conflict: Russian forces invade after Putin TV declaration," *BBC*, February 24, 2022.

31. Like so many others, I am disturbed by recent Russian actions in Ukraine. I have made five good visits to Russia over the past decade, and am grateful in particular for special visas that allowed me to carry out academic research at the National Library of Russia, the Kunstkamera Museum, and the Institute of Oriental Manuscripts. I do hope to spend more time in these places in coming years with the Russian government's permission. So, my criticism of what I understand to be an injustice is not absent personal affection for the countries and the people on both sides.

32. Andrea Shalal, "Biden warns Putin: Russia will pay 'terrible price' if it invades Ukraine," *Reuters*, December 11, 2021.

33. Ann Saphir, and Lindsay Dunsmuir, "Biden's Fed nominees back U.S. inflation fight," *Reuters*, February 3, 2022.

34. My thanks to Olga Garber for laying out these details.

35. Adam Isacson, "Weekly U.S.-Mexico Border Update: Remain in Mexico restarts, drug seizures, caravans," *WOLA*, December 3, 2021; Nick Miroff, and Kevin Sieff, "Mexico to allow US 'Remain in Mexico' asylum policy to resume," *The Boston Globe*, December 2, 2021; Zachary Stieber, "Biden Administration Blames Delay in Restarting 'Remain in Mexico' Program on Mexico," *Epoch Times*, September 17, 2021. In August of 2021, the U.S. Supreme Court upheld a lower court's ruling that Biden's ending of MPP was "arbitrary and capricious," and thus in violation of federal law. However, the ordered resumption of the policy, now requiring renegotiation with Mexico, did not occur immediately. By December, Mexico had agreed to reinstitute a modified version of the program which among other things required legal counsel be provided to asylum seekers.

36. Edgar Moreno, and Edgar H. Clemente, "New migrant caravan sets off from southern Mexico border," *Associated Press*, November 18, 2021; Melanie Sun, "2,000-Person Caravan Surges Past Mexican Riot Police Near Guatemala Border," *Epoch Times*, October 24, 2021.

37. "FACT SHEET: The Biden Administration Blueprint for a Fair, Orderly and Humane Immigration System," White House Briefing Room, July 27, 2021.

38. Fred Lucas, "Why Illegal Immigrants Are Being Released Without Court Dates," *Daily Signal*, June 25, 2021; Nick Miroff, "At border, record number of migrant youths wait in adult detention cells for longer than legally allowed," *Washington Post*, March 10, 2021. "Under catch and release, when the Border Patrol issues a notice to appear for a future date in immigration court, the overwhelming majority of illegal immigrants do not complete the court and adjudication process ... ," "The entire system is turned on its head with catch and release. This is the definition of open borders ... . This is just an indication of a system in collapse."

39. Kyle Morris, "White House responds to migrant transport: 'No such thing as secret flights;'" Gina Martinez, "Leaked video shows illegal migrants landing at Westchester airport on secret charter flight - one of DOZENS carried out on orders of Biden administration: 'The government is betraying the American people,'" *Daily Mail*, January 27, 2022.

40. Mark Moore, "Nearly a thousand illegal immigrants held under a bridge in Texas, video shows," *New York Post*, August 2, 2021.

41. Callie Patteson, "10K+ illegal migrants mass in Texas as Biden FAA bans news drones," *New York Post*, September 17, 2021.

42. Ibid.

43. A friend who works for DHS, name withheld. Personal correspondence, July 28, 2021.
"Many here believe that non-citizen voting has allowed for very liberal city council
members to get voted in to office in small cities that sit on the border with Mexico like San
Ysidro, Chula Vista, Otay, National City and Palm City. All those cities are here in San
Diego County and are separately incorporated but frequently act together in 'Brown Soli-
darity'. The same holds true for local school boards here that are almost hysterical in their
support for Critical Race Theory. Our public schools along the border are inundated with
kids from Mexico whose parents drive them to the border where they simply walk across
on the Obama era 'Friendship Bridge' to where school buses wait to pick them up on the
U.S. side, and off to school they go. Their parents don't pay taxes to support the school
districts and the kids are almost impossible to discipline, many of whose parents are
involved in some way with the Cartels in Tijuana. This creates a huge tax burden for the
parents of American kids, causing massive overcrowding in classrooms and physical
bullying of white kids who are often blamed for just about anything because the school
administrators are brown or black liberals and white people are bad ... .

"Bonita Middle-School is now notorious for its violence. California gives money to
school districts based on numbers of students in a district so the illegal kids don't get
reported and expelled by the administration for the purpose of increasing State funding. If
a whistleblower does speak up, it ends their career in education, at least in California. My
church has its own State accredited school district, Christian School District located in El
Cajon, that has become an island of sanity but now unfortunately overwhelmed by
applications for admittance. More than a year's waiting list to get in for every grade K
through 12.

"Officials on local water boards, water boards that are very important here in the west,
are also elected. Not very political as far as elected positions go but are often used as spring
boards to more public and partisan elected positions, like city council positions and school
boards. Getting voted on to the water board one or two times shows whatever party you
are affiliated with that you are electable and gives you campaign experience so the party
leaders are more likely to fund and support your campaigns for higher office. The noncitizen vote is crucial in most of these low level elections because most of the Americans
who are residents of the water districts live out in the back country and are white and
usually conservative so illegals who live in the canyons and park areas, which are of course
no longer safe, can turn an election in favor of an otherwise unelectable leftist candidate.
In such small communities even two votes can change an election.

"The effect on these small communities is the disenfranchisement of the majority of
citizen voters and ultimately an adverse influence on how their children are educated,
often against their own race, history and economic interests. Because these communities
are usually only a few hundred people who have even fewer lawful voters, sometimes as
few as 100, there is little to no interest in investigating allegations of voter fraud by either
the State or Federal DOJs. Not politically useful or cost effective enough to investigate so
the liberals grind away at the most basic level of our democracy. I'm not joking when I say
it's really quite remarkable how the huge fires we have out here can literally change the
voting demographics of some communities when the canyons and parks burn out. You get
the picture. What's so irritating is that liberal politicians here don't at all try to hide it,
sometimes even smirking into the camera when a local news reporter brings up voter
fraud. They usually respond with the racist, conspiracy nut, white supremacist, crazy white
cowboys who live in festering inbred ignorance out in the woods baloney.

"Most of the illegal aliens who cross over here in San Diego County come from countries that are socialist and have been that way since the 1930s so they naturally tend to vote
left. Democrats are eager to pick these 'voters' up and are really good at making Republicans and conservatives, especially white conservatives, appear to be of the same character
as the political elites they ran away from in their countries of origin. In many Latin American countries the lighter your skin, or the more 'Spanish' you look the higher your social
status and greater the opportunities for advancement. The browner you look, or the Indio
skin color, or as locals more precisely put it, 'if you have a cactus in your face' the lower
your social status so the connection, however fallacious, works on illegals.

"The closer you get to the border the fewer rights white people have but no one will
speak up. Crime against whites has escalated over the years so that now in parts of Southeast and East San Diego it's not safe for white people to be there after dark, including the
police. Whites have closed up businesses and moved to other parts of the county where

they are still safe. It's somewhat like being white in South Africa, if you even say the word 'white' in connection with just about anything while in a border community like Otay or San Ysidro, people will literally draw back in fear or anger as if somehow you have said something dangerous and repulsive...

"One stand out for focused anger here is white, Evangelical Protestants and in particular the women in that group. They are the most likely to experience physical assault from non-white people when in south and southeast San Diego, especially if they are at all physically attractive. Assaults usually are by other non-white women who try to cut up the faces of the white women or by non-white men who will just beat them down. Democrats here are really good at contrasting 'Del Sur' or southern brown Roman Catholics with 'Del Norte' or northern White Protestants and beating the drum of revisionist history regarding the westward expansion of the United States. Many Mexicans and what we term OTMs or Other Than Mexican, a term used by ICE to create statistical data on countries of origin so CBP can return illegals if they get a deportation order, also have a grudge against 'White America' and see voting illegally as a revolutionary act of defiance. That's a big draw used by more educated and elitist American Latinos to get illegals to vote. This is also popular on local college campuses, especially on Southwestern Community College which is heavily attended by illegals in their early 20's, the rhetoric on voting can sound pretty violent.

"Next we have the small but growing radical leftist group calling itself 'Bronze Nation' which is new but starting to gain popularity. They literally have voter guides, also filled with their racist propaganda which the local media ignores, for illegals that they pass out at CBP Detention during the election cycles when illegals are released from ICE custody. That is until the local police are called and they get ticketed for trespassing on Federal property or leave voluntarily. Bronze Nation wants to forcibly expel anyone who is not of Latino or Hispanic origin from all of the southwest they describe as; Texas, New Mexico, Arizona, and California, which, like the Palestinian PLA they use as a business model, they consider 'occupied territory' and refuse to obey U.S. laws and recognize the Constitution. They want to set up a socialist nation open to only brown people of the correct origin. Blacks and Arabs need not apply but can still be part of the revolution if they are willing to contribute blood and treasure. This appeals to local black separatists who also want a separate nation for only black people. This also appeals to some illegals who want to recreate, in some magical way, an idealized replication of the failed state they ran away from. Crazy but they are out there.

"They all have a similar mindset to the Sovereign Citizen movement but are better organized and far more dangerous. They use the old trope of 'White Law for White America' regarding Federal laws and the Constitution. The perfect storm; race, religion, history and politics, much of which illegals now get connected to for the first time while in ICE custody. Most of them had no idea of the political atmosphere here but now they do. Thank you Kamala Harris, who while still a Senator here in California made it clear she hated white people and said publicly many needed to [be] hunted down and made to pay for unspecified crimes. Radical Roman Catholic priests are all too happy to take part in the Biden Administration's illegal immigrant resettlement program who work with American immigration attorneys who go into Mexico to coach illegal immigrants on what to say to ICE to stay in the U.S. They also get a big dose of who wants them to stay and who wants to keep them out, naturally it's white Republicans vs. inclusive Democratic Socialists so they know who to vote for when the time comes. Oh yeah, throw in coaching on how to get welfare without a local address and you are churning out newly minted Democrats by the thousands.

"To get welfare just get a friend or relative already here with a local address, sign up for welfare and when the checks and your CBT card (Food shopping card) arrive, usually within 90 days, (Hey! Who can't live in a canyon for 90 days to get all that free stuff!?) have your mail forwarded to a P.O. Box you share with 20 or 30 other illegals, (SIDEBAR: Private postal businesses make a fortune in skimming off money from both renting the box for exorbitant fees per customer and also cashing their welfare checks. They also convert U.S. Dollars into Pesos or any other currency and wire it wherever it needs to go, yep, even to the middle-east, AND California now says you can use your CBT to buy alcohol if you are legally able to drink alcohol! Feeling no pain.) and you are good to go far into the future.

"Welfare in California is based on family numbers so if you have a child or children you naturally get more money. So, as long as there is no male over 18 years old in the household (don't worry, no one ever asks about it more than once) you get free money, free food, free school, free medical care, free pre-school education for the kids in whatever language you prefer which is required by law, no taxes, preferential status at the California Department of Employment Development if you 'choose' to work and often free housing. What's not to like? The housing can be, by American standards quite miserable, but it's better than what it was where they started. Just keep voting Democrat and it never stops. Don't worry about not having the right to vote, your candidate will be in office before the truth can be known and then it's too late.

"This narrative is literally what illegals are being told by liberals and other Democrats all in their native language to boot. None of the information being passed along to illegals is itself illegal, ironic as it seems, and nothing can be done about it from a law enforcement perspective. What is truly ironic, ICE is a majority non-white federal agency and most of our non-white personnel despise the Biden/Harris administration.

"Finally, we are releasing illegals into the U.S. who have tested positive for COVID-19, many of whom refuse to take the vaccine shots. We had almost 1200 single females in custody over the last year, housed separately from the men of course, and have released all of them into the wild, many who were never tested for COVID-19 because they have been coached they have the right to refuse any medical treatment and which they almost universally do. They don't want anything standing in the way of release and they have State and local legal aide standing by to make sure it all goes according to plan. We believe that many of them are (were) pregnant and want an anchor baby so no matter what happens they can't be deported because their child is a U.S. citizen. Another reason to 'vote' illegally for politicians who say 'Let them stay.' I'm not sure if any of this is news to you but these are the driving forces all along the southern border for why illegals always vote Democrat. These are things I have grown up with and which are now reaching a critical mass."

44. Abigail Adcox, "Leaked audio reveals DHS secretary's meeting with Border Patrol agents," *Washington Examiner*, January 26, 2022.
45. Patrick Goodenough, "79,678: December Border Encounters With Illegal Migrants Not From Mexico/Northern Triangle Up Tenfold," *CNS News*, January 25, 2022.
46. Ibid.
47. Rebecca Downs, "Kamala Harris Can't Be Bothered with Proper Border Visit, But She Did Go to Honduran President's Inauguration," *Townhall*, January 27, 2022; Steven Nelson, "Kamala Harris says her anti-illegal immigration efforts won't bear fruit 'overnight,'" *New York Post*, January 27, 2022; Fran Beyer, "VP Harris Under Fire for Lack of Attention to Border Crisis," *Newsmax*, September 20, 2021.
48. Harris announced in late 2021 "that she had raised $1.2 trillion from corporations across the globe to invest in Central American countries such as Guatemala, El Salvador, and others." Dale Wilcox, "Kamala's neglect of the border crisis is her greatest failure," *American Thinker*, December 24, 2021.
49. Ibid.
50. "Woman who can't define woman put on Supreme Court," *Ruth Institute*, April 7, 2022.
51. Brown Jackson was celebrated by the administration and national media as the first black woman on the Supreme Court.
52. David Ditch, Mike Gonzalez, Hans von Spakovsky, and Erin Dwinell, "President Biden's 'Equity Action Plans' Reveal Radical, Divisive Agenda," *Heritage Foundation*, May 25, 2022.
53. David Ditch, Mike Gonzalez, Hans von Spakovsky, and Erin Dwinell, "Biden Administration Implements a Racial Spoils System," *Daily Signal*, May 31, 2022.
54. Ibid.
55. Andrew Kerr, "Abortion rights group doxxes Supreme Court Justices, offers stipends for protests," *Washington Examiner*, May 5, 2022.
56. Melissa Quinn, and Scott MacFarlane, "Man arrested near Kavanaugh's home charged with attempting to murder Supreme Court justice," *CBS News*, June 9, 2022.
57. Tierney Sneed, Ariane de Vogue, and Joan Biskupic, "Supreme Court draft opinion that would overturn Roe v. Wade published by Politico," *CNN*, May 3, 2022.
58. John McCormack, "Schumer's Reckless Threats against Kavanaugh and Gorsuch," *National Review*, June 9, 2022.
59. Isaac Schorr, "New York Times Buries Kavanaugh Assassination Attempt on Page A20," *National Review*, June 9, 2022.

60. Houston Keene, "Biden yet to speak on alleged Kavanaugh assassination attempt 2 days after arrest," *Fox News*, June 10, 2022.

61. Ali Zaslav, Jessica Dean, and Ted Barrett, "Senators quickly pass bill to expand security for Supreme Court justices," *CNN*, May 9, 2022.

62. Katelyn Caralle, and Elizabeth Elkind, "Nancy Pelosi insists NO Supreme Court Justives are 'in danger' after Democrats blocked a bill to give them more security - hours after armed man 'threatened to kill Brett Kavanaugh,'" *Daily Mail*, June 9, 2022.

63. Bobby Burack, "AOC Brags She Helped Stop Bill To Protect Supreme Court Justices Following Kavanaugh Assassination Attempt," *OutKick*, June 10, 2022.

64. Òscar Jordà, Celeste Liu, Fernanda Nechio, and Fabián Rivera-Reyes, "Why Is U.S. Inflation Higher than in Other Countries?" *FRBSF Economic Letter*, March 28, 2022.

65. A significant "stimulus" was passed and signed by Donald Trump in mid-2020 as a response to the COVID-19 crisis. As will be discussed further below, the economic damage of the crisis itself, leading to a situation in which such "rescue" was needed in the first place, had been deepened and extended by overreaching restrictions pushed principally by Trump's opponents.

66. Audrey McNamara, "Biden raises social cost of carbon, restoring key climate policy tool slashed by Trump," *CBS News*, February 27, 2021.

67. Emma Newburger, "Biden suspends oil and gas leasing in slew of executive actions on climate change," *CNBC*, January 27, 2021.

68. "Biden suspends oil-drilling leases in Alaska's Arctic refuge," *NBC News*, June 1, 2021.

69. Niina H. Farah, "How Biden's NEPA plan could change the energy sector," *EnergyWire*, October 7, 2021.

70. Madison Hoff, "1 chart compares how much gas prices have skyrocketed in different regions of the US in the last 2 years," *Business Insider*, June 2, 2022.

71. "Average Regular Gas Price Comparison by State," https://www.gasbuddy.com/usa.

72. Matt Dempsey, and Katie Brown, "WATCH: Sec. Chu refuses to retract statement that the goal is to boost price of gas to levels in Europe," U.S. Senate Committee on Environment & Public Works, March 1, 2012.

73. Brad Polumbo, "'Inflation Tax' Will Cost Families This May Thousands This Year, Bloomberg Analysis Warns," *FEE*, April 1, 2022.

74. Tina Moore et al., "Federal agents raid Rudy Giuliani's NYC apartment in Ukraine probe," *New York Post*, April 28, 2021.

75. Zachary Evans, Alan Dershowitz Claims Giuliani Raid Was Political Revenge, Likens U.S. to 'Banana Republic,'" *National Review*, May 3, 2021.

76. "Americans Deserve an Explanation on FBI's Mar-a-Lago Search," *National Review*, August 10, 2022.

77. John Daniel Davidson, "The 2024 Election Is Being Rigged Right Now In Plain Sight," *Federalist*, August 12, 2022.

78. Victor Morton, "Report: FBI sought nuclear documents in Trump raid," *Washington Times*, August 11, 2022.

79. Margot Cleveland, "Four Possible Reasons The FBI Raided A Former President," *Federalist*, August 11, 2022.

80. Keith Griffith, "Washington Post columnist demands CNN retract claim that Steele dossier had been 'partly corroborated' after key source was arrested for lying - as paper corrects its own stories," *Daily Mail*, November 12, 2021.

81. Ibid.; Leia Idliby, "Washington Post's Erik Wemple Takes CNN and MSNBC to Task Over Steele Dossier Coverage: 'A Reckoning is Years Overdue,'" *MSN*, November 9, 2021; Carmine Sabia, "Major Arrest Made in Durham Investigation As Federal Authorities Nab Dossier Source," *Conservative Brief*, November 4, 2021.

82. Daniel Mitchell, "Hillary Clinton's 38-Year History of Sleaze and Corruption," *People's Pundit Daily*, October 29, 2016; Kimberly A. Strassel, "Grifters-in-Chief: The Clintons don't draw sharp lines between their 'charity' and personal enrichment," *Wall Street Journal*, October 27, 2016. "A Hillary Clinton presidency will be built, from the ground up, on self-dealing, crony favors, and an utter disregard for the law. This isn't a guess. It is spelled out, in black and white, in the latest bombshell revelation from WikiLeaks. It comes in the form of a memo written in 2011 by longtime Clinton errand boy Doug Band, who for years worked simultaneously at the Clinton Foundation and at the head of his lucrative consulting business, Teneo."

83. "'One of the greatest scandals in American history': Mark Levin's 'silent coup' claims are finally confirmed," *Blaze*, March 4, 2019.

84. Michael Dimock, and John Gramlich, "How America Changed During Donald Trump's Presidency," *Pew Research*, January 29, 2021.

85. Matea Gold, "The campaign to impeach President Trump has begun," *Washington Post,* January 20, 2017.

86. A selection of the alleged grounds includes: "1) obstruction of justice; 2) violations of the Foreign Emoluments Clause and Domestic Emoluments Clause of the United States Constitution; 3) conspiring with others to: (a) commit crimes against the United States involving the solicitation and intended receipt by the Donald J. Trump campaign of things of value from a foreign government and other foreign nationals; and (b) conceal those violations; 4) advocating illegal violence, giving aid and comfort to white supremacists and neo-Nazis, and undermining constitutional protections (sic) of equal protection under the law; 5) abusing the pardon power; 6) recklessly threatening nuclear war against foreign nations, undermining and subverting the essential diplomatic functions and authority of federal agencies, including the United States Department of State, and engaging in other conduct that grossly and wantonly endangers the peace and security of the United States, its people and people of other nations, by heightening the risk of hostilities involving weapons of mass destruction, with reckless disregard for the risk of death and grievous bodily harm; 7) directing or endeavoring to direct law enforcement, including the Department of Justice and the Federal Bureau of Investigation, to investigate and prosecute political adversaries and others, for improper purposes not justified by any lawful function of his office, thereby eroding the rule of law, undermining the independence of law enforcement from politics, and compromising the constitutional right to due process of law; 8) undermining the freedom of the press; 9) cruelly and unconstitutionally imprisoning children and their families; and 10) making and directing illegal payments to influence the 2016 election." "Why Impeachment?" impeachdolnaldtrumpnow.org (Accessed February 1, 2022)

87. For example, concerning point 9, illegal entry to the United States is a felony offense, and the law provides for illegal border crossers to be detained and prosecuted or returned to the nation of their citizenship. If critics are concerned about enforcement of the law being "cruel," they should take the matter up with Congress, not blame the President who is legally obligated to apply the law as written and approved by the American voters *via* their elected representatives.

88. For example, regarding allegation number 7, Trump's critics who expressed outrage at the President's firing of FBI director James Comey, citing "the independence of law enforcement from politics," betrayed a lack of awareness of the constitutional role and powers of the presidency. The FBI and other agencies are not independent of the president. The president is the nation's chief law enforcement officer; he is answerable to the people for the enforcement of the laws of the land, and the directors of the agencies are answerable to him. Neither the FBI nor the CIA nor any other government agency have oversight of the President. As with any other sitting president, Trump could fire and replace a federal agency director such as Comey at any time and for any reason.

89. Sam Dorman, "Trump's top advisers wanted him to fire Comey early on: book," *Fox News*, September 8, 2020.

90. The details of the alleged 2016-2017 palace intrigue are extensive and beyond the scope of this book. For a brief discussion, see Joe Saunders, "Reporter Calls Out Meeting Where Obama, Comey Were 'Hatching' Plot Against Trump," *Western Journal*, May 12, 2020.

91. Republican disruptors like Trump and Reagan have always faced difficulties in a wide and entrenched bureaucracy generally hostile to their agenda. The previous administration's political appointees are usually replaced upon accession of a new president, and the President has plenary constitutional authority to remove any subordinate. He is accountable only to the American people *via* elections or impeachment; he is not accountable to oversight by his subordinates.

92. Natalie Andrews, "Pelosi Opposes Pursuing Impeachment of Trump: House speaker says such a move would be too divisive," *Wall Street Journal,* March 11, 2019; Jonathan Turley, "Why Pelosi hates impeachment," *Hill*, March 12, 2019.

93. Eli Lake, "The FBI Scandal," *Real Clear Politics,* January 24, 2020; Harsanyi, David, "The FISA Scandal Is about Corruption, Not 'Sloppiness,'" *National Review*, April 2, 2020.

94. David Folkenflik, "Arrest of Steele dossier source forces some news outlets to reexamine their coverage," *NPR*, November 12, 2021; "Trump-Russia Steele dossier analyst charged with lying to FBI." *BBC*, November 5, 2021.

95. Marshall Cohen, "The Steele dossier: A reckoning," *CNN*, November 18, 2021.

96. Jeff Poor, "Mark Levin: 'There is more evidence of voter fraud than there was ever evidence of Russian collusion,'" *Breitbart*, November 7, 2020.

97. Piven, Frances Fox, and Richard A. Cloward, *Poor People's Movements: Why They Succeed, How They Fail* (New York:Vintage Books, 1979). ix-x, xxiv. "Of course, historical developments frustrated Marx's prediction: expanding capitalist production did not create a revolutionary proletariat. Still, the basic mode of dialectical analysis underlying the failed prediction—the idea that the struggles of ordinary people are both formed by and directed against institutional arrangements—is correct." "Our usage deviates from sociological custom but it is consistent with classical Marxist definitions of the working class. Our usage also deviates from the current fashion on the left of referring to impoverished, and underemployed working-class groups as 'lumpen proletarians,' a fashion we find not only offensive for its denigrating implications but also an abuse of Marx, who meant the term to refer to deviant and criminal elements from all classes."

98. Alan Reynolds, "What Marx Got Right about Redistribution—That John Stuart Mill Got Wrong," *FEE*, February 15, 2016.

99. Ibid., 332-4.

100. Piven, Frances Fox and Richard Cloward. "The Weight of the Poor: A Strategy to End Poverty." *The Nation*, May 2, 1966. Emphasis original.

101. Ibid.

102. Tim Hains, "FLASHBACK, 2018: Joe Biden Brags At CFR Meeting About Withholding Aid To Ukraine To Force Firing Of Prosecutor," *RealClearPolitics*, September 27, 2019.

103. Sher Sieve, "Hillary Protector AG Lynch Refuses to Release New Clinton emails to FBI," *Canada Free Press*, October 30, 2016; Margaret Knapp, "FLASHBACK—Levin: 'Sect. 793 of Penal Code ... Is What Hillary Clinton Has to Worry About," *CNS News*, August 13, 2015.

104. Bradley A. Smith, "Remember the IRS targeting scandal? No one ever got punished for it." *Washington Examiner*, January 18, 2018; Kelly Phillips Erb, "IRS Targeting Scandal: Citizens United, Lois Lerner And The $20M Tax Saga That Won't Go Away," *Forbes*, June 24, 2016.

105. Richard Nixon's resignation in 1974 pre-empted an almost certain impeachment and removal.

106. Matthew Hendrickson, "Jussie Smollett sentenced to 5 months in jail for staging fake hate crime in downtown Chicago," *Chicago Sun Times*, March 10, 2022.

107. "Timeline of events since Jussie Smollett reported attack," *Associated Press*, December 10, 2021.

108. Hendrickson, "Jussie Smollett."

109. Ebony Bowden, "Washington Post settles $250M suit with Covington teen Nick Sandmann," *New York Post*, July 24, 2020. 16-year-old high schooler Nick Sandmann had been wearing a distinctive red "Make America Great Again" hat while on a field trip to the U.S. Capitol in early 2019, when activist Nathan Phillips got in his face. Phillips' associates apparently filmed and edited the encounter in such a way as to make it appear that Sandmann had approached and was harassing the elderly Phillips. The clip and accompanying (false) story went wild on social media, thanks in part to the Washington Post, CNN, ABC, CBS, The Guardian, The Hill, and NBC negligently amplifying it either without confirming it or while knowing it to be a misrepresentation. The result was a national vilification of the young Sandmann. In July of 2020, the Washington Post settled a $250 million defamation lawsuit with Sandmann. Earlier in the year, CNN agreed to a settlement with him as part of another $250 million claim over their reporting of the incident.

6

OVERVIEW OF THE YEAR

The close of 2019 through early 2021 was a time of general turmoil, across the world and in the United States. There is reason to believe that the trouble, even at a cost of human lives, was intentionally intensified and extended for specific purposes which included the removal of Donald Trump as president of the United States and the advance of certain other geopolitical transformations and objectives (see Chapter 12). Klaus Schwab, Executive Chairman of the World Economic Forum, said essentially this very thing, or at least the latter part.[1] We need not affirm sensational theories to recognize that those with ideological and financial interests seized the moment and acted upon the motto "never let a serious crisis go to waste."[2]

Like many a petty totalitarian before him, Schwab couched his schemes for oppression in euphemisms that mimicked freedom. For example, instead of openly stating his intention to force his religion and metaphysical assumptions down the throat of every man, woman, and child alive, he rather proposed to enforce the diktats of his politburo by way of what he glibly labeled "stakeholder capitalism."[3]

Schwab's so-called "capitalism," however, rejected the core principle of capitalism and of basic justice: *property*. As such, stakeholder capitalism amounted to little more than involuntary servitude repackaged (though now intended to operate on a global scale), since it essentially seized the fruit of labor from every human being, using the same "greater good" argument wielded by southern plantation owners to perpetuate their subjugation of human chattel in the antebellum South. For this reason among others, American Democrats enthusiastically embraced Schwab's stakeholder capitalism, evidently cheered by the prospect of imposing their rule through a "social credit" scheme that excuses even bad behavior so long as individuals obey the masters, and punishes or destroys anyone—no matter how worthy—who does not obey, all in the name of an enlightened-sounding "ESG" (environmental, social and governance).[4]

Actual capitalism—in which the free meeting of buyer and seller, employer and employee in the context of the private contract naturally improves society as sellers strive to win customers by innovating and improving products and services while minimizing costs—was completely subverted within Schwab's (so-called) stakeholder capitalism. Schwab's model insisted that the individual does not own the product of his or her labor. Thus, private property—that is, the accumulated residue of work and trade in a just society—would be regularly seized by those who had nothing to do with its production and have no moral right to it—all in the name of a vague "greater good" as defined by would-be overlords like Schwab and his cronies.

Schwab and his slave-system had not yet subdued the world in 2020, but the shadow of its looming totalitarianism darkened the door of global humanity and gave form to events as they unfolded. I intend the statement to be sobering but not melodramatic. Time will reveal. If not, I will admit my mistake.

2020 Highlights

Events of 2020 included the January 3 killing of Iranian General Qasem Soleimani by a U.S. air strike in Baghdad;[5] the impeachment and acquittal of President Trump, the emergence of the COVID-19 virus; the late February conviction and early March sentencing of Harvey Weinstein for sex crimes; the two worst ever single-day point drops in the Dow Jones Industrial Average on March 9 and 12 (related to global lockdown);[6] the March 13 fatal police shooting of Breonna Taylor in Louisville, Kentucky, after her boyfriend fired at drug-investigating officers thinking that they were intruders;[7] the shooting death in early May of Ahmaud Arbery by civilians followed three weeks later by the death of George Floyd while Minneapolis police officer Derek Chauvin's knee was on his neck for 9 1/2 minutes as Floyd was face down on pavement (which reinvigorated the Black Lives Matter organization and movement and served as the pretext for the emergence of the Defund the Police movement, complete with riots throughout the summer); the declaration by George Floyd protestors of the "Capitol Hill Autonomous Zone" (CHAZ, or alternately CHOP for Capitol Hill Occupied Protest), demanding—among other things—the abolition of the Seattle Police Department and defunding of existing pensions for Seattle Police, in Seattle from June 8 until its abolishment on July 1;[8] Joe Biden's securing of the Democratic presidential nomination and his early

August selection of Kamala Harris as his running mate, the July arrest of Jeffrey Epstein accomplice Ghislaine Maxwell for sex trafficking; the August police shooting of Jacob Blake and further intensification of BLM and Antifa riots nationwide; the August 13 signing on the White House South Lawn of the Abraham Accords peace agreement between the United Arab Emirates, Bahrain, and Israel; the aborted September 17 seige of the White House; the death of Supreme Court Justice Ruth Bader Ginsburg and the confirmation of her successor Amy Coney Barrett; the filing of antitrust lawsuits against Google on October 20;[9] the October 30 subversion of President Trump by Gen. Mark Milley, the November 3 national election and its aftermath (including the filing of many lawsuits); and the creation and early December approval for emergency use of a COVID-19 vaccine developed under President Trump's "Operation Warp Speed." Emergency Use Authorization for the Pfizer vaccine was granted on December 11, and first doses were given December 14;[10] the Moderna vaccine gained approval on December 18, with first doses given December 21.[11] The election period drew to an end with the events of January 6, 2021 at the U.S. Capitol, followed almost immediately by the hasty and unprecedented January 13 second impeachment of Donald Trump which—like the first—resulted in acquittal in the Senate.[12]

Key international events of 2020 included the continuation of pro-democracy protests in Hong Kong that had begun in late 2019, and their suppression by the Chinese Communist Party over the course of 2020;[13] the January 31 completion of the U.K.'s departure from the European Union ("Brexit"); widespread bushfires in Australia in January and February, the March rescheduling of the Tokyo 2020 summer Olympics to 2021 due to the pandemic;[14] rumors of North Korean leader Kim Jong Un's death at the end of April;[15] and the tragic August 4 explosion in the Beirut, Lebanon harbor of a ship loaded with ammonium nitrate, killing nearly 200 and injuring thousands.[16]

Other events of the year included the January 8 announcement on Instagram by Prince Harry and Meghan Markle of their decision to "step back as 'senior' members of the British royal family," dubbed "Megxit;" basketball star Kobe Bryant's January 26 death in a helicopter crash; the Pentagon's public release of purported UFO videos in April;[17] entrepreneur Elon Musk's SpaceX becoming the first private company to send humans into orbit on May 30;[18] the July 17 death of Congressman and civil rights icon John Lewis, the appearance of Asian 'murder hornets' in Washington State;[19] the early August emergence in California and Oregon of the largest complex of wildfires in California history, which burned more than one million acres;[20] the August 28 death of actor Chadwick Boseman at 43 from colon cancer; the October 6 death of singer Eddie Van Halen; and the November 8 death of *Jeopardy!* host Alex Trebek.

With these general highlights having been presented, let us discuss in some detail the two major developments that most impacted the 2020 election: the COVID-19 virus and the events leading up to and including the Black Lives Matter and Antifa riots. We will then briefly discuss the nomination and confirmation of Amy Coney Barrett following Ruth Bader Ginsburg's death, and Gen. Mark Milley's unilateral seizure of presidential power at the end of October. The chapter concludes with the Democratic primary, and the Biden and Trump campaigns.

COVID-19: The context that became pretext

2020 may ultimately be remembered most for COVID-19. The new coronavirus that appeared in Wuhan, China was known of early in January. The virus did not cause wide alarm at the beginning.[21] Its threat and potential to become a pandemic reached the attention of President Trump *via* Sen. Tom Cotton (R-AR) in the final weeks of January, around the time that the first U.S. case of the virus was confirmed. On January 22, Cotton sent a letter to HHS Secretary Alex Azar, encouraging the Trump Administration to consider a ban on travel between China and the United States, and warning that the Chinese Communist regime could be covering up how dangerous the disease really was.

President Trump first spoke with Cotton about the matter on January 29. Two days later, January 31, Trump announced a ban on entry to the U.S. of foreign travelers who had been in China during the previous two weeks.[22] At the time, the ban allowed Americans and permanent residents to continue travel between the two countries. It was thus somewhat less stringent than Sen. Cotton urged. Many of the President's advisors at this early stage were downplaying the threat, and Democrats were paying virtually no attention to it at all.[23] All Democrats' energies seemed bound up in the election year impeachment of Trump. Joe Biden's first explicit remarks about the coronavirus came on January 31, the day of Trump's ban:

> America needs a president they can trust, especially at times of a crisis. You know, we have right now a crisis with the coronavirus, emanating from China. A national emergency, you know, worldwide alerts. The American people need to have a president who they can trust what he says about it, that he is going to act rationally about it. In moments like this, this is where the credibility of a president is most needed, as he explains what we should and should not do. This is no time for Donald Trump's record of hysteria, xenophobia – hysterical xenophobia – and fearmongering to lead the way instead of science.[24]

Observes Robert Farley after reviewing all of Biden's early statements on the matter,

> In some 35 public appearances at campaign rallies, in television interviews or in Democratic debates over the next three weeks in February, Biden was not asked about and did not mention the coronavirus at all.[25]

In July 2020 testimony before Congress, Dr. Anthony Fauci revealed that he had been involved with the decisionmaking behind the China travel ban and the subsequent Europe travel ban. Fauci praised the Trump administration for both moves, and when asked by Representative Steve Scalese whether he thought the China travel ban decision had saved lives, he replied, "Yes, I do."[26]

Even with the travel ban, however, the cat was out of the bag. COVID-19 had jumped the ocean to U.S. shores. It would run its course, and the only question remaining was what that would look like and how its negative effects could be minimized.

Five weeks after Trump's China travel ban, 21 out of the first 46 passengers tested on a Carnival cruise ship came back positive for COVID-19. News of this led to the March 6-21 quarantine of all 3,500 vacationers (many of them elderly) and crewmembers off the California coast. When the dust settled, just over 100 people onboard had contracted COVID-19, and at least eight died.[27] The incident was the first major story surrounding the virus, and it captured national attention as the ship floated off the coast with passengers quarantined pending clearance.

In the midst of the Carnival Cruise episode, COVID-19 was officially declared a pandemic on March 11. President Trump declared COVID-19 a national emergency on March 13, also issuing a travel ban on non-US citizens coming from Europe. Four days later, the one-hundredth U.S. death from COVID-19 was recorded.

Did Democrats imagine Trump's early steps to control the virus' spread merely a disingenuous attempt to distract the world from the climax of their hard-fought impeachment efforts? Perhaps. Apparently realizing that their own early dismissal of the COVID threat had been a miscalculation, Democrat leadership shifted their messaging. In early April, Nancy Pelosi and Adam Schiff announced an investigation into Trump for allegedly having minimized the COVID-19 threat.[28]

"Two Weeks To Flatten The Curve"

On March 16, 2020, the Trump administration issued a 15-day plan under the heading "15 Days to Slow the Spread." It was also called "two weeks to flatten the curve," the curve being the trajectory of new infections. The idea

was to prevent hospitals and other medical facilities from becoming overwhelmed by slowing the rate of infection. The official release read,

> This afternoon, President Trump and the White House Coronavirus Task
> Force issued new guidelines to help protect Americans during the global
> Coronavirus outbreak.
>
> **The new recommendations** are simple to follow but will have a
> resounding impact on public health. While the President leads a nationwide
> response, bringing together government resources and private-sector inge-
> nuity, every American can help slow the virus' spread and keep our most
> high-risk populations safe:
>
> 1. Listen to and follow the directions of your **state and local authorities.**
>
> 2. **If you feel sick, stay home.** Do not go to work. Contact your medical
> provider.
>
> 3. **If your children are sick**, keep them at home. Contact your medical
> provider.
>
> 4. If someone in your household **has tested positive for the Coron-
> avirus**, keep the entire household at home.
>
> 5. **If you are an older American**, stay home and away from other people.
>
> 6. If you are a person with a **serious underlying health condition**—such
> as a significant heart or lung problem—stay home and away from other
> people.[29]

Despite some concerns among those who already sensed a tendency
for overreach, most Americans complied with the plan, including its first
step regarding following the directions of state and local authorities. The
problem, however, was that many of these authorities had more than
simple public health in mind and took advantage of the situation; they did
not stop after fifteen days. In fact, many of them persisted in onerous
restrictions for nearly two years, doing great and in some cases irreversible
damage to businesses, families, schoolchildren, and American society in
general.

COVID-19 by the numbers

COVID-19 ultimately proved more deadly, by a factor of between three and
seven, than other common endemic viruses such as the seasonal flu.[30]
From February 2020 through September 2021, the CDC estimated 146.6
million total infections in the United States, with 921,371 total deaths—or a
little over one-quarter of 1% of the U.S. population. Based upon these estimates, the case fatality rate of COVID-19 in the U.S. during the pandemic to
that point was 146,600,000 ÷ 921,371, or approximately 0.628%.[31] In
November of 2021, a far more infectious variant, Omicron, emerged.

Omicron's relative mildness, combined with a large number of new cases in December 2021 and January 2022, will likely drive down COVID-19's overall case fatality rate, but reliable figures are not readily available at the time of this writing.

Unlike some viruses, COVID-19's death rate was heavily skewed to the elderly. According to the CDC, estimated U.S. deaths from COVID-19 by age category through September of 2021 were as follows:

0-17 years old: 645 deaths from 25,844,005 infections (0.0025% case fatality rate, or one death for every 40,080 infections; 99.9975% recovery rate)

18-49 years old: 60,355 deaths from 75,179,070 infections (0.08% case fatality rate, or one death for every 1,246 infections; 99.92% recovery rate)

50-64 years old: 159,489 deaths from 27,407,088 infections (0.58% case fatality rate, or one death for every 172 infections; 99.42% recovery rate)

65+ years old: 700,882 deaths from 18,012,882 infections (3.8% case fatality rate, or one death for every 25 infections; 96.2% recovery rate)[32]

As can be seen above, fully 93% of all U.S deaths from COVID-19 through September 2021 were among those over 50, with over three quarters of all U.S. COVID-19 deaths during that time period being among those aged 65 and above.

Even among the elderly, COVID-19 was selective. Two factors beyond age appear to have made a significant difference: the presence of comorbidities, and vaccine or natural immunity status. In other words, those who did not have comorbidities such as obesity, a heart condition, or cancer were at tremendously lower risk of dying from COVID-19 than even the raw age category numbers above would suggest. Furthermore, vaccination in some cases made a big difference, particularly for those in higher risk categories.[33]

Regarding both of these facts, CDC director Rochelle Walensky—speaking of a study with a sample size of 1.2 million people who were vaccinated—stated on January 7, 2022 that "[t]he overwhelming number of deaths, over 75 percent, occurred in people who had at least four comorbidities."[34] The outcomes among unvaccinated in terms of relative death between those with, and those without, significant compounded comorbidities, were likely similar. Walensky had been asserting the benefit of vaccination for those in higher risk categories, such as the elderly and those with compounded comorbidities, but the converse of the point is that those without comorbidities are in a much lower-risk situation whether they have had the vaccine or not.

By March of 2022, more than two years after the start of the COVID-19 pandemic, the estimated global death toll was 6,019,085.[35] This amounted to 1/133 of one percent (0.076%) of the world's population.[36] For perspective, the last major pandemic was the Spanish flu in 1918, a time when the world's population was about 1.85 billion, or less than one-quarter that of 2022. The Spanish flu is generally estimated to have killed 25-50 million people globally, or about 1.35-2.7% of the world's population at the time.[37] For comparison, had it occurred in 2020 and killed a comparable proportion of the world's population, the global death toll would have been 107-213 million rather than the 6 million of COVID-19. Assuming the global estimates mentioned above are correct,[38] in terms of actual deaths, the 2020-22 pandemic was therefore about 18-36 times milder than that of 1918.[39]

There is one other aspect of the COVID-19 virus that bears mention in this context, and that is to acknowledge that there were some differences in the relative effects of COVID-19 by race. In particular, there were slight differences in death rates. Deaths among non-hispanic white people and non-hispanic black people both somewhat exceeded their share of the total population—that is to say, more white people and black people who were not hispanic were dying from COVID-19. Meanwhile, deaths among hispanic people and non-hispanic Asian people somewhat lagged behind their share of the total population—that is to say, fewer hispanic and Asian people were dying from COVID-19. When standardized for age categories,[40] however, it was non-hispanic white people and non-hispanic Asian people who lagged in COVID-19 deaths (that is, had fewer deaths than expected), with hispanic and non-hispanic black people having a higher number of deaths than their share of the overall population.

The differences, of course, were likely due to a combination of causes, some natural and some environmental. But members of the American left used them to fan flames of division and racial animosity, casting aspersions on anyone calling for a "return to normal," opposing business closures, rallying against mask or vaccine mandates, or otherwise advocating for personal choice in how to go about life, family, and work. It is easy to see how racial disparities in COVID-19 outcomes would touch a nerve at a time of heightened tensions around race, the videos of the deaths of Floyd, Blake, Taylor, Arbery, and so forth. In this context, such statistics—regardless of the cause—became useful tools in the hands of those who stood to gain politically or otherwise from racial division and mistrust.

Anthony Fauci and "the science"

Dr. Anthony Fauci, director of the National Institute of Allergy and Infectious Diseases, quickly became the official face of public health messaging around COVID-19 in the United States. Despite his having worked with several presidential administrations, few Americans knew who Fauci was at the beginning of the pandemic. This circumstance changed in early 2020, as he was regularly featured in press briefings and began to make the rounds of major news networks and talk shows.

Fauci began to lose the trust of some Americans with his firm advocacy for some policy actions that went beyond what many could see as medically warranted. Within months of the pandemic's start, messaging inconsistencies were noted. In early March of 2020, Fauci warned of the consequences of masks and directed Americans not to buy them or wear them. Later, he supported wearing masks, and eventually he even recommended double-masking. Fauci also adjusted his recommendations regarding vaccination.[41]

Fauci eventually admitted that his decisions were guided by more than mere truth or science. Responding to criticism from the New York Times, he explained that he took public opinion polls into account when crafting comments:

> When polls said only about half of all Americans would take a vaccine, I was saying herd immunity would take 70 to 75%. Then, when newer surveys said 60% or more would take it, I thought, "I can nudge this up a bit," so I went to 80, 85.[42]

Yet Fauci, and along with him many on the American left, had frequently dismissed those who did not agree with him as though they stood against truth. In mid-2021, he even equated his policy opinions with science itself, telling NBC News that "attacks on me, quite frankly, are attacks on science."[43]

Throughout 2020, Fauci strongly criticized any suggesting the COVID-19 virus might have originated in a lab in Wuhan, China. After many months, when that theory finally came to be generally accepted, numerous emails from Dr. Fauci, Dr. Francis Collins, and other high-level government officials revealed that they had been opposing the theory for political reasons involving concern for "international harmony."[44] Such revelations confirmed what many Americans had already discerned about the public messaging: lies had been presented as truth, and the truthful accused of rejecting "science." As Jim Geraghty wrote,

> The world was facing its worst health crisis in a century, and seemingly every American involved in contagious-virus research at the Wuhan Institute of Virology didn't want the public to know what they had been doing. Does that reassure you? Does that make you feel like you can trust high-level U.S. officials to tell you the truth, the whole truth, and nothing but the

truth? Does that make you believe that these officials prioritize "SCIENCE" above all else, or does it make you think that their primary concerns are managing public opinion and protecting their own reputations?[45]

A book by Robert Kennedy severely criticizing Fauci as deeply compromised by divided loyalties and quest for personal gain appeared in November 2021 and became a national bestseller.[46] Kennedy correctly observes that the net effect of the extended lockdowns endorsed by Fauci was economic destruction, shifting wealth upward while destroying many middle income earners,[47] and greatly enriching those already wealthy and connected—especially those connected to government.[48] Among the more alarming allegations made by Kennedy is that Fauci and other powerful gatekeepers used their control of purse strings and grant funding to exert wide political influence over peer-reviewed medical publications to mount a sophisticated smear campaign against alternate treatments that would have lessened the severity of the crisis or the need for mass vaccination. According to Kennedy,

> His [i.e., Fauci's] agency is co-owner of the patent [for the Moderna vaccine] and stands to collect a fortune in royalties. At least four of Fauci's hand-picked deputies are in line to collect royalties of $150,00/year based on Moderna's success, and that's on top of the salaries already paid by the American public.[49]

A full assessment of the merits of Kennedy's many allegations is beyond the scope of this book, but its runaway success was probably an indication that many Americans were suspicious and unsatisfied with standard narratives.

"Never let a good crisis go to waste"

Messaging around COVID-19 quickly became politicized. The major success of Trump's policies in terms of economic growth, historic low unemployment (including the lowest black unemployment in U.S. history), peaceful diplomatic relations developing between Israel and the other nations of the Middle East, and so forth presented a political challenge for Democrats. Accordingly, they worked to make COVID-19 a vehicle for damaging Trump by first destroying the booming economy and then working to undermine Americans' trust that Trump was leading the country in a direction that would make their lives better. Across the nation, Democrat partisans used emergency powers as a pretext for draconian responses to COVID-19, including extended business shutdowns, and onerous restrictions on movement and in-person commerce.

By mid-spring of 2020 it became extremely difficult for even a PhD researcher to locate reliable data, and spin was everywhere. National news and social media breathlessly reported cumulative total COVID-19 cases, cumulative hospitalizations, and cumulative deaths in the United States. Weekly numbers of new cases by age group would have been more helpful, as these would have given a clearer—albeit less dramatic—picture of the real situation.

I specifically noticed that many reports omitted *per capita* death rates. Comparison of raw death numbers between countries like Spain (population about 47 million) or the UK (population about 68 million) and the United States (population about 331 million) were not useful alone, because ten deaths in Spain would be comparable to seventy deaths in the United States in terms of relative populations. News networks, whose clicks and subscriptions fed upon fear and doom, and politicians on the left seeking to inflict maximum harm on Donald Trump, however, were better served by large and growing cumulative figures and a sense that the United States (and thus, really, President Trump) was performing horribly in its handling of COVID, and they created this impression by omitting or obscuring key data that would have shown the real picture.

On my social media feeds, I witnessed a steady stream of Democrat friends excitedly emphasizing that the U.S. had more deaths than any other country, or showing charts ranking countries by aggregate COVID-19 deaths—the United States is the third most populous country in the world after China[50] and India—suggesting that the large number of deaths or hospitalizations in the U.S. represented a catastrophic failure by Donald Trump. Ironically, the "Lacks Context" warning that Facebook scrupulously displayed beneath posts from other perspectives was not shown in these instances. Throughout 2020, CNN constantly displayed a prominent on-screen chryon tallying the total cases and deaths globally and in the United States throughout nearly every show.[51] Per capita death figures were not emphasized by CNN or many other legacy media outlets.

Federal funds and alleged COVID-19 perverse incentives

Confidence in some long-trusted institutions was undermined during 2020. Unfortunately, some public officials and gatekeepers did significant damage by allowing their policies and messaging to become co-opted for what appeared publicly as base partisan purposes. Mandates and policies that appeared to many Americans as overly broad, overbearing, not supported by evidence, inconsistently applied, and arbitrary in nature opened the door to all manner of questions about what was really driving decisions. Among the allegations that gained traction was an assertion that hospitals and medical practitioners were being influenced by financial incentives to inflate COVID numbers, or to recommend more extensive courses of treatment that were not actually necessary.

The degree to which nefarious activity was actually happening at the doctor-patient level, or even at the clinic or hospital level, was probably low. At a time when many ordinary hospital functions and elective procedures had suddenly become constricted, federal payments related to the COVID-19 crisis became an important line item that simply made a difference to employers and hospital budgets as these entities, like everyone else, tried to stay afloat. Federal funds, it is true, incentivized testing of incoming patients for COVID-19 regardless of their chief complaint. Often, however, it was also simply best practice to routinely rapid-test incoming patients for COVID-19, not only as a precaution to prevent further spread within the facility, but also to ensure good patient care and, obviously, not leave potential legitimate reimbursements unused.[52]

Critics, however, alleged that government reimbursements associated with COVID-19 led to a conflict of interest. Rumors spread on social media that doctors or hospitals were miscoding patients who did not have COVID as though they did, leading to falsely elevated nationwide case numbers. FactCheck generally confirmed the dollar amounts—$13,000 in federal funds for treating a COVID-19 patient, and $39,000 for treatment of a COVID-19 patient placed on a ventilator—as the estimated Medicare payments for COVID-19 hospitalizations. FactCheck further confirmed that the government will pay more to hospitals for COVID-19 cases in the following instances: a) an additional 20% on top of ordinary Medicare rates for COVID-19 patients during the public health emergency, and b) reimbursing hospitals for treating uninsured patients with the disease, and doing so at the enhanced (+20%) Medicare rate. Both of these reimbursement schemes stem from the $2 trillion Coronavirus Aid, Relief, and Economic Security ("CARES") Act, which was passed by Congress and signed into law by President Trump on March 27, 2020.[53]

Under the CARES Act, hospitals were not paid for mere diagnosis of patients with COVID-19; they were reimbursed for treatment. This fact alone would not preclude a false diagnosis. Nor would it alone answer for the larger allegation, which is the apparent financial incentive to place a critical patient on a ventilator. I believe it is extremely unlikely that most or any doctors would consciously recommend a course of treatment, such as a ventilator, that the doctor did not truly believe to be in the best interest of the patient's health. Physicians are bound by the Hippocratic Oath to do no harm and to seek the health and well-being of their patients, and most of them take this oath seriously.

Still, there remained the question of whether physicians *ever* leaned in their judgment toward certain more profitable courses of treatment. The reason that physicians are not allowed to take major gifts from pharmaceutical companies speaks to the same issue. If the Oath itself were enough to prevent material influence, then possible conflict of interest in terms of gifts from pharmaceutical companies would also not be a problem. So, there is some inconsistency among those who claim that the medical profession is immune from the lure of financial incentives in terms of government money while simultaneously claiming they are not immune to such from private drug companies.

Higher numbers of cases and deaths from COVID-19 were desirable to some people. Among other things, high numbers:

- Suggested that Trump was handling the crisis poorly
- Validated the severe mitigation measures—such as extended school and business closures, mask mandates, stay at home orders, and travel restrictions—desired by those who for political, financial, or ideological reasons stood to profit from the extreme disruption of society
- Reinforced the case for even more government action and appropriation of funds for intervention at local, state, and federal levels
- Fed a narrative of American failure sought by those who wished to malign the United States and what she stands for— particularly free markets, rule of law, and individual liberty

Mismanagement and abuse of the COVID-19 situation also served as a windfall for government cronies, particularly in the insurance industry, by forcing taxpaying Americans to effectively pay twice for healthcare, without in many cases even receiving the healthcare they were paying for. First, money was disbursed through Medicare Advantage plans to health insurance companies, much of which went to bloated overhead budgets and never even reached a medical provider since doctor visits and non-urgent surgeries were canceled due to the pandemic. Then, taxpayers paid again when they were forced to foot the bill—*via* the Provider Relief Fund and Paycheck Protection Program (together totaling about $165 billion in 2020)—for the damage the draconian government restrictions had done to hospitals and health professionals.[54]

"China Virus"

"COVID-19" is the name for the disease caused by the SARS-CoV2 coronavirus. COVID-19 is an acronym standing for "coronavirus disease of 2019."

COVID-19 was first identified in Wuhan, China, and likely originated in a lab there. There is a chance that emergence of the pandemic might have been controlled or even averted altogether were it not for the malfeasance and cover-up of the Chinese Communist Party (CCP) in the earliest days. At a time when a new generation in the United States was being increasingly raised to think more sympathetically about communism, President Trump, consistently critical of the Chinese regime—though not of the Chinese people—felt the world should be reminded of the contrast between transparent government by the people (the American model) and the authoritarianism of the CCP. Accordingly, he called the virus the "Wuhan Virus" or the "China Virus."

President Trump was quickly denounced by the left, however, for using these terms, which they called "xenophobic."[55] To this day, I admit that I do not understand how a label correctly reflecting a virus' place of origin is xenophobic. It is anecdotally true that some less sophisticated people said unkind things to others of Asian descent as a result of COVID-19's origin in China. However, such comments reflect upon the ignorance of those who equate a regime (the Chinese Communist Party) or a place (China) with an ethnicity or nationality (e.g., the Chinese), and are not the fault of a president or others who accurately applied a term for what is evidently a specific non-xenophobic purpose.

How COVID-19 affected Americans

As already mentioned, COVID-19 quickly became politicized, and the politicization had a shattering effect on the lives of Americans. The economy was disrupted, family businesses that had taken decades to build were lost virtually overnight as sweeping and heavy-handed government mandates devoured lifetimes of loving investment, and the federal government moved to expand government wealth-redistribution schemes to engulf millions more Americans.

In public schools across the nation, children of all ages were forced to wear masks throughout the school day. Many schools were temporarily closed or moved to hybrid or distance learning. In-person graduations—even those ordinarily held outdoors—were canceled that spring, including that of our eldest daughter.

In the Fall of 2020, many public schools went to 100% "distance learning," setting children without a reliable internet connection or without a good working environment at home at a tremendous disadvantage. Distance learning also caused a general loss of motivation and disruption of the momentum of an actual classroom setting. Since schools could not require students to keep their cameras on throughout the day for privacy reasons, many students around the nation developed the bad habit of keeping their cameras off and engaging in other activities throughout the school day despite technically being "in attendance." By the year's end, studies were confirming the alarming level of learning loss that had been predicted to result from such measures, and contemplating the cascading effect that this lost developmental time could have upon a generation of kids, and in particular poor children.[56]

Of all the horrors of the COVID-19 pandemic, however, dying alone— as compelled by out-of-balance medical policies and protocols—may go down in history as one of the greatest tragedies. As COVID-19 progressed, one-size-fits-all policies driven by seemingly tone-deaf officials and administrators forced thousands of people with the virus (many of them elderly) into isolation without so much as a human contact with loved ones—even spouses—who made desperate but futile attempts to be with them before they died.[57]

> It was a heartbreaking decision—a Wheeling family sent their 96-year-old matriarch suffering from COVID-19 to the hospital, knowing she'd likely be alone.
>
> "On her birthday, January 8th, my grandmother passed away at your hospital—surrounded only by God," Margaret Sundstrom wrote in a letter.
> ...
> "Every day, we kept calling and saying: 'Can we visit? Can we visit?'" Graf said. "They just kept saying, 'No, no, no.'"
>
> Calabrese wasn't improving, and the family begged. ...
>
> "They allowed us to stay for about 30 minutes, and you know, then they said we had to leave ... that was about, I don't know, 8:30 at night—and she died at 11."
>
> Not one person from the family Calabrese built was there to hold her hand.[58]

Cuomo nursing home scandal

On March 25, 2020, New York governor Andrew Cuomo issued an order that all New York State nursing homes must accept medically stable residents, and specifically forbade the denial of admission or readmission based solely upon COVID-19 status or suspected status. The result of this order was the tragic spread of the COVID-19 virus among thousands of the people most needing to be protected from it. The death count was enormous. Nursing homes in New York accepted more than 6,300 COVID-positive patients between March 25 and May 10, when Cuomo finally rescinded the advisory.[59]

Furthermore, top aides to Gov. Cuomo altered a state Health Department report to suppress the number of people killed by COVID-19 in the state's nursing homes, by excluding from the tally those patients who had been ill with COVID-19 and later died in hospitals after subsequent transfer. In the end, at least 15,000 long-term care residents died from COVID-

19, far higher than the 6,432 that Cuomo's Health Department had publicized at the time in a report "designed and released to rebut criticism of Cuomo over [his] March 25 directive."[60]

President Trump had quickly acted to get help to New York City amid increasing COVID-19 case numbers in the densely populated metropolis by directing the Navy's hospital ship *Comfort* there. The ship arrived at New York's Pier 90 on March 30.[61] Its mission was to accept non-COVID patients as a means of alleviating the burden on New York City hospitals. *Comfort*, with its approximately 1,200-person crew and 1,000-bed hospital, departed New York on April 30, having treated only 182 patients, of which about 70% had COVID-19.[62] The Javits Center, similarly set up by the Army Corps of Engineers at that time for the crisis with a capacity of 2,500 beds, was also shut down for lack of use. In addition to forcing elderly COVID-positive patients back into nursing homes, Gov. Andrew Cuomo was criticized for failing to avail himself of the two resources.[63]

The fight over masks

Masks and policies around them soon became visible tokens of a cultural divide. Many on the left found masks an opportunity for virtue-signaling—a way to announce to the world, "I am a good person and I care about others"—as well as an excuse to demean and take adverse action against non-conformists. Many others balked at mask requirements—especially outdoors and in well-ventilated areas, or policies satisfied by ineffective cloth masks—as nonsensical. Innumerable arguments ensued, both in public and in private. The term "Karen," coined prior to 2020, refers to a busybody, typically a white woman and often from privilege, who confronts people around her for not behaving the way she wishes. During the pandemic, the term "Karen" was applied to mask proponents as well as mask objectors.[64]

> Republican Kentucky Sen. Rand Paul relayed some advice for non-mask wearers who get confronted in public by hysterical, hypochondriac Karens... [Sen. Paul, a physician, said,] "I think you should back away and say, 'Lady, you are crazy, leave me the hell alone,' but you should not confront her. You should not use violence. Back away and just say look, can you not find some other lunatic friends to hang around with?"[65]

Dr. Paul added his comments about the philosophical divide that such encounters represent, stating,

> Really this is a difference between individualism and collectivism. I have an opinion, but I'm not wanting to enforce it on anybody. I'm not telling you

that you can't wear a mask. I'm just saying don't make me wear a mask when it doesn't work. They don't understand that, that we have a perspective, they have a perspective. But they want to force and ram their perspective down our throat through force. I mean, what kind of people are they? This has brought out the worst in people.[66]

In November of 2021, Republican Glenn Youngkin won the governor's race in Virginia. Youngkin's margin of victory was attributed to the rogue leftist Loudoun County Public Schools (LCPS) board's alleged harm to children, coverup of assaults, implementation of racist admissions and grading policies, and draconian mask mandates and school closures, causing upheaval and learning loss. One of Youngkin's first acts in office was to issue an executive order that took effect January 24, 2022. The order allowed those wishing to wear a mask at school to do so, but provided that those choosing otherwise must go unmolested.[67] However, during the first week after the order took effect, some 30 students who chose not to mask at our local Loudoun County, Virginia high school, Woodgrove High School, were kept out of their classrooms and confined in the school auditorium, "most of them just sitting there looking at their phones,"[68] while only masked students were allowed in class. On at least one day that week, these unmasked students were reportedly given only a 15-minute lunch period instead of the 30 minutes other students received.

Calling the school the previous week to inquire what would be done with students choosing not to wear masks per the governor's order, I was told they would be suspended but that this was a county-wide requirement imposed by the school board, not a decision by the school.

On Wednesday, February 2, 2022, twenty-nine LCPS students were given two-week suspensions for taking off their masks while at school. An unconfirmed but reportedly large number of the students were from Woodgrove.

I stopped by the school office two days later and spoke with an administrator as an informal follow-up inquiry. She declined to confirm the number suspended, but said the suspensions would continue "until those students make a decision to follow the rules and wear a mask at school." When I asked whether the suspensions would become part of students' permanent records, she said that yes, they would, but that LCPS would not be informing colleges or other outside entities of the suspensions. She added, however, that if college applications ask whether the student has ever been subject to disciplinary action or suspension, it will be up to the student to decide how to answer. So, public school administrators were placing honest and perhaps exemplary students into the position of needing to answer "yes" to such a question in a college interview.

The following week, leaked communication revealed that LCPS

Director of Safety and Security, John Clark, had sent an email to school principals on February 1, coaching them on how to request issuance of an official trespass warrant against non-compliant students or parents "refusing to wear a mask or leave the campus," as a way to work around the Loudoun County Sheriff's Office's confirmation that its school resource officers would *not* "enforce a verbal no trespass for peaceful mask non-compliance without a trespass summons/warrant being issued from a magistrate."[69]

The targets of Mr. Clark's email were enrolled students of Loudoun County Public Schools and their taxpaying parents. LCPS' defiance of Governor Youngkin came mere months after the school system had acted as though outgoing Virginia Governor Ralph Northam's executive order that all Virginia schools must *require* masks must not—indeed, could not—be questioned.[70]

Bullying of students and parents by spiteful school administrators was hard for many parents to believe, yet there it was, day in and day out. It seemed evident that the sensible course of action, had school administrators wished to retain the rules at this point, would have been to keep the LCPS policy contravening the Governor's order in place, without enforcing the rule. They took a different path.

On February 16, 2022, a Loudoun County Circuit judge issued a temporary injunction

> immediately halting LCPS's mask mandate for students. Starting … February 17, this order forbids LCPS from enforcing its mask mandate on students. … Any students who were suspended for violating the mask policy will have their suspensions reversed and expunged from their academic record. …
>
> [T]he judge said this mask policy was causing irreparable and ongoing harm, and that enforcing the policy by suspending students was "unreasonable." He also said that Governor Youngkin's original Executive Order No. 2 was valid, LCPS's interpretation of Virginia law was incorrect, and the three parents who are suing LCPS over the mask mandate have a good chance of winning their case.
>
> This was the latest in a series of major developments today. Earlier today, Governor Youngkin signed SB 739 into law, which will allow Virginia parents to opt their kids out of mask mandates. That law went into effect immediately but gave school systems until March 1 to comply. Shortly after that, Dr. Ziegler [the LCPS Superintendent] informed LCPS families and staff about the new law, and announced that LCPS would let students start opting out of masks on Tuesday, February 22. And not long after that, the judge issued his injunction.[71]

Weaponized Policy

Early in the pandemic, many Americans perceived—and resented—that masks were being used by politicians more for their symbolic and political value than for any medical benefit. The first evidence that the authorities might have been playing games with the public was the complete switch, virtually overnight, from early assertions by Dr. Fauci and others that masks would be ineffective against the virus—as was confirmed from years of medical knowledge—to an all-out and virtually breathless endorsement of masks by most of the very same authorities, including Dr. Fauci himself.[72] For Joe Biden's campaign, masks and masking became almost a campaign slogan or hallmark, a way of purporting to show everyone that he was a man of science—and that Trump (who wore them more selectively and not during public appearances) was not.

The CDC was also compromised, recommending without evidence (as discussed in a major article in *The Atlantic*)[73] that all kids two and older should be masked in school. As masks were coming off kids by court order in Virginia schools on February 16, 2022, Congressional Democrats were joining Republicans in grilling CDC Director Rochelle Walensky over the issue. Even at the very moment the CDC was finally signaling its intention to relax its guidance on masking in general, Walensky—despite acknowledging (when pressed) the "limitations" of the debunked Arizona study upon which the CDC policy was openly based—dug in and stated that the CDC had no plans to change their recommendation that all U.S. schools require students (the portion of the population least vulnerable to COVID-19) to wear masks.[74]

Further evidence that the primary value of masks to the authorities was symbolic, even talismanic,[75] was those authorities' near universal acceptance of the types of masks known to be ineffective in the prevention of viral transmission, including cloth masks, bandanas, and so forth. Said a May 2020 article in the prestigious *New England Journal of Medicine*:

> Masks are visible reminders of an otherwise invisible yet widely prevalent pathogen and may remind people of the importance of social distancing and other infection-control measures.
>
> It is also clear that masks serve symbolic roles. Masks are not only tools, they are also talismans that may help increase health care workers' perceived sense of safety, well-being, and trust in their hospitals. Although such reactions may not be strictly logical, we are all subject to fear and anxiety, especially during times of crisis. One might argue that fear and anxiety are better countered with data and education than with a marginally beneficial mask, particularly in light of the worldwide mask shortage, but it is difficult to get clinicians to hear this message in the heat of the current crisis.

Expanded masking protocols' greatest contribution may be to reduce the transmission of anxiety, over and above whatever role they may play in reducing transmission of Covid-19.[76]

There were varying reports and studies about the effectiveness of N95 and KN95 masks in preventing viral transmission, but the most rigorous studies showed that a mere cloth mask had negligible benefit.[77] A scientific Danish study found no statistically significant difference between those recommended to wear a mask and the control group who were not.[78] Unfortunately, many studies measured things other than rates of actual COVID-19 infection, instead focusing upon droplet transmission, COVID *symptoms* (which are not necessarily an indication of COVID infection), and so forth. Furthermore, photographs emerged of politicians, medical personnel, Hollywood elites, and bureaucrats—many of whom had sanctimoniously lectured America about the need to mask around others—all happily bare-faced in comfortable social settings, not following the rules that they were officially imposing on everyone else. Such optics, once perceived by ordinary people, conveyed several messages:

- Those making the rules either 1) don't really believe the virus to be a major threat, or 2) aren't genuinely concerned for people, since their campaigns of shame blamed those with no mask, but not those with cloth masks
- The politicians and bureaucrats really just want social compliance, conformity, and submission
- The once-trusted medical agencies and authorities issuing or endorsing such guidance have been compromised to political interests

Citizens should not have been faulted for drawing the above conclusions any more than a child looking up at the sky should be blamed for thinking it blue.

Ultimately, a growing number of people discerned that mask mandates, like the shaming of the unvaccinated, served the self-interest of the politicians at the cost of inconvenience and discomfort to masses of their constituents. One key benefit of masks to politicians was the creation of a class of scapegoats onto which these politicians could shift responsibility when the virus did what it ultimately was going to do anyway. Geoff Shullenberger put it well:

> It is not difficult to see why mask mandates proved irresistible to politicians. Masks are the perfect form of hygiene theatre, conveying an intuitive sense of safety regardless of demonstrable efficacy at scale. They also offload

responsibility for controlling the pandemic to ordinary people. The over-crowding of ICUs can be blamed on the bad behavior of "anti-maskers", rather than on the allocation of resources by government and hospital CEOs. When cases and deaths spike, it is the fault of the citizenry, not the leadership.[79]

Masking culture varied, often dramatically over even relatively short distances. Throughout the pandemic, our family traveled by air domestically (Seattle, Arizona, and the Grand Canyon, 2020) and internationally (St. Martin, 2021), and observed varying cultures most visually evident in masking. In the summer of 2021, I visited two Costco stores, one near where I live, and the other about 25 miles closer to Washington, DC. On that day, at the first location, I noted probably four or five people wearing masks out of hundreds in the store. Just a few hours later on the same day, at the latter location, I observed nearly the opposite: perhaps a half dozen were unmasked anywhere, even in the parking lot. The feeling inside the two establishments was also completely different. A sense of danger and fear hung in the air of the second store, with the striking visual reminders of contagion on faces at every turn. At that time, I was unaware of any difference in outcome or transmission of COVID-19 between the two areas.[80]

By February of 2022, as already mentioned above with respect to Virginia, mask and vaccine mandates began to fall by the wayside across the nation. COVID-19 appeared to be moving from pandemic to endemic, but had not yet been declared so. Still, politicians likely sensed election season approaching and acted out of an instinct for self-preservation. As one commenter opined,

> It wasn't the suicides. It wasn't the mental health crisis. It wasn't the strug-gling families. It wasn't the domestic violence. It wasn't the developmental delays. It wasn't the closure of businesses. It wasn't the extreme poverty. It wasn't the side effects. It was the polls. That's why they're lifting the mandates.[81]

White House Press Secretary Jen Psaki made a revealing statement in response to the Biden administration's appeal of federal judge Kathryn Kimball Mizelle's April 18, 2022 order overturning the CDC mask mandate on commercial airlines. Psaki said,

> [F]or current and future public health crises, we want to preserve that authority for the CDC to have in the future.[82]

According to this comment from Psaki, preserving the power of unelected bureaucrats to impose a legally binding mask mandate in private spaces was a primary concern of the Biden administration. Yet, for the prior two years, many expressing alarm and worry about such a background agenda were ridiculed.

Vaccines and trust

Americans also noticed apparent manipulation and limitation of public information after observing changing and mixed official messages around COVID-19 mitigation. On March 16, 2020, the Trump administration announced a plan under the modest description of "two weeks to flatten the curve." The stated purpose of the national initiative—entailing lockdowns, masks, and social distancing—had been to slow the spread of the virus in order to prevent overcrowding of hospitals. At the end of the two weeks, however, the message became the need to continue these measures as a means of *stopping* the spread.[83]

An Arab proverb (presumably based upon experience) says that if a camel gets its nose under the edge of a tent, it will be impossible to prevent the rest of the camel from entering. The camel in this case being bureaucratic overreach, "two weeks to flatten the curve" proved to be the nose that became the launching pad for 18 months of school and business closures, onerous restrictions, and widespread economic destruction.[84] Official messaging shifted yet again to an assertion that these measures would now be the "new normal" until a vaccine appeared.[85]

Once the vaccine did appear in late 2020, however, most other measures remained in place in many parts of the country, with school boards and government bureaucrats aided by major media pressing for an extension of precautions. This time, the stated goal was "herd immunity." What would constitute herd immunity? The needed percentage of vaccinated (or COVID-19 recovered) population, like so many other details concerning the pandemic by that point, proved to be a moving target. It was postulated variously at 74% (Center for Communicable Disease Dynamics, December 2020),[86] 65-70% (CDC, May 2021),[87] at least 85% (arbitrary figure of Anthony Fauci following public opinion (see quotation on page 221), December 2020; and the American Medical Association, August 2021),[88] to 90%,[89] to "mythical" (CNBC, August 2021).[90] To be fair, herd immunity would be partly conditioned by vaccine efficacy, which was also uncertain and dependent upon a variety of factors.[91]

Confusing and unclear messaging was everywhere. When an approved vaccine approached, Kamala Harris was asked in an interview whether she planned to get the shot. She answered that if Trump recommended it, she would not get it. Such statements added to many Americans' sense that leaders were allowing their policy preferences to be driven by politics and personal animus, rather than the health and well-being of real people. Citizens weary of mask mandates and business closures were, however, coaxed with promises that the vaccine was 91-96% effective[92] and if they would just get it they could stop wearing masks and get back to normal. However, after many had complied, the story changed and mask mandates returned, even for the vaccinated. In what some perceived as a theater of the absurd, some began to recommend double- or even triple-masking.[93]

When I asked about skipping the second shot of the Pfizer vaccine after reports of adverse symptoms from friends and family members following the second shot, my own doctor told me the first dose is only 2% effective against COVID-19. Many Americans under severe pressure from friends, employers, and government to get vaccinated just wanted clarity. Some asked, "If your vaccine protects you, why do I need it?," and conversely, "If your vaccine does *not* protect you, why do I need it?" These seemed reasonable questions, but were often met with rage rather than answers.

By the date of Joe Biden's inauguration, some 19 million Americans had voluntarily received at least one dose of a COVID-19 vaccine, and fully 3.5 million of these were fully vaccinated. Apparently hoping that some Americans might give him credit for the existence of a vaccine, the Biden White House brazenly tweeted on May 12, 2022, "When President Biden took office, millions were unemployed and there was no vaccine available."[94]

Back in the real word, as vaccination programs progressed, those who for whatever reason had not yet been vaccinated were publicly scapegoated as the cause of ongoing COVID-19 cases and deaths, but this assertion did not make sense to many as it was accompanied by the news that vaccinated people could still get, spread, and even die from COVID-19 (albeit, with reduced risk of the more severe outcomes), and therefore needed to continue other mitigation measures such as masking.[95]

By late 2021, the messaging changed yet again to state that "vaccines are not enough," and Americans should ready themselves for a steady and regular program of booster shots as frequently as every several months, since the variants of COVID-19 can get around a prior vaccination. Such claims became the pretext for ongoing interference of bungling bureaucrats in regular life, such as school and business closures, the continuation of mask mandates, and attempts to make vaccines mandatory in some localities or professions, accompanied by campaigns to exclude the unvaccinated from full participation in society.[96]

In August 2021, talk of a third shot, a booster, began to emerge.

Other Alleged Motivations

The charged atmosphere around COVID-19, coupled with heavy-handed implementation of public policies and draconian demands for total compliance that many could plainly see went beyond what was warranted by the situation—not to mention the obvious suppression of unapproved views and opinions—led many to wonder what else might be going on.

Concerns about manipulation toward transhumanism (by way of, *inter alia*, chemical intervention in human biology) were new to the ears of most and would have been more easily dismissed as science fiction had they not recently been discussed, at times with enthusiasm and at others with cautionary warning, in scientific and political circles.[97]

Some expressed concern that the push for 100% vaccination might have been the pretext for creation of a central government database of private medical information on all Americans.[98] Indeed, when Americans got vaccine shots at any provider participating in the Federal Retail Partnership Program (FRPP), such as Walgreen's Pharmacy, their personally identifiable information was logged and reported to the federal government. Under the program, vaccines were provided to retail pharmacies free of charge in return for collecting and reporting the required patient information.

Hydroxychloroquine and Ivermectin

In the early days of the pandemic, physicians in some countries reported anecdotal success treating COVID-19 patients with early administration of Hydroxychloroquine (HCQ) or Ivermectin. Both medications are readily available, inexpensive, and have been used to treat other ailments for decades. The prospect of such an easy step for diminishing the number of deaths from the virus gave hope to many.

On March 17, 2020, the University of Minnesota began clinical testing of HCQ related to COVID-19. On March 30, the FDA authorized its use for treating COVID. This authorization, however, was rescinded two and a half months later, on June 15, after studies failed to show the drug effective.

Robert Kennedy, however, has looked at the official studies and alleges that they were designed in such a way as to guarantee failure:"[T]heir main trick for ensuring the protocols failed was to wait until late in the disease process before administering HCQ—when it is known to be ineffective."[99] The allegation is serious, with grave implications, and should not be dismissed lightly.

On the other hand, as is often the case in the beginning, a lay public are often susceptible to shortcuts of logic, leading to error. Such seems to have been the situation—at least in part—with Ivermectin. The drug was observed to have the effect of reducing deaths among COVID-19 patients in some countries. From this, some quickly judged it an effective therapeutic for treatment of COVID-19. In the end, Ivermectin was not found to be effective for the treatment of COVID-19 even though its use among populations *that also contained one additional factor* reduced likelihood of death among COVID-19 patients.

By early 2022, peer-reviewed studies found the likely reason that some countries had seen success with Ivermectin in COVID-19 patients. Ivermectin, the research found, resolved a secondary issue that in some instances became life-threatening in the environment of some standard COVID-19 treatments. Specifically, Ivermectin indirectly helped prevent death from COVID-19 among those populations in which threadworm (*Strongyloides stercoralis*) is prevalent. Threadworm affects about 8% of the world's population, and is also common in the countries reporting success. It was in fact the effectiveness in treating *Strongoloides* that led to William Campbell receiving the Nobel Prize for discovering Ivermectin.[100] "The argument is pretty simple. Ivermectin doesn't have an effect on COVID-19 per se. But people infected with COVID-19 get steroids, which can exacerbate latent *Strongyloides* infections."[101]

Thus, steroids can move a latent *Strongyloides* infection into a *Strongyloides* hyperinfection, and this hyperinfection can lead to death. To test the hypothesis that Ivermectin success, when seen, is related to its limitation of *Strongyloides* hyperinfection secondary to steroids, researchers looked through 151 studies cited by a pro-ivermectin website, eliminated the ones that were fraudulent or that were not randomized, and then subjected the remaining twelve to meta-analysis. The results? "[W]hen the studies were stratified by local *Strongyloides* prevalence, a pattern emerged. In areas of high prevalence, Ivermectin appeared to work better, and in areas with low prevalence, it didn't appear to work at all."[102]

Strongyloides is not common in the United States.

Concern among Americans about treatments and policies was contextualized by an observation that policy-making authorities had been politicized, and that their decisions were therefore not guided by singular interest in public health or the well-being of ordinary individuals. Such factors seem obvious: medicine and healthcare are multi-trillion dollar industries in the United States, and embedded in the American consciousness are stories like that of the framed Harrison Ford in the film *The Fugitive*, where a pharmaceutical company had doctored samples in clinical trials to get FDA approval for their multi-billion dollar drug. Although fiction, most Americans intuitively understand that this problem—the potential compromise of medical and research integrity in the pursuit of business interests—is not impossible to imagine in the real world.

Relating such factors and forces to the 2020 pandemic, Kennedy states, "From the outset, hydroxychloroquine (HCQ) and other therapeutics posed an existential threat to Dr. Fauci and Bill Gates' $48 billion COVID vaccine project, and particularly to their vanity drug, remdesivir, in which Gates has a large stake. Under federal law, new vaccines and medications cannot qualify for Emergency Use Authorization (EUA) if any existing FDA-approved drug proves effective against the same malady."[103]

While the prospect that these alternate treatments—if effective—would pose a threat to the personal business interests of people like Fauci or Gates is not in itself evidence that they are indeed effective treatments, such conflicts of interest should be borne in mind by the public as they consider these matters. A balanced assessment of Kennedy's book that does not dismiss it out of hand has been published by Brian Martin.[104]

"97 times more likely to die"

Fear-mongering by public officials—including CDC Director Dr. Rochelle Walensky, installed by Biden on January 20, 2021—was a tragic outcome of the COVID-19 pandemic that resulted in a tremendous decline of public trust in the institutions themselves. Statistics were presented absent relevant and important clarifying details by people like Walensky to support public health policies that were not really warranted by the data.

As information came in, it became evident that the vaccines were indeed effective in lessening the severity of COVID-19 symptoms to the extent of almost entirely preventing its most severe outcome, death. However, this fact alone was insufficient to recommend universal vaccination rather than an emphasis upon vaccinating those populations most vulnerable to the severest consequences in the first place. For a medical procedure to be warranted, the benefits should outweigh the costs or risks. Healthy young people and particularly children were statistically immune from death from COVID-19 even without vaccination.

Yet Joe Biden wrote on Twitter on February 5, 2022, "Here's the deal: Unvaccinated individuals are 97 times more likely to die compared to those who are boosted. Protect yourself and those around you by getting vaccinated and boosted today."

Biden's Tweet was misleading for its lack of context. The weekly COVID-19 death rate from September 19 through December 4, 2021 was about 97 per million unvaccinated Americans, but only about 1 per million vaccinated and boosted Americans. This of course means that during that 11-week period, unvaccinated Americans overall had a 9,999.03/10,000 likelihood of not dying from COVID-19, while those vaccinated and boosted had a 9,999.93/10,000 likelihood of not dying from COVID-19. So, the first thing to note is that the general population was not likely to die from COVID-19.

The next—and even more important—item to note is that Biden and Walensky conspicuously neglected to remind the American public that the overwhelming number of those dying in *both* cases were people in at-risk categories: those over 65 years of age and those with multiple comorbidities. As already shown, even a person over 65 who caught the virus was overwhelmingly likely (96.2%) to survive it...and this group was at greatest risk. It was pretty well known who needed to be vaccinated, but leading Democrats were playing games with statistics.

Thus, Biden and Walensky's "97 times more likely to die if unvaccinated" statement was true when averaged over the entire population, but its omissions created an expectation that people in every age group and category would be dropping like flies if they did not get vaccinated. Such was simply not the case.[105]

Lab leak theory, revisited

The possibility that the COVID-19 virus had either escaped or been purposely leaked from the virology lab in Wuhan, China—a short distance from where the first cases appeared—was first hypothesized in early 2020. In February, the New York Post published a column by Steven W. Mosher asking whether COVID-19 had leaked from the Wuhan virology lab. The column was labeled "false" by Facebook's fact-checkers.[106] Mere mention of the lab leak theory was for more than a year afterward commonly met with derision and ridicule.

By fiercely rejecting the lab leak theory, gatekeepers served their apparent purpose of framing President Trump as a xenophobe for ever suggesting it. Uncritical rejection of the theory by national media and social media also showed political and diplomatic deference to the Chinese Communist regime. Only after Biden was sworn in did they cautiously admit President Trump could have been right.

Eventually, however, the "conspiracy theorists" were vindicated, as the Wuhan lab leak theory, though not necessarily proven, was suddenly taken seriously once again in early 2021.[107] Tim Graham of the Daily Signal related the Washington Post's stunning 2021 admission that those it and others had viciously ridiculed for a year might have been right after all:

> Washington Post "fact-checker" Glenn Kessler posted an article on May 25 [2021] titled "How the Wuhan lab-leak theory suddenly became credible." Kessler's timeline suggested some media figures and media outlets, including two former New York Times science reporters and CBS "60 Minutes," have been warming up to this once-"debunked" thesis since Trump's defeat.
>
> He notes that Sen. Tom Cotton proclaimed during a Jan. 30, 2020, Senate Armed Services Committee hearing: "This coronavirus is a catastrophe on the scale of Chernobyl for China. But actually, it's probably worse than Chernobyl, which was localized in its effect. The coronavirus could result in a global pandemic."[108]

Graham, however, had scathing words for Kessler and his associates for the way they savaged Cotton "for his merely demanding China should have to answer for this." He listed some examples:

"*Tom Cotton keeps repeating a coronavirus conspiracy that was already debunked*," read a February 17, 2020 headline from Kessler's paper, the Washington Post. The Post has since revised the headline to "Tom Cotton keeps repeating a coronavirus fringe theory that scientists have disputed." However, the article still comes up on a search as "Tom Cotton repeats debunked conspiracy theory about coronavirus..." despite a correction notice on the article itself stating that, "The term 'debunked' and The Post's use of 'conspiracy theory' have been removed.")[109]

"*Senator Tom Cotton Repeats Fringe Theory of Conspiracy Origins*," said a February 17, 2020 headline in the New York Times.

"*Tom Cotton is playing a dangerous game with his coronavirus speculation*," declared a February 18, 2020 article by Chris Cillizza at CNN.com.

What Kessler omitted was that he had also been part of the smear operation—a fact that he seemed to gloss over when announcing that the theory might have something to it, after all:

> Kessler also left out of his timeline his own tweet in which he called the theory "virtually impossible," dismissed Sen. Ted Cruz and promoted his shop's explanatory video on Wuhan: "I fear @tedcruz missed the scientific animation in the video that shows how it is virtually impossible for this virus to jump from the lab. Or the many interviews with actual scientists. We deal in facts, and viewers can judge for themselves."
>
> This explicit reversal—this undebunking—exposes the ridiculousness of the media's assertion that they represent facts, truth and science, and aren't emotionally blinded by Trump hatred. It also exposes the "independent fact-checkers" and their clients such as Facebook who squashed this theory because the liberal knee jerked at every presidential utterance of "China virus" and "Wuhan flu."[110]

Concluded Graham, "It's not a mystery why this happened. The Democrats thought the coronavirus was going to be that silver bullet that would remove former President Trump from office. Their arrogant belief that Trump was an ignoramus led them to shame anyone or any theory that Trump endorsed. ... They were willing to embrace the supposed authority of communist China, the China-enabling World Health Organization and the 'prevailing opinion' of the science journals and magazines that endorsed Joe Biden for president."[111]

On July 20, 2021, Senator Rand Paul, a medical doctor, confronted Dr. Anthony Fauci over his earlier congressional testimony that the Wuhan Institute of Virology, which had received funding from the National Institutes of Health with partial oversight from Fauci himself, had not been engaged in gain-of-function research.[112] The lab, it came to light, had indeed been conducting gain-of-function work on bat coronaviruses.[113]

BLM, Antifa, and "Defund the Police" Riots

We now come to the second paradigmatic issue of 2020.[114] Several shootings or deaths of black people in 2020, in most cases unarmed, drew national attention to questions of injustice along racial lines. The tragic deaths of Ahmaud Arbery and George Floyd and the police shootings of Breonna Taylor and Jacob Blake took their place among others in recent memory—such as the 2016 fatal shooting of Philando Castile in front of his girlfriend and her four-year-old daughter during a police stop, and the 2012 fatal shooting of 17-year-old Trayvon Martin.[115] These deaths pulled the heartstrings of the world.

They also occurred and were comprehended in the context of America's history, in which our nation's founding affirmation—that all people[116] are created equal and endowed by their Creator with certain unalienable rights, among which are life, liberty, and the pursuit of happiness—was not substantially lived out by some original signers of the Declaration of Independence and the Constitution. Even the Declaration's author, Thomas Jefferson, personally kept hundreds of people in slavery for another fifty years, used his influence to lure a teenaged Sally Hemings from freedom in France back to spend the rest of her life in bondage in the United States, and eventually liberated only those slaves who were his own children with Hemings. Upon his death, the families who had been kept enslaved by Jefferson were sold off to settle the former president's debts, with parents separated from children and children separated from each other.

Why the hypocrisy? First, there is a difference between knowing (or saying) what is right and *doing* what is right. We must remember that Jefferson also took it upon himself to cut up the Bible, omitting portions supporting the divinity and divine authority of Jesus. Did these grate at Jefferson's rational presuppositions or did they prick his conscience too much? Either way, they were left out of his "Bible."[117] While we must not dismiss the tremendous good Jefferson did by, for example, drafting one of the wisest political documents in the history of the world that would lead —as sure as the sun rises—to the liberation of millions of slaves and to freedom and opportunity for all Americans on a scale never before realized in the world, it ought to surprise few that a man who cut from the Bible might live an inconsistent moral life.[118]

Kidnapping children or adults and binding them to a life of servitude is deeply sinful, unjust, and inhumane. Binding a child born into servitude to such a life is also sinful, unjust, and inhumane. It is absolutely wrong, and everyone who cares about justice should hate the practice and be angered by it.

Some have asserted that slavery was America's "original sin." It was not. First, taking or holding someone in involuntary servitude is a sin, but 1) sin is universal and 2) at no time was slavery ever particular to the United States. There is not a person alive who is not inclined to do wrong, and there is no person who does not do wrong on a daily basis. Some wrongs, like taking or holding others in involuntary servitude, are deeply egregious. But slavery is neither foundational nor essential to the United States. It has been practiced around the world for millennia. People of all races, including so-called white Europeans, have been captured and held in slavery in large numbers. Slavery and racism are not particularly American problems; they are world problems.

The Declaration of Independence was among other things an aspirational document, a measuring stick to which our forebears increasingly sought to conform over time. Our Civil War, in which one-third of a million lives were lost seeking an end to our national pre-existing condition of slavery, led to the abolition of slavery 89 years after our nation's founding. For those whose lives were consumed as by locusts for those 89 years, it was far too long. In the long arc of history, however, it may be considered a short span. And most importantly, American abolition happened with direct moral appeal to the document Jefferson wrote; the Declaration of Independence was a beacon, a road map toward justice and a more perfect union. It has served as a conscience for the United States then and throughout our history, even if it did not sufficiently prick the human conscience of its own author in his personal life and dealings.

Since the deaths of Arbery, Floyd, Taylor, Blake, Castile, and Martin were rarely presented in media as very sad and even unjust occurrences within a truthful context of overall police shootings or similar criminal acts in the United States, many people quickly reached a conclusion that the accused were guilty and that in every instance the root cause was racism. One cannot say that attention to nuance would have changed the overall conclusion in every case, but truth being foundational to justice, the fierce avoidance of nuance by the mobs harmed everyone and ultimately harmed the cause of justice. These poignant situations simply and reflexively became emblematic of an alleged ongoing systemic devaluation of black people's lives, and were presented by BLM and Antifa as Exhibit A in a damning case against America from her very founding.[119]

Public perception mattered greatly. Protests and violent riots broke out around the United States and even around the world, causing billions of dollars' worth of damage to property in the U.S. and inflicting physical harm on many. By early June, after only two weeks of protests that major media reported as being "mostly peaceful,"[120] nineteen people had died, and many more were injured, in violence related to BLM riots.[121]

Ahmaud Arbery

On February 23, 2020, 25-year-old Ahmaud Arbery, a black man, was chased by three white men in two vehicles, then shot to death during a struggle for one of his pursuer's guns, about two miles from his mother's house near Brunswick, Georgia.[122] Just prior to the incident, Arbery had been wandering inside a vacant house that was under construction in the neighborhood. He had taken nothing. A neighbor, retired police officer Travis McMichael, seeing Arbery exit the house and start running, seems to have assumed that the young man (who did not live in that subdivision) was—or might be—connected to some recent break-ins in the neighborhood. Prosecutors later argued that this assumption was made because Arbery was black, rather than the fact that he had been running from the vacant house. However, instead of calling the police, McMichael and his son Gregory grabbed guns and quickly pursued Arbery in their pickup truck. Ahmaud tried for several minutes to evade and escape, changing course multiple times, but was eventually blocked by Travis McMichael, who had by now exited his truck and was holding a rifle. After running around the truck, rather than continuing to run out of the neighborhood, Arbery seems to have approached McMichael and grabbed his gun. As a result, three shots were fired, and Arbery died on the scene.

The latter parts of the incident were filmed on the cellphone of William "Roddie" Byran Jr., another neighbor who joined the pursuit after seeing Arbery running past his house followed by the McMichaels. Bryan, not armed, began filming as he was driving, stating to police that he had hoped to get a picture of Arbery that would help in later identification. It is unlikely that Bryan knew the reason for the pursuit or contemplated that a shooting would result. Police were called after the incident, and statements were taken. Bryan immediately made his cellphone video available to the police.

Authorities did not make arrests in connection with the incident. Then Bryan's cellphone video was published on YouTube and Twitter on May 5. The video went viral, and public outrage ensued. Like most, I remember being deeply disturbed by the video at that time.

The two McMichaels and Bryan were arrested and tried. In November 2021, all three were convicted on multiple murder counts and other charges.[123] Said Rev. Al Sharpton to a gathered crowd shortly after the conviction, "Let the word go forth all over the world that a jury of eleven whites and one black in the Deep South stood up in the courtroom and said, 'Black lives do matter.'"[124] A subsequent federal hate crime guilty plea which would have reduced Travis McMichael's sentence in exchange for an admission of racist motives and a forfeiture of right to appeal was withdrawn by McMichael, so an appeal is once again expected.[125]

George Floyd

On May 25, 2020, 46-year-old George Floyd, a black man, died while—and perhaps because—Minneapolis police officer Derek Chauvin held his knee on Floyd's neck. Three other officers looked on, and a number of onlookers pleaded with Officer Chauvin to remove his knee from Floyd's neck; meanwhile, Floyd himself, facedown on the pavement, was heard saying "Please...I can't breathe." Chauvin's knee remained on Floyd's neck throughout the 9.5-minute ordeal, during the final two minutes of which Floyd was motionless and without a pulse. Passersby recorded video of the incident that quickly went viral online.

Eleven months later, on April 20, 2021, Chauvin was found guilty of all three charges brought against him in the death of Floyd.[126] This verdict, however, followed intimidation and threats if the jury reached the "wrong" verdict. Joe Biden himself had interfered in the case, in defiance of Judge Peter Cahill's instructions.[127] Congresswoman Maxine Waters, in a video she posted on Twitter of her speaking to a crowd that was protesting the April 11 shooting of Daunte Wright, said that she and the crowd were "looking for a guilty verdict" against Chauvin and, "We've got to stay in the streets, and we've got to demand justice. I am hopeful that we will get a verdict that says, 'guilty, guilty, guilty,' and if we don't, we cannot go away. We've got to get more confrontational."[128]

Because of Congresswoman Waters' attempt to influence the jury, Alan Dershowitz said that the judge ought to have granted the motion for a mistrial. Dershowitz also likened Waters' tactics of jury intimidation to those used by the Ku Klux Klan in the 1920s and 1930s: "The Klan would march outside of courthouses and threaten all kinds of reprisals if the jury ever dared convict a white person or acquit a black person."[129]

It is truly unfortunate that the jury who rendered the verdict against Chauvin faced such threats and intimidation and the awareness that national chaos and destruction would break out were they to render a "not guilty" verdict. Because of these tactics, Floyd and his family got a preferred outcome, but were denied a moral victory. The world will now never know whether the jury would have reached a guilty verdict based upon the evidence of the case—that is, whether Chauvin was justly convicted of the crime of which he was accused. While it seems likely to many that he was guilty, as it is, all we know for sure is that the mob got their way.

The trial of the other three officers present at the time of the Floyd incident began in January of 2022. They are charged with using the "color of the law" to deprive Floyd of his civil rights, particularly the "right to be free from a police officer's deliberate indifference to his serious medical needs."[130]

Lafayette Square Riots and Burning of St. John's Church

Protests around the country and at the nation's capital quickly followed publication of the disturbing video of Floyd's final minutes. On May 31, multiple fires were set around Washington, DC; among them was one set in the basement of the historic St. John's Episcopal Church on Lafayette Square across the street from the White House during the BLM protests. The church, built in the early 1800s, was called the church of presidents, in recognition of the fact that every U.S. president beginning with James Madison had attended a church service there.[131]

Although Trump had nothing to do with the Minneapolis Police Department, or Derek Chauvin, or the death of George Floyd, protestors wished to lay the Floyd situation at the feet of the President, whom his opponents had been trying to paint as racist due to his advocacy for equality in immigration (i.e., supporting equal application of laws rather than indulging the soft bigotry of low expectations), his willingness to utter terms like "radical Islamic terrorism," his previous questioning whether Barack Obama was born in the United States, and the fact that some racist groups had voiced support for Trump and he had declined to immediately acknowledge or immediately repudiate them. Throughout his presidency, memes were commonly circulated that labeled acts or situations with an evident negative racial motivation as "Trump's America."

During the Lafayette Square riots from May 30 through June 1, rioters threw bricks, glass bottles, and other projectiles, and repeatedly struck officers; more than 60 officers were injured, and some were hospitalized requiring surgery.[132] On June 1, 2020, President Trump, following a Rose Garden speech in which he vowed to crack down on violent protests, walked over to take a photo on the public sidewalk in front of St. John's church, which had been damaged by fire at the hands of the vandals the night before. This photo session, too, drew immediate criticism from the left and the media.

Despite widespread reporting to the contrary, an investigation by the Office of the Inspector General (OIG) later confirmed that "U.S. Park Police did not clear Lafayette Park and the nearby area of protestors on June 1, 2020, so President Donald Trump could walk from the White House to St. John's Church, but learned of his interest in surveying the site hours after they had already begun planning to clear the area to put up new fencing."[133] The OIG report determined that Park Police acted within their authority to begin clearing Lafayette Square, and that use of pepper spray against protestors by Bureau of Prisons officers, and the use of tear gas by Metropolitan Police officers, occurred in defiance of Park Police orders not to do so.[134] In a statement following the report's release,[135] President Trump said,

> As we have said all along, and it was backed up in today's highly detailed and professionally written report, our fine Park Police made the decision to clear the park to allow a contractor to safely install antiscale fencing to protect from Antifa rioters, radical BLM protestors, and other violent demonstrators who are causing chaos and death to our cities. In this instance, they tried burning down the church the day before the clearing. Fortunately, we were there to stop the fire from spreading beyond the base-ment - and it was our great honor and privilege to do so. Again, thank you to the Inspector General![136]

Jacob Blake Shooting and Demonization of Rittenhouse

On August 23, in Kenosha, Wisconsin, 29-year-old Jacob Blake—a black man—was shot seven times by a police officer during an attempted arrest for an outstanding warrant. The gunshots injured Blake, but he did not die from his wounds.

Because of the warrant, officers were legally required to arrest Blake. Tasers had failed, Blake had physically fought with officers while armed with a knife, and then he tried to get into the driver's side of his minivan as officers yelled "Drop the knife!" Officers had no way of knowing that he was not reaching into the van to retrieve a gun. The officer reached out in an attempt to pull Blake out, and then fired.[137] According to the Kenosha Times:

> The DOJ [Wisconsin Department of Justice] stated that police were called ... by a woman who said her boyfriend was present and was not supposed to be on the premises. ... According to the statement from Matthews [the Police union lawyer], officers were told before they arrived that Blake had a felony warrant for his arrest for a domestic violence incident that included a charge of third-degree sexual assault. Officers who encounter people with active warrants are required to take them into custody. ... "Mr. Blake was not unarmed. He was armed with a knife. The officers did not see the knife initially," Matthews said in his statement. "The officers issued repeated commands for Mr. Blake to drop the knife. He did not comply." Matthews stated that officers went "hands-on" with Blake and two officers used tasers. "Mr. Blake forcefully fought with the officers," including putting one of the officers in a headlock. [138]

To the public, in the context of the Arbery and Floyd incidents, the Blake shooting immediately became another example of a systemic devaluation of black lives. Over the next several nights, Kenosha was torn apart by violent protests of Blake's shooting. On the third night of vandalism, riots, and burning, many protestors were armed. Cars and local businesses were damaged and destroyed.

Good Samaritans from the neighboring areas, frustrated at the injustice of damage and harm to local residents and businesses and other violence going on at the hands of rioters, stepped forward to help protect the community. One of these, 17-year-old Kyle Rittenhouse, had worked as a lifeguard, was trained in advanced life support, and had volunteered hundreds of community service hours. In December 2018, Rittenhouse had begun a Facebook fundraiser for a nonprofit called "Humanize the Badge," which he said sought to "forge stronger relationships between law enforcement officers and the communities they serve." He asked his friends to donate to the organization for his sixteenth birthday.

On the night of August 25, Rittenhouse came equipped with a first aid kit and other supplies. As many people in these riots were armed, Rittenhouse also carried a rifle. He is seen on video prior to the next events explaining that he was there to help, and directing anyone who has been hurt to come to him. Rittenhouse had extinguished fires that were being started in dumpsters by 36-year-old agitator and convicted sex offender Joseph Rosenbaum. Rosenbaum, face concealed, began chasing Rittenhouse, cornering him into a forming mob armed with bats and other weapons. Upon hearing a single shot fired (the fired shot can be seen in the distance on video footage of the incident, with the shooter later identified as 44-year-old Alexander Blaine), Rittenhouse turned to face Rosenbaum, aiming his gun. When Rosenbaum lunged for the barrel of Rittenhouse's rifle, the latter fired four shots. Rittenhouse was forced to flee the scene as the mob began calling for him to be attacked, but Rittenhouse can be heard on camera immediately calling authorities for help after the shooting, "I just shot somebody. I had to shoot him."[139] Rittenhouse ran toward police vehicles as they arrived on the scene. Somebody is heard calling "Cranium[140] that boy. He just shot a man." Rioters chased after Rittenhouse, a protestor struck him in the head and knocked off his hat, and Rittenhouse tripped and fell to the ground. As another protestor attempted to jump on Rittenhouse, Rittenhouse fired two shots into the air. Another protestor then struck Rittenhouse in the back of the head with the edge of a skateboard.[141]

However, Rittenhouse, a 17-year-old white boy wearing a backwards baseball cap and toting an AR-15, meaning to help minimize the damage while BLM and Antifa rioters were trying to "burn it all down" in protest of systemic racism, proved the perfect target of leftist rage. The young man immediately became the latest poster child for "white supremacy" in the United States. Candidate Joe Biden on two occasions "made remarks or promoted a campaign advertisement that strongly suggested Rittenhouse was a white supremacist ... ."[142] One of these times, Biden tweeted a picture of Rittenhouse with the caption, "There's no other way to put it: the President of the United States refused to disavow white supremacists on the debate stage last night."[143]

Rittenhouse was tried in the killings of Rosenbaum and Huber, and the wounding of Grosskreutz, and vindicated with not guilty verdicts on every one of the five charges.[144]

On the very same day as the Rittenhouse verdict, November 19, 2021, a jury in Vero Beach, Florida acquitted A.J. Coffee IV, a black man, of felony murder and attempted murder of a law enforcement officer. Coffee had fired at deputies several times during a 2017 SWAT raid. Police had been there to apprehend Coffee's father Andrew Coffee, III related to suspected drug dealing. Coffee's girlfriend, Alteria Woods, was killed in the crossfire, and Coffee—who had initiated the shootout—was charged with her murder and also with attempted murder of a police officer. Coffee claimed self-defense, saying he had not heard the police announce themselves and had thought he and Alteria had been in danger. Coffee was formerly convicted in 2013 of battery on a police officer and evading arrest after fleeing a traffic stop.[145]

Coffee's acquittal by a jury on the same day as Rittenhouse' acquittal was interesting, given the overall assertion that the justice system is stacked against black men in the United States. While it is only one data point, some suggest it is evidence that the narrative of double standards when it comes to the use of the self-defense plea in court may be unfounded. Though the particular details varied somewhat, Rittenhouse and Coffee— the latter having a prior conviction while the former did not—had both made the same essential defense, and both were successful before their respective juries.[146]

BLM Inc.

Black Lives Matter (BLM) was founded in 2013. It is ideologically intertwined with many causes associated with the American left.

BLM is also fairly openly self-identified as a Marxist organization. Its clenched fist symbol is quite familiar to observers of Marxist and communist movements around the world throughout the 20th century.[147] The same symbol was also embraced by the Black Power movement of the 1960s.[148] The vast majority of Americans wholeheartedly support justice for all. Many of BLM's objectives and strategies, however, go beyond justice, or reject it altogether. These include the abolition of capitalism, which most Americans do *not* support.

BLM co-founder Patrisse Cullors was not ashamed to embrace the Marxist label for BLM when she said, "We actually do have an ideological frame[work]. ... We are trained Marxists. We are super-versed on, sort of, ideological theories."[149] BLM's official platform, published in 2015, contained a specific call to "disrupt the Western-prescribed nuclear family structure."[150]

A large number of Americans who were indignant over injustice against black people, and willing to say so, remained unwilling to support the Black Lives Matter movement on account of its openly Marxist assertions and proposed solutions,[151] as well as all the other ideological baggage it carried and expressed in the language of Marxist liberation theologies.[152] Because the phrase "black lives matter" was identical to the name of the organization, many bristled at demands that they "say the words," because saying the words felt like endorsement of everything the BLM organization wanted to accomplish. However, people fond of the Marxist agenda often refused to accept any statement supporting justice—no matter how explicit —that was not expressed *via* the exact words "black lives matter" as evidence of "white supremacy," that opposed justice for black people.

The phrases "all lives matter" and "blue [i.e., police] lives matter" also came into use following BLM's 2013 founding. Both slogans were severely criticized by BLM advocates as evasions, tacit denials of the specific concerns for justice narrowly asserted by the Black Lives Matter slogan and movement. We need not discuss these in detail here, except to note that the sentiments behind such terms of several years prior persisted in 2020.

In May of 2021, Cullors resigned her post as executive director of BLM amid growing criticism for her purchase of four homes totaling more than $3 million. The organization at that time had over $60 million in assets, some of which were "transferred to BLM Canada to buy a $6 million mansion in Toronto, the former headquarters of Canada's Communist Party."[153] In May of 2020, further reports of inappropriate large-scale financial mismanagement and self dealing by Cullors and other top BLM individuals emerged from tax filings.[154]

Aborted Siege of the White House

"The White House Siege" of Sept. 17, 2020 and following had been advertised as a successor in spirit to the Occupy Wall Street protests of 2011,[155] and was suggested by the same Canadian group, Adbusters, that started Occupy.[156] On July 28, in the wake of the breakup of the first Lafayette Square protests, Adbusters announced the plan on Twitter:

"On September 17, 2020 we will lay siege to The @WhiteHouse for exactly fifty days. ...

Are you ready for #revolution?

This is the #WhiteHouseSiege[157]

The timing of the siege's September 17 start was for it to run through the November 3 election.

Possibly calculating that the siege might have an effect opposite of that its organizers intended, the event was postponed. Ironically, Trump and his supporters, who had been blamed for the siege itself, were also blamed for its cancelation or postponement. The organizing group announced[158] on Twitter minutes before the scheduled assembly,

NOTICE TO ALL PROTESTERS: After intensive talks and multiple considerations, we've decided to cancel the General Assembly scheduled for 12 noon in Lafayette Square. We received MANY threats of death and violence from Trump supporters and white nationalists. #Safety ...

Supreme Court Vacancy Filled by Amy Coney Barrett

Long-serving Supreme Court Justice Ruth Bader Ginsburg died at age 87 on Sept. 18, 2020. Ginsburg was one of five progressives on the bench, the others being Breyer, Kagan, Roberts, and Sotomayor. Trump had already brought the Court to the brink of a conservative majority by his successful confirmation of two nominees, Neil Gorsuch and Brett Kavanaugh.

Democrats harbored a lingering anger that the Republican-controlled Senate, at the direction of Mitch McConnell, declined to consider Obama's nomination of Merrick Garland in 2016. Immediately upon Ginsburg's death, Democrat leadership drew an analogy, announcing in desperation that Trump had no right to nominate a replacement for Ginsburg because it was an election year. However, the Constitution places no such limitation. In 2016 Obama had simply presided over a divided government, and the situation was now different, with the President's party also in control of the Senate. Republicans rightly reminded Democrats that, had they controlled the Senate in 2016, they would not have refrained from filling the vacancy during Obama's final year, but would have nominated and confirmed an even more ideologically leftist candidate than Garland.

Trump nominated Amy Coney Barrett on September 26. Confirmation hearings took place October 12-15, with very little controversy over her qualifications. She was confirmed by the Senate in a 58-42 vote, with not one Democrat in favor, and assumed her place on the Court on October 27.

The Alleged Treason of Gen. Mark Milley

On October 30, 2020, and without consultation with Commander in Chief Donald J. Trump, Chairman of the Joint Chiefs of Staff General Mark Milley secretly made the first of two calls to Chinese General Li Zuocheng of the China's People's Liberation Army. In this call, Milley said,

> General Li, I want to assure you that the American government is stable and everything is going to be okay. We are not going to attack or conduct any kinetic operations against you. ... General Li, you and I have known each other for now five years. If we're going to attack, I'm going to call you ahead of time. It's not going to be a surprise.[159]

The second phone call was made on January 8, 2021. Milley did not mention either of the calls to the President, reportedly due to a belief that the President's mental state had declined following the election.[160] Furthemore, Milley on the latter date apparently took steps to limit President Trump's ability to call for a military strike. These reports, which did not come to light until nearly a year after the first phone call, led retired Lt. Col. Alexander Vindman to tweet, "If this is true GEN Milley must resign. He usurped civilian authority, broke Chain of Command, and violated the sacrosanct principle of civilian control over the military. It's an extremely dangerous precedent. You can't simply walk away from that."[161]

Milley, however, did not act alone. While he obviously would bear full liability for his actions when executing his duties in the chain of command, General Milley's latter actions "followed a call from House Speaker Nancy Pelosi (D-CA) who wanted Milley to stand in the way of Trump taking any military action."[162] In other words, Pelosi herself—by all appearances— had been attempting to orchestrate a military coup against the President.

Democratic Primary

Twenty-nine candidates ran for the Democratic nomination in 2020. Biden's eventual Vice Presidential pick, Kamala Harris, was among them. Harris, recently rated the most liberal member of the Senate,[163] was the fourteenth to drop out of the race on December 3, 2019, "after months of slumping poll numbers."[164] Biden had vowed publicly to make fitness for the role a lower priority than race and sex when choosing his running mate and nominating to the Supreme Court.[165] He fulfilled his promise in both instances.

Joe Biden became the presumptive nominee on April 8, 2020, after Bernie Sanders' exit.

Other major contenders, with dates they dropped out shown in parentheses, were:

- Tom Steyer, billionaire, climate change and impeachment activist (February 29)
- Pete Buttigieg, former mayor of South Bend, Indiana (March 1)
- Amy Klobuchar, Minnesota Senator (March 2)
- Michael Bloomberg, billionaire media executive, former New York City mayor (March 4)
- Elizabeth Warren, Massachusetts Senator (March 5)
- Tulsi Gabbard, Hawaii Congresswoman (March 19)
- Bernie Sanders, Vermont Senator (April 8)[166]

The Democrat presidential primary contest did not draw the level of national interest one might expect to accompany a groundswell of public opposition to President Trump. The Democrat candidate debate on November 18, 2019 set a record low with only 6.51 million watching, lower still than the October 15 debate, which had already set a record low with 8.55 million total viewers.[167] For comparison, the August 6, 2015 Republican presidential primary debate drew 24 million viewers.[168]

The Trump Campaign

President Trump entered 2020 under attack and nearly impeached, but in a strong position politically. His policies had led—pre-COVID—to a booming economy, record low unemployment, a flowering of small business, energy independence for the first time in 70 years[169] (at least as far as U.S. oil consumption was concerned[170]), the advance of peace abroad, an affirmation of equality and rule of law, and a renewed optimism about the possibilities and promises of the American dream for everyone willing to play fair. Possibly due to the above, Trump's popularity among Americans did not dip despite the severe and steady drumbeat emanating from major media, government, and academia. People seemed to trust him because he had kept promises. A survey of U.S. adults conducted September 18-24, 2018, halfway through his first term, showed that Trump got highest marks for the traits "Stands up for what he believes" (68% said it describes him, 24% said it does not), "Able to get things done" (50% said it describes him, 46% said it does not), and "Keeps his promises" (49% said it describes him, 45% said it does not).[171]

Regarding promises kept, one can find positive and negative lists.[172] One list compiled by Sebastian Gorka was presented in the first chapter. Although attempting to separate a politician from his or her constituents by listing broken promises is common in politics, the tactic becomes less effective when the candidate *has* kept many promises. Even his critics admitted that Trump made good on such promises as taking no salary, ensuring funding for historically black colleges, defunding Planned Parenthood, moving the U.S. Embassy in Israel from Tel Aviv to Jerusalem, suspending immigration from terror-prone countries, limiting illegal immigration, saying "Merry Christmas" instead of "Happy Holidays," asking countries we protect to pay a greater portion of the burden for joint defense, using U.S. steel for infrastructure projects, raising tariffs on imported goods, renegotiating NAFTA, reversing Barack Obama's 2016 executive order on guns, reversing Barack Obama's Cuba policy, nominating from a pre-approved list to replace Supreme Court Justice Antonin Scalia, creating a 10% repatriation tax, and canceling the U.S. participation in the Paris climate accord.[173] Trump's faithfulness in keeping of promises angered those who opposed his agenda, and simultaneously made it difficult to accuse him of not following through.

By the election there was relative calm in the Middle East and no Americans had been killed in Afghanistan since January 2020. On September 15, 2020, President Trump hosted and witnessed the signing of the so-called "Abraham Accords," a "declaration of peace, cooperation, and constructive diplomatic and friendly relations" between the State of Israel and the Kingdom of Bahrain, the State of Israel and the UAE, and later between the State of Israel and the Kingdom of Morocco (December 22, 2020) and with Sudan (undated).[174] One year later, the Accords were called a "rare normalization of relations between the Gulf Arab states and Israel."[175] On this occasion, the State of Israel tweeted that the Trump-era deal was "a milestone for peace in the region."[176]

Trump's preferred public communication style remained direct, down-to-earth, and unscripted. Often ridiculed by his detractors, it was loved by many Americans apparently tired of well-groomed politicians talking a good line but not trustworthy to follow through. Using Twitter, Trump circumvented gatekeepers and communicated directly with the people, a fact that threw the gatekeepers and their allies into fits.

Among the most memorable and dynamic features of Trump's 2020 campaign were his rallies. They were many, they were energetic, and they were consistently large to overflowing in attendance.[177] The President made a total of 76 public campaign appearances from September 7 through November 2, closing out his re-election bid with a flurry of activity, conducting fourteen rallies in Michigan, Iowa, and North Carolina scheduled for the three final days prior to November 3.[178]

Despite his extreme unpopularity among the most outspoken Hollywood elites, Donald Trump had open and solid support from a number of key figures in 2020. Among these were Jon Voight, Kirstie Alley, Kid Rock, Scott Baio, Roseanne Barr, Ted Nugent, Isaiah Washington, Dean Cain,

Robert Davi, Kristy Swanson, Chuck Woolery, Stephen Baldwin, Tony Sabato, Jr., Randy Quaid, Samaire Armstrong, and Stacey Dash.[179]

The Biden Campaign

Joe Biden's campaign was quite different in tone and messaging from that of Trump's. His message was largely anti-Trump; Biden promised to undo what Trump had done, and to restore the policies that Trump had reversed. Biden appealed to the legacy of Barack Obama, and obviously retained much of the base that had supported him and the former president. Biden also regularly alleged that Trump and his supporters were racist, bigoted, and xenophobic. The fact that his own running mate, Harris, had strongly and directly insinuated racism against Biden himself—her precise words to him were "I do not believe you are racist ... but"—was quickly airbrushed from the narrative once she joined the ticket.[180]

Biden's "rallies," when he did have them, were tiny affairs. A photograph of one rally held on September 23 in North Carolina showed a total of about fourteen attendees, each one isolated inside a white circle painted on the ground. Inside each circle was a chair and a bottle of water.

Conservatives were alternately puzzled and amused by Joe Biden's lack of campaign activity in the lead-up to Election Day. Biden aides said his low-key approach was intentional, to show a respect for public health guidelines in a time of COVID.[181] Between September 7 and November 2, Biden conducted 52 public appearances, including presidential debates, rallies, and speeches.[182]

By October, Joe Biden enjoyed the endorsement of all the expected celebrities. Among them were Dwayne "The Rock" Johnson, Jay Leno, Bruce Springsteen, Larry David, Jason Alexander, Cardi B, Mark Cuban, Howard Stern, Zooey Deschanel, Jon Stewart, Tom Hanks, Jimmy Buffett, Barbra Streisand, Rob Reiner, Don Cheadle, Drew Carey, George Clooney, Cher, Robert De Niro, Sheryl Crow, Lady Gaga, Robert Redford, Madonna, Ben Affleck, Dustin Hoffman, Neil Young, George Takei, Mark Hamill, Whoopi Goldberg, Julia Louis-Dreyfus, Leonardo DiCaprio, and Willie Nelson.[183]

Biden seemed to be barely trying. He was mocked by Trump and others for hiding in his basement. His public appearances were not grand affairs, and rallies, when they did occur, small. As Matt Viser put it,

> Joe Biden spent months of his presidential campaign safely ensconced in his basement, communicating to the country via a television camera. His convention speech was delivered to a near-empty room in Delaware. His remarks after being declared the 46th president were given before a distanced parking lot full of honking cars.[184]

The Biden/Harris operation might have well been described as a pursed-lipped scowl at everything that defined Donald Trump: free and easy, unafraid, and available to regular people. If they intended a sharp contrast to Trump's dynamism, their utter lack of energy and enthusiasm hit the mark. Political pundits who had noted the failure, historically, of purely negative campaigns (devoid of a clear positive message or agenda) wondered if Biden and Harris, blinded by pure hatred of Trump and his supporters, had miscalculated. Yet, their cool confidence was unnerving. Observed Sharyl Atkisson in *The Hill*,

> Less than six weeks before the election, one of the most profound disappointments among some of Joe Biden's supporters is that he doesn't even seem to be trying...even to some of his cheerleaders, it feels like Biden hasn't even been showing up. From March until the last week in August, according to news reports, Biden made no in-person speeches or campaign appearances.[185]

All this was occurring—or perhaps we should say not occurring—at a time when Trump rallies were huge and growing in both number and attendance. To be sure, Democrats leveraged such rallies in the midst of the pandemic as reckless and irresponsible, labeling them as "super spreader" events. But the optics of the presidential candidate sitting at home, canceling press events day after day, and so forth, seemed highly odd. Atkisson continued,

> Trump looks like he's running circles around Biden. Whether you believe the precise polls or not, wherever you think Trump's popularity stands, there seems to be general agreement that he is gaining ground. Thousands come out and wait in long lines to see him; even when he's not present, there are boat parades and motorcycle parades. He's said to be picking up votes among blacks, Latinos and police unions that traditionally support Democrats. And then there's the Black Lives Matter protests and urban violence — or, as I and many others have come to think of them, the "Get-Out-The-Trump-Vote Brigade."
>
> While Biden apparently spends quiet hours at home, I count 14 in-person rallies on Trump's September schedule so far: New Hampshire, Michigan, Wisconsin, Nevada, Florida, Virginia and Minnesota and multiple trips to Ohio, North Carolina and Pennsylvania. When he speaks, it's always a stemwinder that delights attendees. He never seems to go shorter than an hour; it's often closer to two. In between the all-out rallies, he's stopping by other campaign events, making policy remarks, taking endless questions from the press — and running the country.
>
> Much to his enemies' chagrin, Trump looks like, well, a winner.[186]

Presidential and Vice Presidential Debates

Three presidential debates and one vice presidential debate were scheduled in 2020.

September 29
Trump-Biden

The first debate, viewed by some 73 million people, took place at Case Western Reserve University and Cleveland Clinic in Cleveland, Ohio and was moderated by Chris Wallace.

The debate topics, chosen by Wallace, included filling a Supreme Court vacancy in an election year, Trump's health care plan, whether Biden proposed to end the filibuster in order to pack the Supreme Court, handling the pandemic, the timing of a vaccine, public confidence in a vaccine, Biden's reluctance to reopen the economy and schools, the benefit of masks, differences between the campaigns during COVID, economic recovery, Trump's federal income taxes, higher taxes on the wealthy, the economy, trust on race issues, whether the justice system is fair to African Americans, racial sensitivity training (and whether systemic racism exists), increasing urban homicides, policing and law enforcement, the Portland violent protests, condemnation of white supremacists, climate change, economic impact of climate change plans, mail-in ballots, the potential of a disputed election (and possibility of the Supreme Court settling it), and whether the candidates would refrain from declaring victory and encourage their supporters to wait for the true results.

Joe Biden having been in Washington for decades, his aggressive debate style of interrupting opponents with condescending snickers and grimaces (crafted for the split screen during television broadcast) at the moment they are making a key point, combined with folksy catch phrases like "come on, man," was well known and well rehearsed. His debate tactics were on display against vice-presidential candidate Paul Ryan in 2012. Although scrappy, Biden's combativeness proved effective with the public, the majority of whom judged him the winner against the more cerebral and polite Ryan.[187]

Trump, in apparent anticipation of such a strategy, went on offense. He frequently interrupted, not only his debate opponent, but also moderator Chris Wallace. It seemed to work. Many commentators, especially on the left, criticized Trump as misbehaving. The more gentlemanly Biden, they said, would now need to decide whether to even engage in further such encounters with the childish president.

If President Trump's objective had been to show himself the top dog and leave voters with the impression that Biden was weak, it worked. Biden was thrown off balance and did not come out of the encounter looking strong. Some suggested the President played his hand too aggressively.

In the debate, Trump stood by his right to nominate Amy Coney Barrett to the Supreme Court, stating that he had been elected for four years, not three—and observing that if Obama's party had held the Senate during his final year, Democrats would not have hesitated to confirm their own nominee, a fact that is obviously true.

Regarding the major issue of packing the Supreme Court, as some Democrats were openly advocating despite Americans deeply opposing it, Wallace asked, "Are you willing to tell the American people tonight whether you will pack the Court?" Biden refused to answer, saying only, "Whatever position I take on that, that'll become the issue." When Trump pressed, Biden retorted, "Would you shut up, man?" When pressed further, Biden said, "Keep yapping, man."

On COVID-19 policy. Biden claimed, "We have four percent of the world's population, twenty percent of the deaths." Trump, acknowledging that any death is tragic, replied that the situation would have been far worse with Biden at the helm. Furthermore, he reminded Biden that the blame belongs with China and also that death figures reported by countries like China, Russia, and India could not be trusted.

Asked about projections of wide vaccine availability in summer of 2021, Trump replied, "We can have it a lot sooner, but people like this [indicating Biden] would rather make it political than save lives." Biden smiled ear to ear, looked down, and shook his head. Trump continued, "It is a very political thing." Biden maintained multiple times during the debate that the vaccine would *not* be widely available until sometime in the middle of 2021.

Wallace asked Biden whether his skepticism toward the vaccine might be contributing to public fear of it. Biden deflected to an accusation that Trump had tried to hide the seriousness of COVID-19 from the public at the beginning.

Asked about his reluctance to reopen businesses and schools, Biden said, "Because he doesn't have a plan. If I were running it, I'd know what the plan is." Trump answered merely that the shutdowns were hurting people, and that Biden's plan for continued lockdowns was not wise. Concerning Democrats trying to keep shutdowns going until after the election, Trump said, "They think they're hurting us by keeping it closed. They're hurting *people*."

Asked about masks, Trump said that he was fine with them, and he wore them when he thought he needed to.

Concerning why he was holding big outdoor rallies, Trump said frankly, "People want to hear what I have to say." Asked if he was not worried about COVID, he answered, "Well, so far, we have had no problem whatsoever. We do them outside. We have tremendous crowds ... and Joe does the circles and he has three people sometimes." Biden countered, "He has been totally irresponsible the way that he has handled the social distancing. ... He's a fool on this," to which Trump replied, "If you could get the crowds, you would have done the same thing. But you can't."

Trump's critics had recently alleged that he paid only $750 in federal income tax during the 2016 and 2017 tax years. Asked about it by Wallace, Trump said he had paid millions in taxes during those years.

In answer to Trump's assertions that Biden's policies would hurt the economy, Biden stated that his economic plan would create an additional $1 trillion in economic growth.

Asked by Wallace why the voters should re-elect him, Trump pointed to his accomplishments, which were done "despite the impeachment hoax." He noted that just prior to COVID, the United States had the lowest unemployment in history, that we had been rebuilding the military—including the Space Force—that we had been rebuilding the Veterans' Administration, that about 300 federal judges had been appointed, and perhaps three Supreme Court justices had been placed.

Asked why the voters should elect him, Biden answered that he had gone head to head with Putin, while Trump is "Putin's puppy." He said that we are poor and the billionaires have gotten more wealthy, we are more violent, and we are more divided. Biden accused Trump of disparaging the military.

A few of Biden's memorable statements from the evening included: "Right now, I am the Democratic Party. I am the Democratic Party right now." At one point he called the president "Donald," and he told Trump to "just shush for a minute." Biden told Wallace and the viewers, indicating Trump, "Here's the deal: everything he's saying so far is simply a lie." At another point, Biden said of Trump, "He is not for any people needing healthcare." He also said of Trump, "He has never done a single thing."

Biden made some promises during the debate, among them that he would rejoin the Paris climate accord, that he would "weatherize four million buildings," and that "nobody's going to build another coal fired plant in America."

Concerning the violent riots that raged on in Oregon throughout the summer, Trump asked Biden, "Have you ever called the Democratic Mayor of Portland and said, 'You've got to stop this'?" The former vice president of the United States and presumptive leader of the Democratic Party answered, "I'm not in elected office right now."

A major narrative on the Democrat side was that President Trump was a fascist and intended not to relinquish power. In this narrative, the unspoken assumption was always that Biden was going to win fair and square, and that Trump would refuse to vacate the White House. Such a dream made sense only if the real Donald Trump were replaced with the cartoonish fiction that Democrats seemed to have built in their imaginations. On the Republican side, the chaos created by all the changes to election law by Democrat lawyers and officials, combined with the activities of Zuckerberg and Soros, led to a certain expectation that Democrats planned to obscure the result and then claim victory amid the chaos. With all this as the unstated background, Wallace asked Trump,

> In eight states, election workers are prohibited, currently by law ... from even beginning to process ballots ... until Election Day. That means that it's likely, because there's going to be a huge increase in mail-in balloting, that we are not going to know on election night who the winner is, that it could be days. It could be weeks ... (Trump interjects, "Could be months") ... until we find out who the new president is. Will you urge your supporters to stay calm, to not engage in any civil unrest? And will you pledge tonight that you will not declare victory until the election has been independently certified?

Trump answered, "If it's a fair election, I am 100% on board."

Wallace next posed the same question to Biden, who answered, "Yes, but here's the deal ... it's honest," and then claimed, "No one has established at all that there is fraud related to mail-in ballots, that somehow it's a fraudulent process."

Throughout his presidency, his opponents had steadily tried to portray President Trump as a racist. In particular, a narrative of a growing threat of "white supremacy," supposedly led by and nurtured by Trump himself, was being built in the media.

In service of this leftist conspiracy theory, the president's critics had brought out the "Will you condemn white supremacy?" question. It was a version of the classic lose-lose political "gotcha" question "Senator, have you stopped beating your wife?" No matter how it is answered, and regardless of whether the premise is even true, the politician being asked walks away with a black eye.

Accordingly, the most outrageous moment of the evening was probably when Wallace—revealing his bias—asked Trump,

> You have repeatedly criticized the vice president for not specifically calling out Antifa and other left-wing extremist groups. But are you willing, tonight, to condemn white supremacists and militia groups and to say that they need to stand down and not add to the violence in a number of these cities as we saw in Kenosha and as we've seen in Portland? Are you prepared specifically to do that?

Trump answered, "Sure, I'm willing to do that."

Trump had already condemned white supremacy multiple times, and clearly, and any competent journalist would have known it.[188] The president was rightly indignant.

Wallace's bias comes into further focus when considering the question he should have asked, but didn't:

> Mr. Biden, your 2020 candidacy has been endorsed by prominent neo-Nazi Richard Spencer.[189] You have boasted of your ability to work with segregationists. You are the presidential nominee of the Democratic Party, out of which was founded the KKK. Your party still celebrates racist segregationists Woodrow Wilson and FDR and supports Planned Parenthood, the organization founded by eugenicist Margaret Sanger with a goal of limiting the black population, an organization that to this day focuses its greatest abortion efforts in heavily black areas. **Mr. Biden, will you, *right here and right now*, disavow white supremacy?**

October 7
Pence-Harris

The first and only vice presidential debate of 2020 was held at the University of Utah, in Salt Lake City, and lasted 90 minutes. Susan Page, USA Today's Washington Bureau Chief, moderated. Page's bias in favor of Biden and Harris emerged most brazenly in the final set of questions, which will be discussed below.

The debate covered the pandemic (safety guidelines and vaccine), protocols in event of the physical incapacitation of the president (Trump would be 74, Biden 78), raising taxes on the wealthy, manmade climate change, the Paris Climate Accord, the Green New Deal, relations with China, the North American Free Trade Agreement (NAFTA), the definition of the role of American leadership, the potential overturning of Roe v. Wade, healthcare and pre-existing conditions, and whether justice was served in the case of Breonna Taylor.

Asked what a Biden administration would do about the pandemic, Harris accused Trump of covering up the virus and asked why the U.S. death toll as a percentage of its population was higher than almost every other wealthy nation on earth. Pence reminded her of Trump's immediate travel ban—which Biden opposed, calling it xenophobic and hysterical—when only five U.S. cases were known.

Harris said that Biden had a plan, while Trump did not. Pence replied, "When you read the Biden plan, it looks an awful lot like what President Trump and I and our task force have been doing every step of the way," and followed this with a jab at Biden who has been caught in plagiarism numerous times.

Page asked Pence about a Rose Garden event he attended eleven days prior, after which a number of attendees contracted COVID-19. Pence answered that he and his wife had been at the event, that it was held outdoors as healthcare authorities routinely advise, and that "The difference here is, President Trump and I trust the American people to make choices in the best interest of their health. Joe Biden and Kamala Harris consistently talk about mandates. ... We're about freedom and respecting the freedom of the American people."

Harris employed dramatic nonverbal communication throughout the debate. For much of the time, she maintained raised eyebrows, a slight squint, and pursed lips, and spoke with frequent dramatic head nods while blinking. In addition to some finding it distracting, the cumulative projected effect was a sense that she felt herself superior and intended to overtly condescend to her opponent. Some critics found her smirks and gestures disrespectful to the vice president and overly snarky. Some supporters saw in them a woman projecting strength in a space ordinarily dominated by men. The mild-mannered Pence remained mostly respectful and even at one point complimented Harris and Biden for their many years in public service, a comment that seemed to briefly catch Harris off guard.

At one point Harris made an accusation against Pence, glared at him while pausing for dramatic effect, and then continued. Pence began to ask the moderator if he could respond. Harris turned to him, put up her left hand while nodding her head, and said, "Mr. Vice President, I'm speaking. I'm speaking."

I observed the following comments, three of the four from women, on social media about Harris' overall performance:

- "#Smug. And dishonest."
- "that typical smirk on her face"
- "Her eye rolls are way too much. So full of herself!"
- "That's why I stopped watching."

Asked whether she would take a vaccine if it was approved by the Trump administration, before or after the election, Harris answered that, despite public health professionals' advice to take it (which, absent endorsement from the president, she would do), "If Donald Trump tells us that we should take it, I'm not takin' it." Pence criticized Harris for what he called continuing to undermine confidence in a vaccine, saying, "Senator, I just ask you: Stop playing politics with people's lives."

Several factually false statements were asserted as though they were true during the evening. Two examples from Harris included a claim that there had been a "Muslim ban," and that Trump refused to condemn white supremacists. A third example, from Susan Page, will be mentioned below.

The matter of undermining the independence of the Supreme Court by increasing the number of justices and filling the additional seats during a Democrat administration, known as Court packing and deeply unpopular with the American people, was a major issue of the election since prominent Democrats had been openly advocating for it. Court packing, however, was not raised by Page in any of her questions. At one point during the debate, Pence took the initiative to ask Harris directly whether she and Biden would pack the Supreme Court. Harris refused to answer or to commit not to do so.

On balance, Susan Page was more fair as a moderator than Chris Wallace had been in the first presidential debate. Page's clear leftward bias, however, was evident. Among other things, she made the false claim that "the scientific community has concluded that manmade climate change has made wildfires bigger, stronger, and more deadly and has made hurricanes wetter, slower, and more damaging." Pence, to his credit, did not accept the premise.

Page jumped the shark, however, with her final set of questions to the candidates. First, she said to Harris, "President Trump has several times refused to commit himself to a peaceful transfer of power after the election. If your ticket wins, and President Trump refuses to accept a peaceful transfer of power, what steps would you and Vice President Biden take? What would happen next?" Implicit in this question were assumptions that Biden would win, that it would be an unquestionably honest victory, and that if there were to be any chaos following the election, it was going to be Trump's fault. Harris' answer to the question was unimportant; the rhetorical punch—to slur and sully Donald Trump—was in the question itself.

Turning to Pence, Page then asked, "President Trump has several times refused to commit himself to a peaceful transfer of power after the election. If Vice President Biden is declared the winner and President Trump refuses to accept a peaceful transfer of power, what would be your role and responsibility as vice president? What would you personally do?" The same assumptions were implicit in this question to Pence, with the addition of a threat. Essentially, it was as though Page were standing with her arm around Harris, wagging her finger at Pence, telling him that he had better behave. Pence, again to his credit, did not accept the premise. He reminded Harris that her party had spent the last four years trying to overturn the results of the last election and pointed out that he and Trump had been fighting to prevent the Democrats from changing the rules in order to allow voter fraud.

The inappropriateness of Page's last two questions comes into focus when compared with what she might have—indeed, *should* have—asked:

> Senator Harris, the American people watched as your party refused to accept the results of the 2016 election. Efforts to overturn the election began

in earnest the day after the 2016 election itself, long before President Trump even took office, cost US taxpayers millions of dollars, and dragged on more than three years. Today, Democrats are threatening violence in the street and calling for civil unrest, have "gamed out" the various scenarios, and have hired an army of 600 lawyers to take action if President Trump wins re-election. Will you, Senator Harris, commit *right here and right now* to peacefully accept the will of the people in this election? What will *you* do if Joe Biden refuses to accept the results of this election?

The problem of constant Democrat bias from the Commission on Presidential Debates must be addressed if we are to have fair elections in the United States. I make a recommendation about it at the end of the book.

October 15
Trump-Biden

The second presidential debate—October 15 in Miami, Florida—was canceled when President Trump refused to participate after the debate commission changed to a virtual format about a week before the event. The move to virtual format had been ostensibly driven by President Trump's COVID-19 diagnosis, announced on October 2. Gloating among his detractors was immediate.[190] Although he would have been non-contagious (and was certainly recovering and in good health) by October 15, the live appearance of a strong and healthy recovered 74-year-old president less than two weeks after diagnosis would have been disharmonious with much of the rhetoric on the side of his opponents. His opponents had blamed him all year for his refusal to wear a mask unless necessary and willingness to meet face-to-face with those who wished to meet with him. It seemed the media and organizers now preferred to treat the President as a pariah and source of contagion. NBC News published a chart showing the COVID status of all those who had been in recent close contact with the President.[191] After the cancellation, Biden instead scheduled a televised town hall style event.[192]

October 22
Trump-Biden

The final presidential debate was held at Belmont University in Nashville, Tennessee. It was moderated by NBC News White House Reporter Kristen Welker. The debate covered six major topics: COVID-19 response, national security, race, climate change, leadership, and families.

Welker first asked Trump how he would handle COVID. He answered with results, and stated that a vaccine was coming very soon. He mentioned his own recent infection, telling of his experience, and reminded Biden that COVID is a worldwide problem. Biden stated that 220,000 Americans were dead, and that Trump was responsible for every last one of those deaths. Biden next promised to take care of it, and said he has a plan.

Asked about the vaccine, Trump answered that it would be coming in a matter of weeks, certainly by the end of the year. Pressed concerning which companies would be first, he said Johnson & Johnson, Pfizer, and Moderna were all doing very well. He also shared that the logistics had been prepared to help ensure distribution as soon as a vaccine was available.

Welker asked Biden how he would give Americans confidence in a vaccine once approved. He said, "We're about to go into a dark winter, and he [i.e., Trump] has no clear plan and there is no prospect that there's going to be a vaccine available for the majority of the American people before the middle of next year."

Trump reminded Biden once again that he had declared Trump's quick limitation of travel from China xenophobic, and suggested that—had Biden been in charge—there would be 700,000 Americans dead. He also said that everything Biden was now saying *should* be done was what Trump had *already* been doing.

When Biden accused Trump of claiming that it would be over soon, Trump answered that Americans can't all lock themselves in a basement like Biden, who had "obviously made a lot of money someplace." He said, "By the way, I as the president couldn't do that. I'd love to put myself in the basement or in a beautiful room in the White House and go away for a year and a half and disappear." He mentioned that he knew of the risks during all his meetings, but he did not stop doing his job. He said, "Ninety-nine point nine [percent] of young people recover. Ninety-nine percent of people recover. We can't close up our nation, or you aren't going to have a nation."

When Welker asked Biden about strategy, the latter again laid the American deaths at Trump's feet, and claimed that Trump says, "I take no responsibility." Trump quickly answered, "Excuse me, I take full responsibility. It is not my fault that it came here; it's China's fault. And you know what? It's not Joe's fault that it came here either. It's China's fault."

On the topic of national security, Welker said, "I do want to start with the security of our election. ... Just last night, top intelligence officials confirmed again that both Russia and Iran are working to influence this election. Both countries have obtained U.S. voter registration information, these officials say, and Iran sent intimidating messages to Florida voters."

Biden answered that any country that interferes with U.S. elections would pay a price for interfering with American sovereignty. He said that Russia did not want him to be the next president, "because they know I know them."

Trump said, "Joe got three and a half million dollars from Russia. And it came through Putin because he was very friendly with the former mayor of Moscow, and it was the mayor of Moscow's wife." Trump also stated that he had never taken any money from Russia. Trump also said that one thing Biden and Russia have in common is that they both want Trump to lose. In partial explanation of why this was the case, Trump mentioned his military support for Ukraine and faulted Biden for supporting Russia.

Biden said, "I have not taken a penny from any foreign source, ever, in my life," and that Trump "has a secret bank account with China. ... I have not taken a single penny from any country whatsoever, ever." Biden also said he had released all of his tax returns, twenty-two years' worth, before faulting Trump for not releasing his. "What are you hiding? Why are you unwilling? Foreign countries are paying you a lot. Russia's paying you a lot. China's paying you a lot." Asked by Welker when he would release his taxes, Trump answered, "As soon as the audit is completed. I get treated worse than the Tea Party got treated," with reference to the IRS targeting of Tea Party organizations under Obama.

On the matter of his personal financial affairs, Trump further said, "I was put through a phony witch hunt for three years. It started before I even got elected. They spied on my campaign. No president should ever have to go through what I went through. Mueller and eighteen angry Democrats, and FBI agents all over the place, spent forty-eight million dollars. They went through everything I had, including my tax returns, and they found absolutely no collusion, and nothing wrong. Forty-eight million. I guarantee you if I spent one million on you, Joe, I could find plenty wrong. Because the kind of things that you've done and the kind of monies that your family has taken ... and they say that you get some of it, and you do live very well. You have houses all over the place."

Concerning possible foreign entanglements, Welker asked Biden about Hunter's work in China and Ukraine, "In retrospect, was anything about those relationships inappropriate or unethical?" Biden said simply, "Nothing was unethical," but did not answer whether it was inappropriate. Biden next tried to flip Ukraine corruption onto Trump for "trying to bribe the Ukrainian government to say something negative" about him. However, Biden avoided mention of Ukraine when he said, "My son has not made money, in terms of this thing about China." Biden further stated that nobody else had made money from China but Trump.

Trump, however, turned the conversation back to Ukraine once again, saying, "His son [i.e., Hunter] didn't have a job for a long time ... As soon as he [i.e., Joe] became vice president, Burisma—not the best reputation in the world—I hear they paid him $183,000 a month ... and they gave him a three million dollar up-front payment. And he had no energy experience. That's 100% dishonest."

Biden denied neither the payments nor the job. Rather, he said, "No basis for that. Everybody investigated that. No one said anything he did was wrong in Ukraine." Welker did not press back on him with the fact that many people *were* in fact saying that it was wrong, that it was a conflict of interest, and that it had the appearance of influence peddling. Rather, she moved on to Trump's foreign business dealings, particularly his promotion of his businesses abroad. She specifically asked about a bank account in China, apparently long since closed. Trump answered, "I have many bank accounts, and they're all listed, and they're all over the place. I mean, I was a businessman doing business. The bank account you're referring to, which —everybody knows about it; it's listed—the bank account was ... opened in 2013. It was closed in 2015, I believe. And then, I decided, because I was thinking about doing a deal in China, like millions of other people, and I decided not to do it, and I closed it. ... Then, I decided to run for president, after that ... I closed it before I even ran for president, let alone became president. Big difference. He is the vice president of the United States, and his son, and his brother, and his other brother are getting rich. They're like a vacuum cleaner; they're sucking money every place he goes."

Biden did not answer these allegations. All he said was, "Not true." Welker did not press Biden on any of these points, and Biden did not request the opportunity to answer the allegations.

Helpless

Across the nation, millions of Americans watched with dismay the lead-up to the election, on Election Day, and throughout the aftermath. Many sensed serious problems with the conduct of the election; some under-stood the specifics of what was occurring and had been trying to stop it, but were blocked. For months the game pieces were moved into place—in plain view—to create an environment in which fraud could occur on a scale never before witnessed in the United States. Virtually every one of these changes was occurring outside of the authority of state legislatures. Political and legal commentators, most notably radio host Mark Levin, clearly sounded the alarm over the unconstitutional extra-legislative changes to election law in key states, driven by Democrat activists—partic-ularly the proliferation of unattended ballot drop boxes, expansion of voting by mail, relaxation of ballot security measures such as signature verification, and altering of ballot deadlines and postmark rules.

By February 2020, nine months *before* the November election, a Gallup poll found that fully 59% of Americans said they were not confident in the honesty of U.S. elections. Of 32 nations surveyed, only two, Chile and Mexico, fared measurably worse.[193] Why was Americans' confidence in their own elections so low?

Residual Effects

One result of U.S. events of 2019-2021 was a collapse of trust in the institutions of government and media, and also between and among citizens. Sociologists in time will study the nuance and causes, but certain events clearly shook the confidence of many Americans in the fairness of a government now turned against them, rather than serving them as it should. Stopping abuse of government power against citizens had been a central concern of the American colonists, stemming from their experience of having their rights as citizens arbitrarily abridged by King George. The assertion of natural rights and the proposition that governments have a moral duty to uphold them also had recent political expression going back to the 13th century.[194] Such concerns came to the fore once again in 2020 and 2021.

Over the preceding decade, Americans witnessed an alarming array of double standards and corruption within their own government that reached a tipping point of distrust during and following 2020. Democrats and their allies were excused from prosecution for crimes, while also selectively deploying agencies of government with punitive force against those who threatened their power, as discussed earlier in this book. Examples include the Fast and Furious gun-running scandal under President Obama (2006-2011);[195] the Benghazi scandal and coverup protecting Hillary Clinton and Barack Obama (2012);[196] the IRS targeting of President Obama's political enemies by Lois Lerner and James Koskinen, and their subsequent protection from prosecution (2011-2013);[197] Hillary Clinton's hiding, exposure to espionage, and later destruction, of sensitive government property by illegally routing her official emails through a private server when she was Secretary of State (2013-2014),[198] followed by FBI Director James Comey's recommendation not to prosecute her despite confirming that thousands of compromised emails containing government secrets and at least eight *top secret* messages had been sent or received by Clinton on the servers—and section (f) of the Espionage Act is solely directed at negligence to preclude the excuse that it was "just a mistake";[199] the Justice Department's decision not to prosecute Hillary mere days after Bill Clinton's allegedly coincidental private meeting with Attorney General Loretta Lynch on the Phoenix Airport tarmac (2016);[200] the FISA court scandal authorizing spying on Trump campaign employees and spouses (2016-17);[201] the politicization of the FBI against sitting president Donald Trump under James Comey (2017);[202] and the Hunter Biden laptop coverup (2019-2020).[203]

Someone may object that the above list containing only acts by Democrats betrays bias on my part. I simply answer that I—like most Americans —support everyone being equal before just laws (see "justice" under

"Some Important Terms" at the beginning of this book). I am not calling for a double standard, but pointing out an embarrassingly obvious double standard that already exists.

Demographics of the Candidates' Supporters

In 2020, Donald Trump gained significant ground among nonwhite women, nonwhite men, white women, Americans of Latino descent, and black voters. The last group made a 3 point swing toward Trump as compared to 2016. In fact, "women and people of color" together comprised 57.2% of Trump's 2020 support, up from 54.8% in 2016. The only category in which Trump's support declined slightly in 2020 as compared to 2016 was among white men.[204]

Joe Biden's key support came from higher-earning college-educated white people in or near major cities.[205] As of August 2020, white college graduates overall favored Biden by 61% to Trump's 38%, whereas among white people with no college degree, Biden's support sank to 34% compared to Trump's 64%. Despite significant movement in the demographic toward Trump in 2020, the great majority of black Americans—89%—still supported Biden. Hispanic Americans favored Biden by 63% to Trump's 35%. Asian Americans favored Biden by 67% to Trump's 31%.[206] However, Biden's greatest loss among any ethnic category was in his share of Latino votes, which decreased by 8 percentage points compared to Hillary Clinton's just four years prior. His second greatest deficit was among black Americans, where he lost 3 percentage points compared to 2016, and 7 since 2012.[207]

There is much more that could be said, but this summary of 2020 events adequately sets the stage for further presentation of the major problems of the election.

QUESTIONS

1. Aside from the deaths it caused, what were the effects of COVID-19 on American society in 2020? How, and by whom, was it used for political purposes?

2. What events fed the Black Lives Matter and Antifa movements in 2020? In what way(s), if any, did either movement advance justice? In what way(s), if any, did either movement advance injustice?

3. What do you suppose was the role of China, if any, in the 2020 election? Was President Trump a help or a hindrance to China's global aspira-

tions? Is it possible that China purposely introduced COVID-19 to undermine President Trump? Why or why not?

4. What did General Mark Milley do to seize power from the Commander in Chief? Why is this a problem?

---

1. In July, 2020, Schwab and co-author Thierry Malleret published *COVID-19: The Great Reset*. The authors' apparent thrill at COVID's long-term potential is evident when they write, "the pandemic continues to worsen globally. Many of us are pondering when things will return to normal. The short response is: never...the coronavirus pandemic marks a fundamental inflection point in our global trajectory. Some analysts call it a major bifurcation, others refer to a deep crisis of 'biblical' proportions, but the essence remains the same: the world as we knew it in the early months of 2020 is no more, dissolved in the context of the pandemic. Radical changes of such consequence are coming that some pundits have referred to as 'before coronavirus' (BC) and 'after coronavirus' (AC) era. We will continue to be surprised by both the rapidity and unexpected nature of these changes..." One wonders how Mr. Schwab can have known all these long-term effects mere months into the crisis. Were the objectives he describes *intended* outcomes of sweeping policy reactions bringing economic devastation, permanent closure of small businesses, and decimation of middle-class wealth? Klaus Schwab, and Thierry Malleret, *COVID-19: The Great Reset* (Geneva: Forum Publishing, 2020).

2. "But deep, existential crises also favour introspection and can harbour the potential for transformation." Ibid. 11. Obama White House Chief of Staff Rahm Emanuel famously made the comment, "You never want a serious crisis to go to waste ... it's an opportunity to do things you could not do before." Stewart D. Friedman, "Do Not Waste This Crisis," *Harvard Business Review*, November 25, 2008.

3. Schwab, Klaus, and Peter Vanham, "What is stakeholder capitalism?," *World Economic Forum*, January 22, 2021.

4. "What is Environmental, Social and Corporate Governance (ESG)?," https://www.diligent.com/insights/esg/.

5. Trump's critics quickly condemned the action, anticipating retaliation by Iran. No meaningful retaliation materialized—only a symbolic firing of missiles at a U.S. base in Iraq several days later, harming no Americans. Courtney Kube, and Doha Madani, "Iran retaliates for Gen. Soleimani's killing by firing missiles at U.S. forces in Iraq," *NBC News*, January 7, 2020; "Qasem Soleimani: US kills top Iranian general in Baghdad air strike," *BBC*, January 3, 2020; Karl Vick, "Why the U.S. Assassination of Iranian Quds Force Leader Qasem Soleimani Has the U.S. Bracing for Retaliation," *Time*, January 3, 2020.

6. Steve Burns, "Top Ten Dow Jones Industrial Average Drops in History," New Trader U, March 10, 2020.

7. "Breonna Taylor: What happened on the night of her death?," *BBC*, October 8, 2020.

8. Becca Savransky, "How CHAZ became CHOP: Seattle's police-free zone explained," *Seattle P-I*, June 15, 2020; Christopher F. Rufo, "Anarchy in Seattle," *City Journal*, June 10, 2020; "The Demands of the Collective Black Voices at Free Capitol Hill to the government of Seattle, Washington," Free Capitol Hill, June 9, 2020.

9. Brett Haensel, "Domino effect: Google antitrust case could spell trouble for other tech giants," *Fortune*, October 29, 2020.

10. Ivan Pereira, "US administers 1st doses of Pfizer coronavirus vaccine," *ABC News*, December 14, 2020; "FDA Takes Key Action in Fight Against COVID-19 By Issuing Emergency Use Authorization for First COVID-19 Vaccine," U.S. Food & Drug Administration, December 11, 2020.

11. Sara E. Oliber et al., "The Advisory Committee on Immunization Practices Interim Recommendation for Use of Moderna COVID-19 Vaccine — United States, December 2020," Centers for Disease Control and Prevention, January 1, 2021.

12. It was the first time any federal official was impeached a second time, and the only time that a former president had been tried. This time one Republican, Liz Cheney, joined all House Democrats in supporting impeachment. Had a conviction resulted, it would likely have been overturned on constitutional grounds.

13. Wenxin Fan, "China's Campaign to Crush Democracy in Hong Kong Is Working," *Wall Street Journal*, February 25, 2021; Frank Fang, "Hong Kong Leader Silent After Beijing Says It Reserves Jurisdiction Over National Security Law," *Epoch Times*, June 16, 2020; Jan Jekielek, "Making History: Hong Kong Protest Is An 'Existential Threat' to Communist China - Michael Yon & Erik Fok," *Epoch Times*, December 28, 2019.

14. Kelly Cohen, "Tokyo 2020 Olympics officially postponed until 2021," *ESPN*, March 24, 2020.

15. Jeff McCausland, "Kim Jong Un's appearance put death rumors to rest. But the world was scared for good reason," *NBC News*, May 5, 2020.

16. David Enders, "6 months after Beirut blast: Rebuilding slow, prosecution stalled," *Al Jazeera*, February 3, 2021.

17. "Pentagon releases UFO videos for the record," *BBC*, April 28, 2020.

18. Mike Wall, "SpaceX's very big year: A 2020 filled with astronaut launches, Starship tests and more," *Space.com,* December 28, 2020.

19. Emily Crane, "Hundreds of 'murder hornets' found in huge Washington nest," *New York Post*, August 27, 2021.

20. "California's August Complex Largest Fire in State's History," *NASA*, October 6, 2020; "California and Oregon 2020 wildfires in maps, graphics and images," *BBC*, September 18, 2020.

21. The World Health Organization announced a coronavirus-related pneumonia in Wuhan, China on January 9, 2020, but such announcements are routine.

22. John McCormack, "The Senator Who Saw the Coronavirus Coming," *National Review,* March 31, 2020.

23. Chris White, "De Blasio, NYC Officials Downplayed COVID-19 Threat After Trump Restricted Travel to China. Here are 5 Examples," *The Daily Signal*, March 30, 2020; Adriana Cohen, "Democrats Forget What They Were Saying About Coronavirus In Early 2020," *GOPUSA*, September 11, 2020.

24. Robert Farley, "Biden's Early Statements About the Coronavirus," *FactCheck*, September 21, 2020.

25. Ibid.

26. C. Douglas Golden, "Fauci Shreds Media Narrative, Admits President Trump's COVID Response Saved Lives," *Western Journal*, August 1, 2020.

27. Olga R. Rodriguez, "Cruise ship passengers recall deaths, confusion, quarantine," *AP News*, March 15, 2021; Brady Dennis, Mark Berman, and Hannah Sampson, "21 people test positive for coronavirus on California cruise ship, out of 46 tested so far," *Washington Post*, March 7, 2020.

28. Byron York, "With virus crisis raging, Pelosi and Schiff ramp up new Trump investigations," *Washington Examiner,* April 2, 2020.

29. "15 Days to Slow the Spread," White House, March 16, 2020. Emphasis original.

30. For the 2016-2017 flu season, there were an estimated 38,000 deaths from flu out of 29 million instances of symptomatic illness (case fatality rate=0.13%). For the 2017-2018 flu season, there were an estimated 61,000 deaths from the flu out of 45 million instances of symptomatic illness (case fatality rate=0.14%). For the 2018-2019 season, there were an estimated 34,000 deaths from the flu out of 36 million instances of symptomatic illness (case fatality rate=0.094%). Some flu seasons are more deadly than others; in 2014-15, there were 51,000 deaths from the flu out of 30 million instances of symptomatic illness (case fatality rate=0.17%). Case fatality rate calculations from these CDC statistics are based upon symptomatic illness and do not include very mild cases. My COVID-19 case estimates do attempt to account for non-symptomatic cases, so it seems likely that the comparison is not apples to apples, and if non-symptomatic cases were factored in, the COVID-19 case fatality rate would be far lower than the estimates that follow here. "Influenza (Flu): Past Seasons," *Centers for Disease Control and Prevention*, (page last reviewed October 1, 2020).

31. "Estimated COVID-19 Infections, Symptomatic Illnesses, Hospitalizations, and Deaths in the United States," Centers for Disease Control and Prevention, updated October 2, 2021, https://www.cdc.gov/coronavirus/2019-ncov/cases-updates/burden.html. Some sources, like Wikipedia, were reporting a *global* case fatality rate from COVID-19 of 1.61% and up to 1.77% as late as February 2, 2022, with the explanatory comment, "Per Our world in data (sic), average world countries on September 9, 2021. Depends largely on the age group of the people. 1.77% on 1/10/22." (citing Ritchie, Hannah, et al., "Mortality Risk of COVID-19," *Our World in Data*, August 24, 2021.) Had the U.S. case fatality rate been 1.61-1.77% as Wikipedia reports the overall rate to be, the total number of U.S. deaths from COVID-19 by the

end of September, 2021 would have been 2.35 million to 2.59 million ... approaching *three times* the real number of fewer than 1 million.

32. Ibid.

33. Even without vaccination, the risk of severe health outcomes from COVID-19 to children 0-17 who do not have other health conditions was virtually zero. Indeed, among all people in the United States 0-49 years of age without other health conditions, the risk of mortality was likewise miniscule, approaching zero. So, for those 49 and under, the relative benefit of vaccination, while not zero, was nonetheless far less pronounced than it was for those over 50, and particularly for those over 65.

34. "Fact Check-CDC study found that over 75% of COVID-19 deaths in vaccinated people were among those with at least 4 comorbidities," *Reuters*, January 12, 2022.

35. "WHO Coronavirus (COVID-19) Dashboard," World Health Organization.

36. 6,019,085 ÷ 7,900,000,000 = 0.00076

37. 25,000,000 ÷ 1,850,000,000 = 0.0135, etc.

38. Many underdeveloped countries, some large and densely-populated, reported very small per capita death rates from Covid-19, dozens or even hundreds of times lower than that in the countries with the highest death rates. Nigeria's death numbers were about 15.6 per million, 417 times lower than Peru's 6,501 per million. Johns Hopkins Coronavirus Resource Center, https://coronavirus.jhu.edu/data/mortality. Factors such as climate and average age of the populace in each country may have contributed to lower transmission and death rates in some instances, but it is also possible that different reporting protocols led to underreporting, or that Covid-19 was attributed as primary cause of death in other countries for political or other purposes. The estimates given here may eventually be modified, but at least they provide a benchmark.

39. 0.0135 ÷ 0.00076 = 17.8 and 0.027 ÷ 0.00076 = 35.52. The reason for the great difference in mortality is probably multi-factorial, with differences in hygiene and medicine perhaps adding to the differences in the severity of the two viruses. The point here is to note the variance in actual impact in terms of relative portions of the world population killed.

40. Taking into account (for example) that the percentage of the total number of non-hispanic white people in the older age categories is greater than the percentage of the total number of non-hispanic black people in those age categories, we see that if COVID-19 were to affect two racial groups following the same age trend disparities, more deaths would be expected among the non-hispanic white population than among the non-hispanic black population.

41. Tyler Olson, "Fauci's mixed messages, inconsistencies about COVID-19 masks, vaccines and reopenings come under scrutiny," *Fox News*, February 23, 2021.

42. Ibid.

43. Catherine Schuster-Bruce, "Fauci brushes off GOP criticism and says attacks on him are 'attacks on science' he can debunk 'immediately,'" *Business Insider*, June 10, 2021.

44. Jim Geraghty, "Fauci Team Cared More about 'International Harmony' Than the Truth," *National Review*, January 13, 2022.

45. Ibid.

46. Kennedy, Robert F., *The Real Anthony Fauci: Bill Gates, Big Pharma, and the Global War on Democracy and Public Health* (New York: Skyhorse, 2021).

47. The left's use of public policy to destroy the vast middle class, as a means of shifting the interests of the electorate, is the topic of my forthcoming book, *Wedge*.

48. Kennedy, *Real Anthony Fauci*, xix-xxi.

49. Ibid., 20.

50. Among many other problems with raw numbers, the comparison was not fair because the Chinese Communist regime dramatically understated China's infection and death numbers. Calhoun, George, "Part 1: Beijing Is Intentionally Underreporting China's Covid Death Rate," *Forbes*, January 2, 2022.

51. This death clock disappeared from CNN after the inauguration of Joe Biden on January 20, 2021. Leah Barkoukis, "Now That Biden's President, CNN's COVID-19 Death Counter Appears to Be Gone," *Townhall*, January 21, 2021.

52. Angelo Fichera, "Hospital Payments and the COVID-19 Death Count," *FactCheck*, April 21, 2020.

53. Ibid. FactCheck is a left-leaning source; thus its confirmation of such details which militate against the left's general push to trust the official statements of COVID-19 case counts should be taken as credible.

54. Steffie Woolhandler, "Taxpayers Paid Twice for Healthcare—Private insurers are profiting more than ever during the pandemic," *MedPageToday*, May 25, 2022.

55. Marietta Vazquez, "Calling COVID-19 the 'Wuhan Virus' or 'China Virus' is inaccurate and xenophobic," *Yale School of Medicine*, March 12, 2020.

56. Katie Reilly, "The Learning Gap Is Getting Worse as Schools Rely on Remote Classes, Especially for Students of Color," *Time*, December 8, 2020; Catherine Pearson, "Experts Predict What This 'Lost Year' Will Really Do To Our Kids," *Huffpost*, October 7, 2020; "Estimates of Learning Loss in the 2019-2020 School Year," Center for Research on Education Outcomes, Stanford University, October 2020.

57. L.S. Dugdale, "COVID-19: Lonely Dying and Dying Alone," *Psychology Today*, April 5, 2021.

58. Marie Saavedra, "Wheeling Family Calls On Hospital To Change Policy After 96-Year-Old Matriarch With COVID Dies Alone," *CBS Chicago*, February 4, 2022.

59. "Cuomo Reverses Nursing Home Directive to Take COVID-19 Patients, Requires More Staff Testing," *NBC New York*, May 10, 2020.

60. "State Officials Altered Count Of New York's Nursing Home Deaths," *Associated Press*, March 5, 2021.

61. Adam Jeffery, "Iconic photos of the USNS Comfort arriving in New York, providing a glimmer of hope," *CNBC*, March 30, 2020.

62. J.D. Simkins, "Hospital ship Comfort departs NYC, having treated fewer than 200 patients," *Navy Times*, April 30, 2020.

63. Kristina Wong, "Hundreds of hospital beds left empty on the USNS Comfort and Javits Center during Cuomo's nursing home order," *Breitbart*, February 22, 2021.

64. "Insane Karen Assaults 69 Year Old Man On Plane Because He Took His Mask Off To Eat, FBI Arrested Her," TheProfessional, December 28, 2021, YouTube video, https://www.youtube.com/watch?v=3ObF-NCz9Yg; "Karen goes Completely CRAZY over Couple not wearing Masks," John Talks, December 24, 2020, YouTube video, https://www.youtube.com/watch?v=z5-BjQaQqe4; "Video shows 'Starbucks Karen' upset when asked to put on mask," ABC 10 News, October 19, 2020, YouTube video, https://www.youtube.com/watch?v=9K-jId17l2o.

65. Scott Morefield, "If You're Confronted By A Mask Karen, Rand Paul Has Some Advice," *Townhall*, January 25, 2022.

66. Ibid.

67. The governor's Executive Order 2, making masking optional in Virginia public schools, faced immediate legal challenge. An Arlington County judge found on February 4 that Youngkin did not have authority to supersede local school boards in this matter, and other cases on both sides of the issue were making their way through the courts. A parents' challenge of the Youngkin school mask order was rejected by the Virginia Supreme Court on February 7. Michael Martz, "Virginia Supreme Court rejects Chesapeake parents' challenge of Youngkin school mask order," *Richmond Times-Dispatch*, February 7, 2022.

68. Elizabeth Brubaker, Personal conversation, January 2022.

69. John Clark, "Subject: Tomorrow - Mask Enforcement," Email correspondence, February 1, 2022, 3:23 p.m.. This story made international news: James Gordon, "Loudoun County principals were COACHED on how to obtain trespassing warrants against students trying to enter schools without masks: Woke board has defied Virginia governor's order allowing parents to choose whether kids cover their faces," *Daily Mail*, February 8, 2022.

70. Hayley Milon Bour, "Northam: Masks Required in All Virginia Schools," *Loudoun Now*, August 12, 2021.

71. Caleb Kershner, "Breaking News," Public Statement, Facebook, February 16, 2022, 10:00 p.m.. Kershner was a Loudoun County, Virginia supervisor.

72. Leah Barkoukis, "Fauci Admits Why Americans Were Initially Misled About Wearing Masks," *Townhall*, June 17, 2020; Darragh Roche, "Fauci Said Masks 'Not Really Effective in Keeping Out Virus,' Email Reveals," *Newsweek*, June 2, 2021.

73. David Zweig, "The CDC's Flawed Case for Masks in School," *Atlantic*, December 16, 2021.

74. Robby Soave, "In Leaked Audio, CDC's Rochelle Walensky Privately Confirms She Won't Relax School Mask Guidance," *Reason*, February 16, 2022.

75. "We know that wearing a mask outside health care facilities offers little, if any, protection from infection..." Michael Klompas et al., "Universal Masking in Hospitals in the Covid-19 Era," *New England Journal of Medicine*, May 21, 2020. 2020; 382:e63.

76. Ibid.

77. "cloth masks were associated with only a 5 percent decrease [in COVID-19 symptoms and antibodies]." Yasmin Tayag, "Why Are Americans Still—Still!—Wearing Cloth Masks?," *Atlantic*, October 4, 2021.

78. Henning Bundgaard, "Effectiveness of Adding a Mask Recommendation to Other Public Health Measures to Prevent SARS-CoV-2 Infection in Danish Mask Wearers: A Randomized Controlled Trial," *Annals of Internal Medicine*, March 2021; Jon Miltimore, "New Danish Study Finds Masks Don't Protect Wearers From COVID Infection," *FEE*, November 18, 2020; Kashmira Gander, "Surgical and Cotton Face Masks Ineffective at Blocking SARS-CoV-2 Particles When COVID-19 Patients Cough, Study Finds," *Newsweek*, April 7, 2020.

79. Geoff Shullenberger, "Were masks a waste of time?," *Unherd.com*, February 7, 2022.

80. We visited the second Costco again on February 19, 2022. As before, I saw no mask requirement or even suggestion. Masks were no longer required in Loudoun County public schools, and for the better part of a year virtually no one in the other Costco had been masked. Yet the vast majority of people, about 90% of those inside this store and about half of those in the parking lot, wore masks. Around this time, some local parents reported that their children were afraid to take their masks off at school for fear of being classified as "anti-maskers." One public school boy was reportedly taking photos or videos of other kids who weren't wearing masks and posting them to a social media account. I do not know whether the child faced discipline for bullying.

81. Destiny Gentry, Instagram post. https://ifunny.co/picture/destiny-gentry-wa-lifeandliberty-1s-it-wasn-t-the-suicides-gggmjhzJ9.

82. "Press Briefing by Press Secretary Jen Psaki," White House, April 20, 2022.

83. "CDC calls on Americans to wear masks to prevent COVID-19 spread," Centers for Disease Control and Prevention, July 14, 2020; Karl Dierenbach, "'Flattening The Curve' Has Become A Massive Bait And Switch," *Federalist*, June 29, 2020.

84. Matt Agorist, "Nearly 700 Days Into '2 Weeks To Flatten The Curve' & The Only Thing That's Reduced Is Your Freedom," *The Washington Standard*, January 10, 2022.

85. Emma Reynolds, "Lockdowns shouldn't be fully lifted until coronavirus vaccine found, new study warns," *CNN*, April 9, 2020.

86. Marc Lipsitch, "COVID-19 Vaccines and Herd Immunity," Center for Communicable Disease Dyamics, Harvard University, December 17, 2020.

87. Andrew Jeremijenko et al., "Herd Immunity against Severe Acute Respiratory Syndrome in 10 Communities, Qatar," *Emerging Infectious Diseases*, 27:5 May 2021.

88. Sara Berg, "What doctors wish patients knew about herd immunity," *AMA*, August 27, 2021; Dylan Scott, "Fauci: 85 percent of the US needs to get the Covid-19 vaccine for 'true herd immunity,'" *Vox*, December 15, 2020.

89. Hilary Brueck, "Getting to herd immunity will require 90% of people to be vaccinated against COVID-19, experts say," *Business Insider*, August 27, 2021.

90. Holly Ellyatt, "Here's why herd immunity from Covid is 'mythical' with the delta variant," *CNBC*, August 12, 2021.

91. Kamran Kadkhoda, "Herd Immunity to COVID-19: Alluring and Elusive," *American Journal of Clinical Pathology*, January 5, 2021.

92. "Moderna Says Its COVID Vaccine Is 96% Effective In Protecting 12 To 17-Year-Old Kids," *CBS News*, May 6, 2021; Aimee Picchi, "Pfizer and BioNTech say their vaccine is 91% effective against COVID-19, citing new test data," *CBS News*, April 1, 2021.

93. CNBC showed a graphic citing a January 15, 2021 study showing that double- and triple-masking have respective "efficiency" of 75% and 90%. Joseph Curl, "CNBC Touts TRIPLE-Masking For Best Protection Against COVID-19," *Daily Wire*, January 27, 2021.

94. Daniel Dale, "Fact check: White House tweet falsely claims 'there was no vaccine available' when Biden took office," *CNN*, May 13, 2022.

95. Jon Miltimore, "Spain's First Study on Omicron Finds Vaccinated People Spread COVID at Same Rate as Unvaccinated," *FEE*, February 2, 2022.

96. For a flowchart outlining this progression, see: "'2 Weeks To Flatten the Curve' to 'Vaccinated Only,'" Bright Light News.

97. Christina Lin, "Gene-editing, Moderna, and Transhumanism," *The Times of Israel*, August 5, 2020; Robin McKie, "No death and an enhanced life: Is the future transhuman?," *Guardian*, May 6, 2018; Meghan O'Gieblyn, "God in the machine: my strange journey into transhumanism," *Guardian*, April 18, 2017; Klaus Schwab, "The Fourth Industrial Revolution: what it means, how to respond," *World Economic Forum*, January 14, 2016; Natasha

Vita-More, "Life Expansion: Toward an Artistic, Design-Based Theory of the Transhuman / Posthuman" (PhD diss., University of Plymouth, 2012); Massimo Pigliucci, "The problems with transhumanism," *Psychology Today*, July 7, 2009; Susan Schneider, "Future Minds: Transhumanism, Cognitive Enhancement, and the Nature of Persons," Center for Neuroscience & Society, University of Pennsylvania, July 1, 2008.

98. Samira Said, and Kelly Mena, "Database for Covid-19 vaccination info raises concerns about privacy and vaccine uptake," *CNN*, December 13, 2020.

99. Kennedy, *Real Anthony Fauci*, 23.

100. F. Perry Wilson, "Ivermectin and COVID: Is a Microscopic Worm the Key?," *Medscape*, March 22, 2022.

101. Ibid.

102. Ibid.

103. Kennedy, *Real Anthony Fauci*, 19-20.

104. Brian Martin, "Who's afraid of The Real Anthony Fauci?" https://www.academia.edu/78900507/Whos_afraid_of_The_Real_Anthony_Fauci.

105. D'Angelo Gore, "Latest CDC Data: Unvaccinated Adults 97 Times More Likely to Die from COVID-19 Than Boosted Adults," *FactCheck*, February 9, 2022.

106. "Facebook admits the truth: 'Fact checks' are really just (lefty) opinion," *New York Post*, December 14, 2021.

107. "Covid origin: Why the Wuhan lab-leak theory is being taken seriously," *BBC*, 27 May 2021.

108. Tim Graham, "The Media's Humiliating Incuriosity About Wuhan," *Daily Signal*, May 28, 2021.

109. Paulina Firozi, "Tom Cotton keeps repeating a coronavirus fringe theory that scientists have disputed," *Washington Post*, February 17, 2020. The original headline, which remained up for more than a year, is visible at web.archive.org.

110. Graham, "The Media's Humiliating Incuriosity."

111. Ibid.

112. "Gain-of-function" refers to the process by which bio-engineers alter organisms to strengthen some aspect. Such work can yield useful or beneficial results, such as drought-resistant crops for agriculture. In the discussion of viruses, gain-of-function could involve making them more contagious, more deadly, or both. Teaganne Finn, "Fauci blasts Rand Paul's Wuhan lab funding claim: 'You do not know what you're talking about,'" *NBC News*, July 20, 2021; Tyler Olson, "Fauci, Rand Paul trade 'lying' accusations about gain-of-function research in hearing on Delta variant: Kentucky senator stepped close to the line of accusing Fauci of lying to Congress in previous testimony," Fox News, July 20, 2021; Lori Robertson, "The Wuhan Lab and the Gain-of-Function Disagreement," *FactCheck.org*, May 21, 2021.

113. Emily Crane, "NIH admits US funded gain-of-function in Wuhan — despite Fauci's denials," *New York Post*, October 21, 2021.

114. I discuss this matter second not to downplay its importance, but as a practical matter. Certainly for some Americans the BLM concerns overshadowed everything else, while for others the COVID-19 matters touched their lives more deeply. For most Americans, there was overlap, and both were major issues in 2020.

115. The Black Lives Matter movement had begun in 2013 as a response to the acquittal of Zimmerman in his trial for the killing of Martin. "About," Black Lives Matter, https://blacklivesmatter.com/about/.

116. "Men" in the Declaration of Independence meant all people of every race and sex. The phrase "all men are created equal and endowed by their Creator" refers to the biblical account in Genesis chapter 1:26-27, which says, "Then God said, 'Let Us make **man** in Our image, according to Our likeness; and let **them** rule over the fish of the sea and over the birds of the sky and over the cattle and over all the earth, and over every creeping thing that creeps on the earth.' **God created man** in His own image, in the image of God He created him; **male and female he created them**." (Emphasis added). It was from this first family, according to the Bible, that all people alive today descended. The failure of the United States to affirm full and equal *political* rights—such as the right to vote—for women or those in a state of involuntary servitude, or to politically remove the ongoing infringement of *God-given* (or *natural*) rights of the latter group, in the years immediately following the Constitution's adoption, thus cannot be taken as evidence that the Declaration's affirmation was less than universal. By "men," the Declaration means all human beings.

117. "Thomas Jefferson's Bible," *Smithsonian National Museum of American History*.
118. Jefferson was a rationalist, but God himself exists outside nature. Rejecting the power of God to intervene in nature would also deprive God of authority to set a moral law universally governing human action. Certainly Jefferson understood this. In the matter of slavery, he had a conflict of interest; his own judgment was already compromised, and he was not qualified to serve as arbiter. This probably helps explain his unwillingness to submit to the complete moral authority of the Bible: doing so would have required of him difficult and costly action.
119. My use of the term "alleged" and similar wording in this paragraph should not be taken as indication that I reject the possibility that racism was a contributing factor in any or all of the incidents. Justice, however, requires truth. And those interested in truth are careful to avoid quick and simple conclusions.
120. "CNN became the source of mockery last week after the network ran a ridiculous chryon stating, 'fiery but mostly peaceful protests after police shooting.'" Jon Miltimore, "The Solzhenitsyn Quote That Explains the 'Mostly Peaceful' Violence in America," *FEE*, September 1, 2020.
121. Minnesota: Calvin L. Horton (43); Michigan: Javar Harrell, (21); California: David Patrick Underwood (53) and Robert Forbes (55); Nebraska: James Scurlock (22); Missouri: Barry Perkins (29), Marvin Francois (50) and David Dorn (77); Indiana: Chris Beaty (38) and Dorian Murrell (18); Iowa: Italia Kelly (22) and Marquis M. Tousant (23); Illinois: John Tiggs (32), Jose Gutierrez (28) and Victor Cazares Jr. (27), Kentucky: David McAtee (53), Nevada: Jorge Gomez (25); and two as-yet unidentified males in Pennsylvania (Philadelphia). Jemima McEvoy, "14 Days Of Protests, 19 Dead," *Forbes*, June 8, 2020.
122. Rich McKay, "Factbox: Who was Ahmaud Arbery?," *Reuters*, February 7, 2022.
123. Elliott C. McLaughlin, Devon M. Sayers, Alta Spells, and Steve Almasy, "Guilty verdicts in the trial of Ahmaud Arbery's killers met with relief and joy in Georgia and beyond," *CNN*, November 24, 2021.
124. Ibid. While the facts of the incident and failure to arrest the perpetrators show that serious problems remain, the trial outcome noted by Sharpton also demonstrates that the general population in the Deep South—who comprised the jury—has changed in important ways since the days when the Democratic Party dominated the South.
125. Russ Bynum, "Arbery case hate-crime plea pulled," *Northwest Arkansas Democrat Gazette*, February 5, 2022; Andrew Branca, "Ahmaud Arbery Case: Seven Facts the Jury Will (Probably) Never Hear," *Legal Insurrection*, October 17, 2021.
126. Tucker Higgins, "Former police officer Derek Chauvin found guilty of murder, manslaughter in the death of George Floyd," *CNBC*, April 21, 2021.
127. Jordan Boyd, "Biden Ignores Chauvin Trial Judge's Admonishment About Jury Intimidation And Tampering From Politicians," *Federalist*, April 20, 2021.
128. Cheryl Teh, "Alan Dershowitz accused Maxine Waters of using 'KKK tactics' to intimidate the jury in the Chauvin murder trial," *Business Insider*, April 21, 2021.
129. Ibid.
130. Andy Mannix, and Matt Delong, "What you need to know about the federal trial of three ex-Minneapolis police officers in George Floyd's death," *Star Tribune*, January 20, 2022.
131. Paula Bolyard, "Rioters Burn Historic St. John's Church in D.C., Deface Monuments Across the City," *PJ Media*, June 1, 2020.
132. Brent Scher, "Park Police Releases New Footage of Violent Lafayette Park Protests," *Washington Free Beacon*, June 24, 2020.
133. Stephanie Ebbs, "Police did not clear Lafayette Square so Trump could hold 'Bible' photo op: Watchdog," *ABC News*, June 10, 2021.
134. Ibid.
135. "Review of U.S. Park Police Actions at Lafayette Park," Office of the Inspector General, U.S. Department of the Interior, June 8, 2021; "Review of U.S. Park Police Actions at Lafayette Park (revised version)," Office of the Inspector General, U.S. Department of the Interior, June 2021; Mark Lee Greenblatt, "Statement Regarding Special Review Report," Office of Inspector General, U.S. Department of the Interior, June 8, 2021. *Note: When formatting and preparing the bibliography during final editing (August 10, 2022), I discovered that Inspector General Greenblatt's statement is no longer available. I leave the URL in place for the record.
136. Stephanie Ebbs, and Benjamin Siegel.=, "Police did not clear Lafayette Square so Trump could hold 'Bible' photo op: Watchdog," *ABC News*, June 10, 2021.

137. Rod Dreher, "The Rest Of The Jacob Blake Story," *American Conservative*, August 29, 2020.

138. "Police union releases statement on shooting," *Kenosha News*, August 28, 2020.

139. Ewan Palmer, "The Kyle Rittenhouse Trial Story Explained," *Newsweek*, November 15, 2021.

140. "Cranium" = Kill with a shot to the head.

141. Hannah Nightingale, "BREAKING: Judge rules mob members shot by Kyle Rittenhouse cannot be called 'victims' in court," *Post Millennial*, October 26, 2021.

142. Dan MacGuill, "Did Joe Biden Call Kyle Rittenhouse a 'White Supremacist'?," *Snopes*, November 24, 2021.

143. Ernst Douglas, "Biden links Kyle Rittenhouse to white supremacists; Lin Wood vows to 'rip Joe into shreds,'" *Washington Times*, September 30, 2020.

144. Becky Sullivan, "Why the Kyle Rittenhouse 'not guilty' verdict is not a surprise to legal experts," *NPR*, November 19, 2021.

145. Denise Sawyer, and Jay O'Brien, "Man acquitted of shooting at deputies in raid that led to death of girlfriend," *CBS 12 News*, November 19, 2021.

146. Jack Gist, "Black Man Acquitted on Self-Defense Same Day as Rittenhouse Busts Myth of 'Unjust' Justice System." *Western Journal*, November 21, 2021.

147. Maxim Lott, "BLM clenched-fist symbol has little-known communist history, critics say," *Fox News*, April 15, 2021.

148. Debbie White, "CALL TO ACTION Black Lives Matter fist symbol — what's the meaning behind the Black Power salute?" *Sun*, June 3, 2020.

149. Peter Flaherty, "Where Is the BLM $60 Million?" *Real Clear Politics*, February 9, 2022.

150. Mike Gonzalez, and Andrew Olivastro, "The agenda of Black Lives Matter is far different from the slogan," *New York Post*, July 1, 2020.

151. Brad Polumbo, "Is Black Lives Matter Marxist? No and Yes," *FEE*, July 7, 2020.

152. "We are a collective of liberators ... Our network centers those who have been marginalized within Black liberation movements." "About," Black Lives Matter; Daniel Brubaker, "Liberation Theology," in *Religion and Contemporary Politics: A Global Encyclopedia*, ed. Timothy J. Demy and Jeffrey M. Shaw (Santa Barbara: ABC-CLIO, 2019), vol. 1. 464-467.

153. Flaherty, "Where Is."

154. Natasha Anderson, "REVEALED: BLM founder Patrisse Cullors paid her baby father $970,000 for 'creative services', her brother $840,000 for security, a fellow director $2.1m and reimbursed the organization $73,000 for a charter flight," *Daily Mail*, May 17, 2022.

155. Julio Rosas, "Anti-Trump White House 'Siege' Suffers Major First Day Setback," *Townhall*, September 17, 2020.

156. William A. Jacobson, "Group behind 'Occupy Wall Street' planning 50-day 'White House Siege' through Election Day," *Legal Insurrection*, August 9, 2020.

157. Ibid.

158. Rosas, "Anti-Trump."

159. Libby Emmons, "BREAKING: Milley undermined Trump, told China he would warn them if US would attack," *Post Millennial,* September 14, 2021.

160. Alex Anas Ahmed, "Donald Trump Jr. slams General Milley for 'treasonous coup,'" *Post Millennial,* September 14, 2021.

161. Dominick Mastrangelo, "Vindman calls for Milley's resignation: 'He usurped civilian authority,'" *MSN*, September 15, 2021.

162. Nick Arama, "Talk About a Coup: It Was Pelosi Who Pushed Milley to Act Against Trump," *RedState,* September 14, 2021; ———, "Pelosi Tried to Foment a Military Coup Against Trump," *RedState*, January 9, 2021.

163. Daniel Villareal, "Kamala Harris More Liberal Than Bernie Sanders, Senate Record Analysis Shows," *Newsweek*, August 20, 2020.

164. Alexander Burns, Matt Flegenheimer, Jasmine C. Lee, Lisa Lerer, and Jonathan Martin, "Who's running for President in 2020?," *New York Times*, April 8, 2020.

165. Bob Fredericks, "Joe Biden will choose 'woman of color' as running mate by August," *New York Post*, June 30, 2020; Charlotte Alter, "Joe Biden Definitively Vows to Pick a Woman Vice President," *Time*, March 15, 2020.

166. Ibid.

167. Craig Bannister, "Democrat Debate Ratings Fall to Lowest Level of 2020 Election Cycle, Breaking October's Record Low," *CNS News*, November 21, 2019.

168. Gary Levin, "Republican debate sets ratings record," *USA Today*, August 7, 2015.

169. "Trump Just Achieved," *Investor's Business Daily*.

170. Robert Rapier, "Is The U.S. Energy Independent?" *Forbes*, November 14, 2021.

171. "Trump Gets Negative Ratings for Many Personal Traits, but Most Say He Stands Up for His Beliefs," *Pew Research Center*, October 1, 2018.

172. Paul Bedard, "Trump's list: 289 accomplishments in just 20 months, 'relentless' promise-keeping," *Washington Examiner*, October 12, 2018; "The President Has Kept His Promises - And More;" "Trump-O-Meter," *Politifact*.

173. Ibid.

174. "The Abraham Accords Declaration," U.S. Department of State; "Full text of Israel-Bahrain 'Declaration of Peace,'" *Times of Israel*, September 16, 2020.

175. Zaini Majeed, "Israel Commemorates Abraham Accords; 'Truly Historic Milestone' In Middle East Peace," *Republic World*, September 6, 2021.

176. Ibid.

177. Joe Hoft, "Final 2020 Rally Tally: President Trump Had Largest Crowds at His Rallies in US History - Biden Had Some of the Smallest," *Gateway Pundit*, November 3, 2020; "In Pictures: Trump supporters hold rallies for the president," *BBC*, October 4, 2020.

178. Bill Ruthhart, and Jonathon Berlin, "Campaign trail tracker: Where Trump, Biden and their running mates have traveled in presidential race's final weeks," *Chicago Tribune*, November 5, 2020; Mario Parker, and Jordan Fabian, "Trump to Hold 14 Rallies in Three Days to Close Out Campaign," *Bloomberg*, October 30, 2020.

179. "16 Celebrities Who Supported Trump In 2020 And What They Say About Him Now," *Yahoo!News*, January 7, 2022.

180. "FLASHBACK: Watch Kamala Harris CALL Joe Biden RACIST!," Scott's Sovereignty, August 17, 2020, YouTube video, https://youtu.be/-1HHmyc78hY.

181. Alexandre Jaffe, and Alan Fram, "Biden's low-key campaign style worries some Democrats," *Associated Press*, September 25, 2020.

182. Ruthhart and Berlin, "Campaign trail."

183. Brittany De Lea, "Biden banks on Hollywood support in final days before 2020 election," *Fox News*, November 1, 2020; Fox Van Allen, "Celebrities who support Joe Biden for president," *CBS News*, October 29, 2020.

184. Matt Viser, "Joe Biden spent much of the general election in his basement. Now, he and his aides ponder a very public inauguration," *Seattle Times*, November 21, 2021.

185. Sharyl Atkisson, "When will 'Basement Biden' get in the game?," *Hill*, September 26, 2020.

186. Ibid.

187. Stephanie Condon, "Biden's in-your-face debate style: Just 'Joe being Joe'?," *CBS News*.

188. James S. Robbins, "Trump did condemn white supremacists, too bad so many people won't listen," *USA Today*, October 2, 2020.

189. Jocelyn Grzeszczak, "Richard Spencer Reiterates Support for Biden, Disavows 'Useless' and 'Traitorous' GOP," *Newsweek*, August 25, 2020.

190. Brie Stimson, and Vandana Rambaran, "Trump critics seize on president's positive coronavirus test to mock, lecture," *Fox News*, October 2, 2020.

191. Carol E. Lee, Nigel Chiwaya, Kanwal Syed, and Joe Murphy. "Tracking Covid-19 infections among President Donald Trump's contacts," *NBC News*, October 2, 2020.

192. "October 15 U.S. presidential debate officially canceled after Trump balked," *Reuters*, October 9, 2020.

193. RJ Reinhard, "Faith in Elections in Relatively Short Supply in U.S.," *Gallup*, February 13, 2020.

194. Amanda L. Tyler, "A 'Second Magna Carta': The English Habeas Corpus Act and the Statutory Origins of the Habeas Privilege," 91 Notre Dame L. Rev. 1949 (2016).

195. Paul Sperry, "The scandal in Washington no one is talking about," *New York Post*, May 21, 2016; Ian Tuttle, "El Chapo's Capture Puts 'Operation Fast and Furious' Back in the Headlines," *National Review*, January 22, 2016; Capital Flows, "'Fast And Furious' Just Might Be President Obama's Watergate," *Forbes*, September 28, 2011.

196. John Bickley, "8 Devastating Facts From The Benghazi Report," *Daily Wire*, June 28, 2016; "What We Do Know about the Benghazi Attack Demands a Reckoning," *National Review*, June 28, 2016.

197. Erb, "IRS Targeting."

198. "Clinton Email Scandal: New Revelations Of Cover-Up Spell Trouble For Hillary," *Investor's Business Daily*, September 22, 2016.

199. Andrew McCarthy, "FBI Rewrites Federal Law to Let Hillary Off the Hook," *National Review*, July 5, 2016.

200. Thomas Blow, "EMAIL SCANDAL: Bill Clinton and Loretta Lynch's tarmac meeting: What happened?," *U.S. Sun*, June 14, 2021; Max Kutner, "After Clinton-Lunch Tarmac Meeting, FBI Scranbled to Find and Punish Source, Newly Released Emails Show," *Newsweek*, December 15, 2017.

201. Jerry Dunleavy, "Ex-FBI lawyer gets probation for Carter Page FISA email deception in Durham investigation," *Washington Examiner*, January 29, 2021; Jed Babbin, "The FBI's FISA Frauds: Until this scandal is addressed squarely the FBI's reputation will remain mud," *American Spectator*, December 27, 2019; David Harsanyi, "The Obama's Administration's FISA Abuse Is a Massive Scandal," *National Review*, December 12, 2019.

202. Bill Gertz, "FBI Increasingly Politicized Under Comey and Mueller," *Washington Free Beacon*, December 16, 2017.

203. "Washington Post, New York Times finally admit Hunter's laptop is real — but only to protect Joe Biden some more," *New York Post*, April 1, 2022; Jesse O'Neill, "Laptop connected to Hunter Biden linked to FBI money-laundering probe," *New York Post*, October 21, 2020.

204. Michael Lee, "Data show majority of Trump's 2020 support came from women and people of color," *Washington Examiner*, May 11, 2021.

205. Jake Lahut, "The demographic that won Joe Biden the election: Higher-earning, college-educated white people near major cities," *Business Insider*, December 11, 2020.

206. "The 2020 Trump-Biden matchup," *Pew Research Center*, August 13, 2020.

207. Andrew Prokop, "A new report complicates simplistic narratives about race and the 2020 election," *Vox*, May 10, 2021.

7

NOVEMBER 3 - JANUARY 6

Before the polls opened on November 3, 2020, more than 100 million Americans had already cast ballots *via* early voting and mail-in voting.[1] Although allowed by many states, early voting seems to violate at least the spirit of the Constitution's Same Day Clause, which stipulates a single day for presidential elections—"The Congress may determine the Time of chusing the Electors, and the Day on which they shall give their Votes; which Day shall be the same throughout the United States"—which, together with U.S. Code, Title 3, Section 1 (specifying Tuesday after the first Monday of November the fourth year after every election of a President and Vice President), means that is the only day we may vote for president or vice president. In 2020, it was November 3.[2]

Voting early—sometimes before key information on the candidates or issues has become public—distorts election outcomes. The campaign period is a time for candidates to be cross-examined by each other and exposed to public scrutiny. Opening general voting before Election Day is like letting two thirds of a bored jury in a murder trial give their verdict and go home *before* all witnesses have been called to the stand. The result would be a miscarriage of justice.

Wyoming, Virginia, South Dakota, and Minnesota opened early voting September 18—*six and a half weeks before Election Day*. Vermont, Michigan, Illinois, and Pennsylvania also opened voting in September, followed by Montana (10/2); South Carolina, Nebraska, Maine, Iowa, and California (10/5); Indiana (10/6); Arizona (10/7); Georgia (10/12); Texas and Kentucky (10/13); Tennessee, Rhode Island, and Kansas (10/14); North Carolina (10/15); Washington and Louisiana (10/16); New Mexico, Nevada, and Massachusetts (10/17); North Dakota, Idaho, Florida, Colorado, Arkansas, and

Alaska (10/19); Wisconsin, Utah, and Hawaii (10/20); West Virginia (10/21); New York (10/25); Maryland (10/26); the District of Columbia (10/27); and Oklahoma (10/29).[3]

The Constitution's Same Day Clause has as one of its purposes the prevention of problems that are well known and common in extended elections. These include people moving from one jurisdiction to another and casting multiple votes, intimidation of people who haven't yet voted, and the mining of data to see who has voted for purposes of strategic manipulation. Expanding the voting period also takes much of the election process outside the all-hands-on-deck environment of Election Day, increasing opportunities for mischief. It is difficult enough to recruit volunteers to work the polls on Election Day; when an election is stretched to nearly fifty times in duration, getting citizens to watch or help at all times on all days in all precincts becomes effectively impossible.

Proponents of expanded election times often argue that many people, such as those whose jobs prevent them from getting to the polls on time, are effectively disenfranchised. It is a reasonable concern, and it would be fair to make Election Day every four years a national holiday.

Ultimately, voting is a civic duty, and it is therefore up to each citizen to take action to find a way to vote; it is not the responsibility of government to make voting an easy and mindless task, nor is it appropriate for government to expend resources to try to increase voter participation. Government needs to provide the fair opportunity for all citizens to vote; after that, it is up to the people to decide. Not voting is a valid expression as well.

Timeline

The critical dates from Election Day 2020 through certification in Congress were:

November 3 → November 4 → November 7 →
December 8 → December 14 → December 23 →
January 3 → January 5 → January 6

Let's look at each of these dates, the reasons for their importance, and what actually happened on them. I extend special thanks to Ivan Raiklin, of whom I had heard but had the privilege to meet for the first time after much of this book was written, for patiently walking me through many of the details that follow and giving clarity to the discussion. I also thank John Droz for pointing me toward the important statistical analyses that were conducted and published during this time period. I do not doubt that there will be differing opinions on the value and meaning of the information, but it is preserved here for posterity.

November 3 (Election Day)

The time period from November 3 (the Tuesday after the first Monday in November; in 2020, Election Day fell on November 3) to December 8 was the time that states had to certify. That is, they needed to go through their process of counting, double-checking, running any recounts, and so forth. In order for a presidential candidate to win, he or she must have 1) won the popular vote inside the state, and 2) the election must not be contested. Once an election becomes contested, however, the popular vote in that state is nullified until the matter is properly resolved.

In the event that a contested election cannot be properly resolved—for example, if the election is found to be irredeemably tainted by improper process (i.e., illegally conducted) or other factors—that state would have several options. The first would be to run a second election properly and according to state law. The second would be to decide the assignment of electors by a simple vote in the state legislature. The third (unlikely to be chosen) would be for that state to abstain altogether from the presidential election. The decision of how to resolve the situation presented by an improperly conducted election lies entirely with the state legislature.

Six states—Georgia, Wisconsin, Arizona, Michigan, Pennsylvania, and Nevada—were quickly contested in 2020. That means that the winner of the popular vote in those states should not have been placed into the column of either candidate until the election issues in those states were properly resolved. Setting the electors of these six states off to the side pending resolution, the actual count in the second week of November, therefore, stood at 232 for Donald Trump to 227 for Joe Biden. The basis for this assessment is the U.S. Constitution, Article II, Section 1, Clause 2; and the Electoral Count Act of 1886.

In the instance of a contested election, the range of possible outcomes —and their relative likelihood—can be discerned based upon several factors. **First**, if the makeup of the state legislature (Democrat or Republican) aligns with the popular vote result of the tainted election. **Second**, if the state's secretary of state is of the same party as that of the popular vote winner of the tainted election. **Third**, if the governor of the state is of the same party as that of the popular vote winner of the tainted election. If the political party of all four of these (i.e., popular vote winner, state legislature majority, secretary of state, and governor) align, then the tainted election result must be considered safe, as there is no practical way to correct it. It should be assumed that the result will be certified in Congress on January 6.

But, if there is a divergence in party within a given state during such a situation, it cannot be presumed that the tainted election result will prevail.

Election Night

Although Florida, Iowa, Maine, Minnesota, New Hampshire, North Carolina, and Ohio were also swing states in the 2020 election, the six pivotal states whose elections are suspect were Arizona, Georgia, Michigan, Nevada, Pennsylvania, and Wisconsin.

In summary, at 7:00 p.m. Eastern Standard Time the Associated Press reported that Trump won Kentucky, and Biden Vermont. At 7:15, CNN announced Indiana for Trump. At 7:30, West Virginia was called for Trump, and a few minutes later, Virginia is called for Biden. At 8:00, Trump had taken Alabama, Mississippi, Oklahoma and Tennessee, while Connecticut, Delaware, Illinois, Maryland, Massachusetts, New Jersey and Rhode Island are called for Biden. So far, none of these were surprises. At 8:30, Trump had won Arkansas, and at 8:54, Indiana. At 9:01, Louisiana, North Dakota, Wyoming and Nebraska were called for Trump, while New Mexico and New York were called for Biden. At 9:28, the District of Columbia was called for Biden. At 9:37, Colorado was called for Biden. At 10:00, Kansas went to Trump. At 10:33, Missouri went to Trump, and at 10:57, New Hampshire went to Biden.[4]

In the early hours of November 4, most of America went to sleep shocked by what—by all accounts—looked like an election that, after weeks of polling on endless repeat showing Biden and Harris with a substantial lead, was going strongly in the direction of Donald Trump. By the end of the night, people on the left were dismayed and those on the right were relieved.

It is not that a strong Trump win did not make sense: the enthusiasm around him all year and particularly in the months leading up to the election had been electric. Tens of thousands were attending his rallies. "Trump caravans" had been spontaneously appearing across the country— one comprised of hundreds of vehicles honking and flying American flags, balloons, and Trump banners passed by my own home in northern Virginia the week before the election—and people were lining the streets to support them. A boat parade on Lake Murray in South Carolina honoring Donald Trump over the 4th of July weekend drew approximately 3,000 vessels, twice the number that organizers had expected and possibly, according to Newsweek, breaking a world record.[5] The mood for Trump was exuberant.

Meanwhile, Biden and Harris had, as mentioned above, been almost reclusive throughout the summer, with Biden teased by critics for hiding in his basement, and for calling a tiny crowd of what appeared to be fewer than two dozen people seated inside circles, about 12 feet apart a "rally."

The "Burst Pipe" and Election Night Pause

Morning brought a completely different picture. When Americans woke up, they learned that Joe Biden was now running ahead in not merely a few, but *every single one* of the battleground states. It was now the turn of Democrats to be elated, while Republicans smelled something rotten.

Furthermore, reports of Election Night disruptions and irregularities—all in heavily Democratic areas that seemed a little too convenient—emerged. Prominent among these was news of a burst water main at Atlanta, Georgia's central ballot counting venue, the massive State Farm Arena.[6] The incident was blamed for an abrupt pause in vote counting on election night. Reports of the length of delay in counting ranged from 1.5 to 4 hours. After the fact, documentation of the incident at a site where millions of ballots were being tabulated was scant. No photographs of the affected area were released, some sources stated that it was not a burst pipe but an overflowing urinal in a restroom distant from the location of ballot counting, and that there was never a need for disruption. A text message from Geoffrey Stiles, Vice President of facilities at the Arena, was released under freedom-of-information laws at the request of an astute Georgia voter. In the text message exchange, Stiles called the incident "highly exaggerated ... a slow leak that caused about an hour and a half delay ... we contained it quickly—it did not spread."[7]

The situation became stranger when Fulton Commission Chairman Robb Pitts told the Atlanta Journal-Constitution on the evening of November 3 that the pipe burst at 6:07 a.m. and was repaired within two hours.[8] If Pitts' statement is accurate, one writer asked, "Why would any state send its election workers home at 10:30pm due to a plumbing problem that had been repaired 14 hours earlier? For the same reason several other swing states did so. On November 3, CNN reported, 'Election officials in some states called it a night and planned to resume the count in the morning.' Among them were Pennsylvania, Wisconsin, and Michigan."[9] According to Election Day reports, the plan was to stop scanning absentee ballots at 10:30 p.m., leaving approximately 20,000 absentee ballots to count on the morning of November 4. The final official margin for Biden in Georgia was a mere 11,779.

Heavily Democratic Fulton County is Georgia's largest county. In 2016, Donald Trump won Georgia comfortably, with 51.3% to Hillary Clinton's 45.6%. In Fulton County, however, Hillary Clinton won 69.2% of the vote in 2016.[10]

Fulton County was not alone in pausing ballot counting overnight. Philadelphia stopped around 10:30 p.m.,[11] and others were alleged to have paused as well, although some of the reports were also alleged to be "mostly untrue."[12] As with so many points of fact related to the election, it was difficult to fully trust even formerly solid news media agencies.

November 4

Some prominent fact check sites minimize the claim of the November 4 ballot counting interruption. Politifact rates the claim of ballot counting interruption as mostly false. As was discussed in Chapter 2, many of the major donors to Politifact and its parent, the Poynter Institute, however, are not neutral and include Facebook, TikTok, Craig Newmark, and the Bill and Melinda Gates Foundation.

FactCheck has also purported to refute a number of the major election fraud claims that were circulating in late 2020.[13] However, in so doing, it cites Democrat activist sources such as the November 12 Joint Statement, and so its supposed debunking—while probably not completely without merit—is already suspect and not worth treating here. If fraud were an essential part of my argument, I would deal with it more carefully. Fact-Check's leftward bias has been discussed in Chapter 2.

It is not my purpose to mediate these issues, but to present a general outline without dismissing allegations too cavalierly, and also to let readers know that there was disagreement about the facts.

Victory Asserted Quickly

Supporters of Joe Biden who had pressed Trump for weeks to commit to waiting "until the full results are in before declaring victory" seemed to forget such caution in the days immediately following the election. While the nation still had virtual whiplash from the overnight shift in results from Trump to Biden, and at a moment when the results were still far from certain, Joe Biden and Kamala Harris wasted no time stepping up to the cameras and posturing as though they were the winners. Cheerleaders in national media—including Fox News—seemed happy to help them fortify the public impression of unquestioned victory.

By November 5 and 6, I observed partisans of Biden and Harris on social media taunting their opponents with messages such as, "It's over," and saying that Trump supporters just need to "accept the result," because "the American people have spoken, and they chose Biden and Harris."

Lawsuits

Dozens of lawsuits were filed soon after the election. One was the subject of Chapter 3, and others will be discussed in Chapter 9. Former New York City mayor Rudy Giuliani,[14] Sydney Powell, and Lin Wood were prominent among those bringing legal action and alleging election fraud. Depending upon one's political preferences, these three figures were either maverick heroes representing the last hope for justice to prevail, or the punchline of a joke who were throwing away their formerly sterling reputations as prosecutors. There was very little middle ground.

Despite the large shadow that Giuliani, Powell, and Wood cast across the landscape in the final two months of 2020, I will not be discussing them in great detail in this book. I do believe that history will vindicate, and already is vindicating, their cause. They operated under extreme time pressure and supercharged political criticism. Because of the threat they posed, they became lightning rods for fury from partisans of the left, who were joined by a number of establishment Republicans who quickly pivoted to accept the results amid repeated claims of the "most secure election in American history."

November 7

On Saturday, November 7, the Associated Press called the election for Biden at 11:25 a.m. EST. Kamala Harris posted a video of her calling Biden on the phone and saying, "We did it, Joe!" This video was shared widely.

By November 11, a full week after the election, there was as yet no real projected winner. However, the Associated Press call, helped by support from Fox News, buttressed an impression among many Americans that the election was, indeed, over and unquestionable.

On November 16, 2020, thirteen days after the election, the Pennsylvania Report, the first independent substantive data analysis of the election, was published. It comprised a time series analysis by Dr. Louis Anthony Cix, Jr., a summary of Pennsylvania Country voting anomalies by S. Stanley Young, PhD, a statistical voting analysis of Montgomery and Allegheny Counties and an analysis of "strangely synchronized" Allegheny County absentee ballots by Dr. Eric Quinnell, and others. This report was remarkable in that it was prepared by competent academics with advanced degrees who, with one exception, were willing to put their names on their work. It was also remarkable for the level of analysis it presented less than two weeks after the election.

John Droz, who directed the report's preparation, explained to me how it came about. He said that he was contacted days after the election by a member of Trump's team. He told me that this person said to him, basically, "We've got a bunch of data, we have a sense that there is something wrong with this election, and we wonder if you could take a look at it and see what you find." He asked about time parameters, and they told him and it was a short turnaround for a lot of data. He told them that for this he would need to form a team. They told him to do what he needed.

Droz related to me that one thing he very much appreciated as a scientist was that the Trump team gave him no particular parameters or expectations for the sort of outcome or analysis they wanted. They just said, basically, "look at it and see what jumps out at you." In turn, Droz did the same thing with the other academics that he invited to the analysis. He says that they came from different perspectives, and he just provided them the data (which, he told me, was just a big mess of raw data and files from various sources with very little organization), and said, "see what jumps out at you."

The result was a series of reports, all unique and coming at the data from different angles, but all suggesting that there were real problems. The report was prepared and published, and constitutes the first substantial post-election analysis of the data.

On November 20, 2020, the report "The Small World of Voting Machine Certification" was published. This report highlighted the often incestuous (figuratively speaking) relationships among voting machine companies and the public officials who are involved with securing their lucrative contracts.[15]

After the Pennsylvania report Droz' team began work on data for another state. A week and a half later, November 27, the Michigan 2020 Voting Analysis Report, prepared by mostly the same group of experts, was released. It included a time series analysis of Trump and Biden votes in Michigan, an analysis of Michigan county vote counts that compared the 2016 and 2020 elections and identified nine counties with shifts in vote distribution up to about 54,000± in a state where most counties had shifts of fewer than 3,000 votes (those nine counties together yielded a swing toward Biden of about 190,000 votes from what would be expected if those counties followed a similar pattern to the rest of the state), an analysis of Wayne and Oakland Counties that identified deviations toward Biden well outside their voting history, and several other analyses related to Michigan absentee ballots.[16]

It is beyond my ability to deal with or assess the reports prepared by Droz and his team. Many of them are highly technical. Also, there is no need in this book, which is focused upon the constitutional problems, to do so. The series of reports prepared by Droz and his team are publicly available and can be referenced at election-integrity.info. They have not (to my knowledge) been subjected to a formal process of external peer review, and it would be desirable to do so, but tricky since there is no assurance that peer review in this instance will not be politically biased.

On November 21, 2020, the report "Statistical Evidence of Dominion Election Fraud? Time to Audit the Machines" was published. The study identified what it called the "Dominion effect," and while not concluding that it was nefarious, did determine that the effect would be enough to influence the outcome of elections and concluded that the findings are sufficient to warrant Arizona, Georgia, Nevada, and Wisconsin to allow Republicans to audit the Dominion machines that were used in the 2020 election.[17]

December 8

On the 8th of December, the states have to decide which slates of electors they are going to transmit. Their decision is not binding, but it is a strong recommendation to the states to make this decision.

On December 13, 2020, the Antrim Michigan Forensics Report was published by Allied Security Operations Group, detailing the results of their investigation into the Dominion Voting System. The audit found, among other things, that the Dominion system allowed a flip of some 7,048 Trump votes to Biden on election night in Antrim County, Michigan, and further judged that this flip was not the result of human error as the Antrim County Clerk and Michigan Secretary of State Jocelyn Benson claimed, but because of a machine error built into the voting software designed to create error. In fact, the audit found, "forensic examination of the server for Antrim County from December 6, 2020 consists of 15,676 individual events, of which 10,667, or 68.05% ... were recorded errors."[18]

December 14

On this day, the electors that were picked on the 8th actually vote in the state capitals. They give six copies, which are sent in various directions, and these electoral votes are transmitted over to the federal government— namely to the president of the Senate (in this case, Mike Pence) and/or the national archivist.

On December 16, 2020, Jesse Binnall, under oath, made the following statement to the United States Senate:

> Thank you Mr. Chairman, Ranking Member Peters, and member of the committee.
>
> This year, thousands upon thousands of Nevada voters had their voices cancelled out by election fraud and invalid ballots. Here's how it happened.
>
> On August 3, 2020, after a rushed special session, Nevada legislators made drastic changes to the state's election law by adopting a bill known as AB4. The vulnerabilities of this statute were obvious: it provided for universal mail voting without sufficient safeguards to authenticate voters or ensure the fundamental requirement that only one ballot was sent to each legally qualified voter. This was aggravated by election officials' failure to

clean known deficiencies in their voter rolls. Because of AB4, the number of mail ballots rocketed from about 70,000 in 2016 to over 690,000 this year.

The election was inevitably riddled with fraud and our hotline never stopped ringing. While the media and the Democrats accused us of making it all up, our team began chasing down every lead. Our evidence came both from data scientists and brave whistleblowers.

Here is what we found:

• Over 42,000 people voted more than once. Our experts were able to make this determination by reviewing the list of actual voters and comparing it to other voters with the same name, address, and date of birth. This method was also able to catch people using different first name variations, such as William and Bill, and individuals who were registered both under a married name and a maiden name.

• At least 1,500 dead people are recorded as voting, as shown by comparing the list of mail voters with the social security death records.

• More than 19,000 people voted even though they did not live in Nevada; to be clear, this does not include military voters or students. These voters were identified by comparing the lists of voters with the U.S. Postal Service's National Change of Address database, among other sources.

• About 8,000 people voted from non-existent addresses. Here we cross-referenced voters with the Coding Accuracy Support System which allowed our experts to identify undeliverable addresses.

• Over 15,000 votes were cast from commercial or vacant addresses. Our experts found these voters by analyzing official U.S. Postal Service records that flag non-residential addresses and addresses vacant for more than 90 days.

• Incredibly, almost 4,000 non-citizens also voted, as determined by comparing official DMV records of non-citizens to the list of voters in the 2020 election.

The list goes on. All in all, our experts identified over 130,000 unique instances of voter fraud in Nevada. But the actual number is almost certainly higher. Our data scientists made these calculations not by estimations or statistical sampling, but by analyzing and comparing the list of actual voters with other lists, most of which are publicly available. To put it simply, they explained their methods so that others could check their work. Our evidence has never been refuted, only ignored.

Two Clark County technical employees came forward, completely independent of each other, and explained that they discovered that the number of votes recoded by voting machines and stored on USB drives would change between the time the polls were closed at night until they were reopened the next morning. In other words, votes were literally appearing and disappearing in the dead of night. When we attempted to verify the integrity of these voting machines, we were allowed only a useless visual inspection of the outside of a USB drive. We were denied a forensic examination.

Finally, our investigation also uncovered a campaign to illegally incentivise votes from marginalized populations, by requiring people to prove they voted to receive raffle tickets for gift cards, televisions, and more.

Our determined team verified these irregularities without any of the tools of law enforcement, such as grand jury subpoenas or FBI agents. Instead, we had less than a month to use critical thinking and elbow grease to compile our evidence. When we tried to obtain testimony or documents from Clark County officials they obstructed and stonewalled, literally dodging subpoenas and refusing to release documents. Even the U.S. Postal Service obstructed our discovery efforts. When we filed suit, state officials and even courts delayed proceedings for days, but then offered us merely hours to brief and argue our cases.

Mr. Chairman, these findings are disturbing, alarming and unacceptable in a free society. Our free and fair election tradition is a precious treasure that we are charged with protecting. Government by the consent of the governed is hard to win and easy to lose. Every single time a fraudulent or illegal vote is cast, the vote of an honest citizen is canceled out. Thank you.

On December 17, 2020, the report "Evidence of Fraud in Conjunction with Use of Dominion BMD Machines" was published. This report carries the label "Donaldwon.com," and therefore was evidently prepared by advocates of Trump. However, its methodology is stated and its data presented within the report. Furthermore, its conclusions seem reasonably measured. It found that "analysis of publicly available data shows evidence of possible fraud involving Dominion Voting System's BMD machines and Hart Verity Touch machines," possibly resulting from systematic programming resulting in the "'overperformance' of candidate Biden by approximately 5% in many of the counties in which the machines were used. The increases in votes occurred in hundreds of counties in the U.S."[19] This report is mentioned here for the benefit of readers who may be better qualified than I to assess its merit, and for purposes of a historical record of the analyses that were released during the time period.

December 23

Under the Electoral Count Act, if any state did not send a slate of electors for adjudication by Congress on the 6th of January by the "fourth Wednesday of December" (In 2020, December 23rd), the president of the Senate should send a demand letter back to that state's secretary of state asking them to transmit a letter. It should be noticed that, since this process exists by law, it means that the December 14 deadline for transmittal is not binding. In fact, it would mean that the true deadline for states to transmit electors, under normal circumstances, is always January 6. It also demonstrates that the first moment when any federal officer has any say or input in the process in 2020 was December 23.

Texas et al. v. Pennsylvania et al. (the "Texas lawsuit" of Chapter 3) was filed on December 8, 2020. On December 11, the U.S. Supreme Court ruled that Texas and the other plaintiff states had no standing. The Court's ruling raised the natural questions such as "is there someone else who would have standing? Does another plaintiff have standing? Is it possible that the state legislatures would have standing? Or, are there any other circumstances in which these plaintiffs (Texas and the other plaintiff states) would have standing?"

But, the key question was *why did the Supreme Court rule "no standing"* in the first place? To answer this question, we need to look at the makeup of the Court. Doing this, we find that there were five conservatives (Alito, Coney Barrett, Gorsuch, Kavanaugh, and Thomas), one unknown (Roberts), and three non-conservatives (Breyer, Kagan, and Sotomayor). We know how the three non-conservatives were going to vote: no standing. Now we look next at Chief Justice Roberts. Roberts was appointed by George W. Bush, and the Bush family is a political dynasty that despises Donald Trump and especially objects to Trump's signature embrace of equality and fairness in the area of immigration. Roberts' loyalties lie with the Bushes, he has furthermore many times demonstrated his willingness to depart from a faithful interpretation of the Constitution.

If Chief Justice Roberts had brought this case before the Court, there was existing precedent of the Electoral Count Act's prior application. Contingent elections have been carried out three times in U.S. history under the 12th Amendment. In 1960, Hawaii initially voted for Nixon and then flipped to change the electoral outcome after the certification. In 2000, Bush v. Gore set precedent in which the state legislative body of Florida voted to exercise their Article II, Section 1, Clause 2 authority in order to vote, and sent the Bush electors, with the U.S. Supreme Court making it moot by ruling in a way that ultimately made Bush prevail. There were, furthermore, two legal precedents including a Supreme Court case confirming that the state legislature has plenary authority to determine electors. Add to all this the Tenth Amendment, which states that any powers not explicitly enumerated to the federal government are retained by the states or by the people.

Considering the above, it came as no surprise that Roberts would join the other non-conservatives in voting "no standing." If the Court had taken the Texas case, they would have *had* to—at a minimum—nullify the results in Pennsylvania. And, that would have been the first domino to fall, after which other contested states that had conducted their elections improperly would have followed. What we do not know, and may never know, is which of the five conservatives on the Supreme Court joined the four non-conservatives in curtly dismissing the Texas lawsuit, hiding behind the fig leaf of "no standing."

Raiklin told me, "If I were a Supreme Court justice, and four states joined with Texas in this lawsuit, and five states were suing four, I would find that very compelling to take on as a case. This is a total Article III, no-brainer standing. You can't have any *better* standing than this."

So, the precinct captains certified an illegal election. The county clerks (or commissioners, in some cases), the secretaries of state, the governors that transmitted the electors, all violated the election laws of the state, because the way they ran the election was not in line with the laws passed by the legislatures of those states, who have plenary authority under Article II, Section I, Clause 2. Notice that there is *no mention of fraud* anywhere in this discussion.

But, the Supreme Court ducked. What could happen next? If the states transmit a constitutionally insufficient slate of electors, then the president of the Senate is under a duty and obligation to defend the U.S. Constitution, as per his oath. Mike Pence needed to say, *"Hey, secretary of state of [Arizona, Pennsylvania, Michigan, Georgia, Wisconsin, Nevada], you have to fix what you just did. You have options, and I'm not going to tell you which one you must choose. You can have a brand new election. You can take a roll-call vote in the legislature. Or, you can abstain from the election altogether until you sort out the underlying issues, and at a later date you can transmit your electors. It's up to you. But what you cannot do is submit unconstitutionally appointed electors. You have until January 6."*

Ivan Raiklin tweeted a memo articulating this on December 20, 2020, and it spread quickly. Several days passed with no notable action. On December 23, President Trump retweeted the memo. Mike Pence, however did not transmit a letter instructing those states. When Mike Pence accepted the electors without objection after being informed that the electors were constitutionally insufficient, he arguably broke his oath to defend the Constitution.

After Pence did nothing on December 23, Raiklin began to contact individuals that he knew who would be in the 117th Congress as of noon on January 3, and who would want to join an objection on January 6. He reached out to former judge Mo Brooks, who was already onto it and needed no persuading. Also, he contacted Marjorie Taylor Greene, who was not yet a congresswoman but would be on January 3. Congressman Moore from Alabama joined. Bob Goode came out publicly as the fourth or fifth congressman to state that he planned to object to all six slates of electors. Many members of Congress from the plaintiff states in the Texas lawsuit also joined after seeing the Supreme Court ruled "no standing."

How Is a U.S. President Chosen?

The Constitution's Elections Clause, which gives plenary authority to the state legislatures, has been already discussed above and in Chapter 3. The second important legal guide for the matter at hand is the Electoral Count Act of 1887, which is now 3 U.S. Code § 15. The Act says:

> Congress shall be in session on the sixth day of January succeeding every meeting of the electors. The Senate and House of Representatives shall meet in the Hall of the House of Representatives at the hour of 1 o'clock in the afternoon on that day, and the President of the Senate [i.e., Mike Pence in 2021] shall be their presiding officer. Two tellers shall be previously appointed on the part of the Senate and two on the part of the House of Representatives, to whom shall be handed, as they are opened by the President of the Senate, all the certificates and papers purporting to be certificates of the electoral votes, which certificates and papers shall be opened, presented, and acted upon in the alphabetical order of the States, beginning with the letter A; and said tellers, having then read the same in the presence and hearing of the two Houses, shall make a list of the votes as they shall appear from the said certificates; and the votes having been ascertained and counted according to the rules in this subchapter provided, the result of the same shall be delivered to the President of the Senate, who shall thereupon announce the state of the vote, which announcement shall be deemed a sufficient declaration of the persons, if any, elected President and Vice President of the United States, and, together with a list of the votes, be entered on the Journals of the two Houses. Upon such reading of any such certificate or paper, the President of the Senate shall call for objections, if any. Every objection shall be made in writing, and shall state clearly and concisely, and without argument, the ground thereof, and shall be signed by at least one Senator and one Member of the House of Representatives before the same shall be received. When all objections so made to any vote or paper from a State shall have been received and read, the Senate shall thereupon withdraw, and such objections shall be submitted to the Senate for its decision; and the Speaker of the House of Representatives shall, in like manner, submit such objections to the House of Representatives for its decision; and *no electoral vote or votes from any State which shall have been regularly given by electors whose appointment has been lawfully certified* according to section 6 of this title from which but one return has been received shall be rejected, *but the two Houses concurrently may reject the vote or votes when they agree that such vote or votes have not been so regularly given by electors whose appointment has been so certified.* If more than one return or paper purporting to be a return from a State shall have been received by the President of the Senate, those votes, and those only, shall be counted which shall have been regu-

larly given by the electors who are shown by the determination mentioned in section 5 of this title to have been appointed, if the determination in said section provided for shall have been made, or by such successors or substitutes, in case of a vacancy in the board of electors so ascertained, as have been appointed to fill such vacancy in the mode provided by the laws of the State; but in case there shall arise the question which of two or more of such State authorities determining what electors have been appointed, as mentioned in section 5 of this title, is the lawful tribunal of such State, the votes regularly given of those electors, and those only, of such State shall be counted whose title as electors the two Houses, acting separately, shall concurrently decide is supported by the decision of such State so authorized by its law; and in such case of more than one return or paper purporting to be a return from a State, if there shall have been no such determination of the question in the State aforesaid, then those votes, and those only, shall be counted which the two Houses shall concurrently decide were cast by lawful electors appointed in accordance with the laws of the State, unless the two Houses, acting separately, shall concurrently decide such votes not to be the lawful votes of the legally appointed electors of such State. But *if the two Houses shall disagree in respect of the counting of such votes, then, and in that case, the votes of the electors whose appointment shall have been certified by the executive of the State, under the seal thereof, shall be counted.* When the two Houses have voted, they shall immediately again meet, and the presiding officer shall then announce the decision of the questions submitted. No votes or papers from any other State shall be acted upon until the objections previously made to the votes or papers from any State shall have been finally disposed of.[20]

The Electoral Count Act became law in 1887. Generally, it provided that states had the say in the appointment of their own electors, but that the states had to abide by the Constitutional parameters for doing so. If a state did not run a lawful election or otherwise lawfully appoint their electors, Congress could direct the state to rectify matters. The result of rejecting the electors would have been an excellent national civics lesson. Americans of all ages would have learned that:

- any state legislature can decide the assignment of presidential electors without a statewide election, and that
- a national election cannot be stolen by merely overpowering the system in a few states, and those that try to do so run the risk of throwing the election to the legislature

As a practical matter, most states whose electors were rejected, if they chose to settle the matter by a vote in their state house, would have assigned their electors to Trump since each of those state houses are controlled by Republicans. This is one reason Nancy Pelosi, Chuck Schumer, and others were labeling the option an "effort to overturn the results of the election." They contended that Biden had won those states and that sending the matter back to the state legislatures would have overturned the will of the people. It was a disingenuous point, since the exact issue in those states was that they had conducted their elections in such a way that the number of suspect or illegal votes greatly outnumbered the margin of alleged victory in each case. In other words, the correct term would not be "overturning the results," but "deciding the assignment of electors in states tainted by tampering."

In mid-December of 2020, Representative Mark Meadows forwarded part of a message from attorney Joseph Schmitz developing the legal theory,

> On January 6, 2021, Vice President Mike Pence, as President of the Senate, should call out all the electoral votes that he believes are unconstitutional as no electoral votes at all — in accordance with guidance from founding father Alexander Hamilton and judicial precedence. 'No legislative act,' wrote Alexander Hamilton in Federalist No. 78, 'contrary to the Constitution, can be valid.' The court in Hubbard v. Lowe reinforced this truth: 'That an unconstitutional statute is not a law at all is a proposition no longer open to discussion.' 226 F. 135, 137 (SDNY 1915), appeal dismissed, 242 U.S. 654 (1916).[21]

Democrats fiercely ridiculed those allies of President Trump who saw in the Electoral Count Act one last avenue for redress of election integrity concerns. Although Rob Natelson believes the act to be unconstitutional, it is nevertheless a law that has been in place for nearly a century and a half, unchallenged, and has been applied on more than one occasion. As such, it is appropriate for guidance until it is either repealed or its constitutionality is tested by the Supreme Court.

It is fair at this point to present why Natelson states that the Electoral Count Act is unconstitutional, and he gives at least two reasons. First, the choice of presidential electors is one of a set number of *federal functions* of the state legislatures, and therefore cannot be modified by Congress. As a federal function, the power is furthermore not contingent upon the governor calling the state legislature into session. The legislature gets to act in this particular case because the federal Constitution gives it enumerated power to do so. Second, the Act materially alters the process of handling objections to electoral votes from the process laid out in the Constitution, namely by separating the houses of Congress rather than having them in joint session, which has a real effect on the relative power of senators and representatives in the matter.[22] The Trump team, argues Natelson, was on solid ground in arguing that the Electoral Count Act did not bind Congress, but "the 12th amendment does not clearly determine that the vice president has exclusive authority to count the ballots," and "When the Constitution or law is silent, normal parliamentary procedure is to proceed according to the rules specified by the parliamentary body. That means rules adopted by the joint session of Congress, not by the presiding officer."[23] In other words, had Pence objected, Congress—controlled by Democrats—could have likely overruled him.

It is interesting to observe that arguments from the left that the Electoral Count Act presented no serious possibility on January 6, 2021, and that those who thought it did were nuts and conspiracy theorists, were belied by their later admissions—and legislative attempts to overturn or modify the act—to the contrary.[24] These seemed to demonstrate that President Trump was right when he suggested that Mike Pence had the power in 2021 to act. If Trump was wrong, then why would Democrats later suggest that the Act needed changing? Also, professor John Eastman's argument that the vice president could postpone the electoral vote count for a few days to allow for investigations in disputed states came from a man whom Natelson himself recognizes as a respected constitutional scholar.[25]

The failure of the Supreme Court to take up the matter left those harboring valid concerns about an unlawfully conducted election looking for *any* lawful and orderly way to set things right. Schmitz had extrapolated from the principle articulated by Hamilton the possibility of the Vice President calling out the unconstitutional electoral votes as though they were no votes at all. The theory was, however, not to be tested since Pence—who would certainly have been crucified by Democrats, the media, the institutions, and many within his own party for doing so—apparently did not have the stomach for it or calculated in the moment that the harm to his party and the cause might be greater than the vindication and so chose to refrain.

On December 31, 2020, the "Statistical Voting Analysis of the 2020 NY-22 Congressional Contest" was published.[26]

On January 2, 2021, the "2020 Presidential Election Startling Vote Spikes" report, by Eric Quinnell, Stan Young, Tony Cox, Tom Davis, Ray Blehar, John Droz, and one other, was published. It addressed Arizona, Florida, Georgia, Illinois, Kentucky, Maine, Michigan, Minnesota, Missouri, New Jersey, Ohio, Pennsylvania, Virginia, and Wisconsin. This report looked at unusually large differences between votes received for one presidential candidate or the other at a single time. It analyzed such spikes for both Trump and Biden in each of the above mentioned states. The report did not seek to address what caused the spikes (also called "dumps"), but rather to identify where and when they occurred.[27]

Having failed to get a hearing on the merits at the Supreme Court, the

Trump team argued that electors from those states that conducted unlawful elections—namely (at least) Pennsylvania, Georgia, Michigan, and Wisconsin, and possibly Arizona—could be rejected, returning the matter to those states to resolve one way or another. Congress would not, under such a scenario, tell those states *how* to rectify things. The states would then have had at least three options: first, hold a new election, following the laws set forth by their state legislature; second, appoint their electors by roll call vote of their state legislature; or third, abstain from submitting electors altogether.

Rejecting slates of electors from states that had not conducted their elections in a manner prescribed by their own state legislatures would not have been "overturning an election," as some like Rep. Liz Cheney have disdainfully—and either ignorantly or disingenuously—suggested.[28] It would merely have returned the matter to those states, informing them that they need to follow the Constitution if they wish to participate in the national election. In other words, those states would have needed to make sure that the people's voice was heard and not corrupted or smothered by changes to the process that were not approved by the state legislatures that those people elected for this purpose.

January 3

The 117th Congress began at noon.

January 5

A runoff election for the Senate race in Georgia took place on January 5. The result was that two Democrats, Raphael Warnock and Jon Ossoff, unseated two Republican senators, Kelly Loeffler and David Perdue, and delivered control of the Senate to the Democrats, with Kamala Harris the tie-breaker.

The problem was that many of the people who were actually allowed to vote in the runoff may have been illegal, and the matter had not yet been decided as litigation was pending. The Georgia constitution says that the runoff race is an extension of the general election, and only people that voted legally in the general election are allowed to vote in the runoff. At this time, there was still pending litigation in Georgia to find out whether the people who voted in Georgia in the general election (for example, by drop boxes) had voted legally. Raiklin's memo proposed postponing the runoff pending the outcome of the litigation to determine who was legally allowed to vote. There is more to be said about this matter, but the outcome here, as with the presidential election, was extraordinarily consequential for the entire nation.

On January 5, 2020, the "Edison Timeseries Distribution Analysis in the 2020 Presidential Election" was published by Eric Quinnell. Among its findings were: 1) a total of almost 4 million negative votes occurred between election night (November 3rd) and the final Edison timestamp, 2) 1,006 of the 21,452 datapoints are negative votes, 3) not all negative votes are corrected—e.g. New York deleted 500k+ votes on November 8th, never to be recovered, 4) only two states—Hawaii and Delaware—lack negative votes, 5) Trump had the majority of time-series updates in his favor (6,208 data pairs) vs Biden (4,467 data pairs), 6) Biden averaged 577 votes per time-series update in his favor—the average is dominated heavily by multi-sigma dumps extremely outside the mean, 7) seven states have a skewed tail in favor of Trump (meaning "dumps" dominate in Trump's favor), 8) 38 states have a skewed tail in favor of Biden, and 9) the top 5 of Trump's largest dumps in his favor are a result of negative votes.[29]

On the eve of January 6, momentum was strongly in the direction of rejecting at least some of the electors. On January 5, 2020, the number of House members who had expressed willingness to object to the slates of electors from Arizona and Pennsylvania was 149—and growing by the minute.[30]

January 6

January 6 following a presidential election is the date that Congress certifies the electors from the states. Nancy Pelosi, the Speaker of the House, must have been looking on in dismay at a likely House vote to reject electors from Pennsylvania and Arizona. President Trump had called for a rally on the National Mall that day. Hundreds of thousands of his supporters from around the country showed up. Trump spoke to them near the White House and the Washington Monument in his usual conversational style. He lamented the many problems with the election, talked about the alleged fraud, and generally told those present that he was not going to roll over and affirm something (i.e., a Biden victory) that he knew not to be true because of cheating. However, the proceedings of the January 6 committee and others notwithstanding, I have seen no evidence to support the contention that President Trump ever suggested or incited violence or lawbreaking that day or at any other time. Maybe I have missed something, and if I am ever presented with such evidence, I will revise this conclusion.

Objections

Even in the wake of the January 6 drama and its media coverage, which undoubtedly frightened away some senators and representatives who otherwise intended to join, or may have been persuaded to join, the objections, six U.S. senators (Ted Cruz (TX), Josh Hawley (MO), Cindy Hyde-Smith (MS), John Kennedy (LA), Roger Marshall (KS), and Tommy Tuberville (AL)), and 121 representatives (Robert Aderholt (AL), Rick Allen (GA), Jodey Arrington (TX), Brian Babin (TX), Jim Baird (IN), Jim Banks (IN), Jack Bergman (MI), Stephanie Bice (OK), Andy Biggs (AZ), Dan Bishop (NC), Lauren Boebert (CO), Mike Bost (IL), Mo Brooks (AL), Ted Budd (NC), Tim Burchett (TN), Michael Burgess (TX), Ken Calvert (CA), Kat Cammack (FL), Jerry Carl (AL), Buddy Carter (GA), John Carter (TX), Madison Cawthorn (NC), Ben Cline (VA), Michael Cloud (LA), Andrew Clyde (GA), Tom Cole (OK), Rick Crawford (AR), Warren Davidson (OH), Scott DeJarlais (TN), Mario Díaz-Balart (FL), Byron Donalds (FL), Jeff Duncan (SC), Neal Dunn (FL), Ron Estes (KS), Pat Fallon (TX), Michelle Fishbach (MN), Scott Fitzgerald (WI), Chuck Fleischmann (TN), Scott Franklin (FL), Russ Fulcher (ID), Matt Gaetz (FL), Mike Garcia (CA), Bob Gibbs (OH), Carlos Gimenez (FL), Louie Gohmert (TX), Bob Good (VA), Lance Gooden (TX), Paul Gosar (AZ), Sam Graves (MO), Mark Green (TN), Marjorie Taylor Greene (GA), Morgan Griffith (VA), Michael Guest (MS), Jim Hagedorn (MN), Andy Harris (MD), Diana Harshbarger (TN), Vicky Hartzler (MO), Kevin Hern (OK), Yvette Herrell (NM), Jody Hice (GA), Clay Higgins (LA), Richard Hudson (NC), Darrell Issa (CA), Ronny Jackson (TX), Chris Jacobs (NY), Mike Johnson (OH), Bill Johnson (OH), Jim Jordan (OH), John Joyce (PA), Mike Kelly (PA), Trent Kelly (MS), Doug LaMalfa (CA), Doug Lamborn (CO), Jacob LaTurner (KS), Debbie Lesko (AZ), Billy Long (MO), Barry Loudermilk (GA), Frank Lucas (OK), Blaine Luetkemeyer (MO), Nicole Malliotakis (NY), Tracey Mann (KS), Brian Mast (FL), Kevin McCarthy (CA), Riordan McClain (OH), Mary Miller (IL), Barry Moore (AL), Markwayne Mullin (OK), Troy Nehls (TX), Ralph Norman (SC), Devin Nunes (CA), Jay Obernolte (CA), Steven Palazzo (MS), Gary Palmer (AL), Scott Perry (PA), August Pfluger (TX), Bill Posey (FL), Guy Reschenthaler (PA), Tom Rice (SC), Mike Rogers (AL), Hal Rogers (KY), John Rose (TN), Matt Rosendale (MT), David Rouzer (NC), John Rutherford (FL), Steve Scalise (LA), Pete Sessions (TX), Jason Smith (MO), Adrian Smith (NE), Greg Steube (FL), Tom Tiffany (WI), William Timmons (SC), Jeff Van Drew (NJ), Tim Walberg (MI), Jackie Walorski (IN), Randy Weber (TX), Daniel Webster (FL), Roger Williams (TX), Joe Wilson (SC), Ron Wright (TX), and Lee Zeldin (NY)) voted in favor of an objection to the Arizona slate of electors.

Seven senators (Ted Cruz (TX), Josh Hawley (MO), Cindy Hyde-Smith (MS), Cynthia Lummis (WY), Roger Marshall (KS), Rick Scott (FL), and Tommy Tuberville (AL)) and 137 representatives (Robert Aderholt (AL), Rick Allen (GA), Jodey Arrington (TX), Brian Babin (TX), Jim Baird (IN), Jim Banks (IN), Cliff Bentz (OR), Jack Bergman (MI), Stephanie Bice (OK),

Andy Biggs (AZ), Dan Bishop (NC), Lauren Boebert (CO), Mike Bost (IL), Mo Brooks (AL), Ted Budd (NC), Tim Burchett (TN), Michael Burgess (TX), Ken Calvert (CA), Kat Cammack (FL), Jerry Carl (AL), Buddy Carter (GA), John Carter (TX), Madison Cawthorn (NC), Steve Chabot (OH), Ben Cline (VA), Michael Cloud (LA), Andrew Clyde (GA), Tom Cole (OK), Rick Crawford (AR), Warren Davidson (OH), Scott DeJarlais (TN), Mario Díaz-Balart (FL), Byron Donalds (FL), Jeff Duncan (SC), Neal Dunn (FL), Ron Estes (KS), Pat Fallon (TX), Michelle Fishbach (MN), Scott Fitzgerald (WI), Chuck Fleischmann (TN), Virginia Foxx (NC), Scott Franklin (FL), Russ Fulcher (ID), Matt Gaetz (FL), Mike Garcia (CA), Bob Gibbs (OH), Carlos Gimenez (FL), Louie Gohmert (TX), Bob Good (VA), Lance Gooden (TX), Paul Gosar (AZ), Sam Graves (MO), Mark Green (TN), Marjorie Taylor Greene (GA), Morgan Grifith (VA), Michael Guest (MS), Jim Hagedorn (MN), Andy Harris (MD), Diana Harshbarger (TN), Vicky Hartzler (MO), Kevin Hern (OK), Yvette Herrell (NM), Jody Hice (GA), Clay Higgins (LA), Richard Hudson (NC), Darrell Issa (CA), Ronny Jackson (TX), Chris Jacobs (NY), Mike Johnson (OH), Bill Johnson (OH), Jim Jordan (OH), John Joyce (PA), Mike Kelly (PA), Trent Kelly (MS), David Kustoff (TN), Doug LaMalfa (CA), Doug Lamborn (CO), Debbie Lesko (AZ), Billy Long (MO), Barry Loudermilk (GA), Frank Lucas (OK), Blaine Luetkemeyer (MO), Nicole Malliotakis (NY), Tracey Mann (KS), Brian Mast (FL), Kevin McCarthy (CA), Riordan McClain (OH), Dan Meuser (PA), Mary Miller (IL), Carol Miller (WV), Alex Mooney (WV), Barry Moore (AL), Markwayne Mullin (OK), Greg Murphy (NC), Troy Nehls (TX), Ralph Norman (SC), Devin Nunes (CA), Jay Obernolte (CA), Burgess Owens (UT), Steven Palazzo (MS), Gary Palmer (AL), Greg Pence (IN), Scott Perry (PA), August Pfluger (TX), Bill Posey (FL), Guy Reschenthaler (PA), Tom Rice (SC), Mike Rogers (AL), Hal Rogers (KY), John Rose (TN), Matt Rosendale (MT), David Rouzer (NC), John Rutherford (FL), Steve Scalise (LA), David Schweikert (AZ), Pete Sessions (TX), Jason Smith (MO), Adrian Smith (NE), Lloyd Smucker (PA), Elise Stefanik (NY), Greg Steube (FL), Chris Stewart (UT), Glenn Thompson (PA), Tom Tiffany (WI), William Timmons (SC), Jeff Van Drew (NJ), Beth Van Duyne (TX), Tim Walberg (MI), Jackie Walorski (IN), Randy Weber (TX), Daniel Webster (FL), Roger Williams (TX), Joe Wilson (SC), Robert Wittman (VA), Ron Wright (TX), and Lee Zeldin (NY)) voted in favor of an objection to the Pennsylvania slate of electors.[31]

QUESTIONS

    I. What happened on election night? What was the situation when people went to bed? What had changed when America woke up on the 4th? Can you think of any reason that the counting would have stopped?

2. What were the constitutional deadlines for certification and counting of the electoral votes? How did these deadlines affect the events of the period following the election?

3. How would you describe the arguments of the various lawsuits filed on behalf of Trump? How many lawsuits were there? How many of them were resolved on the merits? For those that were resolved on the merits, what was the outcome?

---

1. Adam Levy, Ethan Cohen and Liz Stark, "More than 100 million ballots were cast before Election Day," *CNN*, November 3, 2020.
2. Rob Natelson, "The Constitution Offers Ways Out of the Election Mess," *Epoch Times*, November 8, 2020.
3. "Early voting dates, 2020," Ballotpedia.
4. "Election Night 2020: Minute-by-minute on the tri-campus," *Observer*, University of Notre Dame, November 4, 2020.
5. Ewan Palmer, "Trump Boat Parade Likely Breaks World Record As Over 3,000 Vessels Turn Up," *Newsweek*, July 7, 2020.
6. Anthony Leonardi, "Burst pipe causes election results to be delayed in Georgia's most populous county," *Washington Examiner*, November 3, 2020.
7. Frank Chung, "'Slow leak': Text messages cast doubt on Georgia officials' 'burst pipe' excuse for pause in counting," *news.com.au*, November 13, 2020.
8. Ben Brasch, "Fulton County election results delayed after pipe bursts in room with ballots," *Atlanta Journal-Constitution*, November 3, 2020.
9. David Catron, "About Atlanta's Election Day Pipe Dream," *American Spectator*, November 13, 2020.
10. Chris Pandolfo, "Report: Election results delayed in Georgia's largest county after water pipe bursts in a room containing ballots: Not good news," *Blaze*, November 3, 2020.
11. Larua Italiano, "Philadelphia stops counting mail-in ballots for the night," *New York Post*, November 3, 2020, 10:38 p.m..
12. "Fact check: List of partly false statements on the 2020 election," *Reuters*, November 10, 2020.
13. Saranac Hale Spencer, "Nine Election Fraud Claims, None Credible," *FactCheck*, December 11, 2020.
14. Giuliani served as Attorney General of the United States from 1981 to 1983 and six years as Mayor of New York City; he was the mayor at the time of the 9/11 attacks that brought down the World Trade Center towers. Giuliani is a serious man with a record of public service at high levels and an absence of scandal.
15. Jeff Carlson, "The Small World of Voting Machine Certification," November 20, 2020.
16. Louis Anthony Cox, Jr. et al., "Michigan 2020 Voting Analysis Report," November 27, 2020.
17. Ben Turner, "Statistical Evidence of Dominion Election Fraud? Time to Audit the Machines," November 21, 2020.
18. "Antrim Michigan Forensics Report," Allied Security Operations Group, December 13, 2020.
19. "Evidence of Fraud in Conjunction with Use of Dominion BMD Machines," *Based Media*, December 17, 2020.
20. "3 U.S. Code § 15 - Couting electoral votes in Congress," Legal Information Institute, Cornell Law School.
21. Daniel Chaitlin, "Jan. 6 committee caught misportraying another text message to Mark Meadows," *Washington Examiner*, December 17, 2021.
22. Rob Natelson, "The Electoral Count Act Is Unconstitutional," *Epoch Times*, March 14, 2022.
23. Rob Natelson, "Sorry, Vice-President Pence can't replace electors on his own," *Independence Institute*, January 3, 2021.
24. Clare Foran, and Manu Raju, "Senators moving 'aggressively' on Electoral Count Act reform, but face long way to go before a deal," *CNN*, February 1, 2022; Libby Cathey, "What is the Electoral Count Act and why does it present problems?," *ABC News*, January 31, 2022.

25. Natelson, "The Electoral Count."
26. Eric Quinnell et al., "Statistical Voting Analysis of the 2020 NY-22 Congressional Contest," December 31, 2020.
27. Eric Quinnell et al., "2020 Presidential Election Startling Vote Spikes," January 2, 2021.
28. Aaron Parsey, "Liz Cheney Says Evidence Shows Trump and Others Knew Plan to Overturn 2020 Election Was Illegal," *People*, April 11, 2022.
29. Eric Quinnell, and Anonymous, "Edison Timeseries Distribution Analysis of the 2020 Presidential Election," January 5, 2021.
30. Ivan Raiklin, Personal interview with Daniel Brubaker, Hamilton, Virginia, May 12, 2022.
31. Zachary Stieber, "Full List: how Members of Congress Voted on Objections to Arizona, Pennsylvania Electoral Results," *Epoch Times*, January 7, 2021; Andrew Solender, "Majority Of House Republicans Vote To Reject Pennsylvania, Arizona Electors," *Forbes*, January 7, 2021.

8

A WRITTEN CONFESSION

On February 4, 2021, a mere two weeks and one day after Joe Biden's inauguration (skipped by Trump), the national media and cultural establishments remained abuzz with the narrative of a January 6 "insurrection." Trump, who had left office without conceding, awaited acquittal by the Senate after his lightning-fast January 13 second impeachment in the House.

It was at this very moment that an article appeared in Time magazine, titled "The Secret History of the Shadow Campaign That Saved the 2020 Election." Judging from the article's tone, its author—Molly Ball—was a hardcore anti-Trump partisan. In it, Ball admits and details, in plain English and with stunning candor, that Republican claims of conspiracy and manipulation of the election *process* by the likes of Mark Zuckerberg, social media gatekeepers, the AFL-CIO, the Democrat Party, and some anti-Trump Republicans—precisely what Trump supporters had been claiming for months in the face of withering and even violent ridicule from the left —were *absolutely true*. Ball now oozed praise for the cleverness of the cheaters. This chapter is a review and analysis of that article.

"Trump was right," Ball wrote of the President's December 2 remark that "Within days after the election, we witnessed an orchestrated effort to anoint the winner, even while many key states were still being counted."[1]

She continued,

There *was* a conspiracy unfolding behind the scenes, one that both curtailed the protests [i.e., of those demanding election integrity] and coordinated the resistance from CEOs [i.e., against a Trump second term]. Both ... were the result of an ... alliance between left-wing activists and business titans ... Both sides would come to see it as a sort of implicit bargain ... in which the forces of labor (sic) came together with the forces of capital to keep the peace and oppose Trump's assault on democracy.[2]

The author, however, did not present the actions of these parties as though they were nefarious. These cheaters were on the side of the good guys. Ball asserted that the true interest of these Trump opponents was merely "ensuring it would be free and fair, credible and uncorrupted," to counter the danger of "an autocratically inclined President." Ball continued to state that "The scenario the shadow campaigners were desperate to stop was not a Trump victory ... [but] an election so calamitous that no result could be discerned at all." There is no indication that Ball saw irony in the statement.

Next, Ball admitted the central complaint of the Texas lawsuit to have been true. The work of these conspirators,

> touched on every aspect of the election. They got states to change voting systems and laws and helped secure hundreds of millions in public and private funding. ... This is the inside story of the conspiracy to save the 2020 election ... It is the story of an unprecedented, creative and determined campaign whose success also reveals how close the nation came to disaster. "Every attempt to interfere with the proper outcome of the election was defeated," says Ian Bassin, co-founder of Protect Democracy ....

Despite claiming to be a nonpartisan endeavor, the Protect Democracy website has a rabid anti-Trump bias.[3] One would be justified in wondering what Bassin meant by preventing interference with "the proper outcome." It is an interesting choice of words, since an election's *outcome* is different from its *process*. An outcome is a specific result: this candidate won, and that candidate lost. What outcome would Bassin have considered "improper" in 2020? I believe the answer is obvious from the context and from the tone of the Protect Democracy website.

Returning to the Time article, Ball told us that the conspirators now wanted the secret history of the 2020 election told. In the remainder of this chapter, we will discuss what she presented.

The Hero and the Problem

A cause needs a founding story, and a founding story needs a hero. Enter senior advisor to the president of the AFL-CIO, Mike Podhorzer, who in the fall of 2019 "became convinced the election was headed for disaster—and determined to protect it."

Who is this Mike Podhorzer? The question is soon answered:

Among Democratic insiders, he's known as the wizard behind some of the biggest advances in political technology in recent decades. A group of liberal strategists he brought together in the early 2000s led to the creation of the Analyst Institute, a secretive firm that applies scientific methods to political campaigns. He was also involved in the founding of Catalyst, the flagship progressive data company.

From the above, we may infer that Podhorzer is a serious Democrat/progressive activist. Podhorzer is listed by Ball under the heading "The Architect." What was the specific nature of the looming "disaster" Podhorzer feared in late 2019? A newsletter sent by Podhorzer in October 2019 expressed concern about Trump himself trying to disrupt the election. He hypothesized what he called the two most likely outcomes: Trump losing and refusing to concede, or Trump winning the Electoral College ("despite losing the popular vote," he hastened to add) by corrupting the voting process in key states.

In other words, Podhorzer envisioned two likely possibilities: Trump loses but won't let go of power, or Trump wins by cheating. He does not seem to have imagined Trump capable of winning fair and square.

The Band of Conspirators

Podhorzer, Ball reported, was soon contacted by other leftist groups including the Fight Back Table—"a coalition of 'resistance' organizations" —who had been gathering local and national liberal activists under a label of Democracy Defense Coalition. Podhorzer "spent months pondering scenarios and talking to experts," before concluding that the main problem with America's decentralized election system was that it "couldn't be rigged in one fell swoop."

"That," Ball stated, "presented an opportunity to shore it up."

Podhorzer began "holding back-to-back Zoom meetings for hours a day with his network of contacts across the progressive universe: the labor movement; the left-wing institutions like Planned Parenthood and Greenpeace; resistance groups like Indivisible and MoveOn; progressive data geeks and strategists, representatives of donors and foundations, state-level grassroots organizers, racial-justice activists and others." By April, hundreds from across the "progressive movement" were attending. The meetings, Ball stated, "became the galactic center for a constellation of operatives across the left." The effort continued to grow, and eventually "reached across the aisle, into the world of Trump-skeptical Republicans appalled by his attacks on democracy."

So far the article reported one of the broadest coalitions of leftist and Democrat organizations and individuals ever assembled, a coalition of some of the most uniformly and fiercely anti-Trump people in the world of Democrats and leftists. Now, Ball stated, they were joined by anti-Trump Republicans.

But, remember that Ball stated the express purpose of the entire effort was to make sure the election was "free and fair, credible and uncorrupted." Did this group of anti-Trump political activists, that soon began meddling with the very process of the election itself, sound like a coalition who didn't care *who* won, so long as the contest was "free and fair, credible and uncorrupted?"

They said they wanted to "save" the 2020 election. Were they truly trying to save the country from a dishonest election—*or just from a Trump victory*? Ball's ironic description of Trump as "autocratically inclined," or of his efforts to ensure election integrity as "plotting," do not suggest journalistic neutrality.

The Plan of Action

Ball described a three-page confidential memo that Podhorzer drafted and titled "Threats to the 2020 Election." In it, he laid out four categories of challenges that he anticipated from Trump:

1. attacks on voters
2. attacks on election administration
3. attacks on Trump's political opponents
4. efforts to reverse the results of the election

Tellingly, all of Podhorzer's anticipated challenges were expected to emanate from Trump. He apparently anticipated no threat to democracy from the Democrats.

Then, Ball said, COVID-19 burst onto the scene, and normal methods of voting "were no longer safe" for voters or volunteers. She bemoaned what she calls "Trump's crusade against mail voting," which, she said, "prevented some states from making it easier to vote absentee and for jurisdictions to count those votes in a timely manner." Ball did not detail, exactly, how the President was able to block state legislatures from changing their own election rules. Is it possible that Democrats were merely frustrated that Trump was shining a light in their direction as they moved to circumvent those legislatures and usurp their plenary power?

Whatever unspecified action Trump supposedly took to block the state legislatures from legislating, Ball said that chaos resulted. Democrat strongholds such as Milwaukee and New York, respectively, suddenly had trouble opening the full number of polling places, and counting the votes in a timely manner. Somehow, Ball alleged, it was Trump's fault.

So, Podhorzer's weekly meetings, beginning in April 2020, were effectively uniting this coalition of anti-Trump activists across the nation into a galactic center of leftist operatives. She quoted Maurice Mitchell as describing the nature of the effort as "the litigation space, the organizing space, [and] the political people just focused on the W." What was "the W"? Did it mean "the win"? And if so, for whom?

Seeming to lack self-awareness of the fascistic nature of what she was describing, Ball persisted in detailing the effort under the euphemism "protecting the election." She proudly reported its "unprecedented scale," framing the entire operation as a "liberal alliance," which "reached across the aisle, into the world of Trump-skeptical Republicans appalled by his attacks on democracy."

So, what was this alliance's plan of attack? Job one, we learn, was "overhauling America's balky election infrastructure." Yes, a coalition of devoted partisans of one of the two candidates was going to "save" the election by overhauling the election system itself.

What could possibly go wrong?

Sidebar: Ball's Misguided Accusation

In his 2021 article, "Why Do Most Countries Require Photo Voter IDs? They Have Seen Massive Vote Fraud Problems," John Lott observed several things:

- Virtually all of Europe and nearly all developed countries require in-person voters to use photo IDs to vote.
- The vast majority of countries ban absentee ballots for people living in their country.
- Other countries have discovered widespread voter fraud when safeguards are not in place, and most significantly,
- **Unlike the US, few countries changed their voting rules for the pandemic.** France temporarily allowed sick or at-risk individuals to vote absentee. Poland allowed mail-in ballots for everyone only for 2020. Two cities in Russia allowed mail-in ballots. The rest? In person voting, period.[4]

Molly Ball, in other words, was wrong to criticize Trump for crusading against mail voting. The United States stood basically alone in its hyperventilation over the dangers of in-person voting in 2020, and almost all other countries ban mail-in voting because they have learned from experience that it is dangerous to democracy. That is to say, almost every other country was on the same "crusade" against mail-in voting that Ball alleged Trump to have been on. Furthermore, far from preventing participation,

Mexico saw an average nine percentage point *increase* in voter participation in the three elections *after* implementation of strict anti-fraud rules, compared to the three elections prior to those rules being in place. Lott observed, "As people gained faith in the electoral process, they became more likely to vote."

The Power of Money

The first step in the process of the conspirators' election infrastructure overhaul plot was for the leftists in this coalition to give money to the mostly nonpartisan people administering the elections. This money was directed toward pushing absentee voting by sending out postcards, mailing ballots unsolicited to every single voter in some states, and paying for additional staff and scanners to process the ballots.

The coalition lobbied Congress to direct COVID relief money to elections administration. The resultant CARES Act yielded $400 million in grants to state election administrators. However, Ball said, "It wasn't going to be enough."

Who would help America out of this dire predicament? "Private philanthropy" swooped in to fill the gap and save the day. Foremost among them, Ball informed us, was the Chan-Zuckerberg Initiative, which ponied up $300 million.

Remember, in the states that decided the election—as we have already seen in Chapter 3— the unsolicited mass mailing of absentee ballot applications or ballots is *illegal*. However, one Amber McReynolds of the National Vote at Home Initiative blamed the lack of funding to support these illegal activities upon the federal government: "It was *a failure at the federal level* that 2,500 local election officials were forced to apply for philanthropic grants to fill their needs" (emphasis added).

As of this writing, McReynolds' "nonpartisan" organization's website boasts about their work in the 2020 election:

National Vote at Home Institute (NVAHI) has helped facilitate innovation of vote-at-home systems by offering policy and implementation recommendations, research, and communications support to states across the country. In 2020, the organization:

• Improved election operations in 2020 by providing assistance to numerous state and local election offices in 37 states, with a concentration in the key battleground states of Georgia, Michigan, Pennsylvania, and Wisconsin.[5]

It is interesting that a "nonpartisan" organization innocently pursuing the advance of voting from home across the nation would in 2020 have taken such a keen special interest in the battleground states, strongly concentrating their efforts in specifically those states, and would furthermore celebrate the *outcome* of those efforts (the election of Joe Biden and ouster of Donald Trump) following one of the most controversial elections in U.S. history. Why?

NVAHI's "2020 Retrospective" report advocates for no-excuse mail-in ballots, shaming states that require an excuse for a mail ballot, citing New Jersey as a "Success Story," and reserving highest praise—with a five star rating—for California, with their full vote at home model.[6] These two states are famous for corruption in their elections.[7]

So, Ball continued, the Institute "helped 37 states and D.C. bolster mail voting." But, that was not enough! NVAHI, we learn, regularly deployed canvassers door-to-door to get out the vote. In 2020, NVAHI was not just concerned to make sure people had the *opportunity* to vote by mail; they wanted to make sure that people *did* vote by mail "in key states"—and they did so by sending out ballot applications to 15 million people in those states.

Ball told of heightened skepticism. Black voters did not trust the mail. She did not ask why. Rather, the initiative was pushing voting by mail as a *better* way "to ensure one's vote was counted" than even by voting in person. In fact, she asserted that voting by mail is the *best* way to ensure one's vote is counted.

Meanwhile, there was the matter of whether all this was even legal. Ball related that *Democratic* lawyers were busy battling an "historic tide of pre-election litigation." Wendy Weis of the Brennan Center for Justice bemoaned litigation brought by the Trump campaign to raise doubt about mail voting. Why was it that Democratic lawyers were the only ones engaged in this $800 million—supposedly nonpartisan—effort to ensure a "safe and secure" election?

Suppression of Information

In a section about disinformation, Ball wrote about "Trump's lies and conspiracy theories" without giving any concrete examples, much less a demonstration of why they were unfounded. She told, however, of Laura Quinn, a "progressive operative," who led a "nameless, secret project" to track disinformation and "dangerous lies" online.

Quinn found that arguing with what she called disinformation was not effective, stating that engagement only made the content more likely to appear on searches, to be seen by more people. Having observed multiple news items classified as "disinformation"—most notably the October 2020 New York Post article on the contents of Hunter Biden's laptop as discussed earlier in this book, which was grudgingly admitted to have been true by even the most leftist outlets more than a year after the election—I do wonder if Quinn merely preferred to create an unlevel playing field in which truths inconvenient to her side could be suppressed. In any event, her chosen strategy became application of pressure on platforms to remove content labeled "disinformation" by progressive operative Laura Quinn and her allies.

In November 2019, Ball related, Mark Zuckerberg hosted a dinner at his home for nine individuals who made use of the evening to warn him about the danger of such "falsehoods" spreading unchecked. They evidently applied great pressure to Zuckerberg and others to take action and suppress information that these individuals (presumably all Democrats) and their allies deemed misinformation. And, Zuckerberg was not their only target; Vanita Gupta, who was at the dinner, relates having similarly pressured Twitter CEO Jack Dorsey and others. And she met her reward: immediately upon Biden's inauguration, he nominated Gupta for Attorney General, with the confirmation taking place in April.

Propaganda

But stopping "misinformation" such as Trump's assertion that voting by mail was an invitation to widespread fraud was not enough, Ball said. Podhorzer's coalition also needed an active campaign to affirmatively convince Americans that millions of ballots sent through the mail, often to addresses where people no longer lived, or addressed to individuals who were deceased, or to people known not to vote but whose mailboxes could be easily accessed by nefarious actors, "weren't susceptible to fraud," and furthermore to convince them that "it would be normal if some states weren't finished counting votes on election night."

Put differently, they needed to conduct psychological operations ("psy-ops") on the nation to prepare a critical mass of Americans to disbelieve their own eyes and accept—or, even better, to defend as credible—what this group of leftist operatives was already scheming to perpetrate in November.

One arm of this operation was to be spearhead by Dick Gephardt. The former Democratic congressman gathered a network of former elected officials, military leaders, and others, and began a messaging campaign to the public simultaneous to targeting key secretaries of state, governors, and attorneys general. Gephardt raised $20 million in private money for the effort.

The appearance of nonpartisanship was of obvious importance. Former congressman Zach Wamp, one of the Trump-skeptical Republicans, filled that role.[8] Wamp headed up a group of twenty-two Democrats and an equal number of Republicans through a group that Ball claimed was nonpartisan called Issue One. A glance at Issue One's website quickly reveals it to have a strong Democrat bias, as evidenced (among other things) by the fact that the very first sentence one encounters on its page about the 2020 Election is the claim, "The 2020 election was the most secure in history."[9] It seems an odd position, absent the slightest hesitation or least qualification, for an organization whose ostensible core mission is integrity of democracy, elections, and ethics. The Issue One website gives credence to the partisan January 6 Committee (see discussion in the Introduction to this book), and in fact formally praises what it calls the "Bipartisan Jan. 6 Investigation."

Wamp's subgroup was called the National Council on Election Integrity. It ran ads in six states—presumably the 2020 swing states—and wrote articles in favor of election integrity. Wamp claimed that the group had "rabid" Trump supporters onboard as well, but does not name them.

Two other groups, the Voting Rights Lab and IntoAction—again, both obviously geared toward leftist political objectives, with the former being a project of the New Venture Fund, and stating, "Democracy Donors, a liberal donor group, has listed the Voting Rights Lab as a top organization to fund"[10]—were involved in creating and disseminating the propaganda that "every vote be counted" *via* email, text message, and social media. The message was going to be especially important in the overall push to remove security safeguards such as signature verification. And the campaign was not small: with the help of donors, Ball claimed that this messaging was seen more than one billion times. Tracking polls run by the organization soon found that the campaign was having the desired effect: a late October poll revealed that over 70% of respondents had been imbued with the expectation that there would be no winner known on election night.

Meanwhile, Podhorzer was noting the polls were underestimating Trump's support. He therefore made his data available—prior to Election Day—to the media organizations who would be calling the election. These data, Ball said, alerted them to how much better Trump was likely to do on Election Day than they had expected.

Planning an Uprising in Case of a Trump Victory

Organizers who had been part of the Marxist M4BL movement and the far left Democracy Defense Coalition which included MoveOn, the Working Families Party, People's Action, and Color of Change among a total of more than 150 liberal groups joined, Ball reported, to plan widespread protests if Trump "tried to steal the election." How would they know if Trump tried to steal the election? We are not told. However, Ball described that the coalition would be activated *via* text message as soon as the day after the election—so that they could "flood the streets" if the "coup they feared" materialized.

It is eminently worth pondering what a "coup" by Trump would have looked like on November 4. What was President Trump, the then-current occupant of the White House, going to do to effect such a coup? Occupy the White House? Or were they merely preparing to take to the streets if Trump happened to pull out a victory, with these leftist organizations claiming, without evidence, that he had cheated? It is in such a context that the shrill derision of Trump for making similar claims that the left had stolen the election is interesting. It seems quite evident that this coalition had been planning for months to do exactly that in the face of even a manifestly legitimate Trump victory.

USCC and Christian Organizations Jump in

One week before Election Day, Ball stated that the U.S. Chamber of Commerce—the single largest lobbying group in the United States—reached out to Podhorzer. Ordinarily at odds with Podhorzer and his union, the violent protests and destruction over the previous summer and the threats of further disruption of business if Trump were not ousted had apparently had their desired intimidating effect. The Chamber released a pre-election statement reinforcing the "count every vote" and "don't expect to know the winner on election night" message.

Neil Bradley, the Chamber's executive vice president, now wanted to issue a joint statement with Podhorzer on the matter, pledging shared commitment to "a fair and peaceful election." The statement was crafted and endorsed by some Christian leaders before its release on Election Day under the names of Chamber CEO Thomas Donohue and AFL-CIO president Richard Trumka, along with leaders of the National Association of Evangelicals and the National African American Clergy Network. The statement admirably called for the process to be allowed "to proceed without violence, intimidation or any other tactic that makes us weaker as a nation."[11]

Election Night

Ball next told about Democrat despair on election night. She presented Podhorzer as a calm figure amid the storm who observed exactly what he had expected. He "could tell that as long as all the votes were counted, Trump would lose." Ball did not say "all the legitimate votes," but rather, "all the votes." This detail should be remembered in light of the information in Chapters 3 and 4 and as you read forward through Chapter 9.

The conspirators, Ball reported, gathered for an 11:00 p.m. call on

Zoom. "Hundreds joined; many were freaking out." Podhorzer, however, "presented data to show ... that victory was in hand."

Then, Fox News called Arizona for Biden. Ball explicitly tied this early call by Fox to the earlier relationships cultivated between the conspirators and the news networks and TV anchors.

Still, the coalition were ready to mobilize their mass protests. However, they were careful since they were aware that a poorly timed show of strength could backfire by leading to violence that she stated could give Trump a reason to send in federal troops. The conspirators intended to send a message that "the people had spoken," and not give credence to Trump's claims of a coup. The coalition thus told their national anti-Trump mob to stand down for now. And they did—for the rest of the week.

The plan was now, Ball said, to project a national impression that Biden had won. "Counter their disinfo with our confidence & get ready to celebrate," was the guidance sent around to the conspirators on Friday, November 6. "Declare and fortify our win. Vibe: confident ... NOT passive, anxious."

Remember that the stated goal of the conspirators had been to protect a fair and honest process. However, their "win" was entirely centered around an alleged Biden victory. The integrity of the process seemed merely a talking point from here forward.

Blocking Transparency To Secure Biden Victory

President Trump had been warning of major vote fraud in urban centers for months, all the more so with the massive opportunities that had been opened through the millions of mail-in ballots in circulation and the proliferation of ballot drop boxes concentrated in heavily Democrat areas of swing states. As the nation's attention thus settled upon the hotspots, the task of the coalition of Molly Ball's "conspirators" was to move into a phase of obstructing observers and election integrity groups.

Art Reyes III was on the job. He created a massive text chain to counter the GOP observers at the TCF center in Detroit. The coalition decided to try to claim the moral high ground by demagoguing the "people's right to decide," and—importantly—suggesting that calls for honest elections were really a racial issue aimed at denying black Detroiters their votes. Flooding Wayne County's canvassing board's certification meeting on November 17, activists on Reyes' text chain were part of the mob intimidating William Hartmann and Monica Palmer, calling them racists for asking for answers, threatening violence against them and their families unless they voted to certify, and so forth—as described in their affidavits printed in Chapter 3.

But the election boards were only one prong. The state legislature in Michigan also had a great deal of power in the process. Accordingly, the conspirators did a deep-dive on key lawmakers' personal and political histories and then Issue One ran television ads in Lansing. Never-Trumper Wamp prevailed upon former colleague Mike Rogers to write an op-ed for the Detroit papers calling for officials to "honor the will of the voters." Rogers' piece repeated the "[count] every ballot" mantra; conspicuously absent was the word "legal" in front of the word "ballot." He further framed a failure to ignore election integrity concerns as though taking them seriously would compromise national security by delaying Biden's transition team.[12]

Protect Democracy also targeted three former Michigan governors (two Republicans and one Democrat) and prevailed upon them to issue a joint statement calling for certification of Michigan's electoral votes for Joe Biden without further inquiry. Behind the scenes, John Engler (one of the three) made phone calls to major donors and others who could apply pressure to lawmakers on the matter.

Ball described the standoff as one between "pro-democracy forces" and "a Trumpified Michigan GOP," implying that Trump supporters were against democracy itself. On the side of the alleged "anti-democracy" GOP were the powerful Ronna McDaniel and former Education Secretary Betsy DeVos—both influential, and the latter a member of a billionaire family. Having already labeled McDaniel and DeVos as standing against democracy, Ball proceeded to imply that these two or their allies might corruptly influence the outcome. Nowhere did she acknowledge a valid concern over election integrity or address any of the issues that were raised and that have been discussed elsewhere in this book.

Ball concluded her article with a description of the final effort to intimidate the state canvassing board into certifying the election. After a livestream and Twitter hashtag drew thousands to the certification meeting, Republican Aaron Van Langevelde folded under the pressure, giving the necessary third vote to certify. The other Republican abstained.

The other states in question—Pennsylvania, Wisconsin, and the others—followed suit by certifying their electors.

January 6: The Final Hurdle

On January 6, Congress was to meet to count the electors from the states. President Trump had called those supporting him to gather on the National Mall that day for a rally. As Ball described it, Trump addressed the crowd and "peddled the lie that lawmakers or Vice President Mike Pence could reject states' electoral votes." Then, she said, the crowd "sacked the building" after Trump had told them to go to the Capitol and "fight like hell." After thus framing the events, she stated that it was Trump's "final attack on democracy, and once again, it failed."

Molly Ball's Final Analysis

Ball concluded by claiming that "Democracy won in the end," and "[t]he will of the people prevailed."

QUESTIONS

1. Why do you suppose Americans who voted for Trump found the content of Molly Ball's article so frustrating?

2. Ball described the effort to "save" the election as *bipartisan*, meaning that people from both parties were participating in the effort. Does "bipartisan" mean "neutral"? If they were given the choice between a *fair* election and a Biden victory, which do you feel would have been the top priority of the participants in this effort that Ball calls a "conspiracy"?

3. Do you believe that Ball would have written this article praising the effort and all of the participants if the 2020 election had been perfectly fair and secure but Trump had emerged the winner? Why or why not?

---

1. Molly Ball, "The Secret History of the Shadow Campaign That Saved the 2020 Election," *Time*, February 4, 2021.

2. Ibid. Emphasis added.

3. One of the first features appearing on the website, for example, is a link to a featured project whose title is "Securing Consequences for the January 6th Insurrection." The term "insurrection" applied to January 6th is not correct. What happened on January 6th at the Capitol was a rally, and a very small subset of the rally-goers participated in a riot. The term "insurrection" refers to a planned and coordinated attempt to overthrow a government. An insurrection would have involved weapons, and it would not have dispersed peacefully. To date, the only guns that were documented at the Capitol on January 6 were those in the hands of police or other government officials. Yet, the first sentences on the aforementioned page read, "On January 6, 2021, a violent mob staged one of the most significant insurrections against the United States since the Civil War. Donald J. Trump and his allies rallied this mob of thousands of his supporters behind the repeatedly debunked lie that the 2020 presidential election was stolen and summoned them to Washington, D.C. on January 6. He then incited those supporters to storm the U.S. Capitol." https://protectdemocracy.org/project/securing-consequences-for-the-january-6th-insurrection/. (6/15/22).

4. John R. Lott, Jr., "Why Do Most Countries Require Photo Voter IDs? They Have Seen Massive Vote Fraud Problems," *Crime Prevention Research Center*, May 18, 2021.

5. "About Us: Our Impact," National Vote At Home Institute.

6. "Vote at Home Policy Actions: 2020 Retrospective," National Vote At Home Institute. 4-8.

7. Joel B. Pollak, "Voter Fraud Leads To Reversed Result In California Local Government Election," *Breitbart*, May 31, 2022; Fred Lucas, "Exclusive: 3 Plead Out in California Election Fraud Case as Councilman's Trial Proceeds," *Daily Signal*, January 25, 2022; Hans von Spakovsky, "Latest Alleged Election Fraud in California May Have Changed Election Outcome," *Daily Signal*, August 24, 2021; "New election ordered in race marred by voter fraud charges," *Associated Press*, August 19, 2020; Dana Wefer, "New Jersey Elections Are the Lifeblood of State's Political Corruption," *Independent Voter News*, March 9, 2017.

8. Chris Butler, "Zach Wamp Praises Liz Cheney, Trashes Donald Trump," *Tennessee Star*, December 25, 2021; Chris Butler, "Report: Former Tennessee Congressman and Zach Wamp Helped Remove Donald Trump from White House," *Tennessee Star*, February 8, 2021.

9. https://issueone,org/issues/elections-voting/2020-election/. (6/28/22).

10. https://www.influencewatch.org/organization/intoaction/; "Voting Rights Lab." https://www.influencewatch.org/organization/voting-rights-lab/.

11. "AFL-CIO, Chamber of Commerce, National Faith Leaders Call for Votes to Be Counted," AFL-CIO, November 3, 2020.

12. Mike Rogers, "Opinion: Certify election results to preserve democracy," *Detroit News*, November 21, 2020.

9

DENIAL OF REQUESTS FOR INVESTIGATION OR REDRESS

This was a black letter law case .... These justices sat in their conference room and had a long talk, not so much about the law in the Constitution but of our politics and the political ramifications of what would happen to their institution, which is now being threatened. And I think they made a terrible decision, and I think history will judge it that way.[1]

— MARK R. LEVIN, CONCERNING THE U.S. SUPREME COURT'S DECEMBER 8, 2020 REJECTION OF THE REPUBLICAN LAWSUIT TO UNDO PENNSYLVANIA'S CERTIFICATION OF THE ELECTION

The abdication by some courts, including the U.S. Supreme Court, of the duty to render judgment on the merits of many of the election cases was a missed opportunity in 2020. At key junctures, the judiciary dismissed cases on technicalities without comment upon the material concerns. In many instances, writes Steven J. Mulroy, "the courts were too quick to rule that plaintiffs lacked standing. These rulings resulted in unjustified sweeping rulings that voters were not injured even if their legal votes were diluted by states accepting illegal votes; that campaigns did not share interests with the voters who supported them; and that only state legislatures, and not Electoral College nominees," had standing to sue under the Electors Clause. "All this threatens to create dangerous precedent which would improperly prevent full consideration of the merits of future meritorious voting rights and election suits."[2]

The dilemma here is vitally important. On the one hand, it is true that rule of law does not prevail if the courts are not respected as the arbiters.

Rep. Liz Cheney's claim that "the most conservative of conservative principles is reverence for the rule of law. ... Those who refuse to accept the rulings of our courts are at war with the Constitution" is a powerful statement.[3] But, what happens when the courts refuse to rule on a matter for illegitimate reasons—such as a guess by the court that a just ruling will cause social or political problems? Would that be justice? The answer is "no."

While our legal system is designed with a requirement (for example) that a person bringing a lawsuit must have "standing" (that is, they must have a personal stake or interest in the matter about which they are bringing a suit), and this requirement serves the important functions of preventing the courts from being overburdened and avoiding third party busybody interference in the affairs of others, some of these situations in 2020—the Texas lawsuit being a good example—exposed a real problem: If *this* plaintiff has no standing, then who does? And, how then can the governed ever hope for resolution of such a matter?

In the end, a sense that justice has not prevailed in the election is betrayed not merely by the traction gained by ongoing claims of a "rigged election" by Donald Trump and his supporters, but also by the post-election statements and actions of Joe Biden and *his* supporters, who seem to "protest too much." Wrote Bob Anderson,

> The courts have always served as a pressure-relief valve on our internal disagreements. [...] The election is over. There has been an inauguration. So why did ABC's George Stephanopoulos feel the need to berate a U.S. senator and his audience with the demand, "Can't you just say the words: This election was not stolen?" Why must he shout, "There were 86 challenges filed by President Trump and his allies in court. All were dismissed!" Perhaps the answer lies in the details of those cases....[4]

The loud and frequent repetition of partial facts, avoiding context, may serve a near-term political purpose for interested parties. However, as the epigraphic quotation from George Washington at the front of this book states, "[T]ruth will ultimately prevail where pains is taken to bring it to light." In this case, the slightest scrutiny reveals a quite different narrative:

> In reality, there were 28 unique cases filed across the six contested states by President Trump or others on his behalf. Twelve were filed in Pennsylvania, six in Georgia, and two or three in each of the other states. Of course, there was also the lawsuit filed by the state of Texas against the state of Pennsylvania that had the potential to change the outcome. So let's call it 29. ... To be sure, that is still a lot of cases. [... But] review of them shows that ... few were ever considered on the merits.[5]

Doubtless some judges, having observed the fate awaiting helpers of the President, were afraid. Perhaps others rationalized that they did the nation a service by leaving these cans of worms unopened. However, the courts' failure to faithfully and timely answer these urgent questions did the opposite. Every obstruction of efforts at transparency, exclusion of poll watchers, instance of midnight ballot processing after watchers had gone home or comingling late ballots with timely ones, and so on—naturally fed suspicion. Together, they formed a mountain of lingering doubt that is profoundly damaging to the fabric of American society.

The 2020 Court Cases

Joe Biden partisans made much of the un-elaborated fact that so many of the lawsuits brought by Trump and the RNC "failed." The picture is distorted by omission of detail. In some cases, pro-Biden propagandists such as Marc Elias further distorted the picture by treating appeals as separate from the original case, so that (for example) a single case which was won by Trump on the second appeal would be treated as two losses and one win.[6] The ultimate just ruling by a higher court, however, is the moral victory, and it is appropriate to look at this as a single and solid legal win for the one who prevails, and a rebuke for the other. The overridden victories in lower courts are mostly irrelevant.

While it is true that a slight majority of the total ninety-two lawsuits to which Trump or the GOP (counting the original filing and any appeals as a single case) were a party went against them, most of the losses—forty-one as of February 2022—were dismissed on technicalities such as standing, timing or jurisdiction, rather than the merits.[7]

Of those thirty 2020 election lawsuits involving Trump or the Republican Party so far decided on the merits, a supermajority of 73.3% (that is, twenty-two) went in favor of Trump and/or the RNC. *Only eight* of the 2020 presidential election lawsuits were so far lost by Trump or his allies on the merits. In terms of all ninety-two lawsuits, the DNC or Biden allies won only 8.7% on the merits, while Trump and his allies won 24% on the merits —with most of the rest dismissed on technicalities having nothing to do with the substance of the case.

In stark contrast to these facts, a tally of lawsuit results posted on Twitter by Democrat lawyer Marc Elias, since deleted,[8] was one of the most widely-referenced sources bolstering a narrative of staggering Trump losses in court.[9] It was Elias who commissioned the fraudulent Steele dossier and used it in his own attempt to overturn the 2016 presidential election.[10] That and other dishonest activities led to his formal sanction by the 5th Circuit Court.[11] He and his law firm, Perkins Coie, were behind many of the activities to subvert the election laws as detailed in Chapter 3.

Elias' involvement in these matters are discussed at length elsewhere, including by Mollie Hemingway in her book *Rigged*.

Elias tweeted on May 29, 2022, "The Trump campaign lost 64 of 65 post-election lawsuits." Just a few days later, on June 4, 2022, he tweeted, "Since their humiliating defeats in court following Trump's loss in 2020, Republican lawyers and operatives have been looking for new ways to subvert our elections. They have endless resources and a single focus." Since in neither tweet did he link sources to back up his claims, it is not clear on what he was basing these numbers.

The entire universe of 2020 election lawsuits is not the center of this book, but it is good to make a quick summary of those cases that were heard. Particularly, the GOP's strong record for prevailing in these lawsuits related to election integrity—when those cases were not thrown out on a technicality—should be understood.

The summaries below generally follow the helpful compilation of data by John Droz, Jr., which can be referenced at https://election-integrity.info/2020_Election_Cases.htm, and draw heavily from the Stanford-MIT Healthy Elections Project, many of whose case descriptions I closely paraphrase below.[12] Within each category, the suits are listed in chronological order of initial filing. Also, documentation was not easy to locate in every lawsuit.

Donald Trump / GOP Losses on the Merits

The following eight 2020 election cases were lost by Donald Trump or the GOP, or mostly lost, on the merits.

Pennsylvania Democratic Party v. Boockvar was filed on July 10, 2020. Neither Trump nor the GOP were a party. It was, rather, one of the 2020 "friendly lawsuits" that Pennsylvania Secretary of State, Democrat Kathy Boockvar, would have happily settled while the court would not necessarily have been aware of any collusion between the plaintiff and defendant. In the suit, the Pennsylvania Democratic Party used COVID-19 as an excuse to demand 1) that ballot drop boxes should be permitted (even though forbidden by law), 2) that mail-in and absentee ballots postmarked by 8:00 p.m. on Election Day and received by the Uniformed and Overseas Citizens Absentee Voting Act (UOCAVA) deadline must be counted, 3) that boards must contact voters whose mail-in or absentee ballots contain facial defects, and allow an opportunity to cure them by the UOCAVA deadline, 4) a declaration that "naked" ballots—that is, those lacking a secrecy envelope—must be "clothed" and not excluded from counting, and 5) a declaration that a residency requirement for poll watchers does not violate the law. On September 14, the Supreme Court of Pennsylvania 1) ruled that the law permits drop boxes, 2) purported to change the law by extending the absentee and mail-in ballot received-by deadline to 5:00 p.m. on November 6, 2020 if postmarked by 8:00 p.m. on November 3, 2020, 3) ruled that the poll watcher residency requirement is constitutional, 4) denied the request that the Board of Elections be required to contact individuals whose mail-in or absentee ballots contained a minor facial defect and provide an opportunity to cure the defects, and 5) denied the request to count ballots returned without the secrecy envelope instead of invalidating them. It was a mixed victory for the Democratic Party, but their main prize was counting of late ballots, despite such not being permitted by Pennsylvania law. On October 19, 2020, the Republican Party of Pennsylvania sued Kathy Boockvar concerning this prior lawsuit, seeking an emergency stay that would uphold Pennsylvania law and prohibit counting of ballots received late. In a 4-4 split on the very same day, the Court failed to grant the requested stay, allowing the earlier ruling to stand. On October 28, the United States Supreme Court, *relying upon a promise that Pennsylvania would keep the late-received ballots in question separate for further consideration,* decided in a 4-4 split (with Justice Barrett not participating) to narrowly deny expedited review of the Pennsylvania Supreme Court's decision. At the same time, Justices Alito, Thomas, and Gorsuch filed a statement that "there is a strong likelihood that the [PA] Supreme Court decision violates the Federal Constitution." On November 6, the Republican Party of Pennsylvania, pointing out that the election boards are not required to follow the Secretary of State's directions, that the Secretary of State may (as indeed occurred) change her mind, and that it is not clear that all sixty-seven county boards of elections in the state *are* following the directions, asked the Supreme Court to order the individual election boards to separate ballots received after the deadline and through November 6. On that same day, Justice Alito ordered all absentee ballots received after the 8:00 p.m. deadline on November 3 be kept separate, and that if they are counted, their tally be kept separate. On February 22, 2021, review of the lower court decision was denied. This was technically a partial victory for Donald Trump and the GOP, but the actual result was that the ballots were not kept segregated and therefore it became (as feared) impossible to tell whether Joe Biden actually won Pennsylvania with legally counted on-time ballots. This outcome appears to have been the objective of Boockvar and the Pennsylvania Democratic Party all along.

Donald J. Trump for President, Inc. v. Philadelphia County Board of Elections was filed on October 1, 2020. Election officials in Philadelphia had not been allowing campaign poll observers at on-site early voting polling locations, and the Trump campaign complained that such denial was a violation of Pennsylvania statute. The court found on October 9 that—*despite the fact that polling was happening there*—the Philadelphia Board of Election's satellite offices do not count as polling places under the Election

Code, and that therefore poll observers had no right to be present. On October 23, the ruling was upheld upon appeal to the Pennsylvania Commonwealth Court.

Kraus v. Cegavske was filed on October 23, 2020. The suit was brought by the Nevada Republican Party and Donald Trump's re-election campaign. Their complaint was that watchers were not being allowed meaningful observation of the verification of mail-in ballots, including the opportunity to observe all parts of the verification process and be close enough to verify data including seeing voter signatures. Absent such access, the work of watchers is pointless, because they do not have the necessary information to fulfill their role and challenge the counting of any suspect ballot. They asked the court to immediately stop the county's ballot processing and counting. On October 29, 2020, the court ruled that the plaintiffs lacked standing because they had not proven injury. However, the court continued to rule on the merits, and found that the plaintiffs had presented no proof of an equal protection violation and that the law did not require Clark County to provide the level of observation the plaintiffs sought. On November 3, 2020, Kraus, Donald J. Trump for President, and the Nevada Republican Party appealed, seeking a stay on the lower court's decision which allowed duplication of mail-in ballots without observation and the use of artificial intelligence to authenticate ballots. Later that same day, the Nevada Supreme Court granted the request to expedite the appeal and gave a deadline of 4:00 p.m. on November 5 for filing and serving an opening brief, but denied the request for an emergency stay to stop the county from processing the ballots in question. The decision also upheld the lower court's concern about lack of standing, and denied the request to immediately stop the county from counting. On November 5, the appellants filed an emergency motion for a seven-day extension. On November 10, the Nevada Supreme Court granted a motion to dismiss since the parties reached a settlement agreement to allow more poll observers. This was thus a symbolic victory for Trump and the GOP, but it absolutely failed to address the many ballots that were counted without proper observation during the week following the election and before the agreement was reached.

In re Enforcement of Election Laws and Securing Ballots Cast or Received After 7:00 p.m. on November 3, 2020 was filed on November 4, 2020 by the Georgia Republican Party and Donald J. Trump, who wanted Georgia law to be enforced in order to safely store absentee ballots received by the Chatham County Board of Elections after 7:00 p.m. on Election Day. Georgia law makes it illegal to count ballots received after 7:00 p.m. on Election Day, and the Trump team was concerned that the Democrats were going to count such ballots anyway. The Trump team was asking that all ballots received on time be secured and accounted for, so that they could be distinguished from late-arriving ballots pending further deliberation on the matter. The court ruled on November 5 that the suspect ballots were valid.

Donald J. Trump for President, Inc. v. Montgomery County Board of Elections was filed on November 5, 2020. In it, the Trump team objected to the counting of some 600 absentee ballots that failed to include all the required information (signature, address, and/or date) on the outer declaration envelope. The Trump Team said that counting such ballots violated two sections of Pennsylvania election law. The court agreed on November 13 with the Montgomery County Board of Election's interpretation of the law, that voters are not required to provide their addresses on the declaration envelope. The 592 ballots in question were to be counted.

Donald J. Trump for President, Inc. v. Bucks County Board of Elections was filed on November 9, 2020. In it, the Trump team complained that the Bucks County Board of Elections was accepting mail-in ballots with date or address defects, or with unsealed secrecy sleeves, as valid. On November 19, the court held that the Pennsylvania Supreme Court has spoken on the matter, and that address, date, or secrecy envelope are not mandated by the law. Upon appeal, the court agreed that going forward, ballots must be securely sealed, but held that (among other things) since it cannot be determined that the voters did *not* seal the envelopes, and that the instructions only told voters to place the ballots into the secrecy envelope and did not specify that it needed to be sealed, the 69 ballots under question would be counted.

Law v. Whitmer was filed in Nevada on November 17, 2020. It was brought by Nevada presidential electors (that is, voters) for Donald Trump. They brought several complaints, including 1) an allegation of widespread voting systems malfunctions specifically due to the Agilis machine and also more generally, 2) an allegation that voting drives in Nevada to encourage Native Americans to vote depicted Biden-Harris promotional material, and 3) that the Agilis machine being used to verify signatures only in Clark County but not in other Nevada counties led to a violation of the Constitution's guarantee of equal protection. They sought the invalidation of votes cast by those recruited by the tainted voting drive, and the certification of Donald Trump as the winner of Nevada. On December 4, 2020, the court pointed out that identical issues had been litigated before in Kraus *v.* Cegavske, but continued to rule on the merits, stating that there was no *proof* of machine malfunctions, improper votes, election board malfeasance, or vote manipulation, and dismissed the case with prejudice. On December 8, 2020, the Nevada Supreme Court upheld the lower court's decision.

Washington v. Trump was filed in Washington, D.C. on August 17, 2020, in the Ninth Circuit. The 120-page complaint was brought by the states of

Washington, Colorado, Connecticut, Illinios, Maryland, Michigan, Minnesota, Nevada, New Mexico, Oregon, Rhode Island, Vermont, Wisconsin, and Virginia, against Donald Trump, DeJoy, and the United States Postal Service (USPS). The states complained that the USPS had made the following changes to their mail service without seeking a required advisory opinion from the Postal Regulatory Commission (PRC) that harmed the interests of the states: 1) elimination of overtime, 2) instructing mail carriers to leave mail behind, 3) decommissioning sorting machines, 4) removing mailboxes, 5) reducing operating hours, and 6) changing how election mail is classified and charged. These states claimed a sovereign interest in conducting elections the way they wish (presumably including extensive mail-in voting), a proprietary interest in the mail system (since the states are extensive users of it), and an interest in protecting their citizens' fundamental right to vote (including, presumably, by mail if the state chooses to allow such an option). The states complained that the Trump administration had talked about the risk of fraud with mail-in voting. The states made eight requests: 1) that the defendants be compelled to seek the advisory opinion from the PRC, 2) that if they do not do so, the changes should be deemed unlawful and barred, 3) the actions of the USPS has violated the "time, place and manner" clause by interfering with the states' ability to determine the manner of their elections, 4) the actions of the defendants have violated Article II Section 1 of the Constitution by interfering with the method chosen by the states to appoint presidential electors, 5) that there has been violation of the states' retained powers under the 10th Amendment, 6) citizens' constitutional right to vote (sic) has been violated by creating an undue burden, 7) the actions violate the 5th Amendment's Equal Protection (sic—this is found in the 14th Amendment) and Due Process clauses, and finally 8) the actions violate the Rehabilitation Act by discriminating against voters with disabilities and making it more difficult to vote by mail. On September 17, the court granted the request for a preliminary injunction against the USPS policy changes. The court, among other things, expressed an opinion that the changes had been made without authority and for partisan purposes. On October 2, the court made a clarification concerning the delay of mail delivery trips. On October 30, the court ordered the USPS to take extraordinary measures when necessary to deliver ballots by Election Day, and to carry out certain daily reporting to the court from November 1-10.

Donald Trump / GOP Victories on the Merits

The following twenty-two cases were won by Donald Trump or the GOP on their merits.

Donald Trump or GOP Successfully Suing

Jefferson v. Dane County, No. 2020AP000557-OA, filed March 27, 2020, Wisconsin. Mark Jefferson and the Republican Party of Wisconsin sued Dane County and its Clerk, Democrat Scott McDonell, who on March 25 posted guidance on Facebook suggesting that all Dane County voters could declare themselves "indefinitely confined" due to illness, thereby avoiding the legal requirement to submit proof of identification when requesting an absentee ballot. The Wisconsin Supreme Court on March 31 ruled in favor of the GOP and granted a temporary restraining order requiring McDonell to remove misleading information concerning absentee ballots.[13]

Ritchie v. Polis, No. 2020CV31708, No. 20CA983, No. 20SC453, filed May 18, 2020, Colorado, Denver District Court. On May 15, 2020, Colorado's Democrat governor, Jared Schutz, issued an executive order to suspend the law requiring a petition circulator to be in the physical presence of an elector when signing. Those who sued asked the court to stop the governor from suspending these requirements. After the District Court denied the request on May 27, the Colorado Supreme Court on July 1, 2020 reversed that decision, agreeing with the GOP's assertion that the governor could not do away with the legal requirement that ballot initiatives must be signed in the presence of the petition circulator.

Republican National Committee v. Newsom, No. 2:20-cv-01055, 2020 WL 3430243 2020 WL 3074351, filed May 24, 2020, California, Ninth Circuit. California's Democrat governor, Gavin Newsom, issued an order to send mail-in ballots to all California voters for the November general election. Two suits—one by the RNC, the National Republican Congressional Committee (NRCC) and the California Republican Party, and the other by Judicial Watch on behalf of former Rep. Darrell Issa—said that Newsom's plan violates the Constitution because it usurps the legislature's powers (one of the same arguments made by the Texas Lawsuit as discussed in Chapter 3). They specifically alleged violations of the Electors Clause, the Elections Clause, the right to vote, and the Equal Protection Clause. The case was withdrawn by the RNC plaintiffs on July 9 because Newsom's order was superseded by legislative action (AB 860) on June 18, 2020.

Daunt v. Benson, No. 1:20-cv-522-RJJ-RSK, filed June 9, 2020, Michigan, Western District Court. The petitioners sued Democrat Secretary of State Jocelyn Benson for Michigan to clean up or purge their voter rolls. On January 28, 2021, the State agreed to do so, scheduling 177,000 voter registrations for cancellation "because the state has reason to believe the voter has moved away from the registration address," and the case was voluntarily dismissed on February 16, 2021.[14]

RNC v. Weipert, No. 06521CVCV081957, filed August 10, 2020, Iowa District Court, Johnson County. Democrat Travis Weipert, Johnson County

Auditor, sent voters absentee ballot applications prepopulated with some of the voter information. The RNC asked that he be stopped from using the prepopulated forms, many of which had already been sent, and to contact voters and inform them that the forms cannot be used. On September 12, 2020, the court held that Weipert did not have the authority to send prepopulated absentee ballot request forms, and that the RNC and Trump campaign would be irreparably harmed if those forms—many already sent, filled out, and returned—were counted. Weipert was required to contact each voter who submitted such a form and tell them that the form is null and void.

RNC/Trump v. Miller, No. 06571EQCV095986, was filed August 10, 2020, Iowa District Court. The auditor of Linn County had taken action to mail prepopulated ballots to every active registered voter. The plaintiffs argued that pre-populating ballots should not be allowed. The court on August 27 ruled in favor of Trump and the GOP, granted the requested injunction, and told Iowa counties to send blank ballots. The county auditors appealed to the Iowa Supreme Court on September 16, and on the same day that court deferred to the lower court.[15]

RNC v. Gill, No. 03971EQCV193154, No. 20-1169, filed on August 14, 2020, Iowa. The Woodbury County auditor sent voters absentee ballot applications prepopulated with some of their voter information. The RNC sued for a temporary injunction against the county, and the Iowa District Court of Woodbury County granted it, citing irreparable harm posed by inconsistent absentee voting procedures and the risk of fraud as a result of prepopulated ballot request forms. The court further found that "defendants knowingly violated Iowa Code Section 53.2(2)(a), pertaining to vote by mail distribution." The decision was affirmed by the Iowa Supreme Court, which upheld the trial court's injunction after Gill appealed.[16]

Texas v. Hollins, No. 2020-52383, No. 14-20-00627-CV, Nos. 20-0715 and 20-0729, filed August 31, 2020, Texas District Court, Harris County. The Harris County Clerk, Democrat Chris Hollins, wanted to mail applications for mail ballots to every registered voter in the county. Texas claimed that doing so would increase fraud and exceeds Hollins' statutory authority. On October 7, 2020, the Texas Supreme Court determined that the law does not authorize a county clerk to send mail-in ballots to voters who have not requested them, and that a clerk doing so anyway would result in an irreparable injury to the state. It ordered that the opinions of the trial and appellate courts denying the temporary injunction be reversed and sent the case back to the trial court for entry of a temporary injunction.

Carson et al. v. Simon, No. 0:20-cv-02030, No. 20-3139, filed September 22, 2020, Minnesota, Eighth Circuit. The Minnesota Secretary of State, Democrat Steve Simon, entered into a consent decree to not enforce Minnesota's Election Day deadline for receiving ballots. Those suing sought to stop this decree on grounds that it conflicts with state law, federal law, and the U.S. Constitution. On October 29, 2020, a three-judge panel of the Eighth Circuit reversed a lower court's order denying the request, and granted a preliminary injunction to stop Simon from extending the deadline for ballot receipt. The court further ruled that Simon's extension likely violated Article II of the U.S. Constitution since the action was taken without legislative authorization. The court further ruled that, even though this decision came only five days before the election, the Purcell principle (which prevents disturbing the status quo during an election) was not violated by the decision, stating, "the Minnesota Legislature set the status quo, the Secretary upset it, and it is [the court's] duty, consistent with Purcell, to at least preserve the possibility of restoring it." The court further directed the Secretary of State to "identify, segregate, and otherwise maintain and preserve all absentee ballots" arriving by mail after 8:00 p.m. on Election Day. Simon announced his disagreement with the court's decision, saying he would not seek a stay of the decision but that "[w]e absolutely reserve the right to make every argument after Election Day..."[17] On October 30, 2020, the District Court ordered Simon to identify, segregate, and otherwise maintain and preserve all absentee ballots received after the deadline for ballot receipt stipulated by Minnesota law.

Reed v. Virginia Department of Elections, No. CL20-622, filed October 9, 2020, Frederick Circuit Court. The Virginia State Board of Elections wanted to accept absentee ballots received up to three days after Election Day without a postmark, in violation of Virginia law. The Court issued a consent decree on January 13, 2021, permanently banning ballots without postmarks from being accepted after Election Day.

PILF v. Boockvar, No. 1:20-cv-01905, filed October 15, 2020, Middle District Court of Pennsylvania. A post-resolution statement from the Public Interest Legal Foundation said "Prior to the initiation of the lawsuit, the Foundation provided the Commonwealth with the names of **at least 21,000** deceased registrants who remained on the voter rolls less than a month before the pivotal 2020 election. PILF's data revealed that 9,212 of these deceased registrants had been dead for at least five years, 1,990 had been dead for at least ten years, and 197 had been dead for at least twenty years. In addition, hundreds of these registrants showed *post-death* voting credits for the 2016 and/or 2018 elections." In the voluntary settlement, Pennsylvania "agreed to compare its full voter registration database against the Cumulative Social Security Death Index in order to identify dead voters. Pennsylvania then agreed to direct all county election commissions to remove the names of dead voters."[18]

Nevada Republican Central Committee v. Clark County, No. A-20-823821OW, filed October 27, 2020, Nevada District Court, Clark County. The Nevada Republican Party and Donald Trump's re-election campaign asked the Court to compel Clark County, Nevada to grant immediate access to complete copies of extensive public records related to (among other things) images of voters' signature on ballots for the general election; their signatures on file; the names, party affiliation and shifts of members of the counting board; detailed policy documents, training materials, and the names of employees involved with every aspect of poll watching, ballot processing, and security. On November 2, 2020, the request was granted for the documents in existence at the time of the petitioner's request, but it denied it concerning the documents yet to be produced.

Donald Trump for President v. Simon, No. A20-1362, was filed October 28, 2020, Minnesota Supreme Court. Democrat Secretary of State Steve Simon, issued a rule pursuant to an agreement between himself and private parties that election officials will accept and count mail-in ballots cast and postmarked on or before Election Day but received by 8:00 p.m. within seven days of Election Day. The Trump campaign sought to stop Democrats' intended counting of late ballots, or late postmarked ballots, and so forth. The Supreme Court decided in favor of Trump and granted the injunction, ordering the sequestration of late ballots.

Donald J. Trump for President v. Gloria, No. A-20-824153-C, was filed on November 3, 2020, in Nevada district court. The President's team requested an extension of voting time, until 8:00 p.m., at polling locations that were affected by voting machine malfunctions. The Nevada District Court on the same day decided in favor of Trump and the GOP, ordering extended poll hours.

Donald J. Trump for President, Inc. v. Kathy Boockvar et al., No. 602 MD 2020, filed November 4, 2020, in Pennsylvania. Democrats had been pushing to allow proof of ID to be provided by mail-in voters until November 12, many days after the election. The Commonwealth Court of Pennsylvania on November 12 agreed with Trump and granted the injunction against counting ballots that were received without proof of ID.

Donald J. Trump for President, Inc. v. Benson, No. 1:20-cv-01083, filed November 11, 2020, Michigan, Sixth Circuit. The Trump campaign alleged that Wayne County and Democrat Secretary of State Jocelyn Benson violated Michigan election law by not permitting challengers to observe the conduct of the election and processing of ballots, and that they had pre-dated ballots not eligible to be counted. The Trump campaign sought for Wayne County not to certify their results. On November 19, the case was voluntarily dismissed, and the Wayne County results not certified.

Favorito v. Cooney, No. 2020CV343938, filed December 23, 2020, Georgia Superior Court, Fulton County. A Fulton County tabulation observer and several hand count operators sued, saying that they 1) detected a sudden unexplained 20,000 vote increase for Biden and filed a report that went unanswered; 2) observed boxes of ballots containing mostly Biden votes, and 3) that they believed cast ballots were fraudulent because they did not contain creases that would have been present if the ballots had been mailed. They also alleged that staff's retrieval and scanning of suitcases full of ballots following the departure of some staff and reporters when a water main in the State Farm Arena broke violated Georgia law. The petitioners alleged equal protection and due process violations against those voters who had their votes counted in the State Farm Arena on the night of November 3, 2020, and requested an order permitting them to inspect and scan all mail-in ballots for the general election. The request was granted on May 21, 2021.

VoterGA v. Gwinnett County Board of Registrations and Elections, No. 20-A-08626-2, filed December 30, 2020, Superior Court, Gwinnett. The election integrity group, VoterGA, alleged improper ballot counting and sued for opportunity to inspect about 100 ballot images, which were not under seal, did not disclose any personally identifying information about any elector nor link any specific elector to any specific vote, and did not require disclosing any passwords, encryption codes, or other security information, after the Gwinnett Board refused to make these records available. VoterGA sought a declaratory judgment in their favor, and an injunction instructing the Gwinnett Board to allow VoterGA to inspect the requested ballot images. On January 24, 2022, the court granted access to VoterGA.

Genetski & Michigan GOP v. Benson, No. 20-216-MM, filed January 20, 2021, Michigan Court of Claims. Michigan law requires voters to sign applications for absent voter ballots in order to receive a ballot, and to sign their absent voter ballot return envelopes in order for their ballot to be counted. Furthermore, Michigan law requires that signatures be checked against those contained in the qualified voter file (QVF) or those that appear on the "master registration card," and it requires that signatures on applications or ballots that do not "agree sufficiently" with those on file must be rejected. Democrat Secretary of State Jocelyn Benson, however, stated that signature review "begins with the presumption that" the signature is valid. Benson's guidance further instructed clerks to look for "redeeming qualities" and to treat the signature as valid if any can be found. Allegan County Clerk Robert Genetski sued Secretary Benson, alleging that her guidance will allow invalid votes to be counted. On March 9, 2021, the Court broadly agreed with the plaintiffs, and knocked down the defendants on point after point. Among many other things, the Court said,

> nowhere in this state's election law has the Legislature indicated that signatures are to be presumed valid, nor did the Legislature require that signatures are to be accepted so long as there are any redeeming qualities in the application or return envelope signature as compared with the signature on file. Policy determinations like the one at issue—which places a thumb on

the scale in favor of a signature's validity—should be made pursuant to properly promulgated rules under the APA or by the Legislature.[19]

The court, while denying Genetski's request for an additional audit, granted his request to strike down Benson's "rule," declaring that it was issued in violation of the Administrative Procedures Act and is therefore invalid.

Donald Trump or GOP Successfully Defending

Mi Familia Vota v. Hobbs, No. 2:20-cv-01903, No. 20-16932, was filed on September 30, 2020 in Arizona. Using the excuse of COVID-19, the pro-Democrat organization active in registering new voters seeking to circumvent the Arizona legislature, sued the Secretary of State to remove the existing legal deadline for registration of 29 days before the general election. The suit succeeded in Arizona District Court, but was struck down by the 9th Circuit Court of Appeals, a GOP and Trump win.

Pierson v. Stepien, No. 1:20-cv-09266, filed November 4, 2020, Southern District of New York. Elizabeth Pierson sued Matthew Morgan and Bill Stepien, both of the Trump campaign, claiming that Wisconsin's policy allowing wealthy parties to pay created an uneven playing field and gave rise to an Equal Protection violation. She alleged that ordering recounts was a "scorched earth tactic to sow discord and paranoia." She also alleged other things about the defendants' personal psychology, asserting (for example) that they knew that no amount of recount could overcome the margin of victory, and that their intent is to merely undermine the validity and legitimacy of the presidential election overall. On November 13, 2020, the claim filing having been found to have deficiencies that were not corrected after notification by the court, the case was closed without prejudice.

Maricopa v. Fann, No. CV2020-016840, filed December 29, 2020, Superior Court of Arizona, Maricopa County. The County sued Republican Karen Fann, president of the Arizona Senate, and Republican Eddie Farnsworth, Chairman of the Arizona Senate Judiciary Committee, to declare two legislative subpoenas issued to the Board related to the November 2020 election illegal and unenforceable. The case became very involved, with back-and-forth, but basically the County strongly resisted providing all the requested election materials and access to the election equipment, complaining that it was too much of a burden. A Senate vote to hold the County officials in contempt failed by one vote. The Court ruled in favor of the Senators, declaring that they have the right to issue subpoenas and to enforce those subpoenas, that they can find a person who does not comply guilty of a misdemeanor, hold them in contempt, and have them arrested by the sergeant-at-arms. It further found that the subpoenas were properly issued for a valid legislative purpose, since the legislature is vested by the Arizona Constitution with the power to enact "laws to secure the purity of elections and guard against abuses of the elective franchise."

Lawsuits Not Decided on the Merits

Thirty-nine cases were either dismissed on a technicality or withdrawn or consolidated. All these are listed below, some with discussion. Mention here does not imply that the dismissal was inappropriate in all or any of the cases; it merely emphasizes that the loss was based upon something other than a full consideration of the merits of the case. Some of the cases below may yet be appealed.

Curtin et al. v. Virginia State Board of Elections, No. 1:20-cv-00546 (E.D. Va.), 2020 WL 2817052, was filed on May 13, 2020 in Virginia, Fourth Circuit. The plaintiffs, several Virginia voters, claimed harm from allowing a person without disability or illness to vote absentee despite not actually being ill or disabled. The State Board of Elections had issued guidance that any "Voters may choose reason '2A My disability or illness' for absentee voting in the May and June 2020 elections due to COVID-19." In so doing, plaintiffs alleged, the board directed and encouraged voters to make a false statement, punishable as a Class 5 felony. The plaintiffs raised and listed many problems that arise with widespread absentee balloting, including vote buying, coercion, and fraud (including theft of ballots from mailboxes largely targeting impoverished minorities, the opportunity for undue influence upon voters, impersonation of voters, duplicate voting), and problems of inconsistent receipt of ballots by voters, among many other issues. The case was dismissed on May 29, 2020 under the laches (timeliness) technicality.

Davis v. Benson et al., No. 20-000099-MM (Mich. Ct. Claims), was filed on May 28, 2020 in Michigan. Robert Davis, a registered voter in Wayne County, Michigan, complained that Michigan Secretary of State Jocelyn Benson's action of mailing unsolicited absentee ballot applications to all registered voters in Michigan violates Michigan law and two clauses of the Michigan Constitution. This complaint was also made in the Texas lawsuit and is discussed in Chapter 3. On June 18, the court denied Davis' request for an injunction against Benson, claiming, among other things, that Mr. Davis did not show irreparable harm. The case went through appeals. It was ultimately dismissed on October 30, 2020 on both procedural grounds and failure to demonstrate a likelihood of success on the merits.

Donald J. Trump for President, Inc. v. Boockvar, No. 2:20-cv-00966, filed June 29, 2020, Pennsylvania, Third Circuit. Concerning the claims that using drop boxes is not permitted by the Pennsylvania constitution, that Secretary Boockvar's guidance to accept mail-in ballots where the signature does not match is unconstitutional, and that Pennsylvania's restriction that poll watchers must be resident in the county where they watch is unconstitutional. The court ruled lack of standing, and dismissed the case without prejudice on October 10.

Donald J. Trump for President v. Cegavske, No. 2:20-cv-01445, filed August 4, 2020, Nevada, Ninth Circuit. The plaintiffs complained that a recently-passed bill expanding the use of mail-in and absentee voting in elections impacted by a pandemic or other disaster would result in fraud and dilution of the votes of in-person voters. It was not heard on the merits, but was dismissed for lack of standing on September 9, 2020.[20]

Reed-Pratt v. Winfrey, No. 20-12129 (E.D. MI.), was filed August 8, 2020. Leigh Reed-Pratt sued over alleged violations of her procedural and substantive due process rights connected to Detroit City Clerk Janice Winfrey, the Detroit Election Commission and the Detroit Department of Elections mailing unsolicited absentee voter applications to voters in Detroit contrary to state law. The case was dismissed as moot on January 19, 2021.

Donald J. Trump for President v. Murphy, No. 3:20-cv-01753, filed August 18, 2020, New Jersey, Third Circuit. Phil Murphy, Democrat governor of the famously corrupt state of New Jersey, took it upon himself to change the state's election law by executive order, mandating that the November 3 elections will be all mail, that all active voters will automatically receive mail-in ballots, that ballots postmarked on or before Election Day will be counted even if they are received after Election Day, and that all in-person ballots will be cast as provisional ballots. The Trump campaign complained and asked for an injunction. The complaint was modified September 11 to add a request concerning establishment of drop boxes. On October 22, the court dismissed the case for lack of standing.

Election Integrity Project of Nevada v. Nevada, No. A-20-820510-C (Nev. Dist. Ct., Clark Cnty.), was filed by Election Integrity Project of Nevada and Nevadan Sharron Angle on September 1, 2020. The plaintiffs challenged AB4, a recently enacted piece of legislation, alleging that the law—which required mailing of absentee ballots to all registered voters; the acceptance of ballots lacking a postmark if received by 5 p.m. on the third day after Election Day; allowed counting of mailed ballots to begin fifteen days *before* Election Day, does not require signatures to match—violates both the Nevada and U.S. constitutions on equal protection and other grounds. It was not decided on the merits. Rather, the case was first dismissed in district court partly because the judge stated that, while there might have been serious problems with the election, calling for a new election instead of just certifying what they had already, no matter how flawed, would be a "shocking ask." An attorney representing the Nevada State Democratic Party and the Democratic National Committee in the case, arguing for certification of the results, said, "It is well-established that the simple act of one or two or even more acts of actual voter fraud, that's not a basis for overturning an election. That's not a basis for striking down a law."[21]

Martel v. Condos, No. 5:20-cv-00131 (D. Vt.), No. 5:20-cv-00131 (D. Vt. filed Sept. 4, 2020), was filed on September 4, 2020 in Vermont. It was brought against Vermont Secretary of State James Condos by five Vermont registered voters. Their complaint was that actions of the defendant were causing their votes to be diluted by illegal votes. The complaint quoted from *Reynolds v. Sims* (1964), that the right to vote "is more ... than the right to mark a piece of paper and drop it in a box or the right to pull a lever in a voting booth. ... It also includes the right to have the vote counted at full value without dilution or discount." It was dismissed on September 16, 2020 for lack of standing, stating that the plaintiffs did not demonstrate their specific harm as compared to other voters, stating, among other things, that "only those specifically disadvantaged by the unconstitutional scheme have standing. A vote cast by fraud or mailed in by the wrong person ... has a mathematical impact on the final tally and thus on the proportional effect of every vote, but no single voter is specifically disadvantaged."[22]

Lamm v. Bullock, No. 6:20-cv-00067 (D. Mont.), was filed in Montana on September 9, 2020. The plaintiffs complained that Montana Governor Stephen Bullock's expansion of mail-in voting without involvement from the state legislature, and Secretary of State Corey Stapleton's implementation of this rule change, were illegal under the First and Fourteenth Amendments and Article I, Section IV, clause 1 of the Constitution of the United States, as well as 42 U.S.C. § 1983. Although paying lip service to the merits, the court seemed to gloss over the constitutional issues by, among other things, defining a governor's veto (conferred upon him legislatively) as being included within what the Constitution means by the term "legislature"—notwithstanding Montana law's explicit prohibition of conducting a regularly scheduled federal, state, or county election by mail ballot. The decision further states that "the use of mail ballots present no significant risk of fraud."[23]

Monmouth County Republican Committee v. Way, No. MON-L-003019-20 (N.J. Super. Ct., Monmouth Cnty.), No. 3:20-cv-13914 (D.N.J.), was filed in New Jersey on September 24, 2020. It was consolidated with another case on October 5, 2020.

Moore v. Circosta, No. 4:20-cv-00182 (E.D.N.C.), was filed on September 26, 2020, in North Carolina, Fourth Circuit. Its complaint, like so many others, was that vote-by-mail leads to fraud and/or vote dilution and constitutional violations of the Equal Protection and Elections Clauses of the U.S.

Constitution. The District Court on October 14, 2020 found that the plaintiffs had established a likelihood of success on their Equal Protection challenges, stating that "This court believes the unequal treatment of voters and the resulting Equal Protection violations as found herein should be enjoined. Nevertheless, ... this court is of the opinion that it is required to find that injunctive relief should be denied at this late date, even in the face of what appear to be clear violations."

In re November 3, 2020 Gen. Election, No. 149 MM 2020, filed October 4, 2020, Pennsylvania state court. This case dealt with whether Pennsylvania law allows invalidation of mail-in ballots based upon signature comparisons. It was dismissed by the U.S. Supreme Court on February 22, 2021.

Hotze v. Hollins, No. 20-20574 (U.S. Court of Appeals, Fifth Circuit), was filed on November 2, 2020. Dismissed for lack of standing on the same day.

In re Canvassing Observation, No. 7003, filed November 3, 2020, Pennsylvania Court of Common Pleas, Philadelphia County. The Trump campaign complained that poll observers were not permitted to be sufficiently close to the vote counting. Court decisions went back and forth but settled in favor of the election administrators when it was dismissed on February 22, 2021.

Donald J. Trump for President, Inc. v. Benson, No. 1:20-cv-01083, filed November 4, 2020, Michigan, Sixth Circuit. The Trump campaign alleged that state law was violated by failure to allow observers access, and sought to stop counting. It was ruled moot since not filed until 4:00 p.m. on the day after the election, and after the votes had been counted. The problem of observers being denied access, then, was not addressed by the court. Writes Anderson, "So we are left with the memory of the videos of vote counters clapping as Republican observers were evicted and of covers being placed over windows. The judge on this case also said Michigan Secretary of State Jocelyn Benson bore no legal responsibility for video monitoring of drop boxes nor of [sic] making video from such surveillance available, despite a recently passed law requiring surveillance of all drop boxes installed after Oct. 1."[24]

Donald J. Trump for President, Inc. v. Philadelphia County Board of Elections, No. 2:20-cv-05533-PD, filed November 5, 2020 in Pennsylvania, Third Circuit. Donald Trump asked for an injunction to stop counting unless Republican observers were allowed to monitor it. The complaint claimed that the Board of Elections was ignoring an Order requiring Republican observers to be present.

Donald J. Trump for President Inc. v. Hobbs, No. CV2020-014248, filed on November 7, 2020 in Arizona. The suit against the Democrat Secretary of State Katie Hobbs and Maricopa County Recorder, Democrat Adrian Fontes, alleged that election day in-person voters were induced to override electronic tabulators' ballot rejection which classified their ballots as an "overvote," resulting in those ballots being disqualified and not counted, whereas early votes and some other election day votes were not treated the same way. It alleged that such tabulator overrides potentially caused thousands of voters across Maricopa County to be disenfranchised and were outcome determinative in the election for President of the United States in Arizona and/or other contested offices in Maricopa County. On November 16, 2020, it was dismissed as moot with the court claiming that the affected votes could not have influenced the outcome.

Donald J. Trump for President v. Boockvar, No. 4:20-cv-02078, filed November 9, 2020, Pennsylvania. Concerned poll watching related to absentee ballots. Dismissed for lack of standing, November 27, 2020.

Costantino v. Detroit, No. 20-014780-AW, was filed on November 9, 2020. The plaintiffs were Wayne County voters in Michigan who alleged election misconduct, including that workers for the City of Detroit processed and counted ballots from voters whose names were not in the Qualified Voter File; told election workers not to verify signatures on absentee ballots, to backdate them, and to process them regardless of their validity; and on a daily basis leading up to the election, coached voters to vote for Joe Biden and the Democrat party. The plaintiffs asked for an audit and an injunction against certification of the election results. The Court denied the injunction on November 13, 2020, believing that the allegations, among other things were speculative and overly general.

In re Canvass of Absentee and Mail-In Ballots of November 3 General Election, No. 20110894, filed November 10, 2020, Pennsylvania Court of Common Pleas, Philadelphia County. Concerned issues such as observer access, signature verification standards, and notice to cure defective ballots related to vote-by-mail. Dismissed as moot by the U.S. Supreme Court, February 22, 2021.

Lin Wood v. Raffensperger, No. 1:20-cv-04651-SDG (N.D. Ga.), was filed in Georgia on November 13, 2020. The plaintiff complained that Georgia's Secretary of State, Brad Raffensperger, illegally entered into a litigation settlement with the Georgia Democratic Party that resulted in disparate treatment of ballots that caused a constitutional violation of the Equal Protection Clause. It was dismissed for lack of standing and then dismissed on appeal to the U.S. Supreme Court as moot, since the election had passed.

Kelly v. Pennsylvania, No. 620 MD 2020, filed November 21, 2020, Pennsylvania Commonwealth Court. Claimed that the no-excuse absentee voting rule passed by the state legislature in 2019 violated Section 14 of the Pennsylvania Constitution. Dismissed for timeliness (*laches*) by Pennsylvania Supreme Court. Dismissed by U.S. Supreme Court without comment. Discussed further below.

Kistner v. Simon, No. A20-1486 (Minn. Sup. Ct.), was filed on November

24, 2020 in Minnesota. The plaintiffs complained that the Minnesota State Canvassing Board had, among other things, illegally removed scrutiny of absentee ballots by suspending the witness requirement stipulated by Minnesota law. It was dismissed by the Minnesota Supreme Court on December 4, 2020 for timeliness (*laches*).

Wood v. Raffensperger, No. 2020CV342959 (Ga. Super. Ct., Fulton Cnty.), was filed in Georgia on November 25, 2020. The plaintiff, the president of the Georgia Voters Alliance, alleged that Georgia officials violated the state constitution and state law by accepting money from the Center for Tech and Civic Life (i.e., the Zuckerberg-Chan money) to help run the election, and by (among other things) counting illegal votes. The court dismissed the case on December 8, 2020, saying that Georgia election law does not allow for either the governor or secretary of state to be named as defendants in an election contest. Thus, it did not consider the substantive complaint.

Pearson v. Kemp, No. 1:20-cv-04809-TCB (N.D. Ga.), was filed on November 25, 2020 in Georgia. The plaintiffs alleged that software and hardware from Dominion Voting Systems led to a fraudulent ballot-stuffing campaign in several Georgia counties. The case was dismissed for jurisdiction before being voluntarily withdrawn after appeal to the U.S. Supreme Court.

King v. Whitmer, No. 2:20-cv-13134-LVP-RSW (E.D. Mich.), was filed on November 25, 2020 in Michigan. Plaintiffs complained that poll observers were denied the opportunity to meaningfully observe, that election workers altered or forged ballots, and that unqualified ballots were counted. The case was dismissed for timeliness before being dismissed as moot by the U.S. Supreme Court on December 12, 2020.

Johnson v. Benson, No. 162286 (Mich. Sup. Ct.), was filed on November 26, 2020 in Michigan. The plaintiffs, Black Voices for Trump, complained that Michigan officials did not allow meaningful poll observation, told election workers to count unqualified ballots, and allowed grant funding for the election from Mark Zuckerberg. They also alleged that election workers duplicated and/or forged ballots. The case was dismissed on December 9, 2020 for jurisdiction and as moot.

Mueller v. Jacobs, No. 2020AP1958-OA (Wis. Sup. Ct.), was filed on November 27, 2020 in Wisconsin. The petitioner was a Wisconsin voter who complained that the use of ballot drop boxes by Wisconsin was illegal. The case was dismissed as moot on December 3, 2020.

Hahn v. Simon, No. A20-1654 (Clay County District Court), was filed in Minnesota on November 30, 2020. It was dismissed on January 13, 2021 for timeliness and jurisdiction.

Ward v. Jackson, No. CV2020-015285, was filed on November 30, 2020 in the Arizona Superior Court, Maricopa County. Dr. Kelli Ward, an Arizona voter, claimed that (among other things) observers were not present for the replication of damaged ballots, in violation of state law. She requested an audit and that the election results be annulled. Many parties intervened, including the Lincoln Project and the Democrat Secretary of State Katie Hobbs. The Arizona Supreme Court on December 8, 2020 upheld the Superior Court's ruling. The U.S. Supreme Court on February 22, 2021 denied Ward's petition for review. Dr. Ward has written a book on the topic of the Arizona audit that includes much first-hand account.[25]

Trump v. Evers, No. 2020AP1971-OA, filed December 1, 2020, Wisconsin Supreme Court. This suit alleged that municipal clerks in Milwaukee and Dane Counties had, in violation of state election law, issued absentee ballots without the required written application; illegally completed missing information on ballots; absentee ballots provided without voter identification; and ballots wrongly accepted from voters claiming "indefinite confinement" status. It furthermore claimed that Madison, Wisconsin's "Democracy in the Park" event violated state election laws.[26] The case was dismissed on December 3, 2020 on a jurisdiction technicality. Opines Anderson, "A divided Wisconsin Supreme Court refused to hear the lawsuit, sidestepping a decision on the merits of the claims and instead ruling the case must first wind its way through lower courts—an effective death sentence given the timing."[27]

Braun v. Simon, No. 62-CV-20-5602 (Ramsey Cty.), was filed on December 1, 2020 in Minnesota. The plaintiffs argued, among other things, that the Minnesota Secretary of State's decision to dispense with the witness requirement for absentee ballots violated the Equal Protection Clause and separation of powers. The case was dismissed with prejudice (meaning the plaintiffs are not allowed to re-file the case) on December 18, 2020. No explanation was given.

Feehan v. Wisconsin Elections Commission, No. 2:20-cv-1771 (E.D. Wis.), was filed on December 1, 2020 in Wisconsin. The plaintiff alleged various election violations that affected the integrity of the Wisconsin election. It was dismissed for standing and mootness on December 9, 2020, and for the same reasons by the U.S. Supreme Court on March 1, 2021.

Trump v. Wisconsin Elections Commissions, No. 2:20-cv-01785 (E.D. Wis.); No. 20-3414 (7th Cir.); No. 20-883 (Sup. Ct.), filed December 2, 2020 in Wisconsin. Donald Trump argues that the defendants, local Wisconsin election officials, undermined the election by (among other things) ignoring legal limits on mail-in balloting, creating ballot drop boxes, failing to provide enough access to poll observers, wrongly allowing election workers to alter ballots, and purporting to overturn state laws requiring voters to provide information on the mail-in ballot envelope. The 7th Circuit Court dismissed it on *laches* and failed to rule on the constitutional question. The Supreme Court on March 8, 2021 declined review of the lower court's decision.

Bowyer v. Ducey, No. 2:20-cv-02321-DJH (D. Ariz.), was filed on December 12, 2020 in Arizona. Plaintiffs were Arizona voters and one candidate for Arizona presidential elector, and they complained, among other things, of partisan interference in the election process by Maricopa County ballot dispute referees; absence of chain of custody for Dominion backups; and errors in the Dominion machines themselves. The court ruled lack of standing on December 9, 2020.

Trump v. Biden, No. 2020CV007092 (Wis. Super. Ct., Milwaukee Cnty.); No. 2020AP2038 (Wis. Sup. Ct.), filed December 3, 2020 in Wisconsin. In this case, Trump complained that the Wisconsin Elections Commission (WEC) "made choices explicitly contradicting what [the] statutes required and then, either on WEC's advice or on their own volition, municipal clerks chose not to follow the absentee voting statutes." It argued for over-turning the findings and conclusions of the Dane County and Milwaukee County Canvassing Boards based upon their failure to follow the law concerning the administration of absentee voting. The case was substantial, citing many specific violations of Wisconsin statutes that tainted the election by allowing ballots to be counted that were not legal to count. On December 14, 2020, the Wisconsin Supreme Court held that "the Campaign is not entitled to the relief that it seeks," and dismissed the claims concerning the several categories of ballots challenged as either meritless or failing due to timeliness of the claim (*laches*). Trump appealed to the U.S. Supreme Court on December 29, but the Court declined to hear it.

Trump v. Raffensperger, No. 2020CV343255 (Ga. Ct., Fulton Cnty.); No. S21M0561 (Ga. Sup. Ct.), was filed on December 4, 2020. In it, President Trump and a Georgia voter alleged violations of the Georgia Election Code and the state constitution, allowing unqualified people to vote, sending unsolicited absentee ballots to voters, and other actions. They requested a new presidential election. On December 12, 2020, it was dismissed by the Georgia Supreme Court for lack of jurisdiction.

Metcalfe v. Wolf, No. 636 MD 2020 (Penn. Commonw. Ct.), filed December 4, 2020. This suit claimed that "'approximately 144,000 to 288,000 completed mail-in and/or absentee ballots' in Pennsylvania may have been illegal based on testimony from a U.S. Postal Service contractor," who claimed to have been hired to drive a truck of what he believed to have been many completed mail-in ballots from New York to Pennsylvania. "The complaint also alleged there was 'evidence' of ballots that were backdated at a postal facility in Erie." The suit was dismissed on a technicality, as Pennsylvania state election code required filing "within 20 days of the alleged violation," which would have been November 23.[28]

Burk v. Ducey, No. CV202001869 (Ariz. Super. Ct., Pinal Cnty.), No. CV-20-0349-AP/EL (Ariz. Sup. Ct.), was filed December 7, 2020. Dismissed for lack of standing. The Arizona Supreme Court dismissed her appeal on standing and filing deadlines for election challenges.

Trump v. Toulouse Oliver, No. 1:20-cv-01289 (D.N.M.), was filed on December 14, 2020 in New Mexico, Tenth Circuit. President Trump sought to prevent New Mexico's electors from voting for president and vice president, alleging the state violated the Electors Clause by allowing voters to return ballots at ballot drop boxes. The case was not heard on the merits, but was voluntarily withdrawn by President Trump on January 11, 2021.

Trump v. Kemp, No. 1:20-cv-05310-MHC (N.D. Ga.), was filed on December 31, 2020 in Georgia, Eleventh Circuit. In it, President Trump requested an emergency injunction to decertify Georgia's election results, alleging that the way Georgia conducted the election violated the Electors Clause. The court dismissed the case for lack of standing.

Cases Not Yet Decided

Election Integrity Fund v. Benson, No. 20-000169-MM (Mich. Ct. Claims), was filed on August 24, 2020 in Michigan. It challenged Michigan Secretary of State Jocelyn Benson's action in allowing people to apply for absentee ballots online, a system that fails to comply with Michigan law and invites fraud.

Donald J. Trump for President et al. v. Bullock et al., filed September 2, 2020, Montana, Ninth Circuit. Democrat governor of Montana Steve Bullock, took it upon himself to override the Montana state legislature by issuing an executive order granting universal vote by mail balloting. The Trump campaign argued that the system is especially vulnerable to abuse and fraud and that only the state legislature has the authority to enact universal vote by mail. On September 30, 2020, the district court stated that the threat of mail-in voter fraud in Montana is "a fiction." The court invoked the Purcell principle, which states that courts should not change election rules immediately prior to an election, and denied the request. It was consolidated with the Lamm case.

Ziccarelli v. Allegheny County Board of Elections — This suit was filed on November 12, 2020. The Allegheny County Board of Elections had decided to accept 2,349 mail-in ballots containing an undated voter verification, despite the state legislature having set out a requirement that voters casting mail-in ballots "'shall fill out, date, and sign' the declaration." According to state law, the plaintiffs argued, these ballots did not meet the legal requirements to be counted. However, despite the court agreeing that the law required the voter to date their declaration, the court ruled that the ballots could be counted anyway, as the Allegheny County Board of Elections wished to do.[29]

Michigan Welfare Rights Organization v. Trump, filed on November 20,

2020 in Washington, D.C., federal court. The suit was brought by Detroit voters and a state chapter of a union. They allege that the Trump campaign's pressure on government officials to not certify election results amounts to an attempt to disenfranchise Black voters and thus constitutes a violation of the Voting Rights Act.

Other Election Lawsuits and Discussion

Boland v. Raffensperger, No. 2020CV343018 (Ga. Ct., Fulton Cty.). This lawsuit meant to address an alleged 90% drop in the mail-in ballot rejection rate from 1.53% in prior elections, to a mere 0.15% in the 2020 general election. This reduction in rejected ballots means that there were likely *thousands* of ballots (which in any other election would have been disqualified because the signatures did not match or due to other problematic factors) that were counted in 2020. The lawsuit also raised the question of whether some 20,000 people who did not live in the state cast votes in Georgia, where Biden's alleged margin of victory was only 12,000 votes.[30]

The lawsuit was filed November 30, 2020. It was dismissed on December 8, 2020, on grounds that the named defendants were "improper parties," that the suit was barred by laches (meaning that the suit was not filed in a timely manner), that the one bringing the suit—Georgia Secretary of State Brad Raffensperger—was not a candidate and therefore lacked standing, and for other reasons. The case was appealed on December 14, 2020, on grounds that the superior court judge lacked authority to rule in an election contest. The appeal was denied on the same day.[31]

The substance of the lawsuit—the enormously reduced ballot rejection rate and the matter of non-residents voting—was not considered by the court.

Kelly v. Pennsylvania, mentioned briefly above, was one of the most consequential cases, with one of the most egregious outcomes, of 2020. It deserves more extensive discussion here.

In 2019, the Pennsylvania General Assembly wanted to implement no-excuse absentee voting. In order to do so, two steps would be required. The first was an amendment to the Pennsylvania Constitution. Toward this end, the process of proposing such an amendment was initiated. Second, the General Assembly would need to pass a law actually instituting no-excuse absentee voting.

For the constitutional amendment to pass, it would need to be approved by a majority of the members of both the Pennsylvania Senate and House, *in two separate legislative sessions*. Then, the proposed amendment would need to be put forward as a ballot question for approval by Pennsylvania voters. Only then would the amendment take effect. However, the proposed amendment, in fact, has neither been approved by both House and Senate in two consecutive legislative sessions, nor has it been submitted to the voters for their approval.

Now we come to the problem that the Kelly lawsuit was seeking to correct. Passing an amendment is hard and takes time. The Pennsylvania General Assembly, deciding not to wait for it but to just do what they wanted, passed and implemented their desired no-excuse absentee voting through a law called Act 77. However, since step one—the constitutional amendment—has never occurred, Act 77 *is not legal*. The General Assembly knew this, but in 2020 Democrats in Pennsylvania used the COVID-19 pandemic as an excuse to take shortcuts, pretend the law was valid, and implement the policy anyway. Said the lawsuit:

> Rather than abide by the arduous, but mandated, process for amending the Pennsylvania Constitution to implement no-excuse absentee voting, the Pennsylvania General Assembly neglected this lawful mechanism entirely and instead attempted to bypass amending the Pennsylvania Constitution by fundamentally overhauling [the] Commonwealth's voting system through the enactment of a general law. In so passing Act 77, Respondents disenfranchised the entire Pennsylvania electorate, who were entitled to a constitutionally-mandated vote to approve this sweeping change to absentee voting before it was implemented.[32]

The Kelly lawsuit sought to declare Act 77 unconstitutional and to stop certification of the state's election results. On November 25, the Commonwealth Court agreed with Kelly and granted the request to stop the certification of any remaining election results.

The cheaters, however, were not going to give up so quickly. They appealed to the Pennsylvania Supreme Court. Kelly's argument for the Court to uphold the lower court's decision read, in part:

> Act 77 is the Commonwealth's latest attempt to override through legislation the protective limitations on absentee voting contained in the Pennsylvania Constitution, as interpreted by the Pennsylvania Supreme Court over the last 158 years. The Pennsylvania Supreme Court's holdings regarding Article VII of the Pennsylvania Constitution make clear that there are two, and only two, constitutionally-permissible methods of voting : 1) offering your ballot *in propria persona* at the polling place on Election Day; and 2) exceptions to the first method limited to those persons qualifying under the absentee voting provision, Article VII, § 14 of the Pennsylvania Constitution.
>
> Respondents have begun the steps necessary to certify the results of the Election, which was undertaken pursuant to an unconstitutional, no-excuse absentee voting scheme. Absent intervention by this Court, Respondents will complete the process of certifying the results of an election, and poten-

tially cast electoral college votes for president and vice president, conducted in a manner which the Pennsylvania Supreme Court has long rejected as unconstitutional.

The Pennsylvania Commonwealth Court, finding that Petitioners were likely to succeed on the merits of this case (App. p.26), issued emergency preliminary injunctive relief to prevent irreparable injury to the Petitioners and all Pennsylvania voters. [But, r]ather than provide clarity and address this vitally important, and valid constitutional question on the merits, the Pennsylvania Supreme Court exercised its extraordinary jurisdiction to take over the case and dismiss it on the basis of laches. In so doing, the Pennsylvania Supreme Court violated Petitioners' right to petition and right to due process, guaranteed by the First and Fourteenth Amendments of the U.S. Constitution, respectively, by closing all avenues of relief for past and future harms. Petitioners request this Court to extend the same preliminary injunctive relief initially granted by the Commonwealth Court of Pennsylvania and to further strike down Act 77 as an unconstitutional, *ultra vires* act of the Pennsylvania General Assembly pursuant to the Pennsylvania and U.S. Constitutions.[33]

On November 28, however, the left-leaning Pennsylvania Supreme Court vacated the injunction and dismissed the case with prejudice, citing timeliness (laches) owing to the fact that Act 77 had been passed more than a year prior to the filing of the suit and that millions of voters had already cast mail-in votes in the 2020 election.

In order to understand the problem with the timeliness technicality, called *laches*, which means the case was brought too late (i.e., the plaintiffs should have brought the case before the election), we need to consider what the left-leaning Pennsylvania Court would have ruled if Kelly had, in fact, done so. The answer is that they would have ruled "no standing," because there has been no harm done yet. In other words, this was a no-win situation ... there was no way to get justice in the face of the leftist Pennsylvania Supreme Court.[34]

Kelly then appealed to the U.S. Supreme Court, who would have been hard pressed to disagree with the plaintiff. The Court, however, shrunk from reviewing the case, curtly dismissing it on December 8 without any comment as to why:

Application (20A98) denied by the Court.[35]

As Mark Levin tweeted on December 9, 2020, concerning the U.S. Supreme Court's refusal to take the case on appeal, "The Court ducked. Has nothing to do with [laches]. Nothing to do with safe harbor. Nothing to do with ambiguity about the PA constitution. The Court issued a one sentence order without a word of explanation. Unless it takes up the case when the petitioners file as a writ on the merits, it'll be a disastrous precedent for decades to come. The Supreme Court acted with far less authority in Bush v. Gore in 2000. It's that simple."[36]

The legal provision for choosing presidential electors in absence of a lawfully conducted election (that is, when the will of the people of the state has not been lawfully discerned) is for the state legislature to assign electors. What ought to have happened in Pennsylvania, given the circumstances of an election conducted in grievous defiance of Pennsylvania's constitution, was for the U.S. Supreme Court to have upheld the injunction of further steps by Pennsylvania authorities to perfect the certification of the election, and return the decision to the state legislature, where authority to assign electors under such a circumstance resides.

> The partisan members of the Pennsylvania Supreme Court were never going to allow the Kelly complaint to be resolved on its merits. ... the Pennsylvania Supreme Court protected the partisan outcome of the electoral tally that it favors — nothing more.[37]

Swept Under The Rug

In the course of writing this chapter, I reviewed thousands of pages of material, including many of the legal filings and arguments. Most people will not do that, but you can if you wish. If you do, I believe you would, like myself, come away deeply frustrated by the many serious grievances left unanswered by the courts. Concerns related to officials playing fast and loose with election laws are not minor, nor were they in the balance self-serving sophistry on the part of Trump and his allies. In my observation, most were real, substantive, and extensive. In many cases they were obvious and blatant violations of completely unambiguous election statutes. Unjustified arbitrary changes to election rules and administration clearly had a serious impact upon the outcome of the 2020 election.

While the above-noted twenty-two vindications are obvious moral victories, as a practical matter they are for the moment consolation prizes for President Trump. The effect of the overall disposition of the 2020 election lawsuits was that acts of lawlessness, numerous and harmful, were merely swept out of view. Truth swept out of view, however, is still truth.

Vindication Begins

Several additional lawsuits were filed in 2021 and 2022 seeking to address the issues of 2020. Among them was a set of suits filed in May 2022 by the Thomas More Society on behalf of Wisconsin voters challenging the use of drop boxes in the cities of Milwaukee, Madison, Racine, Kenosha, and Green Bay, seeking a declaratory judgment ruling that the use of unmanned absentee drop boxes is illegal under Wisconsin law.[38] The suits were filed following the refusal of the Wisconsin Elections Commission to begin investigations into the defendant cities, even after Waukesha County Circuit Court Judge Michael Boren declared that "there is no statutory authority" in Wisconsin for drop boxes or ballot harvesting.[39]

Not long after the filing of that lawsuit, the Wisconsin Supreme Court on July 8, 2022 ruled on a 2021 lawsuit filed by the Wisconsin Institute for Law & Liberty addressing the same core issues, finding that unmanned drop boxes are illegal under Wisconsin law. Although not yet addressing the matter of ballot harvesting, the ruling was a major vindication and what appeared to be a scathing rebuke of the nonprofit organization Center for Tech and Civic Life (CTCL) funded by Meta CEO Mark Zuckerberg, which pressed for and achieved the implementation of drop boxes in Democrat areas of Wisconsin. Wisconsin received about $10.1 million in CTCL grants during the 2020 election, with nine of the ten "largest per capita grants" being received by cities that Joe Biden won.[40] In a statement, the Thomas More Society said that the Supreme Court Decision was the "tip of the iceberg," which involved coordination by the CTCL "with the blessing of the Wisconsin Elections Commission."[41]

QUESTIONS

1. What is the meaning of the word "stonewall"? What investigations into the conduct or outcomes of the 2020 election were stonewalled? Who stonewalled them? Why do you suppose they did so?

2. Would you be comfortable with ballots and other election records being destroyed in September-November 2022, before there has been a full forensic audit in many of the states that decided the 2020 election?

3. Do you believe that not wanting to undermine confidence in our election system is a valid reason for avoiding investigation of serious allegations of fraud or other misconduct?

---

1. Miller, Andrew Mark, "Mark Levin: Supreme Court 'ducked' on Pennsylvania election case and is 'hiding under the proverbial table,'" *Washington Examiner*, December 9, 2020.

2. Mulroy, Steven J., "Baby & Bathwater: Standing in Election Cases After 2020," Dick. L. Rev. 9. (2021).

3. Jeremy Herb, and Annie Grayer, "Liz Cheney strikes defiant tone in floor speech on eve of her expected ousting from House GOP leadership," *CNN*, May 12, 2021.

4. Bob Anderson, "Courts Repeatedly Refused To Consider Trump's Election Claims On The Merits," *Federalist,* March 11, 2021.

5. Ibid.

6. Zoe Tillman, "Trump And His Allies Have Lost Nearly 60 Election Fights In Court (And Counting)," *BuzzFeed News*, December 14, 2020; Louis Jacobson, and Amy Sherman, "Donald Trump has lost dozens of election lawsuits. Here's why," *Politifact*, December 10, 2020; Matthew S. Schwartz, "Trump's Legal Losses Come Fast and Furious," *NPR*, December 5, 2020.
7. John Droz, Jr., "2020 Presidential Election Lawsuits — the Facts," Election-Integrity.info.
8. https://twitter.com/marceelias/status/1336751110334377986
9. Alison Durkee, "Trump And The GOP Have Now Lost More Than 50 Post-Election Lawsuits," *Forbes*, December 8, 2020.
10. Isabel Vincent, "BLM hires Clinton aide who paid for Steele dossier to sort shady finances," *New York Post*, February 17, 2022.
11. Audrey Unverferth, "5th Circuit Keeps Sanctions On Democrat Russia Hoax Lawyer Marc Elias," *Federalist*, July 8, 2021.
12. "COVID-Related Election Litigation Tracker," Stanford-MIT Healthy Elections Project.
13. Droz, John Jr., "2020 US Presidential Election Related Lawsuits," https://election-integrity.info/2020_Election_Cases.htm.
14. "Secretary Benson continues to bolster election security," Michigan Secretary of State, January 28, 2021.
15. Republican National Committee v. Miller, No. 06571 EQCV095986 (Iowa Dist. Ct., Linn Cnty.), COVID-Related Election Litigation Tracker. https://healthyelections-case-tracker.stanford.edu/detail?id=189.
16. "Republican National Committee v. Gill, No. 03971 EQCV193154 (Iowa Dist. Ct., Woodbury Cnty.)," *Healthy Elections Case Tracker,* Stanford-MIT Healthy Elections Project; "2020 US Presidential Election Related Lawsuits," https://election-integrity.info/2020_Election_Cases.htm
17. https://healthyelections-case-tracker.stanford.edu/detail?id=264
18. "Lawsuit To Remove Dead Voters In Pennsylvania Ends With Win For Election Integrity," *Public Interest Legal Foundation*, April 7, 2021.
19. "Genetski v. Benson, No. 20-216-MM in The Court of Claims For The State of Michigan"
20. "2020 US Presidential Election Related Lawsuits," https://election-integrity.info/2020_Election_Cases.htm.
21. Riley Snyder, "Judge rejects 'shocking ask' of new election over voter fraud claims brought by Sharron Angle and affiliated group," *Nevada Independent*, November 20, 2020.
22. "Order on motion for preliminary injunction and on motion to dismiss," Martel v. Condos, September 16, 2020.
23. *Trump v. Bullock,* Order, September 30, 2020.
24. Anderson, "Courts Repeatedly Refused To Consider Trump's Election Claims On The Merits."
25. Ward, Kelli, *Justified: The Story of America's Audit.*
26. Anderson, "Courts Repeatedly Refused To Consider Trump's Election Claims On The Merits."
27. Ibid.
28. Ibid.
29. Ziccarelli v. Allegheny County Board of Elections, No. GD-20-11654 2020.
30. Anderson, "Courts Repeatedly Refused To Consider Trump's Election Claims On The Merits."
31. *COVID-Related Election Litigation Tracker,* Stanford-MIT Healthy Elections Project. https://healthyelections-case-tracker.stanford.edu/detail?id=403
32. Kelly v. Pennsylvania. 10-11.
33. Mike Kelly, et al., v. Commonwealth of Pennsylvania, et al., "Emergency Application for Writ of Injunction Pending the Filing and Disposition of a Petition for a Writ of Certiorari."
34. Tim Hains, "Levin: Why Pennsylvania Mail-in-Ballot Changes Are Unconstitutional," *RealClearPolitics*, December 7, 2020.
35. https://www.supremecourt.gov/search.aspx?filename=/docket/docketfiles/html/public/20a98.html
36. Mark R. Levin, Twitter post, December 9, 2020, https://twitter.com/marklevinshow/status/1336669753000292358.
37. Shipwreckedcrew, "Has the Penn Supreme Court Invited Scrutiny and Rebuke By Relying on 'Laches' to Dismiss an Inconvenient Complaint?" *RedState*, December 1, 2020.

38. Shawn Fleetwood, "Wisconsin Voters Sue Democrat Cities Over Illegal Drop Boxes In 2020 Election," *Federalist*, May 27, 2022; "Voter Lawsuits Filed Against Election Officials in Wisconsin's Five Largest Cities," Thomas More Society (Press Release), May 25, 2022.
39. Dan O'Donnell, "Wisconsin Judge Bans Ballot Drop Boxes, Says Election Officials Broke The Law," *Federalist*, January 17, 2022.
40. Shawn Fleetwood, "Wisconsin Supreme Court Drops Hammer On 2020 Election Shenanigans: 'Ballot Drop Boxes Are Illegal' Under Wisconsin Law," *Federalist*, July 8, 2022.
41. "Wisconsin Supreme Court Decision Banning Absentee Ballot Drop Boxes is 'Tip of the Iceberg,'" Thomas More Society (Press Release), July 8, 2022.

10

A FALSE RESULT

I n the United States, the will of the people in a presidential election is expressed *via* two essential components. If you take away either one, then the result is not the will of the people. The components are:

   1. A lawful process
   2. An honest vote count

It is not enough just to get the necessary number of votes if those votes were not received according to the law.

In the 2020 election, there is cause to believe that the American people did not have the second, but we *know* that the American people did not have the first.

Millions of illegal mail-in ballots were received and counted.

Millions of ballots received outside the election dates and times set by state legislatures—also illegal—were counted

Millions of ballots received in illegally placed drop boxes were counted

In addition to the above ballots, all ballots in any of the fifty states that were carried at any time by a private person who received money for doing so (for example, a "mule," as cataloged in the D'Souza film *2000 Mules*) were also categorically illegal. Based upon geotracking, official surveillance video, and other evidence, D'Souza—in partnership with Katherine Englebrecht and Gregg Phillips—conservatively estimate that hundreds of thousands of illegal trafficked ballots were counted. These ballots had the involvement of multiple identified Democrat activist 501(c)3 nonprofit organizations. These ballots alone are many times the margin of Biden's alleged victory.

While we cannot now identify which ballots were counted illegally since ballots have no unique marks connecting them to the voter, nor a time stamp telling when they were received or counted, we have the use of our reason. It is my feeling that the only way that the 2020 election could represent an actual victory for Joe Biden in those states—in the midst of such heavy, coordinated, widespread, and extensive interference with the election on the part of Democrats and their allies—would be if team Trump had also been interfering, and with similar effectiveness. Yet, I am unaware of any serious accusation of coordinated voter fraud or election fraud on the part of Trump or his partisans in the 2020 election. Furthermore, if there had been any such activity, I suspect that it would have been exposed and displayed on endless repeat by media eager to paint him as a cheater. It would also have been investigated by the Biden Justice Department eager to further harm a political opponent. Neither of these happened.

So no, there was likely no significant voter fraud or election fraud favoring Trump in 2020, but reason and data both suggest a significant amount of voter fraud and election fraud favoring Joe Biden, with suspect vote tallies in heavily Democratic areas and populations far exceeding the margin of alleged Biden victory in every single swing state.

Following are summaries of the situation in each of the six contested states at the time of this writing:[1]

Arizona

Approximately 300,000 votes are disputed in Arizona. Reported issues include ballot trafficking (exposed by True The Vote's investigation of cellphone data as presented in *2000 Mules*), noncitizen voting, and other problems. Biden's official margin of victory in Arizona was 10,457 (0.3%). Arizona has eleven electoral votes.

Georgia

Up to 300,000 votes are disputed in Georgia. Reported issues include ballot trafficking (also documented by True The Vote and presented in *2000 Mules*), significant numbers of apparently ineligible voters (including some deceased voters), ballots counted without observation, and lack of verification of absentee ballots. Biden's official margin of victory in Georgia was 11,779 (0.25%). Georgia has sixteen electoral votes.

Michigan

About 270,000 votes are disputed in Michigan. Reported issues include eyewitness reports of illegal ballot handling, audits performed by the same county staff who performed the elections, obstruction of further audits, and others. Biden's official margin of victory in Michigan was 154,188 (2.8%). Michigan has sixteen electoral votes.

Nevada

At least 130,000 votes are disputed in Nevada. Reported issues include more than 42,000 people voting more than once, 1,500 deceased persons voting, 8,952 more votes than records show as the number of people having voted, obstruction of audits, and voter address irregularities. Biden's official margin of victory in Nevada is 33,596. Nevada has six electoral votes.

Pennsylvania

Approximately 500,000 votes are disputed in Pennsylvania. Reported issues include poor and illegal security procedures for mail-in ballots, 170,830 more votes than people recorded as having voted, a single large and question-able batch of 580,000 ballots that went 99.5% to Biden, missing chain of custody documentation, and other issues. The forensic audit process was begun, but was subsequently stonewalled by Senate President Jake Corman, who replaced Doug Mastriano with Chris Dush after Mastriano insisted that he didn't want a "glorified recount" but an actual forensic audit.[2] In December of 2021 came evidence in the form of whistleblower videos capturing Delaware County officials plotting to fabricate missing election data from the prior year (one bragging to the other that the local Democrat district attorney "owes him"). Earlier videos from the same county captured officials "destroying elec-tion materials or blocking out 'derogatory' information in the copies made in response to the Right to Know Request."[3] Biden's official margin of victory in Pennsylvania was 81,660 votes (1.2%). Pennsylvania has twenty electoral votes.

Wisconsin

Approximately 221,323 votes are disputed in Wisconsin. Reported issues include illegal use of absentee ballot drop boxes, election bribery in the amount of $8.8 million by the Center for Tech and Civic Life in the cities of

Milwaukee, Madison, Racine, Kenosha and Green Bay, up to 200,000 ballots counted without independent observation, approximately 226,000 absentee ballots tainted by illegal solicitation and invalid applications, incomplete or altered ballot certificates, and 205,000 voters removed from the rolls in the months following the election (i.e., were these ineligible on Election Day, and if so, how many voted?), failure to send required special voting deputies to nursing homes and a resultant 100% voting rate in many including ineligible or incapacitated residents voting, failure by the WEC to record noncitizens in the WisVote voter database which allowed noncitizens to vote.[4] Biden's official margin of victory in Wisconsin was 20,682 (0.6%). Wisconsin has ten electoral votes.

Wake up and smell the Autocrats

Unless the American people understand that not everyone in their country *believes* in free and fair elections, we will never have an actual free and fair election again. Anyone can claim victory if they have personal power to rewrite the rules in the middle of the contest. But we have a rule book in the United States and it cannot be arbitrarily changed by political partisans who don't happen to be elected representatives operating through the legislative process. Our rule book is a Constitution and the body of laws that were certified by the people through their elected representatives.

The 2020 election was not run by the book. Our Constitution is not a secret. It has been around a long time and is publicly available for anyone who wants to read it. As Americans, we need to link arms to address these structural problems. Furthermore, those who illegally conspired to compromise the 2020 election should be dealt with, prosecuted to the fullest extent of the law.

---

1. The summaries in this section are based partly upon information contained at electionfraud20.org.
2. Monroe, Nick. "Pennsylvania 2020 election audit slated to go ahead amidst management shift." *The Post Millennial*, August 25, 2021; Murphy, Jan. "Pa. senator blasts GOP leadership for 'stonewalling' his pursuit of an election audit." *PennLive*, August 20, 2021.
3. Cleveland, Margot. "New Videos Capture Pennsylvania Officials Hiding Evidence Of Alleged Election Fraud." *The Federalist*, December 21, 2021.
4. "Second Interim Investigative Report On the Apparatus & Procedures of the Wisconsin Elections System," Wisconsin Office of the Special Counsel, March 1, 2022.

11

THE SECOND IMPEACHMENT OF PRESIDENT TRUMP

President Trump Refuses to Accept the Results of the 2020 Election

— HOUSE IMPEACHMENT TRIAL MEMORANDUM,
JANUARY 2021

Thus reads the heading of the first section of the "Statement of Facts" in the Memorandum that accompanied the second impeachment of President Trump. The President's opponents were angered most by his simple failure to agree with their assertions that Biden had won the 2020 election.

An *obviously* false claim—one that everyone knows to be false—does not typically lead to deep rage. There is often no need to even waste one's breath on a reply. A ridiculous accusation can sometimes be ignored; not so with a credible allegation.

Trump's was, arguably, a credible allegation. Had a Biden victory been clear and transparent in 2020, Democrats would not have been so infuriated by Trump's refusal to agree that Biden had won. They could have calmly dismissed President Trump as a sore loser, and Americans—seeing that all the legal safeguards against fraud had remained in place during the election, that vote-by-mail so liable to fraud had not occurred widely, that poll watchers had not been ejected from polling places, that signature verification of absentee ballots had been properly carried out, that unattended drop boxes had not been selectively placed in Democrat-dominated parts of swing states that then went for Biden, that chain-of-custody was attested in all cases, and so forth—would have acknowledged a generally uncontroversial Biden victory.

This is not what happened, and Democrats had no one to blame but themselves. Stuck without a real answer, and frustrated at being made to lie in the bed they had made, Democrats were left to lash out at the boy who dared to say out loud that the emperor had no clothes.

Put somewhat more graphically, Trump's cardinal sin in 2020 seems to have been his refusal to stop blowing the rape whistle as America was being violated. Meanwhile, Democrats were caught in the act, frantically telling Trump to just shut up about it. As is so often the case, when Trump was not intimidated by the attacker's repeated threats that "nobody's going to believe you," Democrats blamed the victim.

A Breathless Narrative of "Insurrection"

Declining to affirm as "true" a statement that one knows or has reason to believe false is not a federal crime in the United States—at least not yet.[1] So, President Trump's political enemies were going to need another excuse if they wished to impeach him again. They found it in the events of January 6, responsibility for which they sought to lay at the President's feet rather than at their own.

The events of January 6, including their misrepresentation in hyperbolic reporting by national media and partisan Democrats was soberly presented earlier in this book. However, the information and perspective available to reasonable observers even one month later was not plainly evident in the days immediately following the events. Democrats acted with great speed, and their two-step strategy involved:

1. Painting January 6 as an "insurrection," and greatly magnifying and spinning the damage, injury, and loss of life that occurred
2. Portraying Trump as having intentionally caused the events

The Memorandum accordingly went on to claim "Donald J. Trump's incitement of insurrection against the Republic he swore to protect"[2] stating:

> The House of Representatives has impeached him for that constitutional offense. To protect our democracy and national security—and to deter any future President who would consider provoking violence in pursuit of power —the Senate should convict President Trump and disqualify him from future federal officeholding.[3]

The House Memorandum is characterized by haste and woeful lack of precision. I have delayed discussion of the second impeachment until the end of this book because knowledge of what happened during the election is required if one wishes to understand why President Trump refused to concede in the first place, and why he kept talking about these matters publicly.

Some of Trump's critics have condescendingly declared him a narcissist. Since 100% of humans have narcissistic traits, presumably those critics mean that they specifically believe him to have Narcissistic Personality Disorder (NPD), which affects between 0.5 and 2% of people. Narcissism is a clinical term, and I doubt that most who have labeled Trump with it are licensed in psychology or have a doctor-patient relationship with him in order to properly render such a diagnosis. If any of them do have such credentials and have diagnosed Trump clinically in the context of such a relationship, that information would be protected by patient privacy laws. So, while it is not impossible that they are right, in my observation the word is often wielded merely as a convenient term of derision against a strong-willed and self-assured person—usually a man—with whom the one applying the label happens to disagree or whom such a person finds personally annoying. In other words, the common use of the term "narcissist" as an epithet is facile.

However, speculations of narcissism might be a distraction. Those who concluded that Trump's refusal to concede the election was about him and his ego might have forgotten that the most important people in any election are the citizens who voted and who deserve to have their voice heard and reflected in government. Trump often reminded his supporters, "They are not after me; they are after you. I'm just standing in the way." In not accepting the official results that he knew or had reason to believe were false, and demanding an honest election, Trump was insisting upon justice not for himself, but for the American people.

I also delayed discussion of the second impeachment in order to bring the poor character and judgment of every member of the House who on January 13, 2021 voted to impeach and every member of the Senate who on February 13 voted (albeit unsuccessfully) to convict into proper focus. Republicans and independents who joined Democrats in voting to impeach Trump this second time were:

House (Voted to Impeach)
Liz Cheney, Anthony Gonzalez, Jaime Herrera Beutler, John Katko, Adam Kinzinger, Peter Meijer, Dan Newhouse, Tom Rice, Fred Upton, David Valadao

Senate (Voted to Convict)
Richard Burr, Bill Cassidy, Susan Collins, Angus King, Lisa Murkowski, Mitt Romney, Bernie Sanders, Ben Sasse, Pat Toomey

The Accusation

Readers may be excused for finding the Memorandum, as the congressional proceeding that it summarized, to be thoroughly vapid and partisan, and it is hardly worth quoting at length here except for the purpose of showing this vapidity. In that spirit, let's look at a few excerpts and then conclude. The Memorandum dramatically states,

> Since the dawn of the Republic, no enemy—foreign or domestic—had ever obstructed Congress's counting of the votes. No President had ever refused to accept an election result or defied the lawful processes for resolving electoral disputes. Until President Trump.

While it may be true that no enemy had obstructed Congress' counting of the votes, and that no president had ever refused to accept an election result, it is not evident that Trump is an enemy, nor that his refusal to accept the election result is unjust. It is also not evident that Trump obstructed Congress.

Glaringly, the Memorandum failed to state that most U.S. elections have been conducted lawfully, that in most U.S. elections the actual winner was certified in the end, or that the 1960 and 2020 elections were exceptions in which the losing candidate (in both cases the Democrat) appears to have been installed. It is true that President Trump is the first to not accept an election result. However, absent acknowledgement that his refusal came on the heels of an election, the execution of which was intentionally compromised on a large scale by his political opponents, the moral import of that fact cannot be properly understood.

Further Observations

The Memorandum states, "As it stormed the Capitol, the mob yelled out 'President Trump Sent Us,' 'Hang Mike Pence,' and 'Traitor Traitor Traitor.'"[4] A mob, however, does not yell out. Individual people yell.

With evident intent to embellish the facts in order to strengthen their case for impeachment, the Memorandum states, "Five people—including a Capitol Police officer—died."[5] The memorandum thus implies, falsely, that five people died as a result of the events on January 6. The matter has been discussed earlier in this book.

Begging the question, the authors of the Memorandum repeatedly refer to the January 6 events as an "insurrection" and refer to those involved as "insurrectionists." Insurrection has a legal meaning that includes coordinated planning and intent to overthrow a government. However, neither has been demonstrated concerning Trump or his supporters.

Begging the question, the authors of the Memorandum state that, "After losing the 2020 election, President Trump refused to accept the will of the American people. He spent months asserting, without evidence, that he won in a 'landslide' and that the election was 'stolen.'"[6] The authors of the Memorandum, however, assume that Trump actually lost the 2020 election, that his resistance was a refusal to accept—rather than an affirmation of—the will of the American people, and that he had no evidence that he had won in a landslide. If their idea of what constituted evidence differed from that of Trump and his supporters, that would be one thing. As it is, the Memorandum's inclusion of specimen after specimen of desperate hyperbole fatally detracts from any moral weight that it might otherwise have carried.

Of course, the Senate acquitted President Trump. He is not disqualified from future officeholding, nor is he convicted of that of which he was accused.

---

1. Canada, the UK, and other countries have in recent years criminalized the speaking of some statements of truth. The First Amendment of the United States' Constitution prohibits any such limitation of speech. https://judiciary.house.gov/uploadedfiles/house_trial_brief_fi nal.pdf (3/1/22).

2. United States House of Representatives, *TRIAL MEMORANDUM OF THE UNITED STATES HOUSE OF REPRESENTATIVES IN THE IMPEACHMENT TRIAL OF PRESIDENT DONALD J. TRUMP*, by Jamie Raskin et al.

3. Ibid.

4. Ibid. 1.

5. Ibid.

6. Ibid. 2.

12

WHY 2020?

M otive, means, and opportunity on their own are not evidence of criminal activity. However, when we see an entire category of people who share a motive suddenly singing in perfect unison (extended voting hours, vote by mail, etc.) and working overtime to advocate for the creation and expansion of means and opportunity, we should take note.

In 2020, Democratic operatives in government bureaucracies, on election boards, in media, and in academia coordinated to remove obstacles to voter fraud and election fraud, hinder transparency, and enlist the participation—financial and otherwise—of powerful industry and technological gatekeepers who would have the ability to help. In 2020, billionaire George Soros broke his own record, channeling more than $50 million into Democratic campaigns and causes in the months prior to the election.[1] Likewise, in 2020 Mark Zuckerberg and Priscilla Chan—under the pretext of "safety" —dedicated more than one-third of a billion dollars into helping Biden and the Democrats win the 2020 election, while Facebook's one-sided "fact checking" and other algorithmic manipulations doubtless accounted for an untold fortune of in-kind additional donations. Why?

Of course, the biggest difference between 2016 and 2020 was the incumbency of Donald Trump. What was so fundamentally different about Donald Trump that caused such panic among the elites? In the words of Roger Kimball,

> The central fact to appreciate about Donald Trump is that he was elected president without the permission, and over the incredulous objections, of the bipartisan oligarchy that governs us. That was his unforgivable offense.

Trump was the greatest threat in history to the credentialed class and the globalist administrative state upon which they feed. Representatives of that oligarchy tried for four years to destroy Trump. Remember that the first mention of impeachment came 19 *minutes* after his inauguration, an event that was met not only by a widespread Democratic boycott and hysterical claims by Nancy Pelosi and others that the election had been hijacked, but also by riots in Washington, D.C. that saw at least six policemen injured, numerous cars torched, and other property destroyed.[2]

The bottom line was that Trump was disrupting the apple cart. No president of any party was supposed to *actually* move the U.S. embassy to Jerusalem. No president was supposed to unabashedly support and increase U.S. oil production, while also actually reducing all kinds of government regulations on American people and American businesses. No president was supposed to throw a wrench into the left's "progress" toward global socialism by withdrawing from the Paris Climate Accord or by taking a meaningful stand against placing Iran on the path to nuclear weapons. Perhaps most significantly, no president was supposed to actually buck the steady inch-by-inch concession of American sovereignty within her own borders. That is the sort of thing that Republican presidents are supposed to grandstand about, but they are not really supposed to stop it.

Rogue Government

Democrats really, really, wanted to win in 2020. They really, really thought they *should* win in 2020. They evidently thought that the need to win was of greater importance than the need to play by the rules. So, they bent the rules and claimed victory.

But that is not how democracy works. In fact, it is how democracy dies. Americans are today faced with an existential crisis. Pirates have seized control of the United States Government. The institutions designed for checks and balances have been either weakened and torn down, or commandeered by a carefully-placed minority ready to uphold such subversion. And the pirates have raised the sails to gather speed, while steering us into the reefs. That the American people rightfully own this vessel is small consolation when they no longer control it. Meanwhile, the people's personal property is daily plundered by these brigands through unchecked waste, unfair and exorbitant taxation, costly and overbearing regulations, unjust entitlement programs, and thieving property redistribution schemes. What's left is being devoured by inflation or burnt up in the gas tank just to drive to work and pick up the kids from school. Furthermore, some of the marauders are actually voicing an intention to confiscate the people's means of personal defense and protection.

What avenues remain for reassertion of citizens' rightful control? Must Americans henceforward resign themselves to the whims and preferences, so-called "election" after so-called "election," of these marauders who mean now to rule them with an iron fist? Or, will they choose a different direction?

---

1. Soellner, Mica. "George Soros contributes record $50M to back 2020 Democratic efforts." *Washington Examiner*, July 27, 2020.
2. Kimball, Roger, "The January 6 Insurrection Hoax," *Imprimis*, Volume 50, Number 9 (September 2021).

13

CONCLUSION

On July 8, 2022, the Wisconsin Supreme Court ruled that the 2020 election in Wisconsin was unlawful, and its results illegitimate. Although the opinion applied more broadly than presidential elections, stating categorically that drop boxes are illegal in the state, the majority opinion affirmed the assertion that has been the focal point of this book: Only state legislatures have the power to set rules in a presidential election, and a presidential election conducted under rules set by other people or bodies is not legitimate.[1]

In 2020, multiple U.S. states disenfranchised their own citizens by allowing laws passed by those citizens through their state legislatures to be overridden by petty partisans of candidate Joe Biden. In the ensuing election, these activities caused legal votes to become diluted by those cast in manners not allowed by law. All these changes were pushed by partisans of Joe Biden, and all of them favored Joe Biden. The actions of these states did not end with the disenfranchisement of their own citizens, but caused electors for U.S. president and vice president to be chosen that influenced the outcome of the national election. These electors, the fruit of those states' unconstitutional infringement of the Electors Clause, the Elections Clause, and the 14th Amendment's guarantee of equal protection, disenfranchised *every* U.S. citizen by devaluing their votes for president and tipping the election in favor Joe Biden.

If a college student shows up an hour after the final exam has ended, he has missed the exam and must accept the result, unless the only person with authority to show him grace (the professor) decides to extend it. The student, being enrolled in the class, had the *right* to take the exam and to receive a grade for it. But the student had *no right* to expect that he could take the exam outside the parameters set by the professor.

State legislatures, elected by the residents of their states, have sole ("plenary") power to set the rules for conduct of elections. State legislatures can, and often do, change the rules through the legislative process. But nobody else (e.g. the governor, the secretary of state, etc.) has the right or power to do so. Changes to election laws that are made by parties other than the state legislature are not legal changes, and when the election comes around, it is still the case that only the rules set by the state legislatures are valid, no matter what anyone else says.

In 2020, millions of people in key states cast ballots that were not legally countable. Yet, these ballots *were* counted, and we know based upon the vote breakdowns for different methods of ballot return that they strongly favored Joe Biden. The number of illegally counted ballots exceeded the margin of Biden's victory over Trump many times over.

But if changes are made to state election laws against the explicit provisions of existing law, isn't it the job of the state legislatures to step in and reassert that the law they passed is the law of the state? The answer to this question is, I sense, no. If the law was clear and unambiguous to begin with, then there is no need for the state legislature to come back in and say, essentially, "Hey guys, we really mean it." Of course they really mean it! That is why they went to the trouble of proposing, debating, amending, and passing the laws in the first place! Laws do not need to be passed through the legislature a second time in order to be valid. Furthermore, it is not the job of the legislatures to see that the laws are followed. That is the job of the executive and the judiciary. The executive and judiciary, however, do not get discretion to create new laws or to change existing ones.

What We Know For Certain

One fact that is now beyond doubt is that *it cannot be confirmed that Joe Biden won the 2020 election*. And, while it may or may not be now possible to state with scientific certainty that Donald Trump won, all the available evidence strongly recommends that conclusion. Indeed, the likelihood that Biden was chosen by the people—that is, without resort to ballots that were illegally counted—approaches zero.

Consider the following scenario: A child is caught with his hand in the cookie jar. Crumbs surround his mouth, lay on his shirt, and are on the floor in front of where he is standing. But, can it be *proven* scientifically that he took a cookie? Perhaps, since there is still a cookie inside his mouth. Looking up at mom, the boy chews ... and swallows. The evidence is now gone! But, would it really be so unreasonable to reach a conclusion about what happened?

Democrats around the country chewed and swallowed the cookie in 2020 by way of evasive maneuvers, insistence upon "counting every vote" while knowing that mail-in ballots, after separated from the ballot envelope, would be impossible to tie to a fraudulent voter, failure to keep late-received ballots separate for later consideration, and so forth. The high bar for scientific certainty is very important in a laboratory, and it is possible to expect in the hard sciences—even if it is today widely neglected by many people who claim to "follow the science." However, when key data has been withheld or where other barriers to a controlled system prevent scientific certainty, a reasoned assessment of available evidence is nonetheless often both possible and sufficient. Indeed, courts of law do not require scientific certainty of guilt, but rather set the standard as "beyond a reasonable doubt." So, in the current environment it is similarly not necessary to require an examination of the illegally counted ballots—a task that has mostly been rendered impossible by those who apparently reasoned that they could protect a contrived outcome by chewing and swallowing—in order to see what has happened and to discern the true outcome.

If Joe Biden was truly on his way to a clean and fair victory, would it not have been in the best interest of him and his supporters to just go with that by keeping everything in full view?

Breaking Down the Electoral Tallies

The official tally of electoral votes in 2020 was **306** for Joe Biden, and **232** for Donald Trump.

Following is a summary of the salient points from the preceding chapters, particularly Chapters 3 and 9:

In Georgia, the acceptance criteria for absentee ballots were illegally relaxed in direct defiance of Georgia's statutory requirements, even while the *number* of absentee ballots, as well as their *proportion* of the total number of ballots, increased dramatically in 2020. The policy decision to ignore the laws concerning signature verification and other criteria for counting absentee ballots resulted in a greatly-reduced rejection rate of only 0.37%, versus the 6.42% rejected in 2016 when the law was followed. Meanwhile, former Vice President Biden had nearly double the number of absentee votes as President Trump. If (as would have happened had the law been followed), the rejection rate had remained similar to what it had been in 2016, Trump would have carried the State of Georgia by approximately 13,000 votes. And, this is the case even if the only thing considered is the rejection rate. But we also know about the mules operation, the drop boxes, and other shenanigans—which also clearly worked (illegally) in Joe Biden's favor. Joe Biden was judged the winner in Georgia only after rules and procedures were changed to cause tens of thousands of votes not legally qualified to count (i.e., they ought to have been rejected following fraud-prevention criteria) to be counted. And, it is perfectly safe to say without the slightest reasonable doubt (i.e., the courtroom standard) that Donald J. Trump won the state of Georgia. Notice that the determination can be made without any reliance upon investigation of actual voter fraud, election fraud, voting machine malfunctions, or other issues.

Shifting *only Georgia's* sixteen electoral votes over to Donald Trump, the new Electoral College tally stands at **290** Biden to **248** Trump.

Let us turn to Wisconsin. The Wisconsin Supreme Court ruled on July 8, 2022 that unattended drop boxes are illegal under Wisconsin law. This means that they were illegal in 2020. More than 500 drop boxes, most of them unmanned and therefore illegal, were placed around Wisconsin with a concentration in heavily Democratic areas. Ballots not legally received are not legal to count. Democrats who instructed voters to use them essentially disenfranchised those voters; it is not the fault of Republicans or of Trump—the law was clear all along and those such as the WEC who negligently advised voters to cast their ballots in an illegal manner bear the blame. Every ballot received in an unmanned drop box was not legal to count. Biden and Harris received 317,270 votes in Milwaukee County alone (Trump and Pence received 134,357). Not all these ballots were returned in an unmanned drop box, but those that were should not have been counted. Milwaukee County is only one of five major heavily Democrat areas where such illegal drop boxes were concentrated. The official margin of victory for Biden in Wisconsin was a mere 20,682. It is therefore possible to say beyond any reasonable doubt that Donald Trump won the state of Wisconsin. Notice that the determination can be made without any reliance upon investigation of actual voter fraud, election fraud, voting machine malfunctions, or other issues.

Now also shifting *Wisconsin's* ten electoral votes over to Donald Trump, the new Electoral College tally stands at **280** for Biden to **258** for Trump.

Let us turn our attention to the state of Pennsylvania. Pennsylvania law requires that absentee ballots meet certain basic criteria in order to be counted, such as being signed and having a signature that reasonably matches that of the voter's signature on file. Historically, a certain percentage of mail-in ballots are rejected under these criteria, and in 2016 that number was 0.95% or 2,534 ballots. However, Democrat Secretary of State Kathy Boockvar in apparent coordination by way of friendly lawsuits from Democrat partisans, relaxed the standards in 2020, so that very few mail-in ballots were rejected that by law should not have been counted, at the same time as more than ten times as many mail-in ballots were received in the state. Furthermore, 118,426 Pennsylvania mail-in ballots were reported as being returned before the date that they were even mailed to the voter, or one day after being mailed to the voter (both of these are impossibilities), or without a date at all. These constitutionally tainted ballots already exceed the official margin of victory, but that is not where it ends, as Boockvar also decided, in another friendly lawsuit with the Pennsylvania Democratic Party to accept ballots received three days after the legal deadline of 8:00 p.m. on Election Day, and declared that even ballots received without a postmark must be presumed to have arrived on time. Boockvar's later claim that this illegal change only affected 10,000 ballots is meaningless, since she herself refused (in defiance of the U.S. Supreme Court) to keep the late-received ballots separate from all the others. The official margin of victory for Biden in Pennsylvania was 81,660. It is therefore possible to say beyond any reasonable doubt that Donald Trump won the Commonwealth of Pennsylvania. Notice that the determination can be made without any reliance upon investigation of actual voter fraud, election fraud, voting machine malfunctions, or other issues.

Now also shifting *Pennsylvania's* twenty electoral votes over to Donald Trump, the new Electoral College total stands at **260** for Biden to **278** for Trump. And Donald Trump is the solid victor before we have even considered Michigan, Nevada, and Arizona ... all of which, likely also would have fallen into Donald Trump's column were it not for the shenanigans that have been discussed at length throughout this book. Nor are these all the states that might have been in play; others that had serious issues which may have affected the outcome were Virginia, New Mexico, New Hampshire, and Nebraska. Absent full forensic audits prior to the destruction of evidence in September 2022 (or later if that deadline is extended by law), none of these states should be assumed beyond doubt given the enormous mess of the 2020 election. Note that this is not a claim that any of those states *did* go for Trump; it is only to say that, according to my research, things are far less certain than is being represented.

As an exception, I should note that in the above calculations I have not included Arizona with its ten Electoral College votes. Biden's official margin of victory in Arizona was a minuscule 10,457 votes (out of 3,387,326), and the problems in that state, including obstruction of meaningful audits, are enormous. I believe that most reasonable people understand that Arizona was carried handily by Donald Trump in 2020, but because my argument in this book is based upon the process changes, particularly in the defendant states named in the Texas lawsuit, I have chosen to leave Arizona aside from the calculation.

Getting justice for the citizens of the United States requires addressing the constitutional and election integrity problems in *every* state, including Arizona. I have only outlined selected states as a start, to help readers understand how overwhelming and decisive was the probable Trump victory.

Six Red Flags

A fair-minded person might ask whether concerns over the integrity of a particular election are not driven by a partisan bias. Why are we concerned about 2020, and where was similar concern from us in 2016?

First, in 2020 there was an exponential increase in voting by mail, with more than 41% of all ballots in the United States in 2020 received by mail.

Second, an enormous number of Americans voted before Election Day. In most cases, in-person early voting was permitted by state law even though this seems to violate the Constitution's same day clause. The potential for compromise of election integrity, of course, is greater when voting is spread out over many days or weeks, and also the suppression of important information that voters need to hear which often emerges nearer the election and after early voters have sealed their decision is similar to allowing jurors to render their verdict and go home before all the evidence and testimony has been presented.

Third, voter ID checks and signature and address verification checks that are required by law in many states were relaxed or discarded in swing states at the direction of officials who acted outside of their authority.

Fourth, chain of custody was deeply compromised in many of the most crucial locations in key states.

Fifth, ballot drop boxes were illegally placed, with an uneven concentration in Democrat areas, and often lacked 24-hour staffing as would be required by law for any location accepting ballots. *Ballots received in an illegal manner are not legal to count.*

Sixth, electronic voting systems were widely used, thumb drives were carried and inserted, vote-switching from Trump to Biden was observed, and more was reported or deduced, and the appearance of compromise at many points has yet to be answered to the satisfaction of many Americans. The onus is upon the authorities and on the voting machine companies to demonstrate that the election was not compromised. It is not the responsibility of Americans without access or technical expertise to prove compromise—it is the responsibility of the authorities to prove integrity to the public in a way that the public can understand and verify or reasonably trust.

All the peculiarities of the conduct of the 2020 general election, in other words, moved our systems away from well-known best practices for protecting election integrity. Under such circumstances, if 2020 did not see massive levels of election fraud and vote fraud, it would have been only because everyone, including all the hard-core election operatives who have been cheating for decades, were for some reason perfectly honest for a change.

In 2020, with Democrats serving as gatekeepers in the pivotal urban areas and precincts that turned the election, the bank vault was left wide open for weeks, with security cameras figuratively (and, in some instances, literally) turned off, and keys to the safe and deposit boxes sitting at an unmanned table. Is it really reasonable to believe that the usual political operative suspects refrained from taking advantage of the situation out of the goodness of their hearts and the high level of their moral character?

One Detailed Recap

Following is a review of the information that has been discussed in the foregoing pages concerning just one state, as an example. In Michigan, the Secretary of State unilaterally abrogated Michigan election statutes concerning absentee ballot applications and signature verification, while simultaneously doing away with protections designed to deter voter fraud. Secretary Benson launched a program in June of 2020 allowing absentee ballots to be requested online *without* signature verification as expressly required under Michigan law, which says "a clerk or assistant clerk shall not deliver an absent voter ballot to an applicant who does not sign the application."

> Secretary Benson's unconstitutional modifications of Michigan's election rules resulted in the distribution of millions of absentee ballot applications without verifying voter signatures as required by MCL §§ 168.759(4) and 168.761(2). This means that *millions* of absentee ballots were disseminated in violation of Michigan's statutory signature-verification requirements.[2]

Furthermore, local election officials in Wayne County made a conscious and express policy decision to break the law concerning the opening, counting, and recording of absentee ballots, and also to ignore Michigan's statutory signature verification requirements for absentee ballots.

> Jesse Jacob, a decades-long City of Detroit employee assigned to work in the Elections Department for the 2020 election testified that:
>   'Absentee ballots that were received in the mail would have the voter's signature on the envelope. While I was at the TCF Center, I was instructed not to look at any of the signatures on the absentee ballots, and I was instructed not to compare the signature on the absentee ballot with the signature on file.'[3]

Former Vice President Biden received 68% of the vote in Wayne County, and therefore materially benefited from these illegal changes to Michigan's election law.

Statewide, former Vice President Biden's official margin of victory in Michigan was 146,007 votes. In Wayne County alone, 174,384 votes were not tied to a registration number for the City of Detroit.

> The extra ballots cast most likely resulted from the phenomenon of Wayne County election workers running the same ballots through a tabulator multiple times, with Republican poll watchers obstructed or denied access, and election officials ignoring poll watchers' challenges....[4]

Given all these problems, one might ask how the election in Michigan was even certified? It looks as though Democratic partisans got it done through old-fashioned bullying and threats of violence against Canvassing Board officials:

> On November 17, 2020, the Canvassers Board deadlocked 2-2 over whether to certify the results of the presidential election based on numerous reports of fraud and unanswered material discrepancies in the county-wide election results. A few hours later, the Republican Board members reversed their decision and voted to certify the results after severe harassment, including threats of violence.
>
> The following day, the two Republican members of the Board *rescinded their votes* to certify the vote and signed affidavits alleging they were bullied and misled into approving election results and do not believe the votes should be certified until serious irregularities in Detroit votes are resolved.[5]

Defenders of the 2020 election results as certified, with claims that "there is no widespread election malfeasance," are placing the proverbial cart before the horse. It is quite easy to make such a claim, but in a matter as consequential as a United States presidential election, a statement like this should be subject to meaningful testing. The authors of the U.S. Election Integrity Recommendations Report frame the matter well:

> No one can say that: "there was no widespread election malfeasance in 2020" unless a statistically significant number of forensic audits are performed by independent experts. **Suspiciously, the same people who are making this unsupported assertion, are those who are adamantly opposing the forensic audits.**
>
> The narrative that: "there was no widespread election malfeasance in 2020" is almost certainly false, based on these three facts:
>
> a) Numerous bipartisan experts have already indicted the US system as having major liabilities (Appendix A). To find out that the 2020 election results accurately reflect citizens' wishes, would not only be unexpected, but

it would undermine the conclusions and competence of these independent experts.

b) There are multiple statistical analyses of various 2020 Presidential election results that have concluded that these results are extremely unlikely to occur naturally. (See first section of this list.)

c) In the rare cases where voter and machine 2020 results have been forensically investigated, substantial irregularities have been revealed. (For example, see the second and third sections of this list.)[6]

Freudian slip

At the front of this book Joe Biden's statement made on October 4, 2020 is quoted: "We have put together, I think, the most extensive and inclusive voter fraud organization in the history of American politics."[7] A generous reading of this statement would suggest that he *meant* to indicate that he and his team were working on *preventing* voter fraud. In light of the contents of this book and other evidence, however, I am inclined to believe that Biden wittingly or unwittingly revealed a truth in that statement, a truth that would explain the rather nonchalant attitude that he and Kamala Harris took toward campaigning in the lead-up to the election: they knew that the fix was in, and that they could rest easy knowing that they were going to ultimately be declared the winners.

In light of the foregoing, it is a true shame that the United States Supreme Court declined to consider the Texas lawsuit, which presented them the perfect opportunity to weigh in on these matters so central to the question of whether the American people will ever be able to regain self governance after the events of 2020. Unfortunately, this question remains unresolved as the only remaining safeguard against the loss of the people's authority to the will of those who would rule over them—the Supreme Court—appears missing in action. If the people are left without recourse against an obviously illegal election, the question becomes: what happens next?

One who rules as the result of a false election is a usurper and a tyrant. When the voice of the people is not reflected in government, self governance does not exist. The 2020 election having been seized by illegal maneuvering for Joseph R. Biden, the United States is not under self governance at the time of this writing.

Now it comes down to the American people to decide whether and how to correct the serious matter before us, to right this ship. If we do not, then sadly the American experiment is now over, having died in its youth at the hands of enemies, following decades of internal cultural weakening,[8] and from self-inflicted wounds.

As we work together to set things right, honesty is essential. The answer to injustice is justice. We do not repay evil for evil, and we do not solve cheating by more cheating. The answer to cheating is to shine light and then remove the compromised processes, situations, and people. We must set in place and restore appropriate safeguards.

So, restoration is possible, but there remains very little time to right the ship before we slip into a very unpleasant situation of true oppression and full-blown tyranny.

What Should Have Happened

The true fork in the road concerning the 2020 election was the disposition of the Texas lawsuit. Some have opined that the biggest problem with the Texas lawsuit was that it was brought on December 7, when the constitutional deadline for certifying electors was December 14, a mere week later.[9]

> The real issue, as far as state electors was concerned, should not have been, "Did Trump win rather than Biden win," but was there enough of a mess here to justify either setting up a new snap election or choosing electors themselves. And what was striking about this election is that even though there was a convincing muddle in perhaps six states, not one state legislature—and five of those states had Republican legislatures—manned up and actually did what they were supposed to do under the Constitution: hold hearings on the issue of whether there was a clear winner. And if there was not a clear winner, either call a snap election or choose the electors themselves.[10]

Urgent Correction Needed

The law governing our most precious right that stands upstream from all our other political rights—that is, the right to self governance—must be upheld. Those who break the Constitution's process for selecting a president should not get angry when their claimed victory, resulting from a process that they illegally changed, is doubted or even reversed.

Democrats and those who helped them undermine the election in 2020 must be made to straighten up and fly right. There is a common way of training dogs that rubs their noses in their mess when they urinate or defecate inside the house. While some people do not prefer the method, the point is that it uses a basic principle of negative reinforcement to eliminate undesirable behavior, so that a new and better habit will be formed. People also respond to reinforcement. I believe it is important that those who engaged in misconduct in 2020 to have their noses—figuratively, of course —rubbed in their own mess, while the American people speak to them with a firm "no!"

Separation of powers and their distribution to specific offices (executive, legislative, judicial, state, federal, etc.) must be enforced. We cannot have self governance if we allow the rogue exercise of power, or its delegation to unelected parties that cannot be held accountable by the voting citizens.

The sovereignty of the American citizen must be reaffirmed. If foreign nationals wish to become citizens, to become American, they should be encouraged to go through the arduous process of doing so and applauded and welcomed into the American family when they have succeeded. But those who have not done this absolutely must not ever vote in U.S. national elections.

Illegitimate Guests in the White House

For nearly eighteen months as of the time of publication, Joe Biden has occupied the White House and wielded the power of the executive branch during what was almost certainly Donald Trump's second term as President of the United States.

The facts and analyses presented in the preceding pages establish that Joe Biden and Kamala Harris were certified and sworn into the offices of President and Vice President of the United States on January 20, 2021 only after a number of illegal votes many times the margin of victory in the states of Arizona, Georgia, Pennsylvania, Wisconsin, Nevada, and Michigan were added to the tallies. Because of Democrats' own decisions, it *cannot be known* that Joe Biden and Kamala Harris would have prevailed as is alleged.

Therefore, while Joe Biden is procedurally the president, having been certified, confirmed, and inaugurated, he cannot be said to be the *rightful* president. The 2020 election was a false election because it was an illegally conducted election in key states, as the Wisconsin Supreme Court has now confirmed. Joe Biden and Kamala Harris cannot be asserted to have been the choice of the American people.

The foregoing assertions are, I believe, unassailable. I welcome criticism and have no doubt that I will receive it.

The Grave Compounded Effects of False Elections

In 2009, Democrats passed the "Affordable Care Act," also known as "Obamacare," only because they had the vote of Al Franken in the Senate. They would not have been able to get the legislation to President Obama's desk without him. Yet an 18-month study found after the fact that at least 341 felons in heavily Democrat Minneapolis-Saint Paul voted illegally in the election that Franken won by only 312 votes. If Franken did not win, his vote should not have been available for Democrats to rely upon, and the

United States should not have ever seen Obamacare become the law of the land. Today, we know that there is a strong likelihood that Franken was an illegitimate senator. However, all the official actions that he took while occupying that office, including his Obamacare vote, have continued to reverberate through this nation. Obamacare was not reversed when Franken's legitimacy was cast into doubt. Nor would Obamacare have been overturned even if Franken's election was proven beyond all doubt to have been a fraud.

Turning to 2020, at the beginning of this book I listed some of the immediate effects of Joe Biden's presidency. While it is true that his executive orders can be undone by a successor, the impact of his actions have now become part of U.S. and world events that will be felt for many decades. And, even though legitimately elected presidents, senators, and congresspeople also make bad policy decisions, the difference is that they are actually representatives chosen by the people. We have already mentioned the tragic retreat in Afghanistan, the virtual undoing—in a matter of days—of twenty years' investment of lives and treasure in the interest of our national security and of justice, that then led to disasters in Ukraine and possibly Taiwan. Add to this tragedy the appointment in 2022 of a radical leftist, Ketanji Brown Jackson, to the U.S. Supreme Court, destruction of businesses and livelihoods and personal savings, and many other terrible effects.

If or when Biden is removed, will businesses lost be reinstated and the lost revenue recuperated? Will Jackson's appointment be rescinded? Will the innocent lives lost in Afghanistan and Ukraine be restored, and the Taliban once again dethroned and the U.S. position in that situation restored? No. There is a constitutional mechanism for impeaching a Supreme Court justice, but it has been used only once in our nation's history. Jackson, who in her confirmation hearings refused to affirm the basis for (among other things) the abolition of slavery, that is, the proposition that individual natural rights exist, could be undermining justice on the Court for 30 years. Likewise, other developments are now irreversible in whole or in part.

---

1. Fleetwood, Shawn, "Wisconsin Supreme Court Drops Hammer On 2020 Election Shenanigans: 'Ballot Drop Boxes Are Illegal' Under Wisconsin Law," *Federalist*, July 8, 2022.
2. State of Texas v. Commonwealth of Pennsylvania, State of Georgia, State of Michigan, and State of Wisconsin (Supreme Court of the United States, 2020). 26.
3. Ibid. 27.
4. Ibid. 28.
5. Ibid. 29.
6. Black, Jared et al. "U.S. Election Integrity Recommendations Report" https://election-integrity.info/Recommendations_Report.pdf
7. Schwartz, Ian, "Biden: We Have Put Together The Most Extensive And Inclusive Voter Fraud Organization In The History Of American Politics," *Real Clear Politics*, October 24, 2020.

8. Contributing factors to the weakening and balkanization of the American people are worth noting. Among of them are a century-long subversion and erosion of the principles upon which the nation was founded, and of some of the key checks and balances that were first set in place. This harmful erosion has happened simultaneous to a good movement toward realization of other principles such as the affirmation of life, liberty, and the pursuit of happiness, for example, that was denied to those unjustly held in involuntary servitude, which situation persisted another 90 years until the end of the Civil War fought over the matter, and whose other vestiges in terms of Jim Crow, the affirmation of Civil Rights, and so forth, took further effort to uproot. But, while the abolition of involuntary servitude and the unequal protection of citizens before the law has been a movement *toward* greater realization of our nation's good founding principles, other trends have moved us further *away* from those good founding principles. Among these, ironically, the groundwork was laid partly by the assertion of federal authority (albeit toward a good end, in that case) by the first Republican president, Abraham Lincoln. Amassing of federal power has continued since that time. To take another example, the Revenue Act of 1913 established an income tax and set the stage for eventual emergence of the likes of Bernie Sanders half a century later, and Alexandria Ocasio-Cortez half a century after that. Until 1913, the federal government had no business knowing the amount of any person's earnings or accumulated wealth. The moral foundation of such prohibition is found in the 8th and 10th Commandments, which affirm property rights and forbid coveting. The Revenue Act, however, invited Americans to break the commandment not to covet (e.g., hating the rich as a political category, and seeing their wealth as a sin in its own right) and encouraged stealing (e.g. voting to reduce taxation for oneself and raise it for those with more ... essentially voting money out of others' pockets). The Act thus stands opposed to life, liberty, and the pursuit of happiness. Indeed—wealth being the result of every person's honest labor, free exchange, and industry—the involuntary redistribution of wealth frankly *undid* the abolition of involuntary servitude. That this happened within mere decades of the abolition of slavery—and at the hands of the very people who fought so hard to preserve slavery in the first place!—is no coincidence.

9. Natelson, Rob II. "What did Trump's legal team do wrong?" Interview by Jon Caldara. IITV, December 31, 2020.

10. Ibid.

14

WHAT NOW?

At noon on January 20, 2021, control of one-third of the United States government was placed into the hands of a man apparently not chosen by the American people, after much illegal manipulation of the election by his supporters. This man was inaugurated, having cleared the procedural hurdles to occupy the office, but only after key checks and balances were suppressed by a variety of shenanigans.

Americans now have two major problems: A likely usurper in the White House plus an elections system that has been successfully corrupted by bad actors in the Democrat Party. They are now making a final push to pour concrete into the mold they built in 2020, to repeat the process in every future election.

What can U.S. citizens, defrauded of their right to self governance by those who seized the 2020 election, do?

Americans' Goodness Weaponized Against Them

Preference for orderly resolution of grievances is an American attribute. Today's crisis exists as a result of deliberate actions by people who do not share such respect for order, who pay only lip service to the Constitution, and who in truth care nothing for the people's voice. They think and act as autocrats, caring only about their own agenda (*the end justifies the means*). They must not be permitted to continue in their subjugation of the United States.

Ironically, it is respect for laws and for orderly resolution of grievances that restrained indignant Americans even until now. The patience of the American Revolution—suffering evils while they are sufferable—is our heritage.[1] Americans at their best fight passionately for truth and justice while refraining from vengeance.

Americans' respect for authority and assumption of good in others, however, has been used against them. In 2020, many citizens begged their representatives—including the Supreme Court—to equitably resolve these matters. Since these parties have failed to properly address the election integrity issue, Americans today stand as a people abused, ongoing victims of tyranny in a nation that was until recently free and self-governing.

40-State Call For 50-State Audit

Following publication of the Arizona audit results, a letter signed by 159 legislators representing forty states, dated November 23, 2021, called for a full fifty-state forensic audit of the 2020 election.

Letter from State Legislators to the American People Reference the 2020 Election

To the citizens of the United States of America,

We the undersigned state legislators of the United States are vested with the plenary power by our US Constitution (Article 2 Section 1 Clause 2) to oversee the election of the president of the United States.

It has come to our attention from an audit of 2.1 million ballots in Arizona complemented by an in-depth canvass of votes in Arizona, as well as through multiple different data reviews of voting by independent experts; that our representative republic suffered a corrupted 2020 election.

In addition to Arizona, sworn affidavits have accumulated from many states detailing rampant corruption and mismanagement in the election process. Fraud and inaccuracies have already been shown through multiple audits and canvasses in multiple states, as well as through lawsuits challenging the validity of election results in several counties in multiple states.

We have come to the conclusion that all 50 states need to be forensically audited. Voter rolls should be scrubbed with a canvass of the voters to ensure future integrity of our elections.

If results from these measures prove an inaccurate election was held, as has been shown in Arizona, and is being shown in many other states; then it is clear that certification of many electors was improperly rendered in January 2021 of the November 2020 United States presidential election.

We call on each state to decertify its electors where it has been shown the elections were certified prematurely and inaccurately.

If it is shown that either Joe Biden would receive fewer than 270 tallied electoral votes, or Donald Trump would receive more than 270 electoral votes, then we call for the US House of Representatives to convene and vote per the US Constitution by means of one vote per state to decide the rightful winner of the election in accordance with the constitutional process of choosing electors.

This is our historic obligation to restore the election integrity of the vote as the bedrock of our constitutional republic.

If we do not have accurate and fair elections, we do not have a country.[2]

What Is A Full Forensic Audit?

Nowhere in the legislators' letter is the term "forensic audit" defined. The details are profoundly important.

A full forensic audit investigates, in depth, three categories:

1. The voter (e.g. "Did only legally eligible citizens vote, and did they vote only once?")
2. The machine (e.g. "Did the voting machines accurately report all ballots received, without any changes?")
3. The ballot process (e.g. "Did third parties illegally change or delete any legitimate ballots, or add ballots? Were all legal ballots counted? Were all illegal ballots prevented from being counted?").[3]

Note that *none of the questions listed in these three categories are answered by an election recount, or by election canvassing, or by election certification.*[4] A full forensic audit would answer all of them. Following the helpful article by John Droz (which contains more excellent detail), I summarize each below.

The Voter

The Binnall Report, given to the U.S. Senate on December 16, 2020, is an example of a *voter forensic audit*. By checking actual voters and comparing them to a list of other voters with the same name, address, and date of birth, Binnall's audit team found that more than 42,000 people in Nevada voted more than once in the 2020 election. Using Social Security death records, they found at least 1,500 dead people recorded as voting in Nevada. Comparing the U.S. Postal Service's National Change of Address database and other sources to lists of actual voters, they found that more than 19,000 people voted in Nevada who do not live in Nevada. Cross-referencing voters with the Coding Accuracy Support System, they found that about 8,000 people voted in Nevada from non-existent addresses. Analyzing official U.S. Postal Service records that flag non-residential addresses and addresses vacant for more than 90 days, they found that over 15,000 votes were cast from commercial or vacant addresses in Nevada. Comparing official DMV records of noncitizens to the list of actual voters in the 2020 election, they found that nearly 4,000 noncitizens voted in Nevada.[5]

The Machine

Russell James Ramsland, Jr.'s 23-page report, published December 13, 2020 and discussed above in Chapter 7, is a good example of a *machine forensic audit*. Ramsland's audit team tested the integrity of the Dominion Voting System, reviewing the machines, the software, and the data of the tabulations throughout the process. The audit team concluded with their opinion that the Dominion Voting System was "intentionally and purposefully designed with inherent errors ... [generating] an enormously high number of ballot errors. The electronic ballots are then transferred for adjudication. The intentional errors lead to bulk adjudication of ballots with no oversight, no transparency, and no audit trail. ... Based on our study, we conclude that The Dominion Voting System should not be used in Michigan. We further conclude that the results of Antrim County should not have been certified."[6] They also concluded, "Secretary of State Jocelyn Benson's statement on November 6, 2020 that '[t]he correct results always were and continue to be reflected on the tabulator totals tape ...' was false."[7] The audit report, worth reviewing in its entirety, is stunning for its detailed findings, and even more stunning for the fact that so many Americans remain unaware of it despite it having been published prior to the certification of the 2020 election.

The Ballot Process

One judge, New York State Supreme Court Justice Scott DelConte, did investigate the process question for the 2020 election in one district. A *ballot process forensic audit* (alternately called a *ballot handling* or a *ballot administration* forensic audit) looks into the matter of whether third parties illegally changed or deleted any legitimate ballots or added ballots. Among other things, the judge made mention of significant number of uncounted ballots (citing two separate instances), disputed ballots that were lost track of, administratively rejected ballots that were not reported, failure to record and/or adjudicate candidates' objections to particular sets of ballots, mishandling of about 1,500 affidavit ballots, and a miscalculated vote tally that flipped a local race.[8] While DelConte's exercise was not a full process audit, it is an example of the sort of thing that is meant by a ballot process audit.

A Ticking Clock

States are legally required to preserve ballots and election records for only twenty-two months. Those who perpetrated this crime against our nation have been stonewalling forensic audits, hoping to reach the moment when records can be destroyed on or around September 3, 2022. Formal action should be taken immediately to stop the destruction of those records under these extraordinary circumstances.

The Way Back

My best hope would be that, the moment I publish this book, the authorities (having been made aware of the crime and of the identity of the culprits) will rush out, cuff the villains, and rescue the victim tied to the tracks (i.e., the American people) from the oncoming train—but, I know it is a pipe dream. Among other things, the villains in this case are great in number, powerful, sometimes seeded throughout the federal bureaucracy, and are aided by technocrats and other private interests. Still, there are things we can and must do to right this ship.

The fifty-state full forensic audit of the 2020 presidential election demanded by the legislators in the letter above should be the top administrative priority of Americans at this juncture. Beyond that, there are three general categories of issues to be addressed: the matter of justice in *this election*, the matter of systemic election integrity in *all elections*, and the matter of *general culture dynamics* that have recently enabled a movement toward totalitarianism inside the United States.

Above and before all the suggestions I make below, I believe that all kinds of Americans need to get on our knees and pray, in a spirit of love and without malice toward any of our fellow citizens. We should turn from our many sins (this is not primarily an exercise in finger-pointing, but rather for individual humble reflection), ask God for wisdom to do what is right, and beg him to help this nation.[9]

Righting The Immediate Wrong

Justice in the first category is important and demands at least three things:

First, the presumption of victory in 2020 cannot be toward the candidate whose partisans got him to the position by extensive illegal maneuvers and manipulations, preventing transparency and flooding the system with illegally counted votes many times the margin of victory in the states that decided the election. *Donald Trump should be politically restored to the office of president,* so that he may serve out what is left of his second term. I suggest

—based upon my overall argument in this book, particularly Chapters 1, 3, and 8—that this restoration is justified completely apart from the results of audits which may or may not occur.

There is a perfectly legal way for President Trump to be restored by political means and fulfill at least the final part of his second White House term. If Republicans retake both houses of Congress in November 2022, the House could (since the position may be filled by any private citizen) elect Donald Trump speaker on January 2, 2023, and would—if subsequent steps are carried out successfully—remain speaker for only seventeen days, during which time he would preside over the impeachment in the House of Joe Biden (on six articles) and Kamala Harris (on three articles). If the Senate then convicts both Biden and Harris, Donald Trump would be re-elevated to the presidency—since the speaker is third in line. Furthermore, if the vote to convict occurred one second after 12:00 p.m. on January 20, 2023, there would be less than half of the current presidential term remaining, meaning Trump would be left an option to run again in 2024. That way, in theory at least, he could spend the remainder of the term unraveling some of the damage done by Biden, and then continue to help move the country in a good direction after 2024 if re-elected.

Note that what is proposed above is a thoroughly legal and constitutional political process. It will be up to the American people to decide whether or not they wish to give the House and Senate majorities required to accomplish such a thing in November 2022, and to let their elected representatives know whether or not they expect such a process to be carried out. The U.S. Capitol Switchboard telephone number is listed at the front of this book under "ATTENTION."

Importantly, everyone should remember that the circumstance in which Joe Biden now sits is entirely of his own making and that of the illegal actions of his supporters. It did not need to be this way. If Biden, Harris, or their partisans wish to complain, they should lament their own bad decisions. Had they won their positions in a constitutionally sound manner, they would not be facing the current prospect of removal.

I have heard some who agree the election was false say, "Well, yes, that is too bad, but I really don't think that we should fight to get Trump back into office." Such individuals are essentially saying that some people (i.e., Donald J. Trump or those who supported him) don't deserve justice. But we are not supposed to have second-class citizens in this country; it is a bedrock American principle that *everyone* is owed justice. Those who would allow the disenfranchisement of all Americans to stand—who say that "what's done is done"—are basically suggesting that thieves should be allowed to keep property they stole, and we should just put better locks on the doors for next time. In other words, they propose that the subversion of the people's will as expressed in their federal Constitution and duly passed state laws—and all of its dire consequences —should be allowed to stand and be exploited by the cheaters for another two years. Along with allowing it to stand would come a certain perception, in the United States and abroad, that what happened wasn't really *that* bad. Once again, this matter is not up to me; it is up to the American people. I am only expressing my view of the moral and ethical situation before us.

Donald Trump worked faithfully as president, kept his campaign promises, and ran an honest and clean re-election campaign. *If* it is true that he was the choice of Americans in 2020, then everyone is owed his second term. If Mr. Trump remains willing to serve, then justice demands that he be restored so long as there is a legal mechanism for accomplishing that restoration. If someone says, "I didn't like his tweets," or, "I think there are better candidates out there," as an excuse to allow the injustice to stand, then they are no better than the tyrants. Either we uphold the will of the people, or we do not have self-government. There really is, in my view, no other option. Insisting upon restoration is not equal to treating Donald Trump as a "god" any more than ruling for the wronged party in court is the equivalent of declaring that party a "god." It is merely seeing justice done. As stated earlier, this matter is bigger than either Donald Trump or Joe Biden. It is about the American people and upholding their right to self rule.

Second, a special counsel must be appointed to investigate the Biden family dealings, not only to expose any personal corruption, but to reveal in what ways foreign actors may have exerted influence upon U.S. elections and elected personnel at the highest levels of government. Such an investigation must not be vengeful, but rather just, open, and fair. Many people in Washington have a vested interest in preventing such a special counsel, so it will not happen unless citizens demand it.[10]

Third, all who criminally interfered with the conduct of the 2020 election must be criminally prosecuted. Furthermore, those in authority who stood by and let it happen when they had both the power and the moral obligation to stop it should be exposed to public shame.[11] The political and/or prosecutorial (as the case may be) fates of all these individuals ought to serve as a warning to others.

Restoring Election Integrity In General

In the second category, the following ten things are needed.

First, do your best to think critically. Don't believe everything that sounds right, and don't throw out everything that sounds a little crazy. Take care to check that something is true before sharing it on social media. Build for yourself a reputation for being trustworthy. Use your head, and do your best to test everything.

Second, Americans must stop listening to those who lie to them, gaslight them, fail to check sources, and call them names if they step out of line. Tune out CNN, ABC, MSNBC, CBS, the New York Times, the Washington Post and NPR.[12]

Third, we must learn from our mistakes. Americans must insist upon meaningful federal and state legislative changes that genuinely improve election integrity. These changes should include actions prior to Election Day, on Election Day, and after the polls close on Election Day. Seeking justice requires that *actual changes be made*. Simply talking about what went wrong while doing nothing to actually set it right is not justice. Here are some sensible and strong federal and state recommendations from independent experts:

Prior to Election Day

- Election laws and regulations may not be changed within 180 days prior to that election.
- Primary elections should be closed. (A closed primary means that only voters registered in a particular party are eligible to vote for candidates in that party.) It is common practice for members of the other party to vote in an open primary for the weakest candidate (who they think will be easier to defeat in the general election); this system does not serve the people since it tends to disqualify the best candidates prior to the general election. A closed primary prevents sabotage by members of the other party.
- Absentee voting should be allowed only in specialized circumstances, such as hospitalized, in a nursing home, out of the district during the election, etc. It should be illegal to send out unsolicited absentee ballot request forms. *Approximately 75% of European countries have essentially banned absentee voting.*
- Drop boxes should be illegal.
- Ballot harvesting should be illegal, because ballot harvesting exposes the voters to abuse such as harvesters "losing" ballots that they do not like. *Note: The Americans with Disabilities Act* has a loophole that allows ballot harvesting. This loophole should be closed.
- It should be illegal for any state, county or precinct to accept third-party election-related funds. If donations from the KKK or Russia to "assist" a state, county or precinct with an election would be unacceptable, then why would donations from Mark

Zuckerberg or any other partisan individual be alright? Managing elections is a core responsibility of government. The process should not ever be tainted by private money as it was in 2020

- Election Day should be a national holiday.
- Absentee voting is a privilege. Federal law should mandate that all absentee ballots must be received by (or, alternately, postmarked by) Election Day.
- Any individual providing voter assistance to more than one voter (such as due to the voter being disabled) should be required by law to complete a form, to be filed with election officials, and provide their photo ID, the names of the persons they helped, and the reason(s) they provided assistance.
- Photo ID should be required in order to vote.
- It should be illegal for any voting machine to have any capability, *even if that capability is temporarily disabled*, to connect to the internet.
- Election Day voting should end at 5:00 p.m., local time. If Election Day is a national holiday, this rule should not prevent anyone from voting, and it would allow election workers to count all ballots on Election Night.

After Close of Polls on Election Day

- All absentee and early-voting ballots should be tabulated, and reported, prior to any Election Day ballots.
- Election observers should always be allowed complete access to the election process, without minimum distance requirements. The access should extend to pre-Election Day activities as well.
- Fixing deficient ballots (or mail-in envelopes) must be restricted and must be completely transparent. They should only be cured or adjudicated in very limited circumstances and every one that is must be fully documented—with the records available for public inspection.
- Absentee and in-person totals should be reported separately.
- Sample forensic audits should be automatic.
- Chain of custody must be maintained for all ballots and voting equipment for at least twenty-two months. A paper ballot (not an image) must be on record for every vote cast. Conveyance documents (envelopes, signature cards, etc.) and ballots should be stamped with identical unique codes. After verifying the voter's signature, the envelopes should be saved in a secure location, and the barcode elsewhere. Where feasible, custody

and control of ballots and of conveyance documents should be held by the state attorney general's office. In the case of a forensic audit, the envelope and ballot can be reconnected under controlled circumstances to assure privacy of votes.

- Negative vote tabulations (e.g. Edison) must be prohibited without detailed transparent supporting data.
- All eligible U.S. citizens should be automatically registered to vote.
- Every state should be required by law to annually update their election rolls, for the purpose of adding new eligible residents (due to age, citizenship status, moving into the state, etc.) and for deleting prior voters who are no longer eligible (due to death, moving out of state, etc.).
- Rules and processes for preventing noncitizens from voting must be tightened. It is a crime for any noncitizen to vote in a U.S. federal election.
- A national toll-free phone number and website should be established for citizens to report possible improper election actions. Complaints should be automatically routed to the appropriate state. Each state should have an independent ombudsman, overseen by the state's attorney general, to investigate election irregularities. All complaints should be publicly available online, with only the filer's personal information redacted. All such complaints should be presented and reviewed by each state's legislature before certification of their election results. The state's attorney general should file a formal written report to the state legislature at least three (3) days prior to the legislature voting on certification of their election results.
- Consider complete elimination of the use of electronic voting machines (EVMs).
- A federal law should be passed requiring state recall rules to be consistent with state election rules. For example, if an official ID is required in order to sign a recall petition, then an official ID should be required to vote in an election.[13]

Fourth, citizens should insist upon states doing meaningful post-election audits. Considering that we have yet to carry out a thorough investigation of the 2020 election that involves, at a minimum, conducting forensic audits (as described above, "What Is A Full Forensic Audit?") of select precincts within select counties within key swing states (a manageable undertaking), we actually *do not know* with any scientific certainty whether the 2020 election was "safe and secure."

Fifth, Americans should insist upon 1) an Election Day (not election week or election month); 2) a movement away from electronic voting systems and back to paper ballots counted and recorded at the polling precinct, then preserved for audit; and 3) prohibition of vote-by-mail, except for those who specifically request in each election to vote absentee with a valid reason.

Sixth, Americans must reject the Commission on Presidential Debates which has tipped the playing field toward the Democratic Party in election after election by its choice of left-leaning moderators who then adopt a Democrat narrative when crafting questions. Each party should sponsor and host an equal number of debates, choosing its own moderator, and should ask whatever questions they want, phrased in whatever way they wish, of the candidates.

Seventh, Americans should remember the "too many to imprison" principle. The woke establishment today relies upon Americans abandoning each other. Stop playing along with them. Even that friend or colleague with whom you disagree has the right to be heard. When you see injustice such as the silencing of political opponents (remember, political opponents should be *answered*, not silenced), speak up on their behalf. Call your congressperson and complain. Tell your friends and colleagues that you don't agree. Move your alliances and your business to those places where people do not support tyranny and injustice.

Eighth, Section 230—which has been widely abused by internet and technology companies as a shield for overtly manipulating opinions and selectively regulating the flow of information to exert partisan influence on U.S. elections—should be amended to explicitly remove legal immunity from internet providers and tech companies in any instance of editing not involving sexually explicit or vulgar materials.

Ninth, Americans should disempower social media gatekeepers by reducing reliance upon their electronic devices, and renewing the habit of gathering and talking directly to friends and neighbors. Direct, old-fashioned speech or correspondence cannot be so easily snatched away at a moment's notice, or manipulated by others.

Tenth, but not least, Americans across the nation should follow the recommendation of Col. John Mills by creating leaders at the county level and taking back the following six institutions (or their equivalents): 1) the election registrar, 2) the election board, 3) the county council (board of supervisors), 4) the school board, 5) the sheriff's office, and 6) the state prosecuting attorney.[14] The best way to make an actual impact is to see that these six institutions follow the will of local citizens. If Americans of goodwill across the nation would roll up their sleeves and retake these institutions, more honest elections would follow and other problems diminish.

General Cultural Dynamics

The path that the United States has gone down recently is leading toward tragic situations experienced in many other parts of the world over the past century. Since we have the benefit of the repeated experience of others, there is no reason that we should fail to learn and choose a different direction, before it is too late. Allusion was made early in this book to the writings of Hannah Arendt. To those who have sounded the alarm could be added many others, including the late George Orwell. In all cases, language and the flow of information have been key in the gradual erosion of basic human freedoms, leading to a state of tyranny and subjugation.

First, Americans must understand that they are at war and are being groomed for submission. They ought take special care to not adopt the enemy's language:

- Note that terms like "equity," "the rich," "fair share," "diversity," "whiteness," and "privilege" are the language of hate. Choose not to participate. Racism is not the solution to racism. Hate and coveting hurts everyone. Dogmatic emphasis on difference drives people apart when they actually have so much in common.
- Reject the false premise that truth does not exist. Avoid saying "my truth" or "your truth." Just say "truth." Avoid saying "gender"; people have a sex (male or female), so use "sex." There's no need to be rude—in fact, kindness is beautiful—but justice doesn't exist without truth.
- Don't excuse perpetrators by shifting blame to third parties. Those who commit crimes are responsible.
- Don't blame victims. When bystanders blame a victim, they finish the job begun by the attacker. It all but guarantees that bullying will continue. Tell victim-blamers to stop.
- Never apologize for speaking truth without malice. Recognize when tears have been weaponized to keep you silent. Those who silence you by claims that your words harm them are in the wrong, not you. Do not self-censor. The appearance that everyone agrees with the prevailing narrative today is the spiraling result of millions of people keeping quiet in the name of peace, or not rocking the boat, or preserving the relationship —but it is an illusion. Speaking your conscience is an act of love and will give others courage to do the same.
- A phobia is a clinical diagnosis. Unless rendered in a context of an established doctor-patient relationship, a suggestion of (something)-phobia or being a (something)-phobe is

meaningless. Furthermore, if a licensed psychologist *does* diagnose someone, for example, as an "islamophobe" or a "homophobe" or a "transphobe," that diagnosis is protected in the United States by HIPAA laws and cannot be publicly disclosed by medical professionals without express consent of the patient. If you hear anyone referred to as any of these things, politely ask the speaker how they came to be in possession of that sensitive medical information.

Second, we must address the problem of our public schools. There are many such problems to be taken up, including the fact that federal involvement in education is not permitted by the Constitution, but meanwhile, one of the most basic problems has been the replacement of critical thinking skills by rote learning in national K-12 curricula. A lack of such skills does not benefit those children—it benefits those with authoritarian aspirations who intend to rule over them. Failing to reinforce critical thought will do great harm to everyone and weaken our country. The matter should be urgently addressed.

Fallen Soldiers

As I researched this book, I was sobered to observe the number of good people, many with distinguished records of achievement and public service, who virtually overnight came to be tarred as crazies, and were hurt, shunned, fired from jobs, and viciously maligned, even by those who ought to have been their friends. Their sin? Caring enough to speak honestly about what they could sense in their hearts and see with their eyes, trying to stop a crime in progress. My listing their names is not endorsement of everything they said about the election. It was the so-called "fog of war;" everyone got things wrong. But, in the final analysis, I expect that these people will be generally vindicated, as even now appears to be happening. In my estimation, they showed far better character than others who took fashionable positions to avert the wrath of the mob.

The list is incomplete, but I propose many Americans owe an apology to the following people, who in the end were probably more correct on the election than their critics:

Christian Adams, Esq.; Steve Bannon; Ken Blackwell; Ken Cuccinelli, Esq.; Matt DePerno, Esq.; Lou Dobbs; Dr. John Eastman; Rudy Giuliani; Mollie Hemingway; Cleta Mitchell, Esq.; Jenny Beth Martin; Dr. Peter Navarro; Sidney Powell, Esq.; Lin Wood; and of course, Donald Trump

Final Comments

You are under attack. Today, the weapons are mostly words and threats (such as job loss or reputational damage), but the conquest is real and the people doing it will soon bring ruthless violence against you, your family, and your friends if you do not reinforce the safeguards against tyranny that were wisely handed down to all of us by those who designed our system of government. We will lose before the actual fighting has even begun if we don't understand right now that we are already in a major war.

Above all, please stop believing that what you do won't make a difference. The world needs you. I did a little by laboring over this book, trying to communicate as clearly and helpfully as I was able. What will you do?

A friend recently shared the statement, "If you leave your children a world where you never stood up, they'll inherit a world where they can't." I do hope that we will remember this together. We really should work to preserve the blessings of liberty for those who come after us.

———————

QUESTIONS

1. What was the essential problem with the 2020 election? What will be the consequences for the American people of failing to address it? What will be the consequences for the rest of the world?

2. What is the "ticking clock" referenced at the beginning of this book and in this chapter?

3. Which of the action steps listed in this chapter do you believe are most important, and why? Thinking of the tendency for centralized government to get out of control and evade accountability to the sovereign citizen, why is civic engagement important?

———————

1. "...[E]xperience hath shewn, that mankind are more disposed to suffer, while evils are sufferable, than to right themselves by abolishing the forms to which they are accustomed." United States Declaration of Independence.
2. "Update: 187 Legislators From 39 States Write A Letter Calling For A 50-State Audit."
3. Adapted from Droz, John, "Post-Election Audits: Verifying Election Integrity," June 22, 2021.
4. Ibid.
5. "Witness Statement of Jesse Binnall," Senate Homeland Security and Governmental Affairs Committee. December 16, 2020.
6. "Antrim Michigan Forensics Report," Allied Security Operations Group. December 13, 2020.
7. Ibid.
8. Weiner, Mark, "9 ways election officials failed in Brindisi-Tenney House race, judge says." ; Decision and Order on Ballot Challenges, Tenney v. Oswego County Bd. of Elections et al., January 29, 2021; Tenney v. Oswego County Bd. of Elections et al. (Sup. Ct. Oswego Cty. 2020)
9. I appreciate those who are atheists, and fully affirm the right of everyone—including those who assert that God is not there—to believe as they wish. While my suggestion to pray is an open invitation, in the context of freedom, to something that I believe is essential.

10. Halon, Yael. "Levin calls for special counsel to investigate Biden family: 'We need to know what the hell is going on'." *Fox News*, April 3, 2022.

11. By "exposed," I do not here mean threats or intimidation; I mean mere public criticism. As I write these words, the private homes of several Supreme Court justices are being picketed mere miles from where I sit by people who are trying to influence the outcome of a particular decision whose draft was leaked for the very purpose of such undue influence. This is the first time in U.S. history that a draft Supreme Court opinion has been leaked. Intimidation of judges in an effort to influence their decision is never appropriate. Public discussion and pointed criticism of bad decisions and unethical actions after the fact, however, is entirely appropriate.

12. Yes, I know that I have cited CNN and many other discredited media sources in this book. I've usually done so with the purpose of demonstrating that even compromised and partisan media sources admit some of the points that are being discussed. In other cases, I have found useful information that I judged worthy of presenting to you. It is not that CNN, or NPR, or PBS, or MSNBC never have some information of value; it is that we now know that they *cannot be trusted* to tell the truth. So, use them with utmost caution and skepticism.

13. Black, Jared et al. "U.S. Election Integrity: Recommendations Report," April 22, 2021 (rev. August 1, 2022). 10-12.

14. Personal conversation. John Mills, May 19, 2022.

BIBLIOGRAPHY

Aaker, Jennifer, and Victoria Chang. "Obama and the Power of Social Media and Technology." *Stanford Graduate School of Business,* Case M-321, August 27, 2009. https://www.gsb.stanford. edu/faculty-research/case-studies/obama-power-social-media-technology.

"Video shows 'Starbucks Karen' upset when asked to put on mask." ABC 10 News. October 19, 2020. YouTube video. https://www.youtube.com/watch?v=9K-jId17I2o. (4/13/22).

Adcox, Abigail. "Leaked audio reveals DHS secretary's meeting with Border Patrol agents." *Washington Examiner*, January 26, 2022. https://www.washingtonexaminer.com/news/leaked-audio-reveals-dhs-secretarys-tense-meeting-with-border-patrol-agents. (4/19/22).

"AFL-CIO, Chamber of Commerce, National Faith Leaders Call for Votes to Be Counted." AFL-CIO, November 3, 2020. https://aflcio.org/press/releases/afl-cio-chamber-commerce-national-faith-leaders-call-votes-be-counted. (6/28/22).

Agorist, Matt. "Nearly 700 Days Into '2 Weeks To Flatten The Curve' & The Only Thing That's Reduced Is Your Freedom." *Washington Standard*, January 10, 2022. https://thewashingtonstandard.com/nearly-700-days-into-2-weeks-to-flatten-the-curve-the-only-thing-thats-reduced-is-your-freedom/. (5/23/22).

Ahmed, Alex Anas. "Donald Trump Jr. slams General Milley for 'treasonous coup.'" *Post Millennial,* September 14, 2021. https://thepostmillennial.com/trump-jr-slams-general-milley-coup. (5/23/22).

Aitken, Peter. "Conservatives, others claim Twitter removed thousands of followers." *Fox News*, January 9, 2021. https://www.foxnews.com/politics/conservatives-celebrities-claim-twitter-removed-thousands-followers. (6/28/22).

Akan, Emil. "COVID-19 Relief Measures Make US Tax System 'More Progressive': Tax Foundation." *Epoch Times*, August 22, 2021. https://www.theepochtimes.com/covid-relief-measures-make-us-tax-system-more-progressive_3960227.html.

Alter, Charlotte. "Joe Biden Definitively Vows to Pick a Woman Vice President." *Time*, March 15, 2020. https://time.com/5803677/joe-biden-woman-vice-president/.

"Antrim Michigan Forensics Report." Allied Security Operations Group. December 13, 2020. https://www.depernolaw.com/uploads/2/7/0/2/27029178/antrim_michigan_forensics_report_%5B121320%5D_v2_%5Bredacted%5D.pdf.

"2019 Allsides Google 'Top Stories' Bias Audit." *Allsides*, (6/29/22). https://www.allsides.com/news-source/google-news-media-bias.

Anderson, Bob. "Courts Repeatedly Refused To Consider Trump's Election Claims On The Merits." *Federalist,* March 11, 2021. https://thefederalist.com/2021/03/11/courts-repeatedly-refused-to-consider-trumps-election-claims-on-the-merits/. (7/27/22).

Anderson, Monica. "Americans divide on whether Trump should be permanently banned from social media." *Pew Research Center,* May 5, 2021. https://www.pewresearch.org/fact-tank/2021/05/05/americans-divided-on-whether-trump-should-be-permanently-banned-from-social-media/.

Anderson, Natasha. "REVEALED: BLM founder Patrisse Cullors paid her baby father $970,000 for 'creative services', her brother $840,000 for security, a fellow director $2.1m and reimbursed the organization $73,000 for a charter flight." *Daily Mail*, May 17, 2022. https://www.dailymail.co.uk/news/article-10823779/New-tax-filings-reveal-BLM-founder-Patrisse-Cullors-spent-foundations-funds.html. (5/19/22).

Andrews, Natalie. "Pelosi Opposes Pursuing Impeachment of Trump: House speaker says such a move would be too divisive." *Wall Street Journal,* March 11, 2019. https://www.wsj.com/articles/pelosi-opposes-pursuing-impeachment-of-trump-11552338051.

Andrzejewski, Adam. "Staggering Costs—U.S. Military Equipment Left Behind In Afghanistan." *Forbes*, August 23, 2021. (5/31/22).

"Arizona Sham 'Audit' E-course." *American Oversight*, June 7, 2022. https://www.americanover sight.org/arizona-sham-audit-e-course. (6/8/22).

"The Arizona Senate's Partisan Audit of Maricopa County Election Results." *American Oversight*, updated March 2, 2022. https://www.americanoversight.org/investigation/the-arizona-senates-partisan-audit-of-maricopa-county-election-results. (6/8/22).

Arama, Nick. "Pelosi Tried to Foment a Military Coup Against Trump." *RedState,* January 9, 2021. https://redstate.com/nick-arama/2021/09/14/talk-about-a-coup-it-was-pelosi-who-pushed-milley-to-act-against-trump-n442936. (5/23/22).

———. "Talk About a Coup: It Was Pelosi Who Pushed Milley to Act Against Trump." *RedState,* September 14, 2021. https://redstate.com/nick-arama/2021/09/14/talk-about-a-coup-it-was-pelosi-who-pushed-milley-to-act-against-trump-n442936.

Arendt, Hannah. *The Origins of Totalitarianism.* New York: Harcourt, Inc., 1976.

"New election ordered in race marred by voter fraud charges." *Associated Press*, August 19, 2020. https://apnews.com/article/ced07318e9fb6a95c5f6cab606de1df8. (6/28/22).

"State Officials Altered Count Of New York's Nursing Home Deaths." *Associated Press*, March 5, 2021. https://wskg.org/state-officials-altered-count-of-new-yorks-nursing-home-deaths/. (2/16/22).

"Timeline of events since Jussie Smollett reported attack." *Associated Press*, December 10, 2021. https://abcnews.go.com/Entertainment/wireStory/timeline-events-jussie-smollett-reported-attack-83350284. (4/17/22).

Atkisson, Sharyl. "When will 'Basement Biden' get in the game?" *Hill*, September 26, 2020. https://thehill.com/opinion/campaign/518180-when-will-basement-biden-get-in-the-game/. (6/6/22).

Austin, Michael. "Five Left-Wing Lies That Twitter Refuses To Fact-Check." *Western Journal*, August 19, 2020. https://www.westernjournal.com/5-left-wing-lies-twitter-refuses-fact-check/. (3/22/22).

———. "Poll: The Majority of Likely Voters Now Believe Cheating Impacted the Results of the 2020 Election." *Western Journal*, June 11, 2020. https://www.westernjournal.com/poll-majority-likely-voters-now-believe-cheating-impacted-results-2020-election/.

Babbin, Jed. "The FBI's FISA Frauds: Until this scandal is addressed squarely the FBI's reputation will remain mud." *American Spectator*, December 27, 2019. https://spectator.org/the-fbis-fisa-frauds/. (5/23/22).

Bader, Phillip. "A shocking 61% of Americans want more restrictions on free speech. Here's why they're dead wrong." *Pacific Legal Foundation,* November 25, 2019. https://pacificlegal.org/a-shocking-61-of-americans-want-more-restrictions-on-free-speech-heres-why-theyre-dead-wrong/.

Baker, Brent. "Washington Examiner's 'Liberal Media Scream' With the MRC's Assessment." *MRC*, July 18, 2022. https://www.newsbusters.org/blogs/nb/brent-baker/2022/07/18/washing ton-examiners-liberal-media-scream-mrcs-assessment. (7/20/22).

Baldor, Lolita C., and Robert Burns. "US drone strike kills 2 Islamic State members in Afghanistan." *Associated Press*, August 27, 2021. https://chicago.suntimes.com/2021/8/28/22645980/us-afghanistan-drone-strike-islamic-state. (2/16/22).

Ball, Molly. "The Secret History of the Shadow Campaign That Saved the 2020 Election." *Time*, February 4, 2021. https://time.com/5936036/secret-2020-election-campaign/. (5/27/22).

"Early voting dates, 2020." Ballotpedia. (5/18/22).

Bandler, Aaron. "5 Things You Should Know About How Al Gore Lost The 2000 Election." *Daily Wire*, October 21, 2016. https://www.dailywire.com/news/5-things-you-should-know-about-how-al-gore-lost-aaron-bandler. (4/4/22).

Bannister, Craig. "Democrat Debate Ratings Fall to Lowest Level of 2020 Election Cycle, Breaking October's Record Low." *CNS News*, November 21, 2019. https://cnsnews.com/blog/craig-bannister/democrat-debate-ratings-fall-lowest-level-2020-election-cycle-breaking. (6/6/22).

Barkoukis, Leah. "Fauci Admits Why Americans Were Initially Misled About Wearing Masks." *Townhall*, June 17, 2020. https://townhall.com/tipsheet/leahbarkoukis/2020/06/17/fauci-masks-n2570789. (5/23/22).

———. "Now That Biden's President, CNN's COVID-19 Death Counter Appears to Be Gone."

Townhall, January 21, 2021. https://townhall.com/tipsheet/leahbarkoukis/2021/01/21/cnns-covid-death-count-is-gone-n2583502. (5/23/22).

"Biden sets to work on reversing Trump policies with executive orders." *BBC,* January 21, 2021. https://www.bbc.com/news/world-us-canada-55738746. (4/1/22).

"California and Oregon 2020 wildfires in maps, graphics and images." *BBC,* September 18, 2020. https://www.bbc.com/news/world-us-canada-54180049. (5/23/22).

"Covid origin: Why the Wuhan lab-leak theory is being taken seriously." *BBC,* 27 May 2021. https://www.bbc.com/news/world-asia-china-5726811.

"In Pictures: Trump supporters hold rallies for the president." *BBC,* October 4, 2020. https://www.bbc.com/news/election-us-2020-54405735. (5/16/22).

"Pentagon releases UFO videos for the record." *BBC,* April 28, 2020. https://www.bbc.com/news/world-us-canada-52457805.

"Qasem Soleimani: US kills top Iranian general in Baghdad air strike." *BBC,* January 3, 2020. https://www.bbc.com/news/world-middle-east-50979463. (2/16/22).

"Trump claims millions voted illegally in presidential poll." *BBC,* November 28, 2016. https://www.bbc.com/news/world-us-canada-38126438. (4/14/22).

"Trump-Russia Steele dossier analyst charged with lying to FBI." *BBC,* November 5, 2021. https://www.bbc.com/news/world-us-canada-59168626. (4/1/22).

"Ukraine conflict: Russian forces invade after Putin TV declaration." *BBC,* February 24, 2022. https://www.bbc.com/news/world-europe-60503037 (2/24/22).

Beamon, Todd. "Rand Paul Slams Liz Cheney as 'Never Trumper' Amid Twitter Rift." *Newsmax,* September 12, 2019. https://www.newsmax.com/newsfront/elizabeth-cheney-never-trumper-gop-war-hawk/2019/09/12/id/932443/. (6/7/22).

Becker, Bernie. "Conservative groups sue Holder over Tea Party targeting." *Hill,* May 29, 2013. https://thehill.com/policy/finance/302403-tea-party-groups-sue-holder-irs-over-targeting.

Bedard, Paul. "Mark Levin smashes 1M sold for *American Marxism,* top 2021 book." *Washington Examiner,* September 23, 2021. https://www.washingtonexaminer.com/washington-secrets/mark-levin-smashes-1m-sold-for-american-marxism-top-2021-book.

———. "Trump's list: 289 accomplishments in just 20 months, 'relentless' promise-keeping." *Washington Examiner,* October 12, 2018. https://www.washingtonexaminer.com/tag/donald-trump?source=%2Fwashington-secrets%2Ftrumps-list-289-accomplishments-in-just-20-months-relentless-promise-keeping. (5/23/22).

Benen, Steve. "Why an out-of-control president raged through a cringe-worthy debate." *MSNBC,* September 30, 2020. https://www.msnbc.com/rachel-maddow-show/why-out-control-presi dent-raged-through-cringe-worthy-debate-n1241541. (4/20/22).

Berg, Sara. "What doctors wish patients knew about herd immunity." *AMA,* August 27, 2021. https://www.ama-assn.org/delivering-care/public-health/what-doctors-wish-patients-knew-about-covid-19-herd-immunity. (5/23/22).

Berenson, Tessa. "Donald Trump Calls on Russia to Hack Hillary Clinton's Emails." *TIME,* July 27, 2016. https://time.com/4426272/donald-trump-hillary-clinton-russia-emails/. (4/5/22).

———. "President Trump Pulls U.S. Out of 'Defective' Iran Nuclear Deal." *Time,* May 8, 2018. https://time.com/5269746/donald-trump-iran-nuclear-deal-macron/. (5/26/22).

Berkovitz, Will. "Afghan allies in hiding, executed in the street — Jewish people know this haunting story." *USA Today,* September 9, 2021. https://www.yahoo.com/news/afghan-allies-hiding-executed-street-080012479.html. (4/19/22).

Bernhard, Matthew, Allison McDonald, Henry Meng, Jensen Hwa, Nakul Bajaj, Kevin Chang, and J. Alex Halderman. "Can Voters Detect Malicious Manipulation of Ballot Marking Devices?" University of Michigan and The Harker School. https://jhalderm.com/pub/papers/bmd-verifiability-sp20.pdf.

Bernstein, Brittany. "Biden Announces Plan to Require Large Companies to Mandate COVID Vaccines." *National Review,* September 9, 2021. https://www.nationalreview.com/news/psaki-stay-tuned-for-federal-requirements-for-large-employers-on-covid-19-vaccine-mandates/.

Bertrand, Natasha. "Hunter Biden story is Russian disinfo, dozens of former intel officials say." *Politico,* October 19, 2020. https://www.politico.com/news/2020/10/19/hunter-biden-story-russ ian-disinfo-430276. (3/21/22).

Beyer, Fran. "VP Harris Under Fire for Lack of Attention to Border Crisis." *Newsmax,* September

20, 2021. https://www.newsmax.com/politics/harris-border-czar-social-media-mexico/2021/09/20/id/1037202/. (4/19/22).

Bickley, John. "8 Devastating Facts From The Benghazi Report." *Daily Wire*, June 28, 2016. https://www.dailywire.com/news/10-devastating-facts-benghazi-report-james-barrett. (5/23/22).

"About." Black Lives Matter. https://blacklivesmatter.com/about/. (2/16/22).

Blake, John. "There's a sobering truth to Trump's racist tweets that we don't like to admit." *CNN*, July 15, 2019. https://www.cnn.com/2019/07/15/us/trump-tweets-two-americas-blake/index.html. (4/20/22).

"'One of the greatest scandals in American history': Mark Levin's 'silent coup' claims are finally confirmed." *Blaze*, March 4, 2019. https://www.theblaze.com/levintv/one-of-the-greatest-scandals-in-american-history-mark-levins-silent-coup-claims-are-finally-confirmed.

"BleachBit 'stifles investigation' of Hillary Clinton." *BleachBit.org*, August 25, 2016. https://www.bleachbit.org/news/bleachbit-stifles-investigation-hillary-clinton. (4/5/22).

Bloom, Arthur. "Of Course The FBI Was Infiltrating January 6 Groups." *The American Conservative*, June 22, 2021. https://www.theamericanconservative.com/articles/of-course-the-fbi-was-infiltrating-january-6-groups/. (5/23/22).

Blow, Thomas. "Email Scandal: Bill Clinton and Loretta Lynch's tarmac meeting: What happened?" *U.S. Sun*, June 14, 2021. https://www.the-sun.com/news/3079610/bill-clinton-loretta-lynch-tarmac-meeting/. (5/23/22).

Bokhari, Allum. "10 Times Google's Far-Left, Anti-Trump Bias Was Exposed." *Breitbart*, August 28, 2018. https://www.breitbart.com/tech/2018/08/28/10-times-googles-far-left-anti-trump-bias-was-exposed/. (6/29/22).

———. "'Joe Biden Corruption' trends on Google—but Google whitewashes autocomplete suggestions." *Breitbart*, October 28, 2020. https://www.breitbart.com/tech/2020/10/28/google-joe-biden-corruption-burisma-autocomplate/. (5/23/22).

Bolyard, Paula. "Rioters Burn Historic St. John's Church in D.C., Deface Monuments Across the City." *PJ Media*, June 1, 2020. https://pjmedia.com/news-and-politics/paula-bolyard/2020/06/01/breaking-rioters-burn-historic-st-johns-church-in-d-c-deface-monuments-across-the-city-n474820. (5/23/22).

Bonchie. "The FBI Admits to Having Informants at January 6th Protest." *RedState*, September 25, 2021. https://redstate.com/bonchie/2021/09/25/the-fbi-admits-to-having-informants-at-january-6th-protest-n447808. (5/23/22).

Borter, Gabriella, Joseph Ax, and Joseph Tanfani. "School boards get death threats amid rage over race, gender, mask policies." *Reuters*, February 15, 2022. https://www.reuters.com/investigates/special-report/usa-education-threats/?fbclid=IwAR0M-P7wRjRMfCuAldIbOizQy04gPurXhxBM-_g7Z_QUi-3u0BmroawiCs.

Bossie, David. "Jan. 6 committee abusing its power." *Washington Times*, January 31, 2022. https://www.washingtontimes.com/news/2022/jan/31/jan-6-committee-abusing-its-power/. (7/29/22).

Bour, Hayley Milon. "Northam: Masks Required in All Virginia Schools." *Loudoun Now*, August 12, 2021. https://loudounnow.com/2021/08/12/northam-masks-required-in-all-virginia-schools/. (5/23/22).

Bovard, James. "The Coming 'January 6' Train Wreck." *The American Conservative*, July 22, 2021. https://www.theamericanconservative.com/articles/the-coming-january-6-train-wreck/. (5/25/22).

Bowden, Ebony. "Washington Post settles $250M suit with Covington teen Nick Sandmann." *New York Post*, July 24, 2020. https://nypost.com/2020/07/24/washington-post-settles-250m-suit-with-covington-teen-nick-sandmann/. (4/17/22).

Bowden, John. "Twitter CEO Jack Dorsey: I 'fully admit' our bias is 'more left-leaning.'" *Hill*, August 18, 2018. https://thehill.com/policy/technology/402495-twitter-ceo-jack-dorsey-i-fully-admit-our-bias-is-more-left-leaning. (3/22/22).

Boyd, Jordan, "Biden Ignores Chauvin Trial Judge's Admonishment About Jury Intimidation And Tampering From Politicians," *Federalist*, April 20, 2021. https://thefederalist.com/2021/04/20/biden-ignores-chauvin-trial-judges-admonishment-about-jury-intimidation-and-tampering-from-politicians/. (2/16/22).

———. "Corporate Media Is Hating On Musk's Twitter Bid Because They Hate Free Thought."

Federalist, April 19, 2022. https://thefederalist.com/2022/04/19/corporate-media-is-hating-on-musks-twitter-bid-because-they-hate-free-thought/. (7/20/22).

———. "Federal Judge Releases BLM Capitol Rioter Without Bail." *Federalist*, January 17, 2021. https://thefederalist.com/2021/01/07/federal-judge-releases-blm-capitol-rioter-without-bail/. (5/25/22).

———. "Ridiculous AP 'Fact Check' Claims School Boards Association Didn't Ask Biden To Label Parents As 'Domestic Terrorists.'" *Federalist*, October 6, 2021. https://thefederalist.com/2021/10/06/ridiculous-ap-fact-check-claims-school-boards-association-didnt-ask-biden-to-label-parents-as-domestic-terrorists/. (4/5/22).

———. "Twitter Allows Actual Hacked Doxxing of Freedom Convoy Donors After Censoring Hunter Biden Reporting." *Federalist*, February 16, 2022. https://thefederalist.com/2022/02/16/twitter-allows-actual-hacked-doxxing-of-freedom-convoy-donors-after-censoring-hunter-biden-reporting/. (3/22/22).

Boyle, Matthew. "Exclusive — True the Vote conducting massive clandestine voter fraud investigation." *Breitbart*, August 24, 2021. https://www.truethevote.org/news-posts/the-breitbart-article-true-the-vote-update.

Branca, Andrew. "Ahmaud Arbery Case: Seven Facts the Jury Will (Probably) Never Hear." *Legal Insurrection*, October 17, 2021. https://legalinsurrection.com/2021/10/ahmaud-arbery-case-seven-facts-the-jury-will-probably-never-hear/. (5/23/22).

Brasch, Ben. "Fulton County election results delayed after pipe bursts in room with ballots." *Atlanta Journal-Constitution*, November 3, 2020. https://www.ajc.com/news/atlanta-news/fulton-election-results-delayed-after-pipe-bursts-in-room-with-ballots/4T3KPQV7PBEX3JVAIGJBNBSVJY/.

Braynard, Matthew. "Expert Report of Matthew Braynard." https://cdn.factcheck.org/UploadedFiles/BraynardReport.pdf.

"Debunking the Voter Fraud Myth." *Brennan Center*, January 31, 2017. https://www.brennancenter.org/our-work/research-reports/debunking-voter-fraud-myth. (7/20/22).

Brennan, Margaret, and Christina Ruffini. "U.S. preparing to withdraw all personnel from Ukraine capital within 48 hours, sources say." *CBS News*, February 13, 2022. https://www.cbsnews.com/news/ukraine-us-withdraws-personnel/.

"'2 Weeks To Flatten the Curve' to 'Vaccinated Only.'" Bright Light News. https://brightlightnews.com/2-weeks-to-flatten-the-curve-to-vaccinated-only/. (8/10/22).

Brooks, Daryl M., and Stephen Martino. *37 Days: The disenfranchisement of a Philadelphia poll worker*. Independently published, 2020.

Brown, Elizabeth Nolan. "January 6 Defendant Who Says He Thought He Was Allowed in Capitol Beats Charges." *Reason*, April 7, 2022. https://reason.com/2022/04/07/january-6-defendant-who-says-he-thought-he-was-allowed-in-capitol-beats-charges/. (4/7/22).

Brown, Hayes. "Trump crams one more racist policy into his final days as president: Even on his way out, Trump continues to place white people's grievances over national security." *MSNBC*, November 24, 2020. https://www.msnbc.com/opinion/trump-crams-one-last-racist-policy-his-final-days-president-n1248736. (4/20/22).

Brown, Lee. "Taliban has billions in US weapons, including Black Hawks and up to 600K rifles." *New York Post*, August 20, 2021. https://nypost.com/2021/08/20/us-left-billions-in-weapons-in-afghanistan-with-black-hawks-in-talibans-hands/.

Brubaker, Daniel. "Democrats to America: 'You'd better put some ice on that.'" *danielbrubaker.com*, November 11, 2020. https://www.danielbrubaker.com/social-and-political/rule-of-law/democrats-to-america-youd-better-put-some-ice-on-that/.

———. "Liberation Theology," in *Religion and Contemporary Politics: A Global Encyclopedia*, ed. Timothy J. Demy and Jeffrey M. Shaw. Santa Barbara: ABC-CLIO, 2019, vol. 1. 464-467.

Brubaker, Elizabeth. Personal conversation. January 2022.

Brueck, Hilary. "Getting to herd immunity will require 90% of people to be vaccinated against COVID-19, experts say." *Business Insider*, August 27, 2021. https://www.businessinsider.com/delta-variant-herd-immunity-90-percent-2021-8?op=1. (2/16/22).

Bundgaard, Henning. "Effectiveness of Adding a Mask Recommendation to Other Public Health Measures to Prevent SARS-CoV-2 Infection in Danish Mask Wearers: A Randomized

Controlled Trial." *Annals of Internal Medicine*, March 2021. https://www.acpjournals.org/doi/10. 7326/M20-6817. (5/23/22).

Burack, Bobby. "AOC Brags She Helped Stop Bill To Protect Supreme Court Justices Following Kavanaugh Assassination Attempt." *OutKick*, June 10, 2022. https://www.outkick.com/aoc-brags-she-helped-stop-bill-to-protect-supreme-court-justices-following-kavanaugh-assassination-attempt/. (6/10/22).

Burk, Eric. "Virginia School Board Association Withdraws from National Association that Asked Biden to Use Federal Agencies to Respond to Threats." *Virginia Star*, November 23, 2021. https://thevirginiastar.com/2021/11/23/virginia-school-board-association-withdraws-from-national-association-that-asked-biden-to-use-federal-agencies-to-respond-to-threats/. (4/5/22).

Burns, Alexander, Matt Flegenheimer, Jasmine C. Lee, Lisa Lerer, and Jonathan Martin. "Who's running for President in 2020?" *New York Times*, April 8, 2020. https://www.nytimes.com/interactive/2019/us/politics/2020-presidential-candidates.html. (5/23/22).

Burns, Robert. "Pentagon admits deadly Kabul strike was an error." *Associated Press,* September 17, 2021. https://apnews.com/article/pentagon-calls-deadly-kabul-strike-an-error-25e2b83a9a0ae9a95d1aac71fe5f4ca7. (4/19/22).

Burns, Steve. "Top Ten Dow Jones Industrial Average Drops in History." New Trader U, March 10, 2020. https://www.newtraderu.com/2020/03/10/top-ten-dow-jones-industrial-average-drops-in-history/. (2/16/22).

Butler, Chris. "Report: Former Tennessee Congressman and Zach Wamp Helped Remove Donald Trump from White House." *Tennessee Star*, February 8, 2021. https://tennesseestar.com/2021/02/08/report-former-tennessee-congressman-and-nevertrumper-zach-wamp-helped-remove-donald-trump-from-white-house/. (6/28/22).

———. "Zach Wamp Praises Liz Cheney, Trashes Donald Trump." *Tennessee Star*, December 25, 2021. https://tennesseestar.com/2021/12/25/zach-wamp-praises-liz-cheney-trashes-donald-trump/. (6/28/22).

Bynum, Russ. "Arbery case hate-crime plea pulled." *Northwest Arkansas Democrat Gazette*, February 5, 2022. https://www.nwaonline.com/news/2022/feb/05/arbery-case-hate-crime-plea-pulled/. (5/23/22).

Byrne, Patrick. *The Deep Rig: How Election Fraud Cost Donald J. Trump the White House, By a Man Who did not Vote for Him.* Independently published. 2021.

Calhoun, George. "Part 1: Beijing Is Intentionally Underreporting China's Covid Death Rate." *Forbes*, January 2, 2022. https://www.forbes.com/sites/georgecalhoun/2022/01/02/beijing-is-intentionally-underreporting-chinas-covid-death-rate-part-1/?sh=478892ae4352. (4/12/22).

Camarota, Steven A.. "Illegal Immigrants Get $10.5 Billion from Child Tax Credit in Reconciliation; More than Previously Estimated: Illegals with both U.S.-born & illegal immigrant children will benefit, as will recent border-crossers." *Center for Immigration Studies*, November 9, 2021. https://cis.org/Camarota/Illegal-Immigrants-Get-105-Billion-Child-Tax-Credit-Reconciliation-More-Previously.

Campbell, Colin. "Barbara Walters to Donald Trump: 'Are you a bigot?'." *Business Insider*, December 8, 2015. https://www.businessinsider.com/barbara-walters-donald-trump-muslim-plan-bigot-2015-12?op=1. (7/20/22).

Caralle, Katelyn. "Antony Blinken rejects comparison of Afghanistan to Saigon and blames 'inability of Afghan security forces' for Taliban takeover as Republicans say the buck stops with Biden." *Daily Mail*, August 15, 2021. https://www.dailymail.co.uk/news/article-9895577/Blinken-blames-inability-Afghan-forces-Taliban-takeover-GOP-says-buck-stops-Biden.html. (5/31/22).

Caralle, Katelyn, and Elizabeth Elkind. "Nancy Pelosi insists No Supreme Court Justices are 'in danger' after Democrats blocked a bill to give them more security - hours after armed man 'threatened to kill Brett Kavanaugh.'" *Daily Mail*, June 9, 2022. https://www.dailymail.co.uk/news/article-10900319/House-Dems-BLOCK-security-Supreme-Court-justices-arrested-man-threatening-Kavanaugh.html. (6/10/22).

Carlson, Jeff. "The Small World of Voting Machine Certification." November 20, 2020. https://themarketswork.com/2020/11/20/the-small-world-of-voting-machine-certification/.

Carlson, Tucker. "Tucker Carlson: Government agents may have helped organize the Jan. 6

Capitol riot." *Fox News*, June 16, 2021. https://www.foxnews.com/opinion/tucker-carlson-government-agents-helped-organize-capitol-riot?fbclid=IwAR2Arm6-uxkxDHYX7HP5C1Tog AzIbNSgpOgR4i1iDbE-bOWfN2uO6BSEpP8. (2/25/22).

Carr, Brendan. "Twitter Suppresses Speech by Calling It 'Manipulated Media': Imagine going after LBJ's 'Daisy Girl' ad lest viewers think the girl actually died in a nuclear strike." *Wall Street Journal*, March 17, 2020. https://www.wsj.com/articles/twitter-suppresses-speech-by-call ing-it-manipulated-media-11584485145. (7/20/22).

Caspani, Maria, and Julia Harte. "New York City mandates COVID-19 vaccine for teachers in largest U.S. school district." *Reuters*, August 23, 2021. https://www.reuters.com/world/us/new-york-city-mandates-covid-19-vaccine-public-school-teachers-staff-mayor-2021-08-23/.

Cathey, Libby. "What is the Electoral Count Act and why does it present problems?" *ABC News*, January 31, 2022. https://abcnews.go.com/Politics/electoral-count-act-present-problems/story? id=82396332. (5/18/22).

Catron, David. "About Atlanta's Election Day Pipe Dream." *American Spectator*, November 13, 2020. https://spectator.org/pipe-burst-georgia-election/.

Caulfield, Mike, Kayla Duskin, Stephen Prochaska, Scott Philips Johnson, Annie Denton, Zarine Khazarian, and Kate Starbird. "The rise of 'trafficking' language in ballot collection narra-tives." *Center for an Informed Public*. University of Washington, April 30, 2022. https://www.cip. uw.edu/2022/04/30/ballot-trafficking-collection-narratives/.

Cavallaro, Olivia. "As Expected, Biden Administration Now Pushing Forced Vaccinations Following FDA Approval of Pfizer Jab." *Christianity Daily*, August 24, 2021. https://www.chris tianitydaily.com/articles/13023/20210824/as-expected-biden-administration-now-pushing-forced-vaccinations-following-fda-approval-of-pfizer-jab.htm.

Caygle, Heather, Burgess Everett, and Kyle Cheney. "Trump repeats debunked voter fraud claim at meeting with Hill leaders." *Politico*, January 23, 2017. https://www.politico.com/story/2017/01/donald-trump-fraud-claims-234083.

"Texas Social Worker Charged With 134 Counts Involving Election Fraud." *CBS DFW*, November 6, 2020. https://dfw.cbslocal.com/2020/11/06/texas-social-worker-charged-counts-election-fraud/.

"Moderna Says Its COVID Vaccine Is 96% Effective In Protecting 12 To 17-Year-Old Kids." *CBS News*, May 6, 2021. https://www.cbsnews.com/sanfrancisco/news/moderna-covid-vaccine-teens-kids-trial-effective/. (5/18/22).

"Obama's ACORN Connection To Voter Fraud." *CBS News*, October 14, 2008. https://www. cbsnews.com/news/obamas-acorn-connection-to-voter-fraud/. (4/1/22).

"Trump On North Korea Missile Launch: 'We Will Take Care Of It'." *CBS News*, November 28, 2017. https://www.cbsnews.com/newyork/news/north-korea-ballistic-missile/. (5/26/22).

"Trump's 'covfefe' tweet sparks confusion on social media." *CBS News*, May 31, 2017. https://www. cbsnews.com/news/trump-covfefe-tweet/. (6/28/22).

"CDC calls on Americans to wear masks to prevent COVID-19 spread." Centers for Disease Control and Prevention, July 14, 2020. https://www.cdc.gov/media/releases/2020/p0714-ameri cans-to-wear-masks.html. (5/23/22).

"Estimated COVID-19 Infections, Symptomatic Illnesses, Hospitalizations, and Deaths in the United States." Centers for Disease Control and Prevention, updated October 2, 2021. https:// www.cdc.gov/coronavirus/2019-ncov/cases-updates/burden.html.

"Influenza (Flu): Past Seasons." Centers for Disease Control and Prevention, (page last reviewed October 1, 2020). https://www.cdc.gov/flu/about/burden/past-seasons.html. (5/23/22).

"Estimates of Learning Loss in the 2019-2020 School Year." Center for Research on Education Outcomes, Stanford University, October 2020. https://credo.stanford.edu/sites/g/files/sbiyb j6481/f/short_brief_on_learning_loss_final_v.3.pdf.

Chaitlin, Daniel. "Jan. 6 committee caught misportraying another text message to Mark Mead-ows." *Washington Examiner*, December 17, 2021. https://www.washingtonexaminer.com/news/house/jan-6-committee-caught-misportraying-another-text-message-to-mark-meadows. (4/17/22).

Chakraborty, Barnini. "FBI informants had bigger role in Whitmer kidnap plot than thought: report." *Washington Examiner,* July 21, 2021. https://www.washingtonexaminer.com/news/fbi-informants-bigger-role-whitmer-kidnap-plot. (5/23/22).

Chamlee, Virginia. "Ginni Thomas Might Get a Jan. 6 Subpoena: 'Hope It Doesn't Get to That'." *People*, July 25, 2022. https://people.com/politics/ginni-thomas-might-get-jan-6-subpoena/. (7/29/22).

Chapman, Steve. "Donald Trump is a profoundly incompetent president." *Chicago Tribune*, June 7, 2017. https://www.chicagotribune.com/columns/steve-chapman/ct-donald-trump-incompetent-president-chapman-perspec-20201010-column.html. (4/20/22).

Chappell, Bill. "Architect Of The Capitol Outlines $30 Million In Damages From Pro-Trump Riot." NPR, February 24, 2021. https://www.npr.org/sections/insurrection-at-the-capitol/2021/02/24/970977612/architect-of-the-capitol-outlines-30-million-in-damages-from-pro-trump-riot. (5/25/22).

Cheney, Kyle. "Capitol Police provided more than 14,000 hours of Jan. 6 footage to lawmakers." *Politico*, March 29, 2021. https://www.politico.com/news/2021/03/29/capitol-police-jan6-footage-478439. (5/25/22).

Cheney, Liz. Twitter post, June 10, 2022, 2:45 p.m., https://twitter.com/RepLizCheney/status/1535332409738153984.

Cho, Winston. "Twitter's Case Against Elon Musk Might Be Tougher Than Expected." *Hollywood Reporter*, July 15, 2022. https://www.hollywoodreporter.com/business/business-news/twitter-case-lawsuit-elon-musk-1235180919/. (7/20/22).

Cillizza, Chris. "What is 'Trump Derangement Syndrome' - and do you have it?" *CNN*, July 20, 2018. https://www.cnn.com/2018/07/09/politics/trump-derangement-syndrome/index.html. (3/18/22).

Clapper, Jim, Mike Hayden, Leon Panetta, John Brennan, Thomas Finger, Rick Ledgett, John McLaughlin, Michael Morell et al. "Public Statement on the Hunter Biden Emails." October 19, 2020. https://www.politico.com/f/?id=00000175-4393-d7aa-af77-579f9b330000. (3/21/22).

Clark, John. "Subject: Tomorrow - Mask Enforcement." Email correspondence. February 1, 2022, 3:23 p.m..

Cleveland, Margot. "Four Possible Reasons The FBI Raided A Former President." *Federalist*, August 11, 2022. https://thefederalist.com/2022/08/11/four-possible-reasons-the-fbi-raided-a-former-president/.

———. "Joe Biden's Voicemail To Hunter Means It's Time To Appoint A Special Counsel." *Federalist*, June 29, 2022. https://thefederalist.com/2022/06/29/joe-bidens-voicemail-to-hunter-means-its-time-to-appoint-a-special-counsel/. (7/1/22).

———. "Whistleblower Videos Capture Pennsylvania Election Officials Destroying Evidence." *Federalist*, November 19, 2021. https://thefederalist.com/2021/11/19/whistleblower-videos-capture-pennsylvania-election-officials-destroying-evidence/.

Cohen, Adriana. "Democrats Forget What They Were Saying About Coronavirus In Early 2020." *GOPUSA*, September 11, 2020. https://www.gopusa.com/democrats-forget-what-they-were-saying-about-coronavirus-in-early-2020/. (4/6/22).

Cohen, Kelly. "Tokyo 2020 Olympics officially postponed until 2021." *ESPN*, March 24, 2020. https://www.espn.com/olympics/story/_/id/28946033/tokyo-olympics-officially-postponed-2021. (5/23/22).

Cohen, Marshall. "The Steele dossier: A reckoning." *CNN*, November 18, 2021. https://www.cnn.com/2021/11/18/politics/steele-dossier-reckoning/index.html.

Collins, Ben, and Brandy Zadrozny. "Twitter permanently suspends President Donald Trump." *NBC News*, January 8, 2021. https://www.nbcnews.com/tech/tech-news/twitter-permanently-bans-president-donald-trump-n1253588. (3/22/22).

Concha, Joe. "CNN, MSNBC say 'racist' more than 1,100 times regarding Trump 'go back' tweet since Sunday." *Hill*, July 16, 2019. https://thehill.com/homenews/media/453300-cnn-msnbc-say-racist-636-times-regarding-trump-go-back-tweet-since-sunday/. (4/20/22).

Condon, Stephanie. "Biden's in-your-face debate style: Just 'Joe being Joe'?" *CBS News*, https://www.cbsnews.com/news/bidens-in-your-face-debate-style-just-joe-being-joe/. (6/7/22).

"The Child Tax Credit: Legislative History." *Congressional Research Service*, Updated December 23, 2021. https://crsreports.congress.gov/product/pdf/R/R45124.

Coren, Anna, Sandi Sidhu, Abul Basir Bina, and Hilary Whiteman. "The Taliban knocked on her door 3 times. The fourth time, they killed her." *CNN*, August 18, 2021. https://edition.cnn.com/2021/08/17/asia/afghanistan-women-taliban-intl-hnk-dst/index.html. (4/19/22).

Corsi, Jerome R. *The Obama Nation.* New York: Threshold Editions, 2008.

———. *Where's the Birth Certificate? The Case That Barack Obama Is Not Eligible To Be President.* New York: WND Books, 2011.

Cox, Chelsey. "Fact check: Claim that voting noncitizens affected 2020 election outcome is unverified." *USA Today*, November 19, 2020. https://www.usatoday.com/story/news/factcheck/2020/11/19/fact-check-claim-voting-noncitizens-2020-election-unverified/6237115002/. (4/17/22).

Cox, Chelsey, Matthew Brown, David Jackson, Savannah Behrmann, Michael Collins, N'dea Yancey-Bragg, Joey Garrison, Michelle Shen, Ella Lee, and Ledyard King. "Jan. 6 review: Biden blasts Trump in speech, Dick Cheney hailed in surprise Capitol visit for ceremony." *USA Today*, January 7, 2022. https://www.usatoday.com/story/news/politics/2022/01/06/january-6-capitol-riot-live-updates/9046664002/. (2/25/22).

Cox, Louis Anthony Jr., Tom Davis, S. Stanley Young, Eric Quinnell, Robert Wilgus, Thomas Davis, and William M. Briggs. "Michigan 2020 Voting Analysis Report." November 27, 2020. https://election-integrity.info/MI_2020_Voter_Analysis_Report.pdf.

Crane, Emily. "The cost of the Afghanistan war: Lives, money and equipment lost." *New York Post*, August 31, 2021.

———. "Hundreds of 'murder hornets' found in huge Washington nest." *New York Post*, August 27, 2021. https://nypost.com/2021/08/27/hundreds-of-murder-hornets-found-in-huge-washington-nest/. (5/23/22).

———. "NIH admits US funded gain-of-function in Wuhan — despite Fauci's denials." *New York Post*, October 21, 2021. https://nypost.com/2021/10/21/nih-admits-us-funded-gain-of-function-in-wuhan-despite-faucis-repeated-denials/. (4/7/22).

Crilly, Rob. "Trump under pressure to condemn violence after his supporters attack Capitol." *Washington Examiner*, January 6, 2021. https://www.washingtonexaminer.com/news/donald-trump-pressure-condemn-violence-capitol-twitter-rage. (5/25/22).

Crilly, Rob, and Ariel Zilber. "As Biden repeats claim that 'nobody could have known' Afghan Army would collapse, bombshell transcript from July reveals he pressured Afghan President Ghani to create 'perception' Taliban wasn't winning 'Whether It's True Or Not.'" *Daily Mail*, August 31, 2021. https://www.dailymail.co.uk/news/article-9945031/Biden-told-Afghan-President-needed-change-perception-Talibans-rapid-advance.html?fbclid=IwAR3Z7n8NhGNaPFhUi_ZoCn7ye_tGQkuvwcP8GqeeJmBOWsihhs6IyXgU-lY.

Crowder, Steven, "Exposed: Wikipedia's Bias Tested and Proven! | Louder with Crowder," January 27, 2022. YouTube video. https://www.youtube.com/watch?v=Iv7s_ydrdHE.

Crowley, Michael, and Tyler Pager. "Trump Urges Russia to hack Clinton's email." *Politico*, July 27, 2016. https://www.politico.com/story/2016/07/trump-putin-no-relationship-226282. (4/5/22).

Curl, Joseph. "CNBC Touts Triple-Masking For Best Protection Against COVID-19." *Daily Wire*, January 27, 2021. https://www.dailywire.com/news/cnbc-touts-triple-masking-for-best-protection-against-covid-19. (2/16/22).

"Joint statement from Elections Infrastructure Government Coordinating Council & the Election Infrastructure Sector Coordinating Executive Committees." Cybersecurity and Infrastructure Security Agency, November 12, 2020. https://www.cisa.gov/news/2020/11/12/joint-statement-elections-infrastructure-government-coordinating-council-election. (5/25/22).

Dale, Daniel. "Fact check: White House tweet falsely claims 'there was no vaccine available' when Biden took office." *CNN*, May 13, 2022. https://www.cnn.com/2022/05/13/politics/fact-check-white-house-no-vaccine-available-tweet/index.html. (5/18/22).

Daley, Kevin. "Conservative activist talks to the Free Beacon about her work and her husband, Supreme Court justice Clarence Thomas." *Washington Free Beacon*, March 14, 2022. https://freebeacon.com/courts/exclusive-ginni-thomas-sets-the-record-straight-on-january-6/. (7/29/22).

Damore, James. "Google's Ideological Echo Chamber." July 2017. https://s3.documentcloud.org/documents/3914586/Googles-Ideological-Echo-Chamber.pdf. (6/29/22).

Davidson, John Daniel. "The 2024 Election Is Being Rigged Right Now In Plain Sight." *Federalist*, August 12, 2022. https://thefederalist.com/2022/08/12/the-2024-election-is-being-rigged-right-now-in-plain-sight/.

Davis, Jack. "Watch the Blatantly Satirical Video Trump Posted That Twitter Has Labeled

'Manipulated Media.'" *Western Journal*, June 19, 2020. https://www.westernjournal.com/watch-blatantly-satirical-video-trump-posted-twitter-labeled-manipulated-media/. (3/22/22).

Davis, Sean. "During January 6 Hearing, Schiff Doctored Text Messages Between Mark Meadows And Rep. Jim Jordan." *Federalist*, December 15, 2021. https://thefederalist.com/2021/12/15/during-january-6-hearing-schiff-doctored-text-messages-between-mark-meadows-and-rep-jim-jordan/. (6/28/22).

———. "Read The Google Diversity Memo That Everyone Is Freaking Out About," *Federalist*, August 8, 2017. https://thefederalist.com/2017/08/08/read-the-google-diversity-memo-that-that-everyone-is-freaking-out-about/. (6/29/22).

De Lea, Brittany. "Biden banks on Hollywood support in final days before 2020 election." *Fox News*, November 1, 2020. https://www.foxnews.com/politics/biden-celebrity-endorsements-2020-election. (5/16/22).

Dempsey, Matt, and Katie Brown. "Watch: Sec. Chu refuses to retract statement that the goal is to boost price of gas to levels in Europe." U.S. Senate Committee on Environment & Public Works, March 1, 2012. https://www.epw.senate.gov/public/index.cfm/2012/3/post-d06a83f9-802a-23ad-421c-d407d1d706d2.

Brady Dennis, Mark Berman, and Hannah Sampson. "21 people test positive for coronavirus on California cruise ship, out of 46 tested so far." *Washington Post*, March 7, 2020. https://www.washingtonpost.com/health/dozens-of-passengers-on-a-stranded-cruise-ship-are-infected-by-coronavirus-that-number-could-soon-grow/2020/03/06/17cf1974-5fdb-11ea-b014-4fafa866bb81_story.html.

DeSoto, Randy. "Levin Calls for Special Counsel to Investigate 'Corrupt' Biden Family, Says AG Garland Cannot Be Trusted." *Western Journal*, April 6, 2022. https://www.westernjournal.com/levin-calls-special-counsel-investigate-corrupt-biden-family-says-ag-garland-cannot-trusted/. (6/8/22).

Dierenbach, Karl. "'Flattening The Curve' Has Become A Massive Bait And Switch." *Federalist*, June 29, 2020. https://thefederalist.com/2020/06/29/flattening-the-curve-has-become-a-massive-bait-and-switch/. (5/23/22).

diGenova, Joseph E.. "The Politicization of the FBI." *Imprimis*, vol. 47, no. 2 (February 2018). https://imprimis.hillsdale.edu/the-politicization-of-the-fbi/.

Dimock, Michael, and John Gramlich. "How America Changed During Donald Trump's Presidency." *Pew Research*, January 29, 2021. https://www.pewresearch.org/2021/01/29/how-america-changed-during-donald-trumps-presidency/.

Dinan, Stephen. "Judge approves $3.5 million settlement from IRS to tea party groups." *Washington Times,* August 9, 2018. https://www.washingtontimes.com/news/2018/aug/9/judge-approves-35-million-settlement-irs-tea-party/.

Ditch, David, Mike Gonzalez, Hans von Spakovsky, and Erin Dwinell. "Biden Administration Implements a Racial Spoils System." *Daily Signal*, May 31, 2022. https://www.dailysignal.com/2022/05/31/biden-administration-implements-a-racial-spoils-system/. (6/1/22).

———. "President Biden's 'Equity Action Plans' Reveal Radical, Divisive Agenda." *Heritage Foundation*, May 25, 2022. https://www.heritage.org/progressivism/report/president-bidens-equity-action-plans-reveal-radical-divisive-agenda. (6/1/22).

Doherty, Carroll. "Key takeaways on Americans' growing partisan divide over political values." *Pew Research Center*, October 5, 2017. https://www.pewresearch.org/fact-tank/2017/10/05/take-aways-on-americans-growing-partisan-divide-over-political-values/.

Domonoske, Camila. "2 Activists Who Secretly Recorded Planned Parenthood Face New Felony Charges." *NPR*, March 29, 2017. https://www.npr.org/sections/thetwo-way/2015/07/15/423212004/undercover-video-targets-planned-parenthood. (4/1/22).

Doornbos, Caitlin. "DoD Inspector General Launches Investigation into Kabul Drone Strike that Killed 10 Civilians." *Stars and Stripes,* September 24, 2021. https://www.stripes.com/theaters/us/2021-09-24/kabul-drone-strike-investigation-afghanistan-dod-inspector-general-3005041.html. (4/19/22).

Dorman, Sam. "Trump's top advisers wanted him to fire Comey early on: book." *Fox News*, September 8, 2020. https://www.foxnews.com/politics/trump-advisers-comey-clinton.

Dougherty, Jon. "Bomber who killed 13 U.S. soldiers at Kabul airport released from Bagram prison by Taliban thanks to Biden's plan; report." *BizPacReview*, September 20, 2021. https://

www.bizpacreview.com/2021/09/20/bomber-who-killed-13-u-s-soldiers-at-kabul-airport-released-from-bagram-prison-by-taliban-thanks-to-bidens-plan-report-1137062/. (4/19/22).

Downs, Rebecca. "Kamala Harris Can't Be Bothered with Proper Border Visit, But She Did Go to Honduran President's Inauguration." *Townhall*, January 27, 2022. https://townhall.com/tipsheet/rebeccadowns/2022/01/27/kamala-harris-cant-be-bothered-with-proper-border-visit-but-she-did-go-to-hondura-n2602482. (4/19/22).

Dreher, Rod. "The Rest Of The Jacob Blake Story." *American Conservative*, August 29, 2020. https://www.theamericanconservative.com/dreher/kenosha-kyle-rittenhouse-the-rest-of-the-jacob-blake-story/. (2/18/22).

Droney, Pat. "New court filings show FBI had at least 12 'informants' in Whitmer 'kidnapping' plot." *Law Enforcement Today*, July 22, 2021. https://www.lawenforcementtoday.com/new-court-filings-show-fbi-had-at-least-12-informants-in-whitmer-kidnapping-plot/. (5/23/22).

———. "Thousands of cops were injured, over $2 billion in damage during Floyd riots. Where are the 'congressional hearings'?" *Law Enforcement Today*, July 28, 2021. https://www.lawenforcementtoday.com/thousands-of-cops-were-injured-over-2-billion-in-damage-during-floyd-riots-where-are-the-congressional-hearings/. (5/25/22).

Droz, John Jr.. "2020 US Presidential Election Related Lawsuits." https://election-integrity.info/2020_Election_Cases.htm.

———. "2020 Presidential Election Lawsuits — the Facts." https://election-integrity.info/2020_Election_Lawsuits.pdf. (7/26/22).

Dugdale, L.S. "COVID-19: Lonely Dying and Dying Alone." *Psychology Today*, April 5, 2021. https://www.psychologytoday.com/us/blog/the-lost-art/202104/covid-19-lonely-dying-and-dying-alone. (5/23/22).

Dunleavy, Jerry. "Ex-FBI lawyer gets probation for Carter Page FISA email deception in Durham investigation." *Washington Examiner*, January 29, 2021. https://www.washingtonexaminer.com/news/durham-investigation-kevin-clinesmith-probation. (5/23/22).

———. "Jan. 6 committee highlights Barr calling Trump fraud claims 'bulls***.'" *Washington Examiner*, June 13, 2022. https://www.washingtonexaminer.com/politics/committee-highlights-barr-trump-fraud-claims. (6/14/22).

Durkee, Alison. "Trump And The GOP Have Now Lost More Than 50 Post-Election Lawsuits." *Forbes*, December 8, 2020. https://www.forbes.com/sites/alisondurkee/2020/12/08/trump-and-the-gop-have-now-lost-50-post-election-lawsuits/?sh=df9017829606. (7/26/22).

Ebbs, Stephanie. "Police did not clear Lafayette Square so Trump could hold 'Bible' photo op: Watchdog." *ABC News*, June 10, 2021. https://abcnews.go.com/Politics/police-clear-lafayette-park-area-trump-hold-bible/story?id=78171712. (3/15/22).

Ebbs, Stephanie, and Benjamin Siegel. "Police did not clear Lafayette Square so Trump could hold 'Bible' photo op: Watchdog." *ABC News*, June 10, 2021. https://abcnews.go.com/Politics/police-clear-lafayette-park-area-trump-hold-bible/story?id=78171712. (3/15/22).

Egan, Lauren. "Barr says no evidence of widespread fraud, defying Trump." *NBC News*, December 1, 2020. https://www.nbcnews.com/politics/white-house/barr-says-no-evidence-widespread-voter-fraud-defying-trump-n1249581. (7/20/22).

Eggers, Eric. *Fraud: How the Left Plans to Steal the Next Election*. Washington, DC: Regnery, 2018. 7-8.

Ekins, Emily. "Is Cancel Culture Real? New Poll Says Americans Are Self-Censoring: Nearly a third of Americans are afraid for their jobs." *National Interest*, July 26, 2020. https://nationalinterest.org/blog/reboot/cancel-culture-real-new-poll-says-americans-are-self-censoring-165471. (2/25/22).

———. "Poll: 62% of Americans Say They Have Political Views They're Afraid to Share." *Cato Institute*, July 22, 2020. https://www.cato.org/survey-reports/poll-62-americans-say-they-have-political-views-theyre-afraid-share. (2/25/22).

Elder, Larry. "Twitter Permanently Bans Trump. Why Do Hillary Clinton, Jimmy Carter, Harry Reid Get a Pass?" *Daily Signal*, January 21, 2021. https://www.dailysignal.com/2021/01/21/twitter-permanently-bans-trump-why-do-hillary-clinton-jimmy-carter-harry-reid-get-a-pass/.

Ellyatt, Holly. "Here's why herd immunity from Covid is 'mythical' with the delta variant." *CNBC*, August 12, 2021. https://www.cnbc.com/2021/08/12/herd-immunity-is-mythical-with-the-covid-delta-variant-experts-say.html. (5/23/22).

————. "Russian forces invade Ukraine." *CNBC*, February 24, 2022. https://www.cnbc.com/2022/02/24/russian-forces-invade-ukraine.html. (7/20/22).

Emmons, Libby. "Breaking: Milley undermined Trump, told China he would warn them if US would attack." *Post Millennial,* September 14, 2021. https://thepostmillennial.com/breaking-milley-undermined-trump-told-china-he-would-warn-them-if-us-would-attack. (5/23/22).

————. "Gaetz, Greene call on FBI to release 14,000 hours of footage from Jan 6." *Post Millennial,* September 27, 2021. https://thepostmillennial.com/gaetz-greene-fbi-14000-footage-jan-6. (5/25/22).

Enders, David. "6 months after Beirut blast: Rebuilding slow, prosecution stalled." *Al Jazeera,* February 3, 2021. https://www.aljazeera.com/news/2021/2/3/six-months-after-beirut-port-explosion-rebuilding-slow-reconstruction-stalled.

English, Nellie. "'Donald wants a participation trophy': Even GOP pundits are mocking Trump for being a sore loser." *Front Page Live,* November 12, 2020. https://frontpagelive.com/2020/11/12/trump-throws-a-tantrum/. (5/25/22).

Erb, Kelly Phillips. "IRS Targeting Scandal: Citizens United, Lois Lerner And The $20M Tax Saga That Won't Go Away." *Forbes,* June 24, 2016. https://www.forbes.com/sites/kellyphillipserb/2016/06/24/irs-targeting-scandal-citizens-united-lois-lerner-and-the-20m-tax-saga-that-wont-go-away/?sh=6c875469bcd1. (2/16/22).

Ernst, Douglas. "Biden links Kyle Rittenhouse to white supremacists; Lin Wood vows to 'rip Joe into shreds.'" *Washington Times,* September 30, 2020. https://www.washingtontimes.com/news/2020/sep/30/biden-links-kyle-rittenhouse-to-white-supremacists/. (2/18/22).

Evans, Zachary. "Alan Dershowitz Claims Giuliani Raid Was Political Revenge, Likens U.S. to 'Banana Republic.'" *National Review*, May 3, 2021. https://www.nationalreview.com/news/alan-dershowitz-labels-u-s-banana-republic-after-giuliani-raid/.

"Working to Stop Misinformation and False News." Facebook/Meta, April 7, 2017. https://www.facebook.com/formedia/blog/working-to-stop-misinformation-and-false-news. (4/1/22).

Fan, Wenxin. "China's Campaign to Crush Democracy in Hong Kong Is Working." *Wall Street Journal,* February 25, 2021. https://www.wsj.com/articles/chinas-campaign-to-crush-democracy-in-hong-kong-is-working-11614268174. (5/23/22).

Fang, Frank. "Hong Kong Leader Silent After Beijing Says It Reserves Jurisdiction Over National Security Law." *Epoch Times,* June 16, 2020. https://www.theepochtimes.com/hong-kong-leader-silent-after-beijing-says-it-reserves-jurisdiction-over-national-security-law_3389854.html. (5/23/22).

Farah, Joseph. "Who was the first 'birther'." *WND,* August 3, 2022. https://www.wnd.com/2022/08/first-birther/. (8/4/22).

Farah, Niina H. "How Biden's NEPA plan could change the energy sector." *EnergyWire,* October 7, 2021. https://www.eenews.net/articles/how-bidens-nepa-plan-could-change-the-energy-sector/. (6/4/22).

Farley, Robert. "Biden's Early Statements About the Coronavirus." *FactCheck,* September 21, 2020. https://www.factcheck.org/2020/09/bidens-early-statements-about-the-coronavirus/. (4/6/22).

————. "Fact check: Trump claims massive voter fraud; here's the truth." *USA Today,* January 26, 2017.

"How to report in-kind contributions." Federal Election Commission. https://www.fec.gov/help-candidates-and-committees/filing-reports/in-kind-contributions/. (7/24/22).

"Surprise! Facebook Blacklists Trending Topics And Conservative News Outlets." *Federalist,* May 3, 2016. https://thefederalist.com/2016/05/03/surprise-facebook-blacklists-trending-topics-and-conservative-news-outlets/.

"Noncitizens, Voting Violations and U.S. Elections." *Federation for American Immigration Reform*, July 2020. https://www.fairus.org/issue/societal-impact/noncitizens-voting-violations-and-us-elections. (4/17/22).

Feldman, Noah. "By not conceding, Trump is doing extraordinary harm to America's democracy and Constitution." *Print,* November 20, 2020. https://theprint.in/world/by-not-conceding-trump-is-doing-extraordinary-harm-to-americas-democracy-and-constitution/542635/. (5/25/22).

————. "Comment: Trump's refusal to concede is legal; and damaging." *HeraldNet,* November 13,

2020. https://www.heraldnet.com/opinion/comment-trumps-refusal-to-concede-is-legal-and-damaging/. (5/25/22).

Feuerherd, Ben. "Hunter Biden's pal sentenced to prison for role in fraud scheme." *New York Post*, February 28, 2022. https://nypost.com/2022/02/28/devon-archer-sentenced-for-role-in-hunter-biden-fraud-scheme/. (3/2/22).

Ferrechio, Susan. "Wisconsin probe finds 2020 election riddled with nursing home voting fraud: 100% turnout in some facilities." *Washington Times*, March 2, 2022. https://www.washington times.com/news/2022/mar/2/wisconsin-probe-finds-2020-election-riddled-nursin/. (8/4/22).

Fichera, Angelo. "Hospital Payments and the COVID-19 Death Count." *FactCheck*, April 21, 2020. https://www.factcheck.org/2020/04/hospital-payments-and-the-covid-19-death-count/. (2/13/22).

"What Is Electoral and Voter Fraud?" *FindLaw*, last updated March 18, 2020. https://www.findlaw. com/voting/how-u-s--elections-work/what-is-electoral-and-voter-fraud-.html.

Finn, Teaganne. "Fauci blasts Rand Paul's Wuhan lab funding claim: 'You do not know what you're talking about.'" *NBC News*, July 20, 2021. https://www.nbcnews.com/politics/congress/ fauci-blasts-rand-paul-s-wuhan-lab-funding-claim-you-n1274489. (2/16/22).

Firozi, Paulina. "Tom Cotton keeps repeating a coronavirus fringe theory that scientists have disputed." *Washington Post*, February 17, 2020, https://www.washingtonpost.com/politics/ 2020/02/16/tom-cotton-coronavirus-conspiracy/. (6/16/22).

Fisher, Anthony L. "Trump is an incompetent, conspiracy theory-pushing liar who puts Americans' lives at risk." *Business Insider Nederland*, September 16, 2020. https://www.businessin sider.nl/trump-is-an-incompetent-conspiracy-theory-pushing-liar-who-puts-americans-lives-at-risk/. (4/20/22).

Flaherty, Peter. "Where Is the BLM $60 Million?" *Real Clear Politics*, February 9, 2022. https://www. realclearpolitics.com/articles/2022/02/09/where_is_the_blm_60_million_147160.html. (5/23/22).

Flood, Brian. "Minnesota newspaper lists over 360 local businesses destroyed by riots." *Fox News*, June 30, 2020. https://www.foxnews.com/media/minnesota-newspaper-lists-over-360-local-businesses-destroyed-by-riots-with-maps-specific-details-of-damage.

Flood, Brian, and Nikolas Lanum. "ABC, NBC, CBS, CNN, MSNBC ignore voicemail Joe Biden allegedly left for Hunter Biden on business dealings." *Fox News*, July 8, 2022. https://www. foxnews.com/media/abc-nbc-cbs-cnn-msnbc-voicemail-joe-biden-hunter-biden-business-dealings. (7/23/22).

Flows, Capital. "'Fast And Furious' Just Might Be President Obama's Watergate." *Forbes*, September 28, 2011. https://www.forbes.com/sites/realspin/2011/09/28/fast-and-furious-just-might-be-president-obamas-watergate/?sh=57f24dbd752a. (5/23/22).

Flynn, Karen Hobert, and Pamela Smith. "Commentary: Why voting systems must be as secure as the U.S. power grid." *Reuters*, August 17, 2016. https://www.reuters.com/article/us-security-internet-voting-commentary-idUSKCN10S08G. (8/5/22).

Flynn, Michael. "Gen. Flynn Exclusive: 10 Indisputable Facts on the 2020 Election That Argue for Audits." *Western Journal*, July 30, 2021. https://www.westernjournal.com/gen-flynn-exclu sive-10-indisputable-facts-2020-election-argue-audits/. (5/26/22).

Folkenflik, David. "Arrest of Steele dossier source forces some news outlets to reexamine their coverage." *NPR*, November 12, 2021. https://www.npr.org/2021/11/12/1055030223/the-fbi-arrests-a-key-contributor-to-efforts-trying-to-link-trump-with-russia. (4/1/22).

Foran, Clare, and Manu Raju. "Senators moving 'aggressively' on Electoral Count Act reform, but face long way to go before a deal." *CNN*, February 1, 2022. https://www.cnn.com/2022/02/ 01/politics/electoral-count-act-reform/index.html. (6/20/22).

"18 Former ACORN Workers Have Been Convicted or Admitted Guilt in Election Fraud." *Fox News*, December 23, 2015. https://www.foxnews.com/politics/18-former-acorn-workers-have-been-convicted-or-admitted-guilt-in-election-fraud. (4/1/22).

Fox News. "College student who questioned Brian Stelter speaks out." April 8, 2022. https:// youtu.be/-6iZDcvhYZo.

"Presidential Election Results." *Fox News*. https://www.foxnews.com/elections/2020/general-results. (2/16/22).

"'Watters' World' on Democrats' power grab propaganda, border crisis." *Fox News*, October 4,

2021. https://www.foxnews.com/transcript/watters-world-on-democrats-power-grab-propa ganda-border-crisis. (5/23/22).

Fredericks, Bob. "Joe Biden will choose 'woman of color' as running mate by August." *New York Post*, June 30, 2020. https://nypost.com/2020/06/30/joe-biden-to-pick-woman-of-color-as-running-mate-by-august/.

"The Demands of the Collective Black Voices at Free Capitol Hill to the government of Seattle, Washington." Free Capitol Hill, June 9, 2020. https://medium.com/@seattleblmanon3/the-demands-of-the-collective-black-voices-at-free-capitol-hill-to-the-government-of-seattle-ddaee51d3e47.

Freed, David. "The First U.S. General to Call Trump a Bigot." *Atlantic*, June 22, 2020. https://www.theatlantic.com/politics/archive/2020/06/ricardo-sanchez-general-racism-military-trump/613279/. (7/20/22).

Freeman, Brian. "Trump: I Have Not Conceded 2020 Election." *Newsmax*, June 22, 2021. https://www.newsmax.com/politics/trump-election-fraud-biden/2021/06/22/id/1025990/. (5/25/22).

French, Lauren. "IRS knew of tea party targeting." *Politico*, May 11, 2013. https://www.politico.com/story/2013/05/irs-knew-tea-party-targeted-in-2011-091214.

Frey, William H. "Turnout in 2020 election spiked among both Democratic and Republican voting groups, new census data shows." Brookings Institute, May 5, 2021. https://www.brook ings.edu/research/turnout-in-2020-spiked-among-both-democratic-and-republican-voting-groups-new-census-data-shows/. (7/29/22).

Friberg, John. "Investigation on Abbey Gate Bombing HKIA August 2021." *Afghan Report*, February 5, 2022. https://afghan-report.com/news/abbey-gate-bombing/. (5/31/22).

Stewart D. Friedman. "Do Not Waste This Crisis." *Harvard Business Review*, November 25, 2008. https://hbr.org/2008/11/dont-waste-this-crisis.html.

Friedman, Uri. "The Damage Will Last." *Atlantic*, November 27, 2020. https://www.theatlantic.com/ideas/archive/2020/11/trumps-refusal-to-concede-wasnt-some-sideshow/617215/. (5/25/22).

Fund, John. "More Acorn Voter Fraud Comes to Light." *Wall Street Journal*, May 9, 2009. https://www.wsj.com/articles/SB124182750646102435. (4/1/22).

———. "Non-Citizens Are Voting." *National Review*, October 30, 2014. https://www.nationalre view.com/2014/10/non-citizens-are-voting-john-fund/. (3/16/22).

———. *Stealing Elections: How Voter Fraud Threatens Our Democracy, (Second edition)*. New York: Encounter Books, 2008.

Fund, John, and Hans von Spakovsky. *Our Broken Elections: How the left changed the way you vote*. New York: Encounter Books, 2021.

———. *Who's Counting? How fraudsters and bureaucrats put your vote at risk*. New York: Encounter Books, 2012.

Funke, Daniel. "Fact-checking false claims about the 2020 election." *Politifact*, November 19, 2020. https://www.politifact.com/article/2020/nov/20/fact-checking-false-claims-about-2020-elec tion/. (7/20/22).

Fuzzy Slippers. "Republican and Conservative Leaders Condemn Capitol Hill Violence." *Legal Insurrection*, January 6, 2021. https://legalinsurrection.com/2021/01/republican-and-conserva tive-leaders-condemn-capitol-hill-violence/. (4/17/22).

Galofaro, Claire. "America's bellwethers crumbled in aligning with Trump in '20." *ABC News*, November 18, 2020. https://abcnews.go.com/Politics/wireStory/americas-bellwethers-crum bled-aligning-trump-20-74280253. (5/26/22).

Gamboa, Suzanne, and Julia Ainsley. "Trump administration starts 'remain in Mexico' policy in El Paso, Texas." *NBC News*, March 20, 2019. https://www.nbcnews.com/news/us-news/trump-administration-starts-remain-mexico-policy-el-paso-texas-n985641. (5/26/22).

Gander, Kashmira. "Surgical and Cotton Face Masks Ineffective at Blocking SARS-CoV-2 Parti cles When COVID-19 Patients Cough, Study Finds." *Newsweek*, April 7, 2020. https://www.newsweek.com/surgical-cotton-face-masks-ineffective-blocking-sars-cov-2-particles-when-covid-19-patients-1496476. (5/23/22).

Gannon, Kathy. "Taliban official: Strict punishment, executions will return." *Associated Press*, September 23, 2021. https://apnews.com/article/religion-afghanistan-kabul-taliban-22f5107f1dbd19c8605b5b5435a9de54. (4/19/22).

Garamone, Jim. "Trump Signs Law Establishing U.S. Space Force." U.S. Department of Defense,

December 20, 2019. https://www.defense.gov/News/News-Stories/Article/Article/2046035/trump-signs-law-establishing-us-space-force/. (5/26/22).

Garrison, Joey. "Biden unleashes a year's worth of anger at Trump in Jan. 6 speech, blasting him as an undemocratic liar." *USA Today*, January 6, 2022. https://www.usatoday.com/story/news/politics/2022/01/06/biden-trump-capitol-attack/9114614002/. (2/25/22).

Gartner, John. "Mental Health Professionals Declare Trump is Mentally Ill And Must Be Removed." (Petition). https://www.change.org/p/trump-is-mentally-ill-and-must-be-removed?. (3/18/22).

Geller, Pamela. "Report: Raffensperger Launches Intimidation Campaign Against Election Whistleblowers in Georgia." *Geller Report*, July 10, 2021. https://gellerreport.com/2021/07/raffensperger-vicious-traitor.html/. (7/20/22).

Gelman, Andrew. "Election 2008: what really happened." *Statistical Modeling, Causal Interference, and Social Science* (Columbia University), November 5, 2008. https://statmodeling.stat.columbia.edu/2008/11/05/election-2008-what-really-happened/. (4/1/22).

Gentry, Destiny. Instagram post. https://ifunny.co/picture/destiny-gentry-wa-lifeandliberty-1s-it-wasn-t-the-suicides-gggmjhzJ9.

George, Liz. "Biden Admin gave Taliban a list of American, Afghan evacuees' names: Politico." *American Military News,* August 26, 2021. https://americanmilitarynews.com/2021/08/biden-admin-gave-taliban-a-list-of-american-afghan-evacuees-names-politico/. (4/19/22).

Geraghty, Jim, "Fauci Team Cared More about 'International Harmony' Than the Truth." *National Review,* January 13, 2022. https://www.nationalreview.com/the-morning-jolt/fauci-team-cared-more-about-international-harmony-than-the-truth/. (4/13/22).

Gertz, Bill. "FBI Increasingly Politicized Under Comey and Mueller." *Washington Free Beacon*, December 16, 2017. https://freebeacon.com/national-security/fbi-increasingly-politicized-comey-mueller/. (5/23/22).

Gist, Jack. "Black Man Acquitted on Self-Defense Same Day as Rittenhouse Busts Myth of 'Unjust' Justice System." *Western Journal*, November 21, 2021. https://www.westernjournal.com/black-man-acquitted-self-defense-day-rittenhouse-busts-myth-unjust-justice-system/. (3/10/22).

Glum, Julia. "Trump Is Out of Control and 'Spiraling Down Into Paranoia,' Says His 'Art of the Deal' Ghostwriter." *Newsweek*, October 11, 2017. https://www.newsweek.com/trump-mortal-danger-art-deal-682450. (4/20/22).

Gohmert, Louie, Paul Gosar, Bob Good, Marjorie Taylor Greene, and Matt Gaetz. "The Tyrannical Treatment of Jan. 6 Prisoners Is a Threat to Our Democracy." *Epoch Times*, November 4, 2021. https://m.theepochtimes.com/the-tyrannical-treatment-of-jan-6-prisoners-is-a-threat-to-our-democracy_4080664.html. (5/25/22).

Gold, Matea. "The campaign to impeach President Trump has begun." *Washington Post,* January 20, 2017. https://www.washingtonpost.com/news/post-politics/wp/2017/01/20/the-campaign-to-impeach-president-trump-has-begun/.

Goldberg, Bernard. "It's Worse Than Bush Derangement Syndrome." *RealClear Politics*, January 3, 2017. https://www.realclearpolitics.com/articles/2017/01/03/its_worse_than_bush_derangement_syndrome__132696.html#!. (8/5/22).

Golden, C. Douglas. "Fauci Shreds Media Narrative, Admits President Trump's COVID Response Saved Lives." *Western Journal*, August 1, 2020. https://www.westernjournal.com/fauci-shreds-media-narrative-admits-president-trumps-covid-response-saved-lives/. (4/13/22).

———. "Insider Documents Show Anti-Trump Google Employees Wanting To Rig Search Results." *Western Journal*, September 21, 2018. https://www.westernjournal.com/anti-trump-google-rig-results/. (6/28/22).

Golding, Bruce. "'Huge integrity test': Calls for action as Biden voicemail reveals he knew of Hunter China deals." *New York Post*, June 28, 2022. https://nypost.com/2022/06/28/calls-for-action-as-biden-voicemail-reveals-he-knew-of-hunter-china-deals/. (7/23/22).

Gonzalez, Mike, and Andrew Olivastro. "The agenda of Black Lives Matter is far different from the slogan." *New York Post*, July 1, 2020. https://nypost.com/2020/07/01/the-agenda-of-black-lives-matter-is-far-different-from-the-slogan/. (3/10/22).

Goodenough, Patrick. "79,678: December Border Encounters With Illegal Migrants Not From Mexico/Northern Triangle Up Tenfold." *CNS News*, January 25, 2022. https://www.cnsnews.

com/article/international/patrick-goodenough/79678-december-border-encounters-illegal-migrants-not/. (4/19/22).

Goodman, Jack, Christopher Giles, Olga Robinson, and Jake Horton. "US Election 2020: The 'dead voters' in Michigan who are still alive." *BBC*, November 14, 2020. https://www.bbc.com/news/election-us-2020-54874120

Goodwin, Michael. "Hunter biz partner confirms email, details Joe Biden's push to make millions from China: Goodwin." *New York Post*, October 22, 2020. https://nypost.com/2020/10/22/hunter-biz-partner-confirms-e-mail-details-joe-bidens-push-to-make-millions-from-china/. (5/23/22).

Gordon, James. "Loudoun County principals were Coached on how to obtain trespassing warrants against students trying to enter schools without masks: Woke board has defied Virginia governor's order allowing parents to choose whether kids cover their faces." *Daily Mail*, February 8, 2022. https://www.dailymail.co.uk/news/article-10487399/amp/Loudoun-public-schools-official-coached-principals-WARRANTS-stop-unmasked-students-school.html. (5/23/22).

Gore, D'Angelo. "Latest CDC Data: Unvaccinated Adults 97 Times More Likely to Die from COVID-19 Than Boosted Adults." *FactCheck*, February 9, 2022. https://www.factcheck.org/2022/02/scicheck-latest-cdc-data-unvaccinated-adults-97-times-more-likely-to-die-from-covid-19-than-boosted-adults/. (2/21/22).

Gorka, Sebastian. *The War for America's Soul*. Washington, D.C.:Regnery, 2019. 176-182.

Graham, David A., Adrienne Green, Cullen Murphy, and Parker Richards. "An Oral History of Trump's Bigotry." *Atlantic*, June 2019. https://www.theatlantic.com/magazine/archive/2019/06/trump-racism-comments/588067/. (4/20/22).

Graham, Tim. "The Media's Humiliating Incuriosity About Wuhan." *Daily Signal*, May 28, 2021. https://www.dailysignal.com/2021/05/28/the-medias-embarrassing-incuriosity-about-wuhan/. (3/2/22).

Gray, Melanie. "Businesses and bystanders feeling pain of George Floyd riots." *New York Post*, May 30, 2020. https://nypost.com/2020/05/30/black-latino-businesses-in-minneapolis-feel-pain-of-looting/. (5/25/22).

Grayer, Annie, and Jeremy Herb. "McCarthy pulls his 5 GOP members from 1/6 committee after Pelosi rejects 2 of his picks." *CNN*, July 21, 2022. https://www.cnn.com/2021/07/21/politics/nancy-pelosi-rejects-republicans-from-committee/index.html. (7/25/22).

Greenblatt, Mark Lee. "Statement Regarding Special Review Report." Office of Inspector General, U.S. Department of the Interior, June 8, 2021. https://www.doioig.gov/site-page/statement-inspector-general-mark-lee-greenblatt-regarding-special-review-report-review-us.

Griffith, Keith. "Washington Post columnist demands CNN retract claim that Steele dossier had been 'partly corroborated' after key source was arrested for lying - as paper corrects its own stories." *Daily Mail*, November 12, 2021. https://www.dailymail.co.uk/news/article-10196961/Washington-Post-columnist-demands-CNN-retract-corroboration-claim-Steele-dossier.html. (4/19/22).

Grzeszczak, Jocelyn. "Richard Spencer Reiterates Support for Biden, Disavows 'Useless' and 'Traitorous' GOP." *Newsweek*, August 25, 2020. https://www.newsweek.com/richard-spencer-reiterates-support-biden-disavows-useless-traitorous-gop-1527555. (6/23/22).

"Twitter says Trump ban is permanent—even if he runs for office again." *Guardian*, February 10, 2021. https://www.theguardian.com/us-news/2021/feb/10/trump-twitter-ban-permanent-social-media. (3/22/22).

Gurman, Sadie, and Rebecca Davis O'Brien. "Barr Worked to Keep Hunter Biden Probes From Public View During Election." *Wall Street Journal*, December 10, 2020. https://www.wsj.com/articles/barr-worked-to-keep-hunter-biden-probes-from-public-view-during-election-11607653188. (6/14/22).

Haensel, Brett, "Domino effect: Google antitrust case could spell trouble for other tech giants." *Fortune*, October 29, 2020. https://fortune.com/2020/10/29/google-antitrust-duckduckgo-search-engine-fortune-brainstorm/.

Hains, Tim. "Flashback, 2018: Joe Biden Brags At CFR Meeting About Withholding Aid To Ukraine To Force Firing Of Prosecutor." *RealClearPolitics*, September 27, 2019. https://www.realclearpolitics.com/video/2019/09/27/flashback_2018_joe_biden_brags_at_cfr_meet ing_about_withholding_aid_to_ukraine_to_force_firing_of_prosecutor.html. (4/19/22).

Hanneman, Joseph M.. "Babbitt Tried to Stop Attack on Capitol Speaker's Lobby, Video Shows." *Epoch Times*, January 19, 2022. https://www.theepochtimes.com/babbitt-tried-to-stop-attack-on-capitol-speakers-lobby-video-shows_4216934.html. (5/23/22).

———. "Police Beating of Unconscious Trump Supporter Was 'Objectively Reasonable,' Department Rules." *Epoch Times*, February 15, 2022. https://www.theepochtimes.com/police-beating-of-unconscious-rosanne-boyland-was-objectively-reasonable-department-rules_4267104. html?utm_source=ref_share&utm_campaign=bn-cc. (5/16/22).

Hansen, Claire. "How Much of Trump's Border Wall Was Built?" *U.S. News and World Report*, February 7, 2022. https://www.usnews.com/news/politics/articles/2022-02-07/how-much-of-president-donald-trumps-border-wall-was-built. (5/26/22).

Hansen, Tayler. "Capitol Offense: The Ugly Truth Behind The Five Deaths From January 6th and 7th." Substack. January 27, 2022. https://taylerhansen.substack.com/p/capitol-offense-the-ugly-truth-behind?s=r. (5/16/22).

Harsanyi, David. "I know first-hand how looters can crush a family's dreams." *New York Post*, June 5, 2020. https://nypost.com/2020/06/05/i-know-first-hand-how-looters-can-crush-a-familys-dreams/. (5/25/22).

———. "The FISA Scandal Is about Corruption, Not 'Sloppiness.'" *National Review*, April 2, 2020. https://www.nationalreview.com/2020/04/fbi-inspector-general-report-fisa-scandal-about-corruption-not-sloppiness/.

———. "The Obama's Administration's FISA Abuse Is a Massive Scandal." *National Review*, December 12, 2019. https://www.nationalreview.com/2019/12/the-obamas-administrations-fisa-abuse-is-a-massive-scandal/. (5/23/22).

Hasen, Richard L. *Election Meltdown: Dirty Tricks, Distrust, and the Threat to American Democracy*. New Haven: Yale University Press, 2020.

Haughey, John. "Researcher Featured in '2000 Mules' Documentary Explains How Local Election Fraud Was Grown to National Scale." *Epoch Times*, May 1, 2022. https://www.theep ochtimes.com/mkt_eet/researcher-featured-in-2000-mules-documentary-explains-how-local-election-fraud-was-grown-to-national-scale_4437085.html. (5/18/22).

Hemingway, Mollie. *Rigged: How the Media, Big Tech, and the Democrats Seized Our Elections*. Washington, D.C.: Regnery, 2021.

Hendrickson, John. "Are You Going to Vote for a Bigot?" *Esquire*, August 23, 2016. https://www.esquire.com/news-politics/videos/a47944/donald-trump-bigot/. (7/20/22).

Hendrickson, Matthew. "Jussie Smollett sentenced to 5 months in jail for staging fake hate crime in downtown Chicago." *Chicago Sun Times*, March 10, 2022.

Herb, Jeremy, and Annie Grayer. "Liz Cheney strikes defiant tone in floor speech on eve of her expected ousting from House GOP leadership." *CNN*, May 12, 2021. https://www.cnn.com/2021/05/11/politics/cheney-house-floor-remarks/. (6/6/22).

Higgins, Tucker. "Former police officer Derek Chauvin found guilty of murder, manslaughter in the death of George Floyd." *CNBC*, April 21, 2021. https://www.cnbc.com/2021/04/20/derek-chauvin-trial-verdict.html. (2/16/22).

Hoff, Madison. "1 chart compares how much gas prices have skyrocketed in different regions of the US in the last 2 years." *Business Insider*, June 2, 2022. https://www.businessinsider.com/how-much-gas-prices-gone-up-compared-two-years-ago-2022-6?op=1. (6/4/22).

Hoft, Joe. "Final 2020 Rally Tally: President Trump Had Largest Crowds at His Rallies in US History - Biden Had Some of the Smallest." *Gateway Pundit*, November 3, 2020. https://www.thegatewaypundit.com/2020/11/final-2020-rally-tally-president-trump-largest-crowds-rallies-us-history-biden-smallest/. (5/16/22).

Hosenball, Mark, and Sarah N. Lynch. "Exclusive: FBI finds scant evidence U.S. Capitol attack was coordinated - sources." *Reuters*, August 20, 2021. https://www.reuters.com/world/us/exclu sive-fbi-finds-scant-evidence-us-capitol-attack-was-coordinated-sources-2021-08-20/. (3/1/22).

Hsu, Spencer. "Justice Dept. calls Jan. 6 'Capitol Attack' probe one of largest in U.S. history, expects at least 400 to be charged." *Washington Post*, March 12, 2021. https://www.washington post.com/local/legal-issues/capitol-attack-investigation-largest/2021/03/12/5c07b46c-833d-11eb-9ca6-54e187ee4939_story.html. (4/17/22).

———. "Jan. 6 riot caused $1.5 million in damage to Capitol — and U.S. prosecutors want defendants to pay." *Washington Post*, June 3, 2021. https://www.washingtonpost.com/local/legal-issues/capitol-riot-defendants-pay-damages-restitution/2021/06/03/74691812-c3ec-11eb-93f5-ee9558eecf4b_story.html. (5/25/22).

Hudson, Jerome. "Illegal alien sitcoms from actress Gina Rodriguez headed to CBS and CW." *Breitbart*, September 17, 2017. https://www.breitbart.com/entertainment/2017/09/07/illegal-alien-sitcoms-actress-gina-rodriguez-headed-cbs-cw/.

"'No Forgiveness for People Like You' Executions and Enforced Disappearances in Afghanistan under the Taliban." *Human Rights Watch*, November 30, 2021. https://www.hrw.org/report/2021/11/30/no-forgiveness-people-you/executions-and-enforced-disappearances-afghanistan. (5/31/22).

Husebø, Wendell. "Report: Peter Navarro Handcuffed At Airport And 'Frogmarched' To The Courthouse." *Breitbart*, June 3, 2022. https://www.breitbart.com/politics/2022/06/03/report-peter-navarro-handcuffed-at-airport-and-frogmarched-to-the-courthouse/. (7/29/22).

Hutzler, Alexandra. "2 People Who Died at Capitol Riot Died of Natural Causes, Medical Examiner Rules." *Newsweek*, April 7, 2021. https://www.newsweek.com/2-people-who-died-capitol-riot-died-natural-causes-medical-examiner-rules-1581804. (5/16/22).

Ibrahim, Nur. "Did Kamala Harris Say Protests Are 'Not Gonna Let Up, and They Should Not'?" *Snopes*, October 7, 2020. https://www.snopes.com/fact-check/kamala-harris-protests/. (4/17/22).

Idliby, Leia. "Washington Post's Erik Wemple Takes CNN and MSNBC to Task Over Steele Dossier Coverage: 'A Reckoning is Years Overdue.'" *MSN*, November 9, 2021. https://www.msn.com/en-us/news/politics/washington-post-s-erik-wemple-takes-cnn-and-msnbc-to-task-over-steele-dossier-coverage-a-reckoning-is-years-overdue/ar-AAQvxgn. (4/19/22).

Ingram, David. "Elon Musk has a plan for Twitter. It may scare away users and advertisers." *NBC News*, April 15, 2022. https://www.nbcnews.com/tech/tech-news/elon-musk-twitter-speech-rules-users-advertisers-rcna24613. (7/20/22).

"Clinton Email Scandal: New Revelations Of Cover-Up Spell Trouble For Hillary." *Investor's Business Daily*, September 22, 2016. https://www.investors.com/politics/editorials/clinton-email-scandal-revelations-of-cover-up-spell-trouble-for-hillary/. (5/23/22).

"Go Figure: Federal Revenues Hit All-Time High Under Trump Tax Cuts." *Investor's Business Daily*, October 16, 2018. https://www.investors.com/politics/editorials/trump-tax-cuts-federal-revenues-deficits/. (5/26/22).

"Trump Just Achieved What Every President Since Nixon Had Promised: Energy Independence." *Investor's Business Daily*, December 7, 2018. https://www.investors.com/politics/editorials/energy-independence-trump/. (5/16/22).

Isacson, Adam. "Weekly U.S.-Mexico Border Update: Remain in Mexico restarts, drug seizures, caravans." *WOLA*, December 3, 2021. https://www.wola.org/2021/12/weekly-u-s-mexico-border-update-remain-in-mexico-restarts-drug-seizures-caravans/. (4/19/22).

Jacobs, Emily. "CNN staffer tells Project Veritas network played up COVID-19 death toll for ratings." *New York Post*, April 14, 2021. https://nypost.com/2021/04/14/cnn-staffer-tells-project-veritas-network-played-up-covid-19-death-toll-for-ratings/.

Jacobson, Louis, and Amy Sherman. "Donald Trump has lost dozens of election lawsuits. Here's why." *Politifact*, December 10, 2020. https://www.politifact.com/article/2020/dec/10/donald-trump-has-lost-dozens-election-lawsuits-her/. (7/26/22).

Jacobson, William A. "Group behind 'Occupy Wall Street' planning 50-day 'White House Siege' through Election Day." *Legal Insurrection*, August 9, 2020. https://legalinsurrection.com/2020/08/group-behind-occupy-wall-street-planning-50-day-white-house-siege-through-election-day/. (2/18/22).

Jaffe, Alexandre, and Alan Fram. "Biden's low-key campaign style worries some Democrats." *Associated Press*, September 25, 2020. https://apnews.com/article/election-2020-virus-outbreak-ruth-bader-ginsburg-delaware-elections-9282e7a189e965b124f1fc31c857903e. (6/7/22).

Jeffery, Adam. "Iconic photos of the USNS Comfort arriving in New York, providing a glimmer of hope." *CNBC*, March 30, 2020. https://www.cnbc.com/2020/03/30/iconic-photos-of-the-usns-comfort-arriving-in-new-york-provides-a-glimmer-of-hope.html. (2/16/22).

Jekielek, Jan. "Making History: Hong Kong Protest Is An 'Existential Threat' to Communist China - Michael Yon & Erik Fok." *Epoch Times*, December 28, 2019. https://www.theep

ochtimes.com/making-history-hong-kong-protest-is-an-existential-threat-to-communist-china-michael-yon-eric-fok_3195237.html. (5/23/22).

Jeremijenko, Andrew, Hiam Chemaitelly, Houssein H. Ayoub, Moza Alishaq, Abdul-Badi Abou-Samra, Jameela Ali A.A. Al Ajmi, Nasser Ali Asad Al Ansari, et al.. "Herd Immunity against Severe Acute Respiratory Syndrome in 10 Communities, Qatar." *Emerging Infectious Diseases*, 27:5 May 2021. https://wwwnc.cdc.gov/eid/article/27/5/20-4365_article.

"Karen goes Completely Crazy over Couple not wearing Masks." John Talks. December 24, 2020. YouTube video. https://www.youtube.com/watch?v=z5-BjQaQqe4. (4/14/22).

Johns Hopkins Coronavirus Resource Center. https://coronavirus.jhu.edu/data/mortality. (3/10/22).

Johnson, Andrew. "N.C. Board Finds More than 35K Incidents of 'Double Voting' in 2012." *National Review Online*, April 2, 2014. https://www.nationalreview.com/corner/nc-state-board-finds-more-35k-incidents-double-voting-2012-andrew-johnson/. (7/31/22).

Johnson, Brad. "Texas Rejected Use of Dominion Voting System Software Due to Efficiency Issues." *Texan*, November 19, 2020. https://thetexan.news/texas-rejected-use-of-dominion-voting-system-software-due-to-efficiency-issues/. (7/20/22).

Johnson, Ron. "Letter to Attorney General The Honorable William P. Barr and Federal Bureau of Investigation Director The Honorable Christopher A. Wray." *United States Senate Committee on Homeland Security and Governmental Affairs,* January 8, 2020. https://www.hsgac.senate.gov/imo/media/doc/2020-1-08%20RHJ%20to%20AG%20Barr%20and%20Director%20Wray%20re%20Sharyl%20Attkisson%20Hacking.pdf.

Jones, Tim. "Court won't review Obama's eligibility to serve." *Chicago Tribune*, December 8, 2008. https://www.chicagotribune.com/nation-world/chi-obama-birth-certificate1dec08-story.html. (4/5/22).

Jordà, Òscar, Celeste Liu, Fernanda Nechio, and Fabián Rivera-Reyes. "Why Is U.S. Inflation Higher than in Other Countries?" *FRBSF Economic Letter*, March 28, 2022. https://www.frbsf.org/economic-research/publications/economic-letter/2022/march/why-is-us-inflation-higher-than-in-other-countries/. (5/23/22).

Jose, Andrew. "Dem Rep Pleads Guilty to Mass Voter Fraud: Thousands of Dollars Paid to Crooked Judges." *Western Journal*, June 8, 2022. https://www.westernjournal.com/dem-rep-pleads-guilty-mass-voter-fraud-thousands-dollars-paid-crooked-judges/. (7/20/22).

"FBI Finds 30 Pages of Clinton-Lynch Tarmac Meeting Documents - Wants Six Weeks to Turn Over Docs." *Judicial Watch*, October 13, 2017. https://www.judicialwatch.org/fbi-finds-30-pages-clinton-lynch-tarmac-meeting-documents-wants-six-weeks-turn-docs/

"Judicial Watch: U.S. Capitol Police Tell Federal Court January 6 Disturbance Videos Are Not Public Records." *Judicial Watch* (Press Release), August 20, 2021. https://www.judicialwatch.org/judicial-watch-u-s-capitol-police-tell-federal-court-january-6-disturbance-videos-are-not-public-records/. (5/25/22).

Justice, Tristan. "Liz Cheney Was A Primary Culprit Of Spreading Fake News On Russian Bounties To Undermine Trump." *Federalist*, April 16, 2021. https://thefdrlst.wpengine.com/2021/04/16/liz-cheney-was-a-primary-culprit-of-spreading-fake-news-on-russian-bounties-to-under-mine-trump/. (6/7/22).

Kadkhoda, Kamran. "Herd Immunity to COVID-19: Alluring and Elusive." *American Journal of Clinical Pathology*, January 5, 2021. https://www.ncbi.nlm.nih.gov/pmc/articles/PMC7929447/. (5/23/22).

Kaminsky, Gabe. "Virginia Superintendents Group Did Not Consult Members Before Issuing Letter Slamming Youngkin's Policies On CRT, DEI." *Daily Wire*, March 15, 2022. https://www.dailywire.co/news/virginia-superintendents-group-did-not-consult-members-before-issuing-letter-slamming-youngkins-policies-on-crt-dei. (3/16/22).

Kaplan, Rebecca. "More than $30 million needed for Capitol repairs and new security after assault, officials say." CBS News, February 24, 2021. https://www.cbsnews.com/news/capitol-repairs-and-new-security-30-million-after-assault-official-says/. (5/25/22).

Kaplan, Talia. "Ken Starr: 2020 election may be remembered as one 'where the ultimate results are called into question.'" *Fox News,* November 5, 2020. https://www.foxnews.com/politics/ken-starr-2020-election-ultimate-result-called-into-question.

Keene, Houston. "Biden yet to speak on alleged Kavanaugh assassination attempt 2 days after arrest." *Fox News*, June 10, 2022. https://www.foxnews.com/politics/biden-kavanaugh-assassi nation-attempt-arrest. (6/10/22).

———. "Conservatives blast Facebook over sudden decision to end ban on COVID origin posts: Rep. Banks quipped, 'The "Ministry of Truth" admits a mistake! Amazing!.'" *Fox Business*, May 27, 2021. https://www.foxbusiness.com/politics/conservatives-blast-facebook-covid-origin-ban. (5/31/21).

———. "Dem Sen. Tim Kaine rips Biden admin's claim that nobody forecasted rapid Afghanistan fall." *Fox News*, September 14, 2021. https://www.foxnews.com/politics/tim-kaine-biden-admin-afghanistan-fall.

Kelly, Julie. "20 Questions for Nancy Pelosi About January 6." *American Greatness*, July 5, 2021. https://amgreatness.com/2021/07/05/20-questions-for-nancy-pelosi-about-january-6/. (7/21/22).

———. "A January 6 Detainee Speaks Out." *American Greatness*, July 22, 2021. https://amgreat ness.com/2021/07/22/a-january-6-detainee-speaks-out/. (6/6/22).

———. "Capitol Investigation Seeks to Criminalize Political Dissent: The government's response to the January 6 melee isn't about justice. It's about partisan retribution and revenge. And the consequences will be disastrous." *American Greatness*, March 15, 2021. https://amgreatness. com/2021/03/15/capitol-investigation-seeks-to-criminalize-political-dissent/. (5/25/22).

———. *January 6: How Democrats used the Capitol protest to launch a war on terror against the political right.* New York: Bombardier. 2022.

Kennedy, Robert F. *The Real Anthony Fauci: Bill Gates, Big Pharma, and the Global War on Democracy and Public Health.* New York: Skyhorse. 2021.

"Police union releases statement on shooting." *Kenosha News*, August 28, 2020. https://www. kenoshanews.com/news/local/police-union-releases-statement-on-blake-shooting/arti cle_140a3c34-d0b4-5a78-b838-e2ace80cf8dc.html#tracking-source=home-trending. (5/23/22).

Kerr, Andrew. "Abortion rights group doxxes Supreme Court Justices, offers stipends for protests." *Washington Examiner*, May 5, 2022. https://www.washingtonexaminer.com/abortion-rights-group-doxxes-scotus-justices-offers-stipends-for-protests. (6/10/22).

Kershner, Caleb. "Breaking News." Public Statement. Facebook, February 16, 2022, 10:00 p.m..

Keshel, Seth. "The Battle for the Largest Counties." *Election Fraud At A Glance.* Updated September 9, 2021. https://electionfraud20.org/in-detail/battle-for-largest-counties/. (6/8/22).

———. "The Ten Points To True Election Integrity." *ElectionFraud20*, January 10, 2022. https:// electionfraud20.org/seth-keshel-reports/#statement-by-donald-j-trump. (5/26/22).

Kessler, Glenn. "Donald Trump's bogus claim that millions of people voted illegally for Hillary Clinton." *Washington Post,* November 27, 2016.

Kheel, Rebecca. "Billions in US weaponry seized by Taliban." *Hill*, August 21, 2021. https://thehill. com/policy/defense/568493-billions-in-us-weaponry-seized-by-taliban.

King, Ryan. "Bannon calls for new Jan. 6 committee to deliver 'crushing blow' to Democrats." *Washington Examiner*, July 22, 2022. https://www.washingtonexaminer.com/news/steve-bannon-calls-new-panel-jan-6-deliver-crushing-blow. (7/29/22).

Kittle, M.D. "Conservative Groups Targeted in Lois Lerner's IRS Scandal Receive Settlement Checks." *The Daily Signal,* January 11, 2019. https://www.dailysignal.com/2019/01/11/conserva tive-groups-targeted-in-lois-lerners-irs-scandal-receive-settlement-checks/.

Klompas, Michael, Charles A. Morris, Julia Sinclair, Madelyn Pearson, and Erica S. Shenoy. "Universal Masking in Hospitals in the Covid-19 Era." *New England Journal of Medicine*, May 21, 2020. 2020; 382:e63. https://www.nejm.org/doi/full/10.1056/NEJMp2006372.

Knapp, Margaret. "Flashback—Levin: 'Sect. 793 of Penal Code … Is What Hillary Clinton Has to Worry About." *CNS News*, August 13, 2015. https://www.cnsnews.com/blog/margaret-knapp/ levin-sect-793-penal-codeis-what-hillary-clinton-has-worry-about. (2/16/22).

Kovac, Steven. "Election Watchdog Finds 137,500 Ballots Trafficked in Wisconsin." *Epoch Times*, New York/DC Edition, March 30, 2022.

Kranz, Michal. "'This is not going to end well': Trump's friends and allies are worried he's spiraling out of control — and they say this time is different." *Business Insider*, March 4, 2018. https://www.businessinsider.com/trump-spiraling-out-of-control-according-to-friends-2018-3?op=1. (4/20/22).

Krayden, David. "Former Navy Seal Who Killed Bin Laden Claims Taliban Are Torturing Families Of Afghans Allies 'Before They Cut Their Heads Off.'" *Daily Caller,* September 9, 2021.

https://dailycaller.com/2021/09/09/rob-oneill-taliban-torturing-families-afghans-allies/?_s=vy5fsglubzurbejj7i4d. (4/19/22).

Krieg, Gregory. "It's official: Clinton swamps Trump in popular vote." *CNN*, December 22, 2016.

Kube, Courtney, Carol E. Lee, and Josh Lederman. "U.S. troops to leave Syria as President Trump declares victory over ISIS." *NBC News*, December 19, 2018. https://www.nbcnews.com/news/us-news/u-s-troops-leave-syria-president-trump-declares-victory-over-n949806. (5/26/22).

Kube, Courtney, and Doha Madani. "Iran retaliates for Gen. Soleimani's killing by firing missiles at U.S. forces in Iraq." *NBC News*, January 7, 2020. https://www.nbcnews.com/news/world/u-s-base-iraq-comes-under-attack-missiles-iran-claims-n1112171. (2/16/22).

Kutner, Max. "After Clinton-Lunch Tarmac Meeting, FBI Scrambled to Find and Punish Source, Newly Released Emails Show." *Newsweek*, December 15, 2017. https://www.newsweek.com/loretta-lynch-bill-clinton-tarmac-meeting-details-comey-749995. (5/23/22).

Lahut, Jake. "The demographic that won Joe Biden the election: Higher-earning, college-educated white people near major cities." *Business Insider*, December 11, 2020. https://www.businessinsider.com/higher-earning-college-educated-white-voters-biden-election-2020-12?op=1. (5/16/22).

Lake, Eli. "The FBI Scandal." *Real Clear Politics,* January 24, 2020. https://www.commentary.org/articles/eli-lake/the-fbi-scandal/.

Lancaster, Jordan. "Philadelphia City Commissioners Say They Are Investigating After Video Allegedly Shows GOP Poll Watcher Getting Kicked Out Of Polling Place." *Daily Caller*, November 3, 2020. https://dailycaller.com/2020/11/03/philadelphia-city-commissioners-investigating-video-shows-gop-poll-watcher-kicked-out-polling-place/?fbclid=IwAR2bhRoXfYcoQ_uc2BsU7Ss1Rurol Rb5Ijzkj JNMYSOXpcP-QNTWorfUl6I. (4/17/22).

Lee, Carol E., Nigel Chiwaya, Kanwal Syed, and Joe Murphy. "Tracking Covid-19 infections among President Donald Trump's contacts." *NBC News*, October 2, 2020. https://www.nbcnews.com/news/us-news/tracking-covid-19-infections-among-president-trump-s-contacts-n1241877. (6/7/22).

Lee, Michael. "Data show majority of Trump's 2020 support came from women and people of color." *Washington Examiner*, May 11, 2021. https://www.washingtonexaminer.com/news/data-show-majority-trump-support-women-people-color-2020. (5/16/22).

Lee, Trymaine, Andrew Rafferty, and Corky Siemaszko. "America Gives Trump an Earful at 'Not My President's Day' Rallies." *NBC News*, February 20, 2017. https://www.nbcnews.com/news/us-news/america-gives-trump-earful-not-my-president-s-day-rallies-n723371. (4/1/22).

"3 U.S. Code § 15 - Couting electoral votes in Congress." Legal Information Institute, Cornell Law School. https://www.law.cornell.edu/uscode/text/3/15. (5/18/22).

"47 U.S. Code § 230 - Protection for private blocking and screening of offensive material." Legal Information Institute (Cornell University). https://www.law.cornell.edu/uscode/text/47/230. (3/22/22).

Lemon, Jason. "Liz Cheney's Chances of Beating Trump-Backed Harriet Hageman in Wyoming." *Newsweek*, May 28, 2022. https://www.newsweek.com/liz-cheney-harriet-hageman-wyoming-republican-house-primary-1711035. (6/7/22).

———. "Who Is Juan Guaidó? Trump Officially Recognizes Venezuela's National Assembly Leader As 'Interim President'," *Newsweek*, January 23, 2019. https://www.newsweek.com/juan-guaido-trump-recognizes-venezuela-president-1302318. (7/20/22).

Leonardi, Anthony. "Burst pipe causes election results to be delayed in Georgia's most populous county." *Washington Examiner*, November 3, 2020. https://www.washingtonexaminer.com/news/burst-pipe-causes-election-results-to-be-delayed-in-georgias-most-populous-county.

Leonhardt, David, and Ian Prasad Philbrick. "Donald Trump's Racism: The Definitive List, Updated." *The New York Times*, January 15, 2018. https://www.nytimes.com/interactive/2018/01/15/opinion/leonhardt-trump-racist.html?mtrref=duckduckgo.com&gwh=2DA4E5D3869AFE14C195D6F003669A13&gwt=pay&assetType=PAYWALL. (4/20/22).

Levin, Gary. "Republican debate sets ratings record." *USA Today*, August 7, 2015. https://www.usatoday.com/story/life/tv/2015/08/07/republican-debate-sets-rating-record/31297777/. (6/6/22).

Levin, Mark R.. *Mark Levin Show,* September 28, 2021.

———. "The Rule of Law." *National Review*, November 13, 2000. https://www.nationalreview.com/2000/11/rule-law-mark-r-levin/. (8/5/22).

———. Twitter post. December 9, 2020. https://twitter.com/marklevinshow/status/1336669753000292358.

Levine, Jon. "Confessions of a voter fraud: I was a master at fixing mail-in ballots." *New York Post*, August 29, 2020. https://nypost.com/2020/08/29/political-insider-explains-voter-fraud-with-mail-in-ballots/. (6/6/22).

———. "Ginni Thomas to 'clear up misconceptions' about role to Jan. 6 committee." *New York Post*, June 18, 2022. https://nypost.com/2022/06/18/ginni-thomas-cant-wait-to-testify-before-jan-6-committee/.

Levy, Adam, Ethan Cohen and Liz Stark. "More than 100 million ballots were cast before Election Day." *CNN*, November 3, 2020. https://www.cnn.com/2020/11/03/politics/100-million-votes/index.html. (5/18/22).

Levy, Michael. "United States presidential election of 2000." *Britannica*. (4/5/22).

"Biden's connection to China: Peter Schweizer." *Life, Liberty & Levin (Fox News)*. January 24, 2022. https://video.foxnews.com/v/6293289712001?playlist_id=5736530682001&fbclid=IwAR1jh9nqrGg87h3IXbdg9DrtZ-XPAvprq8fOjoB7A7TKVV9dROEJhOJBEg#sp=show-clips.

Linan, Ali. "Texas sues Biden for education memo labeling parents 'domestic terrorists.'" *Herald Banner*, March 4, 2022. https://www.heraldbanner.com/news/texas-sues-biden-for-education-memo-labeling-parents-domestic-terrorists/article_6913d054-9bde-11ec-8bc7-ebc3693cc3af.html. (4/5/22).

Lindsay, James M.. "The 2020 Election by the Numbers." *Council on Foreign Relations*, December 15, 2020. https://www.cfr.org/blog/2020-election-numbers.

Lin, Christina. "Gene-editing, Moderna, and Transhumanism." *The Times of Israel*, August 5, 2020. https://blogs.timesofisrael.com/gene-editing-moderna-and-transhumanism/. (4/20/22).

Lipsitch, Marc. "COVID-19 Vaccines and Herd Immunity." Center for Communicable Disease Dyamics, Harvard University, December 17, 2020. https://ccdd.hsph.harvard.edu/2020/12/17/covid-19-vaccines-and-herd-immunity/. (5/23/22).

Liptak, Kevin. "Trump defends honoring racists in monument debate." *CNN*, July 1, 2020. https://www.cnn.com/2020/06/30/politics/donald-trump-racist-monuments/index.html. (4/20/22).

Liptak, Kevin, and Kaitlan Collins. "Trump denies racist tweets were racist." *CNN*, July 15, 2019. https://edition.cnn.com/2019/07/15/politics/donald-trump-racist-tweets-democrats/index.html. (4/20/22).

Lizza, Ryan, Rachel Bade, Tara Palmeri, and Eugene Daniels. "POLITICO Playbook: Double trouble for Biden." *Politico*, September 21, 2021. https://www.politico.com/newsletters/playbook/2021/09/21/double-trouble-for-biden-494411. (5/23/22).

LoBianco, Tom. "Trump falsely claims 'millions of people who voted illegally' cost him popular vote." *CNN*, November 28, 2016.

Logan, Bryan. "Trump repeats debunked claim that voter fraud caused him to lose popular vote to Hillary Clinton." *Business Insider*, January 23, 2017.

Lott, John R. Jr. "Heed Jimmy Carter on the Danger of Mail-In Voting." *Wall Street Journal*, April 10, 2020. https://www.wsj.com/articles/heed-jimmy-carter-on-the-danger-of-mail-in-voting-11586557667.

———. "Why Do Most Countries Require Photo Voter IDs? They Have Seen Massive Vote Fraud Problems." *Crime Prevention Research Center*, May 18, 2021. https://ssrn.com/abstract=3849068. (6/15/22).

Lott, Maxim. "BLM clenched-fist symbol has little-known communist history, critics say." *Fox News*, April 15, 2021. https://foxnews.com/politics/black-lives-matter-antifa-clenched-fist-symbol-communist-history. (3/10/22).

Lucas, Fred. "Exclusive: 3 Plead Out in California Election Fraud Case as Councilman's Trial Proceeds." *Daily Signal*, January 25, 2022. https://www.dailysignal.com/2022/01/25/exclusive-3-plead-out-in-california-election-fraud-case-as-councilmans-trial-proceeds/. (6/28/22).

———. "Facebook Extends Its Ban of Trump to 2 Years or More." *Daily Signal*, June 4, 2021. https://www.dailysignal.com/2021/06/04/facebook-extends-its-ban-of-trump-to-2-years-or-more/.

———. "Why Illegal Immigrants Are Being Released Without Court Dates." *Daily Signal*, June 25, 2021. https://www.dailysignal.com/2021/06/25/why-illegal-immigrants-are-being-released-without-court-dates/. (4/19/22).

Luckhurst, Toby. "Taliban 'carrying out door-to-door manhunt.'" *BBC News*, August 15, 2021. https://www.bbc.com/news/live/world-asia-58219963?at_campaign=64&at_custom1=%5Bpost+type%5D&at_custom2=twitter&at_medium=custom7&at_custom4=6733B2A4-FDF5-11EB-A785-C3F4BDCD475E. (4/19/22).

Lyman, Brianna. "Democrats Are Desperate To Brand Voting Integrity Measures As 'Racist' Suppression." *Daily Caller*, July 8, 2021. https://dailycaller.com/2021/07/08/voting-integrity-laws-voter-suppression-racism-georgia-arizona-ballot-harvesting/. (5/26/22).

Lynch, Conor. "Yes, Donald Trump is an incompetent buffoon — but he's still a major threat to democracy." *Salon*, June 11, 2017. https://www.salon.com/2017/06/11/yes-donald-trump-is-an-incompetent-buffoon-but-hes-still-a-major-threat-to-democracy/. (4/20/22).

MacGuill, Dan. "Did Joe Biden Call Kyle Rittenhouse a 'White Supremacist'?" *Snopes*, November 24, 2021. https://www.snopes.com/fact-check/kyle-rittenhouse-biden/. (2/18/22).

Machera, Peter. "If You Don't Want To Use Google's Biased Search Engine, Try This." *Federalist*, April 23, 2021. https://thefederalist.com/2021/04/23/if-you-dont-want-to-use-googles-biased-search-engine-try-this/. (6/28/22).

Mackey, Robert. "John Sullivan, Who Filmed Shooting of Ashli Babbitt in Capitol, Detained on Federal Charges." *Intercept*, January 14, 2021. https://theintercept.com/2021/01/14/capitol-riot-john-sullivan-ashli-babbitt/. (5/25/22).

Majeed, Zaini. "Israel Commemorates Abraham Accords; 'Truly Historic Milestone' In Middle East Peace." *Republic World*, September 6, 2021. https://www.republicworld.com/world-news/middle-east/israel-commemorates-abraham-accords-truly-historic-milestone-in-middle-east-peace.html. (5/23/22).

Malloy, Allie. "Trump signs 'Right to Try Act' aimed at helping terminally ill patients seek drug treatments." *CNN*, May 30, 2018. https://www.cnn.com/2018/05/30/politics/right-to-try-donald-trump/index.html. (5/26/22).

Malone, Scott, and David Ingram. "Despair and introspection on U.S. coasts after Trump win." *Reuters*, November 9, 2016.

Mannix, Andy, and Matt Delong. "What you need to know about the federal trial of three ex-Minneapolis police officers in George Floyd's death." *Star Tribune*, January 20, 2022. https://m.startribune.com/minneapolis-police-officers-federal-civil-rights-trial-thao-keung-lane-derek-chauvin-george-floyd/600136916/. (2/18/22).

Manskar, Noah. "Jack Dorsey says blocking Post's Hunter Biden story was 'total mistake'—but won't say who made it." *New York Post*, March 25, 2021. https://nypost.com/2021/03/25/dorsey-says-blocking-posts-hunter-biden-story-was-total-mistake/. (3/22/22).

Maqbool, Aleem. "Guantanamo Bay: In a courtroom, just feet away from 9/11 suspects." *BBC News*, September 12, 2021. https://www.bbc.com/news/world-latin-america-58527700. (6/24/22).

Marcus, David. "Biden introduces door-to-door vaccination effort." *New York Post*, July 6, 2021. https://nypost.com/2021/07/06/biden-introduces-door-to-door-vaccination-effort/.

Margolis, Matt. "Five Things Democrats Could Do To Convince Us They Don't Want Widespread Voter Fraud." *PJ Media*, June 20, 2021. https://pjmedia.com/news-and-politics/matt-margolis/2021/06/20/five-things-democrats-could-do-to-convince-us-they-dont-want-wide spread-voter-fraud-n1455844. (5/26/22).

Martin, Brian. "Who's afraid of The Real Anthony Fauci?" https://www.academia.edu/78900507/Whos_afraid_of_The_Real_Anthony_Fauci. (5/27/22).

Martinez, Gina. "Leaked video shows illegal migrants landing at Westchester airport on secret charter flight - one of DOZENS carried out on orders of Biden administration: 'The government is betraying the American people.'" *Daily Mail*, January 27, 2022. https://www.dailymail.co.uk/news/article-10448165/Leaked-video-shows-illegal-migrants-landing-Westchester-airport-secret-charter-flight.html. (4/19/22).

Martz, Michael. "Virginia Supreme Court rejects Chesapeake parents' challenge of Youngkin school mask order." *Richmond Times-Dispatch*, February 7, 2022. https://richmond.com/news/state-and-regional/govt-and-politics/virginia-supreme-court-rejects-chesapeake-parents-chal lenge-of-youngkin-school-mask-order/article_af297d59-f567-5577-90aa-53a13e1cf97d.html. (5/23/22).

Mastrangelo, Dominick. "Vindman calls for Milley's resignation: 'He usurped civilian authority.'"

MSN, September 15, 2021. https://www.msn.com/en-us/news/politics/vindman-calls-for-milleys-resignation-he-usurped-civilian-authority/ar-AAOsUbf. (3/15/22).

McBride, Jessica. "Dominion Voting Systems: Glitch, Clinton Tie Cause Scrutiny in 2020 Election." *Heavy*, December 18, 2020. https://heavy.com/news/dominion-voting-systems-glitch-clinton-pelosi-michigan-georgia/.

McCann, Steve. "So Much Evidence that January 6, 2021 was a Calculated Set-Up." *American Thinker*, July 13, 2021. https://www.americanthinker.com/articles/2021/07/so_much_evidence_that_january_6_2021_was_a_calculated_setup.html. (5/23/22).

McCarthy, Andrew. "FBI Rewrites Federal Law to Let Hillary Off the Hook." *National Review*, July 5, 2016. https://www.nationalreview.com/corner/fbi-rewrites-federal-law-let-hillary-hook/. (5/23/22).

McCaughey, Betsy. "Democrats Reject Work Ethic, Embrace Freeloaders." *Epoch Times*, December 29, 2021. https://www.theepochtimes.com/democrats-reject-work-ethic-embrace-freeloaders_4183690.html.

McCausland, Jeff. "Kim Jong Un's appearance put death rumors to rest. But the world was scared for good reason." *NBC News*, May 5, 2020. https://www.nbcnews.com/think/opinion/kim-jong-un-s-appearance-put-death-rumors-rest-world-ncna1199886.

McClallen, Scott. "Over 7,000 affidavits delivered to Michigan lawmakers claim election fraud." *Washington Examiner*, June 18, 2021. https://www.washingtonexaminer.com/politics/over-7-000-affidavits-delivered-to-michigan-lawmakers-claim-election-fraud. (7/20/22).

McCormack, John. "Schumer's Reckless Threats against Kavanaugh and Gorsuch." *National Review*, June 9, 2022. https://www.nationalreview.com/2022/06/schumers-reckless-threats-against-kavanaugh-and-gorsuch/. (6/10/22).

———. "The Senator Who Saw the Coronavirus Coming." *National Review,* March 31, 2020. https://www.nationalreview.com/2020/03/the-senator-who-saw-the-coronavirus-coming/.

McEvoy, Jemima. "14 Days Of Protests, 19 Dead." *Forbes*, June 8, 2020. https://www.forbes.com/sites/jemimamcevoy/2020/06/08/14-days-of-protests-19-dead/?sh=76ee6fd14de4. (2/20/22).

McGrath, Matt. "Climate change: US formally withdraws from Paris agreement." *BBC*, November 4, 2020. https://www.bbc.com/news/science-environment-54797743. (5/26/22).

McKay, Rich. "Factbox: Who was Ahmaud Arbery?" *Reuters*, February 7, 2022. https://www.reuters.com/world/us/who-was-ahmaud-arbery-2022-02-07/. (5/23/22).

McKeever, Amy. "No modern presidential candidate has refused to concede. Here's why that matters." *National Geographic,* November 8, 2020. https://www.nationalgeographic.com/history/article/no-modern-presidential-candidate-refused-to-concede-heres-why-that-matters. (5/25/22).

McKie, Robin. "No death and an enhanced life: Is the future transhuman?" *Guardian*, May 6, 2018. https://www.theguardian.com/technology/2018/may/06/no-death-and-an-enhanced-life-is-the-future-transhuman. (4/20/22).

McLaughlin, Elliott C., Devon M. Sayers, Alta Spells, and Steve Almasy. "Guilty verdicts in the trial of Ahmaud Arbery's killers met with relief and joy in Georgia and beyond." *CNN*, November 24, 2021. https://www.cnn.com/2021/11/24/us/ahmaud-arbery-killing-trial-wednesday-jury-deliberations/index.html. (5/23/22).

McNamara, Audrey. "Biden raises social cost of carbon, restoring key climate policy tool slashed by Trump." *CBS News*, February 27, 2021. https://www.cbsnews.com/news/carbon-social-cost-raised-by-biden/. (6/4/22).

Meadows *v.* Pelosi (1:21-cv-03217). https://drive.google.com/file/d/1TgAg2wjKEZVwYvCLg_wkhqxXefN-gYHp/view.

Metzger, Bryan. "FBI finds no evidence that Trump and his allies were directly involved with organizing the violence of the Capitol riot: report." *Yahoo!News*, August 20, 2021. https://news.yahoo.com/fbi-finds-no-evidence-trump-153636457.html. (4/17/22).

Michel, Adam. "In 1 Chart, How Much the Rich Pay in Taxes." *Heritage Foundation*, March 3, 2021. https://www.heritage.org/taxes/commentary/1-chart-how-much-the-rich-pay-taxes.

"Report on the November 2020 Election in Michigan." Michigan Senate Oversight Committee. https://misenategopcdn.s3.us-east-1.amazonaws.com/99/doccuments/20210623/SMPO_2020ElectionReport_2.pdf. (6/1/22).

Miller, Andrew Mark. "Democratic senators warned of potential 'vote switching' by Dominion

voting machines prior to 2020 election." *Washington Examiner*, November 13, 2020. https://
www.washingtonexaminer.com/news/democratic-senators-warned-of-potential-vote-switch
ing-by-dominion-voting-machines-prior-to-2020-election. (7/20/22).

———. "Mark Levin: Supreme Court 'ducked' on Pennsylvania election case and is 'hiding
under the proverbial table.'" *Washington Examiner*, December 9, 2020. https://www.washing
tonexaminer.com/news/mark-levin-supreme-court-ducked-on-pennsylvania-election-case-
and-is-hiding-under-the-proverbial-table.

Miller, Joshua Rhett, and Miranda Devine. "Voicemail indicates Joe Biden knew of hunter deals
with 'spy chief of China'." *New York Post*, June 27, 2022. https://nypost.com/2022/06/27/voice
mail-shows-joe-biden-knew-of-hunters-china-dealings-report/. (7/23/22).

Millhiser, Ian. "New study confirms that voter ID laws are very racist." *ThinkProgress*, February 17,
2017. https://archive.thinkprogress.org/new-study-confirms-that-voter-id-laws-are-very-racist-
c338792c3f04/. (5/26/22).

Millman, Andrew, and Casey Gannon. "Man who said January 6 was 'magical' acquitted in US
Capitol riot case." *CNN*, April 6, 2022. https://www.cnn.com/2022/04/06/politics/magical-
acquitted-us-capitol-riot/index.html. (4/7/22).

Miltimore, Jon. "New Danish Study Finds Masks Don't Protect Wearers From COVID Infection."
FEE, November 18, 2020. https://fee.org/articles/new-danish-study-finds-masks-don-t-protect-
wearers-from-covid-infection/. (5/23/22).

———. "Spain's First Study on Omicron Finds Vaccinated People Spread COVID at Same Rate
as Unvaccinated." *FEE*, February 2, 2022. https://fee.org/articles/spain-s-first-study-on-
omicron-finds-vaccinated-people-spread-covid-at-same-rate-as-unvaccinated/. (5/18/22).

———. "The Solzhenitsyn Quote That Explains the 'Mostly Peaceful' Violence in America."
FEE, September 1, 2020. https://fee.org/the-solzhenitsyn-quote-that-explains-the-mostly-
peaceful-violence-in-america/. (3/10/22).

Miranda, Leticia. "First came a pandemic. Then, looting. Small businesses pick up the pieces as
their debt mounts." *NBC News*, June 4, 2020. https://www.nbcnews.com/business/business-
news/first-came-pandemic-then-looting-small-businesses-pick-pieces-their-n1224776.
(5/25/22).

Miranda, Marvin. "Rafael Agustin: the uniquely American writer redefining the American
story." *LA Weekly*, May 31, 2018. https://www.laweekly.com/rafael-agustin-the-uniquely-ameri
can-writer-redefining-the-american-story/.

Miroff, Nick. "At border, record number of migrant youths wait in adult detention cells for longer
than legally allowed." *Washington Post*, March 10, 2021. https://www.washingtonpost.com/
national/unaccompanied-minors-detention-cells/2021/03/10/a0d39390-81c6-11eb-bb5a-ad9a91
faa4ef_story.html. (4/19/22).

Miroff, Nick, and Kevin Sieff. "Mexico to allow US 'Remain in Mexico' asylum policy to resume."
The Boston Globe, December 2, 2021. https://www.bostonglobe.com/2021/12/02/nation/mexico-
allow-us-remain-mexico-asylum-policy-resume/. (4/19/22).

"Voting by mail and absentee voting." *MIT Election Data and Science Lab*, March 16, 2021. https://
electionlab.mit.edu/research/voting-mail-and-absentee-voting.

Mitchell, Daniel. "Hillary Clinton's 38-Year History of Sleaze and Corruption." *People's Pundit
Daily*, October 29, 2016. https://www.peoplespunditdaily.com/policy/2016/10/29/hillary-clin
tons-38-year-history-sleaze-corruption/. (4/6/22)

Moloney, William. "Has the FBI demolished Democrats' insurrection narrative about Jan. 6?"
Hill, August 25, 2021. https://thehill.com/opinion/white-house/569269-has-the-fbi-demol
ished-democrats-insurrection-narrative-about-jan-6. (5/25/22).

Monahan, Kevin, Cynthia McFadden, and Didi Martinez. "Online and vulnerable': Experts find
nearly three dozen U.S. voting systems connected to the internet." *NBC News*, January 10,
2020. https://www.nbcnews.com/politics/elections/online-vulnerable-experts-find-nearly-
three-dozen-u-s-voting-n1112436. (8/4/22).

Moore, Mark. "Nearly a thousand illegal immigrants held under a bridge in Texas, video shows."
New York Post, August 2, 2021. https://nypost.com/2021/08/02/nearly-a-thousand-illegal-immi
grants-held-under-a-bridge-in-texas/. (4/19/22).

Moore, Tina, Larry Celona, Kevin Sheehan, Ben Feuerherd, and Bruce Golding. "Federal agents raid Rudy Giuliani's NYC apartment in Ukraine probe." *New York Post*, April 28, 2021. https://nypost.com/2021/04/28/federal-agents-raid-rudy-giulianis-nyc-apartment/.

Morefield, Scott. "If You're Confronted By A Mask Karen, Rand Paul Has Some Advice." *Townhall*, January 25, 2022. https://townhall.com/tipsheet/scottmorefield/2022/01/25/if-youre-confronted-by-a-mask-karen-rand-paul-has-some-advice-n2602364. (4/13/22).

Moreno, Edgar, and Edgar H. Clemente. "New migrant caravan sets off from southern Mexico border." *Associated Press*, November 18, 2021. https://news.yahoo.com/migrant-caravan-begins-southern-mexico-161101914.html. (4/19/22).

Morris, Emma-Jo, and Gabrielle Fonrouge. "Smoking-gun email reveals how Hunter Biden introduced Ukrainian businessman to VP dad." *New York Post*, October 14, 2020. https://nypost.com/2020/10/14/email-reveals-how-hunter-biden-introduced-ukrainian-biz-man-to-dad/. (5/23/22).

Morris, Kyle. "White House responds to migrant transport: 'No such thing as secret flights.'" https://www.foxnews.com/politics/white-house-responds-migrant-transport-no-such-thing-as-secret-flights. (4/19/22).

Morton, Victor. "Kayleigh McEnany Twitter account locked." *Washington Times*, October 14, 2020. https://www.washingtontimes.com/news/2020/oct/14/kayleigh-mcenany-twitter-account-locked/. (6/6/22).

———. "Report: FBI sought nuclear documents in Trump raid." *Washington Times*, August 11, 2022. https://www.washingtontimes.com/news/2022/aug/11/fbi-sought-nuclear-documents-trump-raid-report/.

Mulroy, Steven J.. "Baby & Bathwater: Standing in Election Cases After 2020." Dick. L. Rev. 9. (2021).

Murica, Lizzy. "VP Candidate Kamala Harris chilling interview about BLM riots: 'They're not gonna stop. And they should not.'" *Law Enforcement Today*, August 30, 2020. https://www.lawenforcementtoday.com/kamala-harris-about-riots-theyre-not-gonna-stop-and-they-should-not/. (5/25/22).

Nagesh, Ashitha. "US election 2020: Why Trump gained support among minorities." *BBC*, November 22, 2020. https://www.bbc.com/news/world-us-canada-54972389.

"California's August Complex Largest Fire in State's History." *NASA*, October 6, 2020. https://www.nasa.gov/image-feature/goddard/2020/californias-august-complex-largest-fire-in-states-history. (5/23/22).

Natelson, Rob. "Sorry, Vice-President Pence can't replace electors on his own." *Independence Institute*, January 3, 2021. https://i2i.org/sorry-vice-president-pence-cant-replace-electors-on-his-own/. (6/20/22).

———. "The Constitution Offers Ways Out of the Election Mess." *Epoch Times*, November 8, 2020. https://www.theepochtimes.com/the-constitution-offers-ways-out-of-the-election-mess_3570136.html. (6/22/22).

———. "The Electoral Count Act Is Unconstitutional." *Epoch Times*, March 14, 2022. https://www.theepochtimes.com/the-electoral-count-act-is-unconstitutional-congress-should-stop-wasting-time-reforming-it_4334762.html. (6/20/22).

"Ballot Collection Laws." National Conference of State Legislatures. https://www.ncsl.org/research/elections-and-campaigns/vopp-table-10-who-can-collect-and-return-an-absentee-ballot-other-than-the-voter.aspx.

"Americans Deserve an Explanation on FBI's Mar-a-Lago Search." *National Review*, August 10, 2022. https://www.nationalreview.com/2022/08/americans-deserve-an-explanation-on-fbis-mar-a-lago-search/.

National School Boards Association. Letter to Joseph R. Biden. September 29, 2021. https://www.documentcloud.org/documents/21094557-national-school-boards-association-letter-to-biden.

"Biden's Desperate COVID Overreach." *National Review*, September 9, 2021. https://www.nationalreview.com/2021/09/bidens-desperate-covid-overreach/.

"What We Do Know about the Benghazi Attack Demands a Reckoning." *National Review*, June 28, 2016. https://www.nationalreview.com/2016/06/benghazi-scandal-hillary-clinton-state-department-obama-administration-house-committee/. (5/23/22).

"About Us: Our Impact." National Vote At Home Institute. https://voteathome.org/about-us/. (6/21/22).

"Vote at Home Policy Actions: 2020 Retrospective." National Vote at Home Institute.

Navarro, Peter. *In Trump Time: A journal of America's plague year.* St. Petersburg: All Seasons Press. 2021.

———. "The Navarro Report." https://www.dropbox.com/s/584r7xtnngauc4t/The%20Navarro%20Report%20Vol%20I%2C%20II%2C%20III%20-%20Feb.%202%2C%202021.pdf?dl=0.

Nazaryan, Alexander. "Trump's incompetent presidency is succeeding despite itself." *CNN,* June 18, 2019. https://www.cnn.com/2019/06/18/opinions/trump-administration-revolving-door-incompetence-nazaryan/index.html. (4/20/22).

"Cuomo Reverses Nursing Home Directive to Take COVID-19 Patients, Requires More Staff Testing." *NBC New York,* May 10, 2020. https://www.nbcnewyork.com/news/local/cuomo-reverses-nursing-home-directive-to-take-covid-19-patients-requires-more-staff-testing/2410533/. (3/15/22).

"Biden suspends oil-drilling leases in Alaska's Arctic refuge." *NBC News,* June 1, 2021. https://www.nbcnews.com/business/energy/biden-suspends-oil-drilling-leases-alaska-s-arctic-refuge-n1269270. (6/4/22).

Neidig, Harper. "Judge: Bannon can argue to throw out contempt charges after conviction." *Hill,* July 27, 2022. https://thehill.com/regulation/3576385-judge-bannon-can-argue-to-throw-out-contempt-charges-after-conviction/. (7/29/22).

Nelson, Steven. "Biden orders federal workers to get COVID vaccine or submit to testing." *New York Post,* July 29, 2021. https://nypost.com/2021/07/29/biden-orders-fed-workers-to-get-covid-vaccine-or-submit-to-tests/.

———. "Kamala Harris says her anti-illegal immigration efforts won't bear fruit 'overnight.'" *New York Post,* January 27, 2022. https://nypost.com/2022/01/27/kamala-harris-says-illegal-immigration-wont-be-fixed-overnight/. (4/19/22).

———. "Psaki claims Biden didn't discuss business with Hunter — despite docs that suggest otherwise." *New York Post,* July 9, 2021. https://nypost.com/2021/07/09/psaki-claims-biden-didnt-discuss-business-with-hunter-despite-docs-that-show-otherwise/. (5/23/22).

———. "Psaki won't defend claim Post's Hunter Biden laptop scoop was 'Russian plant'." *New York Post,* March 17, 2022. https://nypost.com/2022/03/17/psaki-ignores-posts-hunter-biden-laptop-scoop-verification/. (5/23/22).

"Washington Post, New York Times finally admit Hunter's laptop is real — but only to protect Joe Biden some more." *New York Post,* April 1, 2022. https://nypost.com/2022/04/01/new-york-times-finally-admit-hunters-laptop-is-real-but-only-to-protect-joe-biden/. (5/22/23).

"Across the world, Shock and Uncertainty at Trump's Victory." *New York Times,* November 9, 2016.

"Facebook admits the truth: 'Fact checks' are really just (lefty) opinion." *New York Post,* December 14, 2021. https://nypost.com/2021/12/14/facebook-admits-the-truth-fact-checks-are-really-just-lefty-opinion/. (5/29/22).

"One year later, The Post's Hunter Biden reporting is vindicated — but still buried." *New York Post* (Editorial Board), October 12, 2021. https://nypost.com/2021/10/12/one-year-later-the-posts-hunter-biden-reporting-is-vindicated-but-still-buried/. (5/23/22).

"Spies who lie: 51 'intelligence' experts refuse to apologize for discrediting true Hunter Biden story." *New York Post,* March 18, 2022. https://nypost.com/2022/03/18/intelligence-experts-refuse-to-apologize-for-smearing-hunter-biden-story/. (3/21/22).

"Fact-Checking the First 2020 Presidential Debate." *New York Times,* September 29, 2020. https://www.nytimes.com/live/2020/09/29/us/debate-fact-check. (6/6/22).

Newburger, Emma. "Biden suspends oil and gas leasing in slew of executive actions on climate change." *CNBC,* January 27, 2021. https://www.cnbc.com/2021/01/27/biden-suspends-oil-and-gas-drilling-in-series-of.html. (6/4/22).

"Breaking MRC Poll: Majority of Voters Believe Media Hope Shutdown Hurts Trump Reelection." *NewsBusters,* June 9, 2020. https://www.newsbusters.org/blogs/nb/nb-staff/2020/06/09/breaking-mrc-poll-majority-voters-believe-media-hope-shutdown-hurts. (6/6/22).

"Liz Cheney Endorses Trump; Rips 'Felon' Hillary." *Newsmax,* August 12, 2016. https://www.newsmax.com/Politics/liz-cheney-endorse-trump-rips/2016/08/12/id/743406/. (6/7/22).

"Trump asked for more security on Jan 6 and was ignored, memo confirms | American Agenda on Newsmax," Newsmax TV, December 6, 2021. YouTube video. https://www.youtube.com/watch?v=3ov40RVVptE. (4/17/22).

Nightingale, Hannah. "Breaking: Judge rules mob members shot by Kyle Rittenhouse cannot be called 'victims' in court." *Post Millennial*, October 26, 2021. https://thepostmillennial.com/breaking-judge-rules-mob-members-shot-by-kyle-rittenhouse-cannot-be-called-victims-in-court. (5/23/22).

Nolan, Lucas. "Google Hides Popular Hillary Clinton Health Searches." *Breitbart*, August 30, 2016. https://www.breitbart.com/tech/2016/08/30/google-hides-popular-hillary-clinton-health-searches/. (6/28/22).

———. "Read Elon Musk's Letter To Twitter Calling Off $44 Million Buyout." *Breitbart*, July 9, 2022. https://www.breitbart.com/tech/2022/07/09/read-elon-musks-letter-to-twitter-calling-off-44-billion-buyout/. (7/20/22).

———. "Social Justice Warriors Furious As Internal Google Manifesto Slams Company For Political Intolerance." *Breitbart*, August 7, 2017. https://www.breitbart.com/tech/2017/08/07/sjws-furious-as-internal-google-manifesto-slams-company-for-political-intolerance/. (6/28/22).

Norman, Adrian. *The Art of the Steal*. Eleven Press. 2020.

"LIVE Russian attack on Ukraine: Number of reported casualties rises, EU prepares massive sanctions." *Norway Today*, February 24, 2022. https://norwaytoday.info/news/putin-launches-attack-explosions-reported-in-kyiv-and-ukraine/. (2/24/22).

Noyes, Rich. "Special Report: The Stealing of the Presidency, 2020." *MRC Newsbusters*, November 24, 2020. https://www.newsbusters.org/blogs/nb/rich-noyes/2020/11/24/special-report-stealing-presidency-2020. (5/23/22).

O'Gieblyn, Meghan. "God in the machine: my strange journey into transhumanism." *Guardian*, April 18, 2017. https://www.theguardian.com/technology/2017/apr/18/god-in-the-machine-my-strange-journey-into-transhumanism. (4/20/22).

Denyse O'Leary. "Google Engineer Reveals Search Engine Bias." *Mind Matters News*, July 27, 2019. https://mindmatters.ai/2019/07/google-engineer-reveals-search-engine-bias/.

O'Neil, Tyler. "17 VA Scandals Before Trump's Reform Bill." *PJ Media*, June 28, 2017. https://pjmedia.com/news-and-politics/tyler-o-neil/2017/06/28/17-va-scandals-before-trumps-reform-bill-n52204. (5/26/22).

O'Neill, Jesse. "Laptop connected to Hunter Biden linked to FBI money-laundering probe." *New York Post*, October 21, 2020. https://nypost.com/2020/10/21/hunter-biden-laptop-linked-to-fbi-money-laundering-probe-report/. (5/23/22).

"Election Night 2020: Minute-by-minute on the tri-campus." *Observer*, University of Notre Dame, November 4, 2020. https://ndsmcobserver.com/tag/election-2020/.

"Limestone County Social Worker Charged With 134 Felony Counts Involving Election Fraud." Office of Attorney General of Texas Ken Paxton, November 6, 2020. https://www.texasattorneygeneral.gov/news/releases/limestone-county-social-worker-charged-134-felony-counts-involving-election-fraud.

"Colorado Secretary of State's Office Adopts Emergency Rules for Voting Systems." Office of Colorado Secretary of State Jena Griswold, June 17, 2021. https://www.sos.state.co.us/pubs/newsRoom/pressReleases/2021/PR20210617Rules.html.

"Review of U.S. Park Police Actions at Lafayette Park." Office of the Inspector General, U.S. Department of the Interior, June 8, 2021. https://www.doioig.gov/reports/review/review-us-park-police-actions-lafayette-park.

"Review of U.S. Park Police Actions at Lafayette Park (revised version)." Office of the Inspector General, U.S. Department of the Interior, June 2021. https://www.oversight.gov/sites/default/files/oig-reports/DOI/SpecialReviewUSPPActionsAtLafayetteParkPublic.pdf.

"Inslee issues proclamation requiring vaccination for most state employees, health and long-term care workers." Office of Washington Governor Jay Inslee, August 9, 2021. https://www.governor.wa.gov/news-media/inslee-issues-proclamation-requiring-vaccination-most-state-employees-health-and-long.

Oliber, Sara E., Julia W. Gargano, Mona Marin, Megan Wallace, Kathryn G. Curran, Mary Chamberland, Nancy McClung, et al. "The Advisory Committee on Immunization Practices Interim Recommendation for Use of Moderna COVID-19 Vaccine — United States, December 2020." Centers for Disease Control and Prevention, January 1, 2021. https://www.cdc.gov/mmwr/volumes/69/wr/mm695152e1.htm. (2/16/22).

Ollstein, Alice, Arjun Kakkar, and Beatrice Jin. "The 17 things Joe Biden did on Day One: Through executive orders, he overturned Trump's policies—and started making his own." *Politico*, January 21, 2021. https://www.politico.com/interactives/2021/interactive_biden-first-day-executive-orders/. (4/1/22).

Olson, Tyler. "Fauci, Rand Paul trade 'lying' accusations about gain-of-function research in hearing on Delta variant: Kentucky senator stepped close to the line of accusing Fauci of lying to Congress in previous testimony." Fox News, July 20, 2021. https://www.foxnews.com/politics/fauci-walensky-masks-virus-rules-delta-covid-spread-senate-hearing. (2/16/22).

———. "Fauci's mixed messages, inconsistencies about COVID-19 masks, vaccines and reopenings come under scrutiny." *Fox News*, February 23, 2021. https://www.foxnews.com/politics/faucis-mixed-messages-inconsistencies-about-covid-19-masks-vaccines-and-reopenings-come-under-scrutiny. (4/13/22).

Overby, Peter. "IRS Apologizes For Aggressive Scrutiny Of Conservative Groups." *National Public Radio*, October 27, 2017. https://www.npr.org/2017/10/27/560308997/irs-apologizes-for-aggressive-scrutiny-of-conservative-groups.

Ozimek, Tom. "Biden Says Next Month's Child Tax Credit Payments 'Just the First Step' as He Seeks to Make Benefit Permanent." *Epoch Times*, June 22, 2021. https://www.theepochtimes.com/biden-says-next-months-child-tax-credit-payments-just-the-first-step-as-he-seeks-to-make-benefit-permanent_3868766.html.

Paine, Thomas. *Common Sense, Together with The American Crisis.* Norwalk: Easton Press, 1994.

Palma, Bethania. "Obama Encouraged 'Illegal Aliens' to Vote." *Snopes*, November 6, 2016. https://www.snopes.com/fact-check/obama-encouraged-illegal-aliens-to-vote/.

Palmer, Ewan. "The Kyle Rittenhouse Trial Story Explained." *Newsweek*, November 15, 2021. https://www.newsweek.com/kyle-rittenhouse-tial-story-explained-verdict-kenosha-1649267. (3/15/22).

———. "Trump Boat Parade Likely Breaks World Record As Over 3,000 Vessels Turn Up." *Newsweek*, July 7, 2020. https://www.newsweek.com/trump-boat-parade-world-record-lake-murray-1515891.

Pandolfo, Chris. "Report: Election results delayed in Georgia's largest county after water pipe bursts in a room containing ballots: Not good news." *Blaze*, November 3, 2020. https://www.theblaze.com/news/georgia-election-results-delayed-pipe-burst.

Panreck, Hanna. "Progressive activists, media pundits react to Elon Musk's Twitter takeover: 'No good will come of this.'" *Fox News*, April 5, 2022. https://www.foxnews.com/media/progressive-activists-media-pundits-elon-musk-twitter-takeover. (7/20/22).

Parker, Mario, and Jordan Fabian. "Trump to Hold 14 Rallies in Three Days to Close Out Campaign." *Bloomberg*, October 30, 2020. https://www.bloomberg.com/news/articles/2020-10-30/trump-campaign-rallies. (5/16/22).

Parsey, Aaron. "Liz Cheney Says Evidence Shows Trump and Others Knew Plan to Overturn 2020 Election Was Illegal." *People*, April 11, 2022. https://people.com/politics/liz-cheney-evidence-shows-trump-plan-illegal-reverse-2020-election/. (5/17/22).

Patteson, Callie. "10K+ illegal migrants mass in Texas as Biden FAA bans news drones." *New York Post*, September 17, 2021. https://nypost.com/2021/09/17/thousands-of-immigrants-wait-for-asylum-under-texas-bridge/. (4/19/22).

"Trump signs bill to fund veterans medical care program." *PBS*, August 12, 2017. https://www.pbs.org/newshour/politics/trump-signs-bill-fund-veterans-medical-care-program. (5/26/22).

Pearson, Catherine. "Experts Predict What This 'Lost Year' Will Really Do To Our Kids." *Huffpost*, October 7, 2020. https://www.huffpost.com/entry/lost-year-students-kids-coronavirus_l_5f7ca334c5b60c6bcc62f2d1. (5/23/22).

Pereira, Ivan. "US administers 1st doses of Pfizer coronavirus vaccine." *ABC News*, December 14, 2020. https://abcnews.go.com/US/us-administer-1st-doses-pfizer-coronavirus-vaccine/story?id=74703018. (2/16/22).

"The 2020 Trump-Biden matchup." *Pew Research Center*, August 13, 2020. https://www.pewresearch.org/politics/2020/08/13/the-2020-trump-biden-matchup/. (5/16/22).

"The Partisan Divide on Political Values Grows Even Wider: Sharp shifts among Democrats on aid to needy, race, immigration." *Pew Research Center*, October 5, 2017. https://www.pewresearch.org/politics/2017/10/05/the-partisan-divide-on-political-values-grows-even-wider/.

"Trump Gets Negative Ratings for Many Personal Traits, but Most Say He Stands Up for His Beliefs." *Pew Research Center*, October 1, 2018. https://www.pewresearch.org/politics/2018/10/01/trump-gets-negative-ratings-for-many-personal-traits-but-most-say-he-stands-up-for-his-beliefs/. (5/23/22).

Picchi, Aimee. "Pfizer and BioNTech say their vaccine is 91% effective against COVID-19, citing new test data." *CBS News*, April 1, 2021. https://www.cbsnews.com/news/covid-vaccine-pfizer-biontech-91-percent-effective/. (5/18/22).

Pigliucci, Massimo. "The problems with transhumanism." *Psychology Today*, July 7, 2009. https://www.psychologytoday.com/us/blog/rationally-speaking/200907/the-problems-transhumanism. (4/20/22).

Piven, Frances Fox, and Richard A. Cloward, *Poor People's Movements: Why They Succeed, How They Fail.* New York:Vintage Books, 1979.

———. "The Weight of the Poor: A Strategy to End Poverty." *The Nation*, May 2, 1966. https://www.thenation.com/article/archive/weight-poor-strategy-end-poverty/. (4/24/22).

"140 Officers were Injured in Capitol Riot." *Police*, January 28, 2021. https://www.policemag.com/592586/140-officers-were-injured-in-capitol-riot-officials-say. (5/25/22).

"Trump-O-Meter." *Politifact*. https://www.politifact.com/truth-o-meter/promises/trumpometer/. (5/23/22).

Pollak, Joel B.. "FBI Arrests Peter Navarro One Day After He Vows To Impeach Biden." *Breitbart*, June 3, 2022. https://www.breitbart.com/politics/2022/06/03/fbi-arrests-peter-navarro-one-day-after-he-vows-to-impeach-biden/. (7/29/22).

———. "Pollak: Mark Meadows' Lawsuit Could End the January 6 Committee." *Breitbart*, December 9, 2021. https://www.breitbart.com/politics/2021/12/09/pollak-mark-meadows-lawsuit-could-end-the-january-6-committee/. (7/25/22).

———. "Voter Fraud Leads To Reversed Result In California Local Government Election." *Breitbart*, May 31, 2022. https://www.breitbart.com/politics/2022/05/31/voter-fraud-leads-to-reversed-result-in-california-local-government-election/. (6/28/22).

Polumbo, Brad. "George Floyd Riots Caused Record-Setting \$2 Billion in Damage, New Report Says. Here's Why the True Cost is Even Higher." *Foundation for Economic Education,* September 16, 2020. https://fee.org/articles/george-floyd-riots-caused-record-setting-2-billion-in-damage-new-report-says-here-s-why-the-true-cost-is-even-higher/. (5/25/22).

———. "'Inflation Tax' Will Cost Families This May Thousands This Year, Bloomberg Analysis Warns." *FEE*, April 1, 2022. https://fee.org/articles/inflation-tax-will-cost-families-this-many-thousands-this-year-bloomberg-analysis-warns/. (5/23/22).

———. "Is Black Lives Matter Marxist? No and Yes." *FEE*, July 7, 2020. https://fee.org/articles/is-black-lives-matter-marxist-no-and-yes/. (5/18/22).

Poor, Jeff. "Mark Levin: 'There is more evidence of voter fraud than there was ever evidence of Russian collusion.'" *Breitbart*, November 7, 2020. https://www.breitbart.com/clips/2020/11/07/mark-levin-there-is-more-evidence-of-voter-fraud-than-there-was-ever-evidence-of-russian-collusion/.

Porterfield, Carlie. "Google Will Slash Some Autocomplete Suggestions For Political Searches Ahead Of Presidential Election." *Forbes*, September 10, 2020. https://www.forbes.com/sites/carlieporterfield/2020/09/10/google-will-slash-some-autocomplete-suggestions-for-political-searches-ahead-of-presidential-election/.

Prokop, Andrew. "A new report complicates simplistic narratives about race and the 2020 election." *Vox*, May 10, 2021. https://www.vox.com/2021/5/10/22425178/catalist-report-2020-election-biden-trump-demographics. (5/16/22).

Quinn, Melissa, and Scott MacFarlane. "Man arrested near Kavanaugh's home charged with attempting to murder Supreme Court justice." *CBS News*, June 9, 2022. https://www.cbsnews.com/news/nicholas-roske-brett-kavanaugh-attempted-murder/. (6/10/22).

Quinnell, Eric, and Anonymous. "Edison Timeseries Distribution Analysis of the 2020 Presidential Election." January 5, 2021. https://election-integrity.info/TimeSeries-Distributions.pdf.

Quinnell, Eric, Stan Young, Tony Cox, Tom Davis, Ray Blehar, John Droz, and Anonymous Expert. "2020 Presidential Election Startling Vote Spikes." January 2, 2021. https://election-integrity.info/Vote_Spikes_Report.pdf.

Quinnell, Eric, Stan Young, Ray Blehar, Tom Davis, and John Droz. "Statistical Voting Analysis of the 2020 NY-22 Congressional Contest." December 31, 2020. https://election-integrity.info/NY-22nd-2020-Report.pdf.

Raiklin, Ivan. Personal interview with Daniel Brubaker, Hamilton, Virginia. May 12, 2022.

Rapier, Robert. "Is The U.S. Energy Independent?" *Forbes*, November 14, 2021. https://www.forbes.com/sites/rrapier/2021/11/14/is-the-us-energy-independent/?sh=24f57c051387. (5/16/22).

"Election Integrity: 62% Don't Think Voter ID Laws Discriminate." *Rasmussen Reports*, April 13, 2021. https://www.rasmussenreports.com/public_content/politics/general_politics/april_2021/election_integrity_62_don_t_think_voter_id_laws_discriminate.

"Voters Don't Trust Media Fact-Checking." *Rasmussen Reports*, September 30, 2016. https://www.rasmussenreports.com/public_content/politics/general_politics/september_2016/voters_don_t_trust_media_fact_checking. (6/28/22).

Reilly, Katie. "The Learning Gap Is Getting Worse as Schools Rely on Remote Classes, Especially for Students of Color." *Time*, December 8, 2020. https://time.com/5918769/coronavirus-schools-learning-loss/. (5/23/22).

Reimann, Nicholas. "Trump's Changing Stance On Jan. 6 Attack—From Condemning Rioters To Backing 'Protest.'" *Forbes*, January 6, 2022. https://www.forbes.com/sites/nicholasreimann/2022/01/06/trumps-changing-stance-on-jan-6-attack-from-condemning-rioters-to-backing-protest/?sh=5c69d26921a8. (5/25/22).

Reinhard, RJ. "Faith in Elections in Relatively Short Supply in U.S." *Gallup*, February 13, 2020. https://news.gallup.com/poll/285608/faith-elections-relatively-short-supply.aspx. (5/23/22).

"Excerpts of call between Joe Biden and Ashraf Ghani July 23." *Reuters*, August 31, 2021. https://www.reuters.com/world/excerpts-call-between-joe-biden-ashraf-ghani-july-23-2021-08-31/.

"Fact Check: Clarifying video of poll watcher being turned away in Philadelphia." *Reuters*, November 3, 2020. https://www.reuters.com/article/uk-factcheck-poll-watcher-philadelphia-t-idUSKBN27K009. (4/17/22).

"Fact Check-CDC study found that over 75% of COVID-19 deaths in vaccinated people were among those with at least 4 comorbidities." *Reuters*, January 12, 2022. https://www.reuters.com/article/factcheck-walensky-study-idUSL1N2TS0S2. (5/23/22).

"Fact check: Kamala Harris said she supports protests, not 'riots', in Late Show clip." *Reuters*, October 29, 2020. https://www.reuters.com/article/uk-factcheck-kamala-harris-late-show-rio-idUSKBN27E34P. (4/17/22).

"Fact check: List of partly false statements on the 2020 election." *Reuters*, November 10, 2020. https://www.reuters.com/article/uk-factcheck-list-statements-2020-electi-idUSKBN27Q2NI.

"October 15 U.S. presidential debate officially canceled after Trump balked." *Reuters*, October 9, 2020. https://www.reuters.com/article/us-usa-election-debate-idUSKBN26U2M7. (6/7/22).

Reynolds, Alan. "What Marx Got Right about Redistribution—That John Stuart Mill Got Wrong," *FEE*, February 15, 2016. (7/1/22).

Reynolds, Emma. "Lockdowns shouldn't be fully lifted until coronavirus vaccine found, new study warns." *CNN*, April 9, 2020. https://www.cnn.com/2020/04/09/world/lockdown-lift-vaccine-coronavirus-lancet-intl/index.html. (5/18/22).

Richman, Jesse T., Gulshan A. Chattha, and David C. Earnest. "Do non-citizens vote in U.S. elections?" *Electoral Studies* 36 (2014): 149-157.

Robbins, James S. "Trump did condemn white supremacists, too bad so many people won't listen." *USA Today*, October 2, 2020. https://www.usatoday.com/story/opinion/2020/10/02/trump-and-white-supremacy-he-did-condemn-and-has-repeatedly-column/5883336002/. (6/21/22).

Robertson, Lori. "The Wuhan Lab and the Gain-of-Function Disagreement." *FactCheck*, May 21, 2021. https://www.factcheck.org/2021/05/the-wuhan-lab-and-the-gain-of-function-disagreement/. (2/16/22).

Robinson, Eugene. "Opinion: Trump is spinning out of control. We must stop pretending otherwise." *Washington Post*, October 17, 2019. https://www.washingtonpost.com/opinions/trump-is-in-a-tailspin--and-dragging-the-country-down-with-him/2019/10/17/63f3767a-f121-11e9-8693-f487e46784aa_story.html. (4/20/22).

Roche, Darragh. "Fauci Said Masks 'Not Really Effective in Keeping Out Virus,' Email Reveals." *Newsweek*, June 2, 2021. https://www.newsweek.com/fauci-said-masks-not-really-effective-keeping-out-virus-email-reveals-1596703. (5/23/22).

Rodriguez, Olga R.. "Cruise ship passengers recall deaths, confusion, quarantine." *AP News*, March 15, 2021. https://apnews.com/article/travel-san-francisco-coronavirus-pandemic-califor nia-united-states-9b4eb9ac5b43dd890331f7939e205bb9. (5/23/22).

Rodrigo, Chris Mills. "Parler says it alerted FBI to threats before Capitol riot." *Hill,* March 26, 2021. https://thehill.com/policy/technology/545163-parler-says-it-alerted-fbi-to-threats-before-capitol-riot/. (5/23/22).

———. "Trump signs criminal justice overhaul." *Hill*, December 21, 2018. https://thehill.com/ homenews/administration/422517-trump-signs-criminal-justice-reform-bill/. (5/26/22).

Roff, Peter. "Al Franken May Have Won His Senate Seat Through Voter Fraud." *US News And World Report*, July 20, 2010. https://www.usnews.com/opinion/blogs/peter-roff/2010/07/20/al-franken-may-have-won-his-senate-seat-through-voter-fraud. (7/20/22).

Rogers, Mike. "Opinion: Certify election results to preserve democracy." *Detroit News*, November 21, 2020. https://www.detroitnews.com/story/opinion/2020/11/22/opinion-certify-election-results-preserve-democracy/6364273002/. (6/28/22).

Rosas, Julio. "Anti-Trump White House 'Siege' Suffers Major First Day Setback." *Townhall*, September 17, 2020. https://townhall.com/tipsheet/juliorosas/2020/09/17/white-house-siege-suffers-first-day-set-back-n2576411. (2/18/22).

Rose, Jonathan, and Keith Griffith. "'What are the Kingdom's views on journalistic freedom of speech?' Elon Musk socks it to Saudi prince Twitter shareholder for trying to block his hostile takeover bid." *Daily Mail*, April 14, 2022. https://www.dailymail.co.uk/news/article-10718427/ amp/Elon-Musk-tries-buy-Twitter-41billion-Tesla-CEO-offers-54-20-share.html. (6/28/22).

Rosiak, Luke. Twitter post, March 15, 2022, 1:48 p.m. https://twitter.com/lukerosiak/status/ 1503790281275195396.

Roy, Siddharthya, and Richard Miniter. "Taliban kill squad hunting down Afghans—using US biometric data." *New York Post*, August 27, 2021. https://nypost.com/2021/08/27/taliban-kill-squad-hunting-afghans-with-americas-biometric-data/. (4/19/22).

Rufo, Christopher F.. "Anarchy in Seattle." *City Journal*, June 10, 2020. https://www.city-journal. org/antifa-seattle-capitol-hill-autonomous-zone.

Rufus, Anneli. "Voter Fraud and the Mentally Disabled: Were mentally disabled Minnesotans 'coached' to vote for certain candidates?" *Psychology Today*, November 2, 2010.

"Woman who can't define woman put on Supreme Court." *Ruth Institute*, April 7, 2022. https:// ruthinstitute.org/press/woman-who-cant-define-woman/. (4/7/22).

Ruthhart, Bill, and Jonathon Berlin. "Campaign trail tracker: Where Trump, Biden and their running mates have traveled in presidential race's final weeks." *Chicago Tribune*, November 5, 2020. https://www.chicagotribune.com/politics/ct-viz-presidential-campaign-trail-tracker-20200917-edspdit2incbfnopchjaelp3uu-htmlstory.html. (6/7/22).

Rutz, David. "CNN's Powers: All Trump Supporters Are Racist." *Washington Free Beacon*, November 18, 2018. https://freebeacon.com/politics/cnns-powers-all-trump-supporters-are-racist/. (4/20/22).

Saavedra, Marie. "Wheeling Family Calls On Hospital To Change Policy After 96-Year-Old Matriarch With COVID Dies Alone." *CBS Chicago*, February 4, 2022. https://chicago.cbslocal. com/2022/02/04/covid-hospital-visitor-policy-matriarch-dies-alone/. (2/17/22).

Sabia, Carmine, "Major Arrest Made in Durham Investigation As Federal Authorities Nab Dossier Source." *Conservative Brief*, November 4, 2021. https://conservativebrief.com/arrest-53959/. (4/19/22).

Sadeghi, McKenzie. "Fact check: Trump repeats false claim that Pelosi rejected request for National Guard ahead of Jan. 6." *USA Today*, December 16, 2021. https://www.usatoday.com/ story/news/factcheck/2021/12/16/fact-check-no-trump-request-10000-guard-troops-jan-6/ 8929215002/. (5/23/22).

Said, Samira, and Kelly Mena. "Database for Covid-19 vaccination info raises concerns about privacy and vaccine uptake." *CNN*, December 13, 2020. https://www.cnn.com/2020/12/13/poli tics/coronavirus-vaccination-database/index.html. (5/18/22).

Salas-Rodriguez, Israel. "Deadly Scene: Who was Kevin Greeson?" *The Sun*, January 7, 2021. https://www.thesun.co.uk/news/13681360/kevin-greeson-capitol-riots-trump-proud-boys/. (5/16/22).

Samuelsohn, Darren. "Republicans tell Trump to quit claiming rigged election." *Politico,* October 11, 2016.

Saphir, Ann, and Lindsay Dunsmuir. "Biden's Fed nominees back U.S. inflation fight." *Reuters,* February 3, 2022. https://www.reuters.com/business/fed-nominees-back-its-inflation-fighting-agenda-2022-02-03/. (4/19/22).

Saunders, Joe. "Reporter Calls Out Meeting Where Obama, Comey Were 'Hatching' Plot Against Trump." *Western Journal,* May 12, 2020. https://www.westernjournal.com/reporter-calls-meeting-obama-comey-hatching-plot-trump/. (4/20/22).

Savransky, Becca. "How CHAZ became CHOP: Seattle's police-free zone explained." *Seattle P-I,* June 15, 2020. https://www.seattlepi.com/seattlenews/article/What-is-CHOP-the-zone-in-Seattle-formed-by-15341281.php.

Sawyer, Denise, and Jay O'Brien, "Man acquitted of shooting at deputies in raid that led to death of girlfriend." *CBS 12 News,* November 19, 2021. https://cbs12.com/news/local/man-acquitted-of-shooting-at-deputies-in-raid-that-led-to-death-of-girlfriend. (3/10/22).

Saxena, Vivek. "Gen. Milley claims Ukraine capital Kyiv would fall within 72 hours of Russian invasion: report." *BizPacReview,* February 6, 2022. https://www.bizpacreview.com/2022/02/06/gen-milley-claims-ukraine-capital-kyiv-would-fall-within-72-hours-of-russian-invasion-report-1197660/.

———. "Witness testimony describes how Dominion took over Georgia voting machines remotely during election." *BPR,* December 9, 2020. https://www.bizpacreview.com/2020/12/09/witness-testimony-describes-how-dominion-took-over-georgia-voting-machines-remotely-during-election-1003795/. (7/20/22).

Scarborough, Rowan. "Hunter Biden Burisma payments detailed in Treasury Department reports." *Washington Times,* September 30, 2020. https://www.washingtontimes.com/news/2020/sep/30/hunter-biden-burisma-payments-detailed-treasury-de/. (5/23/22).

Schapiro, Rich, Anna Schecter, and Chelsea Damberg. "Officer who shot Ashli Babbitt during Capitol Riot breaks silence: 'I saved countless lives'." *NBC News,* August 26, 2021. https://www.nbcnews.com/news/us-news/officer-who-shot-ashli-babbitt-during-capitol-riot-breaks-silence-n1277736. (5/25/22).

Scher, Brent. "Park Police Releases New Footage of Violent Lafayette Park Protests." *Washington Free Beacon,* June 24, 2020. https://freebeacon.com/latest-news/park-police-release-new-footage-of-violent-lafayette-park-protests/. (5/23/22).

Schlapp, Mercedes. Twitter post, June 7, 2022, 12:29 p.m. https://twitter.com/mercedesschlapp/status/1534210933467357184.

Schneider, Gregory S. "All 133 Virginia school superintendents urge Youngkin to scrap tip line and content policy." *Washington Post,* March 12, 2022. https://www.msn.com/en-us/news/us/all-133-virginia-school-superintendents-urge-youngkin-to-scrap-tip-line-and-content-policy/ar-AAUWj8V. (3/16/22).

Schneider, Susan. "Future Minds: Transhumanism, Cognitive Enhancement, and the Nature of Persons." Center for Neuroscience & Society, University of Pennsylvania, July 1, 2008. https://repository.upenn.edu/cgi/viewcontent.cgi?article=1037&context=neuroethics_pubs. (4/20/22).

Schor, Elana. "Sen. Lankford criticizes Trump's false voter fraud allegations." *Politico,* November 28, 2016.

Schorr, Isaac. "New York Times Buries Kavanaugh Assassination Attempt on Page A20." *National Review,* June 9, 2022. https://www.nationalreview.com/news/new-york-times-buries-kavanaugh-assassination-attempt-on-page-a20/. (6/10/22).

Schreckinger, Ben. "Hunter Biden's prosecutor rejected moves that would have revealed probe earlier." *Politico,* July 16, 2021. https://www.politico.com/news/2021/07/16/hunter-biden-probe-prosecutor-499782.

Schulkin, Peter A.. "Child Tax Credits for Illegal Immigrants." *Center for Immigration Studies,* November 8, 2021. https://cis.org/Child-Tax-Credits-Illegal-Immigrants.

Schumaker, Erin. "New 'medical freedom' law outlaws requiring COVID-19 vaccine to access public spaces." *ABC News,* July 26, 2021. https://abcnews.go.com/Health/medical-freedom-law-outlaws-requiring-covid-19-vaccine/story?id=79062604.

Schuster-Bruce, Catherine. "Fauci brushes off GOP criticism and says attacks on him are 'attacks on science' he can debunk 'immediately.'" *Business Insider*, June 10, 2021. https://www.busi nessinsider.com/fauci-attack-on-science-gop-criticism-2021-6?op=1. (4/13/22).

Schwab, Klaus. "The Fourth Industrial Revolution: what it means, how to respond." *World Economic Forum*, January 14, 2016. https://www.weforum.org/agenda/2016/01/the-fourth-indus trial-revolution-what-it-means-and-how-to-respond/. (4/20/22).

Schwab, Klaus, and Thierry Malleret. *COVID-19: The Great Reset*. Geneva: Forum Publishing, 2020.

Schwab, Klaus, and Peter Vanham. "What is stakeholder capitalism?" *World Economic Forum*, January 22, 2021. https://www.weforum.org/agenda/2021/01/klaus-schwab-on-what-is-stake holder-capitalism-history-relevance/. (8/4/22).

Schwartz, Ian. "Greenwald: FBI Involvement IN Capitol Riot Not A 'Crazy Conspiracy Theory,' This Is What They Do." *Real Clear Politics*, June 18, 2021. https://www.realclearpolitics.com/ video/2021/06/18/greenwald_fbi_involvement_in_capitol_riot_not_a_crazy_conspiracy_theo ry_this_is_what_they_do.html#!. (5/23/22).

———. "WH's Psaki: 'We're Flagging Problematic Posts For Facebook That Spread Disinforma tion." *RealClearPolitics*, July 15, 2021. https://www.realclearpolitics.com/video/2021/07/15/psak i_were_flagging_problematic_posts_for_facebook_that_spread_disinformation.html. (3/22/22).

Schwartz, Matthew S.. "Trump's Legal Losses Come Fast and Furious." *NPR*, December 5, 2020. https://www.npr.org/2020/12/05/943535299/trumps-legal-losses-come-fast-and-furious. (7/26/22).

Scott, Dylan. "Fauci: 85 percent of the US needs to get the Covid-19 vaccine for 'true herd immu nity.'" *Vox*, December 15, 2020. https://www.vox.com/coronavirus-covid19/2020/12/15/22176555/ anthony-fauci-covid-19-vaccine-herd-immunity-goal. (5/23/22).

"Flashback: Watch Kamala Harris Call Joe Biden Racist!" Scott's Sovereignty, August 17, 2020. YouTube video. https://youtu.be/-1HHmyc78hY.

Seipel, Arnie. "Trump Makes Unfounded Claim That 'Millions' Voted Illegally For Clinton." *NPR*, November 27, 2016.

Shalal, Andrea. "Biden warns Putin: Russia will pay 'terrible price' if it invades Ukraine." *Reuters*, December 11, 2021. https://www.reuters.com/world/biden-warns-putin-russia-will-pay-a-terri ble-price-if-it-invades-ukraine-2021-12-11/. (7/1/22).

Shaw, Mitchell. "Comey: Trump Was Not Under Investigation." *New American*, June 8, 2017. https://thenewamerican.com/comey-trump-was-not-under-investigation/. (7/29/22).

Shearer, Rob. "Rob Shearer: What a PA Democrat's election system audit found." *Broad and Liberty*, October 13, 2021. https://broadandliberty.com/2021/10/13/rob-shearer-what-a-pa-democrats-election-system-audit-found/. (5/26/22).

Shelbourne, Mallory. "Trump claims voter fraud without evidence, says 'I won the popular vote.'" *Hill*, November 27, 2016.

Sherman, Amy. "'Send your postcards to 5 key states to decertify fraud' in the 2020 election." *PolitiFact*, August 16, 2022.

Shullenberger, Geoff. "Were masks a waste of time?" *Unherd.com*, February 7, 2022. https:// unherd.com/2022/02/were-masks-a-waste-of-time/?=frlh.

Sieve, Sher. "Hillary Protector AG Lynch Refuses to Release New Clinton emails to FBI." *Canada Free Press*, October 30, 2016. https://canadafreepress.com/article/hillary-protector-ag-lynch-refuses-to-release-new-clinton-emails-to-fbi. (2/16/22).

Sigalos, MacKenzie. "Yes, your boss can fire you if you refuse to get a Covid (sic) vaccine." *CNBC*, December 7, 2020. https://www.cnbc.com/2020/12/07/covid-vaccine-update-your-boss-can-fire-you-if-you-refuse-the-coronavirus-shot.html.

Simcox, Robin. "Did Trump Really Beat ISIS?" *Heritage Foundation*, January 28, 2018. https://www. heritage.org/middle-east/commentary/did-trump-really-beat-isis. (5/26/22).

Simkins, J.D. "Hospital ship Comfort departs NYC, having treated fewer than 200 patients." *Navy Times*, April 30, 2020. https://www.navytimes.com/news/your-navy/2020/04/30/hospital-ship-comfort-departs-nyc-having-treated-fewer-than-200-patients/. (2/16/22).

Singman, Brooke, and Adam Shaw. "Hunter Biden requested keys for new 'office mates' Joe Biden, Chinese 'emissary' to CEFC chairman, emails show." *Fox News*, December 12, 2020. https://www.foxnews.com/politics/hunter-biden-requested-keys-new-office-mates-joe-biden-chinese-emissary-cefc-chairman. (7/23/22).

"'Smoking gun' emails reveal alleged meeting between Joe Biden and Ukrainian company." *Sky News*, October 15, 2020. https://www.skynews.com.au/world-news/smoking-gun-emails-reveal-alleged-meeting-between-joe-biden-and-ukrainian-company/video/4861a303e6ba16a971b16c76bba16809. (5/23/22).

Slater, Tom. "Why Elon Musk has rattled them: His attempted takeover of Twitter has revealed just how terrified the liberal elites are of freedom of speech." *Spiked*, April 15, 2022. https://www.spiked-online.com/2022/04/15/why-elon-musk-has-rattled-them/?fbclid=IwAR3Xbl BOZqM3J7ywgxFr-FsVBXl1Z-LDmgd7_QpR2YeLxOhUNnPvUuZJvq8. (6/28/22).

Smith, Bradley A. "Remember the IRS targeting scandal? No one ever got punished for it." *Washington Examiner*, January 18, 2018. https://www.washingtonexaminer.com/remember-the-irs-targeting-scandal-no-one-ever-got-punished-for-it. (2/16/22).

Smith, Lee. *The Permanent Coup: How Enemies Foreign and Domestic Targeted the American President*. New York: Center Street. 2020.

———. *The Plot Against the President: The True Story of How Congressman Devin Nunes Uncovered the Biggest Political Scandal in US History*. New York: Center Street. 2019.

Smith, Tovia. "They believe in Trump's 'Big Lie.' Here's why it's been so hard to dispel." *NPR*, January 5, 2022. https://www.npr.org/2022/01/05/1070362852/trump-big-lie-election-jan-6-fami lies. (4/5/22).

"The Women's March, 2017." *Smithsonian National Museum of American History*. https://american history.si.edu/creating-icons/women's-march-2017. (4/1/22).

"Thomas Jefferson's Bible." *Smithsonian National Museum of American History*. https://americanhis tory.si.edu/jeffersonbible/. (4/16/22).

Sneed, Tierney, Ariane de Vogue, and Joan Biskupic. "Supreme Court draft opinion that would overturn Roe v. Wade published by Politico." *CNN*, May 3, 2022. https://www.cnn.com/2022/05/02/politics/roe-v-wade-supreme-court/index.html. (6/10/22).

Snyder, Riley. "Judge rejects 'shocking ask' of new election over voter fraud claims brought by Sharron Angle and affiliated group." *Nevada Independent*, November 20, 2020. https://thenevadaindependent.com/article/judge-rejects-shocking-ask-of-new-election-over-voter-fraud-claims-brought-by-sharron-angle-and-affiliated-group. (8/10/22).

Soave, Robby. "In Leaked Audio, CDC's Rochelle Walensky Privately Confirms She Won't Relax School Mask Guidance." *Reason*, February 16, 2022. https://reason.com/2022/02/16/cdc-rochelle-walensky-masks-schools-covid-leaked-audio/. (2/18/22).

Solender, Andrew. "Majority Of House Republicans Vote To Reject Pennsylvania, Arizona Electors." *Forbes*, January 7, 2021. https://www.forbes.com/sites/andrewsolender/2021/01/07/major ity-of-house-republicans-vote-to-reject-pennsylvania-arizona-electors/?sh=23d3e20d6957. (5/17/22).

Solomon, John. "Trump gave order to 'make sure' Jan. 6 rally was 'safe event,' Pentagon memo shows." *Just The News*, July 22, 2022. https://justthenews.com/government/congress/trump-gave-explicit-order-about-jan-6-rally-make-sure-it-was-safe-event-dod. (7/22/22).

Spencer, Robert. "13 Americans Killed in Kabul: 'We did it, Joe!'" *Frontpage Mag*, August 27, 2021. https://robertspencer.org/2021/08/13-americans-killed-in-kabul-we-did-it-joe. (4/19/22).

Spencer, Saranac Hale. "Nine Election Fraud Claims, None Credible." *FactCheck*, December 11, 2020. https://www.factcheck.org/2020/12/nine-election-fraud-claims-none-credible/.

Sperry, Paul. "Naming the Capitol Cop Who Killed Unarmed Jan. 6 Rioter Ashli Babbitt." *Real Clear Investigations*, July 7, 2021. https://www.realclearinvestigations.com/articles/2021/07/07/naming_the_capitol_cop_who_killed_jan_6_rioter_ashli_babbitt_779601.html. (5/25/22).

———. "The scandal in Washington no one is talking about." *New York Post*, May 21, 2016. https://nypost.com/2016/05/21/the-scandal-in-washington-no-one-is-talking-about/. (5/23/22).

———. "Why a Judge Has Georgia Vote Fraud on His Mind: 'Pristine' Biden Ballots That Looked Xeroxed." *Real Clear Investigations*, June 8, 2021. https://www.realclearinvestigations.com/arti cles/2021/06/08/why_a_judge_has_georgia_vote_fraud_on_his_mind_pristine_biden_ballot s_that_look_xeroxed_779795.html.

Stableford, Dylan. "Trump issues stunning, baseless claim that 'millions' voted illegally." *Yahoo!news*, November 27, 2016.

"COVID-Related Election Litigation Tracker." Stanford-MIT Healthy Elections Project. https://

healthyelections-case-tracker.stanford.edu; https://creativecommons.org/licenses/by/4.0/legal code.

Stark, Philip B.. "There is no Reliable Way to Detect Hacked Ballot-Marking Devices." University of California, Berkeley, August 21, 2019. https://www.stat.berkeley.edu/~stark/Preprints/bmd-p19.pdf.

Starr, Michael. "Herein 'Lies' the Tale of Baghdad Bob." New York Post, April 9, 2003. https://nypost.com/2003/04/09/herein-lies-the-tale-of-baghdad-bob/ (8/3/22).

Starr, Penny. "Lawyer: Ginni Thomas Will Not Testify Before January 6 House Committee." Breitbart, June 29, 2022. https://www.breitbart.com/politics/2022/06/29/lawyer-ginni-thomas-will-not-testify-before-january-6-house-committee/. (7/29/22).

Starr, Stephen. "US election result: Why the most accurate bellwether counties were wrong." BBC News. 27 November, 2020. https://www.bbc.com/news/election-us-2020-55062413.

State of Georgia. Certificate of Ascertainment (Amendment and Re-Certification), December 7, 2020. https://www.archives.gov/files/electoral-college/2020/ascertainment-georgia.pdf.

Steinbuch, Yaron. "US volunteer claims Taliban beheaded boys ages 9 and 10 in Afghanistan." New York Post, September 15, 2021. https://nypost.com/2021/09/15/ex-us-officer-claims-taliban-beheaded-two-children-in-afghanistan/. (4/19/22).

Stevenson, Struan. "Taliban's windfall from U.S. withdrawal: $83B in weapons." United Press International, September 20, 2021. https://www.upi.com/Voices/2021/09/20/Afghanistan-with drawal-US-weapons-left-behind/7181632140222/. (4/19/22).

Stieber, Zachary. "Biden Administration Blames Delay in Restarting 'Remain in Mexico' Program on Mexico." Epoch Times, September 17, 2021. https://www.theepochtimes.com/biden-adminis tration-blames-delay-in-restarting-remain-in-mexico-program-on-mexico_4003133.html. (4/19/22).

———. "Clinton Campaign, DNC Misreported Opposition Research as Legal Services: FEC." Epoch Times, April 28, 2022. https://www.theepochtimes.com/clinton-campaign-dnc-misre ported-opposition-research-as-legal-services-fec_4434080.html. (7/24/22).

———. "Full List: how Members of Congress Voted on Objections to Arizona, Pennsylvania Electoral Results." Epoch Times, January 7, 2021. https://www.theepochtimes.com/mkt_app/full-list-how-members-of-congress-voted-on-objections-to-arizona-pennsylvania-electoral-results_3647448.html.

Stimson, Brie, and Vandana Rambaran. "Trump critics seize on president's positive coronavirus test to mock, lecture." Fox News, October 2, 2020. https://www.foxnews.com/politics/trump-critics-seize-on-presidents-positive-coronavirus-test-to-mock-lecture. (6/7/22).

Strach, Kim, Marc Burris, and Veronica Degraffenreid. "Presentation to Joint Legislative Elections Oversight Committee," North Carolina State Board of Elections, April 2, 2014. https://wwwcache.wral.com/asset/news/state/nccapitol/2014/04/02/13534230/SBOE_JointCommit tee_April_2014.pdf.

Strassel, Kimberly A. "Grifters-in-Chief: The Clintons don't draw lines between their 'charity' and personal enrichment." Wall Street Journal, October 27, 2016. https://www.wsj.com/articles/grifters-in-chief-1477610771. (4/6/22).

Sullivan, Becky. "Why the Kyle Rittenhouse 'not guilty' verdict is not a surprise to legal experts." NPR, November 19, 2021. https://www.npr.org/2021/11/19/1057422329/why-legal-experts-were-not-surprised-by-the-rittenhouse-jurys-decision-to-acquit. (2/18/22).

Sun, Melanie. "2,000-Person Caravan Surges Past Mexican Riot Police Near Guatemala Border." Epoch Times, October 24, 2021. https://www.theepochtimes.com/2000-person-caravan-surges-past-mexican-riot-police-near-guatemala-border_4065478.html. (4/19/22).

Swenson, Ali. "Fact-checking '2000 Mules,' the movie alleging ballot fraud." Denver Post, May 8, 2022. https://www.denverpost.com/2022/05/08/2000-mules-fact-check/. (5/18/22).

———. "Kamala Harris said protests should continue, not riots." Associated Press, October 8, 2020. https://apnews.com/article/fact-checking-afs:Content:9579800331. (4/17/22).

Swoyer, Alex. "Supreme Court orders Pennsylvania to segregate late ballots." Washington Times, November 6, 2020. https://www.washingtontimes.com/news/2020/nov/6/supreme-court-orders-pennsylvania-segregate-late-b/. (4/8/22).

Takala, Rudy. "Mark Levin Savages 'Pathetic' Rep. Kinzinger: 'Full-Fledged Never Trumper."

Mediaite, January 1, 2021. https://www.mediaite.com/news/mark-levin-savages-pathetic-rep-kinzinger-full-fledged-never-trumper/. (6/7/22).

Tayag, Yasmin. "Why Are Americans Still—Still!—Wearing Cloth Masks?" *Atlantic,* October 4, 2021. https://www.theatlantic.com/health/archive/2021/10/why-americans-wear-cloth-masks/620296/. (5/24/22).

"Breonna Taylor: What happened on the night of her death?" *BBC,* October 8, 2020. https://www.bbc.com/news/world-us-canada-54210448.

Teh, Cheryl. "Alan Dershowitz accused Maxine Waters of using 'KKK tactics' to intimidate the jury in the Chauvin murder trial." *Business Insider,* April 21, 2021. https://www.businessinsider.com/alan-dershowitz-accused-maxine-waters-of-using-kkk-tactics-2021-4. (2/17/22).

"Australia to withdraw staff from Kiev embassy." *Teletrader News,* February 12, 2022. https://www.teletrader.com/australia-to-withdraw-staff-from-kiev-embassy/news/details/57271363?ts=1644811032665

Terruso, Julia. "He organized a bus of Trump supporters from Pa. for 'the first day of the rest of our lives.' He died in Washington." *Philadelphia Inquirer,* January 7, 2021. https://www.inquirer.com/news/pennsylvania/washington-protest-trump-capitol-pennsylvania-ben-philips-20210107.html&outputType=app-web-view. (5/16/22).

Terry, Miles. "President Obama's IRS Scandal: Seven Years & Counting." *American Center for Law and Justice,* accessed October 1, 2021. https://aclj.org/free-speech/president-obamas-irs-scandal-seven-years-counting.

"Insane Karen Assaults 69 Year Old Man On Plane Because He Took His Mask Off To Eat, FBI Arrested Her." TheProfessional. December 28, 2021. YouTube video. https://www.youtube.com/watch?v=3ObF-NCz9Yg. (4/14/22).

Tillman, Zoe. "Trump And His Allies Have Lost Nearly 60 Election Fights In Court (And Counting)." *BuzzFeed News,* December 14, 2020. https://www.buzzfeednews.com/article/zoetillman/trump-election-court-losses-electoral-college. (7/26/22).

"Full text of Israel-Bahrain 'Declaration of Peace.'" *Times of Israel,* September 16, 2020. https://www.timesofisrael.com/liveblog_entry/full-text-of-israel-bahrain-peace-declaration/. (5/23/22).

Trivers, Robert. *Social Evolution.* Menlo Park: Benjamin/Cummings Publication Company, 1985.

"Trump et al. v. Twitter, Inc. et al.," *Unicourt.* https://unicourt.com/case/pc-db5-trump-et-al-v-twitter-inc-et-al-950772.

"'Trump Heights': A symbol of US shift on Mideast policy." *Times of Israel,* October 20, 2020. https://www.timesofisrael.com/trump-heights-a-symbol-of-us-shift-on-mideast-policy/. (5/26/22).

"Trump Twitter Archive v2," http://www.thetrumparchive.com.

Trump v. Bullock, Order, September 30, 2020, https://electionlawblog.org/wp-content/uploads/MT-Trump-20200930-decision.pdf.

Turley, Jonathan. "Why Pelosi hates impeachment." *Hill,* March 12, 2019. https://thehill.com/opinion/judiciary/433630-why-pelosi-hates-impeachment.

Turner, Ben. "Statistical Evidence of Dominion Election Fraud? Time to Audit the Machines." November 21, 2020. https://www.fraudspotters.com/statistics-about-dominion-election-fraud/.

Tuttle, Ian. "El Chapo's Capture Puts 'Operation Fast and Furious' Back in the Headlines." *National Review,* January 22, 2016. https://www.nationalreview.com/2016/01/fast-furious-obama-first-scandal/. (5/23/22).

Tyler, Amanda L.. "A 'Second Magna Carta': The English Habeas Corpus Act and the Statutory Origins of the Habeas Privilege." 91 Notre Dame L. Rev. 1949 (2016). https://scholarship.law.nd.edu/ndlr/vol91/iss5/7.

"Civilian unemployment rate." U.S. Bureau of Labor Statistics. https://www.bls.gov/charts/employment-situation/civilian-unemployment-rate.htm. (5/26/22).

U.S. Department of Justice. *Re: United States v. Jacob Chansley Criminal Case No. 21-cr-003 (RCL).* Channing D. Phillips, July 15, 2021, 7. https://s3.documentcloud.org/documents/21054932/9-3-21-jacob-chansley-plea-agreement.pdf.

"The Abraham Accords Declaration," U.S. Department of State. https://www.state.gov/the-abraham-accords/. (5/23/22).

"FDA Takes Key Action in Fight Against COVID-19 By Issuing Emergency Use Authorization for First COVID-19 Vaccine." U.S. Food & Drug Administration, December 11, 2020. https://www.fda.gov/news-events/press-announcements/fda-takes-key-action-fight-against-covid-19-issuing-emergency-use-authorization-first-covid-19. (2/16/22).

"Devon Archer Sentenced To A Year And A Day In Prison For The Fraudulent Issuance And Sale Of More Than $60 Million Of Tribal Bonds." United States Attorney's Office, Southern District of New York. February 28, 2022. https://www.justice.gov/usao-sdny/pr/devon-archer-sentenced-year-and-day-prison-fraudulent-issuance-and-sale-more-60-million. (3/2/22).

"H.Res.503 - Establishing the Select Committee to Investigate the January 6th Attack on the United States Capitol." United States Congress, June 28, 2021. https://www.congress.gov/bill/117th-congress/house-resolution/503/text.

"Misuse of position and government resources." United States Department of Justice. https://www.justice.gov/jmd/misuse-position-and-government-resources. (3/22/22).

Unverferth, Audrey. "5th Circuit Keeps Sanctions On Democrat Russia Hoax Lawyer Marc Elias." *Federalist*, July 8, 2021. https://thefederalist.com/2021/07/08/5th-circuit-keeps-sanctions-on-democrat-russia-hoax-lawyer-marc-elias/. (7/26/22).

"Georgia Lawmaker Wants Sect. of State Brad Raffensperger Investigated After Ballot Audit Fraud Allegations." *USA Features News*, July 15, 2021. https://usafeatures.news/2021/07/15/georgia-lawmaker-wants-brad-raffensperger-investigated-after-ballot-audit-fraud-allegations/. (7/20/22).

Van Allen, Fox. "Celebrities who support Joe Biden for president." *CBS News*, October 29, 2020. https://www.cbsnews.com/pictures/celebrities-who-support-joe-biden-for-president/. (5/16/22).

Vassar, Ryan. *Letter from Ryan Vassar to Mr. Keith Ingram, Director of Elections, Texas Secretary of State*. Letter, November 4, 2019. https://www.sos.texas.gov/elections/forms/sysexam/oct2019-vassar.pdf. (7/20/22).

Vazquez, Marietta. "Calling COVID-19 the 'Wuhan Virus' or 'China Virus' is inaccurate and xenophobic." *Yale School of Medicine*, March 12, 2020. https://medicine.yale.edu/news-article/calling-covid-19-the-wuhan-virus-or-china-virus-is-inaccurate-and-xenophobic/. (5/23/22).

Vazquez, Meagan. "Trump leans into racist rhetoric and downplays violence against Black Americans." *CNN*, July 14, 2020. https://www.cnn.com/2020/07/14/politics/donald-trump-police-brutality/index.html. (4/20/22).

Vespa, Matt. "Here's How Many Biden Voters Would Have Bolted from Joe If The Media Did Their Job." *Townhall*, November 28, 2020. https://townhall.com/tipsheet/mattvespa/2020/11/28/heres-how-may-biden-voters-who-would-have-bolted-from-joe-if-the-media-did-their-n2580624. (5/23/22).

Vick, Karl. "Why the U.S. Assassination of Iranian Quds Force Leader Qasem Soleimani Has the U.S. Bracing for Retaliation." *Time*, January 3, 2020. https://time.com/5758250/qasem-soleimani-iran-retaliation/. (2/16/22).

Villareal, Daniel. "Kamala Harris More Liberal Than Bernie Sanders, Senate Record Analysis Shows." *Newsweek*, August 20, 2020. https://www.newsweek.com/kamala-harris-more-liberal-bernie-sanders-senate-record-analysis-shows-1524481. (6/7/22).

Vincent, Isabel. "BLM hires Clinton aide who paid for Steele dossier to sort shady finances." *New York Post*, February 17, 2022. https://nypost.com/2022/02/17/blm-hires-clinton-aide-marc-elias-who-paid-for-steele-dossier/ (7/26/22).

Viser, Matt. "Joe Biden spent much of the general election in his basement. Now, he and his aides ponder a very public inauguration." *Seattle Times*, November 21, 2021. https://www.seattletimes.com/nation-world/joe-biden-spent-much-of-the-general-election-in-his-basement-now-he-and-his-aides-ponder-a-very-public-inauguration/. (6/6/22).

Vita-More, Natasha. "Life Expansion: Toward an Artistic, Design-Based Theory of the Transhuman / Posthuman" PhD diss., University of Plymouth, 2012.

Vlamis, Kelsey. "Elon Musk accuses Twitter of rushing its lawsuit along at 'warp speed' after two months of 'foot-dragging' on providing bot data." *Business Insider*, July 15, 2022. https://www.businessinsider.com/elon-musk-accuses-twitter-of-delaying-bot-data-rushing-lawsuit-2022-7?op=1. (7/20/22).

von Spakovsky, Hans, "Latest Alleged Election Fraud in California May Have Changed Election

Outcome," *Daily Signal*, August 24, 2021. https://www.dailysignal.com/2021/08/24/the-latest-alleged-election-fraud-in-california-may-have-overturned-an-election/.

———. Interview in *2000 Mules*, (2022), digital.

Wall, Mike. "SpaceX's very big year: A 2020 filled with astronaut launches, Starship tests and more." *Space.com,* December 28, 2020. https://www.space.com/spacex-astronaut-starship-launches-2020-milestones. (5/23/22).

"Facebook, Censorship and Political Speech: The problem at hand isn't politically incorrect content that might offend American liberals. It entails covert, fraudulent and often illegal campaigns to manipulate public opinion ahead of elections around the world." *Wall Street Journal*, November 18, 2019. https://www.wsj.com/articles/facebook-censorship-and-political-speech-11574097326. (4/1/22).

Waller, J. Michael. "'A small number of extremists': Capitol Police video will show that January 6 was not an insurrection." *Center for Security Policy*, September 28, 2021. https://centerforsecuritypolicy.org/a-small-number-of-extremists-capitol-police-video-will-show-that-january-6-was-not-an-insurrection/. (5/25/22).

———. "How can Trump be so stupid?" *Week*, August 17, 2017. https://theweek.com/articles/718732/how-trump-stupid. (4/20/22).

Wefer, Dana. "New Jersey Elections Are the Lifeblood of State's Political Corruption." *Independent Voter News*, March 9, 2017. https://ivn.us/2017/03/09/new-jersey-elections-lifeblood-states-political-corruption/. (6/28/22).

Welsh, Rich. "Rep. Gosar Holding Press Conference Calling on DOJ to Release 14,000 Hours of Video Footage of January 6 at the Capitol." *RPW Media*, July 27, 2021. https://richpwelsh.com/2021/07/27/rep-gosar-holding-press-conference-calling-on-doj-to-release-14000-hours-of-video-footage-of-january-6-at-the-capitol/. (5/25/22).

White, Chris. "De Blasio, NYC Officials Downplayed COVID-19 Threat After Trump Restricted Travel to China. Here are 5 Examples." *The Daily Signal*, March 30, 2020. https://www.dailysignal.com/2020/03/30/de-blasio-nyc-officials-downplayed-covid-19-threat-after-trump-restricted-travel-to-china-here-are-5-examples/. (4/6/22).

White, Debbie. "Call To Action Black Lives Matter fist symbol — what's the meaning behind the Black Power salute?" *Sun*, June 3, 2020. https://www.thesun.co.uk/news/11761639/black-lives-matter-fist-symbol-meaning-black-power-salute/. (3/10/22).

"15 Days to Slow the Spread." White House, March 16, 2020. https://trumpwhitehouse.archives.gov/articles/15-days-slow-spread/. (4/13/22).

"Executive Order Protecting the Nation from Foreign Terrorist Entry into the United States." White House, January 27, 2017. https://trumpwhitehouse.archives.gov/presidential-actions/executive-order-protecting-nation-foreign-terrorist-entry-united-states/. (5/26/22).

"Path out of the Pandemic: President Biden's COVID-19 Action Plan." White House. https://www.whitehouse.gov/covidplan/

"President Trump Announces U.S. Withdrawal From the Paris Climate Accord." White House, June 1, 2017. https://trumpwhitehouse.archives.gov/articles/president-trump-announces-u-s-withdrawal-paris-climate-accord/. (5/26/22).

"Press Briefing by Press Secretary Jen Psaki." White House, April 20, 2022. https://www.whitehouse.gov/briefing-room/press-briefings/press-secretary-jen-psaki-april-20-2022/?fbclid=IwAR2QrnferQbd8_mzcYjJ8N-MmPco499EieB1VxSSZ6fanygVo2e1-W9kLY. (4/24/22).

"Fact Sheet: The Biden Administration Blueprint for a Fair, Orderly and Humane Immigration System." White House Briefing Room, July 27, 2021. https://www.whitehouse.gov/briefing-room/statements-releases/2021/07/27/fact-sheet-the-biden-administration-blueprint-for-a-fair-orderly-and-humane-immigration-system/. (4/1/22).

Whitley, Rob. "Is 'Trump Derangement Syndrome' a Real Mental Condition?" *Psychology Today*, January 4, 2019. https://www.psychologytoday.com/us/blog/talking-about-men/201901/is-trump-derangement-syndrome-real-mental-condition. (3/18/22).

Widburg, Andrea. "It looks as if there was massive election fraud in Fulton County, Georgia." *American Thinker,* July 15, 2021. https://www.americanthinker.com/blog/2021/07/it_looks_as_if_there_was_massive_election_fraud_in_fulton_county_georgia.html. (6/1/22).

"Wikipedia:About." Wikipedia. https://en.wikipedia.org/wiki/Wikipedia:About. (4/1/22).

Wilcox, Dale. "Kamala's neglect of the border crisis is her greatest failure." *American Thinker*,

December 24, 2021. https://www.americanthinker.com/blog/2021/12/kamalas_neglec t_of_the_border_crisis_is_her_greatest_failure.html. (4/19/22).

Williams, David, and Mark Nicol. "Military translator, 30, who helped US soldiers in Afghanistan is beheaded by the Taliban sparking new alarm for the interpreters left as the West withdraws." *Daily Mail*, July 25, 2021. https://www.dailymail.co.uk/news/article-9819559/ amp/Military-translator-30-helped-soldiers-Afghanistan-beheaded-Taliban.html. (4/19/22).

Wilson, F. Perry. "Ivermectin and COVID: Is a Microscopic Worm the Key?" *Medscape*, March 22, 2022. https://www.medscape.com/viewarticle/970567. (4/13/22).

"Second Interim Investigative Report On the Apparatus & Procedures of the Wisconsin Elections System." Wisconsin Office of the Special Counsel, March 1, 2022.

Withnall, Adam. "Donald Trump greets American hostages released by North Korea as they touch down on US soil." *Independent*, May 10, 2018. https://www.independent.co.uk/news/ world/americas/trump-north-korea-us-hostages-release-arrive-america-kim-jong-un-a8344281.html. (5/26/22).

Wolf, Tom. "U.S. Election was 'most secure in American history' Federal Agency says." https:// www.governor.pa.gov/newsroom/u-s-election-was-most-secure-in-american-history-federal-agency-says/. (5/25/22).

Wolfe, Jan. "Trump wanted troops to protect his supporters at Jan. 6 rally." *Reuters*, May 12, 2021. https://www.reuters.com/world/us/congresswoman-says-trump-administration-botched-capi tol-riot-preparations-2021-05-12/. (4/17/22).

Wong, Kristina. "Hundreds of hospital beds left empty on the USNS Comfort and Javits Center during Cuomo's nursing home order." *Breitbart*, February 22, 2021. https://www.breitbart.com/ politics/2021/02/22/hundreds-of-hospital-beds-left-empty-on-the-usns-comfort-and-javits-center-during-cuomos-nursing-home-order/. (2/16/22).

———. "January 6 Show Trial: Liz Cheney Omits Exculpatory Phrase While Quoting Trump— 'Go Home With Love And Peace'." *Breitbart*, June 10, 2022. https://www.breitbart.com/politics/ 2022/06/10/cheney-omits-trump-january-6-tweet-go-home-love-peace/. (6/29/22).

Wong, Queenie. "Trump's tweets blocked for election misinformation still spread to other sites." *CNET*, August 25, 2021. https://www.cnet.com/news/politics/trumps-tweets-blocked-for-elec tion-misinformation-still-spread-to-other-sites/. (7/20/22).

Woolhandler, Steffie. "Taxpayers Paid Twice for Healthcare—Private insurers are profiting more than ever during the pandemic." *MedPageToday*, May 25, 2022. https://www.medpagetoday. com/opinion/second-opinions/98916. (6/2/22).

Woolley, John T., and Gerhard Peters. "Biden in Action: the First 100 Days." *American Presidency Project*, April 30, 2021. https://www.presidency.ucsb.edu/analyses/biden-action-the-first-100-days. (4/1/22).

"WHO Coronavirus (COVID-19) Dashboard." World Health Organization. https://covid19. who.int. (3/10/22).

"Report names Capitol Police officer as shooter of Ashli Babbitt." *World Tribune*. July 8, 2021. https://www.worldtribune.com/report-names-capitol-police-officer-as-shooter-of-ashli-babbitt/. (5/23/22).

"Blinken: 100 U.S. citizens in Afghanistan want to leave." *Yahoo News US*, September 13, 2021. https://www.msn.com/en-us/news/other/blinken-100-us-citizens-in-afghanistan-want-to-leave/vi-AAOp2al. (5/31/22).

"16 Celebrities Who Supported Trump In 2020 And What They Say About Him Now." *Yahoo!News*, January 7, 2022. https://news.yahoo.com/16-celebrities-trump-supporters-him-190946443.html. (5/16/22).

"FBI investigation into January 6 becomes largest in FBI history." *Yahoo!News*, May 25, 2021. https://news.yahoo.com/fbi-investigation-january-6-becomes-161956975.html. (5/25/22).

"Trump Administration Rolls Back the Clean Power Plan." *Yale Environment 360*, August 21, 2018. https://e360.yale.edu/digest/the-trump-administration-rolls-back-the-clean-power-plan. (5/26/22).

York, Byron. "With virus crisis raging, Pelosi and Schiff ramp up new Trump investigations." *Washington Examiner*, April 2, 2020. https://www.washingtonexaminer.com/opinion/colum nists/with-virus-crisis-raging-pelosi-schiff-ramp-up-new-trump-investigations. (5/23/22).

———. "When 1,099 felons vote in race won by 312 ballots." *Washington Examiner*, August 6, 2012.

https://www.washingtonexaminer.com/york-when-1-099-felons-vote-in-race-won-by-312-ballots. (7/20/22).

York, Erica. "Summary of the Latest Federal Income Tax Data, 2020 Update." *Tax Foundation,* February 20, 2020. https://taxfoundation.org/summary-of-the-latest-federal-income-tax-data-2020-update/.

Zaslav, Ali, Jessica Dean, and Ted Barrett. "Senators quickly pass bill to expand security for Supreme Court justices." *CNN,* May 9, 2022. https://www.cnn.com/2022/05/09/politics/supreme-court-justices-security-senate-vote/index.html. (6/10/22).

Zweig, David. "The CDC's Flawed Case for Masks in School." *Atlantic,* December 16, 2021. https://www.theatlantic.com/science/archive/2021/12/mask-guidelines-cdc-walensky/621035/. (2/18/22).

"Average Regular Gas Price Comparison by State." https://www.gasbuddy.com/usa.(5/23/22).

"The President Has Kept His Promises - And More," https://www.priestsforlife.org/pdf/trump-kept-promises.pdf. (5/23/22).

"US Unemployment Rate by Month." https://www.multpl.com/unemployment/table/by-month. (5/26/22).

"What is Environmental, Social and Corporate Governance (ESG)?" https://www.diligent.com/insights/esg/.

"Why Impeachment?" https://impeachdonaldtrumpnow.org. (Accessed February 1, 2022)

INDEX

Note: Discussion questions on any topic are listed first among the subheadings. Bold page numbers indicate broad discussion of a topic. Where a reference points to an endnote, its page number is followed by "n" (for *note*), followed by the number of the endnote in which the reference occurs.

Made in the USA
Middletown, DE
11 October 2022

12317223R00275